Lecture Notes of the Institute for Computer Sciences, Social Informatics and Telecommunications Engineering 357

More information about this series at http://www.springer.com/series/8197

Qihui Wu · Kanglian Zhao ·
Xiaojin Ding (Eds.)

Wireless and Satellite Systems

11th EAI International Conference, WiSATS 2020
Nanjing, China, September 17–18, 2020
Proceedings, Part I

Springer

Editors
Qihui Wu
Nanjing University of Aeronautics
and Astronautics
Nanjing, Jiangsu, China

Kanglian Zhao
Nanjing University
Nanjing, China

Xiaojin Ding
Nanjing University of Posts
and Telecommunications
Nanjing, China

ISSN 1867-8211 ISSN 1867-822X (electronic)
Lecture Notes of the Institute for Computer Sciences, Social Informatics
and Telecommunications Engineering
ISBN 978-3-030-69068-7 ISBN 978-3-030-69069-4 (eBook)
https://doi.org/10.1007/978-3-030-69069-4

This Springer imprint is published by the registered company Springer Nature Switzerland AG
The registered company address is: Gewerbestrasse 11, 6330 Cham, Switzerland

Preface

We are delighted to introduce the proceedings of the 11th edition of the European Alliance for Innovation (EAI) International Conference on Wireless and Satellite Systems (WiSATS 2020 formerly PSATS). This conference brought together researchers, developers and practitioners around the world who are leveraging and developing wireless and satellite technology for a smarter global communication architecture. The theme of WiSATS 2020 was "Intelligent Wireless and Satellite Communications for Beyond 5G".

The technical program of WiSATS 2020 consisted of 91 full papers. The conference main track was organized into 5 sessions. Aside from the high-quality technical paper presentations, the technical program also featured three keynote speeches and six technical workshops. The three keynote speakers were Dr. Sastri Kota (Associate Fellow of AIAA) from SoHum Consultants, USA, Professor Geoffrey Ye Li (Fellow of IEEE) from the School of Electrical and Computer Engineering, Georgia Tech, USA and Professor Tony Q.S. Quek (Fellow of IEEE) from Singapore University of Technology and Design, Singapore. The 6 workshops organized were (1) High Speed Space Communication and Space Information Networks (HSSCSIN), (2) Integrated Space and Onboard Networks (ISON), (3) Intelligent Satellite Operations, Managements and Applications (ISOMA), (4) Intelligent Satellites in Future Space Networked System (ISFSNS), (5) Satellite Communications, Networking and Applications (SCNA), (6) Satellite Internet of Things, Trusted Data Sharing, Secure Communication (SIOTTDSSC). The HSSCSIN workshop aimed to address the requirements challenges and promising new technology of broadband communications in future space information networks. The ISON workshop aimed to gain insights into research and development of future integration of onboard and space networks. The ISOMA workshop aimed to discuss the development, operation, management and application of future intelligent satellites. The ISFSNS workshop focused on the role of intelligence and networking in future space systems. The SCNA workshop aimed to achieve a deeper understanding of the future of satellite communications and networking and their applications in a connected world. The SIOTTDSSC workshop aimed to gain understanding of the architecture of satellite-based IoT and the guarantee of security in such networks.

Coordination with the steering chairs, Imrich Chlamtac, Kandeepan Sithamparanathan, Mario Marchese, Weixiao Meng and Min Jia, was essential for the success of the conference. We sincerely appreciate their constant support and guidance. It was also a great pleasure to work with such an excellent organizing committee team for their hard work in organizing and supporting the conference. In particular, the Technical Program Committee, led by our TPC Co-Chairs, Prof. Zhili Sun, Prof. Guangxia Li, Prof. Kanglian Zhao and Prof. Min Jia, completed the peer-review process of technical papers and made a high-quality technical program. We are also grateful to the Conference Managers, Barbora Cintava and Radka Pincakova, for their support and to all the authors who submitted their papers to the WiSATS 2020 conference and workshops.

We strongly believe that the WiSATS conference provides a good forum for all researchers, developers and practitioners to discuss all scientific and technological aspects that are relevant to wireless and satellite technology. We also expect that future WiSATS conferences will be as successful and stimulating, as indicated by the contributions presented in this volume.

Qihui Wu
Biaobin Jin
Qing Guo
Jian Guo
Jun Yang

Conference Organization

Steering Committee

Imrich Chlamtac	University of Trento, Italy
Kandeepan Sithamparanathan	RMIT, Australia
Mario Marchese	University of Genoa, Italy
Weixiao Meng	Harbin Institute of Technology, China
Min Jia	Harbin Institute of Technology, China

Organizing Committee

Honorary Chairs

Zhicheng Zhou	Chinese Academy of Engineering, China
De Ben	Chinese Academy of Engineering, China

General Chairs

Qihui Wu	Nanjing University of Aeronautics and Astronautics, China
Biaobin Jin	Nanjing University, China

General Co-chairs

Qing Guo	Harbin Institute of Technology, China
Jian Guo	Beijing Institute of Spacecraft System Engineering, China
Jun Yang	The Sixty-Third Research Institute, National University of Defense Technology, China

TPC Chair and Co-chairs

Zhili Sun	University of Surrey, UK
Guangxia Li	Jiangsu Collaborative Innovation Center for Satellite Communications and Navigation, China
Kanglian Zhao	Nanjing University, China
Min Jia	Harbin Institute of Technology, China

Sponsorship and Exhibit Chair

Wei Sheng	Nanjing China-Spacenet Satellite Telecom Co., Ltd., China

Local Chair

Lu Lu   Jiangsu Collaborative Innovation Center for Satellite
Communications and Navigation, China

Workshops Chair

Xiongwen He   Beijing Institute of Spacecraft System Engineering,
China

Publicity and Social Media Chair

Guohua Kang   Nanjing University of Aeronautics and Astronautics,
China

Publications Chair

Xiaojin Ding   Nanjing University of Posts and Telecommunications,
China

Web Chair

Peng Li   Nanjing University of Information Science
and Technology, China

Posters and PhD Track Chair

Shaochuan Wu   Harbin Institute of Technology, China

Panels Chair

Xuanli Wu   Harbin Institute of Technology, China

Demos Chair

Xin Liu   Dalian University of Technology, China

Tutorials Chairs

Gongliang Liu   Harbin Institute of Technology, China
Wei Wu   Harbin Institute of Technology, China

Technical Program Committee

Li Yang   Dalian University, China
Huaifeng Shi   Nanjing University of Information Science
and Technology, China
Zhiguo Liu   Dalian University, China
Debin Wei   Dalian University, China.
Yuanming Ding   Dalian University, China
Xiaojin Ding   Nanjing University of Posts and Telecommunications,
China

Tao Hong	Nanjing University of Posts and Telecommunications, China
Chen Zhang	Nanjing University of Posts and Telecommunications, China
Peng Li	Nanjing University of Information Science and Technology, China
Jiao Feng	Nanjing University of Information Science and Technology, China
Mingyu Li	Chongqing University, China
Changzhi Xu	Xi'an Branch of China Academy of Space Technology, China
Bingcheng Zhu	Southeast University, China
Yi Jin	Xi'an Branch of China Academy of Space Technology, China
Jin Guang	National University of Defense Technology, China
Panpan Zhan	Beijing Institute of Spacecraft System Engineering, China
Shasha Zhang	Beijing Institute of Spacecraft System Engineering, China
Jun Yan	Nanjing University of Posts and Telecommunications, China
Yuqing Li	Harbin Institute of Technology, China
Xiye Guo	National University of Defense Technology, China
Wenbin Gong	Innovation Academy for Microsatellites of CAS, China
Rong Lv	The 63rd Research Institute, National University of Defense Technology, China
Lei Yang	National University of Defense Technology, China
Yang Guannan	Nanjing University of Finance & Economics, China
Xiongwen He	Beijing Institute of Spacecraft System Engineering, China
Hongjun Zhang	Beijing Institute of Spacecraft System Engineering, China
Xin Liu	Beijing Institute of Spacecraft System Engineering, China
Ke Li	Beijing Institute of Spacecraft System Engineering, China
Hongyan Li	Xidian University, China
Bo Li	Harbin Institute of Technology at Weihai, China
Weidang Lu	Zhejiang University of Technology, China
Dapeng Wang	Institute of Software Chinese Academy of Sciences, China
Lixiang Liu	Institute of Software Chinese Academy of Sciences, China
Kai Liu	Beihang University, China
Guofeng Zhao	Chongqing University of Posts and Telecommunications, China

Xin Hu   Beijing University of Posts and Telecommunications,
                          China
Shuaijun Liu   Institute of Software Chinese Academy of Sciences,
                          China
Xiaorong Zhu   Nanjing University of Posts and Telecommunications,
                          China
Xu Bao   Jiangsu University, China
Junyu Lai   University of Electronic Science and Technology
                          of China, China
Ci He   The 54th Research Institute of China Electronics
                          Technology Group Corporation, China
Dingde Jiang   University of Electronic Science and Technology
                          of China, China
Guohua Kang   Nanjing University of Aeronautics and Astronautics,
                          China
Yunhua Wu   Nanjing University of Aeronautics and Astronautics,
                          China
Xiaozhou Yu   Dalian University of Technology, China
Xiaoqiang Di   Changchun University of Science and Technology,
                          China
Changhong Hu   Changchun Institute of Optics, Fine Mechanics
                          and Physics, CAS
Ligang Cong   Changchun University of Science and Technology,
                          China
Hui Qi   Changchun University of Science and Technology,
                          China
Yining Mu   Changchun University of Science and Technology,
                          China
Yonglian Sun   Nanjing Tech University, China
Xianfeng Liu   National University of Defense Technology, China
Wenfeng Li   Nanjing University, China
Yuan Fang   Nanjing University, China
Shulei Gong   Nanjing University, China
Dongxu Hou   Nanjing University, China
Zhibo Yan   Nanjing University, China

Contents – Part I

Contents – Part II

**International Workshop on Intelligent Satellites in Future Space
Networked System**

**International Workshop on Integrated Space and Onboard
Networks (ISON)**

**International Workshop on High Speed Space Communication
and Space Information Networks**

**International Workshop on Satellite Network Transmission
and Security (SNTS)**

International Workshop on Satellite Internet of Things, Trusted Data sharing, Secure Communication

Main Track

Simulation System for Space Debris Intelligent Detecting

Feng Shi[1]([⊠]), Yuee Chang[2], Donglei He[1], Kunpeng Wang[3], and Huaifeng Li[1]

[1] Beijing Institute of Spacecraft System Engineering, Beijing 100094, China
shifeng2251@qq.com
[2] Key Laboratory of Photoelectronic Imaging Technology and System, Ministry of Education,
School of Optoelectronics, Beijing Institute of Technology, Beijing 100081, China
[3] Beijing Institute of Tracking and Telecommunications Technology, Beijing 100094, China

Abstract. Space debris has become a major potential safety hazard to the on-orbit spacecraft, which must be considered when launching a spacecraft. A simulation verification system which ground-based and can simulate the debris detecting onboard was established. The system consists of three sub-systems. The background generation sub-system could ensure maximum coverage of the debris targets by adjusting parameters such as satellite orbit, satellite attitude, optical load observation angles, and observation direction. The target identification and tracking sub-system could improve the ratio of track recognition and accuracy by adjusting the detection capability of optical load, switching target recognition and trajectory tracking algorithm. The orbit cataloging sub-system, the processing method of cataloging data can be determined by the process of determining the initial orbit, associating the initial orbit and determining the orbit accurately etc. The system will lay a foundation for updating and enriching the debris cataloging library in the future.

Keywords: Debris intelligent detecting · Simulation system · Target identification and tracking · Orbit cataloging

1 Preface

With the developing of space technology, space activities of human are continual more and more. And at the same time, artificial spacecraft was launched in the space more and more. Risks of collide between spacecraft are increasing simultaneously. Safety operation of spacecraft faces serious threaten. Therefore, technologies of space collision warning, space evasive operation, space debris removal etc. have been carrying out by space superpower countries. The base research of those technologies is detecting and cataloging space targets effectively [1–5].

Research on space debris cataloging is inadequate in China now. Simulation system for space debris intelligent detecting was established in this paper. The system is consisted of background generation sub-system, target identification and tracking sub-system, and orbit cataloging sub-system. The functions of the system are carried out by

© ICST Institute for Computer Sciences, Social Informatics and Telecommunications Engineering 2021
Published by Springer Nature Switzerland AG 2021. All Rights Reserved
Q. Wu et al. (Eds.): WiSATS 2020, LNICST 357, pp. 3–8, 2021.
https://doi.org/10.1007/978-3-030-69069-4_1

inputting the parameters and total control manage. The system can be used to simulate the procedure of debris detecting in space. This integrated simulation system is aimed at verifying the feasibility of the space debris catalog system. The research will lay a foundation for updating and enriching the debris cataloging library in the future.

2 Background Generation Sub-system

Background generation sub-system could achieve the functions to simulate the real sky, including stars, space debris, sun, moon, etc. and to simulate starry sky shot by satellite camera system and put out the image data as projection.

The functions of the sub-system are mainly achieved by image simulator. To develop image simulator, development of optic-coupling system, development of micro-mirror array and driver, and development of controlling system are all carried out. Beyond that, development of landscape-simul computing is also achieved.

In brief, based on Multi-Coordinary transforming and Julian Day computing algorithm, we have realized a dynamical and synchronized landscape generating of aerospace fragments and stars. Our work could serve as data provider of discussing of key parameters of observing, recognizing and labeling aerospace fragments.

3 Target Identification and Tracking Sub-system

Data receiving and processing is critical for target identification and tracking sub-system. Structure of the sub-system is showed in Fig. 1. The sub-system consists of receiving system, data processing and display system, and calibration system. The sub-system can achieve the functions such as simulation of optical load on space debris image acquisition process, obtaining the trajectory data by extracting the debris target in the space debris and analyzing the trajectory.

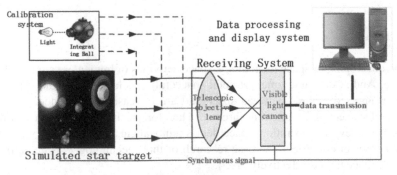

Fig. 1. Structure of target identification and tracking sub-system

Data processing and display system processes the data obtained from receiving system. The first step is image subtraction. The second step is image denoise. The third step is star debris target recognition. The forth step is debris trajectory tracking. And then, the trajectory data will be passed to cataloging system.

Subtract star target recognition method and interframe difference recognition method are used together in star debris recognition algorithm for take advantages of these two methods. Combination of two method will guarantee quickness and accuracy in targets recognition. First, use interframe difference recognition method. If effective data cannot be obtained, subtract star target recognition method follows. After analyzing, centroid error limits at 0.5 pixel in Interframe difference recognition method. The error is about 0.021 mrad under condition of $4° \times 4°$ FOV.

For guarantee trajectory tracking identification accurately, trajectory tracking algorithm integrated advantages of two methods which are search method based on centroid domain and algorithm based on mean shift target tracking. Trajectory tracking algorithm use these two method together.

After trajectory tracking identification accurately, trajectory description is carried out. Trajectory description method use 3D curve display function in Teechart. The character of the method is coordinates of any target are visible at any time. The coordinates are azimuth, elevation angle and time. Schematic diagram of target identification and tracking result showed in Fig. 2.

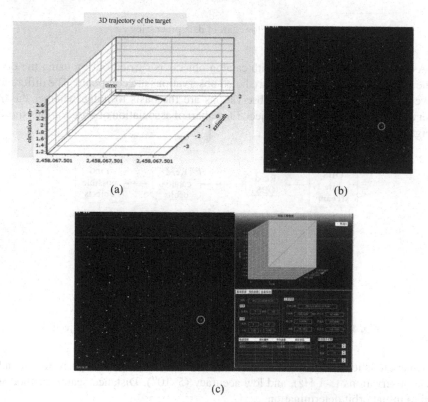

Fig. 2. Schematic diagram of trajectory simulation: (a) 3D display result; (b) Circle the target from FOV; (c) identification

4 Orbit Cataloging Sub-system

Orbit cataloging sub-system could simulate new-found debris cataloging and maintain existing debris cataloging. Also could match obtained cataloging data in database to decide how to deal with it, then update the database. Data processing flowchart of orbit cataloging sub-system showed in Fig. 3.

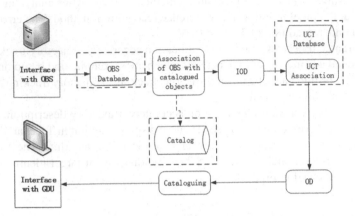

Fig. 3. Flowchart of data processing

Association of observations with catalog objects is carried out by using the orbits of the catalogued objects, and the predicted observations are computed. The differences between the computed and true observations are the basis to judge whether the true observations are of a catalogued object. Flowchart of association of observations showed in Fig. 4.

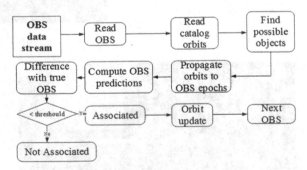

Fig. 4. Flowchart of association of observations with catalog objects

Characteristic of very short-arc (VSA) is short length (may be only several seconds), dense observations (>1 Hz), and low accuracy (5–10″). Distance search method was used to initial orbit determination.

Track Association is given by two independent tracks (IODs), and to determine whether they are of the same object. For the VSA IOD solutions, the errors of IOD elements are usually very large, so the track association is very difficult. To solve this problem, a geometrical approach is applied which based on geometrical distances to achieve track association. Simulation experiment of track association for space targets under a large scale nearly circular orbit were carried out. This approach was studied carefully. Track Association of SBSS IOD solutions are showed in Table 1. Track Association of ground EO array IOD solutions are showed in Table 2. Performance assessment shows the approach is high true positive rate, high computing efficiency, resilient on the errors of the semi major axis, sensitive to the eccentricity errors. When two IOD solutions are less than 24 h apart, the track association success rate is more than 80%.

Table 1. Track association—SBSS IOD solutions

Pairs from same objects			Pairs from different objects		
Association number		Rate	Association number		Rate
Total	15060	100.00%	Total	35690415	100.00%
Correct	12551	83.34%	Correct	35533470	99.56%

Table 2. Track association—ground EO array IOD solutions

	<3 day		<2 day		<1 day	
Same object pairs	35,100		25132		11252	
Correct	30287	86.26%	22043	87.71%	10255	91.14%
Wrong	4813	13.74%	3089	12.29%	265	8.86%
Different object Pairs	46332919		32424093		16277733	
Correct	46159605	99.63%	32305591	99.63%	16235490	99.74%
Wrong	173314	0.37%	118502	0.37%	42243	0.26%
Mean separation time (min)	1095		1741		438	

Debris cataloguing was carried out based on simulation data of detecting and track association result. A summary of cataloguing new objects using the SBSS simulation data is given in the Table 3. The results shows, When an object has three or more IOD solutions, the cataloguing success rate is more than 80%. When an object has four or more IOD solutions, the cataloguing success rate is more than 90%. It was showed that more numbers of observation, the more feasibility of orbit cataloging will be achieved. The procedure of this paper to processing the data is designed reasonable and is easy to be realized. Meanwhile, the cataloging success rate of the approach is high.

Table 3. Cataloguing new objects test using the SBSS simulation data

Number of IOD solutions	Number of objects	Number of catalogued objects	Success rate (%)
>=3	559	466	83.36%
>=4	328	309	94.21%

5   Conclusion

Simulation system for space debris intelligent detecting was established. The system is illustrated particularly, including three sub-system. We have realized a dynamical and synchronized landscape generating of aerospace fragments and stars, star debris recognition algorithm, trajectory tracking algorithm, IOD of very short-arc (VSA) angles data, track association etc. Target identification and tracking, initial orbit determination were both carried out to ensure the study of debris cataloguing. Simulation system established in this paper, the track association success rate is more than 80% when two IOD solutions are less than 24 h apart. The cataloguing success rate is more than 80% when an object has three or more IOD solutions. The rationality of the space debris intelligent detecting system could be verified by this simulation system. This simulation system also could be an important method of demonstrate key technology for orbit cataloging. The simulation system will lay a foundation for updating and enriching the debris cataloging library in the future.

References

1. Li, C., Ouyang, Z., Heng, D.: Space debris and space environment. Quat. Sci. J. **22**(6), 540–551 (2002)
2. Huang, B.: Space Environment Engineering. National Defense Industry Press, Beijng (1993)
3. Stansbery, G.: Orbital Debris Research in the United States, NASA Orbital Debris Program Office, 1–19 June 2009
4. Barton, D.K., Brillinger, D., El-Shaarawi, A.H.: Final Report of the Haystack Orbital Debris Data Review Panel. NASA, Technical Memorandum 4809 (1998)
5. Monthly Number of Objects in Earth Orbit by Object Type: NASA Orbital Debris Quarterly News 8 (2013)

Traffic Prediction Based Capacity Pre-assignment Scheme for Low Latency in LEO Satellite Communication Systems

Jingyu Tang, Guangxia Li, Dongming Bian[✉], and Jing Hu

PLA Army Engineering University, Nanjing 210001, China
biandm_satlab@163.com

Abstract. Low latency is an important index in LEO satellite communication systems, while the satellite capacity "application-assignment" scheme based on the DVB-RCS2 standard in the return channel causes a long round-trip delay. To improving the quality of experience (QoE), in this paper, a more aggressive capacity pre-assignment scheme combining traffic prediction and free capacity assignment (FCA) is proposed. The network control center (NCC) predicts traffic for every return channel satellite terminal (RCST) and assigns capacities in advance without capacity requests. Several FCA strategies based on multi-frequency time division multiple accesses (MF-TDMA) in the physical layer are analyzed as a compensatory capacity assignment method to deal with the inaccuracy of traffic prediction. Simulation results show that the proposed FCA strategies have better performance than existing FCA strategies.

Keywords: LEO satellite communication systems · Low latency · Network traffic · Traffic prediction · Self-similar model · Free capacity assignment · FARIMA · ARIMA

1 Introduction

As a part of the upcoming sixth-generation (6G) mobile communication network, the low earth orbit (LEO) satellite communication network will play an important role in the future for providing global coverage [1]. According to the 6G white paper [2], 6G will focus on the quality of experience (QoE), which has higher requirements in latency. However, satellite communication has inherent inferiority in latency, even it is the LEO satellite system. Generally speaking, the transmission delay in packet-based networks including access delay, propagation delay, and processing delay. The processing delay is relative to the processing performance and congestion control, which accounts for a tiny minority of the whole transmission delay when the traffic load is low. The propagation delay in LEO satellite communication systems is shortened by routing optimization in the inter-satellite link (ISL) [3]. In this paper, the access delay is what we are interested in.

© ICST Institute for Computer Sciences, Social Informatics and Telecommunications Engineering 2021
Published by Springer Nature Switzerland AG 2021. All Rights Reserved
Q. Wu et al. (Eds.): WiSATS 2020, LNICST 357, pp. 9–20, 2021.
https://doi.org/10.1007/978-3-030-69069-4_2

The second-generation digital video broadcasting return channel via satellite (DVB-RCS) protocol [4] defines the medium access scheme for the return channel (uplink channel) via satellite adopts a multi-frequency time division multiple access (MF-TDMA) approach. As shown in Fig. 1, the return channel satellite terminals (RCSTs) need to apply to the network control center (NCC) for capacity. The NCC periodically processes all the capacity requests (CR) received from RCSTs and runs the dynamic capacity allocation (DCA) algorithm to form a terminal burst time plan (TBTP) which is broadcasted to all the RCSTs through forwarding link. The RCSTs receive the TBTP and transmit signal in the specified time–frequency interval according to the TBTP. This round-trip delay may up to hundreds of milliseconds in LEO satellite communication systems depend on the distance between the RCST and the NCC. One of the problems caused by the round-trip delay is the mismatch between capacity requests and capacity assignments. Capacity assignments always lag behind capacity requests by a round-trip time (RTT). To tackle with the latency, the traffic prediction is used in the DBA for DVB-RCS2 systems [5]. The traffic prediction methods can be roughly divided into two categories: one is relying on proper statistical traffic modeling [6, 7] and the other is using a time series prediction model including ARIMA [8, 9], LSTM [10], BPNN [11], and so on.

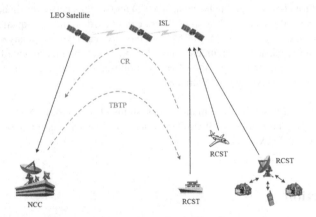

Fig. 1. The return channel via LEO satellites for capacity requests

However, the traffic prediction is inevitably inaccurate, especially when the traffic is relatively random, there will be a large deviation between the predicted traffic and the real traffic. A compensatory capacity assignment must be carried to satisfy the real capacity requests. The DVB-RCS2 standard provides five CR types including continuous rate assignment (CRA), rate-based dynamic capacity (RBDC), volume-based dynamic capacity (VBDC), absolute volume-based dynamic capacity (AVBDC) and free capacity assignment (FCA). Noticing that the FCA is not a true CR and it is trying to allocate the unused capacity to RCSTs. It seems that the FCA can be the compensatory capacity assignment method that assigns additional capacities on the basis of predicted capacity requests to RCSTs to satisfy the real capacity requests. As far as we know, there is no research on combining the traffic prediction and the FCA in the MF-TDMA structure, even the research on the strategy of FCA is rare.

The traffic prediction for DVB-RCS systems mentioned previously is generally carried out by the RCSTs and still need to send CR to the NCC. In this paper, based on the demand assigned multiple access (DAMA) protocol in the link layer and MF-TDMA structure in the physical layer, we propose a more aggressive capacity pre-assignment scheme for low latency in the LEO satellite communication system. The traffic prediction is implemented by the NCC and doesn't need the RCSTs' CR. Several FCA strategies are introduced to satisfy different performance requirements.

The rest of this paper is organized as follows: Sect. 2 introduces the FARIMA model for network traffic simulation and the ARIMA model for traffic prediction. In Sect. 3, several FCA strategies are analyzed from different points of view. Section 4 presents and analyzes the simulation results. Section 5 concludes the paper.

2 Traffic Prediction

2.1 Self-similar Traffic Model

The LEO satellite communication network provides Internet access services. It has been proved that the network traffic is self-similar [12] which has the nature of long-range dependence (LRD). That is to say, when the traffic flow is measured in a large range of time scales, the traffic flow will show self-similar characteristics. The common models for simulating the network traffic including the ON/OFF model [13], FARIMA model [14], FBM model [15], and so on. In fact, in our scheme, the traffic prediction operates in a short range of time scales. Therefore, the traffic model is required to describe both long-range and short-range dependence (SRD) simultaneously. The FARIMA model has better performance in that aspect, hence, we adopt the FARIMA model for its applicability in our simulations to simulate the network traffic. The FARIMA model generates self-similar traffic by driving an ARMA (p, q) process by a fractionally differenced noise FARIMA $(0, d, 0)$, where d is a fractal coefficient and $0 < d < 0.5$. The details of the FARIMA model can refer to [14]. The steps to generate a FARIMA (p, d, q) by definition are as follows:

Step 1: Generating a white noise sequence ε_t with zero mean and variance equal to σ^2.

Step 2: Choosing an approximate value of d and doing fractional differencing on ε_t, we obtain fractional noise ω_t. The fractional differencing filter's unit impulse response is

$$h(n) = (-1)^n \binom{-d}{n} \tag{1}$$

where

$$\binom{-d}{n} = \frac{\Gamma(1-d)}{\Gamma(n+1)\Gamma(1-d-n)} = \frac{-d(-d-1)\cdots(-d-n+1)}{n!} \tag{2}$$

Step 3: Determining the approximate (p, q) combination and driving the ARMA (p, q) by the fractional noise ω_t. Finally, we obtain a FARIMA (p, d, q) series X_t which can simulate the self-similar traffic.

2.2 Traffic Prediction Model

The traffic prediction in our scheme is implemented on the NCC side. The NCC can record the traffic volume from each RCST over a period of time. Therefore, the only information the NCC needs to predict traffic is the previous traffic volume and the traffic prediction belongs to the time series prediction. As mentioned before, the time series prediction model including ARIMA, LSTM, BPNN, and so on. In the scheme we proposed, there are two points we have to note. Firstly, the traffic prediction method should be simple with less computation. The NCC needs to predict traffic for every RCST which leads to a huge computational burden for the NCC. Secondly, even though the network traffic has the LRD, the SRD affects the traffic prediction result much more because of the traffic prediction operates in a short range of time scales. Therefore we adopt the classical ARIMA model for the traffic prediction. Many papers preprocess the traffic before the ARIMA model to predict traffic for more accuracy. Such as Han and Li et al. combine wavelet transform and ARIMA [8, 9], Huang et al. combine ARIMA and artificial neural network (ANN) to deal with the linear part of the historical load data by ARIMA and the nonlinear part of historical load data by ANN [16]. Under the computing power allows, the more prediction accuracy the better. But in this paper, we just use the ARIMA model as long as the model extracts enough information from the traffic time series, and the residual error between real data and predicted data obeys normal distribution which means there is little information that can be extracted from the residual error.

We obtained the real network traffic which is the daily traces at the transit link of WIDE to the upstream ISP (Internet Service Provider) from the *MAWI Working Group of the WIDE Project* [17]. The real traffic packets are counted every 100 ms and it is assumed that all the packets are identical without loss of generality. Figure 2 shows the 200 points of real traffic time series prediction result by the ARIMA method. We can see that the real traffic has strong randomness that the traffic prediction is not enough

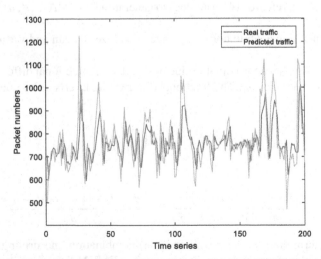

Fig. 2. The real traffic time series prediction result by the ARIMA method

to satisfy the traffic demand. Figure 3 shows the normal distribution fitting of residual error about 1000 points of real traffic time series prediction results. The residual error basically accords with zero mean normal distribution which is a benefit for the analysis of FCA strategies introduced in the next section.

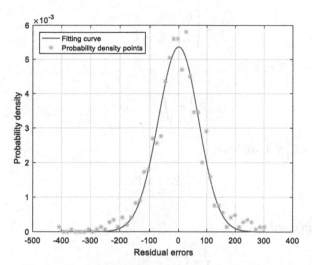

Fig. 3. The normal distribution fitting of residual errors

3 FCA Strategies

After the NCC predicted traffic for the RCSTs, the DCA algorithm calculates the capacity satisfying the predicted traffic demand for each RCST. More concretely, the capacity in the MF-TDMA approach is the timeslot. When there are timeslots remain unused, the unused timeslots can be appropriately assigned to each RCST. Assuming that the capacity assign cycle is a superframe period, for example, 265 ms. Let T_{tot} denotes the total timeslots in a superframe. N_T denotes the number of RCSTs. R_i denotes the average number of packets that the i th RCST can transmit per timeslot depends on channel conditions, where $1 \leq i \leq N_T$. C_i and C_i^* denote the real and predicted number of packets respectively that the i th RCST will transmit, where $\sum_{i=1}^{N_T} \frac{C_i^*}{R_i} < T_{tot}$. σ_i^2 denotes the variance of the residual error of the traffic prediction for the i th RCST and the corresponding residual error distribution is

$$g_i(c) = \frac{1}{\sqrt{2\pi}\sigma_i} e^{-\frac{c^2}{2\sigma_i^2}} \qquad (3)$$

where $c = C_i - C_i^*$. The FCA strategy assigns the unused timeslots into N RCSTs, represented as $X = \{x_1, x_2, ..., x_{N_T}\}$.

3.1 The Strategy of Fairness

A fair FCA strategy is assigning the unused timeslots to the RCSTs to make every RCST has an equal expected satisfaction rate $E[R_s]$. The satisfaction rate for the ith RCST is defined as

$$R_s^i = \begin{cases} 0, & x_i R_i + C_i^* < C_i \\ 1, & x_i R_i + C_i^* \geq C_i \end{cases} \tag{4}$$

Let $x = C_i - C_i^*$ we have

$$E\left[R_s^i\right] = \int_{-\infty}^{x_i R_i} g_i(x) dx \tag{5}$$

Let $E\left[R_s^i\right] = E\left[R_s^j\right]$, we have

$$\frac{x_i R_i}{\sigma_i} = \frac{x_j R_j}{\sigma_j} \tag{6}$$

The X is subjected to

$$\sum_{i=1}^{N_T} \frac{C_i^*}{R_i} + x_i = T_{tot} \tag{7}$$

Combining (6) and (7) we have

$$x_i = \left(T_{tot} - \sum_{j=1}^{N_T} \frac{C_j^*}{R_j} \right) \frac{\frac{\sigma_i}{R_i}}{\sum_{j=1}^{N_T} \frac{\sigma_j}{R_j}} \tag{8}$$

3.2 The Strategy of Minimizing Wasted Timeslots

When the assigned timeslots are far more than the RCSTs require, redundant timeslots are wasted. The more redundant timeslots for some RCSTs, the more likely the assigned timeslots are unsatisfied with other RCSTs. Hence, reducing wasted timeslots is equal to increasing the satisfaction rate. We hope the wasted timeslots to be minimized.

The timeslots waste function is constructed as

$$W(X) = \sum_{i=1}^{N_T} \max \left\{ x_i + \frac{C_i^*}{R_i} - \frac{C_i}{R_i}, 0 \right\} \tag{9}$$

The expected value $W(X)$ is

$$E[W(X)] = \sum_{i=1}^{N_T} \int_{-\infty}^{x_i} (x_i - x) f_i(x) dx \tag{10}$$

where $f_i(x) = g_i(xR_i)$. The problem of minimizing wasted timeslots can be modeled as

$$opt. \min_X \sum_{i=1}^{N_T} \int_{-\infty}^{x_i} (x_i - x)f_i(x)dx$$

$$s.t. \sum_{i=1}^{N_T} \frac{C_i^*}{R_i} + x_i = T_{tot}$$

(11)

Obviously, this problem can be solved by convex optimization method, and the Lagrange function of problem (11) is

$$U(X; \lambda) = \sum_{i=1}^{N_T} \int_{-\infty}^{x_i} (x_i - x)f_i(x)dx + \lambda \left(T_{tot} - \sum_{i=1}^{N_T} \frac{C_i^*}{R_i} - x_i \right)$$

(12)

Let the partial derivative of $U(X; \lambda)$ being zero, we obtain

$$\begin{cases} \int_{-\infty}^{x_i} f_i(x)dx - \lambda = 0 \\ T_{tot} - \sum_{i=1}^{N_T} \frac{C_i^*}{R_i} - x_i = 0 \end{cases}$$

(13)

Combining (13) and $f_i(x) = g_i(xR_i)$ we have

$$x_i = \left(T_{tot} - \sum_{j=1}^{N_T} \frac{C_j^*}{R_j} \right) \frac{\frac{\sigma_i}{R_i}}{\sum_{j=1}^{N_T} \frac{\sigma_j}{R_j}}$$

(14)

Noticing that the result of minimizing expected wasted timeslots is the same as the result of an equal expected satisfaction rate.

3.3 The Strategy of Maximizing Throughput

The throughput for the ith RCST is $\min\{x_iR_i, C_i\}$. We construct the throughput function as

$$M(X) = \sum_{i=1}^{N_T} \min\{C_i^* + x_iR_i, C_i\}$$

(15)

The expected value $M(X)$ is

$$E[M(X)] = \sum_{i=1}^{N_T} \left[\int_{-\infty}^{x_i} xR_if_i(x)dx + \int_{x_i}^{+\infty} x_iR_if_i(x)dx + C_i^* \right]$$

(16)

The problem of maximizing throughput can be modeled as

$$opt. \quad \max_X \sum_{i=1}^{N_T} \left[\int_{-\infty}^{x_i} x R_i f_i(x) dx + \int_{x_i}^{+\infty} x_i R_i f_i(x) dx \right]$$

$$s.t. \quad \sum_{i=1}^{N_T} \frac{C_i^*}{R_i} + x_i = T_{tot} \tag{17}$$

It also can be proved that (17) is a convex problem, and the Lagrange function of problem (17) is

$$V(X; u) = \sum_{i=1}^{N_T} \left[\int_{-\infty}^{x_i} x R_i f_i(x) dx + \int_{x_i}^{+\infty} x_i R_i f_i(x) dx \right] + u \left(T_{tot} - \sum_{i=1}^{N_T} \frac{C_i^*}{R_i} - x_i \right) \tag{18}$$

Let the partial derivative of $V(X; u)$ being zero, we obtain

$$\begin{cases} R_i \int_{x_i}^{+\infty} f_i(x) dx - u = 0 \\ T_{tot} - \sum_{i=1}^{N_T} \frac{C_i^*}{R_i} - x_i = 0 \end{cases} \tag{19}$$

Combining (19) and $f_i(x) = g_i(x R_i)$ we have

$$\begin{cases} x_i = F_i^{-1} \left(1 - \frac{u}{R_i} \right) \\ \sum_{i=1}^{N_T} F_i^{-1} \left(1 - \frac{u}{R_i} \right) = T_{tot} - \sum_{i=1}^{N_T} \frac{C_i^*}{R_i} \end{cases} \tag{20}$$

where $F_i^{-1}(\cdot)$ is the inverse function of $F_i(\cdot)$ and $F_i(\cdot)$ is the cumulative distribution function of $f_i(\cdot)$.

4 Performance Evaluations

The FCA strategies analyzed in Section III can be integrated into two categories. For simplicity, in this paper, the strategies of fairness and minimizing wasted timeslots are abbreviated as FCA-F, and the strategy of maximizing throughput is abbreviated as FCA-MT. For comparison, another two FCA strategies used in the Combined Free/Demand Assignment Multiple Access (CFDAMA) protocol which is a TDMA based access scheme are introduced. In CFDAMA protocols, after demand assignment, the unused timeslots can be assigned to all the ground terminals in round-robin fashion [18] or weighted free assignment fashion [19]. We abbreviate the round-robin fashion FCA as FCA-RR and the weighted free assignment fashion FCA as FCA-WFA. To simulate various network traffics, we generate different FARIMA (p, d, q) sequences plus different traffic mean values C_m to represent the packets sequences the RCSTs transmit. The simulation parameters are shown in Table 1. In the simulations below, we adopt the time average substitute for statistical expectation. The average traffic load is defined as the mean value of timeslots that the RCSTs request and the average traffic load divides total timeslots per superframe T_{tot} for normalization.

Table 1.

Parameter	Value
Network traffic parameter	
White noise sequence variance σ^2	50–500
Fractal coefficient d	0–0.5
ARMA parameter p	0.6–0.9
ARMA parameter (q_1, q_2)	(0.3–0.5, 0.1–0.3)
Traffic mean value C_m	500–5000
Satellite system parameter	
RCSTs number N_T	10, 30, 80
Superframe period	265 ms
Total timeslots per superframe T_{tot}	848
Packets transmitted per timeslot R_i	40–80

Figure 4 compared the expected satisfaction rate of four FCA strategies with the RCSTs number is 10. The min SR and max SR denote the minimum and maximum average satisfaction rate in 10 RCSTs, respectively. The smaller difference between max SR and min SR, the fairer. As we can see, in terms of fairness, the two FCA strategies we proposed significantly better than the FCA-RR and the FCA-WFA. The FCA-F is the fairest that almost all the RCSTs have the same expected satisfaction rate.

Figure 5 compared the throughput of three FCA strategies with the RCSTs number is 10. As analyzed before, the FCA-MT has maximum throughput compare to the other three FCA strategies. In terms of throughput, the FCA-MT > FCA-F > FCA-WFA > FCA-RR.

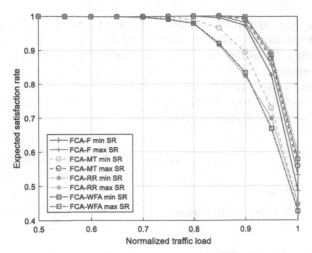

Fig. 4. Fairness comparison between three FCA strategies

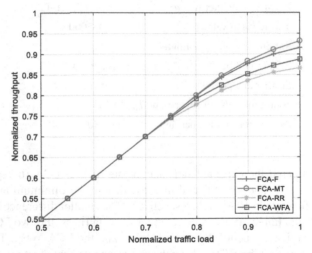

Fig. 5. Throughput comparison between four FCA strategies

Another interesting data is the influence of the number of RCSTs. Figure 6 compared the throughput uses the FCA-MT when the number of RCSTs is 10, 30, and 80. As the number of RCSTs increases, the throughput is descending with the same traffic load. Therefore, to obtain a higher satisfaction rate and throughput, the free capacity must be sufficient and the number of RCSTs should be limited, which means that the scheme we proposed is more suitable for non-high-load scenarios.

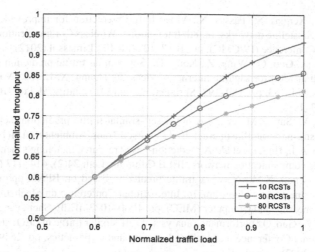

Fig. 6. Throughput comparison between different RCSTs numbers

5 Conclusion

In this paper, a novel capacity pre-assignment scheme combines traffic prediction and FCA is proposed. We adopt the FARIMA model for network traffic simulation and the ARIMA model for traffic prediction. Several FCA strategies are analyzed to appropriately assign unused timeslots based on MF-TDMA in the physical layer. Simulations show that our scheme can achieve a high expected satisfaction rate in non-high-load scenarios, but the throughput is limited in high-load scenarios. In our future work, the traffic will be further classified to make the traffic prediction more accurate which makes our scheme available for high-load scenarios.

References

1. Giordani, M., Zorzi, M.: Non-terrestrial communication in the 6G era: challenges and opportunities. Submitted to the IEEE (2019). https://arxiv.org/abs/1912.10226?context=cs.NI
2. Aazhang, B., Ahokangas, P., Alves, H., et al.: Key drivers and research challenges for 6G ubiquitous wireless intelligence (white paper) (2019)
3. Yan, D., Wang, L.: TPDR: traffic prediction based dynamic routing for LEO&GEO satellite networks. In: 2015 IEEE 5th International Conference on Electronics Information and Emergency Communication, pp. 104–107. IEEE, Beijing (2015)
4. ETSI EN 301 545–2 V1.2.1: Digital Video Broadcasting (DVB); Second Generation DVB Interactive Satellite System (DVB-RCS2); Part 2: Lower Layers for Satellite standard, April 2014
5. Priscoli, F.D., Pompili, D.: A demand-assignment algorithm based on a Markov modulated chain prediction model for satellite bandwidth allocation. Wireless Netw. **15**(8), 999–1012 (2009)
6. Chiti, F., Fantacci, R., Pecorella, T., Giacomelli, L., et al.: An improved dynamic bandwidth allocation scheme based on traffic prediction for DVB-RCS systems. In: The 1st International Conference on Advanced Satellite Mobile Systems ASMS, pp. 254–263. European Space Agency (Special Publication), Frascati (2003)

7. Lygizou, A., Xergias, S., Passas, N.: Video traffic prediction for improved scheduling in joint WiMAX/satellite networks. In: 8th International Wireless Communications and Mobile Computing Conference (IWCMC), pp. 1017–1022. IEEE, Limassol (2012)

8. Han, Y., Li, D., Guo, Q., Wang, Z., Kong, D.: Self-similar traffic prediction scheme based on wavelet transform for satellite internet services. In: Huang, X.-L. (ed.) MLICOM 2016. LNICSSITE, vol. 183, pp. 189–197. Springer, Cham (2017). https://doi.org/10.1007/978-3-319-52730-7_19

9. Li, C., Han, Y., Sun, Z.M., et al.: A novel self-similar traffic prediction method based on wavelet transform for satellite internet. EAI Endorsed Trans. Ambient Syst. 4(14), 1–5 (2017)

10. Han, C., Liu, A.J., Huo, L., et al.: A prediction-based resource matching scheme for rentable LEO satellite communication network. IEEE Commun. Lett. 24(2), 414–417 (2020)

11. Cheng, S.Y., Zhou, X.M.: Network traffic prediction based on BPNN optimized by self-adaptive immune genetic algorithm. In: International Conference on Mechatronic Sciences, Electric Engineering and Computer (MEC), pp. 1030–1033. IEEE, Shengyang (2013)

12. Na, Z., Gao, Z., Guo, Q.: performance analysis of self-similar traffic in LEO satellite network. In: International Conference on Machine Learning and Cybernetics, pp. 2649–2652. IEEE, Hong Kong (2007)

13. Marvi, M., Aijaz, A., Khurram, M.: On the use of ON/OFF traffic models for spatio-temporal analysis of wireless networks. IEEE Commun. Lett. 23(7), 1219–1222 (2019)

14. Liu, J.K., Shu, Y.T., Zhang, L.F., et al.: Traffic modeling based on FARIMA models. In: IEEE Canadian Conference on Electrical and Computer Engineering, pp. 162–167. IEEE, Alberta (1999)

15. Tan, X., Huang, Y., Jin, W.: Modeling and performance analysis of self-similar traffic based on FBM. In: International Conference on Network and Parallel Computing Workshops, pp. 543–548. IEEE, Liaoning (2007)

16. Huang, H.Q., Tang, T.H.: Short-term traffic flow forecasting based on ARIMA-ANN. In: International Conference on Control and Automation, pp. 2370–2373. IEEE Guangzhou (2007)

17. MAWI Working Group Traffic Archive Homepage. https://mawi.wide.ad.jp/mawi/

18. Mitchell, P.D., Grace, D., Tozer, T.C.: Comparative performance of the CFDAMA protocol via satellite with various terminal request strategies. In: IEEE Global Telecommunications Conference, pp. 2720–2724. IEEE, San Antonio (2001)

19. Zhou, X., Wang, Z.J., Cao L.H., She, Y.: Performance of CFDAMA-CFA multiple access protocol via satellite. In: 1st International Symposium on Systems and Control in Aerospace and Astronautics, pp. 1038–1040. IEEE, Harbin (2006)

Distributed Cooperative Positioning Algorithm Based on Message Passing Using Box Particles in UAVs Networks

Lu Lu[1]($\boxtimes$), Mingxing Ke[2], Guangxia Li[1], Shiwen Tian[1], and Tianwei Liu[1]

[1] Institute of Communications Engineering, Army Engineering University of PLA Nanjing, Nanjing, China
lulu_is@163.com

[2] College of Electronic Countermeasures, National University of Defense Technology, Hefei, China

Abstract. Distributed cooperative positioning has become more and more attractive for large-scale unmanned aerial vehicles (UAVs) networks. In this paper, inspired by the box particle filter which combines interval analysis and Monte Carlo methods, a novel distributed cooperative positioning algorithm named Box-Particles Message Passing (BPMP) is proposed. In BPMP, the expressions of messages cannot be obtained in a closed form by belief propagation (BP) algorithm due to the nonlinearity of models and the complexity of computation. Accordingly, we use non-parametric belief propagation (NBP) also known as message passing methodology with a set of box particles to solve the inference problem of cooperative positioning on factor graph (FG) model in a 3-dimensional UAVs network. The proposed BPMP algorithm can reduce the number of particles while maintaining high accuracy. Simulation results demonstrate the effectiveness of proposed BPMP algorithm.

Keywords: UAVs networks · Cooperative positioning · Factor graph · Belief propagation · Box particles · Interval analysis

1 Introduction

The unmanned aerial vehicles (UAVs) networks are increasingly covered in diverse applications such as entertainment, security, surveillance. In these applications, the position information plays a significant role. Traditionally, the position information is provided by Global Navigation Satellite System (GNSS) due to its high performance and global coverage. Currently, the navigation of UVA cluster network is mostly based on the GNSS. However, the performance of navigation can be significantly degraded or nulled in the cities, gorges or indoor scenes. Moreover, GNSS signals can be easily disturbed or deceived by electronic counter-measurement. Therefore, novel navigation technique free of GNSS is needed and the concept of cooperative navigation is proposed [1]. In addition, some UAVs cannot be equipped with GNSS module due to the limits of cost

Q. Wu et al. (Eds.): WiSATS 2020, LNICST 357, pp. 21–34, 2021.
https://doi.org/10.1007/978-3-030-69069-4_3

and energy. In a large-scale UAVs network, it is impossible to manually position and it may lead to a communication bottleneck by a central system. Therefore, distributed structure is preferred for the large-scale networks [2]. As a new and popular method to resolve these problems, distributed cooperative positioning, incorporating peer-to-peer range measurements and exchanging position information between neighboring nodes, has attracted more and more attentions due to its ability to enhance the position accuracy and to improve availability [3].

Various algorithms have been proposed for distributed cooperative positioning. Generally, current methods can be divided into deterministic and probabilistic algorithms. A well-known deterministic algorithm is the least-square (LS) method, considering positioning as an optimization problem. Unlike deterministic algorithm, the probabilistic methods assign probability distributions for the whole space and attempt to avoid the trap of local optima [4].

Probabilistic graphical models such as Bayesian network and Markov random fields provide flexible and appealing tools for solving estimates problems with un-certainty in terms of network structures [5]. There have been several related inference methods under probabilistic graphical models. An attractive approach is the belief propagation (BP), which is also known as message passing or sum–product algorithm. It can efficiently perform exact or approximate marginalization [6]. Currently, the most important branch of BP algorithms is based on parametric messages. The parametric messages exchanged between neighboring nodes are represented by their means and variances [7]. Another branch, using particles to approximate the position distribution, is named non-parametric message passing (NBP) [8]. When the expression of UAV state transition equation and measurement equation is complicated, it is difficult or impossible to use a specific parameter to describe the state information. In this case, the state information can be described by a nonparametric method. In the confidence propagation algorithm, non-parametric belief propagation (NBP), based on particle filter, uses a set of weighted particles to approximate the distribution of states. A distributed cooperative positioning algorithm based on non-parametric belief propagation (NBP) for static networks was proposed in [9] and [10].

Nevertheless, a large number of particles should be used to improve the accuracy of the NBP, which leads to a high computational complexity and introduces communication overhead. Hence, it is strongly demanded to find a method to reduce the number of particles while maintaining high accuracy. As an alternative to the traditional NBP approaches, a novel distributed BPMP algorithm for cooperation positioning is proposed in UAVs networks. With the approximations, all messages passed on factor graph (FG) can be represented in the non-parametric forms with box particles which can significantly reduce computational complexity and improve communication cost.

2   Problem Formulation and System Model

A UAVs network can be divided into two types of UAVs. Those UAVs with known positions are anchor nodes A, while those with unknown positions are agent nodes B, S represents a collection of all UAVs, where $|S| = A + B$, $A = \{a_1, a_2, \cdots, a_n\}$ and $B = \{b_1, b_2, \cdots, b_m\}$. Let $X_i^k = (x_i^k, v_i^k)^T$, $i \in S$ denotes the state of the i - th UAV at time k comprising its position vector $\boldsymbol{x}_i^k \triangleq \left[x_i^k, y_i^k, z_i^k\right]^T$ and velocity vector v_i^k. An example scheme of partial network for UAVs can be seen in Fig. 1.

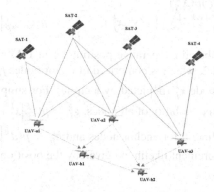

Fig. 1. An example scheme of partial network for UAVs.

In general, the nonlinear state-evolution model of UAV i can be given by

$$X_i^k = \mathrm{F}_i^k(X_i^{k-1}, \boldsymbol{Q}_i^k), i \in S \tag{1}$$

For anchor nodes at time step k, the GNSS observation model is modeled as

$$Y_i^k = G_i^k(X_i^k, b_i^k, \boldsymbol{P}_i^k), i \in A \tag{2}$$

Moreover, all agent nodes perform range measurements with its neighboring UAVs. We assume that the range measurement between node i and j is less than the communication radius R in line-of-sight environment. Consequently, peer-to-peer range measurement at the k th slot can be given as:

$$Z_{ij}^k = H(x_i^k, x_j^k, \boldsymbol{R}^k) = \|x_i^k - x_j^k\| + \boldsymbol{R}^k, i, j \in B \tag{3}$$

where $F(\bullet)$ is the motion state transition function, $G(\bullet)$ and $H(\bullet)$ are nonlinear observation function, $\boldsymbol{Q}_i^k$ represents the system noise, $\boldsymbol{P}^k$ and $\boldsymbol{R}^k$ are the additive white Gaussian noise and $\boldsymbol{R}_{ij}^k = \boldsymbol{R}_{ji}^k$, the $\|\bullet\|$ denotes the Euclidean distance. Within the Bayesian framework, the distributed cooperation positioning in UAVs networks can be substantially formulated as an inference problem on a graphical model.

3 Factor Graph Based and Belief Propagation

Generally, direct marginalization is intractable as the high dimensional integration. To solve this problem, we can employ FG model and BP algorithm for an efficient calculation [6]. Suppose that mobility is modeled as a Markov process, mutually independent for all UAVs, based on the Bayesian criterion and FG, a complex positioning problem in

UAVs networks at time step k can be break down into factors as

$$p(X_S^k | Z^k)$$
$$\propto p(Z^k | X_S^k) p(X_S^k)$$
$$\propto \prod_{i \in S} p(X_i^k | X_i^{k-1}) \prod_{j \in A} p(y_j^k | x_j^k) \prod_{\alpha \in S, \beta \in n(\alpha)} p(d_{\alpha \to \beta}^k | x_\alpha^k, x_\beta^k) \tag{4}$$

A factor graph for distributed cooperative positioning in UAVs network as shown in Fig. 1 is depicted in Fig. 2, which is comprised of factor nodes f_i^k, g_i^k, h_{ij}^k (depicted by a squares) and variable node x_i^k (depicted by a circle). For simplicity, we define $f_i^k \triangleq p(X_i^k | X_i^{k-1})$ represents the mobility of all nodes, $g_i^k \triangleq p(y_i^k | x_i^k)$ represents the pseudo range measurement likelihood for anchor nodes and $h_{ij}^k \triangleq p(d^k | x_i^k, x_j^k)$ represents the peer-to-peer range measurement likelihood given by the positions of agent nodes i and j.

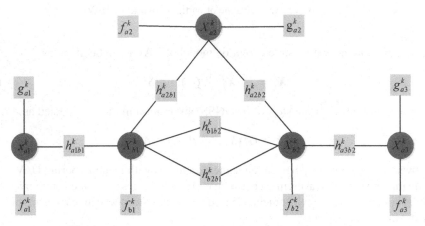

Fig. 2. Factor graph of partial UAVs network at time step k.

BP algorithm, passing messages along the edges between the nodes, is an appropriate tool with the advantage of convenient to get the posterior marginal probability on FG [11]. In BP, at time step k, the message from node i to j at time step k is denoted as

$$m_{ij}^k(x_j) = \int \psi(x_i, x_j) \psi(x_i) \prod_{h \in Neb(i) \backslash j} m_{hi}(x_i) dx_i \tag{5}$$

The belief of node i can be approximated as the posterior marginal $p(x_i | Z)$.

4 Non-parametric Message Passing with Box Particle

Interval analysis is an effective tool to deal with bounded uncertainties [12]. In this section, basic notions of interval analysis and constraints satisfaction problems (CSP) which are also known as consistency techniques are presented firstly. Then, a box-particles message passing (BPMP) algorithm that uses interval analysis method is introduced.

4.1 Basic Notions of Interval Analysis

A real interval denoted $[x]$ in $\mathbb{R}$ is defined as

$$[x] = [\underline{x}, \bar{x}] = \{x \in \mathbb{R} | \underline{x} \le x \le \bar{x}\} \qquad (6)$$

A box $[x]$ is defined as a Cartesian product of n-dimensional intervals can be expressed

$$[x] = [x_1] \times [x_2] \times \cdots \times [x_n] \qquad (7)$$

Where $\mathbb{R}$ is a closed and connected subset, $\underline{x}$ and $\bar{x}$ refer to the lower and upper bound of interval $[x]$ respectively. $|[x]| = \bar{x} - \underline{x}$ denotes the length of an interval $[x]$.

The usual arithmetic operations for intervals are given by [12]

$$[x] \pm [y] = [\underline{x} \pm \underline{y}, \bar{x} \pm \bar{y}] \qquad (8)$$

$$[x] \times [y] = [\min(\underline{xy}, \underline{x}\bar{y}, \bar{x}\underline{y}, \bar{x}\bar{y}), \max(\underline{xy}, \underline{x}\bar{y}, \bar{x}\underline{y}, \bar{x}\bar{y})] \qquad (9)$$

If the interval $[y]$ does not include the 0 value,

$$[x]/[y] = [x] \times [1/\bar{y}, 1/\underline{y}] \qquad (10)$$

Furthermore, elementary functions such as exp, ln, cos and sin, can be simply extended to intervals. All operations on intervals also can be extended to boxes.

In order to accelerate convergence velocity and reduce computational complexity, it is necessary to find inclusion functions $[f]$ approximating the image of $f(x)$ in a reasonable time.

Definition 1 (Inclusion function). Let f be a function from $\mathbb{R}^n$ to $\mathbb{R}^m$. The interval function $[f]$ is an inclusion function from $\mathbb{IR}^n$ to $\mathbb{IR}^m$ for f if

$$f([x]) \subseteq [f]([x]), \forall [x] \in \mathbb{IR}^n \qquad (11)$$

If f is continuous and monotonic, $[f]([x])$ is equal to $f([x])$. However, if f is a no monotonic continuous function, the computation of $[f]$ is usually not straight forward [18].

4.2 Constrains Satisfaction Problem

Another important concept in interval analysis is the constraints satisfaction problem (CSP). The goal of CSP is to find the smallest box $[x'] \subseteq [x]$ constraining the set of all x in the initial domain$[x]$ which satisfies the constraints f. The CSP can be denoted as $\mathbb{C}$ and formulated as follows [13]:

$$\mathbb{C} : (f(x) = 0, x \in [x]) \qquad (12)$$

The solution set of the CSP $\mathbb{C}$ is given by

$$\mathbb{C} = \{x \in [x] | f(x) = 0\} \qquad (13)$$

An contraction designates replacing [x] by a smaller domain $[x']$ such that

$$S \subseteq [x'] \subseteq [x] \tag{14}$$

A simple and efficient contraction algorithm is constraints propagation (CP) method [14] which is independent of nonlinearities.

4.3 Box-Particle Message Passing

The key idea of BPMP is to use weighted box particles instead of weighted point samples representations to approximate the operations of non-Parametric Message on FG models. In BPMP, there are three main components, described as prediction message, update message and cooperative message respectively.

Prediction Message. Considering the box particles $\left\{\left[X_{k-1}^b\right], \omega^b\right\}_{b=1}^B$ representing the state at time step $k-1$, the boxes particles at time step k can be passed through the state transition function.

$$\left[X_k^b\right] = [F]\left(\left[X_{k-1}^b\right], [Q_k]\right), b = 1, \cdots, B \tag{15}$$

Where $[F]$ is an inclusion function for the state transition function F, the system noise is enclosed in $[Q_k]$.

At time step k, the prediction message $M_f(X_i^k)$ is defined as

$$
\begin{aligned}
M_f(X_i^k) &= \int p(X_i^k | X_i^{k-1}) \sum_{b=1}^{B} w_{k-1}^b U_{\left[X_{k-1}^b\right]}(X_i^{k-1}) dX_i^{k-1} \\
&= \sum_{b=1}^{B} w_{k-1}^b \int_{\left[X_{k-1}^b\right]} p(X_i^k | X_i^{k-1}) U_{\left[X_{k-1}^b\right]}(X_i^{k-1}) dX_i^{k-1} \\
&= \sum_{b=1}^{B} w_{k-1}^b U_{[F]}\left(\left[X_{k-1}^b\right], [Q_k]\right)
\end{aligned}
\tag{16}
$$

Where $U_{[x]}$ denotes the uniform distribution of the box $[X]$.

Update Message
The main purpose of this step is to update the predicted box-particles message using the contraction described above at time step k. For anchor node, the contraction can be represented using the intersection between the predicted box $[z_k] = [x_{ki}]$ and the observation box $[\hat{z}_k]$, where $\hat{z}_k$ is the GPS information of anchor nodes at time k.

For agent nodes, let $[\hat{z}_k]$ denote the range measurement between anchor node j and agent node i, the observation is the range measurement, then the predict box updated by

$$\left[\hat{Z}_k\right] = \sqrt{([X_{ki}^b(1)] - X_j(1))^2 + ([X_{ki}^b(2)] - X_j(2))^2 + ([X_{ki}^b(3)] - X_j(3))^2} \tag{17}$$

Therefore, the updated box can be expressed as

$$[R_k] = [\hat{z}_k] \cap [z_k] \tag{18}$$

If $R_k \notin \emptyset$, we can contract $[x_{ki}]$ with $[R_k]$ by CP algorithm [14].

Cooperative Message. The cooperative message $M_{ji}^k(x_i^k)$ can be expressed as

$$M_{ji}^k(x_i^k) = \int \psi(x_j^k, x_i^k) \prod_{h \in Neb(j) \setminus i} m_{hj}(x_j^k) dx_j^k \tag{19}$$

Where $Neb(j) \setminus i$ denotes the set of neighbors of agent node j except node i.

The message $m_{hj}(x_j^k)$ from the node h to the agent node j can be represented using N weighted boxes $\left\{ \left[x_{hij}^{nl} \right], \omega_{hij}^{nl} \right\}_{nl=1}^{N}$.

$$m_{h_l}(x_j^k) = \sum_{nl=1}^{N} \omega_{hij}^{nl} U_{\left[x_{hij}^{nl} \right]}(x_j^k), l = 1, \cdots, L \tag{20}$$

Where L denoted the number of the neighborhood nodes.

Replacing the expression above in that of the message product according algorithm1, we can obtain $M_{ji}(x_j^k)$ as

$$M_{ji}(x_j^k) = \prod_{h \in Neb(j) \setminus i} m_{hj}(x_j^k)$$

$$\propto \prod_{l=1}^{L} \left(\sum_{nl=1}^{N} \omega_{hij}^{nl} U_{\left[x_{hij}^{nl} \right]}(x_j^k) \right)$$

$$\propto \sum_{n=1}^{N} \omega_{h_1j}^{n1} \cdots \omega_{h_Lj}^{nL} U_{\left[x_{h_1j}^{n1} \right]} \cdots U_{\left[x_{h_Lj}^{nL} \right]}(x_j^k) \tag{21}$$

Table 1 describes the algorithm of combining two messages [14, 15].
Then the message $M_{ji}(x_i^k)$ can be given as

$$M_{ji}(x_i^k) = \int \psi(x_i^k, x_j^k) \sum_N \omega^N U_{[x^N]}(x_i^k) dx_j^k \tag{22}$$

For ease of calculation, the $\psi(x_i^k, x_j^k)$ can be transformed into a form through $x_i^k = f(x_j^k, d, \varepsilon)$ according Fig. 3. Then an inclusion function $[f]$ allowing for converting to the expression of tangent square and inscribed square of the annular.

In Fig. 3, the smallest rectangular region represents the position distribution of cooperative node i, the position of node j should fall on the annular. Assume that the ranging measurement between nodes is d, the error is ε, Then the circular region represents the

Table 1. Message combination algorithm.

---

1. Set $\mathbf{x}$ and ω empty, $N = 0$

2. Message 1 and message 2 are represented by $\left\{\left[\mathbf{x}_1^l\right], \omega_1^l\right\}_{l=1}^{L}$ and $\left\{\left[\mathbf{x}_2^u\right], \omega_2^u\right\}_{u=1}^{U}$

3. For $l = 1 : L$

   For $u = 1 : U$

   If, $\left[\mathbf{x}_1^l\right] \cap \left[\mathbf{x}_2^u\right] \neq \varnothing$,

   $-- k = k + 1$

   $-- \left[\mathbf{x}^N\right] = \left[\mathbf{x}_1^l\right] \cap \left[\mathbf{x}_2^u\right]$

   $-- \omega^N = \omega^l \times \omega^u \times \dfrac{\left[\mathbf{x}_1^l\right] \cap \left[\mathbf{x}_2^u\right]}{\left[\mathbf{x}_1^l\right] \cdot \left[\mathbf{x}_2^u\right]}$

   End for

   End for

4. Normalize the weights, $\omega^n = \omega^n / \sum\limits_{n=1}^{N} \omega^n$

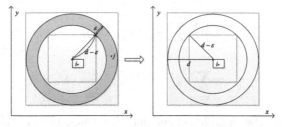

Fig. 3. Projection of ranging model on the XY axis.

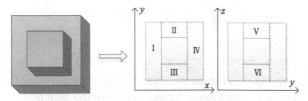

Fig. 4. The diagram of interval partition.

position distribution of the node j. In order to represent the annular region as a box particle, the region is divided into six intervals (Fig. 4).

Let the interval of cooperative node i be expressed as $[\mathbf{x}_i] = [\underline{x}_i, \bar{x}] \times [\underline{y}_i, \bar{y}_i] \times [\underline{z}_i, \bar{z}_i]$ and $[d] = [d - \varepsilon, d], \theta \in [0, \pi]$, then the outer cube area can be expressed as follows

$$
\begin{cases}
[x_b] = [\underline{x}_b, \bar{x}_b] = [x_i] + d \cdot \begin{bmatrix} \cos\theta \\ \sin\theta \end{bmatrix} \\
[y_b] = [\underline{y}_b, \bar{y}_b] = [y_i] + d \cdot \begin{bmatrix} \cos\theta \\ \sin\theta \end{bmatrix} \\
[z_b] = [\underline{z}_b, \bar{z}_b] = [z_i] + d \cdot \begin{bmatrix} \cos\theta \\ \sin\theta \end{bmatrix}
\end{cases} \tag{23}
$$

The inner cube area can be expressed as

$$
\begin{cases}
[x_s] = \left[\underline{x}_i - \sqrt{2}/2(d - \varepsilon), \bar{x}_i + \sqrt{2}/2(d - \varepsilon) \right] \\
[y_s] = \left[\underline{y}_i - \sqrt{2}/2(d - \varepsilon), \bar{y}_i + \sqrt{2}/2(d - \varepsilon) \right] \\
[z_s] = \left[\underline{z}_i - \sqrt{2}/2(d - \varepsilon), \bar{z}_i + \sqrt{2}/2(d - \varepsilon) \right]
\end{cases} \tag{24}
$$

That is, the six intervals divided can be expressed as

$$
\begin{aligned}
&\text{I:} \left[\underline{x}_b, \underline{x}_s \right] \times \left[\underline{y}_b, \overline{y}_b \right] \times \left[\underline{z}_b, \overline{z}_b \right] \\
&\text{II:} \left[\underline{x}_s, \overline{x}_s \right] \times \left[\underline{y}_s, \overline{y}_b \right] \times \left[\underline{z}_b, \overline{z}_b \right] \\
&\text{III:} \left[\underline{x}_s, \overline{x}_s \right] \times \left[\underline{y}_b, \underline{y}_s \right] \times \left[\underline{z}_b, \overline{z}_b \right] \\
&\text{IV:} \left[\overline{x}_s, \overline{x}_b \right] \times \left[\underline{y}_b, \overline{y}_b \right] \times \left[\underline{z}_b, \overline{z}_b \right] \\
&\text{V:} \left[\underline{x}_s, \overline{x}_s \right] \times \left[\underline{y}_s, \overline{y}_s \right] \times \left[\overline{z}_s, \overline{z}_b \right] \\
&\text{VI:} \left[\underline{x}_s, \overline{x}_s \right] \times \left[\underline{y}_s, \overline{y}_s \right] \times \left[\underline{z}_b, \underline{z}_s \right]
\end{aligned} \tag{25}
$$

According to the above formula, the box of node j can be calculated according to the interval of cooperative node i (Table 2).

Table 2. A summary of proposed BPMP algorithm.

Initialize: all UAVs $i \in S$ **in parallel**

---Generate B boxes with the same width and weights $\left\{ \left[\mathbf{X}_0^b \right], \omega_0^b \right\}, \omega_0^b = 1 / N$ for each node

Output: position estimate $\mathbf{X}_i^k$

1. **For time** $k = 1$ **to** K **do**

   $\forall i \in S$ **in parallel do**

2. **Message prediction**

   ---According to prediction message $M_f(x_i^k)$ using (15), get $\left\{ \left[\mathbf{X}_k^b \right], \omega_k^b \right\}_{b=1}^B$

3. **Message update**

   ---Update the prediction message box $\left\{ \left[\mathbf{X}_k^b \right], \omega_k^b \right\}_{b=1}^B$ through the contractions and CP

   algorithm using observation measurement $\left[y_k \right]$, get $\left\{ \left[\mathbf{X}_k^{b\_new} \right], \omega_k^{b\_new} \right\}$.

4. **for iteration** $t = 1 : T$

   for $\forall i \in S$

5. **Cooperative message calculation**

   ---calculate the cooperative message $M_{ji}(\mathbf{x}_i^k)$ boxes according to Algorithm 1and inclusion

   function $\left[f \right]$ using(23) and (24)

6. **end for**

7. **end for**

8. **Belief calculation**

   ---Calculate the belief $b^{(t)}(\mathbf{X}_i^k)$ according to (4) and Algorithm 1

9. **Estimate UAVs' positions using** $\hat{x} = \sum \omega_{k\_bel}^l \left[x_k^l \right]_{bel}$;

---

5 Simulation Results

We evaluate the performance of the proposed BPMP algorithm using Monte Carlo simu-lations. An $100\,\text{m} \times 100\,\text{m} \times 100\,\text{m}$ simulation scenario with 5 anchors (M1, M2,..., M5) and 10 agents (N1, N2,..., N10) is considered. In the simulation scenario, all nodes are randomly scattered and can move independently. For simplicity, ranging measurements are assumed to be performed in line-of-sight environment with 100 m communication range. All results are averaged from 20 independent Monte Carlo simulation runs. We also set the numbers of initial boxes is 10, and the width is 2.

As can be shown in Fig. 5, the true motion trajectories and estimate trajectories using BPMP algorithm of nodes (incluing3 agents and 2 anchors) are convergent.

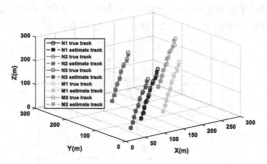

Fig. 5. The true track and estimate track of UAVs.

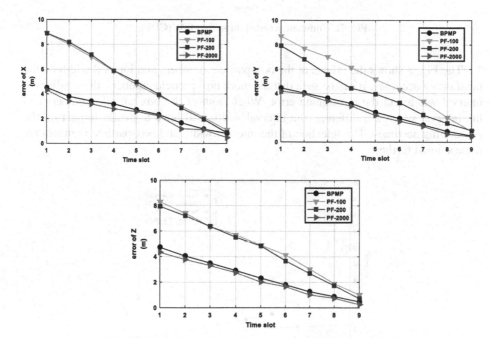

Fig. 6. The estimated error for x, y and z of BPMP and PF.

The Fig. 6 shows the interval error of x, y and z estimated by BPMP, PF-100, PF-200 and PF-2000 respectively. It can be obviously observed that the positioning accuracy of PF and the proposed BPMP algorithm tend to converge with timeslot increasing, and compared with PF, BPMP needs fewer boxes to achieve approximate positioning accuracy, which means the BPMP algorithm need simpler and faster computations and thus more time saving.

According to the Fig. 7, we can see that the positioning accuracy of different positioning algorithms in the UAVs network. The positioning accuracy of BPMP algorithm is better than the particle filter algorithm with fewer particles, and it is close to particle filter algorithm with large number of particles, however, the number of required box particles and resource consumption are significantly reduced.

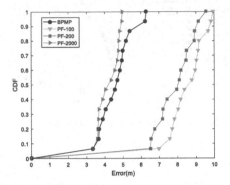

Fig. 7. Cumulative distribution function (CDF).

The Fig. 8 shows the effects of the box-particle numbers and interval width on the positioning accuracy. It can be seen that the more box-particle numbers, the smaller the interval width and the positioning error. When both of the box-particle numbers and the interval width are different, the interval width will have a greater impact on the positioning accuracy. The selection of the interval width and box-particle numbers are to be studied further.

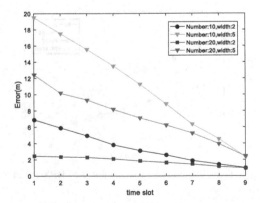

Fig. 8. The effect of the box-particle numbers and the interval width on the positioning accuracy.

6   Conclusion

In this paper, we propose BPMP method based on interval analysis and particles filter to improve the performance of the NBP algorithm. The proposed BPMP algorithm is achieved by box-particles representations of probability quantities to infer on factor graph model for distributed cooperative positioning. Simulation results show that the proposed BPMP algorithm has superior performance compared to PF method BPMP achieves better positioning accuracy with low communication overhead and computational complexity. In the process of message combination, the overlap remains as an issue. Therefore, resampling should be considered to prevent the degradation of box particles. Hence, further research on these problems will be carried out in follow-up work.

Acknowledgements. This work is supported by National Science Foundation of China 61601511.

References

1. Qu, Y., Zhang, Y.: Cooperative localization against GPS signal loss in multiple UAVs flight. J. Syst. Eng. Electron. **22**(1), 103–112 (2011)
2. Sam, S., USman, A.K., Soummya, K., Jose, M.F., M.: Distributed localization: a linear theory. In: Proceedings of the IEEE, vol. 99, pp. 1–20 (2018)
3. Patwari, N., Ash, J.N., Kyperountas, S., Hero, A.O., Moses, R.L., Correal, N.S.: Locating the nodes: Cooperative localization in wireless sensor networks. IEEE Signal Process. Mag. **22**(4), 54–69 (2005)
4. Panagiotis, A., Oikonomou, F., Kai-Kit, W.: HEVA: cooperative localization using a combined non-parametric belief propagation and variational message passing approach. J. Commun. Netw. **18**(3), 397–410 (2016)
5. Koller, D., Friedman, N.: Probabilistic Graphical Models: Principles and Techniques. MIT Press, Cambridge (2009)
6. Kschischang, F.R., Frey, B.J., Loeliger, H.-A.: Factor graphs and the sum-product algorithm. IEEE Trans. Inf. Theory **47**(2), 498–519 (2001)
7. Mauricio, A., Caceres, F.P., Henk, W., Roberto, G.: Hybrid cooperative positioning based on distributed belief propagation. IEEE J. Selected Areas in Commun. **29**(10), 1948–1958 (2011)
8. Lien, J., Ferner, U.J., Srichavengsup, W., Wymeersch, H., Win, M.Z.: A comparison of parametric and sample-based message representation in cooperative localization, Int. J. Navigation and Observation, 1–10 (2012)
9. Ihler, A.T., Fisher, R.L.M., Willsky, A.S.: Non parametric belief propagation for self-localization of sensor networks. IEEE J. Sel. Areas Commun. **23**(4), 809–819 (2005)
10. Danny, B., Alexander, T.I., Harel, A., Danny, D.: A low density lattice decoder via non-parametric belief propagation. In: Conference: Communication, Control, and Computing (2009)
11. Caceres, M.A., Penna, F., Wymeersch, H., Garello, R.: Hybrid cooperative positioning based on distributed belief propagation. IEEE J. Sel. Areas Commun. **29**(10), 1948–1958 (2011)
12. Gning, A., Ristic, B., Mihaylova, L., Abdallah, F.: An introduction to box particle filtering. IEEE Signal Process. Mag. **30**(4), 166–171 (2013)
13. Jaulin, L., Kieffer, M., Didrit, O., Walter, E.: Applied Interval Analysis. Springer, New York (2001)

14. Gning, A., Mihaylova, L., bdallah, F., Ristic, B.: Particle filtering combined with interval methods for tracking applications. Integrated Tracking, Classification, and Sensor Management: Theory and Applications. Wiley, New York (2012)
15. Hiba, H.C., Amadou, G., Fahed, A., Imad, M., Simon, J.: Non parametric distributed inference in sensor networks using box particles messages. Math. Comput. Sci. **8**(3–4), 455–478 (2014)

A Multi-service Traffic Generation System for Emulation of Space Information Networks

Feng Jiang$^{(\boxtimes)}$, Qi Zhang, Yuhang Du, Kanglian Zhao, Wenfeng Li, and Yuan Fang

School of Electronic Science and Engineering, Nanjing University, Nanjing 210023, China
mf1723024@smail.nju.edu.cn

Abstract. Recently, tremendous progress has been made in the research on space information networks, which also inspires the development of general or dedicated emulation systems. As an important part in emulation of the space information networks, the research on traffic generation system is still in the preliminary stage. In view of the insufficient research in this area, a multi-service traffic generation system dedicated for emulation of space information networks is proposed in this paper, which has the characteristics of scale and flexibility. The system is designed based on software-defined networking technology to decouple the traffic generation part from the traffic transmission part, avoiding the complicated configuration problems in emulation of large scale space information networks. At the same time, the traffic generation part of the system uses a variety of business models, which is helpful for the research in future space information networks.

Keywords: Traffic generation · Business model · Space information networks

1 Introduction

With fast research and development in communications, networking and onboard computing technology, the space information networks system are increasing in complexity and scalability, which requires low cost, flexible, high-fidelity experiment and verification before the expansive production and implementation of the system. However, space industry is high-cost and high-risk, which makes it difficult to build testbeds with a bunch of space nodes. Therefore, it is essential to test and verify the performance of the software and the hardware of space information networks through ground emulation platforms [1]. With reference to the test methods of terrestrial networks, traffic generation is an extremely important part of the entire emulation platform. The traffic generator generates data packets with the control of corresponding business models to emulate the data traffic in the scenario under test, which can effectively customize the traffic parameters to meet the test requirements under different network conditions.

There has been a lot of research on traffic generators in the literature. There are also mainstream traffic generators in the open source community. Iperf [2] is a common traffic generator, which is commonly used as a TCP/UDP performance evaluation tool. By tuning various parameters, the maximum bandwidth of TCP and statistics such as

Q. Wu et al. (Eds.): WiSATS 2020, LNICST 357, pp. 35–47, 2021.
https://doi.org/10.1007/978-3-030-69069-4_4

bandwidth, delay, maximum segment, and maximum transmission unit size can be tested. Harpoon [3] is based on the ON/OFF model of heavy-tail distribution to generate self-similar network traffic. Harpoon has two components: a client thread that issues a file transfer request and a server thread that uses TCP or UDP to transfer the requested file. Its self-configuration process uses file records as input to generate the necessary parameters for configuring the network traffic model to generate artificial traffic with near real-time traffic characteristics. D-ITG [4] (Distributed Internet Traffic Generator) can generate IPv4 and IPv6 traffic, as well as network layer, transport layer and application layer traffic. D-ITG can also simulate network delay and support multiple protocols including TCP, UDP, SCTP, ICMP, etc. D-ITG can simulate service traffic such as VoIP and Telnet by modeling a random model of message size and message intervals. And D-ITG also has a logging function. In addition, many companies develop professional hardware-based traffic generators based on their business needs. For example, Breakingpoint by Ixia or Smartbits by Spirent. These professional hardware traffic generation devices can generate up to 10 Gigabit network traffic, and can accurately customize the bandwidth, packet length and number of network data streams. However, these hardware devices are difficult to reflect the diversity of real network data protocols, and are generally very expensive, mainly used for commercial purposes, and are not suitable for the initial stage of network research.

Three different methods are categorized based on the review of the state-of-the-art in network traffic generation [5]: 1) traffic generation based on network model; and 2) traffic generation based on traffic characteristics; and 3) traffic generation based on application protocol. The advantages of the three methods are summarized, which provides important guidance for the subsequent research in the field of traffic generation. The literature [6] designs the FPGEN flow generator based on FPGA. The traffic generator can send data traffic of Poisson model and Markov model. Because the design writes the configuration message of the data stream directly in RAM, the flow rate can reach 2.5 Gps. Later the literature [7] optimizes the design so that the transmission rate could reach 5 Gps, but the shortcoming was that the IP and port number of the data stream could not be flexibly configured. Literature [8] combines software-defined networking (SDN), uses traffic-based virtual network technology and traffic generation technology based on user behavior model, designs and implements a multi-user network traffic generator that can centrally control traffic generation and physical network resources, and can effectively distinguish network traffic.

However, some of the traffic generation tools described above generally can only generate simple TCP/UDP traffic, and the support for business traffic is relatively simple. One of the current development trends of space information network is the development of network services from a single service to multiple services. There are also many studies on traffic generators supporting multiple services in China, but they are all based on terrestrial network. Based on the discussion and summary of the traditional business traffic model and self-similar business traffic model, the literature [9] designs the main modules of the traffic generator such as the analysis module, business traffic module, traffic generator module, timer module, WinSock interface module, etc. And implements a traffic generator supporting multiple services such as voice traffic, video traffic, and M2M traffic. The literature [10] builds a multi-service traffic generator framework based on Qt on the Linux platform, encapsulates the data structure of the business flow, and generates network traffic in a multi-threaded manner. By separately modeling the HTTP service, voice service and video service, the network traffic sequence with its own self-similar characteristics is generated to realize support for multiple services. In addition, the literature also verified the validity and practicability of the model.

The traffic generators mentioned in the above-mentioned domestic and foreign literatures have their applicable scenarios and characteristics, and the research of these traffic generators is mainly for terrestrial networks running TCP/IP network protocol. The space information network is very different from the terrestrial network. The terrestrial network conditions that can run the TCP/IP network protocol are often better, while the communication environment of the space information network is more harsh. Although in low-orbit networks the TCP/IP protocol can still be run directly due to the low orbital height, as the orbital height increases, the operational performance of the TCP/IP protocol in the space information network will be greatly reduced. Therefore, the above-mentioned traffic generator is not suitable for space information networks.

However, at present, there are still insufficient researches on traffic generators suitable for space information networks. The literature [11] develops a DTN traffic generator "DTN-tg" suitable for space information networks. DTN-tg can generate a constant rate of data traffic that conforms to the DTN protocol. The entire working mode is equivalent to adding a client node and a server node at both ends of the network under test. The generated traffic of the client reaches the server node through the network under test to monitor and measure the performance of the DTN node in the network under test. However, this working mode is essentially equivalent to modifying the topology of the network under test. In the DTN node network, node configuration changes are required. Moreover, the traffic generator does not support the generation of multi-service network traffic.

2 System Structure

The literature [1] builds a simulation platform with authenticity, flexibility and reliability for the space information networks. The simulation platform is mainly composed of main control, simulation node, front-end interface and SDN switch. With the idea that the control plane and the data plane are separated from each other, the simulation platform can carry out true and reliable simulation of the protocol architecture, topology information, link characteristics and node performance in the space information network. In addition, through the GUI interface, users can flexibly and conveniently import or modify simulation scene information, start simulation tasks, monitor scene node status, and obtain experimental result reports. However, the simulation platform is lacking in traffic generation, so the traffic generation system designed in this paper is also an improvement of the simulation platform.

The common traffic generation system is mainly to add sending nodes and receiving nodes at both ends of the network under test, so that the sending node and receiving node have a path through the network under test, so that the traffic generated by the sending node circulates in the network under test. To measure various performance indexes of the tested network. This architecture is simple and easy to use, but as the network scale increases, the cumbersome configuration will greatly affect the flexibility of the architecture.

Therefore, based on the consideration of scale and flexibility, this paper designs a more flexible architecture. As shown in Fig. 1.

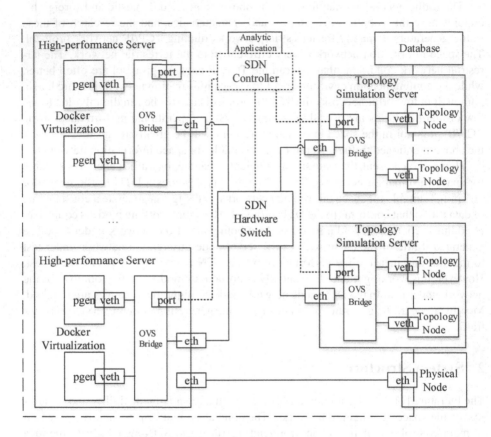

Control Information Transmission Link   ·····················

Simulation Traffic Transmission Link   ·····················

Fig. 1. Architecture diagram of the traffic generation system

The part enclosed by the dotted line in Fig. 1 is the main part of the traffic generation system. It mainly consists of traffic generation nodes (such as pgen in Fig. 1), SDN switches, SDN controllers, etc. Because the system architecture needs to realize large-scale network traffic generation, if a large amount of traffic generation and transmission are implemented in the same server, it will be limited by the server bus speed. Once overload occurs, data loss will occur, affecting the experimental results. Therefore, the traffic generation system adopts a distributed design, placing the traffic generation node in another high-performance server, separating data generation from data transmission, and reducing the load on the server. In addition, the traffic generation system architecture can expand the traffic generation node to multiple high-performance servers, and adopt Kubernetes for cluster management. The unframed part on the right in Fig. 1 is the simulation network part, which can be virtual nodes or physical nodes. In addition, there is a database in the simulation network part, which stores some node information and link information. The simulation network is connected to the virtual switch in the traffic generation system by adding a virtual network port, and the SDN controller is responsible for data forwarding control to realize the interconnection of the two parts. When the traffic generation system is connected to the simulated network, the information of the additional virtual network port will be written into the database as the information of the topology node for subsequent reading and use.

This traffic generation system mainly has three parts of functional design. These are business traffic generation, traffic forwarding control, and network protocol conversion.

The business traffic generation part is implemented in the traffic generation node. First, a traffic model is established according to business characteristics, and then the traffic generation node generates corresponding UDP traffic through Socket network programming and realizes the transmission of the traffic. The third section will introduce the multi-service modeling.

The traffic forwarding control part is implemented by SDN related components. There is an analytic application in the SDN controller in the traffic generation system in this paper, which is used to identify the relationship between the sending and receiving nodes in the parameter configuration file. In addition, the analysis application needs to read the topology node information in the database. After analyzing the obtained information, the source node IP and destination node IP of the injected traffic are discriminated, and the corresponding flow entry information is automatically generated and delivered to the corresponding switch device to ensure that the UDP data traffic generated by the traffic generation node is correct to the corresponding topology node.

The network protocol conversion part is implemented in the topology node part, and is used to process the UDP data packet injected by the traffic generation node. The traffic generation system can be connected to the simulation network of any topology, and supports the operation of different network protocols in the simulation network. For different network protocols in the simulated network, the network protocol conversion will process the received UDP data differently. For the simulation network running the DTN protocol, the relevant experiments in Sect. 4 set the simulation network to run the DTN protocol. First, the topology node acts as the receiving end of UDP traffic. After receiving the UDP data packet, the payload of the UDP data packet is extracted, and the load is encapsulated in accordance with the protocol system running in the simulated network. Finally, a data packet conforming to the simulated network protocol is generated and transmitted in the topology node.

The traffic generation system has the characteristics of low coupling and high flexibility. The low coupling is reflected in the complete decoupling of the traffic generation system and the simulation network. The traffic generation system can be connected to the simulation network of different protocols without modifying any internal configuration. The high flexibility is reflected in the fact that the traffic generation nodes are generated by Docker virtualization, which can achieve lightweight and large-scale deployment, and combine the SDN controller to send flow entries to control the data flow direction, and can flexibly configure the multi-transmission and multi-reception situation between a large number of nodes. It is suitable for large-scale space information network scenarios.

3 Multi-service Modeling

Considering the relative simplicity of the current space information network business, in order to facilitate the establishment of business models, the modeling method used in this paper mainly uses two important characteristics of business traffic: packet interval and packet size. According to the distribution function of packet interval and packet size and other characteristics of business traffic [12], the relevant traffic generation program is realized. At present, the traffic generation system in this paper supports five types of services, namely remote sensing satellite service, voice service, VoIP service, near real-time video service and HTTP service.

The remote sensing business modeling in this paper mainly intercepts the model of the flow acquisition part in the literature [13] and introduces the MMDP process to achieve it. In this experiment, it is assumed that there are four remote sensors in the remote sensing satellite business, so there are five remote sensor states, and each state will only transition to the adjacent state. In addition, the residence time of each state in the remote sensing satellite business conforms to an exponential distribution. At the same time, due to the different usage of remote sensors in various states in the remote sensing satellite business, the corresponding bit rate should also change. In this paper, the basic packet load is set to 50 bytes. According to the current state of use of the remote sensor, the packet load generated by the remote sensing satellite service needs to be increased by a corresponding multiple, so as to indirectly realize the change of the transmission rate. According to the characteristics of the above packets, the algorithm model is established to send a packet of the size of the service characteristics every time interval that conforms to the service characteristics.

In this paper, the traditional modeling method is used to model the voice service, that is, a two-state alternating model is used, which corresponds to the call state and the pause state in voice communication. This model is also called the ON/OFF model. When the model is in the ON state, that is, in the call state, there is traffic generated at this time; when the model is in the OFF state, that is, in the pause state, no traffic is generated at this time. The duration of the ON state and the OFF state conforms to an exponential distribution. In addition, the data traffic generated in the ON state conforms to the Poisson arrival process, that is, the packet interval time conforms to the exponential distribution.

Similar to the traditional voice service, the VoIP service also has two states: active state and inactive state. But unlike the traditional voice service where the two states appear alternately, the VoIP service is modeled using a two-state Markov process. as shown in Fig. 2.

The duration of the active state and the inactive state of the VoIP service conform to the exponential distribution, and their average values are $1/\beta$ and $1/\alpha$, respectively. In the active state, the sending source generates fixed-size packets at specific time intervals. In the inactive state, the sending source generates background data packets with a small amount of data at different specific time intervals. This is different from the traditional

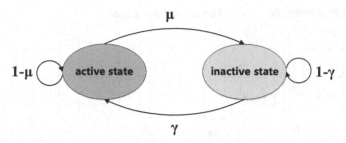

Fig. 2. Markov chain model of VoIP service

voice service. Similar to the heartbeat packet in a long TCP connection, the inactive state tests whether the connection is interrupted by generating a data packet with a smaller amount of data.

Near real-time video service (NRTV) is a type of service that requires high real-time performance. Its QoS requires one-way delay within 10 s, delay jitter as small as possible, and bit error rate less than 1% and so on. The modeling of the NRTV service in this paper is to divide the entire video streaming session into multiple frames. The time interval of arrival of each frame is kept fixed, and each frame can be divided into a fixed number of data packets. The size and arrival interval of these packets conform to the truncated Pareto distribution.

This paper models HTTP business traffic based on web objects. The modeling of HTTP business involves several concepts of web page composition. Suppose an HTTP business process is regarded as a session. When a user runs a web browser, it means that a session starts. When the user disconnects from the Web server, it means that the session ends. Each session contains multiple webpages, meaning that during a session, the user can click on multiple webpages to browse. Each web page will contain multiple objects, these objects can be divided into main objects and embedded objects, and a web page will only have one main object, but there can be multiple embedded objects. The basic flow of the HTTP business model is shown in Fig. 3.

The modeling of HTTP business mainly focuses on the following six parameters: 1) The number of webpages in one session: indicates the number of webpages viewed by the user. 2) The size of the main object in each web page: the main object is a document described by Hypertext Markup Language (HTML), which is the main frame of the entire web page. The size of the main object conforms to the truncated log-normal distribution. 3) Size of embedded objects: embedded objects refer to objects such as pictures, text, and sound embedded in the page frame. The size of the embedded objects also conforms to the truncated log-normal distribution. 4) The number of embedded objects: the number of embedded objects conforms to the truncated Pareto distribution. 5) Reading time: represents the time interval of each webpage, similar to the OFF stage in the ON/OFF model, corresponding to the stage where the user is browsing the webpage. The reading time conforms to the exponential distribution. 6) Parsing time: After sending the main object of the web page to the client, the server will start to send the embedded object part of the web page in sequence after a parsing time. The Parsing time conforms to an exponential distribution.

42   F. Jiang et al.

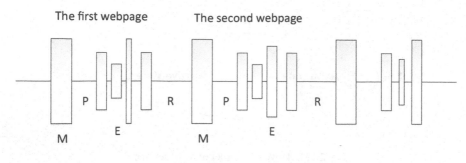

M: main object
P: parsing time
E: embedded objects
R: reading time

Fig. 3. Basic flow of the HTTP business model

4 Experiment

4.1 Architecture Verification

This experiment is to verify that the traffic generation system under this architecture will not adversely affect the performance of the network under test. Two DTN node topology experiments are designed to measure the delivery time under different link conditions. Two sets of comparative experiments were measured separately: changing the size of the packet loss rate under a fixed one-way delay (250 ms), and changing the size of the one-way delay under a fixed packet loss rate (10e−7). Raw means a two-node transmission experiment using the above system architecture, and mod means a normal two-node transmission experiment. The experimental results are shown in Table 1 and Table 2 below.

Table 1. Delivery time changes with packet loss rate under fixed one-way delay

10e−7		10e−6		5 * 10e−6		10e−5	
Raw	Mod	Raw	Mod	Raw	Mod	Raw	Mod
1.7898	1.7228	3.7347	3.4398	4.1696	4.2874	6.2710	6.6519

Table 2. Delivery time changes with one-way delay under a fixed packet loss rate

250 ms		500 ms		1 s		5 s	
Raw	Mod	Raw	Mod	Raw	Mod	Raw	Mod
1.7898	1.7228	2.7454	2.7854	6.5370	6.7838	30.4498	30.9653

The above experimental results indicate that when the traffic generation system adopting this system architecture measures the performance of the network under test, it will not affect the performance of the network under test. To a certain extent, the correct availability of the traffic generation system using this system architecture is verified.

4.2 Related Experiments

The experimental part of this paper adopts a simplified system architecture, and designs a UI interface for interaction. The UI interface is mainly divided into three parts, namely the parameter setting part, the network performance part and the log display part. As shown in Fig. 4,

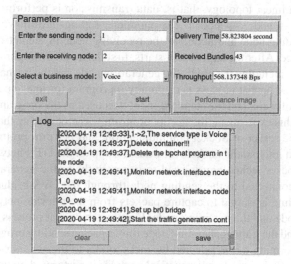

Fig. 4. UI interface

The parameter setting part is composed of three parameter items required for the experiment, which are the sending node number and receiving node number in the tested network, and the traffic service model. The drop-down box for the business model covers the several business models described above. In addition, the OK button in the parameter setting section indicates starting the experiment, and the Exit button indicates exiting the UI interface. The function of the network performance part is to display the relevant performance indicators of the tested network. Specifically, after the end of an experiment, according to the data packet information captured from the network interface of the sending node and the receiving node of the tested network, the three performance indicators of this experiment are counted, which are the delivery time and the number of Bundle and throughput value. In addition, the function of the view performance image button in this part is to display a line graph of each Bundle packet length and a real-time throughput line graph in this experiment. The function of the log display part is to display the experiment process in real time. As the experiment starts, the log display box will show the progress of the experiment in real time. In addition, the progress information will display different colors according to different degrees, general information is displayed in black, key process information is displayed in blue, and error information is displayed in red. At the end of each experiment, the log display box will print out the time of the first Bundle packet sent by the sending node and the time of the last Bundle packet received by the receiving node, and the total size of the bundle packets in the entire network transmission. These statistics can be mutually corroborated with the information in the network performance section. The function of the clear button in the log display part is to clear the contents of the current log box. The function of the save button will save the content displayed in the log display box under the logs folder, with the time as the file name at the time, similar to log2019-12-14-22-12-43.txt.

In this paper, a 4-node space information network is used as the tested network, and the node numbers are identified as 1, 2, 3, and 4, respectively. The space information network adopts a linear topology, that is, data transmission is performed according to node1 → node2 → node3 → node4. The parameter settings are shown in Fig. 4, with node1 as the sending node and node2 as the receiving node in the network under test, using voice service. After the experiment starts, first delete the configuration of the previous experiment, including the old traffic generation node and the bpchat process in the topology node. The bpchat process is originally a program for inter-node communication in the ION software, and the standard input was used as the program input for data transmission. In this experiment, the bpchat program was modified so that it can receive UDP traffic as the server of Socket communication, and perform protocol conversion and encapsulation into bundle packets for transmission on the DTN network under test. Secondly, the Docker technology is used to generate the traffic generation node container, and it is connected to the sending node through the OVS bridge. At the same time, multithreading is started to capture packets from the relevant network interfaces of the sending node and the receiving node. Finally, the bpchat process on the sending node is started, and the traffic generating node runs a packet sending program to transmit UDP traffic conforming to the selected business model to the sending node. After the transmission process is completed, statistical analysis is performed on the captured data packets to display network performance statistics. At this point, a measurement experiment of the flow generation system is ended. Figure 5 is a network performance image obtained in this experiment.

In addition, in order to ensure the accuracy of the traffic collection function in the experiment, this paper simultaneously opens Wireshark in the experiment to capture packets. The captured network interfaces are eth0 of the sending node and eth0 of the receiving node in the topology node. The eth0 is responsible for the transmission of Bundle packets. As can be seen from the captured Bundle packet information, it is true that node 1 (as the sending node) transmitted the bundle packet to node 2 (as the receiving node), which is in accordance with the parameters set in the experiment, and the data packet that has undergone protocol conversion at this time is carried out through the bundle protocol transmission. By filtering bundle packages, you can observe that there are indeed 43 bundle packages displayed, which is consistent with the number of bundle package receptions in the UI interface. Moreover, the start time and end time of the Bundle package also coincide with the log box information. In addition, the load content of the bundle package is also consistent with the load content set in the business model. Through the above comparative analysis, the normal operation of the overall

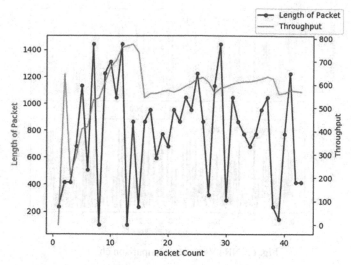

Fig. 5. Network performance image

traffic generation system is ensured, and the accuracy of the relevant module design and operation is verified.

In addition, on the basis of the above experiments, the traffic generation system of this paper is applied to the simulation platform in literature [1]. And a scenario where two ground nodes cannot communicate through a TCP/IP network is simulated, and the space information network is used as a relay network to realize data transmission. The specific experimental realization is that the ground node uploads the relevant UDP service traffic, converts it into Bundle packet and transmits it in the space information network, and finally converts it into UDP packet and sends it to another ground node. In this simulation scenario, there are mainly two nodes representing the ground nodes pgen and recv, and the space information network topology remains unchanged. This experiment separately conducts experiments on the above five types of business traffic. During the experiment, the information of the sending node of UDP traffic and the receiving node of UDP traffic is mainly concerned. In the experiment, Wireshark is used to capture and save the package, and then use Python's pyshark module and matplotlib module to analyze and draw, and get the relevant experiment comparison chart. As shown in Fig. 6.

Figure 6 selects the NRTV service model used. The upper line chart in the figure shows the size distribution of the UDP packets sent by the pgen node to the space information network node. The lower line chart in the figure shows the size distribution of the UDP packets received by the recv node from the space information network node. As can be seen from Fig. 6, the two figures can be completely coincident, indicating that after the UDP data packet sent from the pgen node is transmitted through the space information network, it can be completely restored to the original data packet size and transmitted to the recv node. It is verified that the two terrestrial nodes can be connected through the space information network when the terrestrial network is poor. However, the time attribute of the data packet received by the recv node is inevitably different

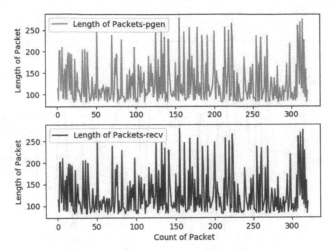

Fig. 6. NRTV service comparison chart

from the sending node. The experimental results show that the traffic generation system designed in this paper can accurately simulate the emergency communication scenario when applied to the simulation platform. Furthermore, it shows that the traffic generation system designed in this paper can effectively access to the simulation platform and undertake the task of traffic generation.

5 Conclusion

This paper studies and analyzes the development status of the traffic generation system, applies emerging network technology, and designs a multi-service traffic generation system architecture suitable for space information networks, which can meet requirements for traffic generation under the large-scale network. The traffic generation system architecture has good low coupling and high flexibility. In addition, in order to solve the problem that the simulation platform cannot simulate business scenarios, the traffic generation system of this paper implements a business traffic module at the traffic generation node, which is used to generate UDP traffic that conforms to the corresponding business characteristics. In addition, this paper has made corresponding verification experiments on the system architecture and operation process, showing that the traffic generation system can be well applied to the simulation platform and undertake the function of traffic generation. The space information network traffic generation system supporting multi-services proposed in this paper has certain reference significance for the subsequent research on multi-service research and traffic generation system in space information networks.

References

1. Lu, T.: An emulation architecture of routing protocol in space information network. Nanjing University (2018)

2. Tirumala, A., Qin, F., Dugan, J., Ferguson, J., Gibbs, K.: iPerf: TCP/UDP bandwidth measurement tool (2005)
3. Sommers, J., Barford, P.: Self-configuring network traffic generation, pp. 68–81 (2004)
4. Botta, A., Dainotti, A., Pescape, A.: A tool for the generation of realistic network workload for emerging networking scenarios. Comput. Netw. **56**(15), 3531–3547 (2012)
5. Wen, O., Zhang, X., Wang, D., Zhang, J., Tang, J.: A survey of network traffic generation. In: International Conference on Cyberspace Technology. IET (2016)
6. Sanh, M., Schmidt, E.G., Giiran, H.C.: FPGEN: a fast, scalable and programmable traffic generator for the performance evaluation of high-speed computer networks. Perform. Eval. **68**(12), 1276–1290 (2011)
7. Wang, X., Wang, Y., Li, P.: An aggregated process-based traffic generator for network performance evaluation. J. Circ. Syst. Comput. **25**, 1650018 (2015)
8. Wang, Z.: The research on virtualization technology of multi-user network traffic generator. Chongqing University of Posts and Telecommunications (2017)
9. Cao, B.: The design and implement of muLti-service traffic generator. Jilin University (2011)
10. Li, K.: Multi-service traffic generator based on Qt. Chongqing University (2016)
11. Amanatidis, T., Malkotsis, A.: DTN-tg A DTN Traffic Generator. In: Koucheryavy, Y., Mamatas, L., Matta, I., Tsaoussidis, V. (eds.) WWIC 2012. LNCS, vol. 7277, pp. 374–379. Springer, Heidelberg (2012). https://doi.org/10.1007/978-3-642-30630-3_35
12. Zhang, X., Wang, W.: Multi-user mixed business modeling and business traffic analysis. Beijing University of Posts and Telecommunications (2008)
13. Zhu, Y., Sheng, M., Li, J.: Traffic Modeling and performance analysis for remote sensing satellite networks. In: 2018 IEEE Global Communications Conference (GLOBECOM), pp. 1–6 (2018)

MininetE: A Lightweight Emulator for Space Information Networks

Tao Lin(✉), Fa Chen, Kanglian Zhao, Yuan Fang, and Wenfeng Li

School of Electronic Science and Engineering,
Nanjing University, Nanjing 210023, China
mf1723029@smail.nju.edu.cn, zhaokanglian@nju.edu.cn

Abstract. With the continuous development of Space Information Networks (SIN), there is an increasing demand for a cost-effective and high-fidelity tool to carry out research on related networking technologies. Neither the real testbed which is expensive nor the simulators which lack realism can meet our requirements. Therefore, this paper introduces MininetE to emulate space networking allowing relatively high-fidelity experiments that can run on the constrained resources of a single laptop. MininetE enhances the well-known Mininet emulator with adequate isolation and implements dynamic topology control with the original SDN capabilities. The validity of MininetE is verified by results of a Delay-/Disruption-Tolerant Networking (DTN) experiment.

Keywords: Space Information Networks · Emulation · Linux namespace · DTN

1 Introduction

Space Information Networks (SIN) [1] are network systems based on space platforms, e.g. various orbit satellites, stratospheric balloons, space probe etc. In the immediate future, SIN will expand into deep space along with the human exploration of other planets in the solar system. Therefore, it is essential to carry out research on new networking techniques as well as evaluate protocols and algorithms for SIN. Compared with terrestrial network, SIN comprise a wide variety of different environments including long propagation delays, frequent link disruptions, channel-rate asymmetry and dynamic changes of the network topology. To this end, an appropriate network experimentation platform is required to support not only accurate link property modeling for space communications, but also space networking technologies such as Delay-/Disruption-Tolerant Networking (DTN) [2].

The currently available approaches of network-related research have their pros and cons. Large scale testbeds (e.g. Emulab, GENI) give researchers the ability to replicate network experiments at the highest possible level of fidelity, but they are expensive and not always readily available for most researchers. Simulators, such as OPNET and NS-3, use mathematical formulas to create a theoretical and entirely abstract model of a network. They lack realism: They

© ICST Institute for Computer Sciences, Social Informatics and Telecommunications Engineering 2021
Published by Springer Nature Switzerland AG 2021. All Rights Reserved
Q. Wu et al. (Eds.): WiSATS 2020, LNICST 357, pp. 48–57, 2021.
https://doi.org/10.1007/978-3-030-69069-4_5

use discrete events to simulate network events such as packet loss and delay in chronological order, and they cannot generate real data flow among the nodes as the realistic network does. Additionally, most emerging networking technologies like DTN, Software Defined Networking (SDN) [3] and Information-Centric Networking (ICN) are not well supported in these simulation tools.

In contrast to simulation, emulation uses actual implementations of protocols and runs real network applications on each virtual node. Emulation aims at accurately reproducing the behavior of a real network and leading to more accurate test results by exploiting as much as possible the same software that would be used on real devices. Emulators can be divided into three major categories by different virtualization methods including full virtualization, para-virtualization and OS-level virtualization [4]. Both full virtualization platforms and para-virtualization platforms provide a high level isolation between virtual nodes but are too heavyweight: the significant consumption of hardware resources limits the emulated network's scale to only a handful of virtual nodes on a single physical machine. By contrast, container-based emulators [5] which leverage OS-level virtualization techniques such as FreeBSD jails, Linux namespaces or OpenVZ are in support of much larger-scale scenarios and are becoming increasingly popular nowadays. This situation can be attributed to containers' ability to consume significantly fewer system resources and instantiate emulated network topologies quickly.

Owing to the features of relatively high fidelity and low overhead offered by container-based emulation, it's an appealing option for testing various network systems and evaluating the performance of protocols. Among these container-based emulators, we eventually choose Mininet [6], an open-source emulator, which permit a variety of network topologies to be emulated on the constrained resources of a single laptop. Mininet provides a straightforward and extensible Python API for arbitrary custom topologies creation and experimentation. Moreover, Mininet integrates well with the Open vSwitch software switch which supports OpenFlow for highly flexible custom routing and Software-Defined Networking. Unfortunately, through our initial experiments we found that Mininet lacked the necessary isolation to support execution of some software (such as ION-DTN and Quagga) which are necessary to emulate SIN. In order to address these issues, this paper presents MininetE, a fork of Mininet extended to support space networking emulation by adding adequate isolation.

The rest of the paper is structured as follows: Sect. 2 presents an overview of Mininet and introduces modifications to the original Mininet. In Sect. 3, the implementation of dynamic topology control is shown in details. In Sect. 4, a sample experiment is presented along with experimental results. At last, a conclusion is given in Sect. 5.

2   MininetE Architecture

The motivation driving us to improve Mininet was that when we performed DTN emulation, we found that Mininet did not support multiple instances of

ION-DTN software on multiple virtual nodes. Afterwards, we set out to start a more in-depth study on why Mininet does not support our needs [7], and then we extend Mininet with a certain components including the following:

- Extensions to the core "mnexec.c" program that provides the container-isolation features.
- Patches and extensions to Mininet Python code, such as Host Class and Net Class.
- Minor modifications to Mininet Python code including definitions and methods of link creation.

In the following subsections, the detailed implementation of MininetE will be introduced in detail.

2.1 Overview of Mininet

Mininet is a widely used container-based emulator when it comes to the experimentation of SDN and the OpenFlow protocol. More than this, by combining lightweight, OS-level virtualization with an extensible CLI and API, Mininet provides a rapid prototyping work flow to customize and create various network topologies.

Figure 1 illustrates a basic network created with Mininet, including virtual hosts, switches, controllers, and links. A host in Mininet is essentially a shell process (e.g. bash) moved into its own network namespace and mount namespace with the unshare system call. Therefore, each host has exclusive network resources, including virtual network interface, network protocol stack and routing tables. Each host has a pipe to the parent Mininet process, mn, which sends commands and monitors output.

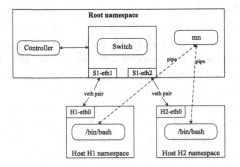

Fig. 1. A Mininet network

Mininet switches are either Open vSwitch instances, Linux bridges, or other types of virtual switch. As for links, a Mininet link is a virtual Ethernet pair (veth pair) which acts like a wire connecting two virtual interfaces. Packets sent through one interface are delivered to the other. The Linux traffic control program (TC) is used to emulate the communication channel by setting link parameters such as packet loss, delay, and channel bandwidth. Last, controllers are just SDN controllers running on the local server or a remote server.

Up to now, many historical networking experiments has been successfully recreated to replicate results, which proves the high fidelity of Mininet.

2.2 Modifications to Mininet

Due to its efficiency and scalability advantages over full-system virtualization and its inherent support for SDN/OpenFlow as mentioned above, we select Mininet as a basis and extend it into the MininetE tool which is capable of instantiating multiple complex networking software instances (e.g. ION-DTN, Quagga and IPsec).

Our first step in the implementation of MininetE is to add necessary isolation to the "mnexec.c" program that uses the Linux unshare system call to create each virtual host. Apart from the namespace isolation (including Network namespace and Mount namespace) provided by Mininet, MininetE adds support for isolation of the Process Identifier (PID) namespace, Inter-Process Communication (IPC) namespace, and the UNIX Timesharing System (UTS) namespace.

Currently, Linux implements six different types of namespaces [8] as shown in Table 1. The purpose of each namespace is to wrap a particular global system resource in an abstraction that makes it appear to the processes within the namespace that they have their own isolated instance of the global resource. Containers implemented with Linux namespaces can provide a group of processes with the illusion that they are the only processes in the system.

Table 1. Summary of namespace isolation

Namespace	Isolate resource	Mininet	MininetE
UTS	Hostname and NIS domain name		✓
IPC	System V IPC, POSIX message queues		✓
PID	Process IDs		✓
User	User and group IDs		*
Mount	Mountpoints and Filesystem	✓	✓
Network	Network devices and Protocol stack	✓	✓

The PID namespace provides processes with an independent set of process IDs (PIDs) from other namespaces. With the introduction of PID namespace, each container can run its own tree of processes and cannot even know of the existence of processes in other PID namespaces. However, processes in the parent PID namespace have a complete view of processes in the child PID namespace, which means that it's convenient to configure and interact with containers by accurate process IDs in the root namespace. The PID namespace is critical for supporting ION-DTN and some common routing daemons, such as Quagga and IPsec, because there is only one daemon permitted without PID namespace isolation. Moreover, Linux's process control mechanism may interfere or even accidentally kill processes in other containers.

The IPC namespace is usually used along with PID namespace. IPC namespace isolates certain interprocess communication resources, namely, semaphores, message queues, and shared memory. By this way, only processes created in the same IPC namespace are visible to each other. On the contrary, within the original Mininet which lacks the support of IPC namespace isolation, two applications in separate virtual hosts may communicate locally via IPC without going over the emulated network. What's more, the IPC namespace is of significant importance for the ION-DTN software to run successfully, because it's a multi-process program which need to make full use of IPC to transfer and exchange information and make this group of processes work together.

UTS namespace provides the isolation of host name and domain name, so that each container can have an independent host name and domain name, which can be regarded as an independent node on the network instead of a process on the host machine. This can be useful for initialization and configuration scripts of these containers based on their names.

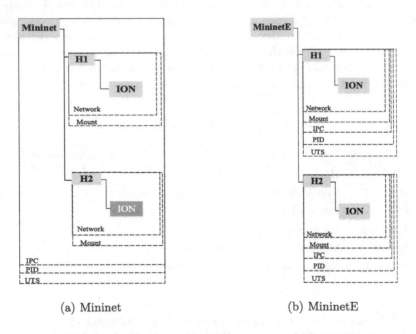

(a) Mininet   (b) MininetE

Fig. 2. Comparison of ION in Mininet and MininetE

Aside from the namespace isolation, we make some corresponding modifications to the python code. In order not to destroy the original functions of

Mininet, we decided to extend this part code of the network element classes (e.g. Host Class and Net Class) instead of modifying them directly.

Additionally, when a link is created in Mininet, a pair of two virtual interfaces are instantiated in one of the connected node's network namespace, and one of the interfaces is transferred to the other node's network namespace. Since we isolate PID namespace, this part of code is invalid because these two nodes don't even know that each other exists. To solve this issue, we firstly create the veth pair in root namespace and then move both endpoints into the corresponding namespaces.

After all the work is done, MininetE is able to run complex networking software such as ION- DTN software and Quagga routing daemons. Figure 2 shows the comparison of networking software running on Mininet and MininetE, using ION-DTN as an example. As illustrated in Fig. 2(a), within Mininet, after the first instance of ION-DTN is started in the virtual host H1, H2 fails in initiating another ION-DTN instance because they share the same PID and IPC namespace. The operating system will report an error and inform you that the ION-DTN software has been launched when you try to do so. By contrast, Fig. 2(b) shows the same two node emulated in MininetE. Since both the IPC and PID namespace are isolated, H1 and H2 is invisible to each other, thus both H1 and H2 can successfully run an instance of ION-DTN without mutual interference. Similarly, it is no big deal for MininetE to execute routing daemon such as Quagga and IPsec in each virtual host, which is far beyond the capability of original Mininet.

3   Dynamic Topology Implementation

Although the Linux traffic control program (TC) is used to emulate link properties such as bandwidth, latency, and packet loss, Mininet can only emulate wired links, because link properties are configured and cannot be changed after a link is created. However, other features such as intermittent space links and dynamically changing topology due to satellite motion, which are essential for space networking emulation, are not supported in Mininet. Fortunately, with its inherent support for SDN/OpenFlow, we develop a scheduling method to control link on-off with the help of SDN controller.

Our topology control scheme is based on a centralized emulation architecture, as shown in Fig. 3. Firstly, all virtual hosts are connected with an Open vSwitch to form a star topology. Then the SDN controller controls link-up/down between hosts by controlling the flow table of the switch. The following describes in detail the implementation process from the dynamic topology description information to the scheduled intermittent connectivity.

Figure 4 shows the flow diagram of the topology control implemented by the SDN controller. At the beginning of the scenario, the link information data is read in advance and stored in the controller cache. Then controller issue the Address Resolution Protocol (ARP) flood flow table. The ARP flood flow table enables all ARP packets passing through the switch to be flooded, so that all nodes can obtain the IP addresses and MAC addresses of neighboring nodes.

Next, the connection flow tables of the static links are issued, which survive the entire emulation period. Meanwhile, the flow table of dynamic link is issued by a timer within the SDN controller. At the time of starting the emulation, a multi-threaded timer is started, and the time points of link on/off are added to the timer structure. When the timer ends, the link connection function or the link disconnection function will be executed to deliver the corresponding connected flow table or delete the corresponding flow table.

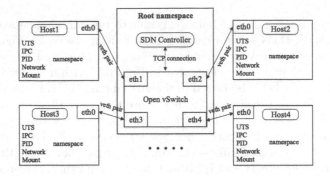

Fig. 3. Centralized emulation architecture

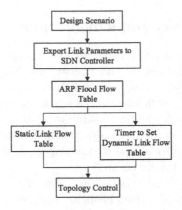

Fig. 4. Dynamic topology control

4   Experimental Validation

MininetE could meet requirements of emulating various networks. It is an ideal emulation tool to provide a credible approach to test and evaluate space networking in a single laptop. In the following subsections, we briefly present a sample work, along with experimental results obtained.

4.1 Specific Scenario

In order to evaluate the reliability of MininetE, we reproduce a DTN experiment presented in [9] with MininetE. The topology of this scenario is shown in Fig. 5. It consists of four DTN nodes: a Moon lander, a satellite orbiting the Moon (SAT), an auxiliary terrestrial Gateway Station (GW), Mission Control Centre (MCC). Intermittent space links are denoted by dotted lines, terrestrial wired links by continuous ones. The purpose of the experiment is to assess the ability of DTN in the deep space communication environment.

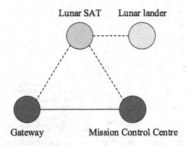

Fig. 5. Topology of the Moon to Earth scenario

Table 2. Contact plan

Link	Contact	Start-Stop time(s)	Speed(downlink)	Latency(s)
Lander-SAT	1	20–40	128 kbit/s	0
	2	100–120	128 kbit/s	0
SAT-GW	1	70–80	1 Mbit/s	1.3
	2	160–170	1Mbit/s	1.3
SAT-MCC		150–180	1 Mbit/s	1.3
GW-MCC		0–180	10 Mbit/s	0

The contact plan and link characteristics are summarized in Table 2. Note that the links between Moon and Earth have a propagation delay of 1.3 s, while the delay of other links is negligible. Besides, losses have been assumed to be negligible on all links.

4.2 Experimental Results

In the scenario summarized above we transfer ten bundles of 50 kB from the Moon lander to the MCC. Figure 6 presents a comparison between some results presented in [9] and those obtained with the MininetE. At the beginning, ten bundles are generated and taken into custody on the Lander. When the first

Lander-SAT contact starts (at 20 s), the first six bundles are transferred to SAT and taken in custody. Then they are transferred to GW when the SAT-GW contact opens (at 70 s), as the GW-MCC link is continuous, they are immediately delivered to the MCC. The rest four bundles are transferred to SAT during the second Lander-SAT contact (begins at 100 s) and taken into custody as before. Finally, they are directly delivered to MCC when the SAT-MCC contact first opens (at 150 s).

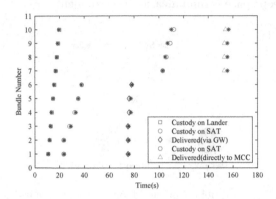

Fig. 6. Bundle transfer from Lander to MCC (Markers: from [9]; x-crosses: MininetE)

5   Conclusion

With MininetE, it is able to run multiple instances of complex network emulation software on each virtual host separately. This, together with our method of dynamic topology control, provides an approach to emulate SIN with accurate link characteristics. Emulation performances prove that MininetE is capable of testing DTN networks. More experiments will be performed in the future to prove that MininetE can meet requirements of emulating various networking techniques.

References

1. Bai, L., de Cola, T., Yu, Q., Zhang, W.: Space information networks. IEEE Wirel. Commun. **26**(2), 8–9 (2019)
2. Burleigh, S., et al.: Delay-tolerant networking: an approach to interplanetary internet. IEEE Commun. Mag. **41**(6), 128–136 (2003)
3. Kreutz, D., Ramos, F.M., Verissimo, P.E., Rothenberg, C.E., Azodolmolky, S., Uhlig, S.: Software-defined networking: a comprehensive survey. Proc. IEEE **103**(1), 14–76 (2014)
4. Salopek, D., Vasić, V., Zec, M., Mikuc, M., Vašarević, M., Končar, V.: A network testbed for commercial telecommunications product testing. In: 2014 22nd International Conference on Software, Telecommunications and Computer Networks (SoftCOM), pp. 372–377. IEEE (2014)

5. Handigol, N., Heller, B., Jeyakumar, V., Lantz, B., McKeown, N.: Reproducible network experiments using container-based emulation. In: Proceedings of the 8th International Conference on Emerging Networking Experiments and Technologies, pp. 253–264 (2012)
6. Lantz, B., Heller, B., McKeown, N.: A network in a laptop: rapid prototyping for software-defined networks. In: Proceedings of the 9th ACM SIGCOMM Workshop on Hot Topics in Networks, pp. 1–6 (2010)
7. Barnes, J.L., Clark, G.J., Eddy, W.: Cogswel: A network emulator for cognitive space networks. In: 34th AIAA International Communications Satellite Systems Conference, p. 5763 (2016)
8. Biederman, E.W., Networx, L.: Multiple instances of the global linux namespaces. In: Proceedings of the Linux Symposium, vol. 1, pp. 101–112. Citeseer (2006)
9. Caini, C., Fiore, V.: Moon to earth DTN communications through lunar relay satellites. In: 2012 6th Advanced Satellite Multimedia Systems Conference (ASMS) and 12th Signal Processing for Space Communications Workshop (SPSC), pp. 89–95. IEEE (2012)

On the Performance of Packet Layer Coding for Delay Tolerant Data Streaming in Deep Space

Xiaoyu Zhu[✉], Dongxu Hou, Kanglian Zhao, Wenfeng Li, and Yuan Fang

School of Electronic Science and Engineering, Nanjing University, Nanjing 210023, People's Republic of China
mf1723072@smail.nju.edu.cn, kaldon@163.com, {zhaokanglian, yfang}@nju.edu.cn, leewf_cn@hotmail.com

Abstract. This paper presents a research on the performance of packet layer coding for space streaming, which integrates Low Density Parity Check (LDPC) Code into space streaming service. By implementing LDPC code into higher layers, such as bundle layer or transport layer, the space streaming service can achieve stronger error correction capability, which improves the quality of experience of space streaming service. To evaluate the performance of packet layer coding for space streaming, emulation of data streaming in space are conducted. The results of the experiments show that compared with the original transmission scheme, space streaming service with packet layer coding has obvious improvements.

Keywords: Delay/disruption tolerant network · Packet layer coding · Low Density Parity Check Code · Space streaming · Streaming data delivery · Deep space

1 Introduction

With the development of aerospace technology, more and more manned deep space program will be conducted in the future. Compared with the traditional deep space communication service, data transmission of manned space program has higher requirements, especially in space streaming service. In manned exploration missions, the proportion of streaming data transmission will be much larger than that of traditional unmanned programs which require mostly reliable data transmission. However, because of the severe communication conditions in the deep space environment, the space streaming service faces many problems. The characteristics of deep space networks such as long delay and high bit error rate lengthen the delivery time, reduce the transmission success rate, and reduce the transmission efficiency, which greatly affects the quality of streaming service. Therefore, it is getting more and more attention of researchers on how to improve the performance of streaming data delivery in deep space.

Q. Wu et al. (Eds.): WiSATS 2020, LNICST 357, pp. 58–68, 2021.
https://doi.org/10.1007/978-3-030-69069-4_6

To solve this problem, the issue of data streaming in DTN [1–4] (Delay/disruptive tolerant networking) has been studied. In [5], erasure codes were implemented on video streaming system over lossy networks. Furthermore, in [6], the notion of 'substitutable content summary frames' has been introduced. An additional 'summary frame' is added to the original stream to improve the performance of video transmission even in bad condition. And in [7], another transport level mechanism based on coding scheme called Tetrys was proposed. An on-the-fly coding scheme is applied to provide the reliability. In 2013, a new space streaming transmission scheme called Bundle Streaming Service(BSS) was implemented in DTN. BSS can ensure the in-order delivery by a forwarding strategy and guarantee the integrity of the data by retransmitting the lost data. In addition, the Consultative Committee for Space Data Systems (CCSDS) suggested a new idea for video applications in deep space by implementing Real-Time Transport Protocol (RTP) over DTN [9]. However, because of the severe communication conditions, BSS and RTP over DTN both have shortcomings in deep service, such as long stream delivery time and high packet loss rate. Therefore, Forward Error Correction (FEC) codes, such as Reed-Solomon (RS) codes, has been combined with BSS in [10].

This paper conducts further research on the performance of packet layer coding for streaming transmission service in deep Space, by integrating LDPC Code [11] into BSS and RTP over DTN.

The rest of the paper is organized as follows. In Sect. 2, we will introduce the related work briefly. In Sect. 3, the design and implementation of packet layer coding for space streaming are shown in details. In Sect. 4, a typical experiment is conducted and we will analyze the experimental results. At last, a conclusion is given in Sect. 5.

2   Related Work

2.1   Overview of BSS

In order to achieve the goal of streaming data delivery in deep space, BSS was implemented in DTN, which can ensure the in-order delivery in real-time display, and provide the playback function. The stark of BSS is shown in Fig. 1.

The focus of BSS is to balance the relationship between unreliable and reliable transmission. BSS does not adopt a reliable transmission protocol for all data, but only uses the reliable transmission protocol to retransmit the lost packets, and most of the data is sent using an unreliable transmission protocol to guarantee the minimum transmission delay. BSS provides two kinds of transmission services, one of them is best effort service and another is reliable service. First of all, when the data is sent for the first time, it will be transmitted through the best effort service by UDP or green LTP to ensure that the data is sent to the receiving side as soon as possible. During the communication process, if some packets are lost, the reliable service will retransmit the lost packets by TCP or red LTP to ensure the reliability of transmission.

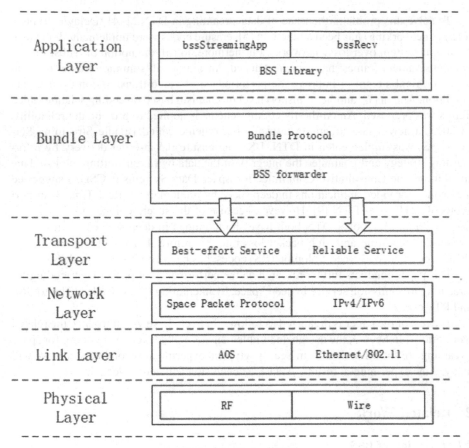

Fig 1. The stack of BSS

2.2 Overview of RTP Over DTN

Besides BSS, a new space streaming transmission scheme called RTP over DTN was proposed by CCSDS in 2018. RTP over DTN is a method of video over DTN using RTP, which can ensure higher quality of video transmission in deep space.

The Real-Time Transport Protocol (RTP) [12] provides a lightweight packet format for the transmission of media-related payloads over IP-based networks. RTP is designed around a fixed 12-byte header, along with a variable-length header extension field, as can be seen in Fig. 2. Amongst other things, this header contains the Payload Type (PT) component, which specifies the type of data which is conveyed in this packet. Additionally, the header contains a timestamp and sequence counters. The last element to be aware of is the marker bit, which specifies that this packet contains "important data", although the definition of importance is left to the payload type.

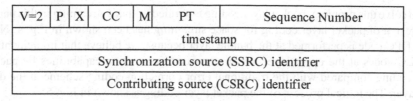

V=2	P	X	CC	M	PT	Sequence Number
timestamp						
Synchronization source (SSRC) identifier						
Contributing source (CSRC) identifier						

Fig 2. The header of RTP [12].

In order to make it apply to deep space, RTP should be implemented over Bundle Protocol (BP) [13]. RTP may be encapsulated into DTN bundles with minimal modification, instead treating the entirety of the RTP packet as a singular bundle. Considering RTP packets have arbitrary sizes, so it can be concatenated, and the following rules should be followed:

- Concatenated packets must have the same marker value. If the marker value changes, a new bundle should be started.
- All RTP payloads in a concatenated bundle must belong to the same media stream & have the same timestamp.
- After the first RTP packet, all headers can be stripped.

Figure 3 shows an example of a concatenated RTP bundle. The state of the Marker bit is shown, while the sequence counters and timestamps are omitted.

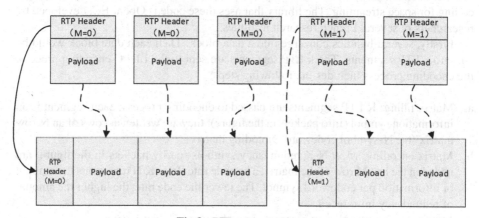

Fig 3. RTP concatenation

3 Packet Layer Coding for Space Streaming

As mentioned above, both of BSS and RTP over DTN have problem with the poor communication conditions in deep space, especially the high bit error rate, which may seriously damage the quality of space streaming service.

To solve this problem, packet layer coding is applied to space streaming in this paper. The design of packet layer coding for space streaming has been shown in Fig. 4. Note that LDPC code is performed at the bundle layer because we believe that implementing the FEC codes at the upper layer has stronger error correction capabilities by packet layer coding compared with the traditional error correction coding scheme at the data link layer. The logical process of the packet layer coding is shown in Fig. 5.

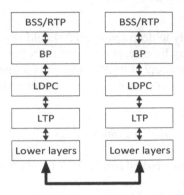

Fig 4. Design of packet layer coding for space streaming [14].

The Staircase LDPC codes, where the parity check matrix could be built by the decoder itself, on the spot, with a quick pseudo-random algorithm, is used in packet layer coding for space streaming. The library that uses these code is OpenFEC, developed by researchers of several French research institutes.

Firstly, several bundles converge into a data block. Then each data block would be cut into k LTP segments. The k LTP segments are sent to the LDPC encoding process, the encoding process includes the following steps:

a. Matrix filling: K LTP segments are passed to encoding process; each segment is an information symbol (Info packets in the figure); they are written as rows of an N-row matrix (the N-symbol codeword, or coding matrix).
b. Matrix encoding: M = N-K redundancy symbols (parity packets in the figure) are added in the last M row of the matrix. The code rate Rc = K/N represents the amount of information per codeword symbol. The lower the code rate, the higher the amount of redundancy introduced.
c. Matrix passing: the N rows are passed one-by-one to lower layers;

On the receiver side, the decoding process includes the following steps:

a. Matrix filling: Let L be the number of packet lost; N-L UDP datagrams arrive; their payload is read and written in an N row matrix (the N codeword at receiver side) leaving gaps (i.e. rows filled by zeros) in correspondence of missing symbols.

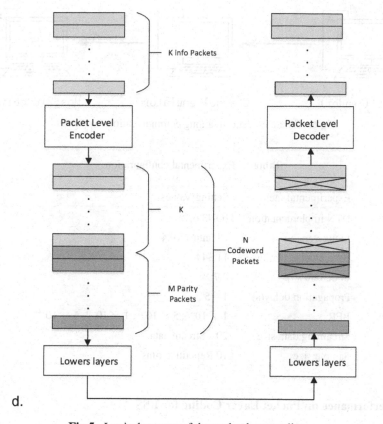

Fig 5. Logical process of the packet layer coding

b. Matrix decoding: The aim of the decoder is to extract the K information symbols (i.e. basically our K LTP segments) from the N-L received symbols. If the decoding is successful, all the first K rows are eventually filled. Put in other words, as the code is systematic, the missing info symbols (two in the figure) are recovered by exploiting the redundancy symbols. Thus, to have a success it is necessary to receive at least K of the N symbols transmitted, whatever they are (information or redundancy);

c. Matrix passing: the first K rows of the matrix, i.e. the info symbols, are read and passed one-by-one to upper layer.

4 Experiment Results

In this experiment, in order to simulate the real deep space communication environment, a two-node experimental scene is constructed, the experimental scene is shown in the Fig. 6.

The Host1 and Host2, represent the sender and receiver respectively. Both of them are equipped with the ION v3.6.1b [15]. And the last computer played the role of channel emulator, which can change the propagation delays and channel error rates. More details of the experimental factors and configuration are shown in Table 1.

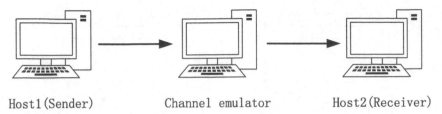

Host1 (Sender)   Channel emulator   Host2 (Receiver)

Fig 6. Emulated data streaming communication experiment

Table 1. Experimental configuration

Experimental factors	Setting/Values
DTN implementation	ION3.6.1b
Linux version	Ubuntu 16.0.4
Each bundle size(bytes)	11,844
Code rate	0.7
Propagation delay(s)	1–15
BER	$1 \times 10^{-7}, 5 \times 10^{-7}, 1 \times 10^{-6}, 5 \times 10^{-6}$
Streaming data size	20 s Stream data
Sample size	10 Repetitive runs

4.1   Performance on Packet Layer Coding for BSS

The following two metrics [8] were introduced to evaluate the performance on packet layer coding for BSS: the stream delivery time (SDT) and the end user's display efficiency (EDE). SDT represents the time of successful trans-mission of all the data to the receiver, and EDE represents the proportion of data successfully transferred for the first time.

In the first part of the experiment, the SDT is used to evaluate the transmission speed of streaming data delivery.

Figure 7 shows the effect of propagation delay on SDT at the same channel bit error rates. According to the results, BSS with LDPC performs better than original BSS in different propagation delay, which means no matter how long the delay is, BSS with LDPC can deliver all the data in a shorter time.

Figure 8 shows the results at different channel bit error rates. When the delay is 1 s, the BSS with LDPC can delivery all the data in 60 s even in bad channel conditions (BER $= 5 \times 10 - 6$), while original BSS takes more time.

In the EDE evaluation, the result in Fig. 9 shows BSS with LDPC can display more streaming data in the receiver than original BSS.

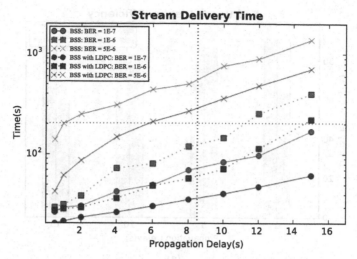

Fig. 7. Experimental result of LDPC-BSS based on SDT respect to delay.

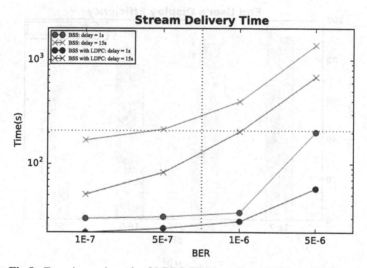

Fig 8. Experimental result of LDPC-BSS based on SDT respect to BER.

4.2 Performance on Packet Layer Coding for RTP Over DTN

The performance on packet layer coding for RTP over DTN is focused on the number of lost packets respect to propagation delay and BER. Table 2, Table 3 show the number of lost packets within the transmission by RTP over DTN with LDPC and RTP over DTN without LDPC.

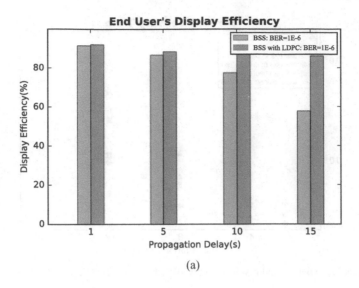

(a)

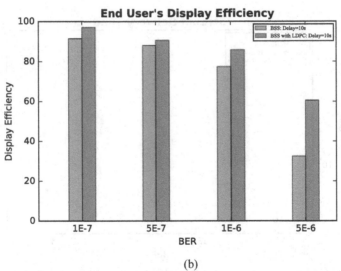

(b)

Fig. 9 Experimental result of LDPC-BSS based on EDE respect to (a) delay (b) BER

It is apparent that packet layer coding can improve the performance of space streaming, including BSS and RTP over DTN. There are some reasons. Compared with original BSS, packet layer coding provides stronger error correction capability, which can avoid retransmission and get stable EDE. When it comes to RTP over DTN, packet layer coding can provide higher quality service by reducing the number of lost packets.

Table 2 Number of lost packets respect to propagation delay (BER = 1E-6)

Delay /s	Lost packets without LDPC	Lost packets with LDPC
1	30	29
6	47	41
10	80	45
15	150	52

Table 3 Number of lost packets respect to BER (Delay = 10 s)

BER/10^{-7}	Lost packets without LDPC	Lost packets with LDPC
1	30	9
5	42	28
10	80	45
50	240	130

5 Conclusion

Based on the emulations in this work, we evaluated the contribution of packet layer coding to streaming data delivery for future deep space applications. And the results of the experiments strongly prove that space streaming with packet layer coding has great advantages for the original space streaming service, no matter in terms of BSS or RTP over DTN. Benefited from stronger error correction capability, packet layer coding ensures the reliability of streaming data delivery and improve the quality of streaming service.

References

1. Cerf, V., Burleigh, S., et al.: Delay-Tolerant Networking Architecture, RFC 4838, IETF (2007)
2. Farrell, S., Cahill, V., Geraghty, D., et al.: When TCP breaks: delay-and disruption-tolerant networking. IEEE Internet Comput. **10**(4), 72–78 (2006)
3. Fall, K.: A delay-tolerant network architecture for challenged internets. Sigcomm03 **33**(4), 27–34 (2003)
4. Burleigh, S., Hooke, A., Torgerson, L., et al.: Delay-tolerant networking: an approach to interplanetary Internet. IEEE Commun. Mag. **41**(6), 128–136 (2003)
5. Zhang, X.J., Peng, X.H.: A testbed of erasure coding on video streaming system over lossy networks. In: International Symposium on Communications and Information Technologies, pp. 535–540. IEEE (2007)
6. Liu, T., Nelakuditi, S.: Disruption-tolerant content-aware video streaming. In: MUL-TIMEDIA 04: Proceedings of the 12th Annual ACM International Conference on Multimedia, pp. 420–423. New York (2004)

7. Tournoux, P.U., Lochin, E., Leguay, J., et al.: Robust streaming in delay tolerant networks. In: IEEE International Conference on Communications, pp.1–5. IEEE (2010)
8. Sotirios-Angelos, L., Scott, C.B., Vassilis, T.: Bundle streaming service: design, implemetation and performance evaluation. Trans. Emerging Tel. Tech. **26**, 905–917 (2015)
9. Draft Recommendation for Space Data System Standards, Real Time Protocol over Delay Tolerant Networking For Video Applications, White Book, February 2018, www.ccsds.org
10. Qian, Q., Zhu, X., Zhao, K., Li, W.: Integration of reed–solomon codes to bundle streaming service (BSS) for deep space Communications. In: Liang, Q., Liu, X., Na, Z., Wang, W., Jiasong, M., Zhang, B. (eds.) Communications, Signal Processing, and Systems: Proceedings of the 2018 CSPS Volume I: Communications, pp. 207–215. Springer , Singapore (2019). https://doi.org/10.1007/978-981-13-6264-4_25
11. Gallager, R.G.: Low-Density Parity-Check Codes . MIT Press, Cambridge (1963)
12. Schulzrinne, H., Casner, S., Frederick, R., et al.: RTP: a transport protocol for real-time applications. Rfc **2**(2), 459–482 (1995)
13. Burleigh, S.C.: Interplanetary Overlay Network Bundle Protocol Implementation (2011)
14. ECLSA enhancements to support the OpenFEC codec library and to take advantage of it characteristic features. https://amslaurea.unibo.it/
15. Burleigh, S.: Interplanetary Overlay Network: an Implementation of the DTN Bundle Protocol. In: Consumer Communications and Networking Conference, 2007, CCNC 2007, 4th IEEE. IEEE (2007).

Virtual Full-Duplex for Two-Way Relaying in SOQPSK Modulation in Small-Scale Satellite Network Application

Alireza Mazinani[1]([⊠]), Vahid Tavakoli[2], and Qiang Gao[1]

[1] School of Electronic and Information Engineering, BeiHang University, Beijing, China
Alireza.mazinani@outlook.com, Lb1425206@buaa.edu.cn
[2] Department of Engineering and Media Technology, IRIB University, Tehran, Iran
vt.tavakoli@gmail.com

Abstract. In this paper, to achieve high network throughput (NT) in the half-duplex mode, a virtual full-duplex multi-hop two-way relay network is developed (VFD-MH-TWRN) using physical network coding (PNC) and SOQPSK modulation for space exploration application in which do not need instantaneous channel state information. In the proposed VFD-MH-TWRN scheme, two full-duplex source nodes exchange their information with the help of multi half-duplex relay nodes. As the main contribution, at first we define a novel data transmission strategy and then analytically derive the end-to-end bit error rate (BER) and, which are validated by the simulation results. It is shown that network throughput is higher than all of the previously defined networks and the simulation results show that the proposed scheme with SOQPSK modulation is close to DF-TWRN the bit error rate and they have similar performance.

Keywords: Multi-hop two-way relay network · Virtual full-duplex · Physical network coding

1 Introduction

Cooperative communication indicates the elements of a communication system that relay signals from one source to another via relays. Recently, relay-based communication networks have utilized small-scale satellites (SSS) known as pico and femto-satellites [1]. The use of SSS as relay nodes can potentially extend radio coverage, enhance link reliability and channel capacity, facilitate deep space and galaxy exploring and perform scientific measurements. SSS has been researched in the Kicksat project [2], in the Edison Demonstration of Small-sat Networks (EDSN) mission [3] and in Femto-satellites at zeroG (an experimental project in ISS). In addition, SSS can be a starting point for next-generation satellite communication and have provided extraordinary access for data collection [4, 5]. So easily can be defined an idea about cooperative communication application in satellite communications especially SSS considering that communication links have used some relay-based cooperative communication. The performance

Q. Wu et al. (Eds.): WiSATS 2020, LNICST 357, pp. 69–80, 2021.
https://doi.org/10.1007/978-3-030-69069-4_7

enhancement of the multi-hop network is so critical in this kind of network and also the two-way relay network (TWRN) can improve the data rate of a cooperative system. Half-duplex (HD) TWR via physical-layer network coding (PNC) transmits only two packets in two-time slots bi-directionally, in contrast with conventional HD TWR, which requires four-time slots [6–9]. Therefore, it improves network throughput and spectral efficiency. Additionally, PNC uses De-Noise and Forward (DNF) protocol to double the throughput of TWR related to Decode and Forward (DF) protocol [7, 9]. Therefore, in a relay-based communication network, SSS can be utilized as a relay and can offer a higher degree of freedom, so the relay-based SSS network is suitable for a lower latency communication in deep space. To realize it, a modulation that can provide power efficiency by offering a more significant improvement in bandwidth efficiency should be selected. Meanwhile, shaped offset quadrature PSK (SOQPSK) [10, 11] is a continuous phase and constant amplitude modulation that is compatible with the existing efficient non-linear class C power amplifier. [5]

In this paper, a Virtual Full Duplex Multi-Hop Two-Way Relay Network (VFD-MH-TWRN) with SOQPSK modulation, which does not need instantaneous channel state information is developed to improve network throughput. In Sect. 2 TWRN and MH-TWRN schemes are presented and in Sect. 3, the system model of L-node M-message VFD-MH-TWRN and transmission schemes are described and then analytically derives its throughput. Section 4 formulates Virtual Full-Duplex Denoise-And-Forward TWR (VFD-DNF-TWR) Scheme, and in Sect. 5, the Bit Error Rate (BER) performance of modulation is analyzed. Then, Sect. 6 presents the simulation results of the proposed scheme. Finally our summary is given in Sect. 7.

2   Two-Way Relay Network Concept

A two-way relay network (TWRN) system is shown in Fig. 1.a, in which source nodes A and B (N_A, N_B) are not directly linked together and instead transmit messages through relay node R using the PNC. All nodes are half-duplex (HD) and are equipped with a single antenna and relay utilize in DeNoise–And–Forward protocol. Therefore, they cannot send and receive simultaneously, so then their mode is alternated in each time slot. Data transmission generally consists of two stages: first one is multiple access (MAC) in which A and B data transmit to the relay simultaneously, and the relay detects

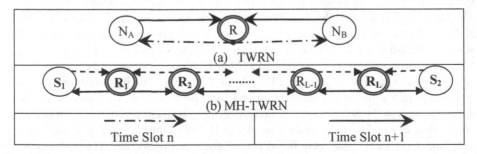

Fig. 1. TWR under PNC and half duplex system.

combined data from superimposed received signal and second one is broadcasting (BC) in which the relay forwards combined data to sources and sources decode new data. The term combined data means when two packet data are XORed with standard PNC. Also MH-TWRN with PNC is shown the in Fig. 1.b in which sources S_i; $i = \{1, 2\}$ are not directly linked together and instead transmit messages through L relay nodes $(R_l, l = 1, \ldots, L)$. Indeed it is extended version of TWRN.

3 System Model

3.1 VFD-MH-TWRN Data Transmission Strategy

We assume the VFD-MH-TWRN shown in Fig. 2.a in which sources S_i; $i = \{1, 2\}$ are not directly linked together and instead transmit messages through L relay nodes $(R_l, l = 1, \ldots, L)$ using the PNC protocol symmetrically. All relays have HD systems that are equipped with a single antenna, and therefore, they cannot send and receive simultaneously so then their mode is alternated in each time slot. Another side, sources have the FD system that are equipped with a two independent antenna, and therefore, they can send and receive simultaneously because of these properties we can name it to virtual full-duplex multi-hop two-way relay network.

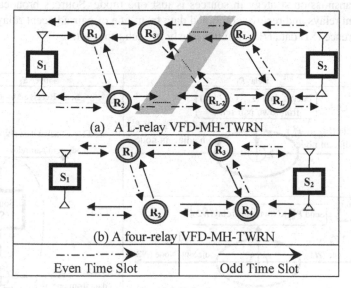

(a) A L-relay VFD-MH-TWRN

(b) A four-relay VFD-MH-TWRN

Even Time Slot   Odd Time Slot

Fig. 2. The schematic of proposed virtual full duplex multi-hop two-way relay network.

Each relay has a limited buffer size that its capacity is equal with only one packet data. Each one of sources can send a packet data in one time slot that transmitted packet by sources S_1 and S_2 in t^{th} time slot, are noted as $P_{s_1}^t$ and $P_{s_2}^t$ ($t = 1, \ldots, N$), respectively and all of the packets have the same length. Each relay can only receive signals from its adjacent nodes and signals received from the non-neighboring are negligible due to the long distance. It is assumed each relay has a neighbor relay that they are pair as $\{(R_1, R_2), (R_3, R_4) \ldots (R_{L-1}, R_L)\}$ in network so in receive mode, each relay received from its pair and two adjacent nodes from two sides. Each pair relay work as complementary, when one of them is in broadcasting (sender) mode, another one is in receiving mode and vice versa. (Number of relays is an odd number). Sources can only receive signals from one of the relays in adjacent pair (source 1 can receive from R_1 or R_2 also, source 2 can receive from R_{L-1} or R_L) in each time slot, and also it receives self-interference (SI) signal from its antenna transmitter simultaneously. The channel properties stay constant state for a frame or packet duration and vary independently from one frame to another as static fading channel (block fading channel).

As illustrated in Fig. 3, data transmission strategy in relays consists of two modes. In Receiver Mode, relay R_l receive combined data from adjacent relays (R_{l-2} and R_{l+2}) and own pair relay R_{l+1} if l is odd or R_{l-1} if l is even sor from source and adjacent relay and own pair relay $\{[S_2, R_{l-2}, (R_{L-1} \ or \ R_L)], [S_1, R_{l+2}, (R_2 \ or \ R_1)]\}$. In transmitter Mode, relay R_l send its combined data ($P_{R_l}^t$) to source and adjacent relay and own pair relay. But data transmission strategy in sources is just one mode. Sources broadcast $P_{S_i}^t$ to pair adjacent relays and receive combined data from one of pair adjacent relays and its self-interference (SI) data ($P_{S_i}^t$)simultaneously in each time slot.

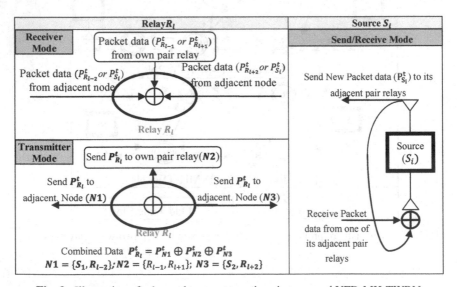

Fig. 3. Illustration of relay and source operations in proposed VFD-MH-TWRN.

In order to simplify and explain all the possible transmission states of VFD-MH-TWRN, a four-relay model is depicted in Fig. 2.b and also a 4-relay 4-message VFD-MH-TWRN is Illustrated in Fig. 4 (where ⊕ is the modulo-2 addition operator). It is obvious, the transmission events at each node are independent of the total number of packets and each relays do not need to extract received data and just need to receive combined data and broadcast it, but sources can decode other source new data by previous received and sent data. (The term combined packet data means when two packet data are XORed with standard PNC) So in case of L-node M-message (packet data) can be easily extended from the same procedure presented in Fig. 4. In generalized VFD-MH-TWRN scheme with L-node M-message that L (the number of relays) is even and the total number of message sequences for exchanging by two sources is symbolized to $2M$, at all, $L/2 + 1$ time slots are required to transmit the one frame so $L/2 + M$ time slots are needed to transmit $2M$ frames mutually.

TS	I/O	Source 1	Relay 1	Relay 2	Relay 3	Relay 4	Source2	I/O
1	I:$P_{S_1}^1$	T: $P_{S_1}^1$	R:			R:	T: $P_{S_2}^1$	I:$P_{S_2}^1$
	-	R: $P_{S_1}^1$	$P_{S_1}^1$			$P_{S_2}^1$	R: $P_{S_2}^1$	-
2	I:$P_{S_1}^2$	T: $P_{S_1}^2$	T:	R:	R:	T:	T: $P_{S_2}^2$	I:$P_{S_2}^2$
	-	R: $P_{S_1}^2 \oplus P_{S_1}^1$	$P_{S_1}^1$	$P_{S_1}^1 \oplus P_{S_1}^2 \oplus P_{S_2}^1$	$P_{S_1}^1 \oplus P_{S_2}^2 \oplus P_{S_1}^1$	$P_{S_2}^1$	R: $P_{S_2}^2 \oplus P_{S_2}^2$	-
3	I:$P_{S_1}^3$	T: $P_{S_1}^3$	R:	T:	T:	R:	T: $P_{S_2}^3$	I:$P_{S_2}^3$
	O:$P_{S_2}^1$	R: $P_{S_1}^3 \oplus P_{S_1}^1 \oplus P_{S_2}^2 \oplus P_{S_2}^1$	$P_{S_1}^3 \oplus P_{S_1}^1 \oplus P_{S_2}^2$	$P_{S_1}^1 \oplus P_{S_2}^2 \oplus P_{S_2}^1$	$P_{S_2}^2 \oplus P_{S_1}^1 \oplus P_{S_2}^1$	$P_{S_2}^3 \oplus P_{S_1}^2 \oplus P_{S_2}^2$	R: $P_{S_2}^3 \oplus P_{S_1}^1 \oplus P_{S_2}^2 \oplus P_{S_1}^1$	O:$P_{S_1}^1$
4	I:$P_{S_1}^4$	T: $P_{S_1}^4$	T:	R:	R:	T:	T: $P_{S_2}^4$	I:$P_{S_2}^4$
	O:$P_{S_2}^2$	R: $P_{S_1}^4 \oplus P_{S_1}^3 \oplus P_{S_2}^2 \oplus P_{S_2}^2$	$P_{S_1}^3 \oplus P_{S_1}^2 \oplus P_{S_2}^2$	$P_{S_1}^3 \oplus P_{S_2}^3 \oplus P_{S_1}^4$	$P_{S_1}^1 \oplus P_{S_2}^3 \oplus P_{S_2}^4$	$P_{S_2}^3 \oplus P_{S_2}^2 \oplus P_{S_2}^2$	R: $P_{S_2}^4 \oplus P_{S_2}^3 \oplus P_{S_2}^2 \oplus P_{S_2}^2$	O:$P_{S_1}^2$
5	-	T:∅	R:	T:	T:	R:	T:∅	-
	O:$P_{S_2}^3$	R: $P_{S_1}^3 \oplus P_{S_2}^3 \oplus P_{S_1}^4$	$P_{S_1}^4 \oplus P_{S_2}^4$	$P_{S_1}^3 \oplus P_{S_2}^3 \oplus P_{S_1}^4$	$P_{S_1}^3 \oplus P_{S_2}^3 \oplus P_{S_2}^4$	$P_{S_1}^4 \oplus P_{S_2}^4$	R: $P_{S_2}^3 \oplus P_{S_2}^3 \oplus P_{S_2}^4$	O:$P_{S_1}^3$
6	-	T:∅	T:	R:∅	R:∅	T:	T:∅	-
	O:$P_{S_2}^4$	R: $P_{S_1}^4 \oplus P_{S_2}^4$	$P_{S_1}^4 \oplus P_{S_2}^4$			$P_{S_1}^4 \oplus P_{S_2}^4$	R: $P_{S_1}^4 \oplus P_{S_2}^4$	O:$P_{S_1}^4$

Fig. 4. A transmission states illustration of 4-Relay 4-message VFD-MH-TWRN.

Then Network Throughput is equal with $\frac{2M}{L/2+M}$ and when the number of messages (M) is much larger than the number of relays (L), it can be achieved an upper limit of the network throughput which is:

$$\lim_{M \gg L} \frac{2M}{L/2 + M} \cong 2; \quad if \ L = 2k, \ k \in \mathbb{N} \tag{1}$$

3.2 SOQPSK Signal Model

It is known that the complex envelope of SOQPSK is defined as follows:

$$s(t; \alpha) = \sqrt{\frac{E_s}{T_s}} exp\left\{ j \sum_i \alpha_i q(t - iT_s) \right\} \tag{2}$$

Where the energy and time duration of symbol are denoted by E_s, T_s respectively and $i \in \mathbb{Z}$ is the discrete-time index and $\alpha = \{\alpha_i\}$ is the transmitted ternary symbol sequence where each symbol has duration T_s where α_i consist of alphabet i.e. $(-1, 0, +1)$ that α_i is come from the true input binary data sequence (b) the b_i take on $\{1, -1\}$ values as follows [11]:

$$\alpha_i = (-1)^{i+1} \frac{b_{i-1}(b_i - b_{i-2})}{2}; \quad (b_i)_{i \in \mathbb{Z}} \in \{1, -1\} \tag{3}$$

And also the phase modulation $\phi(t, \alpha)$ can be expressed as

$$\phi(t, \alpha) = 2\pi h \sum_i \alpha_i q(t - iT_s) \tag{4}$$

That $h = 1/2$ is the modulation index. It is assumed that the signal $s(t; \alpha)$ is full-response [12]. In the appendix 1 is depicted role of previous bits in phase variation in SOQPSK modulation and also is shown phase variation range for the new symbol $\left(\Delta\theta_i \in \left\{\frac{m\pi}{2}, m = 0, 1, -1\right\}\right)$. So we can infer the following the mapping and approximation for phase variation.

$$\theta_{i+1} = \Delta\theta_i(t) + \theta_i$$
$$\theta_i \in \left\{\frac{m\pi}{4}, m = 1, 3, 5, 7\right\}; \quad iT_b \le t \le (i+1)T_b \tag{5}$$

4   A Virtual Full-Duplex Denoise-and-Forward TWR Scheme

As shown in Fig. 2.a, this network consists of two sources and four relays so be defined channels as $S_1 \leftrightharpoons R_1, S_1 \leftrightharpoons R_2, R_1 \leftrightharpoons R_2, R_1 \leftrightharpoons R_3, R_2 \leftrightharpoons R_4, R_3 \leftrightharpoons R_4, S_2 \leftrightharpoons R_3$, $S_2 \leftrightharpoons R_4$, and the RSI channels $S_1 \leftrightharpoons S_1$ and $S_2 \leftrightharpoons S_2$ that their corresponding channels coefficients denoted by

$$h_{S_1R_1}, \ h_{R_1S_1}, \ h_{S_1R_2}, \ h_{R_2S_1}, \ h_{R_1R_2}, \ h_{R_2R_1}, \ h_{R_1R_3}, \ h_{R_3R_1}, \ h_{R_2R_4}, \ h_{R_4R_2}, \ h_{R_3R_4}$$
$$h_{R_4R_3}, \ h_{S_2R_3}, \ h_{R_3S_2}, \ h_{S_2R_4}, \ h_{R_4S_2}$$

All the channel properties and coefficients stay static during one time slot (t), but change from one time slot to another one independently. We suppose the channels between two nodes and the RSI channels are under Rayleigh fading and suppose instantaneous CSI is unknown at any node but long-term (statistics) CSI is known i.e. as $h_{S_iR_j}^t \sim \mathcal{CN}\left(0, \sigma_{S_iR_j}^2\right)$, $i = 1, 2$ and $j = 1, 2, 3, 4$ where $\sigma_{S_iR_j}^2$ denotes the variance as corresponding channel gain in time slot t. The additive white Gaussian noise (AWGN) at each node is indicated by $Z_{Si}^t(n) \sim \mathcal{CN}\left(0, \sigma_{S_i}^2\right) Z_{Ri}^t(n) \sim \mathcal{CN}\left(0, \sigma_{R_i}^2\right)$.

In the odd time slot ($t = 2\ k\text{-}1$, $k \in \mathbb{N}$), sources S_1, S_2 transmit their n^{th} packet symbols to R_1, R_4 respectively and R_2 forwards to R_1, S_1 and R_3 forwards to R_4, S_2 the received symbols in the last time slot. So the received signals at S_1, S_2, R_1, R_4 in t^{th} timeslot can be expressed as

$$y_{S1}^t(n) = \sqrt{E_{R2}} h_{R_2S_1}^t R_2^t(n) + \sqrt{E_{S1}} h_{S_1S_1}^t S_1^t(n) + Z_{S1}^t(n) \tag{6}$$

$$y_{S2}^t(n) = \sqrt{E_{R3}} h_{R_3S_2}^t R_3^t(n) + \sqrt{E_{S2}} h_{S_2S_2}^t S_2^t(n) + Z_{S2}^t(n) \tag{7}$$

$$y_{R1}^t(n) = \sqrt{E_{S1}} h_{S_1R_1}^t S_1^t(n) + \sqrt{E_{R2}} h_{R_2R_1}^t R_2^t(n) + \sqrt{E_{R3}} h_{R_3R_1}^t R_3^t(n) + Z_{R1}^t(n) \tag{8}$$

$$y_{R4}^t(n) = \sqrt{E_{S2}} h_{S_2R_4}^t S_2^t(n) + \sqrt{E_{R3}} h_{R_3R_4}^t R_3^t(n) + \sqrt{E_{R2}} h_{R_2R_4}^t R_2^t(n) + Z_{R4}^t(n) \tag{9}$$

In the even time slot, sources S_1, S_2 transmits their n^{th} packet symbols to R_2, R_3 respectively and R_1 forwards to R_2, S_1 and R_4 forwards to R_3, S_2 the received signal in the last time slot. So the received signals at S_1, S_2, R_2, R_3 can be written as

$$y_{S1}^{t+1}(n) = \sqrt{E_{R1}} h_{R_1S_1}^{t+1} R_1^t(n) + \sqrt{E_{S1}} h_{S_1S_1}^{t+1} S_1^t(n) + Z_{S1}^{t+1}(n) \tag{10}$$

$$y_{S2}^{t+1}(n) = \sqrt{E_{R4}} h_{R_4S_2}^{t+1} R_3^{t+1}(n) + \sqrt{E_{S2}} h_{S_2S_2}^{t+1} S_2^{t+1}(n) + Z_{S2}^{t+1}(n) \tag{11}$$

$$y_{R2}^{t+1}(n) = \sqrt{E_{S1}} h_{S_1R_2}^{t+1} S_1^{t+1}(n) + \sqrt{E_{R1}} h_{R_1R_2}^{t+1} R_1^{t+1}(n) + \sqrt{E_{R4}} h_{R_4R_2}^{t+1} R_4^{t+1}(n) + Z_{R2}^{t+1}(n) \tag{12}$$

$$y_{R4}^{t+1}(n) = \sqrt{E_{S2}} h_{S_2R_3}^t S_2^t(n) + \sqrt{E_{R4}} h_{R_4R_3}^t R_4^t(n) + \sqrt{E_{R2}} h_{R_2R_3}^t R_2^t(n) + Z_{R4}^{t+1}(n) \tag{13}$$

It should mention here, in the tth time slot, source S_i transmit K-bit symbol $b_{si}^t(n) = \left\{ b_{si,K}^t(n) \right\}$ where K index denotes bit index in one symbol and n denote the symbol index in one frame. There are M frames to be transmitted at each source node, so $L/2 + M$ time slots are needed to transmit $2M$ frames mutually. Sources generate SOQPSK signals $S_i^t(n)$ base on $e^{j\theta_i(n)}$ where $\theta_i(n) \in \{ \frac{m\pi}{4}, m = 1, 3, 5, 7 \}$. As mentioned in the previous section, it can be changed to $\pm\frac{\pi}{2}$ or 0 related to the previous one so $\Delta\theta_i$ can be shown as $\Delta\theta_i(n) \in \{ \frac{m\pi}{2}, m = 0, 1, -1 \}$ so $\theta_i^t(n+1) = \Delta\theta_i(n) + \theta_i^t(n)$. Now we want to define two vectors, at first a vector of two successive received signals at the node as $Y = \left[y(n+1)\ y(n) \right]^T$ is defined [13, 14] and the second one is a vector of combined received data at node as $b(n) = b_\alpha(n) \oplus b_\beta(n)$ that α, β denote adjust transmitter nodes. And the mapping from $b_i(n)$ to $\theta_i(n)$ is described by appendix. For simplicity, it is defined these conditions for decoding relay R_1, which these results can be extended to other nodes easily.

$$\mathbb{Y}_{R1}^t(n) = \left[y_{R1}^t(n+1)\ y_{R1}^t(n) \right]^T \tag{14}$$

$$b_{R1}^t(n) = b_{S1}^t(n) \oplus b_{R2}^t(n) \oplus b_{R3}^t(n) \tag{15}$$

So we can rewrite (14) for R_1 as

$$\mathbb{Y}_{R1}^t(n) = \sqrt{E_{S1}} h_{S_1R_1}^t \mathbb{S}_1^t(n) + \sqrt{E_{R2}} h_{R_2R_1}^t \mathbb{R}_2^t(n) + \sqrt{E_{R3}} h_{R_3R_1}^t \mathbb{R}_3^t(n) + \mathbb{Z}_{R1}^t(n) \tag{16}$$

According to the above definition, the related vectors are expressed as $\mathbb{S}_i^t(n) = \left[S_i^t(n+1)\ S_i^t(n) \right]^T$ $(i = 1,2)$ and $\mathbb{R}_2^t(n) = \left[R_j^t(n+1)\ R_j^t(n) \right]^T$ $(j = 1,2,3,4)$ and

$\mathbb{Z}_{Xi}^t(n) = \left[Z_{Xi}^{t+1}(n+1)\, Z_{Xi}^{t+1}(n) \right]^T$ ($X_i = S_i, R_j$) so the covariance matrix (COV(.) is covariance operator) at receiver base on $\mathbb{Y}$ can be calculated as (17) For given $\Delta\theta_{s1}, \Delta\theta_{R2}, \Delta\theta_{R3}$ that $\mathbb{E}(.)$ is expected value operator.

$$COV\left(\mathbb{Y}_{R1}^t(n)\right) = \mathbb{E}\left(\mathbb{Y}_{R1}^t(n).\mathbb{Y}_{R1}^t(n)^T\right)$$

$$= \mathbb{E}\begin{pmatrix} y_{R1}^t(n+1)^2 & y_{R1}^t(n+1).y_{R1}^t(n)^T \\ y_{R1}^t(n).y_{R1}^t(n+1)^T & y_{R1}^t(n)^2 \end{pmatrix}$$

$$= \begin{pmatrix} \mathbb{E}(y_{R1}^t(n+1)^2) & \mathbb{E}(y_{R1}^t(n+1).y_{R1}^t(n)^T) \\ \mathbb{E}(y_{R1}^t(n).y_{R1}^t(n+1)^T) & \mathbb{E}(y_{R1}^t(n)^2) \end{pmatrix} \tag{17}$$

$$\mathbb{E}(y_{R1}^t(n)^2) = \mathbb{E}(y_{R1}^t(n+1)^2$$
$$= E_{S1}\sigma_{S_1R_1}^2 + E_{R2}\sigma_{R_2R_1}^2 + E_{R3}\sigma_{R_3R_1}^2 + \sigma_{R1}^2 \tag{18}$$

$$\mathbb{E}\left(y_{R1}^t(n+1).y_{R1}^t(n)^T\right) = E_{S1}\sigma_{S_1R_1}^2 e^{j\Delta\theta_{s1}(n)}$$
$$+ E_{R2}\sigma_{R_2R_1}^2 e^{j\Delta\theta_{R2}(n)} + E_{R3}\sigma_{R_3R_1}^2 e^{j\Delta\theta_{R3}(n)} \tag{19}$$

$$\mathbb{E}(y_{R1}^t(n).y_{R1}^t(n+1)^T) = E_{S1}\sigma_{S_1R_1}^2 e^{-j\Delta\theta_{s1}(n)}$$
$$+ E_{R2}\sigma_{R_2R_1}^2 e^{-j\Delta\theta_{R2}(n)} + E_{R3}\sigma_{R_3R_1}^2 e^{-j\Delta\theta_{R3}(n)} \tag{20}$$

If it is assumed $b_{R1temp}^t(n) = b_{S1}^t(n) \oplus b_{R2}^t(n) \oplus b_{R3}^t(n) \approx \Delta\theta(n)$ where $\Delta\theta(n) \in \left\{ \frac{m\pi}{4}, m = 1,3,5,7 \right\}$, so at relay R1, result of $b_{R1}^t(n)$ decoding is presented as $\widehat{b_{R1}^t(n)} \approx \Delta\theta_{R1}(n)$ then according to the above equation, base on the de-noising (mapping) function using ML principle which it was mentioned in [15], that relay 1 can use of $\widehat{b_{R1}^t(n)}$ to decode superimposed symbols as is shown in Fig. 4.

$$\widehat{b_{R1}^t(n)} = arg \max_{b_{R1}^t(n)=b_{S1}^t(n)\oplus b_{R2}^t(n)\oplus b_{R3}^t(n)} f\left(\mathbb{Y}_{R1}^t(n)|b_{R1temp}^t(n)\right) \tag{21}$$

Where $f(\mathbb{Y}|b)$ denotes the conditional probability density function (PDF) of $\mathbb{Y}$ when b is given. Then the conditional probability density function (PDF) of $\mathbb{Y}_{R1}^t(n)$ can be calculated as (22) and (23) when $\theta_{s1}(n)$, $\theta_{R2}(n)$ and $\theta_{R3}(n)$, are given according to total probability theorem.

$$f\left(\mathbb{Y}_{R1}^t(n)|b_{R1}^t(n)\right) = \frac{1}{4} \sum_{b_{R1}^t(n)=b_{S1}^t(n)\oplus b_{R2}^t(n)\oplus b_{R3}^t} f\left(\mathbb{Y}_{R1}^t(n)|b_{S1}^t(n), b_{R3}^t(n), b_{R2}^t(n)\right) \tag{22}$$

$$f\left(\mathbb{Y}_{R1}^t(n)|b_{S1}^t(n), b_{R3}^t(n), b_{R2}^t(n)\right) = \frac{1}{\pi^2 |COV(\mathbb{Y}_{R1}^t(n))|} e^{-\mathbb{Y}_{R1}^t(n)^T COV(\mathbb{Y}_{R1}^t(n))^{-1} \mathbb{Y}_{R1}^t(n)}$$

$$\tag{23}$$

5 Performance Analysis

In this section, we use symbol error rate (SER) to performance analysis under the DNF-TWR scheme. Then base on total probability theorem, and mapping signal to its phase (it is mentioned above) so the PDF of $\mathbb{Y}_{R1}^t(n)$ conditioned on $\Delta\theta_{R1}(n)$ is presented with (24).

$$f\left(\mathbb{Y}_{R1}^t(n)|\Delta\theta_{R1}(n) = \pi/4\right) =$$

$$1/4\{f\left[\mathbb{Y}_{R1}^t(n), COV_{\pi/4,\pi/4,7\pi/4}\left(\mathbb{Y}_{R1}^t\right)\right]+$$

$$f\left[\mathbb{Y}_{R1}^t(n), COV_{\pi/4,7\pi/4,\pi/4}\left(\mathbb{Y}_{R1}^t\right)\right]f\left[\mathbb{Y}_{R1}^t(n), COV_{7\pi/4,\pi/4,\pi/4}\left(\mathbb{Y}_{R1}^t\right)\right]$$

$$f\left[\mathbb{Y}_{R1}^t(n), COV_{3\pi/4,7\pi/4,7\pi/4}\left(\mathbb{Y}_{R1}^t\right)\right]+f\left[\mathbb{Y}_{R1}^t(n), COV_{7\pi/4,7\pi/4,3\pi/4}\left(\mathbb{Y}_{R1}^t\right)\right]+$$

$$f\left[\mathbb{Y}_{R1}^t(n), COV_{7\pi/4,3\pi/4,7\pi/4}\left(\mathbb{Y}_{R1}^t\right)\right]+\left[\mathbb{Y}_{R1}^t(n), COV_{5\pi/4,5\pi/4,7\pi/4}\left(\mathbb{Y}_{R1}^t\right)\right]+$$

$$f\left[\mathbb{Y}_{R1}^t(n), COV_{5\pi/4,7\pi/4,5\pi/4}\left(\mathbb{Y}_{R1}^t\right)\right]+f\left[\mathbb{Y}_{R1}^t(n), COV_{7\pi/4,5\pi/4,5\pi/4}\left(\mathbb{Y}_{R1}^t\right)\right]+$$

$$\left[\mathbb{Y}_{R1}^t(n), COV_{5\pi/4,3\pi/4,\pi/4}\left(\mathbb{Y}_{R1}^t\right)\right]+f\left[\mathbb{Y}_{R1}^t(n), COV_{5\pi/4,\pi/4,3\pi/4}\left(\mathbb{Y}_{R1}^t\right)\right]+$$

$$f\left[\mathbb{Y}_{R1}^t(n), COV_{3\pi/4,5\pi/4,\pi/4}\left(\mathbb{Y}_{R1}^t\right)\right]+\left[\mathbb{Y}_{R1}^t(n), COV_{3\pi/4,\pi/4,5\pi/4}\left(\mathbb{Y}_{R1}^t\right)\right]+$$

$$f\left[\mathbb{Y}_{R1}^t(n), COV_{\pi/4,5\pi/4,3\pi/4}\left(\mathbb{Y}_{R1}^t\right)\right]+f\left[\mathbb{Y}_{R1}^t(n), COV_{\pi/4,3\pi/4,5\pi/4}\left(\mathbb{Y}_{R1}^t\right)\right]+$$

$$f\left[\mathbb{Y}_{R1}^t(n), COV_{3\pi/4,3\pi/4,3\pi/4}\left(\mathbb{Y}_{R1}^t\right)\right]\} \tag{24}$$

That $COV_{\theta_{S1},\theta_{R2},\theta_{R3}}\left(\mathbb{Y}_{R1}^t(n)\right)$ is covariance matrix of $\mathbb{Y}_{R1}^t(n)$ conditioned by $b_{S1}^t(n)$, $b_{R2}^t(n)$ and $b_{R3}^t(n)$ when they are mapped to $\theta_{S1}(n)$, $\theta_{R2}(n)$ and $\theta_{R3}(n)$, and it can be rewritten for another state of $\Delta\theta_{R1}(n)$: $f(\mathbb{Y}_{R1}^t(n)|\Delta\theta_{R1}(n) = 3\pi/4)$, $f(\mathbb{Y}_{R1}^t(n)|\Delta\theta_{R1}(n) = 5\pi/4)$ and $f(\mathbb{Y}_{R1}^t(n)|\Delta\theta_{R1}(n) = 7\pi/4)$. Now we can define SER base on phase as

$$P_{SER\pi/4,R1} = P(\Delta\theta_{R1}(n) \neq \pi/4|\Delta\theta(n) = \pi/4)$$
$$P_{SER3\pi/4,R1} = P(\Delta\theta_{R1}(n) \neq 3\pi/4|\Delta\theta(n) = 3\pi/4)$$
$$P_{SER5\pi/4,R1} = P(\Delta\theta_{R1}(n) \neq 5\pi/4|\Delta\theta(n) = 5\pi/4)$$
$$P_{SER7\pi/4,R1} = P(\Delta\theta_{R1}(n) \neq 7\pi/4|\Delta\theta(n) = 7\pi/4) \tag{25}$$

So finally SER in the relay 1 is presented in (26).

$$P\left(\widehat{b_{R1}^t(n)} \neq b_{R1temp}^t(n)\right)$$
$$= 1/4\{P_{SER\pi/4,R1} + P_{SER3\pi/4,R1} + P_{SER5\pi/4,R1} + P_{SER7\pi/4,R1}\} \tag{26}$$

Considering that this structure embraces all of structured named virtual full duplex two-way relay network Fig. 2.a so it easily can develop this method to use for all nodes in the network (including relays and sources) in this structure.

6 Simulation and Results

Finally, we simulate the proposed scheme and show simulation results. In the simulation, it is assumed $E_{S1} = E_{S2} = E_{R1} = E_{R2} = E_{R3} = E_{R4} = E$ and all of the channel variances are equal with σ^2. It is assumed Rayleigh fading channel, AWGN and always relay node located on the middle of line connecting two sender node or center of three sender node. BER means the error probability of decoding at sources and system SNR refers to $\gamma = \frac{E}{2\sigma^2}$.

In Fig. 5, we compare the simulated BER of DF-TWRN with DQPSK and DNF-TWRN with SOQPSK modulation. It can be observed that the BER performance of with DNF-TWR is closed to that of DF, and BER becomes smaller with the increase of SNR. The simulation results show that the BER performance of DF-TWRN scheme and DNF-TWRN scheme are similar while Network Throughput has increased.

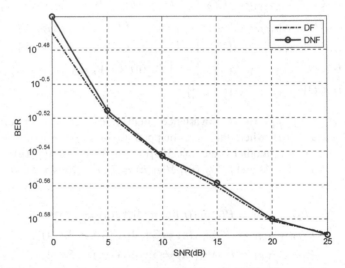

Fig. 5. BER of DF-TWR and DNF-TWR with SOQPSK modulation.

7 Summary

In this paper has proposed a virtual full-duplex de-noise and forward two-way relaying (VFD-DNF-TWRN) scheme with SOQPSK modulation, which does not need instantaneous channel state information (CSI). In the proposed scheme, two full-duplex source nodes exchange their information with the help of multi half-duplex relay node. It has shown that network throughput is higher than all of the previously defined networks and the simulation results show that the proposed scheme with SOQPSK modulation can is close to DF-TWRN the bit error rate and they have similar performance.

Appendix

See Table 1.

Table 1. Relation previous bits and symbol phase variation for SOQPSK

a_i	i	$(-1)^{i+1}$	I a_{i-2}	Q a_{i-1}	I a_{i-1}	Q a_{i-2}	$i\text{-}1^{th}$ phase state.	a_i	IQ New	i^{th} phase state	α	Ph.diff $(i,i\text{-}1)$
I	even	−1	00				$\pi/4$	0	00	$\pi/4$	0	0
I	even	−1	00				$\pi/4$	1	10	$3\pi/4$	1	$\pi/2$
Q	odd	1			00		$\pi/4$	0	00	$\pi/4$	0	0
Q	odd	1			00		$\pi/4$	1	01	$7\pi/4$	−1	$-\pi/2$
I	even	−1	01				$7\pi/4$	0	01	$7\pi/4$	0	0
I	even	−1	01				$7\pi/4$	1	11	$5\pi/4$	−1	$-\pi/2$
Q	odd	1			01		$7\pi/4$	1	01	$7\pi/4$	0	0
Q	odd	1			01		$7\pi/4$	0	00	$\pi/4$	1	$\pi/2$
I	even	−1	10				$3\pi/4$	1	10	$3\pi/4$	0	0
I	even	−1	10				$3\pi/4$	0	00	$\pi/4$	−1	$-\pi/2$
Aa	odd	1			10		$3\pi/4$	0	10	$3\pi/4$	0	0
Q	odd	1			10		$3\pi/4$	1	11	$5\pi/4$	1	$\pi/2$
I	even	−1	11				$5\pi/4$	1	11	$5\pi/4$	0	0
I	even	−1	11				$5\pi/4$	0	01	$7\pi/4$	1	$\pi/2$
Q	odd	1			11		$5\pi/4$	1	11	$5\pi/4$	0	0
Q	odd	1			11		$5\pi/4$	0	10	$3\pi/4$	−1	$-\pi/2$

References

1. Perez, R.T., Subbarao, K.: A survey of current femtosatellite design, technologies, and mission concepts. J. Small Satell. **5**(3), 467–482 (2016)
2. Manchester, Z., Peck, M.: Kicksat: a crowd-funded mission to demonstrate the worlds smallest spacecraft. In: Proceedings AIAA/USU Conference on Small Satellites (2013)
3. Hanson, J., Chartres, J., Sanchez, H.: The EDSN intersatellite communications architecture. In: Proceedings 28th Annual AIAA/USU Conference on Small Satellites (2014)
4. Barnhart, D.J., Vladimirova, T.: very-small-satellite design for distributed space missions. J. Spacecr. Rocket **44**(6), 1294–1306 (2007)
5. Radakrishnan, S.B., Edmonson, W.W., Afghah, F., Rodriguez-Osorio, R.M., Pinto, F.: Survey of inter-satellite communication for small satellites systems: physical layer to network layer view. IEEE Commun. Surv. Tutorials **18**(4), 2442–2473 (2016)
6. Popovski, P., Yomo, H.: Bi-directional amplification of throughput in a wireless multi-hop network. In: Proceedings IEEE 63rd Vehicular Technology Conference, vol. 2, pp. 588–593 (2006)
7. Popovski, P., Yomo, H.: The anti-packets can increase the achievable throughput of a wireless multi-hop network. In: Proceedings IEEE International Conference on Communications, vol. 9, pp. 3885–3890 (2006)
8. Wang, G., Xiang, W., Yuan, J.: Multihop compute-and-forward for generalised two-way relay channels. Trans. Emerg. Telecommun. Technol. **26**(3), 448–460 (2015)
9. Mazinani, A., Gao, Q.: Orthogonal OQPSK modulation with physical layer network coding systems over two-way relay. In: 2018 IEEE International Conference Computing Communication Engineering Technology, pp. 28–33 (2018)
10. Anderson, J.B., Aulin, T., Sundberg, C.-E.: Digital Phase Modulation. Plenum Press, New York (1986)
11. Li, L., Simon, M.K.: Performance of coded OQPSK and MIL-STD SOQPSK with iterative decoding. IEEE Trans. Commun. **52**(11), 1890–1900 (2004)
12. Perrins, E., Kumaraswamy, B.: Decision feedback detectors for SOQPSK. IEEE Trans. Commun. **57**(8), 2359–2368 (2009)
13. Fan, J., Li, L., Zhang, H., Chen, W., Member, S.: Denoise-and-forward two-path successive relaying with DBPSK modulation. IEEE Wirel. Commun. Lett. **2337**(c), 1–4 (2016)
14. Fan, J., Li, L., Zhang, H.: Full-duplex denoise-and-forward two-way relaying with DBPSK modulation. In: Proceedings 8th International Conference on Wireless Communications and Signal Processing (WCSP), pp. 1–5 (2016)
15. Katti, B.-S.: XORs in the air: practical wireless network coding. IEEE/ACM Trans. Netw. **16**(3), 497–510 (2008)

Enhanced Contention Resolution Diversity Slotted ALOHA in Satellite-Based IoTs Using Sparse Code Multiple Access

Bo Zhang[1], Yue Li[1], YunLai Xu[1], and Zhihua Yang[1,2]($\boxtimes$)

[1] Communication Engineering Research Center, Harbin Institute of Technology
(Shenzhen), Shenzhen, Guangdong, China
{18s152602,xuyunlai}@stu.hit.edu.cn, liyue1234566@126.com,
yangzhihua@hit.edu.cn
[2] Pengcheng Laboratory, Shenzhen, Guangdong, China

Abstract. As a efficient random access scheme, contention resolution diversity slotted ALOHA (CRDSA) improves the system throughput greatly, although deadlock problem limits the maximum throughput of system. To address this issue, in this paper, a non-orthogonal multiple access (NOMA) technique is proposed with random access (RA) scheme for supporting multiple terminals access in satellite IoT-oriented networks, by utilizing a code domain NOMA called Sparse Code Multiple Access (SCMA). In the proposed scheme, the throughput is mainly improved by physical (PHY) decoding and iterative decoding. Through mathematical analysis, the throughput lower bound of our scheme is shown and the simulated result proves the proposed scheme is efficient in enhancing RA throughput.

Keywords: SCMA · CRDSA · Random access · PHY decoding ·
Multiple terminals access

1 Introduction

As the number of Internet of things devices that can be expected to proliferate, existing random access methods need to be improved to better support multi-terminal simultaneous access. Recent research achievements called CRDSA-like random access protocols based on CRDSA [1] have shown great enhancement in the system throughput. CRDSA has been seen as a promising scheme for supporting massive machine type communication terminals(MTC) connectivity in future IoT-oriented satellite networks. Since the former research mainly focus on the MAC layer, theoretically, the throughput have a upper threshold of 1 packet/slot which can be reached only in the situation where no terminal collision occurs, such situation hardly exists in high traffic load communication

Q. Wu et al. (Eds.): WiSATS 2020, LNICST 357, pp. 81–95, 2021.
https://doi.org/10.1007/978-3-030-69069-4_8

networks. When terminals heavily collide in CRDSA scheme, no more packets can be recovered and the deadlock appears (The deadlock is explained in Sect. 2). So shifting focus from MAC layer scheme to a Physical-MAC crossed layer scheme may work better. As a pioneering slotted ALOHA scheme with packets diversity, CRDSA allows multiple terminals to have access into satellite networks simultaneously tolerating channel collision in some extent. The most prominent contribution of CRDSA is the successive iterative interference cancellation (SIC) combined with packets diversity. In CRDSA, once a packet is decoded, its replica's slot location can be found according to the pointer information and thus, with SIC, replica packet can be canceled, enabling further more packets decoding in the replica's slot. However, there exists a deadlock problem in CRDSA which is caused by unrecoverable collision packets, resulting in the peak throughput about 0.55. CRDSA++ [2] is proposed as a enhanced version of CRDSA, which enhance the CRDSA through increasing the number of transmitted replicas, however, the enhancement of CRDSA++ only exits in low load region. Another enhanced CRDSA called irregular repetition slotted ALOHA (IRSA) is proposed in [3], the author describe the interference cancellation process with a bipartite graph model, giving a novel application of bipartite to SIC algorithm, and the throughput of IRSA is about 1.5 times of CRDSA in the same traffic load. The enhancements in [2,3] are brought by different numbers of transmitted packets. Even the schemes mentioned above appear functional, the research are still confined to MAC protocol.

Researches in [4–6] shows power domain and code domain combined CRDSA have great improvement in throughput. The author in [4] devote his research direction in resolving the typical deadlock problem of CRDSA, by localizing all the replicas of a terminal utilizing a correlation based method, and then the replicas are combined to decode the packets. Since [4] is not a pure MAC scheme, assisted by power domain technique, the system can achieve a normalized throughput higher than 1.2. To better solve the deadlock problem, the author in [5] proposes a enhanced scheme based on [4], using shared information about time slots location on which terminals transmit their replicas. Research in [6] named coded slotted ALOHA (CSA) turns to a code domain scheme, relying on the combination of packet erasure correcting codes and SIC, this scheme depends on both packets repetition and coding.

NOMA has been proposed as a promising scheme for 5G mobile communication system, and researches about NOMA have increased greatly in the past several years. The research in [7] utilizes a NOMA technique called PDMA to enhance the CRDSA protocol, introducing a kind of multi-carrier scheme to CRDSA. As a efficient NOMA, the code domain NOMA sparse code multiple access (SCMA) proposed by HuaWei in [8] allows multiple terminals to occupy the same time-frequency resource (RE). The RE occupation and SCMA decoding have been described in [9–11].

In this paper, a SCMA based CRDSA scheme is proposed to solve the traditional deadlock problem in CRDSA and improve the system throughput performance. In the scheme, sporadical terminals randomly choose a codebook at the transmitter, and the terminals will physically sent two copies of the same MAC packet like CRDSA. And at the receiver we mainly focus on PHY layer decoding and iterative decoding between MAC layer and PHY layer. Based on the decoding process, lower bound throughput of the proposed scheme is analyzed. We also show that our scheme improve the throughput greatly compared to traditional CRDSA.

The system model is introduced in Sect. 2. Details about our proposed packets decoding scheme are explained in Sect. 3, and complexity and throughput analysis are shown in Sect. 3 and simulation results are presented in Sect. 4.

2   System Model

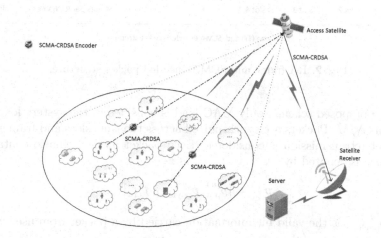

Fig. 1. Multi-type terminal random access model.

The physical communication model used in this paper is shown in Fig. 1. The ellipse enclosed by the light dotted line represents the satellite coverage area, the black dotted line represents the uplink access link, and the black solid line represents the downlink transmission link. The SCMA-CRDSA encoder in the figure is related to the algorithm proposed later in this paper. The satellite can provide access services for different types of wireless terminals in areas it can cover. Considering the energy consumption of the satellite itself, the data received at the satellite end will be forwarded to the ground satellite receiving station for processing. After that, the processed data will be sent to the server. We construct a RA communication scenario, in which N MTC terminals share the common uplink channel of the satellite, N is set to be a finite number in the model. Each RA frame is composed of M equal length slots (slot length is T_S while frame length is $T_F = M \cdot T_S$), and the terminal randomly choose two slots send their packets according to CRDSA. Deadlock in CRDSA is as shown in Fig. 2, the only single packet in slot 5, denoted by PK3 (PK3 in the figure refers to packet from terminal 3), is recovered first. Then according to the SIC in CRDSA, PK2, PK1 and PK6 can be recovered in turn. At the end, only PK4 and PK5 can not be recovered and a deadlock comes into being.

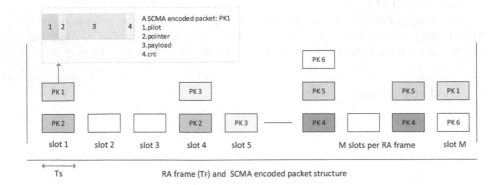

Fig. 2. RA frame and SCMA encoded packet structure.

In the proposed scheme, only MAC load is considered, the system load G is defined as N/M. Packets are synchronized across the time slots and frames, and no packet retransmission is considered. Each packet in the scenario contains k bits, which is denoted by

$$p^{(u)} = [p_{\text{poi}}^{(u)}, p_{\text{payload}}^{(u)}, p_{\text{crc}}^{(u)}] \tag{1}$$

where $p_{\text{payload}}^{(u)}$ is the valid bit information carried by a packet from user u. The head of the packet $p_{\text{poi}}^{(u)}$ contains the pointer bit information that indicates the location of the twins packet. $p_{\text{crc}}^{(u)}$ in the packet is used to check the correctness of payload bits. In order to reduce the influence of noisy channel fading during data transmission, an effective Forward Error Correction(FEC) code is considered. The FEC encoded bits in packets can be denoted by

$$b^{(u)} = [b_{\text{poi}}^{(u)}, b_{\text{payload}}^{(u)}, b_{\text{crc}}^{(u)}] \tag{2}$$

The symbols $b_{\text{poi}}^{(u)}, b_{\text{payload}}^{(u)}, b_{\text{crc}}^{(u)}$ represent the FEC encoded bits corresponding to $b_{\text{poi}}^{(u)}, b_{\text{payload}}^{(u)}, b_{\text{crc}}^{(u)}$ respectively.

The FEC encoded bits will go through a SCMA encoder before being transmitted. Through SCMA encoding, bit data can be allocated to carrier resource blocks in the form of SCMA codewords.

At the receiver, we assume that the receiver is able to recognize slots with a single packet or collision packets, and that the packets in slot can be recognized by adding pilot sequence. The structure of RA frame with SCMA encoded packets is shown in Fig. 2. Based on the RA frame and packet encoding structure, receiver perform a series of decoding processing, decoded packets will be CRC checked and successfully decoded packets can be used to SIC.

3 Proposed PHY Layer Assisted MAC Layer Scheme

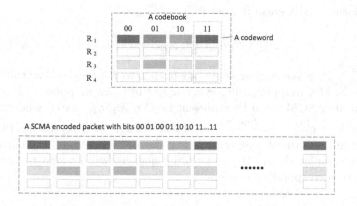

Fig. 3. A codebook and a SCMA encoded packet.

In this section, our proposed scheme and system performance evaluation are described detailedly. First, let us review the original SCMA [8]. In SCMA, the SCMA encoding of a packet is to map the bit information directly to complex number sequence through the selected codebook. The codebook is actually a sparse matrix, as shown in Fig. 3, each row of the sparse matrix represents a carrier. The non-zero row of the matrix represents that the terminal that chooses the codebook occupies the corresponding carrier, and the all-zero row represents that the carrier is not occupied by the terminal, while each column stands for a series of bits in the form of codeword (The codeword, as shown in Fig. 3, is a sparse complex vector). The correspondence between these bits and codewords depends on the modulation mode, taking QPSK modulation for example, the modulation order $O=4$, then every $log_2(O) = 2$ bits is mapped to a codeword. So the codewords of the codebook in Fig. 3 stand for bits 00/01/10/11. R_1, R_2, R_3, R_4 stand for the carriers from 1 to 4 respectively. And after all the bits of a packet are encoded, the structure of a packet can be represented as the way shown in Fig. 3.

The proposed scheme, as a combination of SCMA and CRDSA, focus more on the PHY layer encoding and decoding. In the processing stage, the MAC and PHY layers gain each other. Details are as follows:

3.1 Encoder at the Transmitter

This section describe data processing before transmission. First, a terminal randomly choose the i-th codebook ζ_i from the codebook set $\mathbb{C} = [\zeta_1, \zeta_2, ..., \zeta_i, ..., \zeta_l]$,

l is the total codebook number in codebook set. Once a packet is generated, bit stream of the packet go through FEC encoder(e.g., Turbo encoder), the terminal's coded bits are then mapped to the SCMA codeword according to the selected codebook. The mapping rule follows that every log_2O bits are mapped to a codeword. Bits of a packet from terminal u are represented by $\boldsymbol{b}^{(u)} = [\boldsymbol{b}^{(u)}_{poi}, \boldsymbol{b}^{(u)}_{payload}, \boldsymbol{b}^{(u)}_{crc}]$. Since we don't consider the detailed bits component when perform SCMA encoding, let $\mathbb{B}^{(u)} = \boldsymbol{b}^{(u)}$,

$$\mathbb{B}^{(u)} = [\boldsymbol{b}^{(u)}_{1\cdot log_2O}, \boldsymbol{b}^{(u)}_{2\cdot log_2O}, ..., \boldsymbol{b}^{(u)}_{T\cdot log_2O}] \tag{3}$$

where $\boldsymbol{b}^{(u)}_{T\cdot log_2O}$ is a vector represents bits from T to $T+log_2O$. Now that ,according to the SCMA mapping rule, every log_2O bits are mapped to a codeword, the output after SCMA can be represent by $\mathbb{C} = [\boldsymbol{c}_1, \boldsymbol{c}_2, ..., \boldsymbol{c}_T]$, where $\boldsymbol{c}_T$ stand for the result of $\boldsymbol{c}^{(u)}_{T\cdot log_2O} \xrightarrow{Mapping} \boldsymbol{c}_T$. Each element in $\mathbb{C}$ represents two bits of the packet in the form of a deterministic codeword. Hereto, all the encoder processing are completed, and the codeword sequences will be sent to the receiver according to corresponding carriers.

3.2 Decoder at the Receiver

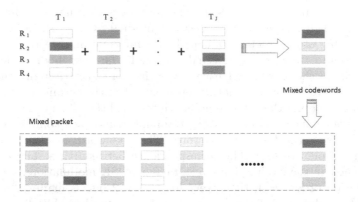

Fig. 4. Superposed signals of a mixed packet.

Physical Decoding. In SCMA-encoded communication systems, since different terminals reuse the same resource (that is, the carrier), the signal received by the receiver is the superposition signal consists of each terminal's codeword. We focus on a certain slot where the received superposition codewords are from J terminals, as shown in Fig. 4, can be written as: $\boldsymbol{R} = [\boldsymbol{r}_1, \boldsymbol{r}_2, ..., \boldsymbol{r}_i, ...\boldsymbol{r}_l]$ (l is the total mixed codewords number in a slot). Where the i-th superposed codeword $\boldsymbol{r}_i$ is represented by

$$r_i = \sum_{j=1}^{J} diag(h_j)x_j + n \tag{4}$$

The signals received by the receiver may be a mixture of hundreds or thousands of codewords form multi-terminal.

The Eq. (4) represents received mixed codeword that have went through different channel and noise. Among the equation, $x_j = [x_{1j}, x_{2j}, x_{3j}, x_{4j}]^T$ ($j = 1, 2, .., J$) is the sparse codeword selected from the corresponding codebook, $x_{mj} = 0(m = 1, 2, 3, 4)$ if the m-th carrier doesn't be occupied by terminal j. And $h_j = [h_{1j}, h_{2j}, h_{3j}, h_{4j}]^T$ represents the channel condition vector between terminal j and receiver, $h_{mj}(m = 1, 2, 3, 4)$ is the channel coefficient on carrier m. The vector $n = [n_1, n_2, n_3, n_4]^T$ is Gaussian noise with variance σ^2.

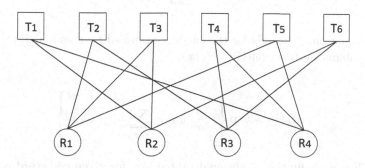

Fig. 5. Factor graph.

Typically, there are 6 terminals (T_1 to T_6) contend for the 4 carriers (R_1 to R_4). Based on the reception model, the relationship between terminals and carriers can be represented by factor graph like Fig. 5. The terminal nodes and carrier nodes are so-called variation nodes (VN) and function nodes (FN). During decoding processing, the mixed packet in a slot is divided into multiple superposed codewords as shown in Fig. 4. Now that decoding of the packet is conducted in parallel, we only need to analyze a specific mixed codeword at the receiver. So the following decoding analysis in section a refers to a mixed codeword.

That We adopt the non-orthogonal technique of SCMA in the physical layer will introduce extra overhead to decoding, so a low-complexity multiple terminal decoding algorithm is required. Here we choose the Message Passing Algorithm (MPA). The MPA algorithm is essentially an iterative update of external information between carrier nodes and terminal nodes just as [12]:

– Information passed from FN nodes to VN node.

$$I_{k \to j}^t(\boldsymbol{x}) \propto \sum_{\tilde{x}_j : \tilde{x}_j = x} \left\{ M_k(\tilde{\boldsymbol{x}}) \prod_{\tilde{j} \in \xi_k \backslash j} I_{\tilde{j} \to k}^{t-1}(\tilde{\boldsymbol{x}}_{\tilde{j}}) \right\} \tag{5}$$

In the equation, $I_{k \to j}^t(x)$ represents external information from FN node k to VN node j, where t stands for current iteration number, $\tilde{x}_j$ is the codeword might sent by terminal j. ξ_k is the set of terminals carried by FN j and the symbol $\backslash$ stands for 'exclude'.

– Information passed from VN nodes to FN node.

$$I_{j \to k}^t(\boldsymbol{x}) = \prod_{\tilde{k} \in \zeta_j \backslash k} I_{k \to j}^t(\boldsymbol{x}_j) \tag{6}$$

In the equation, ζ_j stands for the carriers occupied by terminal j.

– The combination function(CF) $M_k(\tilde{x})$.

$$M_k(\tilde{\boldsymbol{x}}) = \exp\left\{ -\frac{1}{\sigma^2} \left\| y_k - \sum_{j \in \xi_k} h_{k,j} x_{k,j} \right\|^2 \right\} \tag{7}$$

The CF is actually the conditional probability for given codeword combination.

As shown in equations above, the realization process of MPA algorithm is divided into two steps, the first is to update the information of VN node through the factor graph, and the second is to update the information of FN node. When the maximum iteration number is reached, the MPA algorithm will converges. And the output codeword can be judged as:

$$\hat{\boldsymbol{x}} = \max_x \prod_{\tilde{k} \in \zeta_j} I_{k \to j}^{t_{max}}(\boldsymbol{x}) \tag{8}$$

The $\hat{x}$ represents the codeword may sent by terminal j, once the output codeword is obtained, the corresponding bit information can be recovered. Since a terminal's packet contains many codewords, when all the codewords are retrieved, bits in the packet can be recovered. The CRC check is then performed to determine whether the packet has been decoded completely. If the packet passes the CRC check, it can be considered as a collision-free packet and then be used for MAC layer SIC.

As shown in Fig. 6, The MPA algorithm performs much worse than MPA algorithm combined with Turbo coding in BER. So in our scheme the FEC encoding(e.g., Turbo encoding) is indispensable. Channel coding can largely eliminate

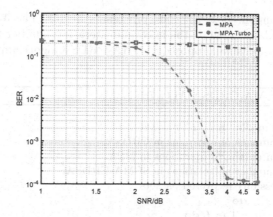

Fig. 6. BER of MPA and MPA-Turbo under low SNR.

the influence of MPA decoding error, which makes it easier to analyze the positive effect brought by introducing SCMA scheme. At low SNR, supposing that there is a lower bound δ of BER in MPA-Turbo scheme, which is achieved when then SNR reaches a certain value. The δ in the MPA-Turbo scheme is approximately equal to 10^{-4} when SNR $= 5\,\mathrm{dB}$.

MAC Decoding. In fact, this section is about the interference cancellation algorithm. In order to perform an iterative decoding process, the receiver will store all the signals, sampled from each frame, in the memory. Just as traditional CRDSA scheme, the SIC decoder's iteration number i_1 is set to 1, the SIC decoding processing will cease when the maximum iteration number I_1 is reached.

At the beginning, because a slot's packets have been tried to be decoded by the physical layer, the packets in this slot may have been completely recovered or may be misunderstood due to codebook collision. If the BER value is far beyond the predefined threshold δ in a slot, the slot is assumed to be bad (It is often caused by terminals' codebook collision), otherwise, this slot is assumed to be good (that is, no collision occurs and more powerful FEC coding can be used to enhance BER performance and the BER can be low enough to ignore), packets in the good slot can be recovered as possible. For easier analyzation, here we assume that the packets in slots with codebook collision are unrecoverable. Then, packets successfully recovered in each slot will be applied to SIC according to the pointer information contained in packet.

The proposed MAC layer decoding scheme relys on interaction between MAC layer and PHY layer essentially, this kind of interaction is reflected as iteration between SCMA decoding and MAC layer SIC processing. At each iteration, the superposed packets are recovered through PHY decoding and then used to SIC. More packets may be recovered through SIC, which makes it's possible that codebook collision disappears in some slot, as a result of collided packets being eliminated by SIC. Once the codebook collision is eliminated, the deadlock will be solved, and then the next iteration processing begins. The iteration number can be represented by i_2, while the maximum iteration number is I_2.

Based analysis above we proposed a SCMA-CRDSA algorithm in Algorithm 1.

Algorithm 1. SCMA-CRDSA ALGORITHM

1: **Initialization:**
2: received mixed in slot: $\boldsymbol{R} = [r_1, r_2, ..., r_i, ...r_l]$
3: I_1: maximum number of iterations in CRDSA.
4: t_{max}: maximum number of iterations in MPA.
5: I_2: maximum number of iterations in SCMA-CRDSA.
6: **Output:** successfully recovered packets
7: **for** i_2 from 1 to I_2 **do**
8:     **for** eachslot from 1 to L **do**
9:         perform message passing algorithm, iteration $t <= t_{max}$, analyze BER in the slot after MPA.
10:        **if** The BER is tolerable compared to δ **then**
11:            This slot is good. Packets in this slot can be recovered to perform SIC.
12:        **end if**
13:    **end for**
14:    perform SIC processing using the packets have just recovered by MPA.
15:    **for** eachslot from 1 to L **do**
16:        search for clean slots
17:        perform SIC processing using the packets have just discovered in clean slots. Iteration number is no more than I_1
18:    **end for**
19: **end for**

3.3 Complexity Analysis

The complexity of traditional CRDSA protocol is mainly related to the SIC iteration number I_1, however, the proposed scheme enhance the system throughput at the cost of introducing extra complexity. The extra complexity comes from MPA decoding at the receiver, which is to the order of M_{d_f}, the modulation order M here is 4, and d_f is the maximum degree of a function node. Complexity of updating a variable node based on the function node is analyzed through the iteration Eq. (2), which needs $M \cdot (d_r + 1) \cdot M^{(d_r - 1)}$ addition terms, $M \cdot (d_r + 2) \cdot M^{d_r - 1}$ multiplication terms and $M \cdot M^{d_r - 1}$ exponential terms. While updating a function node based on the variation node needs $M \cdot (d_c - 2)$, where d_c is the resource number occupied by a terminal. So, among a iteration, the total complexity is $I_2 \cdot (I_1 + O(M^{d_r} \cdot K \cdot d_r \cdot t_{max}))$, where K is the non-zero row numbers in a codebook.

3.4   Throughput Analysis

The throughput T under MAC load G at the iteration i can be derived, like [1], as $T(i|G) = G \cdot P_{pd}(i|G)$, where $P_{pd}(i|G) = P\{$ packet successfully decoded at iteration $i|$MAC load $= G\}$.

The probability P_{pd} can be derived as:

$$P_{pd}(i|G) = 1 - [(1 - P_{pd}^A(i|G)) \cdot (1 - P_{pd}^B(i|G))]$$
$$= 1 - [(1 - (P_{pd}^A(i|G)))^2] \tag{9}$$

where P_{pd}^A and P_{pd}^B correspond respectively to the probability that the twins A and B of the same packet are successfully decoded. In terms of throughput, what the difference in our proposed scheme with CRDSA is that a twins packet may be recovered by SCMA or CRDSA. Here we give a lower bound throughput of the proposed scheme, the lower bound can be achieved after the first iteration.

$$P_{pd}^A(i|G) \geq P_{SCMA} + P_{CRDSA} \tag{10}$$

where P_{SCMA} stands for probability that there is no codebook collision in the slot contains twins A, so P_{SCMA} is computed, as Eq. (13), in the situation that there is no more than $J - 1$ packets collide with A and the $J - 1$ packets also have no codebook collision. J is the total codebook number in the system. The probability that no more than $J - 1$ packets collided with A is represented by P_{col}

$$P_{col} = \sum_{n=1}^{J-1} \binom{N}{n} \cdot p_c^n \cdot (1 - p_c)^{N-n} \tag{11}$$

where $p_c = 1/M$, which stands for the probability that a packet is sent in the slot. The probability that no collision occurs between the V packets in a slot is represented by P_{nocol}

$$P_{nocol} = \frac{J \cdot (J - 1) \cdots (J - V + 1)}{J^V} \tag{12}$$

$$P_{SCMA} = \sum_{n=1}^{J-1} \binom{N}{n} \cdot p_c^n \cdot (1 - p_c)^{N-n} \cdot \frac{(J - 1) \cdots (J - n)}{J^n} \tag{13}$$

while P_{CRDSA} is the probability that twins A is recovered by CRDSA which means twins A suffers from codebook collision.

$$P_{CRDSA} \geq (1 - P_{SCMA}) \cdot P_{SCMA}^a \tag{14}$$

The letter a in Eq. (14) represents the packet number that collide with twins A. The Eq. (14) is interpreted as that twins of the packets collide with twins A are all recovered through SCMA decoding.

4   Numerical Results

In this section, numerical results are presented to evaluate the proposed decoding scheme. First, we simulate our proposed scheme with the performance parameter throughput (measured in useful packets received per slot) vs. load (measured in useful packets transmitted per slot). As other parameters set in [1], each packet's length is 400 bits, and a frame contains 100 slots. The FEC coding we adopted is Turbo with coding rate 1/3.

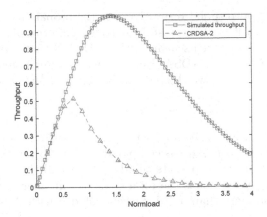

Fig. 7. Simulated result for the SCMA-CRDSA lower bound throughput. $I_1 = 1$, $t_{max} = 5$, $I_2 = 1$, codebook number $J = 6$, SNR $= 5\,\mathrm{dB}$.

In Fig. 7, the lower bound performance of SCMA-CRDSA scheme is shown by Monte Carlo simulation result, which proves that the proposed scheme is efficient. Before the load reaches about 0.7 packets/slot, it can be seen that the throughput of the system keeps increasing linearly as the load value increases. After the load value exceeds 0.7 packets/slot, the throughput growth rate of the system slows down. When the load value reaches about 1.4 packets/slot, the throughput of the system begins to decline. It's when the load reaches about 1.4 packets/slot, the maximum throughput about 1.0 packets/slot is achieved. So the throughput in this proposed scheme is about 2 times of throughput in CRDSA.

The throughput in Fig. 7 is actually the lower bound of our proposed scheme and is the result after the first iteration, so we would like to show the better performance after more iteration processing in Fig. 8. It's obvious that the throughput is enhanced a lot with the increased iteration number. However, when the number of iterations increases to a certain value, the system throughput no longer increases, which is caused by codebook collision and CRDSA deadlocks. In fact, the number of iterations need not be set to a large number, because even if the number of iterations increases later, the throughput performance will not improve significantly, but will lead to higher decoding complexity.

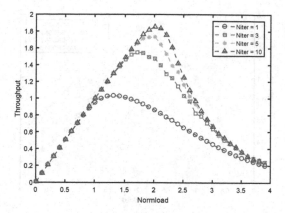

Fig. 8. Throughput of SCMA-CRDSA with iteration number = 1,3,5,10.

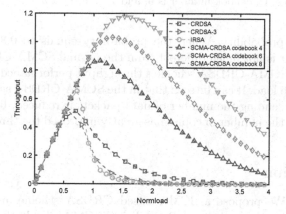

Fig. 9. Throughput of SCMA-CRDSA for codebook number = 4,6,8.

As shown in Fig. 9, with the number of codebooks increasing, throughput performance of the system is greatly improved. The reason for this is that the collision probability of the selected codebook is reduced due to the increase of the codebook number. Although the increasing in the number of codebooks can achieve positive effects, in real communication systems, the number of codebooks cannot be infinite, because the increasing in the number of codebooks also brings more complex decoding problems to the receiver.

Considering that the CRDSA scheme itself will increase the system overhead by sending data packets in multiples, we have adopted a transmission mode where only some of the data packets are repeated. In other words, the user at the transmitter randomly chooses whether to send two identical data packets. During the simulation process, We assume that the packet repetition probability is 0.6, 0.7, 0.8. The SCMA-CRDSA system throughput in these cases is shown in Fig. 10. Overall, the system throughput has better resistance to high load after

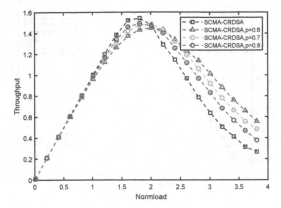

Fig. 10. Throughput of SCMA-CRDSA by sending two packets with different probabilities 0.6, 0.7, 0.8. Codebook number is 6, and $I_1 = 6$, $I_2 = 3$

controlling the probability. When the probability equals to 0.8, the system's peak throughput is not much different from the normal SCMA-CRDSA scheme, but the normal SCMA-CRDSA scheme's throughput performance is significantly worse under high load. It can be seen that in the SCMA-CRDSA scheme, not only the overhead of sending the number of data packets is reduced, but to a certain extent reducing the number of copies has greatly improved the throughput under high load.

5   Conclusion

In this paper, We propose a SCMA based CRDSA scheme and analyze the decoding process at the receiver. By utilizing SCMA, deadlock is more easier to be solved and then throughput of the system is greatly increased compared to traditional CRDSA scheme. And a lower bound of the proposed scheme is derived. The Monte Carlo simulation result proves that our scheme is efficient, enabling to better support multiple terminals access. In fact, we use a more general algorithm in the decoding process, the proposed scheme introduces a relatively high complexity, and the related complexity can be reduced by existing and updated research.

Acknowledgments. The authors would like to express their high appreciations to the supports from the National Natural Science Foundation of China (61871426) and Basic Research Project of Shenzhen (JCYJ20170413110004682) and the Verification Platform of Multi-tier Coverage Communication Network for Oceans (LZC0020).

References

1. Casini, E., De Gaudenzi, R., Del Rio Herrero, O.: Contention resolution diversity slotted ALOHA (CRDSA): an enhanced random access scheme for satellite access packet networks. IEEE Trans. Wirel. Commun. **6**(4), 1408–1419, April 2007

2. Del Rio Herrero, O., De Gaudenzi, R.: A high-performance mac protocol for consumer broadband satellite systems. In: 27th IET and AIAA International Communications Satellite Systems Conference (ICSSC 2009) (2009)
3. Liva, Gianluigi: Graph-based analysis and optimization of contention resolution diversity slotted ALOHA. IEEE Trans. Commun. **59**(2011–02), 477–487 (2011)
4. Bui, H.C., Zidane, K., Lacan, J., Boucheret, M.L.: A multi-replica decoding technique for contention resolution diversity slotted ALOHA. In: 2015 IEEE 82nd Vehicular Technology Conference (VTC Fall) (2015)
5. Zamoum, S., Lacan, J., Boucheret, M., Dupe, J., Gineste, M.: Shared position technique for interfered random transmissions in satellite communications. In: 2018 9th Advanced Satellite Multimedia Systems Conference and the 15th Signal Processing for Space Communications Workshop (ASMS/SPSC), pp. 1–8, September 2018
6. Paolini, E., Liva, M., Chiani, M.: Coded slotted aloha: A graph-based method for uncoordinated multiple access. IEEE Trans. Inf. Theory **61**(12), 6815–6832
7. Zhao, B., Ren, G., Zhang, H.: Random pattern multiplexing for random access in IoT-oriented satellite networks. IEEE Syst. J. 1–12 (2019)
8. Nikopour, H., Baligh, H.: Sparse code multiple access. In: 2013 IEEE 24th International Symposium on Personal Indoor and Mobile Radio Communications (PIMRC) (2013)
9. Jin, L., Zhou, S., Zhang, X., Wang, Y.: Low complexity decoding method for SCMA in uplink random access (2017)
10. Wang, C., Wu, Y., Chen, Yan., Bayesteh, A.: Sparse code multiple access for 5G radio transmission. In: 2017 IEEE 86th Vehicular Technology Conference (VTC-Fall) (2018)
11. Yang, Y., Zhao, Y., Li, D.: SCMA uplink decoding with codebook collision. In: 2017 IEEE 86th Vehicular Technology Conference (VTC-Fall) (2017)
12. Hoshyar, R., Wathan, F.P., Tafazolli, R.: Novel low-density signature for synchronous CDMA systems over AWGN channel. IEEE Trans. Sig. Process. **56**(4), 1616–1626

Bat-Inspired Biogeography-Based Optimization Algorithm for Smoothly UAV Track Planning Using Bezier Function

Jingzheng Chong[1(✉)], Xiaohan Qi[1], and Zhihua Yang[1,2]

[1] Communication Engineering Research Center, Harbin Institute of Technology (Shenzhen), Guangdong, China
{18s152591,qixiaohan}@stu.hit.edu.cn, yangzhihua@hit.edu.cn
[2] Pengcheng Laboratory, Shenzhen, Guangdong, China

Abstract. With the extensive applications of Unmanned Aerial Vehicle (UAV), traditional approaches such as Artificial Potential Field and A-star for UAV track planning are usually limited by their low efficiency and easy failure, especially in the three-dimensional complex environments with obstacles. Moreover, most of these works do not make careful considerations on the fine-grain smooth of track requird heavily by the realistic flight of UAV. Therefore, in this paper, we propose an improved Biogeography-Based Optimization (BBO) algorithm with Bats algorithm (BA), named BIBBO for UAV track planning, which allows a new generating method with continuous Bezier curve by using adaptive-step sampling of control points to smooth original track. The simulation results verify the effectiveness and robustness of the proposed algorithm with shorter and smoother 3-D tracks, compared with typical BBO and BA algorithms.

Keywords: UAV track planning · BBO · BA · Track smoothing · Bezier curve

1 Introduction

In recent years, the UAV has played an increasingly important role in many fields including logistics, patrol and exploration due to its fast, flexible and high-efficiency. The UAV track planning in a known three-dimensional environment is the basis and prerequisite for a series of autonomous control activities of UAV assignment system such as formation control and multi-UAV coordination. However, the original tracks planned contains straight-line segments which generally cannot be followed well by UAV due to the kinematic and dynamic constraints. Therefore, UAV tracks must be smoothed by eliminating right-angled turns in order to make them suitable for UAVs. As discussed above, the track planning and smoothing are important research topics for UAV which received substantial attention.

© ICST Institute for Computer Sciences, Social Informatics and Telecommunications Engineering 2021
Published by Springer Nature Switzerland AG 2021. All Rights Reserved
Q. Wu et al. (Eds.): WiSATS 2020, LNICST 357, pp. 96–108, 2021.
https://doi.org/10.1007/978-3-030-69069-4_9

There are many traditional track planning methods. In [1], a new APF algorithm was put forward to promote UAV to get rid of the local minimum point. Chen et al. apply the A-star algorithm to UAV track planning under the two-dimensional environments in [2]. To avoid slow convergence and poor ability in high dimensional space, the algorithms based on swarm intelligence have attracted the attention of many scholars, including Ant Colony Optimization [3–5], Grey Wolf Optimization [6], Genetic Algorithm [7,8], Particle Swarm Optimization [9,10]. In addition, an improved Rapidly-exploring Random Tree algorithm is proposed in [11], but RRT is a random sampling-based method that doesn't guarantee to be optimal. BA was proposed first by Yang in 2010, which is inspired by the echolocation behavior of bats, and it is potentially more powerful than PSO and GA [12]. BBO algorithm was developed first by Simon in 2008 [13], as a population-based evolutionary algorithm original from the mathematics of biogeography. Upadhyay et al. used BBO algorithm to evaluate the shortest path between load and generating centers in the area [14]. In [15], the BBO algorithm is exploited on the joint transmitter and receiver AS problem. But as far as we know, BBO algorithm is not generally used in the track planning of UAV nowadays.

In order to smooth the track, several methods have been proposed in recent researches. In [16], a novel path smoothing extension is presented, which uses the geometry of hypocycloids to smooth out the sharp and angular turns of the track, but this method smooths leaves the straight paths intact. The quadratic Bezier curve was used for track planning of a UAV ensuring less computational load in [17], but it lacks flexibility since only three control points are used. Therefore, in this paper, a new optimization algorithm named BIBBO is proposed, which improves the BBO algorithm by changing the migration model and mixes it with the BA. The motivation of BIBBO is to address the problems of slow convergence and easy falling into local optimal solutions. Additionally, in order to smooth the original track, we put forward a adaptive-step sampling method to obtain control points for continuous Bezier curve, which can be applied flexibly in different complex scenarios.

The remainder of this paper is organized as follows. The system model and the problem of UAV track planning is introduced in the Sect. 2. Section 3 presents a new optimization algorithm to plan the track. Section 4 presents the idea and steps of the continuous Bezier curve generated by new sampling method. Finally, Sects. 5 and 6 summarize simulation results and research conclusions, respectively.

2 System Model and Problem Formulation

The primary work of track planning is to establish the model of UAV's flight environment. A feasible model of the environment information could improve the efficiency of track planning, and has good visibility in display. We divide the three-dimensional environment into 100 * 200 * 100 points with unit of meters. More points means more accurate of the environment description, then the planning result is more effective. But too many points will enlarge the workload greatly, which will also decrease the entire efficiency. Without loss of generality, the three-dimensional environment can be decomposed into two parts, free points set $\mathcal{F}$ and occupied points set $\mathcal{M}$ respectively. The schematic graph of the three-dimensional environment model is showed in Fig. 1, in which the blue parts are obstacles. $\mathcal{F}$ and $\mathcal{M}$ can be described as follows:

$$\mathcal{F} = \{(x_{F_1}, y_{F_1}, z_{F_1}), (x_{F_2}, y_{F_2}, z_{F_2}) \ldots (x_{F_m}, y_{F_m}, z_{F_m})\} \tag{1}$$

$$\mathcal{M} = \{(x_{M_1}, y_{M_1}, z_{M_1}), (x_{M_2}, y_{M_2}, z_{M_2}) \ldots (x_{M_n}, y_{M_n}, z_{M_n})\} \tag{2}$$

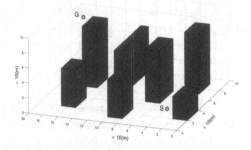

Fig. 1. Environment model (Color figure online)

We suppose that there are a starting point S and a goal point G in the three-dimensional environment as shown in Fig. 1. The optimal track planning is to find a collision-free and short track $\mathcal{T}$ that from S to G under the constrained dynamic properties of UAV flight system. We have two indexes to estimate a track: the length J_L and the hazard level J_R. Typically, these two indexes try to make the track as short as possible and the risk degree as lower as reasonable in the premise of completing the track planning. The definition of $\mathcal{T}$ and J_L can be expressed as follows:

$$\mathcal{T} = \{(x_{T_1}, y_{T_1}, z_{T_1}), (x_{T_2}, y_{T_2}, z_{T_2}) \ldots (x_{T_l}, y_{T_l}, z_{T_l})\} \tag{3}$$

$$J_L = \sum_{i=1}^{l-1} \sqrt{\left(x_{T_{i+1}} - x_{T_i}\right)^2 + \left(y_{T_{i+1}} - y_{T_i}\right)^2 + \left(z_{T_{i+1}} - z_{T_i}\right)^2} \tag{4}$$

For any given point $\mathcal{T}\{i\}(x_{T_i}, y_{T_i}, z_{T_i})$ in $\mathcal{T}$, d_i represents the minimum Euclidean distance from $\mathcal{T}\{i\}$ to the obstacles, which is defined in (5). Therefore, J_R can be described as Eq. (6).

$$d_i = \min\left\{\sqrt{\left(x_{T_i} - x_{B_j}\right)^2 + \left(y_{T_i} - y_{B_j}\right)^2 + \left(z_{T_i} - z_{B_j}\right)^2}\right\}, j \in [1, n] \tag{5}$$

$$J_R = \sum_{i=1}^{l} \frac{1}{d_i} \tag{6}$$

As discussed above, it can be known that the tatal cost function of the track is based on the weighted indexes of the smallest length J_L and the least risk J_R. So we have:

$$J = \tau J_L + (1 - \tau) J_R \tag{7}$$

where J is the weighted sum of cost for the track; $\tau \in (0,1)$ represents the weighting parameter. The choice of τ between 0 and 1 gives the designer certain flexibility to dispose relationships between the threat degree and the track length. When τ is closer to 1, a shorter track is planned with less attention paid to avoid obstacles. On the contrary, when τ is closer to 0, it requires avoiding the obstacles as far as possible on the cost of sacrificing the track length. Besides, we define d_c as the constraint of the track:

$$d_c(\mathcal{T}\{p\}, \mathcal{M}\{q\}) = \sqrt{\left(x_{T_p} - x_{M_q}\right)^2 + \left(y_{T_p} - y_{M_q}\right)^2 + \left(z_{T_p} - z_{M_q}\right)^2} \tag{8}$$
$$\text{for } \forall \mathcal{T}\{p\} \in \mathcal{T}, \forall \mathcal{M}\{q\} \in \mathcal{M}$$

We assume the UAV flight safety radius of η. So the track planning problem can be described as:

$$\min J = \tau J_L + (1 - \tau) J_R$$
$$\text{s.t. } d_c(\mathcal{T}\{p\}, \mathcal{M}\{q\}) > \eta \tag{9}$$

Additionally, in order to make this track meet the flight characteristics and dynamic constraints of the UAV, continuity and smoothness must be taken into account after planning so that the track could be feasible for the flight of UAV, which can be achieved by track smoothing. The detailed description is introduced in Sect. 4.

3   BIBBO Algorithm

The basic BBO algorithm treats every possible solution of the problem as a habitat, and sets the fitness of the each solution to the HSI (Habitat Suitability Index) of the habitat. Each solution is a vector constructed by feasible features called SIV (Suitability Index Variable). Migration process of BBO algorithm is used to replace feasible features in existing solutions, it is an adaptive process. The immigration rate λ and the emigration rate μ are functions of the number of species S in a single habitat as shown in Fig. 2(a). So we have:

$$\begin{cases} \lambda = I \left(1 - \dfrac{S}{S_{\max}}\right) \\[4mm] \mu = \dfrac{ES}{S_{\max}} \end{cases} \tag{10}$$

where E and I represent the maximum emigration rate and maximum immigration rate, respectively; S_{max} is the largest possible number of species that the habitat can hold.

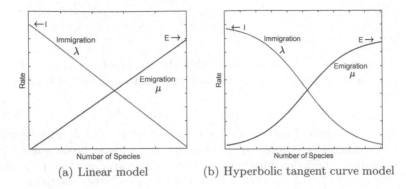

(a) Linear model   (b) Hyperbolic tangent curve model

Fig. 2. Migration model of a single habitat

But in general, the migration model may be more complicated. So we adjusted the migration model by the hyperbolic tangent function to more in line with the law of natural migration. Combining with (10), we can get the new migration model as follow:

$$
\begin{cases}
\lambda_{\text{new}} = \dfrac{I}{2}\left(-\dfrac{k^{S-\frac{S_{\max}}{2}} - k^{S+\frac{S_{\max}}{2}}}{k^{S-\frac{S_{\max}}{2}} + k^{S+\frac{S_{\max}}{2}}} + 1\right) \\[4mm]
\mu_{\text{new}} = \dfrac{E}{2}\left(\dfrac{k^{S-\frac{S_{\max}}{2}} - k^{S+\frac{S_{\max}}{2}}}{k^{S-\frac{S_{\max}}{2}} + k^{S+\frac{S_{\max}}{2}}} + 1\right)
\end{cases}
\tag{11}
$$

The hyperbolic tangent migration curve ($k = 1.4$) as shown in Fig. 2(b), we can see the trend of migration with the number of species is more moderate by using the hyperbolic tangent migration model. When a habitat has less or more species, the migration changes slowly, and moderate numbers of species can cause changes dramatically in migration.

However, the migration process of BBO algorithm is hard to maintain population diversity. Furthermore, the direction of the mutation is uncertain, so the new individual obtained by mutating are not always feasible. Therefore, convergence rate will decrease in the later stage of the BBO algorithm. The BA algorithm can update the solutions by using the historical information recorded and enhance the local search by generating a local new solution around the optimal solution. Introducing the BA update strategy during the migration process of BBO algorithm could improve the exploring ability, and maintain the diversity of the population in BBO algorithm well. The basic update strategy of BA algorithm can be expressed as:

$$
f_i = f_{\min} + (f_{\max} - f_{\min})\,\beta
\tag{12}
$$

$$
v_i^t = v_i^{t-1} + \left(x_i^t - x^*\right) f_i
\tag{13}
$$

$$
x_i^t = x_i^{t-1} + v_i^t
\tag{14}
$$

where $\beta \in (0,1)$ is a random number; x^* is the current global optimal solution; f_i is a frequency value between f_{min} and f_{max}. So we adjust the migration rule of BBO algorithm as follows:

$$v_i^t = v_i^{t-1} + \sigma_1 \left[J\left(H_i\right) - J\left(H_{index}\right) \right] f_i + \sigma_2 \left[J\left(H_i\right) - J\left(H_{best}\right) \right] f_i \tag{15}$$

$$H_{i\_}SIV_j = H_{index\_}SIV_j + v_i^t \tag{16}$$

where J is the total cost of track (habitat) introduced in (7); H_i, H_{index}, H_{best} are the immigrated habitat, the emigrated habitat and the optimal habitat after each iteration, separately; σ_i and σ_2 are constant coefficients. Besides, an optimization check is adopted to ensure the population is always evolving in a more optimized direction. We accept new solution only when the modified habitat H_{new} is better than the original habitat H_i. We transplanted the loudness A_i of bats in BA algorithm into habitats, which will be updated according to the Eq. (17) when a new better habitat is accepted.

$$A_i^{t+1} = \alpha A_i^t \tag{17}$$

where α is the attenuation coefficient of the loudness, and for any $0 < \alpha < 1$, we have:

$$A_i^t \to 0, \text{ as } t \to \infty \tag{18}$$

In addition, we learn from the local search part of BA algorithm to propose a elitism local walk approach, which is different from the general elitism strategy. The global optimal solution H_{best} is called the elite solution, which will be preserved temporarily in next migration process. Meanwhile, there will be a new solution H_{new} generated near H_{best} by Eq. (19), which will be used to replace the elite solution H_{best} only when it has lower total cost, otherwise we abandon it.

$$H_{new\_best} = H_{best} + \epsilon A^I \tag{19}$$

where $\epsilon \in (0,1)$ is a random number; A^I is the average loudness of all the habitats after I times iteration.

Suppose M, N represent the number of habitats and SIVs in one habitat, respectively. Based on the above improvements, we propose a new optimization algorithm named BIBBO, which can be expressed as Algorithm 1.

4   Track Smoothing

Since there are straight-line segments in the three-dimensional UAV track generated by BIBBO algorithm, the original track is usually not smooth. Taking into account the flight characteristics and dynamic constraints of the UAV, if the UAV's flight direction is changed with a large angle frequently, it will be difficult to control UAV stably, which will lead to the UAV hard to follow the track accurately. Therefore, before a track smoother is used to smooth the original track, it is not suitable for the UAV. In this section, a new generating method with Bezier curve is developed to smooth the original track.

Algorithm 1. The Process of BIBBO Algorithm

1: **Begin**
2: *Initialize the H_i, v_i and A_i, define the pulse frequency f_i*
3: **while** *less than the maximum iterations* **do**
4:    **for** $i = 1$ *to* M **do**
5:       *Select H_i with probability λ_{new}*
6:       **for** $j = 1$ *to* N **do**
7:          *Select H_{index} with probability μ_{new}*
8:          *Change the $H_i\_SIV_j$ by equation (16) to generate H_{new}*
9:          **if** H_{new} *is better than* H_i **then**
10:             *Accept the new solution and increase A_i*
11:          **end if**
12:       **end for**
13:    **end for**
14:    *Execute elitism local walk strategy*
15: **end while**
16: **End**

4.1 General Bezier Curve Track Smoothing

Bezier curve is a kind of smooth continuous spline curve. In particular, the basic n-order Bezier curve is defined as:

$$P(t) = \sum_{i=0}^{n} B_{n,i}(t)P_i, t \in [0,1] \tag{20}$$

where P_i represents the coordinates of the i-th control point; $B_{n,i}(t)$ is the Bernstein function of degree n defined as follow:

$$B_{n,i}(t) = \binom{n}{i} t^i (1-t)^{n-i}, i = 0, \ldots, n \tag{21}$$

As shown in Fig. 3(a), the Bezier curve is surrounded completely by the convex hull that built by its control points, as is also applicable in three-dimensional environment. Since the UAV does not have to fly over each control points, so the track smoothed by Bezier curve is feasible.

Recently, track smoothing is mainly achieved by connecting multiple low order Bezier curves. As the Fig. 3(b) shows, a smooth track can be spliced by four two-order Bezier curves. Evidently, it has larger length and more sharp turns compared to the continuous Bezier curve created directly with 6 control points in Fig. 3(a).

Based on the above analysis, it seems that smoothing track by using a continuous Bezier curve is perfect. But the original track is just a poly-line with many redundant points. More control points means higher order of Bezier function and involves more time to calculate or collision check. Since the Bezier curve is only determined by its pivotal control point, we don't need too many extra points to achieve track smoothing. By deleting redundant points, the computing speed

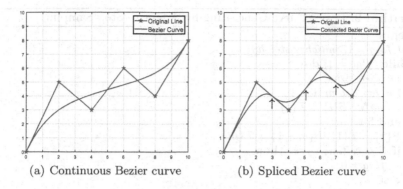

(a) Continuous Bezier curve   (b) Spliced Bezier curve

Fig. 3. Bezier curves with different generating methods

will be greatly improved. However, there is no free lunch. Fewer control points may lead the smoothed track to pass through the edge of the obstacles as showed in Fig. 4.

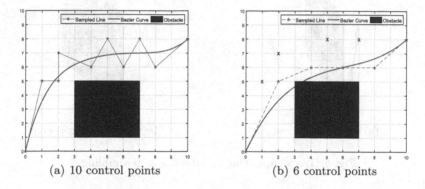

(a) 10 control points   (b) 6 control points

Fig. 4. Comparison of Bezier curves in a same environment

4.2 Bezier Curve with Adaptive-Step Sampling

In order to balance the computing performance and security, so in this section, a new generating method with Bezier curve by using adaptive-step sampling is developed to smooth track. The control points set $\mathcal{B}$ is created by sampling from the $\mathcal{T}$, and then it will be used to generate a Bezier curve which represents the smooth track. The sampling step size h can be adjusted from large to small. The initial value of the step size h generally depends on the complexity of the environment. The Algorithm 2 followed will shows the whole process of this method.

Algorithm 2. Bezier Curve Generating by Adaptive-Step Sampling

1: **Begin**
2: *Set $flag = 1$, initialize step h_0*
3: **while** $(flag = 1)$ **do**
4:     $m=floor(n/h_0)$
5:     **for** $i = 2$ *to* m **do**
6:         $j=i*m$; $\mathcal{B}\{i\} = \mathcal{T}\{j\}$
7:     **end for**
8:     $\mathcal{B}\{1\} = \mathcal{T}\{1\}$; $\mathcal{B}\{m + 1\} = \mathcal{T}\{m\}$
9:     **if** $\mathcal{B}$ *is collision free* **then**
10:         $flag = 0$
11:     **else**
12:         $\mathcal{B} = \emptyset$; *Adjust step to a smaller value*
13:     **end if**
14: **end while**
15: *Using $\mathcal{B}$ to generate Bezier Curve by equation(20)*
16: **End**

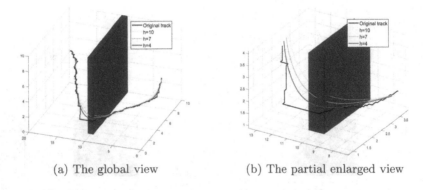

(a) The global view   (b) The partial enlarged view

Fig. 5. Track smoothing by adaptive-step sampling

Figure 5 shows the results of track smoothing by adaptive-step sampling in a three-dimensional environment. From the perspective of a partial enlargement in Fig. 5(b), we can see clearly that when the step h is reduced to 4, the smoothed track no longer passes through the obstacle. This proves that the method which obtain control points by adaptive-step sampling to generate continuous Bezier curve is effective and flexible.

5   Experimental Results

In this section, simulations were designed to prove the efficiency of the approach proposed for UAV smooth track planning in the three-dimensional environment. In order to eliminate the effects of a specific environment, we used two maps of different complexity, each of which was repeated 30 times experiments. All simulations were programmed in a computer running Windows 10 with Intel

Core I3-6100 CPU @3.70 GHz. We set the starting point of (10, 10, 10), and the goal point of (90, 190, 40). The maximum immigration rate I and emigration rate E are both 1. The maximal generation is 50, and the population size is 30. The initial sampling step h_0 is 10.

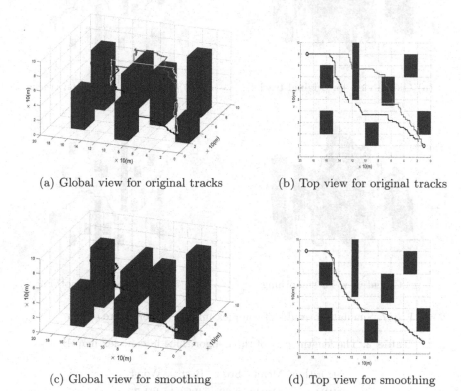

(a) Global view for original tracks   (b) Top view for original tracks

(c) Global view for smoothing   (d) Top view for smoothing

Fig. 6. Simulation results of simple map A (Color figure online)

Table 1. The length costs of three algorithms in simple map A

Algorithm	Mean	Std	Best	Worst
BIBBO	285.24	1.94	282.52	289.37
BA	293.35	17.80	286.95	335.84
BBO	298.67	8.08	289.13	316.23

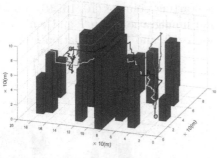

(a) Global view for original tracks

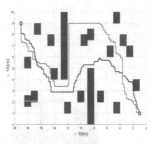

(b) Top view for original tracks

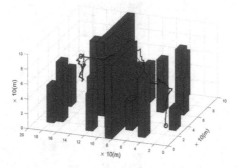

(c) Global view for smoothing

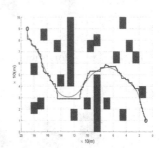

(d) Top view for smoothing

Fig. 7. Simulation results of complex map B (Color figure online)

Table 2. The length costs of three algorithms in complex map B

Algorithm	Mean	Std	Best	Worst
BIBBO	413.49	3.62	408.64	421.75
BA	467.13	34.39	415.78	532.22
BBO	437.33	9.17	419.85	454.56

Figure 6 shows the simulation results of simple map A. In Fig. 6(a) and (b), the line in green, red and black are the original track generated by BBO, BA and BIBBO algorithm separately. Similarly, the simulation results of complex map B are shown in Fig. 7. We can roughly see that the track created by BIBBO algorithm has fewer turns and is shorter than that of the other two algorithms. The detailed comparison of these tracks will be given in the Table 1 and Table 2. Besides, Fig. 6(c)(d) and Fig. 7(c)(d) show that the track (in red) generated by adaptive-step sampling is always smooth and safe even in a complex environment. Besides, the smooth track is very similar with the original track in shape.

According to Table 1 and Table 2, it can be concluded that the track length costs of BIBBO algorithm is always lower than BA and BBO algorithm.

In addition, the standard deviation of BIBBO algorithm is much smaller than that of the other two algorithms, which indicates obviously that the BIBBO algorithm is more stable in different environments.

Figure 8 shows the convergence comparison of the three algorithms, it can be observed that BIBBO algorithm has the faster convergence speed and lower cost compared with the other two algorithms.

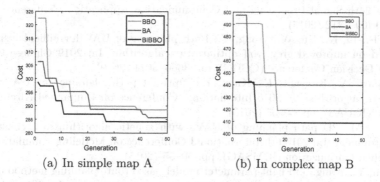

(a) In simple map A   (b) In complex map B

Fig. 8. The convergence of three algorithms in different maps

6   Conclusion

In this paper, we propose an improved BBO algorithm with BA algorithm for UAV track planning, and a new generating method with continuous Bezier curve by using adaptive-step sampling of control points to smooth original track. Simulation results show that our approach can obtain better UAV smooth tracks in different three-dimensional environments. Simultaneously, the effectiveness and robustness of the proposed algorithm is also proved. In the future research we plan to improve the algorithm to work in the environment with dynamic obstacles.

Acknowledgments. The authors would like to express their high appreciations to the supports from the National Natural Science Foundation of China (61871426), the Basic Research Project of Shenzhen (JCYJ20170413110004682) and the Verification Platform of Multi-tier Coverage Communication Network for Oceans (LZC0020).

References

1. Yingkun, Z.: Flight path planning of agriculture UAV based on improved artificial potential field method. In: 2018 Chinese Control And Decision Conference (CCDC), pp. 1526–1530 (2018)
2. Chen, T., Zhang, G., Hu, X., Xiao, J.: Unmanned aerial vehicle route planning method based on a star algorithm. In: 2018 13th IEEE Conference on Industrial Electronics and Applications (ICIEA), pp. 1510–1514 (2018)

3. Zhang, C., Hu, C., Feng, J., Liu, Z., Zhou, Y., Zhang, Z.: A self-heuristic ant-based method for path planning of unmanned aerial vehicle in complex 3-D space with dense U-type obstacles. IEEE Access **7**, 150775–150791 (2019)
4. Konatowski, S., Pawlowski, P.: Ant colony optimization algorithm for UAV path planning. In: 2018 14th International Conference on Advanced Trends in Radioelecrtronics, Telecommunications and Computer Engineering (TCSET), pp. 177–182 (2018)
5. Calik, S.K.: UAV path planning with multiagent ant colony system approach. In: 2016 24th Signal Processing and Communication Application Conference (SIU), pp. 1409–1412 (2016)
6. Ge, F., Li, K., Xu, W., Wang, Y.: Path planning of UAV for oilfield inspection based on improved grey wolf optimization algorithm. In: 2019 Chinese Control And Decision Conference (CCDC), pp. 3666–3671 (2019)
7. Sonmez, A., Kocyigit, E., Kugu, E.: Optimal path planning for UAVs using genetic algorithm. In: 2015 International Conference on Unmanned Aircraft Systems (ICUAS), pp. 50–55 (2015)
8. Cakir, M.: 2D path planning of UAVs with genetic algorithm in a constrained environment. In: 2015 6th International Conference on Modeling, Simulation, and Applied Optimization (ICMSAO), pp. 50–55 (2015)
9. Chen, Y., Wang, S.: Flight parameter model based route planning method of UAV using stepped-adaptive improved particle swarm optimization. In: 2019 5th International Conference on Control, Automation and Robotics (ICCAR), pp. 524–530 (2019)
10. Huang, H., Zhao, D., Zhao L.: A new method of the shortest path planning for unmanned aerial vehicles. In: 2017 6th Data Driven Control and Learning Systems (DDCLS), pp. 599–605 (2017)
11. Li, M., Sun, Q., Zhu, M.: UAV 3-dimension flight path planning based on improved rapidly-exploring random tree. In: 2019 Chinese Control And Decision Conference (CCDC), pp. 921–925 (2019)
12. Yang, X.S.: A new metaheuristic bat-inspired algorithm. Stud. Comput. Intell. **284**, 65–74 (2010)
13. Simon, D.: Biogeography-based optimization. IEEE Trans. Evol. Comput. **12**(6), 702–713 (2008)
14. Upadhyay, S., Chaudhary, A.S., Kumar, M.P., Sharma, M.: Evaluating the shortest path for laying distribution network in a hilly area. In: 2018 8th IEEE India International Conference on Power Electronics (IICPE), pp. 1–5 (2018)
15. Fountoukidis, K.C., Siakavara, K., Goudos, S.K., Kalialakis, C.: Antenna selection for mimo systems using biogeography based optimization. In: 2017 International Workshop on Antenna Technology: Small Antennas, Innovative Structures, and Applications (iWAT), pp. 319–322 (2017)
16. Ravankar, A., Ravankar, A.A., Kobayashi, Y., Emaru, T.: Path smoothing extension for various robot path planners. In: 2016 16th International Conference on Control, Automation and Systems (ICCAS), pp. 319–322 (2016)
17. Jayasinghe, J.A.S., Athauda, A. M. B. G. D. A.: Smooth trajectory generation algorithm for an unmanned aerial vehicle (UAV) under dynamic constraints: Using a quadratic Bezier curve for collision avoidance. In: 2016 Manufacturing and Industrial Engineering Symposium (MIES), pp. 1–6 (2016)

A Three-Level Training Data Filter for Cross-project Defect Prediction

Cangzhou Yuan[1](✉), Xiaowei Wang[1], Xinxin Ke[1], and Panpan Zhan[2]

[1] School of Software, Beihang University, Beijing 100191, China
{yuancz,xiaowei_wang,kexinxin}@buaa.edu.cn
[2] Beijing Institute of Spacecraft System Engineering, Beijing 100094, China
panpan3210@qq.com

Abstract. The purpose of cross-project defect prediction is to predict whether there are defects in this project module by using a prediction model trained by the data of other projects. For the divergence of the data distribution between different projects, the performance of cross-project defect prediction is not as good as within-project defect prediction. To reduce the difference as much as possible, researchers have proposed a variety of methods to filter training data from the perspective of transfer learning. In this paper, we introduce a "project-instance-metric" hierarchical filtering strategy to select training data for the defect prediction model. Using the three-level filtering method, the candidate projects that are most similar to the target project, the instances that are most similar to the target instance, and the metrics with the highest correlation to the prediction result are filtered out respectively. We compared three-level filtering with project-level filtering, instance-level filtering, and the combination of project-level and instance-level filtering methods in four classification algorithms using NASA open source data sets. Our experiments show that the three-level filtering method achieves more significant f-measure and AUC values than the single level training data filtering method.

Keywords: Machine learning · Cross-project defect prediction · Transfer learning

1 Introduction

Software defect refers to a kind of problem, error, or hidden functional defect in the computer software or program that destroys the normal operation ability. In the process of software development, the generation of software defects is inevitable. Incorrect understanding of software requirements, unreasonable development process, and immature development technology might lead to defects. Once the defect is produced, the later it is discovered in the software development process, the greater the cost of fixing the defect. At present, software testing, static inspection, and other methods are mainly used to find defects to ensure the quality of software.

© ICST Institute for Computer Sciences, Social Informatics and Telecommunications Engineering 2021
Published by Springer Nature Switzerland AG 2021. All Rights Reserved
Q. Wu et al. (Eds.): WiSATS 2020, LNICST 357, pp. 109–123, 2021.
https://doi.org/10.1007/978-3-030-69069-4_10

Software defect prediction can use machine learning to predict defect-prone modules based on metrics such as software code characteristics. Software testers can reasonably allocate test resources based on the predicted results to detect defects more efficiently and accurately. Most of the researches on software defect prediction is based on within-project defect prediction (WPDP), that is, the historical data used for training prediction models come from the same project. However, in the actual development process, often a new project lacks of historical data. Collecting and labeling training data take a lot of manpower and resources. So it may face the problem of insufficient data to support model training. However, in the actual development process, there is often a new project to be developed, which may cause the problem that data is too insufficient to support model training.

To solve this problem, researchers consider cross-project defect prediction (CPDP) [1–3]. Cross-project defect prediction uses historical data from other projects to train prediction models to predict whether current projects have defects. Due to factors such as project type, development language, developer habits, and so on, the distribution characteristics of training dataset and test dataset are divergent among different projects, which causes dataset shift [4] and seriously affects the performance of prediction model. Currently, researchers mainly use transfer learning to solve this problem. Transfer learning applies the models trained based on the data of a certain project to other different but related projects. Within the research scope of transfer learning, researchers mainly propose the methods to improve the performance of cross-project defect prediction in the aspects of instance and metric, including instance selection, instance weight setting, metric selection and metric mapping, etc.

The method based on instance selection refers to the selection of appropriate instances from the source project to form the model training data according to the software module instances of the target project to realize the cross-project model transferring. The methods based on instance selection mainly include Burak filter [5], Peters filter [6] and riTDS filer [7] which proposed by Peng et al. to select training data on project level and instance level. The above methods are all based on fixed metrics for instance selection, without considering the correlation between metrics and classes. The metric selection method can reduce the impact of irrelevant and redundant metrics on the performance of the defect prediction model. An empirical study is conducted by Qiao et al. [8] on NASA and PROMISE datasets which showed that both the metric subset selection and metric ranking approaches can improve the performance of CPDP.

Both methods are used in CPDP to improve model prediction performance, but few researchers combine the two methods to select training data of prediction model. Therefore, considering the selection of the data for the training defect prediction model from the two aspects of instance selection and metric selection, a three-level filtering strategy is proposed to find the training data that can be used to train the most suitable defect prediction model for the target data. The three hierarchies in the three-level filtering method refer to the project-level, the instance-level and the metric-level respectively. At the project-level filtering, source projects with high similarity to target projects are selected based on distribution characteristics. At the instance-level filtering, the source instances with high similarity to the target instances are selected based on the instances data. At the metric-level filtering, a metric with a high correlation with the predicted result is selected. To evaluate this strategy, we will focus on the following research issues:

RQ1: How does our strategy perform on each classifier compared to other strategies?

RQ2: Which classifier performs best by our strategy in cross-project defect prediction?

RQ3: Is our strategy practical in specific datasets?

The rest of the paper is organized as follows: Sect. 2 discusses the related work. Afterward, a detailed description of the three level filtering approach are presented in Sect. 3. We evaluate these strategies in a case study in Sect. 4. Section 5 discusses our strategies based on results. Finally, a summary of our strategies is persented and the directions for future work are discussed in Sect. 6.

2 Related Work

To our knowledge, the first research to conduct a feasibility analysis of cross-project defect prediction was completed by BriandL et al. [9]. Based on two midsize Java systems in the same environment, they conducted cross-project defect prediction experiments using logistic regression and MARS (Multivariate Adaptive Regression Splines). The results show that the accuracy of cross-project defect prediction is not as good as that of within-project defect prediction, but the performance of cross-project defect prediction is better than chance.

The method of instance selection mainly selects training data from project level and instance level. Herbold [10] proposed two strategies for project filtering based on the distribution characteristics of metrics, namely EM clustering and the nearest neighbor algorithm. The authors performed experiments on 44 datasets from 14 open-source projects. The results show that the two strategies can effectively improve the performance of cross-project defect prediction, but there is still some gap with within-project defect prediction. Kawata et al. [11] considered the noisy instances in cross-projects improve performance by using density-based spatial clustering of applications with noise (DBSCAN) filter approach. Can Cui et al. [12] proposed iForest filter which is an unsupervised machine learning approach to simplify the training data for CPDP to improve the model performance. This method uses path length to judge abnormal and normal instances, not distance or density. iForest filter uses a fixed size of sub-instances to conduct a small number of trees.

He et al. [13] studies from the perspective of metric selection and selects the subset of minimized metric elements through iterative selection. Amasaki et al. [14] used unsupervised learning to remove irrelevant and redundant metrics from the target project.

From the above related studies, the selection methods of training data mostly focus on only one related aspect, and few studies combine the two aspects of instance and metric. In our work, we combined them to implement source project data selection at the project-level and instance-level, and to remove redundant metrics at the metric-level to reduce the complexity of the model. Thus, the three-level Filtering approach is proposed to improve the performance of the defect prediction model.

3   Methodology

In the actual software development process, due to the lack of sufficient training data for newly developed projects or the high cost of data labeling, the economic benefits of software defect prediction are low and the feasibility is poor. Therefore, transfer learning is used to solve the problem of insufficient data for the target project with the help of the model trained based on the label data of the source project. Due to the divergence of data distribution between source and target projects, the performance of target projects in the prediction model is dramatic. To mitigate the impact of this problem, three level training data filtering method is proposed. First, at the project level, source projects which are the most similar to the target project from multiple candidate projects are filtered. Second, at the instance level, instances that have high distribution similarity to the target project instance from the source project instances are filtered. Third, at metrics level, metrics using feature selection which can identify and selects metrics having high correlation with classes are filtered. The training data of multiple candidate projects are filtered by the three level filtering to form training data. The prediction model is trained with the training data, and the target data is input to the trained model and the prediction result is output. The process of CPDP using three-level filtering are presented in Fig. 1.

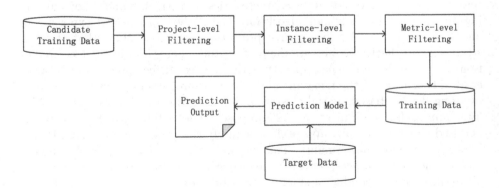

Fig. 1. The process of CPDP using three-level filtering.

3.1 Project-Level Filtering

When filtering projects, source projects that are as similar as the target project type, developer experience, and developer ability as possible are wanted to find. Based on the above requirements, the distribution characteristics of project data are used as the input condition for project similarity judgment including mean, maximum, minimum, standard deviation. The distribution characteristics are determined based on the research of He et al. [15]. Mean can show the central location where project data is relatively concentrated. Maximum and minimum values can show the distribution range of project data. Standard deviation can show how discrete project data is.

In this method, X_{ij} is used to represent the jth metric of the ith instance. The distribution characteristic data of the ith instance is represented as $F_i = \{C_{11}, C_{12}, \ldots C_{jk}\}$, and where C_{jk} is defined as kth distribution characteristics of the jth metric. K-nearest neighbor method based on Euclidean distance of distribution characteristics is used to judge the similarity between projects, that is to calculate Euclidean distance between each candidate source project and the target project separately and select k nearest source projects as the second level source projects. Algorithm 1 gives a detailed description of project-level filtering.

Algorithm 1: The Description of Project-level Filtering

Input:

    candidate project $C\left(\{S_{s(n)}\}_{n=1}^{n=N}\right)$;

    distribution characteristics of target project S_{tc};

    number of desired project k;

    for n=1 to N **do**

        $SM_n = Similarity\left(C\left(S_{tc}\right), C\left(S_{s(n)}\right)\right)$;

    end for ;

    Sort(SM_n, DESC);

    $S_c \leftarrow$ Select(SM_n , k);

    Return S_c;

3.2 Instance-Level Filtering

The candidate training dataset consists of all the instances from the k source projects filtered at project-level filtering. In the instance-level filtering stage, instances with high similarity to the target project dataset are selected from the candidate training dataset. In the existing research, there are two main ways to filter the instance. One is Burak filter [5] and the other is Peters filter [6]. At the instance-level filtering, our approach based on the second method. First, the candidate training set is used as the center for the instance selection so that each instance of the target project forms its own candidate subset. Then choose the instance centered on the instance in the target project. This is equivalent to a second filter, which is the "two-way selection" between the instance of the candidate training set and the instance of the target project. It considers not only the more defective information that may be contained in the candidate training dataset but also the objective requirements that require the prediction model to get better prediction performance on the target dataset. Algorithm 2 gives a detailed description of instance-level filtering.

Algorithm 2: The Description of Instance-level Filtering

Input:

candidate training dataset $NSP = \left\{ X_{source(n)} \right\}_{n=1}^{n=N}$

the instance of the target project S_t;

for i=1 to N **do**

$\quad Array_{target(i)} \leftarrow SelectClosest(X_{source(i)}, S_t)$;

end for ;

while $Array_{target(i)}$ not NULL **do**

$\quad result[i] \leftarrow min(Array_{target(i)})$;

end while ;

Return result[i];

3.3   Metric-Level Filtering

The number of metrics is not directly proportional to the performance of the model. Therefore, metric-level filtering can identify and select a subset of metrics that are highly class-related, which can be regarded as a process of searching and optimizing. The metric-level filtering process includes four parts: the subset generation process, the subset evaluation process, the stopping criterion, and the verification process. The process of metric-level filtering is presented in Fig. 2.

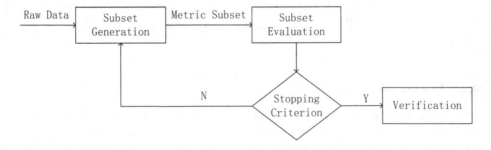

Fig. 2. The process of metric-level filtering.

The generation process of the subset includes the determination of the search starting point, the determination of the direction, and the selection of the search strategy. The starting point of the search is set to the empty set S. As the search progresses, the best metric from the set of metrics that have never been included in S is selected and added to S continuously. The search strategy is set as sequence search, that is, in the search process, metrics are continuously added to the current subset of metrics according to a certain order, so as to obtain an optimized subset of metrics. To determine the order, the method of information gain is used to arrange the order of the metrics. Information gain considers that the more information a feature brings to the classification system, the more important this feature is and the greater the corresponding information gain is. The so-called amount of information is the entropy, which converts the characteristic probability into the degree to which the feature describes the classification results. Entropy is defined as follows:

$$H(X) = -\sum_{i=1}^{n} p(x_i) \log p(x_i) \tag{1}$$

Information gain is the difference between the entropy and the characteristic condition entropy. The information gain from feature T to classification C is defined as follows:

$$IG(T) = H(C) - H(C|T) \tag{2}$$

where $H(C|T)$ is the conditional entropy of classification C under the feature T condition. The information gain represents the degree to which the uncertainty of information decreases when the characteristic T is determined. That is, after the data is classified according to the feature T, the certainty of the classified data is higher than that before the partition.

The method of subset evaluation is generally divided into the filter method and the wrapped method. In the filter method, it generally does not rely on specific learning algorithms to evaluate the subset of metrics. On the contrary, the subsequent learning algorithm is embedded in the metric selection process, in the wrapper method. This method determines its pros and cons by testing the predictive performance of the metric subset on this algorithm, and rarely pays attention to the predictive performance of each metric in the metric subset. Because the evaluation of the filter method has a large deviation from the performance of the subsequent learning algorithm and consider that the current classification performance of cross-project defect prediction is low, the method of embedding the subsequent learning algorithm into the metric selection process is adopted to minimize the performance deviation of the subsequent learning algorithm. The method of information gain is used to determine the search sequence to a certain extent to make up for the shortcoming of the wrapped method's lack of attention to the prediction performance of a single metric.

The stopping criterion is set to complete the search of the metric subset. The result verification is set as the optimal subset of the metric element under the given performance measure.

4 Case Study

Our approach is validated in a case. The experiment is introduced from four aspects: The first is a brief description of data. The second is to introduce the machine learning algorithm used in the experiment. The third is about evaluation performance measures. Finally, the results of the experiment are given.

4.1 Data Setup

The data used in our experiment is part of the NASA metrics data program (MDP) data sets. The repository currently contains 13 module-level data sets explicitly intended for software metrics research [16]. Each dataset contains static code metrics and defect labels for the module. The module here refers to a function or method. Static code metrics used in the NASA metrics data program include lines-of-code (LOC), Halstead, and McCabe-based measures. The development languages used in the NASA metrics data program include C, C++, JAVA, Perl. Considering the impact of the development language on project similarity, we selected data sets in 13 module-level data sets in which the development language is C as our experimental data. Table 1 gives details of the experimental dataset.

Table 1. NASA MDP Data Sets.

Project	# Instance	# Metric	# Defect-prone	% Defect-prone
CM1	344	37	42	12.21%
MC2	127	39	44	34.65%
PC1	759	37	61	8.04%
PC2	1585	36	16	1.01%
PC3	1125	37	140	12.44%
PC4	1399	37	178	12.72%

4.2 Prediction Models

Naive Bayes classifier is a simple statistical learning classifier based on the assumption of feature independence. This assumes that for a given class variable, one particular feature is independent of the others. Naive Bayes classifier has the advantage that other classifications do not. Lewis [17] describes Naive Bayes as a classifier based on Baye's theorem and it decomposed as

$$p\left(C_k|\mathbf{x}\right) = \frac{p\left(C_k\right)p\left(\mathbf{x}|C_k\right)}{p(\mathbf{x})} \tag{3}$$

where $\mathbf{x} = (x_1, \ldots, x_n)$ is a vector of characteristic attributes of the sample data. C_k is k possible outcomes and in our case, it could be 0 or 1.

K-nearest neighbor (K-NN) algorithm is an instance-based classification algorithm. The basic idea is to select the most recent sample in the same attribute class as the training feature. It is usually decided by a majority vote.

The advantage of defect prediction models based on Logistic Regression is that it is easy to understand and realize and it is meaningful for defect rough judgment, but it is easy to unfit and has low classification accuracy.

Random Forests are an ensemble learning method for classification, regression, and other tasks that operates by constructing a multitude of decision trees at training time and outputting the class that is the mode of the classes (classification) or mean prediction (regression) of the individual trees. Random decision forests correct for decision trees' habit of overfitting to their training set.

4.3 Performance Measures

The software defect prediction model refers to the binary problem of whether the software module contains defects, so the performance evaluation index of the classification model in the field of machine learning can be applied to the evaluation of the prediction model. For the sake of simplicity, this study describes the performance evaluation indicators of the prediction model in this paper based on the confusion matrix [18]. Table 2 shows the confusion matrix with four defect prediction results. Here, true positive (TP), false negative (FN), false positive (FP) and true negative (TN) is the number of defective instances that are predicted as defective, the number of defective instances that are predicted as non-defective, the number of non-defective instances that are predicted as defective, and the number of non-defective instances that are predicted as non-defective, respectively.

Table 2. Confusion Matrix.

	Predicted Defective	Predicted non-defective
Actual defective	true positive (TP)	false negative (FN)
Actual non-defetive	false positive (FP)	true negative (TN)

With the confusion matrix, the following performance evaluation measures are adopted, which are commonly used in the defect prediction studies. Table 3 shows the calculation formula of the used performance evaluation measures for defect prediction. Recall,pd [19] is defined as the ratio of the number of defective instances that are correctly classified as defective to the total number of defective instances.

Precision [20] is defined as the ratio of the number of modules that are correctly predicted as defective to the number of modules that are predicted as defective.

The value of AUC (Area Under the Curve) [21] is the area under the roc curve. ROC (Receiver Operating Characteristic) curve is a graphical method to describe the relationship between the real case rate, pd, and false-positive case rate, pf in the classification model. AUC considers the classifier's classification ability for both positive and negative examples, and can still make a reasonable evaluation of the classifier in the case of imbalanced samples.

F-measure comprehensively considers recall and precision. It is defined as the harmonic mean of recall and precision, which comprehensively considers the overall performance of the model on recall and precision, and can comprehensively reflect the performance of the model. It is widely used in cross project defect prediction research, such as [22,23].

Therefore, the comprehensive indicators AUC and f-measure are used to evaluate the performance of each strategy in our experiments.

Table 3. Performance Evaluation Measures.

Measure	Defined as
Recall (pd)	$\frac{TP}{TP+FN}$
Precision	$\frac{TP}{TP+FP}$
AUC	The area under the ROC curve
f-measure	$\frac{2 \times Precision \times Recall}{Precision+Recall}$

4.4 Results

Based on six data sets (CM1, MC2, PC1, PC2, PC3, PC4), four classifiers (KNN, LR, NB, RF) are used to compare the results of the four strategies under f-measure and AUC in our experiments. The experimental results are shown using project-level filtering, instance-level filtering, the filtering method which combined project-level and instance-level, and three-level filtering respectively in the Fig. 3. Besides, under each strategy, the average value of f-measure and AUC on six data sets using four different classifiers was counted in the Table 4. When the same algorithm is used on the same data set and the same performance measure is used as the judgment standard, the percentage of each strategy with the best performance in all experiments is calculated. The results are shown in the Table 5. As a whole, the three-level filtering strategy achieves better prediction performance than the other three strategies. Naive Bayes classifier performs better using our strategy.

Under the strategy we proposed, the f-measure and AUC measure values of each classifier on each data set are calculated. The statistical data is shown in the Table 6. When we focus on the MC2 dataset, we find that Under the f-measure, the Naive Bayes algorithm is the best. Due to NB has the largest f-measure value and the largest f-measure difference with other classifiers based on MC2.

Considering economic benefits and other factors, software defect prediction has not been widely used in engineering practice. Rahman F et al. [21] proposed that the recall value determines the practical validity of the software defect prediction model. Shell et al. [24] pointed out that the recall value of human

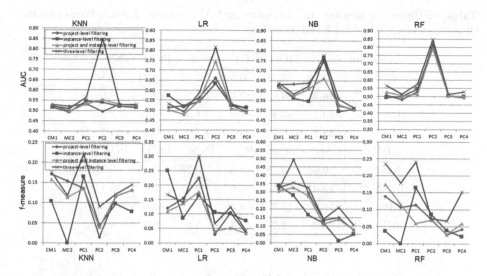

Fig. 3. Results of different strategy on the performance of different prediction models.

Table 4. For f-measure and AUC, the average values of four strategies on six data sets using KNN, LR, NB, RF.

f-measure	Project-level fltering	Instance-level filtering	Project-level and istance-level fltering	Three-level fltering
KNN	0.12	0.08	0.12	0.14
LR	0.11	0.13	0.09	0.14
NB	0.24	0.16	0.21	0.24
RF	0.08	0.06	0.08	0.16
AUC				
KNN	0.52	0.52	0.53	0.58
LR	0.55	0.55	0.55	0.58
NB	0.61	0.58	0.58	0.61
RF	0.56	0.56	0.56	0.59

Table 5. The percentage of each strategy with the best performance in all experiments.

Strategy	f-measure	AUC
Project-level fltering	20.8%	12.5%
Instance-level filtering	8.33%	20.8%
Project-level and instance-level filtering	4.17%	0
Three-level filtering	66.66%	66.66%

Table 6. Under our strategy, the f-measure and AUC values of Naive Bayes and the change rates(%) of KNN, LR, RF classifiers.

f-measure	CM1	MC2	PC1	PC2	PC3	PC4
NB	0.33	0.35	0.33	0.14	0.21	0.10
KNN	−46.7	−66.8	−32.9	−36.1	−42.5	38.5
LR	−49.1	−60.4	−7.8	−51.9	−40.7	−59.2
RF	−28.2	−49.7	−26.3	−47.4	−68.4	45.7
AUC	CM1	MC2	PC1	PC2	PC3	PC4
NB	0.64	0.58	0.62	0.78	0.56	0.51
KNN	−18.0	−12.5	−8.9	9.3	−5.1	3.1
LR	−16.3	−15.7	−5.0	5.1	−4.6	−0.8
RF	−20.2	−17.7	−14.7	5.9	−9.2	−4.0

code review defect is more than 60%. Therefore, recall of different strategies using different algorithms under a single dataset is calculated, as shown in Fig. 4. It can be seen from the figure that our strategy has obvious improvement under the KNN algorithm.

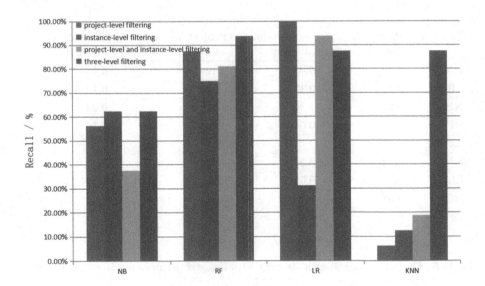

Fig. 4. Recall values of different strategies using different algorithms.

5   Discussion

RQ1: How does our strategy perform on each classifier compared to other strategies?

As is shown in Fig. 3, three-level filtering is the best in most experiments. Even though the performance in individual experiments is not optimal, it is not the worst. Therefore, the proportion of the best performance of each strategy in all the experiments is counted, and the results are shown in the Table 5. The percentage of three-level filtering with the best performance among all experiments is much higher than the other three strategies. According to the Table 4, judging from the average value of different strategies using the same classifier on six data sets for different performance measures, the three-level filtering performed well when using KNN, LR, NB, RF classifiers for defect prediction. The above experimental results can fully prove the superiority of the three-level strategy.

RQ2: Which classifier performs best by our strategy in cross-project defect prediction?

The statistics are shown in the Table 6. NB classifier has absolute advantages in CM1, MC2, PC1, and PC3 data sets. In the PC2 data set, the f-measure of the KNN classifier, LR classifier, and RF classifier is not as good as the NB classifier, but AUC measure is better than Nb, and the improvement range is less than 8%. In the PC4 data set, the LR classifier is better than the NB classifier in performance; the KNN classifier and RF classifier are better than the NB classifier in one measure, and the other measure is worse than NB classifier.

RQ3: Is our strategy practical in specific datasets?

In our limited number of experiments, the recall of the PC2 dataset is best. It can be seen from Fig. 4 that our strategy for the recall using any algorithm is greater than 60%. From this point of view, three-level filtering is feasible in practice.

6   Conclusion

In this work, a three-level training data selection strategy that combines project selection, instance selection, and metric selection is proposed. d. At the same time, the overall performance of the strategy is better than other strategies. The experiment also proves that naive Bayes classifier is more suitable for building a prediction model with simplified training data after three-level filtering. In the limited experimental data set, there is recall value to meet the prediction rate of manual review defects, which further proves that the cross-project defect prediction under three-level strategy has certain practicality.

At present, the recall does not achieve the value of manual review based on most data sets. Our future work will focus on practical validation of methods on more datasets, such as PROMISE.

Acknowledgements. This paper is partly supported by the Pre-research of Civil Spacecraft Technology (No. B0204).

References

1. Zhou, Y., et al.: How far we have progressed in the journey? an examination of cross-project defect prediction. ACM Trans. Softw. Eng. Methodol. **27**, 1–51 (2018)
2. Xu, Z., Yuan, P., Zhang, T., Tang, Y., Li, S., Xia, Z.: HDA: cross-project defect prediction via heterogeneous domain adaptation with dictionary learning. IEEE Access **6**, 57597–57613 (2018)
3. Hosseini, S., Turhan, B., Gunarathna, D.: A systematic literature review and meta-analysis on cross project defect prediction. IEEE Trans. Softw. Eng. **99**, 1–40 (2017)
4. Turhan, B.: On the dataset shift problem in software engineering prediction models. Empir. Softw. Eng. **17**, 62–74 (2012). https://doi.org/10.1007/s10664-011-9182-8
5. Turhan, B., et al.: On the relative value of cross-company and within-company data for defect prediction. Empir. Softw. Eng. **14**, 540–578 (2009). https://doi.org/10.1007/s10664-008-9103-7
6. Peters, F., et al.: Better cross company defect prediction. In: 10th Working Conference on Mining Software Repositories (MSR) (2013)
7. He P., et al.: Simplification of training data for cross-project defect prediction. Computer Science (2014)
8. Yu, Q., Qian, J., Jiang, S., Wu, Z., Zhang, G.: An empirical study on the effectiveness of feature selection for cross-project defect prediction. IEEE Access **7**, 35710–35718 (2019). https://doi.org/10.1109/ACCESS.2019.2895614
9. Briand, L.C., et al.: Assessing the applicability of fault-proneness models across object-oriented software projects. IEEE Trans. Softw. Eng. **28**(7), 706–720 (2002)
10. Herbold, S.: Training data selection for cross-project defect prediction. In: Proceedings of the 9th International Conference on Predictive Models in Software Engineering (2013)
11. Kawata, K., Amasaki, S., Yokogawa, T.: Improving relevancy filter methods for cross-project defect prediction. In: Software Engineering & Advanced Applications, vol. 619. IEEE (2015)
12. Cui, C., Liu, B., Wang, S.: Isolation forest filter to simplify training data for cross-project defect prediction. In: 2019 Prognostics and System Health Management Conference (2019)
13. He, P., Li, B., Liu, X., Chen, J., Ma, Y.T.: An empirical study on software defect prediction with a simplified metric set. Inf. Soft. Technol. **59**, 170–190 (2015)
14. Amasaki, S., Kawata, K., Yokogawa, T.: Improving cross-project defect prediction methods with data simplification. In: Proceedings of the Euromicro Conference on Software Engineering and Advanced Applications (2015)
15. He, Z., Shu, F., Yang, Y., Li, M., Wang, Q.: An investigation on the feasibility of cross-project defect prediction. In: Proceedings Eighth IEEE Symposium on Software Metrics (2012)
16. Gray, D., et al.: Reflections on the NASA MDP data sets. IET Softw. **6**, 549–558 (2012)
17. Lewis, D.D: Naive (Bayes) at forty: the independence assumption in information retrieval. In: European Conference on Machine Learning (1998)
18. Witten, I.H., et al.: Data mining: practical machine learning tools and techniques. ACM Sigmod Rec. **31**, 76–77 (1999)

19. Fawcett, T.: An introduction to ROC analysis. Pattern Recogn. Lett. **27**(8), 861–874 (2006)
20. Buckland, M., Fredric, G.: The relationship between recall and precision. J. Am. Soc. Inf. Sci. **45**, 12–19 (1994)
21. Rahman, F., et al.: Recalling the 'Imprecision' of cross-project defect prediction. In: Proceedings of the ACM SIGSOFT 20th International Symposium on the Foundations of Software Engineering (2012)
22. Nam, Ja., et al.: Transfer defect learning. In: Proceedings of the 2013 International Conference on Software Engineering (2013)
23. Kim, S., Whitehead, E.J., Zhang, Y.: Classifying software changes: clean or buggy? IEEE Trans. Softw. Eng. **34**(2), 181–196 (2008)
24. Shull, F., et al.: What we have learned about fighting defects. In: Proceedings 8th IEEE Symposium on Software Metrics (2002)

A Hierarchical Fault Detection Method for Aerospace Embedded Software

Cangzhou Yuan[1(✉)], Kangzhao Wu[1], Ran Peng[1], and Panpan Zhan[2]

[1] School of Software, Beihang University, Beijing 100191, China
{yuancz,smbody,ran987}@buaa.edu.cn
[2] Beijing Institute of Spacecraft System Engineering, Beijing 100094, China
panpan3210@qq.com

Abstract. Monolithic fault detection methods have low accuracy for comprehensive faults detection, because they can only detect specific type of faults. Therefore, it is necessary to study the combination of fault detection methods to improve the detection accuracy. In this paper, based on the fault propagation on component-based aerospace embedded software architecture, we analyze occur reasons, manifestations and effects of instruction-, component- and system-level faults whose root cause is single event upset (SEU) which is the main reason of aerospace embedded software, and propose a hierarchical fault model to specify characteristics of the three levels faults. And based on the hierarchical fault model, a hierarchical detection method is proposed to combine the three levels monolithic fault detection methods. The experimental results show that the hierarchical fault detection method has higher fault detection accuracy than the monolithic fault detection methods for comprehensive faults detection.

Keywords: Hierarchical fault model · Hierarchical fault detection · Single event upset

1 Introduction

Generally speaking, the execution of space missions has extremely high-reliability requirements for spacecraft hardware and software. However, due to the harsh conditions of strong solar radiation, low temperature, and ion radiation in the space environment, spacecraft hardware and software are likely to be damaged or malfunction, which has extreme risks for the successful execution of space missions [1].

To meet the reliability, safety, and many other requirements of spacecraft software operation, researchers have launched a large number of fault detecting and processing technology researches [1–3], including software fault mechanism, fault detecting, processing methods, and fault processing architecture.

There is strong cosmic radiation in the space environment, which is easy to generate single event upset (SEU) [4], that is, a single high-energy particle in the

© ICST Institute for Computer Sciences, Social Informatics and Telecommunications Engineering 2021
Published by Springer Nature Switzerland AG 2021. All Rights Reserved
Q. Wu et al. (Eds.): WiSATS 2020, LNICST 357, pp. 124–138, 2021.
https://doi.org/10.1007/978-3-030-69069-4_11

universe shoots into the sensitive area of semiconductor devices, which causes the logical state of devices to flip. Once SEU occurs, it may lead to a fault, including silent data corruption (SDC), detected unrecoverable error (DUE), prolong, exception or crash. In this paper, a fault is regarded as a situation where at least one attribute of the system doesn't conform to its expected behavior. When the impact of the fault manifests, the system generates an error [5]. In order to decrease complexity of analysis, we just consider SDC, prolong, exception and crash caused by SEU. It is reasonable to simplify because the hierarchical fault model and hierarchical fault method are adapt to other faults at the instruction-, component- and system-level that the faults we consider can be classified.

Under the harsh conditions, even the redundancy method can not assure 100% detection accuracy. The experimental results of Reis GA et al. [6] show that even if the three redundancy method is used, the SEU can not be detected to 100%. It can be seen that the fault domain caused by SEU is infinite and unpredictable, and the monolithic fault detection method still can be improved.

One way to improve the monolithic fault detection method is to use the comprehensive faults detection method, but there are two challenges: first, how to know the faults contained in the fault domain as fully as possible. It is very convenient for us to design fault detection methods if know what specific faults to be detected, for the specific methods can be used to detect specific faults. Second, how to determine the combination of fault detection methods. As a fault detection method only detects a specific fault domain, if the fault domain of two fault detection methods overlaps greatly, such combination is inefficient.

To solve the first challenge, a hierarchical fault model is established to analyze the fault types and characteristics in the single-particle inversion fault domain, which provides a clear fault target for the hierarchical fault detection method. To solve the second challenge, a hierarchical fault detection method based on the hierarchical fault model is proposed to improve the coverage of the fault domain. The result shows that the hierarchical fault detection method has a higher fault detection rate than the monolithic fault detection methods for comprehensive faults detection.

2   Related Work

Generally speaking, the hierarchical model, the fault propagation model and the fault detection method are three research aspects in fault detection. The hierarchical model focuses on analysing fault in different levels, generally component- and system-level. The fault propagation model focuses on analysing how faults propagate along with instruction dependency, component dependency or other types dependency. The fault detection method focuses on how to detect the target fault in run-time, aiming to high accuracy and cost-effective. In this paper, we try to consider the three aspects comprehensively.

2.1   Hierarchical Model

Based on individual components and components dependency which corresponding to system-level, T. Pitakrat et al. [7] proposed an architecture-aware approach to improve predicition quality. Their result shows that HORA improves the overall area under ROC Curve (AUC) by 10.7% compared to a monolithic approach.

Gao Xiang et al. [8] divided system into serial levels functions to build a network diagram of signal propagation among functions for vulnerable analysis. They regarded system as combination of hierarchical functions.

Kalbarczyk et al. [9] modeled the impact of faults on software behavior by simulating fault propagation at different levels of hardware step by step, including physics-level, transistor-level, logic-level, chip-level and hardware-level.

Savor and Seviora [10] proposed a hierarchical supervisor that has the path-detection layer (PDL) and the base supervisor layer (BSupL) to detect software failures. BSupL receives execution path information from the PDL and checks detail behavior of software.

In our method, we consider instruction-level, component-level and system-level to model SEU propagation.

2.2   Fault Propagation Model

Most fault propagation models are based on fault injection with mathematical analysis and estimation [11]. Researchers often model fault propagation in a probabilistic way for quantitative analysis [12].

Abdelmoez et al. [13] analyzed fault propagation at system design stage based on system states and message. They defined the propagation probability between two components. Hiller et al. [14] introduced the error permeability to represent the propagation probability from a signal to another signal. This paper just analyzes fault propagation between different levels qualitatively, because we only consider how the fault propagates and what it manifests.

Avizienis et al. [15] described the process of system failure caused by component failure. If there is a defect in the code implementation of an internal active component when this part of the code is executed, the error will lead to an internal failure of the component; once the fault reaches the interface of the component, it will cause the component to fail. Based on this process, we think the system fault states caused by SEUes are the same as those caused by defect codes. So that SEU may lead to component or system failure.

Based on empirical observations of error propagations in programs, Guanpeng Li et al. [16] construct a three-level model to capture error propagation at the static data dependency, control flow, and memory levels. This model can predict the overall SDC probabilities and the SDC probabilities of instructions without fault injection, and the accuracy is close to fault injection, while the speed and scalability are better than fault injection. They only studied fault propagation in instruction-level by analyzing each bit's propagation probability. Our approach not only considers how the SEU propagates from instructions to components, but also how propagates from components to systems.

2.3 Fault Detection Method

In instruction-level, signatured instruction streams (SIS) [17] calculates CRC signature of each basic block of code segment, then recalculates signature and check it in run-time. Except for the code segment, the operands of instructions may generate SEU. Error detection by duplicated instructions (EDDI) [18] make another copy of instructions in one thread to cover the code and data segment. But the control flow isn't covered by EDDI. So Reis G et al. [19] proposed software implemented fault tolerance (SWIFT), using signature to cover control flow and redundancy to cover data flow.

In component-level, Huang et al. [20] proposed software rejuvenation, restarting the longest running component based some rules, to prevent software aging [21].

In system-level, Antonio Rodrigues et al. [22] proposed a platform to derive actionable insights from monitored metrics in distributed systems. They can filter out unimportant metrics and infer metrics dependencies between distributed components of the system. The result shows that they can reduce the number of metrics by at least an order of magnitude ($10 - 100$x) and improve existing monitoring infrastructures.

However, the common feature of the above methods is that they only studied fault detection for the faults in one level, without considering their propagation stage, manifestation, and severity. One-level methods cannot process all the faults, so we consider these three levels. The higher level can detect faults not detected by lower level.

3 Hierarchical Fault Model

As one of the main sources of spacecraft software faults, the soft errors caused by SEU will cause various types of software faults. Because of the differences in the propagation stage and manifestation of soft error, it is necessary to establish a hierarchical fault model for different stages and types of software faults caused by soft errors.

Nowadays the design trend of aerospace software architecture is component-based, which makes aerospace software rapidly developed and highly reusable. Because the aerospace software is real time required, it often consists of simple software structure. Sometimes its entire system has little subsystems and components. We do not consider subsystems because the number of subsystems is too little to build analysis in a aerospace software. Based on the architecture elements, aerospace software system can be divided into three levels: instruction, component and system. Instruction is the smallest code that can be executed by CPU. A set of instructions with specific logic rules forms a component. Similarly, a set of components with specific connection rules forms a system.

Because of the uncertainty of SEU, the fault may occur at anywhere, and the lower level fault will propagate along the data or control flow to the higher level and cause higher level fault. Generally, high-level and low-level fault have different manifestations, and higher level the fault occurs on, more serious the harm is. In this paper, a hierarchical fault model is established based on the following two reasons. One is that if the fault is detected at the source when it occurs, the propagation of the fault can be prevented, so as to minimize the harm of the fault. It is easier to distinguish the characteristics and detect of each level fault by using hierarchical fault model. Another is that the fault detection system can also organize hierarchical fault detection methods according to the hierarchical model. The fault detection system architecture is compatible with the aerospace software system architecture, which is instruction, component and system. And it is easy to deploy fault detection system into aerospace software system.

3.1   Instruction-Level Analysis

The first stage is instruction-level, where generates soft errors. There are a large number of high-energy particles in the space environment. These particles come from all kinds of radiation in the universe. When these particles pass through semiconductor devices, they will produce electron-hole pairs. When accumulated to a certain amount, they can reverse the state of logic devices [5]. These logical devices can be registers, cache, memory. The flip of the logical device state is called SEU, and the most direct effect is to cause a bit inversion of the data segment (DS) or code segment (CS).

According to whether it is detected by the system, SEU can be divided into two types, SDC and DUE. SDC refers to the soft errors that are not detected by the system but will affect the system behavior. DUE refers to the soft errors that are detected by the system and may affect the system behavior. The impact of SDC on the system is worse than DUE because it can not be detected. Because instruction-level is the generation stage of soft error, a soft error is in the state of just generated but not started to propagate. If it is detected and recovered when generated, its propagation can be avoided. Since the influence is within the instruction, bit inversion belongs to the instruction-level.

3.2   Component-Level Analysis

When soft errors are not successfully detected or recovered in the generation stage, they may cause exception, prolong, or crash after further propagation along with the data flow or control flow.

Program with soft errors usually enters the wrong control or data flow and then generates exceptions. After the bit of data in control or data, flow is reversed, the program receives the wrong input or produces the wrong output, thus triggering some pre- or post-conditions set by the software developer and resulting in exceptions. For example, if the sign bit of an integer is reversed, the program detects that the data is out of the input range, resulting in data exception.

The cause of prolonging is similar to exception, but just without the data flow. For example, the data controlling the instruction stream increases because of bit inversion, which will increase the time to complete the task. The specific manifestation of prolonging is that the running time of software doesn't meet the expectation, such as no response for a long time, increasing response time, etc.

Exception and prolong can only be detected by monitoring the status of the components. Once they occur, their influence and impact are more serious than SDCs. Because these two types of faults have prevented the components from completing tasks normally or in time, they are component-level faults.

3.3 System-Level Analysis

There are two main reasons for a soft error to cause a crash. First, the soft error changes the value of pointers, resulting in invalid address and causing a crash. Second, the soft error mentioned above occurs in the code segment, resulting in an illegal instruction, then a crash occurs. In Xin Xu and Man-Lap Li's research [23], they injected address fault and found 88% of faults caused crash. Gu et al. [24] studied Linux behavior under soft errors. They found that 95% crash are caused by null pointer, invalid instruction and page fault. The page fault means the kernel tries to access the bad page so it can be classified in invalid address.

The crash causes the components unable to provide function, which may eventually make the whole system crash. Therefore, when the crash occurs, the influence and impact are the largest, which is a system-level fault. The specific manifestation of crash is that the crashed system is stop, means no interaction with environment. So system crash can be detected by monitoring interactions between system and environment.

3.4 Hierarchical Fault Model Proposed

According to the analysis, a model can be built with fault type, effect level and source-critical. Figure 1 shows the model.

We classify type of faults by its generating level and consequence. First at instruction-level, bit inversion on data segment may have no effect, meaning benign fault, and also may cause crash. But bit inversion on code segment will cause crash in most cases, so we put bit inversion (DS) under bit inversion (CS). Second at component-level, an exception means that the component does not function properly but it can be recovered by retrying. And a prolong means that a component can only be recovered by rebooting. That is why we put exception under prolong. Third at system-level, when system crashed, the effect is system level and system can be only recovered by restarting it, so we put crash on the highest position.

It is necessary to consider source-critical. If the source of the fault is not critical, good fault detection methods, which are usually expensive, needn't be implemented, and we can focus on the critical part of the system. The number of source-critical is bigger, the source is more critical. The specific meaning of numbers is depended on the definition of the system. In the implement section, 1 means application that will not affect other applications after failure, 2 means fault detection, isolation, and recovery system which will place the system into an unsafe state after failure and 3 means system critical component which will make system failure when it appears failure.

The effect level is easy to understand. The effect level of bit inversion (DS and CS) can be instruction, component or system because it can just affect one instruction, make an exception of component or crash whole system. The effect level of exception and prolong can be component or system because they can not affect instructions but components and cause components or system failure. The effect level of crash is system. Whenever the crash occurs, the system will fall into stopped state immediately.

If a fault can be modeled with the three dimensions, a more appropriate fault detection method can be used.

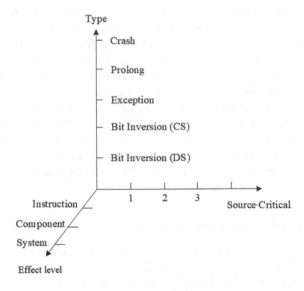

Fig. 1. Hierarchical fault model

4   Hierarchical Fault Detection Method

According to the hierarchical fault model, faults may propagate. If the initial fault can be detected at source and recovery actions are taken, a greater loss can be prevented from the fault propagation, but fault cannot be completely detected by a monolithic fault detection method. Therefore, for the faults caused by bit inversion, we propose the hierarchical fault detection method based on the hierarchical fault model, aiming to detect different types of faults in different propagation stages to improve the accuracy of fault detection.

4.1 Instruction-Level Method

According to the hierarchical fault model, there are two types of bit inversion in the components. One is that the operands of the instruction are reversed, causing the execution path of the program and the function call sequence changed, which may lead to functional failure. The other is that the code segment is reversed and the instruction is changed, resulting in invalid instruction.

For the bit inversion in operands, triple redundancy is used to detect and recover. Two copies of the parameters passed in and condition expressions in the function are created. When the parameter is used, values of the parameter and its two copies are voted, then select the most value. When a branch is encountered, the outputs of the condition expression and its two copies are calculated, then select the most output. In this way, the bit reversal fault can be prevented from propagating. But how to detect it? When voting values of parameters and outputs of condition expressions, it can be checked whether all values or outputs are the same. If not, the bit inversion is detected, then the value or output with the most votes is used to recover the wrong one.

There are remain two questions: why not use double or more redundancy and how to select value and output if all three redundancies are different? First, though the bit inversion can be detected by double redundancy, it can not be recovered. It is cost- and loss-effective if recover the fault when it just occurred. But now, adding just one more redundancy can achieve this goal. Second, it can assume that the probability of bit inversion of one redundancy is P and that when all redundancies occur bit inversion, they must be in different positions each other to simplify our calculation, that is assuming the probability P_d of all redundancies occur in different positions equal to the probability of all redundancies occur bit inversion because that the probability of former is just a little smaller than latter.

According to Aiguo Li et al. [25], the monitoring device experienced 65 times bit reversals in 19 days on orbit. P is calculated about $4\text{e}10^{-5}$ and if there are N-group redundancies, $P_d = P^N$. If $N = 3$, $P_d = 6.4\text{e}10^{-14}$ and $N = 4$, $P_d = 2.56\text{e}10^{-18}$ and so on. If it assume that adding one redundancy will add cost C, then the performance

$$E = \left(1 - P^N\right)/NC \tag{1}$$

which is a minus function. According to the first reason, double redundancy should not be used so we choose triple redundancy which has the best performance. Third, it can be seen that $P_d = 6.4\text{e}10^{-14}$ when $N = 3$, which is a very small number, thus it can assume that bit inversion in all three redundancies will not occur. For the above reasons, we finally choose triple redundancy.

For the bit inversion in the code segment, since the storage area will not change when the code segment is not in a fault state, the check code of code segment can be calculated to detect the change of code segment. We detect the fault by periodically calculating the cyclic redundancy check (specifically CRC-16) code of the code segment. First, starting a thread to calculate the check code regularly, which takes the first value as the standard check value. Then, the thread will calculate the check value of the code segment in cycle T and compare it with the standard check value. If they are the same, no bit reverse occurs; otherwise, a fault is detected.

4.2   Component-Level Method

Soft errors that are not detected within a function can further propagate to cause an exception and prolong. The method of fault detection at the instruction-level can not guarantee that there is no fault at all. At the same time, there are other faults of instruction-level, which lead to the generation of exception and prolong. Therefore, to detect faults which instruction-level can not detect and may lead to exception and prolong at the instruction-level, methods are implemented to detect exception and prolong at component-level.

When an exception occurs, the pre- or post-condition set by developers will be violated, so we can input the checked value and check whether there is any violation according to the pre- or post-condition. If so, an exception occurs. Because there are many kinds of exceptions, the pre- or post-conditions should be defined by developers themselves, to detect any exceptions they want to detect, which caused by the missed soft errors at instruction-level, and to prevent its further propagation.

When the prolong occurs, the specific manifestation is that the program continuously executes the instruction in the loop, while the instruction outside will not be executed and the data beyond the scope of the loop instruction will not be modified. Therefore, the heartbeat mechanism can be used to detect prolong. Each component will send a heartbeat report to the heartbeat detection component every cycle of execution. If the interval between two adjacent heartbeats exceeds the threshold, a prolonged is detected. Due to different space, embedded software have different environments, the timeout time needs to be decided by the developers themselves.

4.3   System-Level Method

Similar to the component-level, soft errors not detected at the component-level may cause a crash. The method of fault detection at component-level can not guarantee that there is no fault at all. At the same time, there are other faults of component-level, which lead to the generation of the crash. Therefore, to prevent the system from permanently stopping due to various possible faults, the method is implemented to detect crash at system-level.

When the crash occurs, the software can not run and can not use a method to detect a crash. So the hardware watchdog is used to detect the crash of the software system. Because hardware watchdog doesn't depend on the services provided by the spacecraft software, when the software crash occurs, it doesn't affect the watchdog. A thread is created to reset the timer of hardware watchdog every cycle of execution, if there is a crash, then the thread will stop and can not reset the timer, which will be zero in a short time. When the timer is zero, the hardware watchdog will be triggered and send a signal, which means that a crash is detected. Others can use this signal to implement some mechanisms of fault recovery. For example, this signal can be used to restart the system automatically or send a crash report to the ground.

5   Implementation

In this section, we implement the hierarchical fault detection method and use fault injection to evaluate its accuracy for comprehensive faults detection. To evaluate accuracy, we use the hierarchical fault detection method to detect comprehensive faults generated by fault injection and compare accuracy with monolithic fault detection methods.

5.1   Target Platform

The hierarchical fault detection method need a target platform to implement it so that it can be sure what the manifestations are of its faults and how to implement the hierarchical detection method on it. The target platform is a spacecraft software middleware, whose architecture is component-based. Every component running on this middleware is a thread, and the middleware supports dynamic loading and unloading components when running. All components follow the publish/subscribe pattern to communicate with each other. There are three reasons why choose the component-based middleware. First, it has no subsystem so that it can be divided into instruction-, component- and system-level, which adapt to the hierarchical fault detection method. Second, it has a well defined and implemented communication mechanism that will help to record the detection result. Third, as a middleware, it shields details of operating system and hardware that are not our concern. The entire middleware will run with Linux on the SPARC hardware.

5.2   Way to Implement the Hierarchical Method

Implement for Bit Inversion on Data Segment. Because this method is instruction-level, it is platform independent. We implement it by insert redundancy code that also adapt to other softwares. For two reasons, we just choose three functions of one of its core components, which means it is very critical to implement this method. First, too much implementation of triple redundancy will affect performance of the middleware and it is time-consuming to implement. It can perform well just implemented on core components to prevent SEU propagating and cause serious effect. Second, it make against for the fault injection if all components implement the method. Because we just inject SEU to cause other faults and triple redundancy can prevent most SEU propagating to cause other faults, it will be inconvenient to evaluate accuracy of other methods.

Implement for Bit Inversion on Code Segment. Because we use CRC16 to calculate the check code, it is necessary to know start address and length of each component and have access to read. Luckily, this middleware provides memory management for its components. Based on the memory management, a component is implemented to calculate the check code of each component with CRC16.

Implement for Exception. For exception detection, we need to know when and where the exception occurs and what exception it is. Components of the middleware will send an exception event when occurs an exception, so we can know the information of this exception. Based on the middleware's event management, a component is implemented to detect exception events.

Implement for Prolong. For prolong detection, we need to know the states of components. Component of the middleware will increase its loop counter by one every loop, which can seen as a heart beat. Based on this rule, a component is implemented to monitor whether the loop counter of each component is increased in a fixed time interval. The interval is set to 10 loops of the heart beat monitor component so that it is neither sensitive too much nor insensitive too much.

Implement for Crash. Crash is a little different. When crash occurs, it is hardware watchdog who detect the crash, not components of the middleware. So we record the detection result by manual according to whether the middleware restarts after crash. To active hardware watchdog, a component is implemented to reset the hardware watchdog timer based on the hardware management of the middleware.

5.3   Fault Injection Method

Fault injection is an effective and convenient method to introduce fault into the middleware. To simulate the SEU propagation process causing bit inversion on data segment and code segment, exception, prolong and crash, the base rule to inject fault is that we just inverse one bit of a random byte. To know what specific fault one injection causes, the random injection is not so 'random'. We design some injections that will cause specific faults known by us, and we will inject faults from the designed injections randomly so that we know what faults we inject.

6   Results

We did a total of five groups of fault injection. In each group, we injected bit inversion (DS), bit inversion (CS), exception event, prolong and crash random, and we recorded the detected numbers of each fault. Table 1 shows the number of fault injected and Table 2 shows the number of fault detected.

Table 1. Number of fault injected in each group

Fault Type	Group 1	Group 2	Group 3	Group 4	Group 5
Bit Inversion (DS)	132	324	238	319	317
Bit Inversion (CS)	58	130	107	113	120
Exception	157	189	114	237	275
Prolong	90	89	80	81	73
Crash	45	70	32	55	38
Total	482	802	571	805	823

Table 2. Number of fault detected each group

Fault Type	Group 1	Group 2	Group 3	Group 4	Group 5
Bit Inversion (DS)	126	309	228	306	302
Bit Inversion (CS)	55	126	101	110	117
Exception	157	189	114	236	275
Prolong	90	89	80	81	73
Crash	45	70	32	55	38
Total	473	783	555	788	805

We calculate the detection accuracy of each fault and the total accuracy of each fault detection method. Figure 2 and Fig. 3 shows the result. We find that average detection accuracy of bit inversion(DS) is about 95.6%. Average detection accuracy of bit inversion(CS) is about 96.2%. Respective average detection accuracy of exception, prolong and crash nearly is or just is 100%. Figure 2 also shows detection accuracy of each monolithic method for their specific fault because in our fault injection design, a fault can only be detected by one specific detection method so that other methods will not introduce errors into detection accuracy of this fault.

Figure 3 shows low accuracy (less 40%) of each monolithic method for comprehensive faults detection. Compared Fig. 2 with Fig. 3, we find that each monolithic fault detection method performs well for its fault but poor for comprehensive faults. The hierarchical fault detection method has about 98% accuracy, much bigger than other monolithic methods. It proves that the hierarchical method can combine monolithic methods at different levels to improve detection accuracy for comprehensive faults detection. And we can reasonably derive that if comprehensive faults only contain one fault, the accuracy of hierarchical method is equal to monolithic one.

7   Discussion

In this section, we want to discuss the inaccuracy of bit inversion detection and accuracy of exception, prolong and crash.

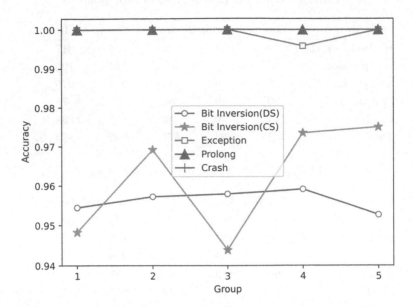

Fig. 2. Each fault detection accuracy of hierarchical detection method

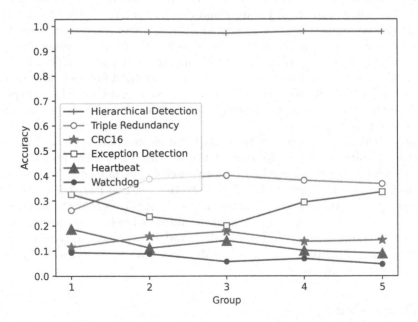

Fig. 3. Comprehensive fault detection accuracy of each detection method

Why Accuracy of Bit Inversion Detection is Not 100%? Because fault injection may occur in any position, some fault may be injected after voting and thus can not be detected by triple redundancy. That is the reason why the detection accuracy of bit inversion(DS) isn't 100%. For the bit inversion(CS), because the CRC check is executed periodically, some fault may be injected after checking and can not be detected.

Why Each Accuracy of Exception, Prolong and Crash Detection is or Nearly is 100%? There are two reasons. One is that exception, prolong and crash are at relatively high levels, where faults are much more easily detected than instruction-level. Another is that the fault injection method can just simulate part of space environment effect and the injection number is maybe little so that detection accuracy of some faults is 100%.

8 Conclusion

We think the reason why a monolithic fault detection method has low accuracy for detection multi-level faults is that the detection coverage of the monolithic fault detection method is too small for the fault domain of multi-level faults. Thus, for the bit inversion fault domain, the hierarchical fault model is proposed to identify what faults the domain has and the hierarchical fault detection method is proposed to increase the detection coverage which leads to increased accuracy. We propose an idea about fault detection that first to build a hierarchical fault to identify faults in a specific fault domain because of fault propagation and second to design hierarchical fault detection method for each fault identified to increase the accuracy.

Acknowledgements. This paper is partly supported by the Pre-research of Civil Spacecraft Technology (No. B0204).

References

1. Tipaldi, M., Bruenjes, B.: Survey on fault detection, isolation, and recovery strategies in the space domain. J. Aerosp. Inf. Syst. **12**, 235–256 (2015)
2. Tang, M., Ning, H., Li, T.: Design and research of FDIR framework for integrated electronic system on satellite (2010)
3. Jiang, L., Li, H., Yang, G.: Research progress of spacecraft autonomous fault diagnosis technology. J. Astronaut. **30**, 13–17 (2009)
4. Li, A., Hong, B., Wang, S.: Research on software vulnerability identification method based on error propagation analysis (2007)
5. Mukherjee, S.: Architecture Design For Soft Errors. Morgan Kaufmann, Burlington (2011)
6. Reis, G.A., Chang, J., August, D.I.: Automatic instruction-level software-only recovery. IEEE Micro **27**, 36–47 (2007)
7. Pitakrat, T., Okanovic, D., Van Hoorn, A., Grunske, L.: An architecture-aware approach to hierarchical online failure prediction. In: International ACM SIGSOFT Conference on Quality of Software Architectures (QoSA) (2016)

8. Xiang, G., Guochang, Z., Xiaoling, L., et al.: Soft-error hierarchical evaluation algorithm of fault vulnerabilities based on sensitive attributes of single event effect. In: IEEE International Conference on Electronic Measurement and Instruments (2015)
9. Kalbarczyk, Z., Ries, G., Lee, M.S., et al.: Hierarchical approach to accurate fault modeling for system evaluation. In: IEEE International Computer Performance and Dependability Symposium (1998)
10. Savor, T., Seviora, E.: Hierarchical supervisors for automatic detection of software failures. In: International Symposium on Software Reliability Engineering (1997)
11. Morozov, A., Janschek, K.: Probabilistic error propagation model for mechatronic systems. Mechatronics **24**, 1189–1202 (2014)
12. Sarshar, S., Simensen, J.E., Winther, R., et al.: Analysis of error propagation mechanisms between software processes. In: Safety and Reliability Conference (2007)
13. Abdelmoez, W.M., Nassar, D., Shereshevsky, M., et al.: Error propagation in software architectures. In: IEEE Computer Society, IEEE International Symposium on Software Metrics (2004)
14. Hiller, M., Jhumka, A., Suri, N.: An approach for analysing the propagation of data errors in software. In: Proceedings of the 2001 International Conference on Dependable Systems and Networks (2001)
15. Avizienis, A., Laprie, J.-C., Randell, B., Landwehr, C.: Basic concepts and taxonomy of dependable and secure computing. IEEE Trans. Dependable Secure Comput. **1**, 11–33 (2004)
16. Li, G., Pattabiraman, K., Hari, S.K., Sullivan, M., Tsai, T.: Modeling soft error propagation in programs. In: IEEE/IFIP(2018)
17. Schuette, M.A., Shen, J.P.: Processor control flow monitoring using signatured instruction streams. IEEE Trans. Comput. **36**, 264–276 (1987)
18. Oh, N., Shirvani, P.P., McCluskey, E.J.: Error detection by duplicated instructions in super-scalar processors. IEEE Trans. Reliab. **51**, 63–75 (2002)
19. Reis, G.A., Chang, J., Vachharajani, N., et al.: SWIFT: software implemented fault tolerance. In: International Symposium on Code Generation and Optimization (2005)
20. Huang, Y., Kintala, C., Kolettis, N., et al.: Software rejuvenation: analysis, module and applications. In: International Symposium on Fault-Tolerant Computing (1995)
21. Cotroneo, D., Natella, R., Pietrantuono, R., et al.: A survey of software aging and rejuvenation studies. ACM J. Emerg Technol. Comput. Syst. (JETC) **10**, 1–34 (2014)
22. Thalheim, J., Rodrigues, A., Akkus, I.E., et al.: Sieve: actionable insights from monitored metrics in distributed systems. In: The 18th ACM/IFIP/USENIX Middleware Conference (2017)
23. Xu, X., Li, M.L.: Understanding soft error propagation using efficient vulnerability-driven fault injection (2012)
24. Gu, W., Kalbarczyk, Z., Iyer, R.K., Yang, Z.: Characterization of linux kernel behavior under errors. In: International Conference on Dependable Systems and Networks (2003)
25. Li, A., Hong, B., Wang, S.: A soft fault correction algorithm for data stream of onboard computer. J. Astronaut. **28**, 1044–1048 (2007)

Research of Improved Genetic Algorithm for Resource Allocation in Space-based Information Network

Wang Rui, Han Xiao-dong$^{(\boxtimes)}$, An Wei-yu, Song Ke-zhen, and Han Huan

Institute of Telecommunication Satellite, China Academy of Space Technology,
Beijing 100094, China
willingdong@163.com

Abstract. Along with the expansion of space-based information network, the task cooperation and resource allocation of access nodes is important issues that need to be addressed in the context of multiple spacecraft access. For the problem of resource dynamic scheduling, based on the present situation and development trend of space-based information network construction, resource allocation on tasks is researched in this paper. Furthermore, network resource allocation model and method of resource dynamic allocation based on genetic algorithm are realized, comprehensively consider the consumption and profit of resources to meet the task demand. By establishing allocation model suitable for space-based network, and using simulated annealing process and adaptive method to design improved genetic algorithm, the advantages and disadvantages are analyzed and simulated. The simulation result indicated the algorithm has good result in improving effectiveness and timeliness of network resource scheduling.

Keywords: Space-based information network · Resource allocation · Genetic algorithm · Simulated annealing

1 Introduction

In the future space information system, there are a large number of spacecraft with complex types. In addition to the large-scale hybrid constellation network which constitutes the space backbone network system, there are still a large number of application spacecraft, such as remote sensing satellite, manned spacecraft, scientific test satellite, etc., which will be the basic unit of the space-based information network, and work together under the deployment of space-based management and control system as managed objects. With the development and scale expansion of this system in the future,

Foundation Items: National Natural Science Foundation of China (no.61972398); Advance Research on Civil Aerospace Technology (no.D010305); National Science and Technology Major Project (no.2017ZX01013101-003).

the difficulty and complexity of space-based information network management are also increasing sharply. Therefore, it is necessary to carry out targeted network resource scheduling and network business management for a variety of space missions. The management of the managed objects in the network has gone far beyond the scope of the traditional equipment monitoring capability, and more emphasis is placed on the cooperative scheduling among multiple types of spacecraft under the unified task specification. In this scene, it is a feasible way to homogenize the functions of the deployable spacecraft into the available resources in the network, and to allocate the resources dynamically and cooperatively based on the mission requirements, so as to meet the requirements of real-time and effectiveness of space-based information network in the future.

The construction of space-based information network in China is conceived in reference [1–3], and aircrafts in different orbits, types and performances, corresponding ground facilities and application systems are described and constructed. Space-based information network has the ability of intelligent information acquisition, storage, transmission, processing, fusion and distribution, as well as high degree of autonomous operation and management capabilities. In reference [4], the architecture of space-based information port is described, and space-based information port satellite is defined as a complex system of "information + network". The multi-source information fusion problem is analyzed, and its process is defined as task planning and resource scheduling, data acquisition, basic algorithm and advanced application. Based on the above scene, the resource allocation problem in space-based information network is a multi-source and multi-type, task-based dynamic scheduling problem. The points of its model and algorithm construction are resource virtualization method, which can eliminate the differences of resource categories in modeling; and the fast dynamic task, resource allocation method to meet the timeliness and accuracy of space-based information network demand.

In terms of resource scheduling algorithm, the concept of satellite contribution degree is proposed in reference [5], and the contribution degree, observation switching rate and relaxation degree are taken as objective functions, and genetic algorithm is used to solve the satellite scheduling strategy; in reference [6], the mixed integer programming model of sensor scheduling is established for the multi-target tracking problem of low orbit early warning system, and the hybrid genetic simulated annealing algorithm is used to optimize the scheduling model In document [7], the problem model is established with the task execution efficiency as the objective function and solved by the quantum genetic algorithm; in document [8], the mathematical model is established with the goal of minimizing the mission completion time and solved by the adaptive genetic algorithm to dynamically schedule the battlefield resources to the platform; in document [9], the conflict resolution model in the satellite ground transmission, and data transmission in the ground transmission are built separately, then different scale scheduling tasks are generated, which are solved by the hybrid algorithm of dynamic programming and genetic algorithm. In reference [10], with the goal of earth observation task planning, the observation element and the receiver element tasks are taken as the way of gene expression, and solved by the genetic simulated annealing algorithm. In reference [11], a hybrid algorithm of genetic and local search is designed to solve the problem of satellite range planning and the matching between satellite task set and time window; in reference [12], a quantum heuristic genetic algorithm is proposed to solve the problem of multi-objective real-time task allocation in multi-sensor environment; in reference [13], a two-stage genetic annealing method is proposed to solve the problem of earth observation satellite scheduling, considering the search efficiency and global search ability of the solution. The above literature analyzes the scheduling and allocation of satellite resources, but its analysis object is mostly based on observation satellite, sensor resources and time window scheduling, not the analysis of space-based information network common resources, so it is not widely applicable.

In order to meet the needs of dynamic resource allocation of space-based information network in the future, this paper studies the cooperation mode and resource allocation method of different types of spacecraft in collaborative tasks. Considering the consumption and profit of resources to meet the needs of tasks, a dynamic resource allocation model of space-based information network is established. According to the characteristics of this model, genetic algorithm and its improved algorithms are used to discuss their application schemes of information network resource allocation.

2   Resource Allocation Model of Space-Based Information Network

The basic architecture of the space-based information network is shown in the figure below. As the control node of the space-based information network, the GEO communication satellite constitutes the space-based backbone network. Other satellites, including remote sensing satellite, navigation satellite, meteorological satellite, communication satellite constellation, as well as various types of spacecraft, such as space station and space telescope, are connected through the inter satellite link as the access node of the backbone network. Other access users also include those operating in the near earth space For example, near space vehicle, airship, UAV, etc. The space-based information network establishes a communication link with the ground station through the GEO communication satellite and communication satellite constellation, and connects to the ground processing center to realize the information interaction with the ground communication network and the ground Internet (Fig. 1).

There are different types of nodes in space-based information network, and the load carried by the nodes has different functions. The backbone network node has strong data processing ability and storage space. By carrying intelligent algorithm, data from other function nodes can be preprocessed. According to the different functions of spacecraft, there are some differences in the types and quantities of resources it can provide. For example, remote sensing satellite has image acquisition and preprocessing functions, communication satellite has communication functions with ground users or other satellites, navigation satellite can provide positioning information, etc. The task is initiated by the ground processing center and sent to the control node of the space-based information network. In the scheduling, different types of spacecraft are required to provide corresponding resources according to their own functions, participate in the task and cooperate to complete it. For example, if the meteorological satellite or remote sensing satellite finds that there is a disaster in a local area by collecting images, the corresponding data will be transmitted to the backbone node of the space-based information network. The backbone node preprocesses and transmits the data on the satellite, then transmits the

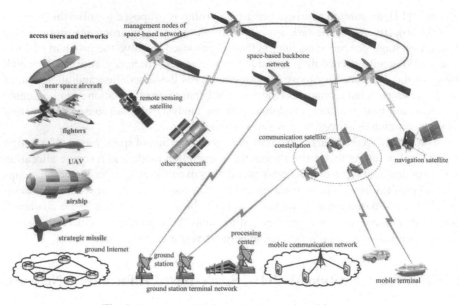

Fig. 1. Space based information network architecture

broadcast information to the communication satellite covering the disaster area, and then broadcasts the disaster details to the ground users through the communication load.

If the number of tasks to be executed sent from the ground is set to M, the task set containing M tasks is set to $T = \{T_1, T_2, \cdots, T_M\}$, and there is N nodes providing resources for task completion as $S = \{S_1, S_2, \cdots, S_N\}$. The $m \times n$ matrix can be used to represent the allocation relationship between resources and tasks. Defined $X = \{x_{ij}\}_{m \times n}$, $x_{ij} = 0/1$ as assignment matrix, we have

$$\sum_{i=1}^{m} x_{ij} = 1 \tag{1}$$

That is, at the same time, each resource can only be allocated to one task. And to ensure that all the proposed tasks be allocated resources to, we have

$$\sum_{i=1}^{m} \sum_{j=1}^{n} x_{ij} = n \tag{2}$$

The process of allocating resources to tasks needs to consider the benefits and consumption of resources, as well as the time held by resources. The use of resources is a unified allocation process, so there is no gain for the spacecraft that provides resources; therefore, the gain is defined as a combination of priority scheduling and the state of the resource-occupying node. The higher the priority of the task, the more necessary it is for the resource-occupying node to participate in the task. At the same time, the working state of the node itself will also affect the effect of participating in the task. For example, if a node acts as resource to provide distributed computing capability, and most of its processor resources have been occupied by other tasks, it may not have enough sufficient computing power to participate in tasks, thus affect the execution of tasks. When task priority is defined as $H = \{H_1, H_2, \cdots, H_M\}$ and node resource occupancy rate is defined as $p = \{p_1, p_2, \cdots, p_N\}$, the benefit of using resources is as follows:

$$a_{ij} = H_i(1 - p_j) \tag{3}$$

About the cost of resource allocation, it is necessary to consider the energy consumption of nodes and the resource occupancy time. The longer the task occupies the resource means resource will be occupied by a specific task, and the lower the probability that the resource will be used by other tasks. Therefore, the energy consumption of a task should be set by the node to prevent it from resource-free state for a long time; at the same time, the longer the occupation time, the higher the cost of using resources. Define the total energy consumed by a node to accomplish a task as e_j, and the cost of using resources is

$$b_{ij} = H_i k_j e_j(1 - c_j^{-t}) \tag{4}$$

k_j is the parameter for node j as energy upper limit and satisfy $H_i k_j \leq 1$, which indicates that the node determines the upper limit of energy consumption according to the priority of the task. c_j is the time attenuation for node j and $c_j > 1$, which are used to express the impact of resource occupancy time to other tasks. The larger of c_j means the resource have stronger timeliness and should be used in shorter time.

In summary, the benefit function of allocating resources to tasks is $f_{ij} = a_{ij} - b_{ij}$, in which the benefit and consumption are the result of normalization of proportion. The goal of optimization is to maximize the total benefit of the allocation relationship between resources and tasks.

In the process of allocation, we need to consider the following situations: 1. the amount of resources provided to a task should be limited; otherwise a task with high priority will incur more overhead, which will block the use of other tasks. Therefore, there is

$$\sum_{j=1}^{n} b_{ij} x_{ij} \leq r_i \tag{5}$$

And r_i is upper limit for a task. When a task uses the resources provided by the node i exceed this limit, it cannot continue to occupy more resources.

2. Some resources need not be used in the execution of certain tasks. For example, in the image acquisition-disaster prediction scenarios illustrated above, it's not need to use the resources provided by reconnaissance satellites, communications satellites that do not cover the communication area. Correspondingly, in the gain function matrix F from resource to task, the corresponding allocation item should be set to 0 to avoid unnecessary resource occupation.

Based on the above constraints, the dynamic resource allocation model of space-based information network can be described as:

$$\max f = \sum_{i=1}^{m} \sum_{j=1}^{n} f_{ij} x_{ij}$$

$$s.t. \sum_{i=1}^{m} x_{ij} = 1$$

$$\sum_{i=1}^{m} \sum_{j=1}^{n} x_{ij} = n$$

$$\sum_{j=1}^{n} b_{ij} x_{ij} \leq r_i \tag{6}$$

3 Solution Algorithm of Model

The resource allocation model established above can be classified as an unbalanced assignment problem due to the unequal number of resources and tasks allocated. It belongs to the problem category of linear programming. Hungarian algorithm (HA) is the basic algorithm for assignment problem. However, a large number of data experiments show that time-consuming of HA is unstable in solving different problems. Even when dealing with some special data, it cannot find its optimal solution because of its non-convergence. At the same time, the Hungarian algorithm has low computational efficiency because of low speed and holding large storage space. For the above reasons, genetic algorithm as substitute algorithm has been widely used.

The main characteristics of genetic algorithm are that it can directly operate the structure object without the limitation of derivation and function continuity; it has the inherent implicit parallelism and better global optimization ability; the probabilistic optimization method can adaptively adjust the search direction without the need of certain rules. At the same time, there are some disadvantages of genetic algorithm: genetic algorithm is a random search method, a large number of calculations take a long time, and it is difficult to meet the scene with high real-time requirements; on the other hand, when the convergence speed is high, it is easy to cause "early-maturing" phenomenon, that is, it may converge to the local optimal solution rather than the global optimal solution, so as to reduce the quality of solution.

Because of the above defects, this paper uses genetic simulated annealing algorithm (GSA) and self-adaptive genetic algorithm (SGA) to solve the problem of resource allocation in space-based information network, compares and analyzes the advantages of the two improved algorithms and the original algorithm. The starting point of simulated annealing algorithm is based on the similarity between the annealing process of physical solid matter and the general combinatorial optimization problem, using the Metropolis criterion to accept the deteriorating solution with probability, so as to avoid the problem of local optimization; but at the same time, substituting the annealing process increases the time of global convergence. The hybrid genetic simulated annealing algorithm combines the advantages of both and improves the efficiency. Unlike traditional genetic algorithm, adaptive genetic algorithm adjusts the probability of adaptation. The goal of this adjustment is to ensure the diversity of the population on the one hand, on the other hand, keep the excellent individuals in the population from being destroyed, avoid the problem that the original algorithm is easy to fall into the local optimization, and improve the global search ability of the algorithm.

(1). Chromosome coding

In the process of assigning resources to tasks, the number of resources is more than the number of tasks, so as to ensure that multiple resources are used by the same task, without the situation that a task cannot be carried out due to no resources available. Therefore, an allocation scheme is defined as an individual in GA, which is an ordered sequence $D = \{D_1, D_2, \cdots, D_j, \cdots, D_N\}, j \in [0, M]$ of N integers to allocate resources j to tasks D_j. If the value of D_j is 0, the resource is not used in the allocation scheme.

(2). Fitness function

The benefit function of resource allocation is selected as the individual fitness function, and the fitness function of the dth individual is expressed as

$$F_d = f_d - f_G \tag{7}$$

Among them, f_G it is the smallest benefit function value of the individual in the current evolution, and the benefit function value f_d is that of the dth individual in the current generation. If the individual benefits greatly, the advantage with the individual of least benefit in the current generation is larger, and the fitness function value is larger.

(3). Individual choosing

The algorithm uses roulette with quintessence selection strategy to simulate natural selection. In order to ensure that the evolution process will not destroy the obtained optimal solution, the strategy of keeping the optimal solution is added on the basis of roulette. This part of the algorithm is described as follows:

Algorithm 1 Individual Choosing Algorithm

For $n = 1 : siz$ **% the number of individual**

Calculate $F_n^{(G)}, F = \text{sum}(F_n^{(G)});$ **% G means generation**

end

$F_1^{(G+1)} = \max(F_n^{(G)});$

$P_1 = F_1^{(G+1)}/F;$

For $j = 2 : siz;$

For $i - 2 : siz$

$r = rand(1);$

$P_i = P_{i-1} + F_i^{(G)}/F;$

if $P_i > r$

$D_j^{(G+1)} = D_i^{(G)};$

else $D_j^{(G+1)} = D_1^{(G+1)};$

end

end

---

(4). Genetic manipulation

Genetic manipulation includes crossover and mutation. Crossover refers to the generation of new individuals by the exchange of the parent individuals' genes in the population, that is, the half of the individuals are crossed with random probability; mutation refers to the random disruption and recombination of their genes, that is, the partial sequences of individuals are replaced with each other with random probability. From the coding design, it can be seen that the target sequence of an individual represents the process of allocating resources to a task, while the total benefit of the allocation scheme is the result of the interaction of the allocation sequence and the benefit function, which has reflected whether a resource can be used for a specific task, so the change of the allocation sequence will not affect the result of whether the node providing the resource is available.

(5). Sampling by Metropolis criterion

In GSA algorithm, the change of individual fitness before and after genetic operation is calculated, and the retention probability is defined as

$$p_{save} = \exp((F^{(G+1)} - F^{(G)})/t) \tag{8}$$

Where T is the current temperature. If $p_{save} > rand(1)$, the new individual is accepted as the current individual. Otherwise, the parent individual is retained as the current individual. At the same time, the operation of $t^{(G+1)} = \alpha t^{(G)}$ as desuperheating is used with the rate of desuperheating α.

(6). Adaptive crossover and mutation

In SGA algorithm, the crossover probability and mutation probability of the population are related to the evolutionary generation. In the early stage of the algorithm, the larger crossover probability and mutation probability are guaranteed to improve the search ability of the optimal solution; in the late stage of the algorithm, the lower probability is to protect the better individuals from being destroyed. Therefore, sine function is introduced into the probability of crossover and mutation to adjust it adaptively, so as to avoid the stagnation of update caused by entering the local optimization when approaching the maximum fitness value. When using SGA algorithm, the crossover probability is defined as:

$$p_{cross}^{(G+1)} = \begin{cases} \frac{(p_{cross1}+p_{cross}^{(G)})}{2} - \frac{(p_{cross1}-p_{cross}^{(G)})}{2} \times \sin(\frac{\pi}{2} \times \frac{F-F_{ave}}{F\max-F_{ave}}), F \geq F_{ave} \\ p_{cross1}, F < F_{ave} \end{cases} \tag{9}$$

And the mutation probability is:

$$p_{vari}^{(G+1)} = \begin{cases} \frac{(p_{vari1}+p_{vari}^{(G)})}{2} - \frac{(p_{vari1}-p_{vari}^{(G)})}{2} \times \sin(\frac{\pi}{2} \times \frac{F-F_{ave}}{F\max-F_{ave}}), F \geq F_{ave} \\ p_{vari1}, F < F_{ave} \end{cases} \tag{10}$$

Where p_{cross1} and p_{vari1} are parameters that vary with evolution generation G:

$$p_{cross1} = p_{cross} + \frac{1}{2 + \lg G} \tag{11}$$

$$p_{vari1} = p_{vari} + \frac{0.1}{2 + \lg G} \tag{12}$$

Where p_{cross} and p_{vari} are the convergence limits of the crossover probability and the mutation probability.

(7). Algorithm flow

The flow chart of GSA and SGA optimization algorithm is as follows (Fig. 2):

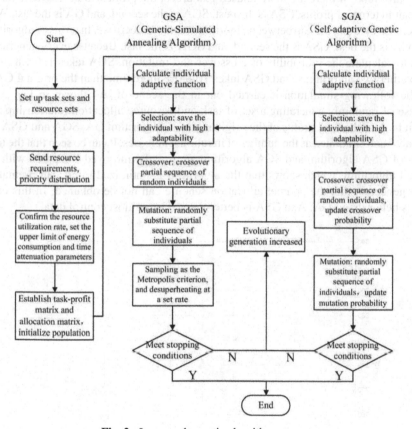

Fig. 2. Improved genetic algorithm process

4 Simulation Results

In the simulation scene of this paper, M cooperative tasks are sent at one time in the space-based information network, N resource nodes are involved in collaboration, the convergence limits of crossover probability and mutation probability are set to =0.6 and =0.8, respectively, the number of individuals is set to 100, the maximum evolution generation is set to 100, the initial temperature is set to 2000, the desuperheating rate is set to 0.95, the upper limit of energy consumption is set to 0.8, the time decay parameter is set to 1.05, and the priority is divided into nine levels.

In order to evaluate the impact of the size and load of space-based information network on the performance of the algorithm, the performance of GSA and SGA are investigated in the scene of task and resource changes. The higher the number of tasks, the higher the load of space-based information network; and the higher the number of resources, the more resources are available, which can better meet the needs of task allocation. Therefore, when the resources can meet the needs of the task, the profit shows an upward trend; if there are more unused resources, the profit will decrease. It can be seen that in terms of profits, GSA is the best, SGA is the second, and GA is the last. With the increase of scale, the gap between algorithms tends to decrease. In terms of algorithm time, GA is the best, GSA is the second, and SGA is the last. Because every generation needs to calculate the probability of crossover and mutation, SGA takes 1.3–1.8 times of the other two algorithms, and GSA takes 10–20% more time than the original GA.

The following simulation is carried out in the scene of. As shown in Fig. 3, in the case of randomly generating a set of task and resource allocation relationship and benefit matrix, the total profits of the original genetic algorithm GA, SGA and GSA are compared and simulated as the number of iterations increases. It can be seen that the total profits of GSA algorithm and SGA algorithm are greatly improved compared with the original algorithm, which shows that the algorithm is optimized to prevent premature convergence, so that the optimal allocation scheme can not be obtained. In this case, GSA is better than SGA. And GSA is better than SGA in most control data.

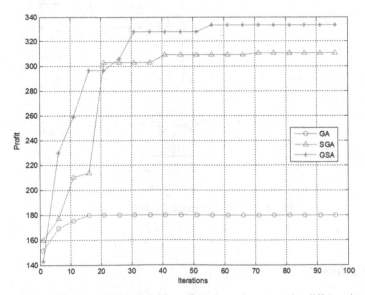

Fig. 3. Profits of GSA and SGA algorithm allocation schemes under different iterations

The simulation in Fig. 4 is the result of adding and averaging 100 randomly generated resource allocation relationships and profit matrices. It can be seen that the total profit of GSA is better than that of SGA.

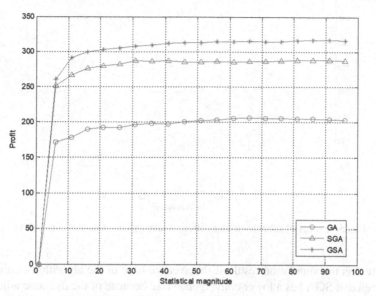

Fig. 4. The profits of GSA and SGA algorithm allocation schemes in random scenes

Figure 5 shows the influence of the range of change on the two improved algorithms after adjustment in the range of profit matrix. By adjusting the upper limit of energy consumption and time decay parameters, the range of energy consumption is adjusted. When the change range is 40 W, the performance of GSA is better than that of SGA; with the decrease of the change range, the performance improvement is gradually reduced, and the performance gap between the two algorithms is also reduced. It can be seen that GSA performance is better for scenes with large energy consumption changes. The energy consumption of space-based information network also fluctuates because of the differences in function and performance of the nodes. In this scene, the adaptability of GSA is better than that of SGA.

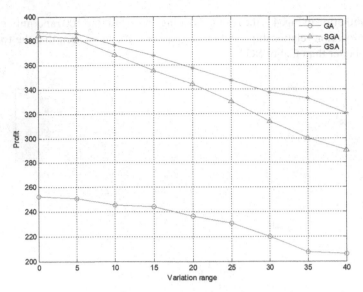

Fig. 5. Profits of schemes under different energy consumption constraints

Figure 6 is the simulation result of the average time of the algorithm execution. It can be seen that SGA has a lower convergence rate because of the dynamic adjustment of crossover and mutation probability in every loop of the algorithm, and its operation time is longer than GSA.

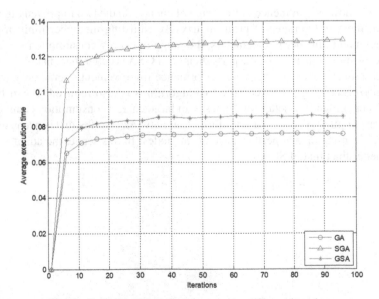

Fig. 6. Operation time of schemes under different iterations

5 Conclusion

In the construction of space-based information network in the future, as the management and control center of space-based information network, GEO satellite constitutes the space-based backbone network, realizes the access of other satellites and spacecraft to the space-based information network, and constructs integrated space-terrestrial information system. This architecture determines that there are many nodes and networks of different types and architectures in the space-based information network. The collaborative tasks initiated on the ground need to realize the dynamic allocation of multi-source and multi-type resources. The virtualization design of resources and the fast resource allocation algorithm are the basis of realizing the rational allocation of resources. Based on the above requirements, this paper studies the application of genetic algorithm in the task resource dynamic allocation of space-based information network. Considering the consumption and profits of resources to meet the task requirements, a dynamic resource allocation model is established. According to the characteristics of the model, the dynamic resource allocation scheme is designed by using improved genetic algorithm And the simulation of scene implementation and algorithm effect is carried out. The results show that the algorithm proposed in this paper has a good effect on improving the timeliness of resource allocation and utilization.

References

1. Min, S.Q.: Preliminary study for space-based integrated information network. In: The 9th Academic Annual Conference of Satellite Communications, China Institute of Communications, pp. 20–29, Beijing (2013)
2. Zhang, N.T., Zhao, K.L., Liu, G.L.: Thought on constructing the integrated space-terrestrial information network. J. Chin. Acad. Electron. Inf. Technol. 10(3), 223–230 (2015)
3. Wu, M.Q., Wu, W., Zhou, B., et al.: Imagine of integrated space-terrestrial information network overall architecture. Satell. Netw. 2016(3), 20–26 (2016)
4. Li, B., Liu, C.Y., Zhang, Y.B.: Space-based information port and its multi-information fusion application. J. CAEIT 12(3), 251–256 (2017)
5. Sun, F., Wang, H.: Research on detection mission scheduling strategy for the LEO constellation to multiple targets. J. Defense Model. Simul. 14(3), 1–17 (2017)
6. Liu, J.Y., Wang, H., Zhou, W.M., et al.: LEO constellation sensor resources scheduling algorithm based on genetic and simulation annealing. Syst. Eng. Electron. 40(11), 2476–2481 (2018)
7. Wan, L.J., Yao, P.Y., Zhou, X.X.: Cooperative task allocation methods in multiple groups using DLS-QGA. Control Deci. 29(9), 1562–1568 (2014)
8. Sun, P., Wu, J.S., Liao, M.C., et al.: Battlefield resource dynamic scheduling model and algorithm based on improved self-adaptive genetic algorithm. Syst. Eng. Electron. 40(11), 2459–2465 (2018)
9. Xiang, Y.W., Zhang, W.Y., Tian, M.M.: Satellite data transmission integrated scheduling and optimization. Syst. Eng. Electron. 40(6), 1288–1293 (2018)
10. Zhang, C., Li, Y.B.: Planning and scheduling method for multi agile satellite coordinated mission. Sci. Technol. Eng. 17(22), 271–277 (2017)
11. Song, Y.J., Zhang, Z.S., Song, B.Y., et al.: Improved genetic algorithm with local search for satellite range scheduling system and its application in environmental monitoring. Sustain. Comput. Inform. Syst. 2019(21), 19–27 (2019)

12. Debanjan, K., Kalpana, S., Varun, S., et al.: A multi-objective quantum-inspired genetic algorithm (Mo-QIGA) for real-time tasks scheduling in multiprocessor environment. Procedia Comput. Sci. **2018**(131), 591–599 (2018)
13. Zhu, W.M., Hu, X.X., Xia, W., et al.: A two-phase genetic annealing method for integrated earth observation satellite scheduling problems. Soft. Comput. **2017**(3), 1–16 (2017)

Switching-Aware Dynamic Control Path Planning for Software Defined Large-Scale LEO Satellite Networks with GEO Controllers

Tingting Zhang[1,3]([✉]), Fan Bai[2,3], Tao Dong[1,3], Jie Yin[1,3], Zhihui Liu[1,3], and Yuwei Su[1,3]

[1] State Key Laboratory of Space-Ground Integrated Information Technology, Beijing Institute of Satellite Information Engineering, Beijing, China
zhangtingting@spacestar.com.cn
[2] Beijing Institute of Spacecraft System Engineering, Beijing, China
[3] China Academy of Space Technology, Beijing, China

Abstract. Recently, to acquire the programmability, flexibility and re-configurability of network, the technologies of software-defined networking (SDN) are utilized to design new architectures for LEO satellite networks, where control plane is realized by several GEO satellites. But in the previous work, it is assumed that each LEO satellites could directly connect with the GEO controllers. This is unreasonable when the LEO data plane is a large-scale LEO satellite constellation, as the number of GEO controllers and antennas of each GEO controller are limited. In this work, we propose a design of software defined large-scale LEO satellite networks with limited GEO controllers, where the communication between GEO control plane and LEO data plane is achieved by limited cross-layer links. In this model, the selection of cross-layer links directly affects the load balance among GEO controllers and the latencies of control paths, which will deeply influence the latency of routing response. Thus, we propose a switching-aware dynamic control path planning scheme to handle this, where we propose a switching-time selection scheme to handle the impact of switching and a multi-objective optimization problem to deal with the selection of cross-layer links, and finally present a particle swarm optimization based algorithm to solve it. Simulation results demonstrate the better performance on reducing the bad influence of switching, optimizing the load balance among controllers and the average latencies of control paths.

Keywords: LEO satellite network · Software-defined networking · Multi-objective optimization component · Particle swarm optimization

1 Introduction

As the fast development of spaceflight technology, the ability of data processing of satellites has been greatly improved. Thus, recently, more and more research communities and industries are considering to achieve a global network service through satellites,

Q. Wu et al. (Eds.): WiSATS 2020, LNICST 357, pp. 153–167, 2021.
https://doi.org/10.1007/978-3-030-69069-4_13

which are called satellite networks. During a satellite network, each satellite is set as a forward node or control node, and connects with other satellites by inter-satellite links (ISLs). Moreover, the satellite backbone network is expected to be designed as a LEO satellite constellation, because of its low-delay and real-time communication. Specially, a series of LEO satellite projects has been launched by some satellite entrepreneurs recently, such as OneWeb, SpaceX [1], which could herald the coming of large-scale LEO satellite networks.

Besides, to acquire the programmability, flexibility and re-configurability of network, the technologies of software-defined networking (SDN) are utilized to design new architectures for satellite networks [1, 2, 4, 5]. In the SDN-based satellite networks, the logically centralized control plane are usually realized by several controllers, in order to avoid the single point of failure and achieve better manageability of the network. Among the different types of satellites, the GEO satellite layer, with stationary position to the ground, wide coverage area, high communication capability and broadcast communication, is regarded as an appropriate layer to deploy the distributed control plane [6].

However, the previous work assumed that each LEO satellite could directly connect with the GEO controllers [6], which is unreasonable in the large-scale LEO satellite network. As the number of GEO controllers and antennas of each GEO controller are limited. For example, the satellite constellation proposed by SpaceX will contain more than 4425 LEO satellites. Suppose that each GEO satellite can hold n antennas pointing to LEO satellites, then it needs $4425/n$ GEO satellites to build direct connection with all LEO satellites. Even if $n = 10$, the number of GEO satellites is about 442, which is a much difficult task in practice. Even though the communication between LEO satellites and GEO controllers is realized by a broadcast control channel, it is also difficult for GEO controllers to provide enough power in order to broadcast to a huge number of LEO satellites. Thus, a practical solution is to select some special LEO satellites to connect with the GEO satellites, and all other LEO satellites communicate with GEO satellites through these special LEO satellites. In this scenario, links between LEO and GEO satellites are called cross-layer links, which will be frequently interrupted and connected by the relative motion of LEO and GEO satellites. Thereby, we need to plan proper cross-layer links before the current cross-layer links are interrupted, and compute control paths for each LEO satellites, which is called switching-aware dynamic control path planning (SADCPP) problem.

In this work, we propose a design of software defined large-scale LEO satellite networks with limited GEO controllers (SDLLSN), where the communication between GEO control plane and LEO data plane is achieved by limited cross-layer links. To handle the SADCPP problem, we propose a switching-aware dynamic control path planning scheme, where a switching-time selection scheme is proposed to handle the impact of switching, a multi-objective optimization problem is presented to deal with the selection of cross-layer links in each time slot. The problem of selecting cross-layer links (SCRLP) with considering the load balance among GEO controllers and the latencies of control paths is NP-hard. Finally we present a particle swarm optimization based algorithm to solve it.

2   Related Work

Software defined satellite networks have been deeply studied in [1, 2, 4–7]. Bao et al. [2] proposed an architecture of software-defined satellite networks, where the logically centralized entity is realized by GEO group. In the architecture presented by Xu et al. [6], the data plane is designed as a LEO satellite constellation, and the control of LEO date plane is realized through several GEO satellites, but it assumed the one-hop connection between GEO controllers and LEO satellites. And all these work are not involved the SADCPP problem.

Besides, there are also some work studying the dynamic topology of satellite network [8–11], but they do not consider the planning of cross-layer with considering the load balance among GEO controllers and the latencies of control paths. To the best of our knowledge, we are the first to study switching-aware dynamic control path planning problem in a large-scale LEO satellite network with limited GEO controllers.

3   System Model

In this section, we first give an architecture for software defined large-scale LEO satellite networks with limited GEO controllers (SDLLSN) and then elaborate the switching-aware dynamic control path planning problem.

3.1   An Architecture for Software Defined Large-Scale LEO Satellite Networks with Limited GEO Controllers

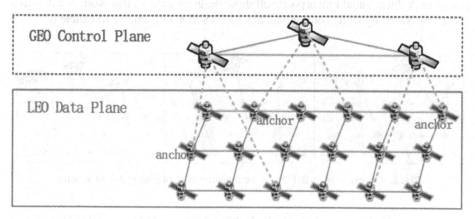

Fig. 1. The architecture of the SDLLSN

The proposed architecture of the SDLLSN is shown in Fig. 1. According to the researches mentioned above, the control plane layer consists of several GEO satellites, which have limited cross-layer links with LEO satellites. Besides, the control plane can be realized by a two-layer hierarchical controller architecture, where it will set each GEO controller just as a domain controller, but additionally deploy multiple super controllers in the ground station, as discussed in [6]. In such scenario, the GEO satellites must have at least one antennas pointing to the ground station such that they can communicate directly with their super controllers. The data plane layer contains an LEO satellite constellation, which can be assumed to be a Walker Delta Pattern constellation such that permanent inter satellite links can be constructed between LEO satellites. Finally, the communication between GEO control plane and LEO data plane is achieved by cross-layer links between the GEO and several LEO satellites, where these LEO satellites are called anchors.

3.2 Problem Formulation

First, note that a control path contains two segments, the direct path from LEO anchors to its GEO controller and the path from any LEO satellite to an anchor. Due to the relative motion between GEO and LEO satellites, the cross-layer links will be interrupted when the GEO and LEO satellites are not accessed. Therefore, antennas of the GEO satellites corresponding to these interrupting links must be re-planned to construct cross-layer links with other LEO satellites. The existing planning strategy make the GEO satellites select the LEO satellite nearest to it. This may result in long control path delays for some LEO satellites to its anchor. In SDLLSN, such long control path delays imply long latencies of responses to routing requests from data plane. Furthermore, the exact time that each cross-layer link is re-planned must also be handled carefully. As if too many cross-layer links are interrupted at the very same time point, it will seriously increase the path delays from LEO satellites to its controller, and thus will aggravate the response delays. Finally, the load balance among controllers is another important problem that has to be considered during the selection of anchors. Therefore, the dynamic control path planning problem should incorporate all these requirements. In this work, we design a switching-aware dynamic control path planning (SADCPP) scheme to handle it.

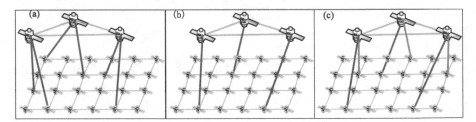

Fig. 2. Overview of switching-aware dynamic control path planning scheme

Now, we start to present how our SADCPP scheme work. In fact, SADCPP scheme consists of two mechanisms, the **TimeSelection** and the **AnchorSelection**. More precisely, the scheme will be run on one of the GEO controllers, which will be deployed these two mechanisms and perform as described in Fig. 2. The **TimeSelection** modular will be activated when the controller starts to re-plan the cross-layer links. Then the **TimeSelection** modular first collects the current state of all cross-layer links from other GEO controllers, and outputs the antennas that will be switched and the time when they will be switched. Then, the **AnchorSelection** modular will be activated to decide an anchor for each switching antenna, distribute controllers for all LEO satellites and compute the control path for each LEO satellite in the next time slot. Besides, the routing computation modular is responsible for planning new control path for LEO satellites that will lose its anchor during the switching. The controller will send all these policies to other controllers and the data plane. Then when the time goes to the point that the switching should be started, each switched antenna will stop the current connection and try to build its next connection depending on the policies it has received. And each LEO satellite will send its routing request through this control path in the next time slot.

Next, before present details of the **TimeSelection** and **AnchorSelection** shemes, we first formalize the SADCPP problem. At first, we model the SDLLSN as a graph $G(t) = \langle V, E(t) \rangle$, where V consists of the GEO satellites V_c and LEO satellites V_s, and $E(t)$ is the link status in time t. In fact, $E(t) = E_c \cup E_s \cup E_{cs}(t)$, where E_c is the set of ISLs between GEO controllers, E_s is the set of ISLs between LEO satellites that keep permanent, and $E_{cs}(t)$ is the cross-layer links between the GEO control plane and LEO data plane. Note that for the LEO data plane, we only consider the permanent ISLs, because we want to avoid the influence of link switching in data plane on the transmission of control message. Furthermore, as the data plane is a LEO satellite constellation where permanent ISLs can be constructed between most of LEO satellites, this assumption is reasonable. Besides, in the following section, we will use $G_c = \langle V_c, E_c \rangle$ to represent the topology of the GEO control plane, $G_s = \langle V_s, E_s \rangle$ denote that of the LEO data plane with permanent ISLs, and set $G(t) = G_s \cup G_c \cup E_{cs}(t)$. The detailed notations and definitions used in this paper are summarized in Table 1.

Table 1. Notations and Definitions

Notations	Definitions	Notations	Definitions
$G(t)$	The topology of network in time t	m	The number of GEO controllers
G_c	The topology of GEO control plane	n	The number of nodes in V_s
V_c	Set of GEO controllers	M	The total number of antennas of all GEO controllers
E_c	Set of ISLs between GEO controllers	c	A controller in V_c
G_s	The topology of LEO data plane without dynamic ISLs	a	An antenna of a GEO satellite
V_s	Set of LEO satellites	S_{anchor}	Set of anchors
E_s	Set of permanent ISLs in LEO data plane	D_{as}	Access data of all GEO satellite with all LEO satellite

For the load balance among controllers, we represent it by the number of LEO switches controlled by each GEO controller. And the measure of load balance uses max–min fairness, which is defined as following:

$$FI = \frac{\min\{num_i\}}{\max\{num_i\}}, i = 1, \ldots, m \tag{1}$$

where num_i is the number of LEO satellites controlled by the i-th GEO controller.

The control path delay is evaluated by average forward times from LEO satellites to their controller. Let L_i^s denote the forward times from i-th LEO satellites to an anchor s. Then the forward times from the i-the LEO satellite to its controller is defined as following:

$$L_i = min_{s \in S_{anchor}}\{L_i^s\} + 1 \tag{2}$$

where S_{anchor} is the set of anchors in LEO data plane.

Then, the problem can be formulated as given $G(t) = G_s \cup G_c \cup E_{cs}(t)$ in time t, we need to give an optimal decision of the following two things:

a. Based on the end time of each link in E_{cs}, decide the time when to switch such that for each GEO controller i, there is at least α_i cross-layer links still working during the switching, which is to guarantee the continuous communication between the GEO control plane and the LEO control plane.
b. The selection of anchors A for the switching antennas to connect in the next time slot such that the average latency of control paths is minimized, and the load balancing index FI is maximized. That is, our optimization objective is,

$$\min L_{ave} = \min \frac{1}{n}\left(\sum_{i=1}^{n} L_i\right) \text{ and } \max FI \tag{3}$$

Subject to:

$$\forall i \in V_c \sum_{j \in V_s} e_{ij} \leq \alpha_i \tag{4}$$

$$\forall j \in V_s \sum_{i \in V_c} e_{ij} \leq \beta_j \tag{5}$$

$$\forall i \in V_c \sum_{j \in V_s} e_{ij} \geq \gamma_i \tag{6}$$

$$\forall j \in V_s L_j \leq \delta \tag{7}$$

$$\forall e \in E_{switching} T_e \geq \sigma \tag{8}$$

$$T_{switching} = \Delta \tag{9}$$

In (4), α_i is the number of antennas in the i-th GEO controller, and then this equation limits the number of cross-layer links built from the i-th GEO controller. Similarly,

Eq. (5) means that the cross-layer links built from the j-th LEO satellites is limited by the number of antennas β_j on it. Equation (6) requires that for every time slot, even during the switching, for the cross-layer links built from the i-th GEO controller, at least γ_i links keep working. Equation (7) means that the forward times of each LEO satellites is limited by δ. In Eq. (8), $E_{switching}$ is the set of cross-layer links that are waiting to be selected for the next time slot, T_e is the continuous time of cross-layer link e after the switching, and then this equation is to make sure that each new cross-layer link can work for an enough long time, that is, at least σ. Equation (9) defines the time needed to process the switching, and this implies that new cross-layer links will start to work in time $t + \Delta$, where t is the end time of this slot.

Then, for the selection of time to switch the cross-link, i.e., the **TimeSelection** mechanism, we will synthesize the end time of all antennas and the constraint of γ_i, which is processed as following:

- First compute the end time of each cross-layer links based on the orbits of GEO and LEO satellites.
- Then arrange all the antennas according to the end time in ascending order. Let $V_{switching}$ be the set of antennas waiting to switch, and $V_{switching}$ is empty at the start of our scheme. Then the sorted time series be defined as $t_1^{a_1}, t_2^{a_2}, \ldots, t_M^{a_M}$, where $t_i^{a_i}$ represents the end time of antennas a_i, and $M = \sum_{i=1}^{m} \alpha_i$ is the number of antennas in all GEO controllers, i.e., the cross-layer links built between the control plane and data plane.
- Set $t_{end} = t_1^{a_1}$, and add a_1 to the set $V_{switching}$.
- For $i = 2, \ldots, M$, do as following:
- If $t_i^{a_i} - t_{end} \geq \Delta'$, break and go to the next step;
- Else, let c be the GEO satellite corresponding to a_i, then if the number of antennas of c in $V_{switching}$ has exceeded γ_c, break and go to the next step; else, add a_i to the set $V_{switching}$.
- Finally, output $V_{switching}$ and $t_{end} = t_{end} - \Delta$.
- For the scheme of setting $V_{switching}$, the reason behind it is that we want the antennas with close end time to be switched at the same moment. This will decrease the frequency of switching, and thus relieve the frequent updating of data plane caused by frequent switching cross-layer links. Thus, the cross-links stopping before $t_{end} + \Delta'$ will be switched at the same moment with the antenna a_1, where the parameter Δ' is used to control the time frequency of switching.
- Next, the selection of appropriate anchors A, i.e., the **AnchorSelection** mechanism, is more complicated. Let $E_{switching}^i$ be the set of LEO satellites that the antenna i can connect with, and N_i be its size. If the size of $V_{switching}$ (denoted by $\mathbb{M}$) is very small, we can use the brute force strategy, that is, for all the combination of switching cross-layer links, respectively compute $\frac{1}{n}(\sum_{i=1}^{n} L_i)$ and FI, and finally select the combination that result in optimal average latency of control paths and load balance index. However, when $\mathbb{M}$ is a little bigger, the complexity of this brute force strategy will become much higher. For example, for a 1584-satellite constellation, when we set $\sigma = 20$ min, N_i is more than 600. Then the complexity of such brute force strategy is $\prod_{i=1}^{\mathbb{M}} N_i$, which is more than $2^{9\mathbb{M}}$. Thus the brute force strategy is not suitable when $\mathbb{M}$ is a little big. Furthermore, note that the problem is a NP-hard combinatorial optimization problem.

Therefore, we propose an optimization algorithm to solve it, called **AS-PSO**, which is presented in the next section.

4 Discrete Particle Swarm Optimization Based Anchor Selection Algorithm

The particle swarm optimization (PSO) [12] is an intelligent, iterative optimization algorithm, which has the advantages of rapid convergence towards an optimum, fast and easy to compute. In this section, we will employ the discrete PSO version to solve the anchor selection problem in SDLLSN.

Let $V_{switching}$ be the set of waiting switching antennas generated by **TimeSelection** mechanism, and use $\mathbb{M}$ denote its size. Let $node_i$ is the set of LEO satellites that can access with the GEO controller corresponding to $a_i \in V_{switching}$ in the next time slot, and satisfies the requirement of Eq. (8). The size of $node_i$ is denoted by $\ltimes_i$. Then, the particle is represented by a $\mathbb{M}$ dimensional vector $\vec{p} = (p_1, p_2, \ldots, p_{\mathbb{M}})$, where p_i is an integer in $[1, \ltimes_i]$ and then $node_i(p_i)$ is the LEO satellite planned to connect with antenna a_i. Let $\bar{V}_{switching}$ denote the antennas that are not switched in the next time slot. Then by merging $\bar{V}_{switching}$ with $\{node_1(p_1), \ldots, node_{\mathbb{M}}(p_{\mathbb{M}})\}$, we obtain a possible anchor combination S_{anchor}. But to decide whether it is a feasible solution, we still need to check the following conditions:

- For each anchor s in S_{anchor}, check if s satisfies the requirement of Eq. (5), i.e., $\sum_{i \in V_c} e_{is} \leq \beta_s$;
- For each LEO satellite i in V_s, check if $(min_{s \in S_{anchor}} \{L_i^s\} + 1) \leq \delta$, where L_i^s is computed by using the shortest path algorithm Dijkstra.

If both of the above two conditions are satisfied, the anchor combination induced by this particle is a feasible solution.

The particle's velocity, local best position, global position and their updating strategies are defined as common discrete- PSO. Besides, we also employ the adaptive parameters approach based on [12] to avoid premature convergence.

Furthermore, for the evaluation of fitness, we still need to select a controller for each LEO satellite, where we propose a load balancing aware clustering (LBAC) scheme to handle it. Then, based on the output of LBAC, we can compute the load balance index FI and the average forward times L_{ave}. Only if both FI and L_{ave} are better, we say that the fitness of this particle is better. Now, we have overview the algorithm AS-PSO, and details of the algorithm are presented in Algorithm 1.

Algorithm 1. Discrete Particle Swarm Optimization Based Anchor Selection Algorithm (AS-PSO)

Input: $G(t), V_{switching}, t_{end}, D_{as}, \mathbb{T}, \mathbb{p}$

Output: S_{anchor}^{op}

1: for each antenna $a_i^c \in V_{switching}$, based on D_{as}, compute $node_i$ such that $\forall s \in node_i, T_{e(c,s)} \geq \sigma$ where $e(c,s)$ is the cross-layer link between LEO node s and GEO controller c.

2: iteratively generate $\mathbb{p}$ particles $\overrightarrow{p_1}, ..., \overrightarrow{p_\mathbb{p}}$ randomly such that each particle corresponds to a feasible solution, and then generate the initial velocity $\overrightarrow{v_1}, ..., \overrightarrow{v_\mathbb{p}}$, local best position $\overrightarrow{p_1}', ..., \overrightarrow{p_\mathbb{p}}'$.

3: for the solution corresponding to each particle, employ the LBAC algorithm to compute the load balance index and average forward times, and record the best values FI^{op}, L_{ave}^{op}, and the global best particle $\overrightarrow{p_{best}}$.

4: **for** $it = 1, ..., \mathbb{T}$ **do**

5:     update the inertia weight.

6:     **for** $\iota = 1, ..., \mathbb{p}$ **do**

7:         update the velocity $\overrightarrow{v_\iota}$ and particle $\overrightarrow{p_\iota}$ by employing the common discrete PSO stratgy.

8:         if $\overrightarrow{p_\iota}$ corresponds to a feasible solution, then compute its fitness values FI^ι, L_{ave}^ι. And then update $FI^{op}, L_{ave}^{op}, \overrightarrow{p_\iota}'$ and $\overrightarrow{p_{best}}$, if these fitness values are better.

9:         if $\overrightarrow{p_\iota}$ does not correspond to a feasible solution, replace $\overrightarrow{p_\iota}$ with a randomly generated particle, and then check and update $FI^{op}, L_{ave}^{op}, \overrightarrow{p_\iota}'$ and $\overrightarrow{p_{best}}$ as above.

10:   **endfor**

11: **endfor**

Finally, for a selection of anchors, we present the LBAC scheme to decide a controller for each LEO satellite .Then for each LEO satellite The LBAC scheme first computes shortest paths from each LEO satellite to all GEO controllers. i, the LBAC counts the control paths whose delay is no more than other control paths, and then add the GEO controllers corresponding to these control paths to the controller set C_i of i-th LEO satellite. If C_i is equal to1, directly set this unique element as the controller of this i-th LEO satellite. After the iteration is completed, iterative all the LEO satellite again. During each iteration$i$, if C_i is greater than1, set the controller of the i-th LEO satellite to be the element in C_i that has controlled the minimal number of LEO satellites. Finally, according to the above clustering result, compute the load balancing index FI and the average latency of control pathsL_{ave}.

Algorithm 2. Load Balancing-Aware Clustering (LBAC) Algorithm

---

Input: a selection of anchors $A_1, \dots, A_m$ respectively for each GEO controllers

Output: FI and L_{ave}

1.1: initialize a series of empty sets $C_1, \dots, C_n$, and parameters $num_1, \dots, num_m$ to 0.

2: **for** $i = 1, \dots, n$ **do**

3:     employ the Dijkstra algorithm to compute the shortest path from the i-th LEO satellite
       to each GEO controller, and computes the shortest path delay as $L_i^1, \dots, L_i^m$.

4:     let $L_i^{min} = \min\{L_i^1, \dots, L_i^m\}$, iteratively check $L_i^1, \dots, L_i^m$, if L_i^j is equal to L_i^{min}, add j to
       C_i.

6:     if the size of C_i is equal to 1, then set the controller of this i-th LEO satellite as the
       unique element of C_i. Suppose the unique controller is in, then update num_{in} as
       $num_{in} + 1$.

6: **endfor**

7: **for** $i = 1, \dots, n$ **do**

8:     **if** the size of C_i is greater than 1 **do**

9:     iteratively check each controller in C_i, and let j is the index of controller such that num_j
       is minimal.

10:     Then set j as the controller of this i-th LEO satellite

11:     **endif**

12: **endfor**

13: finally, compute FI and L_{ave} according to the above clustering result.

---

5   Numerical Simulation and Analysis

In this section, we will present the detail simulation scenario, and then we analyze the numerical simulation results of our SA-DCPP scheme.

5.1   Simulation Setup

In our simulation scenario, the LEO data plane is Walker Delta Pattern constellation introduced by the Starlink project. The parameters comes from the proposal submitted by SpaceX to FCC in 2018, which is presented in the Table 2. In such satellite constellation, each LEO satellite can build permanent ISLs with LEO satellites in its neighbor orbits. Then, for the network topology, each LEO satellite can hold permanent four ISLs with the two satellites in the same orbit and the two satellites in its two neighbor orbits, and one cross-layer ISL with some GEO satellite.

For the GEO control plane, we design six GEO satellites with altitude 35,786 km, and each of them has four antennas pointing to the LEO data plane. Table 3 describes the parameters of them.

To simulate this constellation, we obtain the two-line element sets of the 60 satellites launched by SpaceX, of which the NORAD numbers are from 44235 to 44294U [13]. Then, we analyze the right ascension of the ascending node (RAAN) of the J2000 coordinate system. Finally, the epoch of the seed satellite is set as 27 May 2019 06:14:00.000

Table 2 The parameters of LEO satellite constellation

Parameters	Value	Parameters	Value
Orbital Planes	24	Altitude	550 km
Satellites Per Planes	66	ISLs Per LEO Satellite in LEO Data Plane	2 inter-ISLs, 2 intra-ISLs
Total Satellites	1584	Cross-layer ISLs per LEO Satellite	1
Inclination	53°		

Table 3 The parameters of LEO satellite constellation

Parameters	Value	Parameters	Value
Inclination	0°	ISLs Per GEO satellite in the Control Plane	2
Number of GEO Satellites	6	Cross-layer ISLs per GEO Satellite	4
Altitude	35786 km	Total Cross-layer ISLs	24

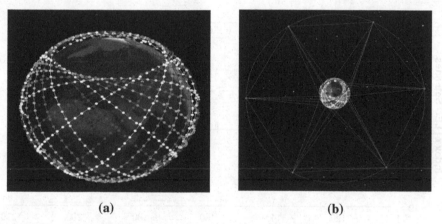

(a)   (b)

Fig. 3 (a) Simulation diagram of LEO satellite constellation and (b) Simulation diagram of cross-layer ISLs

UTC, the RAAN is 160°, the eccentricity is 0°, and other parameters are 0. Then, we can generate the LEO satellite constellation, as shown in Fig. 3(a).

Then, the GEO satellites is simulated, and we can get the time-variant data of the access between GEO and LEO satellites, and the latency of ISLs and cross-layer links. Figure 3(b) shows the cross-layer ISLs at some point. The simulation shows that the number of LEO satellites accessed by a GEO satellite in a time duration 20 min is more than 600, the latency of cross-layer ISLs varies from 117 to 148 ms, and the latency of ISLs between LEO satellites varies from 3.7 ms to 6.1 ms. This implies that if two different ISLs have same forward times, the difference of the path delay between them is small. Thus, we evaluate the optimization objective L_{ave} by the forward times of control paths, instead of the path delay, for which our optimization will be immune to the influence of small difference of control paths.

We simulated the state of our satellite network during 24 h, and recorded the time variant data. Based on these data, we then simulate our SA-DCPP scheme by using MATLAB. The simulation results are presented in the next section.

5.2 Performance Evaluation

Now we analyze the performance of the algorithms on switching-aware, load balance among controllers and control path latencies as follows.

Figure 4 shows the switching of the cross-layer links connected with one GEO satellite during 120 min. In fact, we have simulate for 24 h, and finally generate more than 200 time slots excluding the switching duration. But to clearly demonstrate the results, we only present the results about one GEO satellite during 120 min. The Y-axis is the index of each LEO satellite, and the X-axis is the time from 100 to 220 min. From Fig. 4, we can see that during each switching, every GEO controller still has at least one cross-layer link connected with the LEO data plane, and each cross-layer link can keep working more than 15 min.

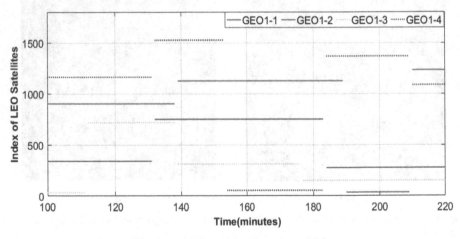

Fig. 4 Switching of the Cross-layer Links

Figure 5 shows the load balance among GEO controllers. The Y-axis is the number of LEO satellites, and the X-axis is the time slot from 0 to 10. And similarly to have a good demonstration, we only Fig. 10 time slots (excluding the switching duration). From Fig. 5, it is obvious that our algorithm can obtain a good load balance, and the worst result is at the first time slot which is influenced by the bad initial selection of anchors. And for most time, the algorithm can achieve best load balance, as shown in Fig. 6.

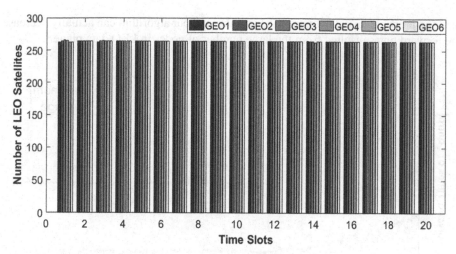

Fig. 5 Load Balance among GEO Controllers

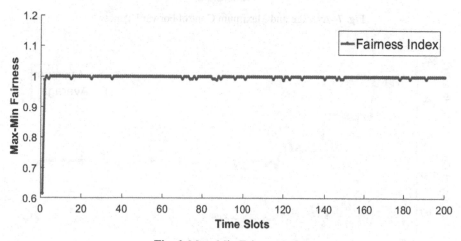

Fig. 6 Max–Min Fairness Index

Figure 7 shows the average and maximum forward times of control path during the 200 time slots (excluding the switching duration). At the first time slot, the maximum forward times from LEO satellites to its controller is 20, and the average forward times is about 7. But after employing our SADCPP scheme, the maximum forward times is decreased to 11 and the average forward times is reduced to about 5. Moreover, to evaluate the control path delay, we further compute the average and maximum control path delays, which is presented in Fig. 8. The propagation delay of ISLs and cross-layer links is evaluated. The results show that after employing our SADCPP scheme, the average control path delay can be reduced to about 155 ms (after the 80-th time slot), and the maximum control path delay is about 186 ms. The long latencies are mainly caused by the long propagation delay of cross-layer links, and our algorithm can actually decrease the forward times resulted from the large number of nodes in LEO data plane.

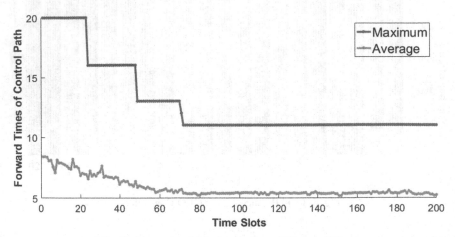

Fig. 7 Average and Maximum Control Forward Times

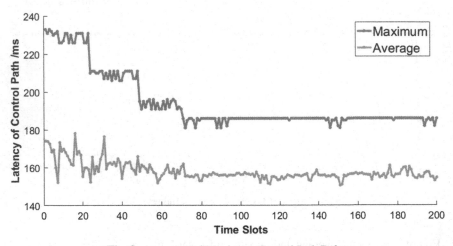

Fig. 8 Average and Maximum Control Path Delay

6 Conclusion

In this work, we propose a practical controller architecture for the software defined large-scale LEO satellite networks, where with considering the limited number and antennas of GEO satellites, we assume that the communication between GEO control plane and LEO data plane is achieved by limited cross-layer links. Then, to plan proper cross-layer links, we propose a switching-aware dynamic control path planning (SADCPP) scheme, consisting of the TimeSelection and the AnchorSelection mechanisms. The TimeSelection can decide the next switching time with maintaining enough cross-layer links in the switching duration and building new cross-layer links that last long enough. Then the AnchorSelection scheme compute proper anchors by employing a heuristic algorithm AS-PSO, which is realized to solve the cross-layer link selection problem with considering the load balance among GEO controllers and the latencies of control paths. Simulation results demonstrate the better performance of our SADCPP scheme on reducing the bad influence of switching, optimizing the load balance among controllers and the control path delays of LEO satellites.

References

1. Majumdar, A.K.: Optical Wireless Communications for Broadband Global Internet Connectivity: Fundamentals and Potential Applications. Elsevier (2018)
2. Bao, J., Zhao, B., Yu, W., et al.: OpenSAN: a software-defined satellite network architecture. ACM SIGCOMM Computer Communication Review. ACM, **44**(4), 347–348 (2014)
3. Tang, Z., et al.: Software defined satellite networks: benefits and challenges. In: IEEE Computers, Communications and IT Applications Conference, pp. 127–132. IEEE (2014)
4. Gardikis, G., et al.: NFV applicability and use cases in satellite networks. In: European Conference on Networks and Communications (EuCNC), pp. 47–51. IEEE (2016)
5. Li, T., Zhou, H., Luo, H., et al.: SERvICE: a software defined framework for integrated space-terrestrial satellite communication. IEEE Trans. Mob. Comput. **17**(3), 703–716 (2017)
6. Xu, S., Wang, X.W., Huang, M.: Software-defined next-generation satellite networks: architecture, challenges, and solutions. IEEE Access **6**, 4027–4041 (2018)
7. Barritt, B.J., Eddy, W.: SDN enhancements for LEO satellite networks. In: 34th AIAA International Communications Satellite Systems Conference (2016). https://doi.org/10.2514/6.2016-5755
8. Li, Y., Wang, Y., Zhang, Q., Yang, Z.: TCDS: a time-relevant graph based topology control in triple-layer satellite networks. In: IEEE Wireless Communications Letters (2019)
9. Bouttier, E., et al.: Analysis of content size based routing schemes in hybrid satellite / terrestrial networks. In: IEEE Global Communications Conference (GLOBECOM), pp. 1-6. IEEE (2016)
10. Sara El Alaoui, Byrav Ramamurthy: Routing Optimization for DTN-Based Space Networks using a Temporal Graph Model. ICC (2016). https://doi.org/10.1109/ICC.2016.7510733
11. Kondrateva, O., et al.: Throughput-optimal joint routing and scheduling for low-earth-orbit satellite networks. In: 14th Annual Conference on Wireless On-demand Network Systems and Services (WONS), pp. 59–66. IEEE (2018)
12. Gang, X.: An adaptive parameter tuning of particle swarm optimization algorithm. Appl. Math. Comput. **219**(9), 4560–4569 (2013)
13. https://www.space-track.org/

Cross-term Suppression in Cyclic Spectrum Estimation Based on EMD

Jurong Hu [✉], Long Lu, and Xujie Li

Hohai University, Nanjing Jiang Su 211100, China
2990693712@qq.com

Abstract. It is inevitable to generate cross term when calculating the cyclic spectrum estimation of complex electromagnetic environment interference signals. Aiming at the problem of cross term in multiple signal cycle spectrum in complex electromagnetic environment, this paper presents a method for cross-term suppression in cyclic spectrum estimation based on empirical mode decomposition (EMD).The effective information of complex electromagnetic environment signals is extracted by compression and reconstruction algorithm, and the effective information is decomposed by empirical mode. results of simulation and experiment show that the proposed method can effectively suppress the cross term.

Keywords: Radar · Cyclic spectrum · Empirical mode decomposition · Cross term

1 Introduction

With the development of communication technology, the distribution of communication base stations is more and more intensive, and the frequency range of communication signals is continuously expanded, which makes the radar [1] more and more interfered by the same frequency communication signals. In the case of same frequency, the jamming of communication signal to radar belongs to compression jamming.

In the electromagnetic space where the radar works, there are interference signals emitted by adjacent radars or hostile radars. Interference signals of various modulation forms, bandwidths and frequencies are superimposed together to form a dense and complex electromagnetic environment. In the electromagnetic environment of radar, the prior information of various radiation sources is unknown, the transmitting waveform is various, and forms [2, 3] of interference signal are various. The research of high precision spectrum estimation method of electromagnetic environment signal is the core of improving radar anti-jamming ability. The mean value, autocorrelation and other statistics of the signal are generally periodic. If the periodicity changes with time, the signal is called cyclic stationary signal, such as communication, radar, remote sensing and other signals [4, 5, 6]. The second order cyclic spectrum has low estimation complexity, fast calculation speed and strong anti-noise capability, which can transform complex nonlinear signals and make them periodic. The second order cyclic spectrum can estimate

© ICST Institute for Computer Sciences, Social Informatics and Telecommunications Engineering 2021
Published by Springer Nature Switzerland AG 2021. All Rights Reserved
Q. Wu et al. (Eds.): WiSATS 2020, LNICST 357, pp. 168–174, 2021.
https://doi.org/10.1007/978-3-030-69069-4_14

and detect the frequency band of interference signal in the electromagnetic environment of MIMO radar better.

In this paper, a spectrum analysis method based on second order cyclic spectrum estimation is studied. It is inevitable to generate cross terms when calculating the cyclic spectrum estimation of complex electromagnetic environment interference signals. Aiming at the problem of cross term in cyclic spectrum estimation, this paper studies the effect of cross-term suppression based on empirical mode decomposition[(EMD), and analyzes the performance of the algorithm through simulation experiment.

2 Cyclic Spectrum Estimation

Radar received signal can be defined as signals and noise. Noise is a random signal with zero mean value, and they are independent of each other. So the signal can be expressed as

$$r(t) = \sum_{i=1}^{m} s_i(t) + n(t) \quad (i = 1, 2, ..., m) \tag{1}$$

where $\sum_{i=1}^{p} s_i(t)$ represent signals and $n(t)$ represents noise.

For formula (1), the second-order hysteresis product of the signal is calculated and expressed as follows

$$q(t) = r(t)r * (t + \tau) \tag{2}$$

where τ is time offset. * is representation conjugate. The statistical average for $q(t)$ is calculated and expressed as follows

$$R_{11}(t, \tau) = E\{r(t)r * (t + \tau)\} \tag{3}$$

$R_{11}(t, \tau)$ is a function of t and τ, called autocorrelation function.

$$R_{11}(t, \tau) = \sum_{p=-\infty}^{\infty} R_{11}(\tau)e^{j2\pi wt} \tag{4}$$

Fourier expansion of Eq. (3) is

$$R_{11}(\tau) = \lim_{T \to \infty} \int_{-T/2}^{T/2} r(t)r * (t+\tau)e^{-j2\pi wt} dt \tag{5}$$

So the cyclic autocorrelation function is expressed as

$$S_{11}(f) = \lim_{T \to \infty} \lim_{\Delta t \to \infty} \int_{-\Delta t/2}^{\Delta t/2} \frac{1}{T} R(t, f + w/2)R * (t, f - w/2)dt \tag{6}$$

$R(f)$ is the Fourier transform of $r(t)$; w is the cycle frequency, and w = p/T_0. T_0 is the period.

3 Cross Term Suppression based on EMD

3.1 Compression and Reconstruction

In order to express a signal more concisely, the signal is usually transformed into a new base or frame. When the number of non-zero coefficients is far less than the number of terms of the original signal, these small number of non-zero coefficients can be called the sparse expression [7, 8] of the original signal.

Collect the signal $r(t)$ at point N. Define $\mathbf{r}$ as the projection coefficient vector of x on the orthogonal basis y. We can use orthogonal basis vectors to represent complex electromagnetic environment signals in space.

$$\mathbf{r} = \sum\nolimits_{ns=1}^{N} \Psi_{ns}\mathbf{a}_{ns} = \Psi\mathbf{a} \tag{7}$$

Ψ is orthogonal basis matrix, and the dimension of Ψ is $N \times N$. The number of non-zero elements in projection coefficient vector a is defined as:

$$K = \|\mathbf{a}\|_0 \tag{8}$$

$$\mathbf{y} = \Phi\mathbf{r} = \Phi\Psi\mathbf{a} = \Theta\mathbf{a} \tag{9}$$

Φ is a $M \times N$ dimensional observation matrix. $\Theta = \Phi\Psi$ is called the recovery matrix.

It is difficult to directly solve the projection coefficient vector $\mathbf{a}$, so it is transformed into $\mathbf{a}'$, the approximate value of matrix $\mathbf{a}$, that is

$$\hat{\mathbf{a}} = \arg\min\|\mathbf{a}'\|_1 \quad s.t. \ \Theta\mathbf{a}' = \mathbf{y} \tag{10}$$

Therefore, the reconstructed signal is

$$\mathbf{r}' = \Psi\mathbf{a}' \tag{11}$$

3.2 Empirical Mode Decomposition

The purpose of EMD algorithm is to decompose the signal with poor performance into a set of Intrinsic Mode Functions (IMF) with good performance. The specific steps of EMD algorithm are as follows:

Step1: The local maximum and minimum points of signal $r(t)$ are found out, and the upper envelope $H(t)$ and the lower envelope $V(t)$ are obtained by cubic spline interpolation.

Step2: Calculate the envelope mean as

$$y_1(t) = \frac{H(t) + V(t)}{2} \tag{12}$$

Step3: The components are obtained by subtracting the envelope mean from the radar received signal.

$$e_1(t) = r(t) - y_1(t) \tag{13}$$

Step4: Whether $e_1(t)$ satisfies the condition of IMF. If not, return to step1 and replace $e_1(t)$ with $r(t)$ for the second screening.

$$e_2(t) = e_1(t) - y_2(t) \tag{14}$$

Repeat k times, until the condition is satisfied, and get the kth component.

$$e_k(t) = e_{k-1}(t) - y_k(t) \tag{15}$$

The first order IMF is

$$b_1(t) = e_k(t) \tag{16}$$

Step5: The remainder of the first order IMF is obtained

$$r_1(t) = r(t) - b_1(t) \tag{17}$$

Step6: Repeat step1 to Step5 with $r_1(t)$ as the new signal. When the residual amount of the nth order IMF is constant or cannot be further decomposed, the EMD algorithm is completed.

$$r_n(t) = r_{n-1}(t) - b_n(t) \tag{18}$$

As is shown in Fig. 1, the improved algorithm is the combination of CS and EMD. We receive electromagnetic environmental signal and get the sparse representation of signal. The signal is compressed and measured, then we reconstruct the signal and conduct EMD, a series of IMF function components are obtained. The cyclic spectrum of each IMF component was calculated separately. The cyclic spectrum of each component is accumulated linearly, so we can get the cyclic spectrum of the original electromagnetic signal.

4 Simulation

In this section, representatives of signal FM and LFM will be selected to simulate the complex electromagnetic environment that radar works in. The carrier frequency of FM signal is 1600 MHz. The amplitude of the carrier signal is 1.0. The initial phase of the carrier signal is 0. The frequency of the baseband signal is 1 MHz. The frequency modulation sensitivity is 14. The amplitude of LFM signal is 0.5. The initial frequency is 0. Signal bandwidth B is 150 MHz. FM slope is 2×10^{12}. It is assumed that the noise in the complex electromagnetic environment is gaussian white noise, and the SNR of radar in complex electromagnetic environment is 20 dB. At this time, the signal model of radar operating complex electromagnetic environment can be expressed as follow.

$$r(t) = s_{FM}(t) + s_{LFM}(t) + n(t) \tag{19}$$

Figure 2 shows cyclic spectrum estimation results of FM and LFM. f is frequency. alfa is cycle frequency. s is cyclic spectrum. Figure 3 shows cyclic spectrum estimation results of FM and LFM based on EMD.

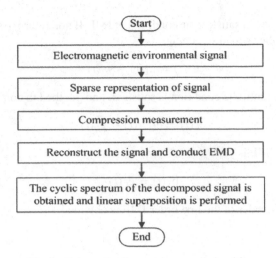

Fig. 1. Schematic diagram improved algorithm

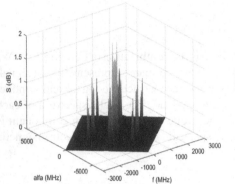

Fig. 2. Cyclic spectrum estimation

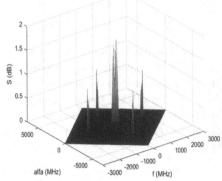

Fig. 3. Cyclic spectrum estimation of FM of FM and LFM and LFM based on EMD

In order to analyze the cyclic spectrum of FM and LFM more clearly, the schematic diagram of cyclic spectrum estimation contour of FM signal and LFM signal in Fig. 2 and the schematic diagram of cyclic spectrum estimation contour based on EMD in Fig. 3 were obtained as follows.

Figure 4 shows that the frequency band of jamming signal FM is –1680 MHz— 1515 MHz, –75 MHz –75 MHz, 1525 MHz –1680 MHz. The frequency band of jamming signal FM is –135 MHz –130 MHz. The frequency band where the cross terms are generated by M and LFM is –905 MHz —685 MHz, 680 MHz –915 MHz.

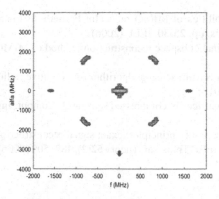

Fig. 4. Cyclic spectrum estimation map contour map

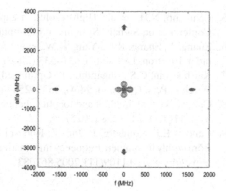

Fig. 5. Cyclic spectrum estimation contour map based on EMD

Figure 5 shows that the frequency band of jamming signal FM is −1670 MHz ~ −1535 MHz, −75 MHz ~ 75 MHz, 1535 MHz ~ 1685 MHz. The frequency band of jamming signal FM is −135 MHz ~ 130 MHz.

Compare Fig. 5 with Fig. 4, the cross term in Fig. 5 was completely suppressed. As the complexity of signal increases, the complexity of cyclic spectrum estimation of signal will increase, and the cross term will also become complex. The improved cyclic spectrum estimation algorithm not only improves the readability of cyclic spectrum estimation of complex electromagnetic environment interference signals, but also effectively eliminates the cross terms.

5   Conclusion

This paper proposes cross term suppression method for cyclic spectrum estimation based on EMD. The cyclic spectrum of common jamming signals such as FM signal and LFM signal is studied emphatically. As the complexity of signals increase, the complexity of cyclic spectrum estimation of signals will increase, and the cross terms will also become more complex. Simulation results show that the proposed method can effectively suppress the cross term of multiple signals in a complex environment and improve the resolution of the self-term.

References

1. Li, J., Stoica, P.: MIMO Radar Signal Processing [M] (2009)
2. White, L.B., et al.: Signal design for MIMO diversity systems. In Conference Record of the Thirty-Eighth Asilomar Conference on Signals, Systems and Computers, 2004, Vol. 1, pp. 973-977. IEEE (2004)
3. Fishler, E., et al.: Spatial diversity in radars—models and detection performance. IEEE Trans. Signal Process. **54**(3), 823–838 (2006)
4. Thameri, M., Abed-Meraim, K., Foroozan, F., Boyer, R., Asif, A.: On the statistical resolution limit (SRL) for time-reversal based MIMO radar. Signal Process. **144**, 373–383 (2018). https://doi.org/10.1016/j.sigpro.2017.10.029

5. Lehmann, N.H., et al.: High resolution capabilities of MIMO radar. In: Fortieth Asilomar Conference on Signals, Systems and Computers, pp. 25-30. IEEE (2006)
6. Zhang, J., Zhang, R.R., Yang, R.W., et al.: Signal subspace reconstruction method of MIMO radar. Electron. Lett. **46**(7), 531–533 (2010)
7. Karthikeyan, C.S., Suganthi, M.: Optimized spectrum sensing algorithm for cognitive radio. Wireless Pers. Commun. **94**(4), 2533–2547 (2017)
8. Gan, H., et al.: Circulant and toeplitz chaotic matrices in compressed sensing. J. Comput. Inf. Syst. **11**(4), 1231–1238 (2015)
9. Candes, E.J., Romberg, J., Tao, T.: Robust uncertainty principles: exact signal reconstruction from highly incomplete frequency information. IEEE Trans. Inf. Theory **52**(2), 489–509 (2006). https://doi.org/10.1109/TIT.2005.862083

Visual Image Downtransmission of Landing Phase for Deep Space Explorers

Cuilian Wang[1(✉)], Yin Li[2], Ke Li[1], and Dong Zhou[1]

[1] Beijing Institute of Spacecraft System Engineering, Beijing 100094, China
cuilian_wang_bit@126.com
[2] DFH Satellite Co. Ltd., Beijing 100094, China

Abstract. Visual image transmission during power descent or landing segment is needed in deep space probes, while the bandwidth of transmission channel is limited and the information transmission rate is low in deep space communication. In view of this contradiction, a rate-adaptive visual image transmission scheme is designed in this paper. Key problems such as frame extraction and playback, frame format identification, joint scheduling are solved. Visual transmission of image under the condition of limited communication rate is realized by the scheme, with the characteristics of real-time performance, rate adaptation, image integrity, etc. At the same time, the concrete implementation and experimental verification of the scheme in engineering are given, which provide reference for the design on spacecraft data management system.

Keywords: Deep space communication · Power descent · Rate adaptation

1 Introduction

The landing camera mounted on deep space probe is installed at the bottom of the lander and perpendicular to the lunar surface. It is used to acquire the image data of the lunar surface in the dynamic descending phase of the probe in real time. The frame rate of the image is not less than 10 frames/s and the peak image transmission rate is higher than 10 Mbps [1]. In order to visualize the landing process of the probe, it is necessary to download the latest image generated by the landing camera as soon as possible. Deep space communication has the characteristics of long communication distance and serious signal attenuation. At the same time, the antenna gain and transmission power of deep space spacecraft are limited, and the signal reaching the ground station is very weak [2]. Therefore, in order to ensure the reliability of long-distance data transmission, the deep space communication rate is generally not too high [3]. At present, the deep space data transmission to ground communication rate is generally below 2 Mbps. Telemetry data, detection data and image data generated by the lander are transmitted to the ground by the relay star after unified routing and coding. The available communication rate for image data does not exceed 500 kbps. In this case, there is a contradiction between the image generation rate and the downlink rate. Therefore, it is necessary to design a

Q. Wu et al. (Eds.): WiSATS 2020, LNICST 357, pp. 175–184, 2021.
https://doi.org/10.1007/978-3-030-69069-4_15

visual image transmission scheme. At the same time, deep space probe is a system with limited resources, so the complexity of project engineering should be reduced as much as possible.

A multiplex memory is designed in the data management subsystem of deep space probe, which is responsible for the joint scheduling, storage and down-transmission of the probe data, image data and telemetry data of the whole device. According to the demand for data transmission in different application scenarios, multiplex memory can realize flexible data flow management. In the power descent section, the storage and transmission requirements of image data are: (1) All the data generated in the power descent section need to be stored in the mass storage. When the detector reaches the lunar surface and the communication channel to the earth is available, the stored data can be selectively played back and transmitted down. (2) During the landing of the probe, the latest image generated by the landing camera is transmitted in real time. There are several schemes to realize visual download of images in the multiplex memory:

Scheme 1: The image data of the landing camera are simultaneously input to the storage channel and the downlink channel. In the data stream design of the memory channel, since the programming rate of the memory chip is higher than the peak input rate of the image, it is not necessary to distinguish the content of the image and can be stored directly by bit stream [4]. However, in the data stream design of the downlink channel, in order to ensure the integrity of the downlink image, the whole image needs to be buffered, then whether the downlink channel is idle or not is judged, and when the channel is idle, data is read from the buffer for downlink. The advantage of this scheme is that it is simple to implement and compatible with the overall data flow of the multiplex memory. Disadvantages are: (1) Due to the need to cache a complete image, when the image is large, the cost of the required hardware resources increases; (2) After an image cache is full, it starts to read the download, which has poor real-time performance.

Scheme 2: The image data of the landing camera is input into the storage channel. The playback mode can be selected as playback by time or playback by address [4, 5]. The above two playback modes require the ground to obtain the storage time or address of the latest image of the landing camera in advance, and inject playback instructions including the playback time or address into the detector. The disadvantages of this scheme are: (1) The application is complicated, which is not conducive to the realization of autonomous storage and playback management; (2) The storage time or address of the latest image can only be accurately estimated on the premise that the input rate of the image is unchanged, and the visual transmission with adaptive rate cannot be realized.

Scheme 3: The image data of the landing camera is stored and transmitted down in the way of recording while playing. At the same time, a special playback mode is designed. In this mode, images are marked with special marks while being stored. During playback, the latest images with special marks are read and downloaded by frame drawing playback [6]. This scheme is compatible with the design state of the lander's multiplex memory, and only one additional information register and a set of latest image storage address registers need to be added to the hardware overhead. This paper focuses on the overall design and key technologies of the scheme.

2 Overall Scheme Design

The landing camera is connected to the multiplex memory through LVDS (Low-Voltage Differential Signaling) interface, and the data content includes high compression ratio image data and low compression ratio image data. The two kinds of data appear at intervals of one picture, and the transmission ratio is variable. The default is 64:1, that is, 64 of 65 images are of low compression ratio and 1 is of high compression ratio.

In order to realize the visual transmission of the image of the landing camera, it is necessary to store all the image data and transmit the high compression ratio image in real time. Considering the design overhead of detector hardware and software resources, the processing of landing camera images should be compatible with the overall design of the multiplex memory. Figure 1 is a design block diagram of a multiplex memory. On this basis, the scheme for realizing the visual transmission of the image of the landing camera is as follows:

(1) The image data sent by the landing camera to the multiplex memory first passes through the image format identification and framing module to separate, segment and distribute the virtual channel identification between the high compression ratio image and the low compression ratio image.

(2) Each high compression ratio image is organized and defined by the Consultative Committee for Space Data System (CCSDS) as an Advanced Orbiting System. AOS) frame format carries out Virtual Channel Data Unit (VCDU) framing on image data, including 1 frame header VCDU, 1 frame tail VCDU and several frame middle VCDU.

(3) The storage combination module performs combination scheduling on the high compression ratio image VCDU and VCDU generated by other loads, and stores the VCDU into a storage carrier after competing for a storage channel.

(4) The playback control module in the storage carrier uses a frame extraction playback method in the power down section to play back the VCDU frame of the high compression ratio image from the storage carrier. The specific work flow is as follows: 1) The storage carrier loads the storage address of the latest image and plays back sequentially from this address; 2) When playing back to the end of a high compression ratio image, completing frame drawing playback of an image; 3) Repeat the above steps to extract and play back the next image.

(5) The screened and filtered high compression ratio image VCDU frame and other real-time downlink frames are sent to the data transmission transponder after downlink combining and encoding.

According to the above processing flow, the key technologies involved in this scheme include frame extraction and playback algorithm, frame format identification method, combined scheduling algorithm, etc.

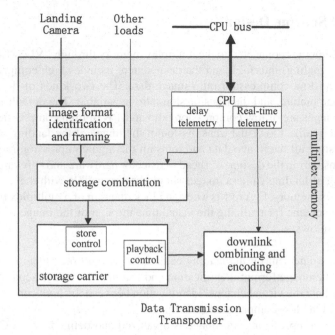

Fig. 1. Design block diagram of a multiplex memory

3   Key Technologies

3.1   Frame Extraction and Playback Algorithm

The frame extraction and playback algorithm is mainly implemented in two modules: storage control and playback control. Figure 2 is the principle block diagram of the frame extraction and playback algorithm. In order to accurately identify a complete high compression ratio image, the data frame after AOS framing needs to design additional information to distinguish VCDU header frame, VCDU tail frame and VCDU intermediate frame of the high compression ratio image, and the additional information needs to be saved at the same time during storage.

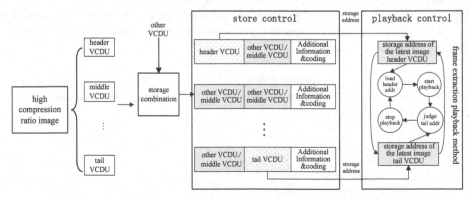

Fig. 2. The block diagram of the frame extraction and playback algorithm

The multiplex memory uses NandFlash as the storage carrier; each page is 2 KB in size and can store two VCDU frames. When storing by page, in addition to the data content of VCDU frame, additional information and coding check bits need to be saved. Because NandFlash is access by a combined schedule mechanism, data stored on that same page may include different VCDU frames generated by various load. Additional information needs to distinguish the data content stored in NandFlash pages. The format design of additional information is shown in Table 1.

Table 1. Format of additional format

Bit	B1:B0	B2:B3	B4:B5
Definition	Number of high compression ratio image frames in this page	Content of the 1st frame	Content of the 2nd frame
Meaning of each state	00: 0 frame	00: header VCDU	00: header VCDU
	01: 1 frame, the 1st frame in this page	01: middle VCDU	01: middle VCDU
	10: 1 frame, the 2nd frame in this page	10: tail VCDU	10: tail VCDU
	11: 2 frames	11: invalid	11: invalid

The playback control module needs to be set to the frame extraction playback mode in the power down section. This mode is different from the traditional sequential playback or site selection playback. It is a playback mode that can run autonomously. Through the autonomous management of playback address loading, playback start and playback stop, the extraction and download of high compression ratio image frames is realized. When the next row number transmission channel is available, the playback control module loads the latest image header frame storage address and sequentially plays back from the address. In the playback process, the additional information stored in the page NandFlash is first read, VCDU frames of non-high compression ratio images are filtered out according to the content of the additional information, and only VCDU frames of high compression ratio images are transmitted to the downlink combining module. When the playback address is equal to the latest image tail frame storage address, playback is stopped. After that, the image header storage address is reloaded. If it is consistent with the previous header address, it is considered that there is currently no new image storage. The playback module continues to wait in the stopped state, and starts a new round of extraction playback flow when the newly loaded header frame address changes.

3.2 Frame Format Identification Method

In the image format identification and framing module, two kinds of image data of the landing camera are distinguished. 1) LVDS signals are converted into byte signals through serial-to-parallel conversion; 2) Sliding matching byte signals; 3) After the frame headers are matched, starting statistics on the length and number of subsequent data blocks; 4) When the length and number of data blocks are consistent with the frame structure shown in Fig. 1, buffer and frame the data, otherwise re-detect the frame header. The two receiving modules adopt exactly the same processing structure, except that the data block length and the numbers of data blocks are designed differently. In the process of FPGA engineering, it can be realized by instantiating two identical modules and setting different parameters.

3.3 Combination Scheduling Algorithm

This scheme involves the combination of two parts: 1) All load (including landing camera) data need to go through unified combination scheduling before storage; 2) Joint dispatching of telemetry data, playback data and other real-time data before downlink. When designing multiple virtual channels, reasonable scheduling algorithm and priority control strategy should be adopted to ensure the data rate matching before and after the channel combination and improve the transmission efficiency. CCSDS recommends a combination scheduling algorithm including [7] fixed priority scheduling algorithm, polling priority scheduling algorithm, residual priority scheduling algorithm, etc. The advantages and disadvantages of the above algorithms are different in different application scenarios and scheduling requirements. This paper designs a priority scheduling algorithm based on working mode according to the storage and downlink requirements of the detector in power descending section, visible arc section and invisible arc section. Different scheduling mechanisms are adopted in different modes, and a combination of fixed priority and polling priority is adopted. The specific design is shown in Table 2.

Table 2. Priority scheduling strategies for different operating modes

Operating mode	Storage priority	Downlink priority
Power decent segment	Fixed priority: 1. Landing camera data 2. Delay telemetry 3. other load data	Fixed priority: 1. Playback data 2. Real-time telemetry 3. other real-time data
Visible segment	Polling priority	Fixed priority: 1. Real-time telemetry 2. Playback data 3. other real-time data
Invisible segment	Polling priority	Downlink prohibition

4 Performance Analysis

4.1 Downlink Real-Time Analysis

The frame extraction and playback algorithm adopted in this scheme updates the storage addresses of the head frame and the tail frame of the image after receiving a complete high compression ratio image data. Considering the worst case, when the latest high compression ratio image is received, the frame extraction playback of the previous image has just started, and the processing delay at this time is the sum of the image receiving time and the input time interval of the two images. The LVDS interface rate of the landing camera is R_{up}, and the frame length of high compression ratio image is L_{imag}, then the receiving time of a high compression ratio image is

$$T_{recv} = L_{imag}/R_{up}$$

The imaging frequency of the landing camera is N frames/s, the interval between two high compression ratio images is K frames, and the time interval is about

$$T_{int} = K/N$$

In the worst case, the processing delay of the image is

$$T_{delay} = T_{recv} + T_{int} = L_{imag}/R + K/N$$

After the download of the nth image is completed, the storage address of the latest image is the storage address of the $(n + 2)^{nd}$ image. After the address is updated, the data content of the $(n + 2)^{nd}$ image is returned and the processing delay is automatically adjusted to T_{recv}. The delay of subsequent image processing is kept at T_{recv}, which meets the requirement of visual transmission.

4.2 Downlink Integrity Analysis

The integrity of image download refers to the complete download of M VCDU frames of a high compression ratio image, and the transmission process is not affected by other events. In the frame-drawing playback mode, the four states of the playback control state machine operate autonomously. The two registers of the head frame storage address and the tail frame storage address of the latest image are refreshed simultaneously only in the stop playback state and not in other states. This processing mechanism can avoid the incompleteness of the downlink image caused by the asynchronous update of the head frame storage address and the tail frame storage address.

4.3 Adaptive Analysis of Downlink Rate

The rate adaptation of this scheme includes two aspects, one is the input rate adaptation of high compression ratio image data, and the other is the downstream rate adaptation of data transmission. The input rate affects the storage efficiency of NandFlash, while the downlink rate affects the reading efficiency of NandFlash. The two rates are decoupled through NandFlash chips. When the high compression ratio image data input rate exceeds the data transmission downlink rate, the storage addresses of the head frame and tail frame of the latest image will cover the storage addresses of the head frame and tail frame of the previous image, so as to ensure that the content of the downlink data is newly generated. Through this way of address real-time coverage, the scheme is not affected by the input rate of image data and the downlink rate of data transmission, and the actual downlink image is the whole image after adaptive extraction.

Set the downlink rate as R_{down}, the downlink VCDU frame length as L_{VCDU}, and the time required to transmit a high compression ratio image is

$$T_{down} = L_{VCDU} * M/R_{down}$$

When R_{down} is 50 kbps and 280 kbps, the time required to download a high compression ratio image is 6.226 s and 1.118 s respectively. When the imaging frequency of the landing camera N is 10 frames/s and the transmission ratios of high compression ratio images and low compression ratio images are 1:8, 1:16, 1:32 and 1:64 respectively, the sequence numbers of images received on the ground are shown in the following table. Under several ratios, the input frequencies of high compression ratio images are 0.8 s/image, 1.6 s/image, 3.2 s/image and 6.4 s/image respectively. As can be seen from Table 3, when the data transmission downlink rate is greater than the image input rate, all high compression ratio images can be transmitted without interval. When the downlink rate of data transmission is less than the input rate of images, the serial numbers of the downloaded images are discontinuous, there is a certain interval between the serial numbers of the two images, and the downloaded images are the latest generated data content.

Table 3. High compression ratio image sequence number under different input ratio and down-transfer rate

Proportion	Image sequence number at downlink rate of 50 kbps	Image sequence number at downlink rate of 280 kbps
1:8	1, 9, 17, 25, 32, 40, 48	1, 2, 3, 4, 5, 6, 7
1:16	1, 5, 9, 13, 17, 20, 25	1, 2, 3, 4, 5, 6, 7
1:32	1, 3, 5, 7, 8, 10, 12	1, 2, 3, 4, 5, 6, 7
1:64	1, 2, 3, 4, 5, 6, 7	1, 2, 3, 4, 5, 6, 7

5   Engineering Implementation and on-Orbit Verification

At present, the scheme has been implemented on FPGA, and the chip model is Xilinx aerospace chip XQR2V3000. The multiplex memory, as an important module of Chang 'e–4 data management subsystem, has been verified on-orbit. On the morning of January 3, 2019, Chang 'e–4 probe began to land, the multiplex memory was set to the frame-drawing playback mode, and the downlink rate was set to 50 kbps. After the landing camera was turned on, the high compression ratio image began to be automatically downloaded and updated about 6.4 s, which successfully realized the visualization of the landing process. Figure 3 is a real shot high compression ratio image transmitted down from the power down section. The on-orbit operation state of Chang 'e–4 shows that under the condition of limited data transmission communication rate, the visual transmission of images in the power descent stage is realized, and the equipment works stably and normally.

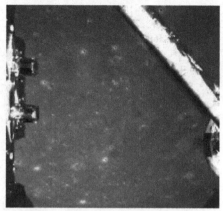

Fig. 3. Downward image of Chang'e–4 probe during power descent

6 Conclusions

This paper designs and implements a visual image transmission scheme with adaptive rate of dynamic descending segment. The scheme recognizes the latest image frame by setting the frame extraction playback mode for extraction playback and downloading. Under the condition of limited data transmission communication rate, it realizes the storage management and visual downloading of the image of the descending camera. It has the characteristics of high real-time, rate adaptation and image integrity.

In the image visualization transmission scheme proposed in this paper, it is required that the low compression ratio image and the high compression ratio image of the landing camera can be distinguished in data format. The following research focuses on designing a general image visualization transmission scheme without limiting the data format of the load image. At the same time, the robustness and scalability of the scheme are further improved, which provides a reference for the design of spacecraft on-board data management subsystem.

References

1. Jia, Y.Z., Zou, Y.L., Xue, C.B., et al.: Scientific objectives and payload allocation of chang 'e-4 mission. J. Space Sci. **38**(1), 118–130 (2018)
2. Wu, W.R., Hui, L., Chen, M., et al.: Design and test of deep space telemetry data transmission system for solar-terrestrial lagrange L2 point exploration. Syst. Eng. Electron. **34**(12), 2559–2563 (2012)

3. Wu, H.T., Jian, J., Gu, S.S., et al.: Data transmission strategy for deep space time-varying channels. Acta Astronautica Sinica **37**(2), 216–222 (2016)
4. Liang, Z.L., Gao, Z.L., Hu, P., et al.: Design and verification of satellite load data storage system for hard X-ray modulated telescope. Spacecraft Eng. **27**(5), 72–77 (2018)
5. Chen, B., Shen, W.H., Zhu, Y., et al.: Design of chang 'e-2 satellite mass storage. Spacecraft Eng. **20**(5), 99–104 (2011)
6. Pei, N., Li, K., Zhao, L.: FPGA-based rate adaptive image extraction algorithm. Mod. Electron. Technol. **36**(19), 58–60 (2013)
7. Xu, Z.H., Dong, Z.H., An, J.S.: FPGA-based design of satellite-borne integrated high-speed data multiplexer. Electron. Des. Eng. **26**(5), 185–188 (2018)

Parameter Estimation of MIMO Radar Based on the OMP Algorithm

Jurong Hu$^{(\boxtimes)}$ and Hanyu Zhou

Hohai University, Nanjing 211100, Jiangsu, China
332930384@qq.com

Abstract. This paper introduces the concept of compressed sensing (CS) into parameter estimation, and proposes a Multiple-input Multiple-output (MIMO) radar parameter estimation algorithm based on the Orthogonal Matching Pursuit (OMP) algorithm. In this algorithm, MIMO radar received signals are represented by joint sparse representation by establishing a sparse base. Then we use the random gaussian observation matrix and the OMP algorithm to reconstruct the target space to finish the estimation of target parameters. Moreover, the algorithm in this paper considers the radar signal model when array error exists, mainly discusses the influence of array amplitude error and phase error on the parameter estimation of MIMO radar based on OMP algorithm. Then the root mean square error (RMSE) of OMP algorithm and Compressive Sampling Matching Pursuit (COSAMP) algorithm are compared when the array error exists. Simulation shows that when the array amplitude and phase error exists, the estimation accuracy of the target's reflection amplitude and target parameters are reduced, and the OMP algorithm has a lower mean square error than the COSAMP algorithm. In conclusion, the proposed algorithm has high precision in parameter estimation. Even when array error exists, the OMP algorithm still has better performance in parameter estimation of MIMO radar target's reflection amplitude, azimuth Angle and pitch Angle than the COSAMP algorithm.

Keywords: Parameter estimation · The OMP algorithm · Amplitude error and phase error of array · MIMO radar

1 Introduction

The concept of MIMO radar and its related signal processing technologies have attracted more and more attention from scholars all over the world. Many scholars have studied the parameter estimation performance of MIMO radar. In recent years, scholars in the field of signal processing began to use the compressed sensing theory, by using the existing classic method (such as transformation coding, optimization algorithm, etc.) to solve the problem of high rate of analog to digital conversion [1–5]. When the sampling frequency is much less than Nyquist sampling rate, it obtains the discrete samples of the signal through random sampling, and then perfectly reconstructs the signal through the non-linear reconstruction algorithm. Paper [6] is based on the sparsity of the target

Q. Wu et al. (Eds.): WiSATS 2020, LNICST 357, pp. 185–193, 2021.
https://doi.org/10.1007/978-3-030-69069-4_16

in the angle-doppler-range domain, by using the CS theory, the paper obtains the joint estimation of the target angle-doppler-range information, so as to realize the super resolution of MIMO radar. Paper [7] utilizes the sparsity of the direction of arrival (DOA) in angular space to estimate the super-resolution parameters of MIMO radar with CS at a low sampling rate. Paper [8] establishes a target information perception model, uses compressed sensing to sample the target echo at a rate lower than Nyquist sampling rate, and extractes target scene information under noise background from a small amount of sampled data.

Both the traditional algorithm and the target reconstruction method based on compressed sensing are premised on the exact known array manifold. However, array errors are often unavoidable in the actual situation, so it is of great practical significance to discuss how to achieve robust target Angle estimation when array errors exist. Paper [9] proves the influence of array model error on the resolution of subspace class algorithms. Paper [10] proposed a global correction method, which comprehensively considered the position, phase and gain errors of array elements, and realized the purpose of simultaneous correction of multiple error parameters, which was relatively consistent with the actual application conditions.

This paper studies parameter estimation based on compressed sensing, mainly discusses the influence of amplitude and phase errors of array elements on the accuracy of target reflection amplitude, azimuth Angle and pitch Angle estimation when using the OMP reconstruction algorithm [11] to estimate the direction of arrival of the target, and compares the estimation performance of parameters based on the OMP algorithm and the COSAMP algorithm [12] when array error exists.

2   System Model

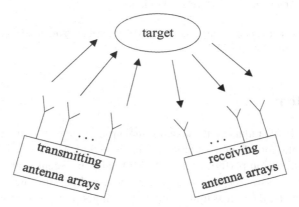

Fig. 1. Structural model of MIMO radar.

We establish a bistatic signal model, in which the transmitting and receiving antenna arrays are equidistant linear arrays, and the transmitting and receiving arrays are remotely separated. The radar system has M transmitting antennas and N receiving antennas. The space between transmitting and receiving antennas is d_t and d_r, respectively. To ensure that the received signal of each receiving signal unit does not have resolution ambiguity, the spacing of receiving array elements should meet the half wavelength condition, that is, $d_r \leq \lambda/2$. Assume that the far field has K objects, the K th object's azimuth is (θ_k, φ_k), and K < MN. θ_k is the direction of departure, and φ_k is the direction of arrival.

For bistatic MIMO radar, when there are multiple targets in space, and the MIMO radar transceiving array contains amplitude-phase error, the received data can be expressed as follows:

$$X_{n-error} = A_{Mr-error}(\varphi_k)\eta A_{Mt-error}^{T}(\theta_k)s + W \tag{1}$$

$A_{Mt-error}(\theta_k) = \Gamma_{Mt}A_{Mt}(\theta_k)$ and $A_{Mr-error}(\varphi_k) = \Gamma_{Mr}A_{Mr}(\varphi_k)$ are the guidance vector matrix with errors in the transmit and receive arrays respectively. $\Gamma_{Mr} = diag[\rho_{Mr1}e^{j\phi_{Mr1}}, \rho_{Mr2}e^{j\phi_{Mr2}}, \ldots, \rho_{Mrn}e^{j\phi_{MrN}}]^{T}$ is diagonal matrix, which represents the amplitude and phase error of N receiving array elements. $\Gamma_{Mt} = diag[\rho_{Mt1}e^{j\phi_{Mt1}}, \rho_{Mr2}e^{j\phi_{Mt2}}, \ldots, \rho_{Mtn}e^{j\phi_{MtM}}]^{T}$ represents the amplitude and phase error of N Transmitting array elements. The ρ_{Mti} and ϕ_{Mti} are the ith a transmitting array amplitude and phase errors respectively.

$A_{Mr}(\varphi_k)$ and $A_{Mt}(\theta_k)$ are the ideal receiving guidance vector and emission guidance vector matrix of K targets, respectively.

$$A_{Mr}(\varphi_k) = [a_{M1}(\varphi_1), a_{M2}(\varphi_2), \ldots, a_{Mr}(\varphi_k)] \tag{2}$$

$$A_{Mt}(\theta_k) = [a_{M1}(\theta_1), a_{M2}(\theta_2), \ldots, a_{Mt}(\theta_k)] \tag{3}$$

$$a_{Mt}(\theta_k) = [1, e^{j2\pi d_t \sin\frac{\theta_k}{\lambda}}, \ldots, e^{j2\pi d_t \sin\theta_k (M-1)/\lambda}]^{T} \tag{4}$$

$$a_{Mr}(\varphi_k) = [1, e^{j2\pi d_r \sin\frac{\varphi_k}{\lambda}}, \ldots, e^{j2\pi d_r \sin\varphi_k (N-1)/\lambda}]^{T} \tag{5}$$

$\eta = [\eta_1, \eta_2, \ldots, \eta_k]^{T}$ is the amplitude of k target reflected signals. S is M orthogonal independent waveforms transmitted by the system. $W \in C^{N \times L}$ is the complex white gaussian noise.

3 Parameter Estimation Principle Based on the OMP Algorithm When Array Error Exists

We discrete each target angle space into $P_1 \times P_2$ directions. Define α as angle P_1 of the signal's direction of departure space. Define β as angle P_2 of the signal's direction of arrival space. $\alpha = [\alpha_1, \alpha_2, \ldots, \alpha_{P_1}]^{T}$, $\beta = [\beta_1, \beta_2, \ldots, \beta_{P_2}]^{T}$.

When the k th goal exists in $(\alpha_{P_1}, \beta_{P_2})$, then $\sigma_{P_1 P_2} = \eta_k$. When $(\alpha_{P_1}, \beta_{P_2})$ have no target, then $(\alpha_{P_1}, \beta_{P_2}) = 0$.

Then the received signal of bistatic uniform linear array MIMO radar when array error exists can be expressed as:

$$X_{n-error} = \sum_{P_2=1}^{P_2} \sum_{P_1=1}^{P_1} A_{Mr-error}(\beta_{P_2})\sigma_{P_1 P_2} A_{Mt-error}^{T}(\alpha_{P_1})s + W \tag{6}$$

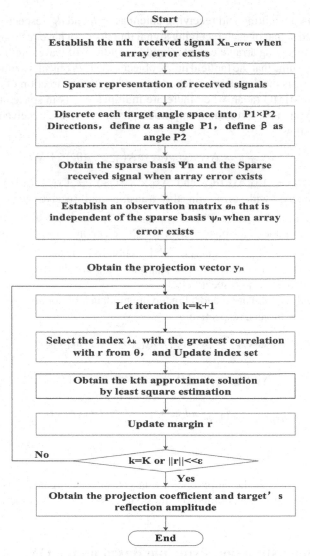

Fig. 2. Flowchart of the algorithm.

Suppose:

$$\psi_n = [A_{Mr-error}(\beta_1)S^T A_{Mt-error}(\alpha_1), \ldots A_{Mr-error}(\beta_{P_2})S^T A_{Mt-error}(\alpha_1), \ldots$$
$$A_{Mr-error}(\beta_1)S^T A_{Mt-error}(\alpha_{P_1}), \ldots, A_{Mr-error}(\beta_{P_2})S^T A_{Mt-error} \qquad (7)$$

And:

$$\sigma = [\sigma_{11}, \ldots, \sigma_{P_21}, \ldots, \sigma_{P_2P_1}, \ldots, \sigma_{P_2P_2}]^T \qquad (8)$$

Then:

$$X_n' = (\psi_n \sigma)^T \qquad (9)$$

The transformation basis matrix $\psi_n(n = 1,2,...L)$ has been determined. It is the sparse basis containing the phase information of the array element, σ is the sparse vector of the signal on the sparse basis. The position of the non-zero element P_2P_1 indicates the target Angle, and its value is the target's reflection amplitude. There are a total of n received signals, and the two-dimensional angle of the target determines the common coefficient structure of these signals. The number of the target is sparsity, and the target's reflection amplitude is the non-zero coefficient of each received signal in the transformation domain. Then take a smooth random gaussian $M \times L$ observation matrix ϕ_n (n = 1,2,...M), it is uncorrelated with transformation basis matrix ψ_n, and M < L. Therefore, the projection vector of the received signal X_n' (n = 1,2,...L) of the nth receiving antenna on the observation matrix ϕ_n is:

$$y_n = \phi_n X_n'^T = \phi_n \psi_n \sigma = \Theta_n \sigma \qquad (10)$$

$\Theta_n(n = 1,2,...M)$ is Perception matrix.

The basic steps of the parameters of the OMP algorithm are as follows:

The input of the OMP algorithm are perception matrix Θ, measurement vector y_n, signal sparsity k and error threshold ε。

The output of the OMP algorithm are residual component $r = y_n(n = 1, 2 ... N)$, index set $\Omega = \phi$, number of iterations k = 1, estimation of signal sparse coefficient $\hat{x}$ and support domain $\hat{\Omega}$。

(1) Select the index λ_k corresponding to the column with the greatest correlation with r from Θ, $\lambda_k = arg\max(\Theta_n^H r)(1 \ll n \ll N)$, Θ_n represents the nth column of the Θ;

(2) Update index set $\Omega = \Omega \bigcup \lambda_k$;

(3) Obtain the approximate solution by least square estimation: $\hat{x}_k = arg\min\left\|y - \Theta_\Omega X_n'\right\|_2$, where $\hat{x}_k$ is the least squares approximate solution of the Kth iteration, Θ_Ω is a matrix consisting of columns indicated by Ω in Θ;

(4) Update margin $r = y_n - \Theta_\Omega - \hat{x}_k$;

(5) Judge whether the iteration satisfies the stopping condition: k = K or $\|r\|_2 \ll \varepsilon$. If it is satisfied, then stop the iteration, output $\hat{x} = \hat{x}_k$ and $\hat{\Omega} = \Omega$. Otherwise, let k = K + 1, and then turn back to the first step.

The index set Ω is determined by the iteration of the OMP algorithm, and Ω represents the position of K non-zero elements, and the values of these elements correspond to the projection coefficient $\hat{x}_k$ (k = 1, 2, ..., K) at this time. The projection coefficients of subspaces formed by observation signal $y_n(n = 1, 2 ... N)$ for K atoms correspond to non-zero elements in $X_n'(n = 1, 2 ... L)$. Therefore, the sparse signal X_n' to be reconstructed can be determined.

4 Simulation

Bistatic MIMO radar, $d_t = d_r \leq \lambda/2$, $M = 6$, $N = 6$. Transmitted signal's coding length is 128 L and the received signal's SNR is 5 dB. DOA and DOD's observation intervals are all $[-90, 90]$. The discrete interval is $5°$ when constructing sparse base. We assume that there are three targets in radar observation space, DOD and DOA are $(-60, -30)$, $(0, 0)$, $(20, 50)$, the reflection amplitudes are 5, 2 and 3, respectively. Random values of the amplitude error of the transmitting element is 2 $(1, M)$, the phase error is $-1 + 2$ $(1, M)$, the amplitude error of the receiving element is 2 $(1, N)$, and the phase error is $-1 + 2$ $(1, N)$.

According to Table 1, on the basis of joint sparse representation of received signals, the weighted OMP algorithm can overcome array noise and achieve accurate estimation of the target's reflection amplitude. When array amplitude and phase errors exist, the accuracy of the algorithm is reduced.

Table 1. Estimation of target reflection amplitude

(DOD,DOA)	Reflection amplitude estimation without Array error			Reflection amplitude estimation with Array error		
	$(-60,-30)$	$(0, 0)$	$(50, 30)$	$(-60, 30)$	$(0, 0)$	$(50, 30)$
r = 1	4.8970	1.8171	2.5170	4.1655	1.7932	3.3294
r = 2	4.8620	1.7851	2.9863	4.2377	1.8326	3.0418
r = 3	4.9603	1.9087	3.2583	3.2743	1.6751	2.6201
r = 4	5.1219	1.9012	2.9426	5.5902	1.4689	2.7151
r = 5	4.8165	1.7412	2.8379	4.2156	1.2983	2.8145
r = 6	4.9714	1.8892	3.2550	4.2846	1.9976	2.6601
Average	4.9381	1.8404	2.9751	4.2945	1.6776	2.6968
Real	5	2	3	5	2	3

As shown in Fig. 1, when SNR = 5 dB, the real position of the target and the estimated position are highly coincident. When the array error exists, the estimation accuracy of the target angle is reduced, and the estimation position of the target is biased.

Figure 2 shows the relationship between the target angle estimation and the signal-to-noise ratio by using the OMP reconstruction algorithm when amplitude and phase error exists or not. The root mean squard error of the target angle estimate used here for comparison takes the average of 3 targets.

It can be more intuitive to see from the Fig. 3, the angle estimation performance curve of the target with the amplitude and phase error is obviously inferior to the angle estimation performance curve when the array has no phase and amplitude error, and the error of the target estimation is large, the estimation accuracy is significantly reduced. When the SNR is increased from 0 to 25 dB at 5 dB intervals, as the signal-to-noise ratio increases, the estimation accuracy becomes higher and higher. The estimated gain performance of the algorithm is obvious between 0 and 10 dB. Continued increase of the signal-to-noise ratio has a lower and lower gain effect on the MIMO radar target parameter estimation. The root mean squard error of the OMP algorithm with array error exists is lower than the root mean squard error of the COSAMP algorithm with array error exists, which indicates that the OMP algorithm used in this paper is better than the COSAMP algorithm in estimating the parameters when array error exists (Fig. 4).

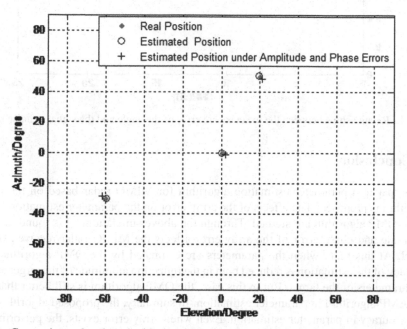

Fig. 3. Comparison of real angle, ideal estimated angle and estimated angle when array error exists

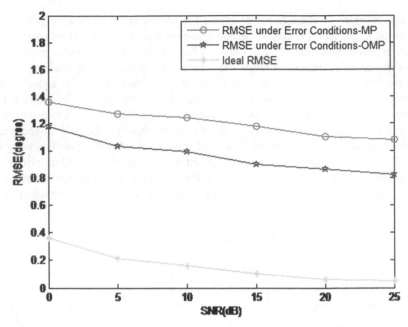

Fig. 4. Relationships between the mean square error of the angle and the signal to noise ratio

5 Conclusion

In this paper, a parameter estimation algorithm for MIMO radar based on the OMP algorithm is proposed. The effects of the array error on the parameter estimation based on the OMP algorithm are studied. Through the above simulations, it is found that the amplitude and phase error of the array error affects the MIMO radar received signal model. At this time, when the parameters are estimated by the OMP algorithm, the accuracy of the estimation is reduced both in the reflection amplitude of the target and in the parameters of the target. But in this case, the OMP algorithm is still better than the COSAMP algorithm in parameter estimation. In summary, the proposed algorithm has high accuracy in parameter estimation. Even when array error exists, the performance of the OMP algorithm in estimating the parameters of MIMO radar target's reflection amplitude, azimuth and elevation angle is better than that of the COSAMP algorithm.

References

1. Fannjiang, A.C.: The MUSIC algorithm for sparse objects: a compressed sensing analysis. Inverse Prob. **27**(3), 035013 (2011)
2. Chang, J., Fu, X., Jiang, W., Xie, M.: Micro-doppler parameter estimation method based on compressed sensing. J. Beijing Inst. Technol. **28**(02), 286–295 (2019)
3. Zhu, C., Zhang, N., Chen, Z., et al.: Parameter estimation for sparse targets in phased-MIMO radar. J. Eng. **2019**(19), 6196–6200 (2019)
4. Wu, H.: Research on Parameter Estimation of DCS-MIMO Radar. Nanjing University of Aeronautics and Astronautics, vol. 12 (2011)

5. Shi, G., Liu, D., Gao, D.: Compressed sensing theory and its research progress. Electron. J. **37**(5), 1070–1081 (2009)
6. Yu, Y., Petropulu, A.P., Poor, H.V.: MIMO radar using compressing sampling. IEEE J. Sel. Topics Signal Process. **4**(1), 146–163 (2010)
7. Yu, Y., Petropulu, A.P., Poor, H.V.: Compressed sensing for MIMO radar. In: IEEE International Conference on Acoustics, Speech and Signal Processing, Taipei, Taiwan, pp. 3017–3020, April 2009
8. He, Y., Wang, K., Zhang, J.: Pseudo-random polyphase code continuous wave radar based on compressed sensing. J. Electron. Inf. **33**(2), 418–423 (2011)
9. Weiss, A.J., Friedlander, B.: Effects of modeling errors on the resolution threshold of the the MUSIC algorithm. IEEE Trans. Signal Process. **42**(6), 1519–1526 (1994)
10. Fitas, N., Manikas, A.: A new general global array calibration method. In: Proceeding of IEEE ICASSP, pp. 73–76 (1994)
11. Fu, W., Jiang, T.: A parameter estimation algorithm for multiple frequency-hopping signals based on compressed sensing. Phys Commun. **37**, 100892 (2019)
12. Lu, D., Sun, G., Li, Z., et al.: Improved CoSaMP reconstruction algorithm based on residual update. J. Comput. Commun. **7**(6), 6–14 (2019)

Time-Division Frequency Measurement and Localization Technology of Single-Satellite in Different Orbits Based on Optimal Observation Position

Hui Ji, Dexin Qu[✉], and Gengxin Zhang

"Telecommunication and Network" National Engineering Research Center, Nanjing University of Posts and Telecommunications, Nanjing 210003, China
qdx@njupt.edu.cn

Abstract. At present, the research on the single satellite frequency measurement and localization technology mainly focuses on the use of multiple satellite observation positions in a single flight orbit to forward the ground target source signals, but there are many limitations in locating the interference source with limited field of view. In this paper, based on the single-orbit single-satellite time-division frequency-measuring localization technology, a localization technology of single-satellite time-division Doppler frequency measurement in different orbits is proposed, which is based on the optimal observation satellite position. Firstly, the positioning model and the positioning equation of the single-satellite time-division Doppler frequency measurement and localization technology in different orbits are constructed. Secondly, a calculation formula for Geometric Dilution of Precision (GDOP) is derived and the optimal model of the observation satellite position is constructed. Finally, based on the positioning process, the minimum positioning error is targeted. Computer simulation results show that the availability and accuracy of the technique are improved significantly in the scene with limited field of view.

Keywords: Single-satellite passive localization · Doppler frequency · GDOP · Position optimization

1 Introduction

As a strong supplement to the ground communication system, satellite communication has been widely used because of its wide coverage and long communication distance. However, in the face of the influence of electromagnetic radiation in the environment, satellite communication will be interfered in the course of work, which makes the communication quality difficult to guarantee, and causes different degrees of influence and economic loss [1]. Therefore, how to accurately find the location of interference source has become an urgent problem in engineering [2, 3].

At present, satellite passive localization technology can rapidly locate the transmitted signals of sea, land and air targets because of its large localization area, good conceal- ment and low interception rate, it plays an important role and has a broad application prospect in both civil and military fields [4, 5]. A method of instantaneous Doppler fre- quency difference passive location is proposed in reference [6]. This method requires the interference source and ground observation stations to see several satellites at the same time. However, the probability of instantaneous multi-satellite visibility is not studied in this paper. If the field of view is limited, the usability of this method is very low. The single-satellite multi-beam localization technology proposed in reference [7, 8] and the single-satellite direction finding and localization technology proposed in reference [9]. They require obtain the Direction of Arrival (DOA) or amplitude of the source sig- nal, and the antenna structure is complex and high cost. The single-orbit single-satellite time-division frequency measurement and localization technology is proposed in refer- ence [10], which can solve the problem of multi-satellite localization being unable to see multi-satellite instantaneously and low positioning availability. However, the positioning error of this method is large in the scene with limited field of view.

In order to solve the problem of low probability and large positioning error under the condition of limited field of view, this paper presents a single-satellite time-division fre- quency measurement and localization technique in different orbits based on the optimal observation position. By constructing the positioning model of single-satellite time- division frequency measurement and localization technology in different orbits, the positioning equation and the calculation formula of geometric dilution accuracy fac- tor are derived, and the optimal positioning model and positioning steps are designed. Aiming at the minimum positioning error, the optimal observation position is obtained to locate the interference source in the scene with limited field of view.

The rest of this paper is organized as follows. In Sect. 2, the positioning model of the technology is presented. The positioning equation and the GDOP formula are derived, and the optimal model of the observation position is established. In Sect. 3, the positioning step of the technology is designed. The simulation results are shown in Sect. 4. Finally, the conclusions are given in Sect. 5.

2 Introduction to Localization Technology

2.1 Positioning Model and Positioning Equation

The single-satellite time-division Doppler frequency measurement and localization tech- nology in different orbits is based on the single-orbit single-satellite time-division fre- quency measurement and localization technology. The difference between the transmit- ted signals received by the same ground station with different Doppler frequency is called Frequency Difference Of Arrival (FDOA). The position of the target is calculated by using the relation between the frequency difference of Doppler's arrival.

The medium-low orbit satellite is far from the earth, so the satellite and the radiation source can be regarded as the particle motion analysis approximately. Figure 1 is a positioning model for single-satellite time-division Doppler frequency measurement and localization technology in different orbits. Suppose that the position of an active geostationary interference source in Earth Centered Earth Fixed (ECEF) is $\mathbf{s} = \begin{bmatrix} x & y & z \end{bmatrix}^{\mathrm{T}}$. The satellites with different orbits fly over the region of visibility at different time intervals, and the observation position at t_j is $\mathbf{s}_{ij} = \begin{bmatrix} x_{ij} & y_{ij} & z_{ij} \end{bmatrix}^{\mathrm{T}}$. The speed of this satellite is $\mathbf{v}_{ij} = \begin{bmatrix} v_{x_{ij}} & v_{y_{ij}} & v_{z_{ij}} \end{bmatrix}^{\mathrm{T}}$, where i is the number of the observing satellite's orbit l_i, where $i \in N^+$, j represents the time interval between the observation time t_j of the observing satellite in orbit l_i and the initial time t_0 of the satellite's entry into the visible region, where $j \in N$.

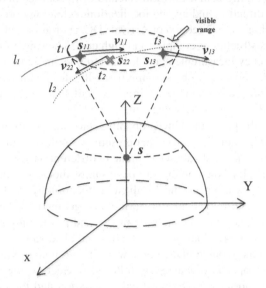

Fig. 1. Positioning model

Assuming that the Doppler frequency measured by observation satellite at different times in different orbits is f_{ij}, and the frequency of the radiation source is known as f_c, the measurement equation is

$$f_{ij} = f_c + \frac{f_c}{c} \cdot \dot{v}_{ij} \tag{1}$$

In the formula, $\dot{v}_{ij} = \left[(x_{ij} - x)v_{x_{ij}} + (y_{ij} - y)v_{y_{ij}} + (z_{ij} - z)v_{z_{ij}} \right]/r_{ij}$ represents the radial velocity of the satellite and the target; $r_{ij} = \sqrt{(x - x_{ij})^2 + (y - y_{ij})^2 + (z - z_{ij})^2}$ represents the relative position of a satellite to a target, where $i \in N^+, j \in N$, c represents the speed at which electromagnetic waves travel.

Taking into account the constraints of the Earth's surface, it is only necessary to obtain three different satellite observation positions are $\mathbf{s}_{\alpha m}, \mathbf{s}_{\beta n}, \mathbf{s}_{\gamma k}$, and corresponding velocities are $\mathbf{v}_{\alpha m}, \mathbf{v}_{\beta n}, \mathbf{v}_{\gamma k}$, as well as Doppler frequencies $f_{\alpha m}, f_{\beta n}, f_{\gamma k}$, which are observed at the corresponding time, where $\alpha, \beta, \gamma \in N^+$, $m, n, k \in N$. The geodetic coordinates of the interference source can be obtained.

$$
\begin{cases}
f_{\alpha m} - f_{\beta n} = \dfrac{f_c}{c} \cdot \left(\dot{v}_{\alpha m} - \dot{v}_{\beta n} \right) \\[2mm]
f_{\alpha n} - f_{\gamma k} = \dfrac{f_c}{c} \cdot \left(\dot{v}_{\alpha m} - \dot{v}_{\gamma k} \right) \\[2mm]
x^2 + y^2 + \dfrac{z^2}{\left(1 - e^2 \right)} = a^2
\end{cases}
\tag{2}
$$

where a is the radius of the earth and e is the first eccentricity of the earth.

2.2 Optimal Model of Observation Satellite Position

Due to the gradual improvement of the satellite system, the number of available satellites is increasing, and the selection of observation positions is becoming more and more complicated. Random selection of satellite observation position will make the positioning effect is not ideal. It is necessary to minimize the location error of the target source by optimizing the selection of observation satellites and their observation positions in different orbits. The optimization objective function can be expressed as

$$
P\left(\left[l_i, s_{ij} \right] \right) = \underset{\left(l_i, s_{ij} \right)}{\text{Min}} \, \| \text{GDOP}(x,y,z) \|
\tag{3}
$$

In the formula, l_i represents the different satellite orbits, i represents the number of orbit, where $i \in N^+$, s_{ij} is the satellite observation position at t_j time on the corresponding orbit l_i. GDOP(x,y,z) is the geometric dilution accuracy factor at the target source s, where $s = \begin{bmatrix} x & y & z \end{bmatrix}^{\text{T}}$, it can be expressed as

$$
\text{GDOP}(x, y, z) = \sqrt{\text{tr}(\boldsymbol{P}_{dX})}
\tag{4}
$$

where P_{dX} is the positioning error covariance matrix, which can be derived from the total differential set of positioning Eq. 5 below.

The positions of the observing satellite are $s_{\alpha m}$, $s_{\beta n}$, $s_{\gamma k}$, the velocities are $v_{\alpha m}$, $v_{\beta n}$, $v_{\gamma k}$, where $\alpha, \beta, \gamma \in N^+$, $m, n, k \in N$, the position of the interference source is $s = \begin{bmatrix} x & y & z \end{bmatrix}^{\text{T}}$, the joint surface equation can be written as

$$
\begin{cases}
f_{\alpha m} = f_c + \frac{f_c}{c} \dot{v}_{\alpha m} = g_1(x, y, z) \\[1mm]
f_{\beta n} = f_c + \frac{f_c}{c} \dot{v}_{\beta n} = g_2(x, y, z) \\[1mm]
f_{\gamma k} = f_c + \frac{f_c}{c} \dot{v}_{\gamma k} = g_3(x, y, z) \\[1mm]
H = \left[\left(1 - e^2 \right) \left(x^2 + y^2 \right) + z^2 \right]^{1/2} - a = g_4(x, y, z)
\end{cases}
\tag{5}
$$

After the total differential, the positioning error is covariance matrix $P_{dX} = \text{E}\left[dX dX^{\text{T}} \right]$, where $dX = \begin{bmatrix} dx & dy & dz \end{bmatrix}^{\text{T}}$. The frequency difference and elevation error is covariance matrix $R_{fH} = \text{E}\left[dU dU^{\text{T}} \right]$, where $dU = \begin{bmatrix} df_{\alpha m} & df_{\beta n} & df_{\gamma k} & dH \end{bmatrix}^{\text{T}}$. The satellite positioning error is covariance matrix $R_{X_{ij}} = \text{E}\left[dX_{ij} dX_{ij}^{\text{T}} \right]$, where $dX_{ij} = $

$[dx_{ij} \ dy_{ij} \ dz_{ij}]^{\mathrm{T}}$. The satellite velocity error is covariance matrix $R_{V_{ij}} = \mathrm{E}\left[dV_{ij}dV_{ij}^{\mathrm{T}}\right]$, where $dV_{ij} = \left[dv_{x_{ij}} \ dv_{y_{ij}} \ dv_{z_{ij}}\right]^{\mathrm{T}}, i = \alpha, j = \mathrm{m}; i=\beta, j = \mathrm{n}; i = \gamma, j = \mathrm{k}$.

The positioning error covariance matrix can be expressed as

$$
P_{dX} = \mathrm{E}\left[dXdX^{\mathrm{T}}\right] = C^{-1}\left(R_{fH} + \sum_{\substack{i=\alpha, j=m; \\ i=\beta, j=n; \\ i=\gamma, j=k;}} C_{X_{ij}} R_{X_{ij}} C_{X_{ij}}^{T} + \sum_{\substack{i=\alpha, j=m; \\ i=\beta, j=n; \\ i=\gamma, j=k;}} C_{V_{ij}} R_{V_{ij}} C_{V_{ij}}^{T} \right) C^{-T} \quad (6)
$$

where $C = \frac{\partial g(s)}{\partial s}$, $C_{X_{\alpha m}} = \frac{\partial g(s)}{\partial s_{\alpha m}}$, $C_{X_{\beta n}} = \frac{\partial g(s)}{\partial s_{\beta n}}$, $C_{X_{\gamma k}} = \frac{\partial g(s)}{\partial s_{\gamma k}}$, $C_{V_{\alpha m}} = \frac{\partial g(s)}{\partial v_{\alpha m}}$, $C_{V_{\beta n}} = \frac{\partial g(s)}{\partial v_{\beta n}}$, $C_{V_{\gamma k}} = \frac{\partial g(s)}{\partial v_{\gamma k}}$, $g(s) = [g_1 \ g_2 \ g_3 \ g_4]^{\mathrm{T}}$.

3   Positioning Process Steps

Through the discussion in Sect. 2, the principle of the technology in this paper has been clarified. When the position of the target source and the lowest visible elevation angle are known, in order to obtain the minimum positioning error corresponding to the optimal observed position, the specific positioning process is as follows:

- Step1: The number of satellites visible to the interference source is N. Obtain the corresponding orbit l_i, the initial time t_0, the flight duration M and the ephemeris data of each satellite.
- Step2: Acquire the selection scheme of observation satellite position. Select two of the N satellites in different orbits as observation satellites. There are C_N^2 selection schemes. The observation interval of each observation satellite is 1 s. If the satellite that needs to acquire two observation positions is the observation main satellite, there are C_{M+1}^2 options for selecting two different observation positions on the observation main satellite and C_{M+1}^1 options for acquiring one observation position on the other observation satellite, a total of $C_N^2 \cdot C_{M+1}^2 \cdot C_{M+1}^1$ observation satellites position selection scheme.
- Step3: Acquire the position and instantaneous velocity of the observation satellite corresponding to each selection scheme, and calculate the observation frequency of each scheme by Eq. 1.
- Step4: Calculate the GDOP of each selection scheme by Eq. 4, Eq. 5 and Eq. 6. Select the minimum value of GDOP at the position of the target source according to the optimal model of the observation position selection. Obtain the optimal observation position and the minimum positioning error of the technology in this paper.

Through the above four steps, the minimum positioning error and the optimal satellite observation position can be obtained by the technology in this paper under the condition of the target source field of view limited. The simulation results and analysis of target source localization using the above method and process will be described in the next section.

4   Simulation Results and Analysis

4.1   Availability Analysis

The minimum elevation angle of the user is 71.57 if the depth of the deep well is 3 m and the diameter of the deep well is 1 m. Taking the four navigation satellite systems as an example, the number of visible satellites under the condition of the target source field of view limited is analyzed using Satellite Tool Kit (STK) software. The global coverage of the four satellite navigation systems by three satellites is shown in Fig. 2, and the global coverage of the four satellite navigation systems by single satellite is shown in Fig. 3. Different colors represent the percentage of visible time of day. Figure 2 shows that in a positioning scenario with a minimum elevation of 71.57, the percentage of a day in which three satellites share a common view instantaneously is less than 40% in most parts of the world. Therefore, the availability of instantaneous three satellites localization method proposed in reference [6] is very low. Figure 3 shows that in the positioning scenario with a minimum elevation of 71.57, the percentage of visible time of single satellite in a day is significantly increased, reaching 100% in some areas. The availability of single-satellite time-division frequency measurement technology is significantly improved compared with instantaneous multi-satellite positioning.

Fig. 2. Global three-satellite coverage of four satellite navigation systems

However, reference [11] shows that the positioning effect of single-orbit single-satellite time-division frequency measurement technology is affected by the frequency

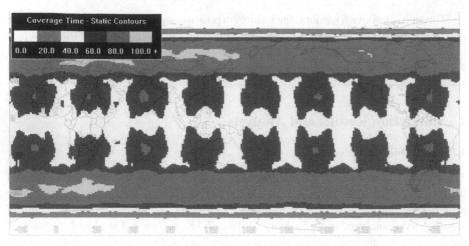

Fig. 3. Global single-satellite coverage of four satellite navigation systems

measurement interval, and the short frequency measurement interval will result in large positioning error. If the target source is located in the flight path of the observation satellite, the positioning error will be further increased. The time-division frequency measurement technique of single satellite in different orbits makes use of the single satellite flying through the visible region at different times to carry out independent observations of the same target source. The time interval between two adjacent frequency measurements is enlarged to improve the positioning accuracy. At the same time, because of the different flight direction and the distribution of sub-satellite points, the observation position selection of different orbits is more flexible.

4.2   Error Analysis

Simulation Parameter Setting
In this paper, the beidou navigation system is used for simulation. The initial time is 29 Nov 2018 21:00:00 (UTCG) and the end time is 29 Nov 2018 22:00:00 (UTCG).STK simulation software is used to obtain the ephemeris data of BeiDou Navigation Satellite System (BDS). If the target source is located in Nanjing (119 E, 32 N, elevation 0 km) and the lowest elevation angle of the user is 45, three satellites will pass through the target source's visible range, namely No. 11, No. 27 and No. 28. The sub-satellite orbits of the three satellites at the global scale are shown in Fig. 4, the sub-satellite orbits of the satellites within the visual range of the target source are shown in Fig. 4. The orbital parameters are shown in Table 1, and during the set time period, all three satellites have 60 min visual time in the target source's visual region (Fig. 5).

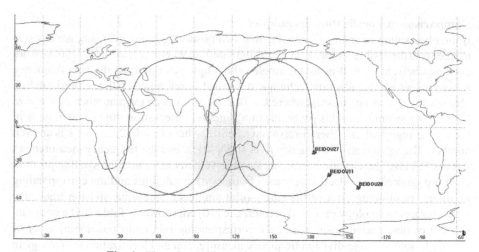

Fig. 4. The sub-satellite orbits of observation satellites

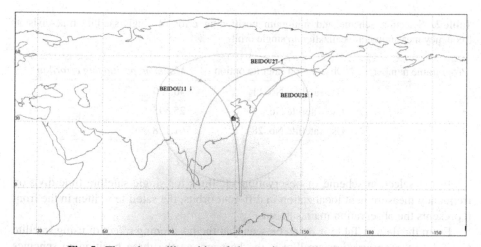

Fig. 5. The sub-satellite orbits of observation satellites in visible region

Table 1. Orbital parameters of satellites

Satellite number	Semi-major axis/km	Eccentricity	Inclination angle/°	Argument of the perigee/°	RAAN/°	True anomaly/°
11	21500	0	55	0	0	0
27	21500	0	55	0	120	253.333
28	21500	0	55	0	120	293.333

Comparison of Localization Techniques

If the observation interval is 2 min, the first two observing moments t_m, t_n are any two moments in the visible region of an observing satellite, where m, $n = 0, 2, \ldots, 60$, m, n are even numbers, $m \neq n$. If using the single-orbit single-satellite time-division frequency measurement and localization technique described in reference [10], the third satellite observation time is any time t_k, where $k = 0, 2, \ldots, 60$, k is an even number, $k \neq m \neq n$. If using the technique in this paper, the third satellite observation time is any time t_k in the visible region of the other observation satellite, where $k = 0, 2, \ldots, 60$, k is an even number. The signal carrier frequency f_c is 406.8 MHz, and the frequency measurement error is 0.2 Hz. The elevation error, the satellite velocity error and the satellite position error are ignored, the selection scheme of observation satellites and the corresponding minimum positioning error of the single-orbit single-satellite time-division frequency measurement technology proposed in reference [10] are shown in Table 2. The optimum scheme of observation position and the corresponding minimum positioning error of the single-satellite time-division frequency measurement and localization technology in different orbits are shown in Table 3.

Table 2. Selection scheme and minimum positioning error of single-satellite time-division frequency measurement localization in single orbit

Programme number	Observation satellite option	*Minimum positioning error*/km
1	Use satellite No. 11	40.550
2	Use satellite No. 27	25.595
3	Use satellite No. 28	61.128

In the selection scheme of observation satellites for single-satellite time-division frequency measurement localization in different orbits, the satellite written in the front represents the observation main satellite.

From the data in Table 2, it can be seen that the positioning effect of using satellite No. 27 as the observation satellite is the best among the three positioning schemes using the single-orbit single-satellite time-division frequency measurement localization technology proposed in reference [10]. The minimum positioning error is 25.595 km, and the positioning effect is not ideal.

From the data in Table 3, it can be seen that the minimum positioning error of all the observation satellite selection schemes using single-satellite time-division frequency measurement and localization technology in different orbits is obviously lower than that of single orbit positioning scheme, the positioning accuracy is greatly improved.

Suppose the first two satellite observation time t_m, t_n are t_0 and t_m. Figure 6 is a comparison of single-satellite time-division frequency measurement and localization schemes between single orbit and different orbits. The positioning effects are compared with the third satellite observation time t_k, where k is the time interval between t_k and t_0, and the programme numbers in the figure are those of the corresponding observation satellite options in Tables 2 and 3.

Table 3. Optimal observation satellite position scheme and its minimum positioning error for single-satellite time-division frequency measurement localization in different orbits

Programme number	Observation satellite option	The time of the observation satellite's position	*Minimum positioning error*/km
1	Use satellites No. 11 and No. 27	The observation time of satellite No. 11 is t_0 and t_M; the observation time of satellite No. 27 is t_M	5.3165
2	Use satellites No. 11 and No. 28	The observation time of satellite No. 11 is $t_{M/2}$, and t_M; the observation time of satellite No. 28 is t_M	6.0549
3	Use satellites No. 27 and No. 11	The observation time of satellite No. 27 is t_0, and t_M; the observation time of satellite No. 11 is t_M	5.0673
4	Use satellites No. 27 and No. 28	The observation time of satellite No. 27 is t_0, and t_M; the observation time of satellite No. 28 is t_M	6.0026
5	Use satellites No. 28 and No. 11	The observation time of satellite No. 28 is $t_{M/2}$, and t_M; the observation time of satellite No. 11 is t_M	7.0755
6	Use satellites No. 28 and No. 27	The observation time of satellite No. 28 is t_0, and t_M; the observation time of satellite No. 27 is t_M	7.6542

From the (a), (b), (c) of Fig. 6, it can be seen that the positioning accuracy can be improved by the introduction of another orbit, and the positioning error is stable. At the same time, the selection of satellite observation time is flexible. The simulation results show that the positioning accuracy is improved by 80.2% compared with the traditional satellite localization technology in single orbit, which can be effectively located by using the single-satellite time-division frequency measurement and localization technology in different orbits based on the optimal observation satellite position under the condition of limited view field.

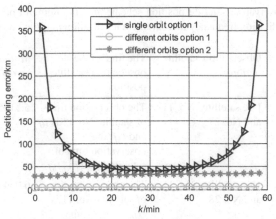

(a) The observation main satellite is satellite No.11

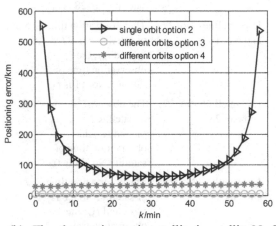

(b) The observation main satellite is satellite No.27

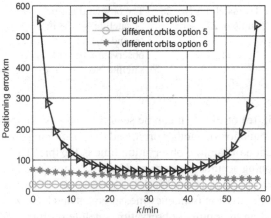

(c) The observation main satellite is satellite No.28

Fig. 6. Comparison of different positioning methods

5 Conclusion

This paper is based on the technology of single-orbit single-satellite time-division frequency measurement and localization. Aiming at the problems of low success rate of multi-satellite localization and poor effect of single-satellite localization in single orbit with limited field of view, a single-satellite time-division frequency measurement and localization technique in different orbits based on the optimal observation position is proposed. Compared with the instantaneous three-satellite localization technology, the positioning accuracy is high and the positioning effect is stable. By comparing the influence of the satellite observation position in different orbits and at different observation times on the positioning accuracy, the selection scheme of the observation satellite is optimized. At the same time, the positioning accuracy of the single-satellite time-division frequency measurement and localization technology in different orbits is significantly improved. It is valuable for the design and application of the localization system in the scene with limited field of view.

Acknowledgement. The work presented in this paper is partially supported by the National Science Foundation of China (No. 91738201).

References

1. Gou, X., Du, P.: Anti-interference technology of satellite communication and its development trend. Commun. World (03), 71–72 (2018)
2. Liu, A., Yuan, L.: Performance analysis of interference location based on Doppler frequency shift of a single satellite. Dig. Commun. World **S2**(10), 80–83 (2013)
3. Hao, B., An, D., Wang, L., et al.: A new passive localization method of the interference source for satellite communications. In: 9th International Conference on Wireless Communications and Signal Processing (WCSP), Nanjing, pp. 1-6 (2017)
4. Huang, J., Zhao, W., Chen, X., et al.: A new passive locating algorithm based on single satellite frequency measurements. Chin. Space Sci. Technol. **39**(04), 11–17 (2019)
5. Wang, D., Wei, S., Wu, Y.: A performance analysis of multi-satellite joint Geolocation. Front. Inf. Technol. Electr. Eng. **17**(12), 1360–1388 (2016)
6. Xu, H., Lu, S., Han, T.: Doppler frequency difference based three-satellite passive algorithm and its precision analysis. J. Astronaut. **31**(07), 1832–1837 (2010)
7. Zhao, F., Zhao, L., Jiang, Y., et al.: Single-satellite multi-beam antenna interference source localization based on frequency reuse. J. Nanjing Univ. Posts Telecommun. (Nat. Sci. Ed.) **39**(02), 41–48 (2019)
8. Zhong, X., Yao, K., Xie, Z., et al.: The method of interference source locating based on multi-beam antenna and analysis of locating accuracy. In: 6th International Conference on Electronics Information and Emergency Communication (ICEIEC), Beijing, pp. 301–305 (2016)
9. Gong, W., Xie, K., Feng, D., et al.: Method and precision analysis of direction-finding and position based on satellites passive location system. J. Electr. Power Sci. Technol. **19**(2), 64–67 (2004)
10. Jiang, D., Xie, D.: Principle and Simulation of single satellite frequency difference passive positioning technology. Ship ECM **40**(02), 16–22 (2017)
11. Pan, L., Li, H.: Single satellite Doppler frequency measurement and location technology based on WGS-84 ellipsoid earth model. Shipboard Electr. Countermeasure **36**(03), 17–21 (2013)

On the Impact of Intrinsic Delay Variation Sources on Iridium LEO Constellation

Amal Boubaker[1,2]([✉]) [iD], Emmanuel Chaput[1], Nicolas Kuhn[3] [iD],
Jean-Baptiste Dupé[3] [iD], Renaud Sallantin[4] [iD], Cédric Baudoin[4],
and André-Luc Beylot[1] [iD]

[1] IRIT Lab, University of Toulouse, Toulouse, France
boubakeramal@gmail.com
[2] TéSA, Telecommunications for Space and Aeronautics, Toulouse, France
[3] Centre National d'Etudes Spatiales (CNES), Toulouse, France
[4] Thales Alenia Space (TAS), Toulouse, France

Abstract. The recent decades have seen an increasing interest in Medium Earth Orbit and Low Earth Orbit satellite constellations. However, there is little information on the delay variation characteristics of these systems and the resulting impact on high layer protocols. To fill this gap, this paper simulates a constellation that exhibits the same delay characteristics as the already deployed Iridium but considers closer bandwidths to constellation projects'.

We identify five major sources of delay variation in polar satellite constellations with different occurrence rates: elevation, intra-orbital handover, inter-orbital handover, orbital `seam` handover and Inter-Satellite Link changes. We simulate file transfers of different sizes to assess the impact of each of these delay variations on the file transfer.

We conclude that the orbital `seam` is the less frequent source of delay and induces a larger impact on a small file transfers: the orbital `seam`, which occurs at most three times during 24 h, induces a 66% increase of the time needed to transmit a small file. Inter-orbital and intra-orbital handovers occur less often and reduce the throughput by approximately ∼8% for both low and high throughput configurations. The other sources of delay variations have a negligible impact on small file transfers, and long file transfers are not impacted much by the delay variations.

Keywords: Satellite constellations · Iridium constellation · CUBIC TCP · Handovers

1 Introduction

Nowadays, satellite constellations have reemerged, due to the need for worldwide high-speed internet coverage that terrestrial solutions fail to deliver. Medium Earth Orbits (MEO) and Low Earth Orbits (LEO) constellations could efficiently

© ICST Institute for Computer Sciences, Social Informatics and Telecommunications Engineering 2021
Published by Springer Nature Switzerland AG 2021. All Rights Reserved
Q. Wu et al. (Eds.): WiSATS 2020, LNICST 357, pp. 206–226, 2021.
https://doi.org/10.1007/978-3-030-69069-4_18

complete their Geostationary Orbits (GEO) counterpart. Many satellite constellation projects are competing with Iridium LEO constellation. While Iridium offers low-speed data communications, constellation projects aim at increasing the throughput provided to the end user (*e.g.*, for collective terminal services).

We provide in this paper a large overview of the constellation projects. They can mainly be divided into two main families: the systems that exploit Inter-Satellite Links (ISLs) (such as Telesat or Starlink) and those who do not (such as OneWeb). Indeed, introducing ISLs enhances the coverage, reduces latency and limits the size of the ground segment. However, this can result in delay variation, which needs to be analysed and whose impact on transport layer needs to be assessed.

The aim of the paper is thus to determine to which extent delay variations caused by the intrinsic characteristics of the satellite constellation topology would affect the performances of CUBIC TCP algorithm, taking Iridium as a representative topology. The contributions of this paper are the following:

- we identify five major sources of delay variation in polar satellite constellations with different ranges of occurrence: elevation, intra-orbital handover, inter-orbital handover, orbital **seam** handover and ISLs changes;
- we measure that the orbital **seam** is the less frequent source of delay and induces the larger impact on a small file transfer;
- we measure that other sources of delay variations have a negligible impact on small file transfers and low impact on long file transfers.

It is worth pointing out that some studies on the impact of the satellite constellations on TCP behaviour have been carried out in the past [25,28]. However, the decomposition of the delay variations into different sources and the impact of each of them on a TCP-based transfer is missing. Moreover, considering some recent evolutions of the TCP stack and the increased throughput offered by the satellite constellations, the conclusions of these papers may be reconsidered.

2   State of the Art of Satellite Constellations Projects

In this section, we present an overview of operating, in-development and satellite constellations, the motivation behind the choice of the Iridium constellation and the different sources of delay variations within the constellation.

2.1   Constellation Projects

The most important information about operating, in-development and upcoming satellite constellations that could come to fruition is outlined in the Table 1. Such systems were proposed mainly for telecommunication purposes, the particular application LEO or MEO constellations we are interested in.

So as we can deduce from the Table 1, by 2020 we would be able to see MEO, LEO to VLEO satellite constellations, from different companies. They are expected to deploy their fleet, mostly with ISLs thus offering more connectivity and mainly in the Ka band hence more usable frequencies and better satellite beams directivity. They should be then able to provide access to broadband services.

Among the existing satellite constellations presented in the Table, we have decided to focus on Iridium's. It is a LEO near-polar constellation, already deployed and has 4 ISLs, which we expect could be used as a representative constellation and would be generalized for the similar in-deployment and future projects.

We will now describe Iridium constellations, focusing on the properties that could jeopardise TCP performance.

2.2   Details on Iridium Satellite Constellation

In the Fig. 1, a scheme of the Iridium topology on an unprojected map, we can distinguish the 6 orbital planes, the 11 satellites per plane and 4 ISLs per satellite.

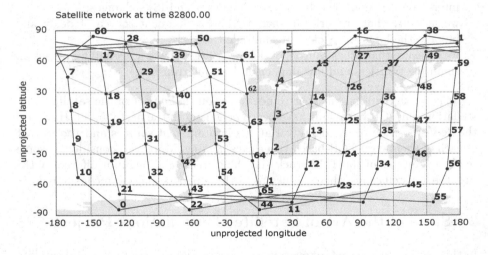

Fig. 1. A plot of Iridium's topology [27] (Color figure online)

An interesting aspect of polar or near-polar satellite constellations is the seam that we can see in the Fig. 2, which is the gap between the last plane of 'ascending' satellites (moving towards north pole) and the counter-rotating (or 'descending' moving away from north pole) satellites [29]. Thus the seam is where ascending and descending planes pass each other [5]. Typically, Iridium's satellites maintain 4 ISLs: 2 intra-plane (in black) in the Fig. 1 that are always maintained and 2 inter-plane intermittent links (in blue). However, the inter-plane links are deactivated close to the poles due to high-speed rotating satellites and on the seam because of counter-rotating overlapping satellites at high speed.

Table 1. Recent satellite constellations [1–4, 6–24]

Operating satellite constellations

Constellation	Operational in	Orbit	ISL	Band	Type of service	# of satellites	# of spots per satellite
- Iridium (Thales Alenia Space, Orbital ATK)	2018	LEO (near-polar 780 km)	4	- Ka (inter-satellite) - L (uplink and downlink)	Low-speed data communications	66 - 6 orbital plans - 11 /plane	- 48 Mobile Satellite Service (MSS) beams +2 (feeder links) - steerable
- O3B 1st Generation (Thales Alenia Space)	2014	MEO (8000 km)	—	Ka	Trunking (cruise ship)	20	- 10 beams /sat - 12 steerable antennas
- Globalstar 2nd Generation (Thales Alenia Space)	2010-2013	LEO (1414 km)	—	L-S-C	Satellite phone and low-speed data communications	24	- 16 spot beams /sat - fixed spot beam

In-development satellite constellations

Constellation	Operational in	Orbit	ISL	Band	Type of service	# of satellites	# of spots per satellite
- O3Bm (O3B 2nd Generation) (Boeing)	2021	MEO (8000 km)	None	Ka	Trunking (cruise ship)	7	4000+ beams /sat (30000 spot beams)

(*continued*)

Table 1. (*continued*)

In-development satellite constellations

	Operational in	Orbit	ISL	Band	Type of service	# of satellites	# of spots per satellite
- OneWeb (OneWeb, Airbus, Virgin)	2020	LEO (1200 km)	None	- Ku (sat user link) - Ka (sat gateway link)	Broadband	- 720 - 18 near-polar orbital planes	- 16 user beams - non-steerable

Upcoming satellite constellations

Constellation	Operational in	Orbit	ISL	Band	Type of service	# of satellites	# of spots per satellite
- Starlink (SpaceX)	2024	2 sub-constellations: - VLEO (335.9-345.6 km) - LEO (1110-1325 km)	—	V	Broadband	- VLEO : 7518 sats - LEO : 4425 sats	- Steerable (phased array)
- Boeing (Boeing Satellite)	2022	LEO	None	V	Broadband	1396-2956	
- LeoSat (Thales Alenia Space)	2022	LEO (1400 km)	4	Ka	Fiber optic-cable-like	78-108	12 steerable spot beams
- Theia (Theia Holdings A, Inc.)	2022	MEO (sun-synchronous 800 km)	—	Ka	EESS (Earth Exploration Satellite Service)	120	
- Telesat Canada (Manufacturer To be defined)	2021	- LEO (polar 1000 km and inclined 1248 km)	max 4	Ka	Fiber optic-cable-like	- 117-512 (120 by 2021) - 6 polar planes: 12+/plane - 5 inclined planes: 9+/plane	45 (16+ steerable user beams & 2 steerable gateway beam)
- ViaSat (Viasat Inc.)	2020	MEO (polar 8200 km)	—	Ka	Broadband	24 (ViaSat 1 & 2) 8 planes	

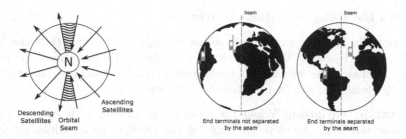

Fig. 2. Position of the orbital `seam` in polar or near-polar satellite constellations, particularly in Iridium and end terminals positions regarding the `seam`

The more ISLs there are, the more candidate routes are available, which introduces delay variations within the constellation. These delay variations have different sources that we will study further in the Subsect. 2.3.

Table 2. Iridium simulation parameters

Parameter	Value
Altitude	780 km
Planes	6
Satellites per plane	11
Inclination (deg)	86.4
Inter-plane separation (deg)	31.6
Seam separation (deg)	22
Intra-plane phasing	yes
Inter-plane phasing	yes
ISLs per satellite	4
Cross-seam ISLs	no

Satellites on both edges of the `seam` maintain two intra-plane links and only one inter-plane link. However, cross-`seam` links are a possible alternative to maintain the links through the `seam`, but for most of the polar or near-polar satellite constellations cross-seam links are turned off due to very large Doppler shifts and hand-offs have to happen more frequently and rapidly which might not allow the satellites to have a synchronized update on the state of the constellation and introduces further delay variation due to the variety and diversity of available paths within the constellation. In Iridium, cross-`seam` links are deactivated.

Table 2 sums up the main characteristics of the Iridium constellation.

2.3   On the Delay Variations in Iridium

LEO constellations are known to have lower propagation delay than the MEO or GEO ones. However, they are subject to higher delay variations due to the movement of satellites with respect to the ground terminal and the constellation's topology itself. This can be broken down into several factors [26]:

1. **Elevation variation:** When the satellite is moving with respect to the ground terminal, the elevation angle of the satellite varies which results in a variation of the ground terminal-satellite slant-range. Thus, resulting in the variation of the propagation delay. This variation could be calculated using a simplified scheme in the Fig. 3a Where :
   - O is the center of earth,
   - U is the position of the terminal on earth,
   - Sat_{min} is the position of the satellite in orbit for a minimum distance with the user on earth and d_{min} is the corresponding distance,
   - Sat_{max} is the position of the satellite in orbit for a maximum distance with the user on earth and d_{max} is the corresponding distance,
   - $\alpha = 8.2°$ is the elevation angle of the maximum distance position for Iridium,
   - and $\alpha = 90°$ is the elevation angle of the minimum distance position,
   - $R_e = 6371\,km$ is the earth's radius,
   - h = 780 km the altitude of the satellite,

   Thus, $d_{min} = h = 780\,km$ where the satellite's nadir point coincides with the user's position and with some trigonometric formulae we get $d_{max} = 2463\,km$. Hence, the propagation delay varies between [2, 6 ms; 8, 2 ms].
2. **Intra-orbital handover delay:** When the satellite drops below the elevation mask of the terminal, the connection is consequently handed over to the following satellite that could be in the same plane and that meets the criterion. For fixed communicating end terminals, this phenomenon occurs every ∼ 10 minutes for Iridium for it has 6 orbital planes and 11 satellites per orbital plane. This results in frequent delay variations.
3. **Inter-orbital handover delay:** The rotation of earth on its axis or the movement of the ground terminal along the longitude make that the coverage of the ground terminal is handed over from the current covering satellite to another one in the adjacent orbital plane. This handover results in a route change and therefore in a delay variation. For fixed communicating end terminals, the inter-orbital handover happens typically every ∼ 2 hours for Iridium.
4. **Seam handover delay:** A particularity of the polar or near-polar satellite constellations is that the satellites in the last and first orbital planes do not have any links with each one another. When satellites on both parts of the seam are sought, route changes occur *e.g.* typically the traffic is rerouted to the satellites that are over the pole. The separation by the seam of two fixed communicating end terminals happens at most three times and at least twice over 24 h, depending on their position with respect to the seam. As for the duration of this phase, it depends on the longitudinal separation of the communicating end terminals.

5. **ISLs changes delay:** For polar or near-polar satellite constellations, inter-orbital links are deactivated at the poles because of high-speed rotating satellites that cross one another. Which dictates rerouting accordingly and thus results in delay changes.

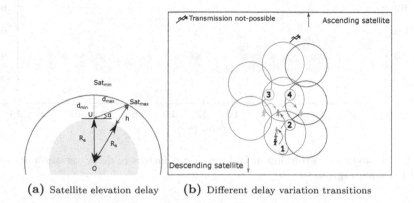

(a) Satellite elevation delay   (b) Different delay variation transitions

Fig. 3. Satellite elevation delay and different delay variations transitions

In the Fig. 3b, we can see the different transitions of 4 out of the 5 sources of delay variations with respect to earth's motion and satellite constellation's topology, for a fixed terminal denoted by a human figure here. The fifth one (ISLs changes) can not be depicted here.

Most of these causes in the satellite constellation have a detrimental impact on the delay variation. In the Fig. 4, the profile of the propagation delay of packets generated from a Constant Bit Rate (CBR) source is shown. The source is a terminal on a boat in the Atlantic Ocean to the destination is in London geographically. They are close enough to have a detailed look on the profile of the Iridium satellite constellation over 24 h based on the delay as a cost metric for route computation. We can clearly see the effect of delay variations in the constellation. The elevation, the intra-orbital handoffs, the inter plane handoffs and the **seam** delay variations, respectively noted by 1, 2, 3 and 4 on the Fig. 4 (and in the text above). Indeed, we can see that the observed values confirm what has been said earlier. Some delay variation factors are frequent but with a low magnitude, while others are less frequent but with more important magnitude. Ergo, TCP should be dealing with each of these different sources of delay variation differently. However, this figure can not show exactly the ISLs changes that are due to the satellites crossing one another in the poles. This delay variation is a result of the hop count change due to routing changes.

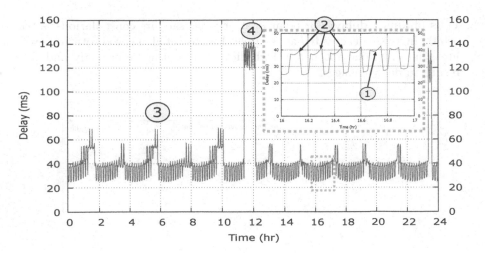

Fig. 4. One-way delay evolution in Iridium. Main factors of delay variation are numbered following Fig. 3

3   Experiment Test Architecture

This section details the characteristics of the experiments that are driven to evaluate the performance of TCP when it faces the delay variations that occur in Iridium.

3.1   Details on the TCP Stack and the Application Layer Data

- TCP stack: In this document, servers exploit CUBIC TCP (default congestion control algorithm in Linux and Windows systems) and clients use SACK with a 3-*Max SACK Blocks*.
- Application layer data: The impact of TCP performance in this context on the end user experience depends on the application that is carried out. In this paper, we consider file transfers of various sizes:
  - 9 kB file: this short file would fit in a 10-packet Initial Window;
  - 15 MB file: this larger file would let TCP get out of slow start;
  - unlimited-bulk file: this unlimited file would let us assess TCP behaviour in congestion avoidance phase.

These file sizes have been chosen in order to analyze the behaviour of TCP in various phases to better understand the impact of delay variations on its algorithm.

For this purpose, we will focus on three delay-sensitive metrics:

- file transfer time for a limited file size because from a *QoE* point of view it is the metric for which delay variation over the satellite constellation has a quantified impact from a user's perspective,
- *cwnd*

- and the instantaneous received throughput for unlimited file size, since it gives a more detailed and refined idea on the behaviour of TCP. In some cases, we also observe other relevant metrics, such as the congestion window or packet sequence number evolution.

3.2 Choice of Iridium Gateway

Assessing the performance when both the terminals' and the gateways' locations vary can make the analysis quite complex. Since several gateways are available, we had to appraise the relevance of choosing one satellite gateway for the rest of the paper.

We have run 50000 simulations. In each run, the terminal is given a random position and downloads at a random time a 9 kB file or a 15 MB file from one of the 7 Iridium gateways.

Figure 5 represents the transfer time for each of the 9 kB and the 15 MB files and for each Iridium gateway. The results illustrate that apart from maximum values that exhibit slight differences, the distribution of the transfer time is quite the same, whatever the position of the gateway.

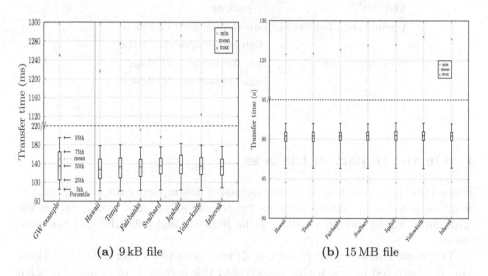

(a) 9 kB file   (b) 15 MB file

Fig. 5. Transfer time for random starting time and terminal positions

We concluded from the results presented in this section that the choice of the Iridium gateway does not matter much. The rest of this paper considers Iridium's gateway at Hawaii.

3.3 Summary of the Simulation Characteristics

The Table 3 sums up the basic characteristics used for all the experiments presented in this paper. Other parameters (simulation start time, file sizes or end terminals positions) will be detailed separately in each following section. Other parameters, related to Iridium, can be found in Table 2.

We define two set of bandwidths (low throughput and high throughput, where there is a factor of 80). Both configurations have been considered in the evaluations and a subset of the results is presented in this paper. In general, the rationale behind this choice is that we want to determine the impact of a constellation with ISLs on TCP and not restrict our conclusions to the sole Iridium.

Table 3. Iridium simulation parameters

Parameter	Value
Tool	NS-2.34
Iridium gateway	Hawaii
Model	Error-free
Cost metric	Hop count
Queue size	BDP
TCP	Sender: CUBIC - Receiver: SACK
TCP IW	10 packets
Up/downlink bandwidth	Low throughput: 1.5 Mbps
	High throughput: 120 Mbps
ISLs bandwidth	Low throughput: 25 Mbps
	High throughput: 2 Gbps

4   On the Impact of the seam

This section is thus dedicated to the analysis of the impact of the **seam** handover delay on a file transmission between two terminals. It also considers the low throughput configuration: results for the high throughput exhibited the same trend.

The **seam** handover delay (number 4) results in important delay variations. This is illustrated in Fig. 4. One objective of this section is to evaluate to what extend the **seam** handover delay is much of an issue for various file sizes.

4.1   On the Impact of the seam on 9 kB Flows

We have run several simulations of a 9 kB file transfer between two terminals: one is the Iridium gateway at Hawaii, which is considered to be the server. The other terminal, the client, is placed in 17 different cities that we chose scattered around the globe to be representative enough to conclude on the results. The starting time of the simulations is chosen randomly within two of the intervals: when the end terminals are not separated by the **seam** and when they are separated by the **seam**. The metric visualized in these simulations is the transfer time of the file, application layer point of view.

Figure 6 represents the time needed to transfer 9 kB for terminals located in different cities, whether they are separated by the **seam** or not. We can clearly see that the mean transfer time when the end terminals are separated by the **seam** is much more important than when they are not separated by the **seam**. For instance, if we take worst and best cases *i.e.* the cities for which the **seam** has had the least and the most impact on the mean transfer time *e.g.* for New Delhi it goes from 124 ms when the terminals are not separated by the **seam** to 144 ms when the terminals are separated by the **seam** which makes a 15.6% increase. However, for Los Angeles the mean transfer time goes from 90 ms when the terminals are not separated by the **seam** to 179 ms when the terminals are separated by the **seam** which makes a 98% increase.

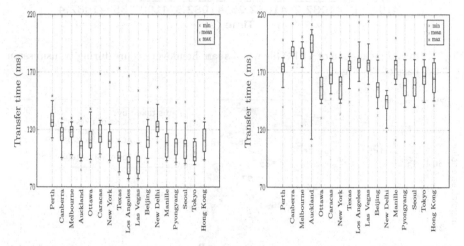

(a) Outside the **seam**, 9 kB file transfer   (b) Separated by the **seam**, 9 kB file transfer

Fig. 6. Transfer time simulations of a 9 kB file

In order to better understand how the **seam** impacts the 9 kB file transfer, we present in Fig. 7 different events for a source terminal on a boat in the Atlantic Ocean communicating to a destination end terminal in London. There are out-of-order ACKs which are due to the fact that the ACKs sent earlier have been through a longer route whereas the ones sent later have been through a shorter one. In the Fig. 8, we can see that ACKs of packets n°0 and n°1 have been through a 1-hop path, right before the two end terminals being separated by the **seam**. When the **seam** separated the end terminals, the ACKs of packets n°2-3 took an 11-hop path. And the ACKs of packets n°4 .. 9 took an 10-hop path.

As opposed to the results presented in Fig. 5, the results presented in Fig. 6 exhibit an important variation. This can be explained by the fact that the

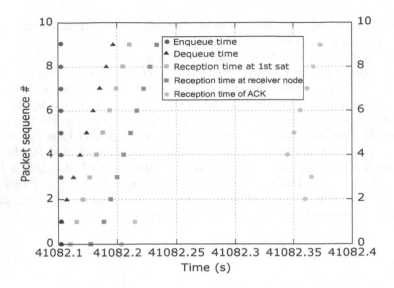

Fig. 7. Data transmission of a 9 kB file when **seam** handover occurs during transmission (4th use case of the Fig. 4)

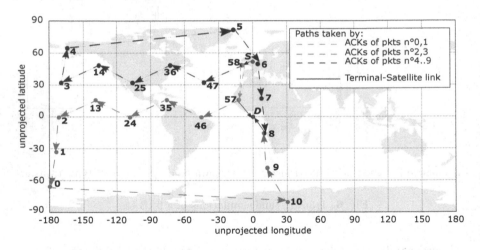

Fig. 8. Paths taken by ACKs of all the packets during a transmission of a 9 kB file when **seam** handover occurs during transmission (4th use case of the Fig. 4) [27]

terminals have random positions and the gateway has a fixed one in the Sect. 3.2 while the terminals and the gateway have fixed positions in this section.

This section has measured that, for a given satellite gateway and whatever the position of the satellite terminal, the **seam** has an important impact on small files transfers.

4.2   On the Impact of the seam on 15 MB Flows

This section focuses on the impact of the seam handover delay for the transmission 15 MB files. We have run several simulations of a 15 MB file transfer,
between two terminals: one is the Iridium gateway at Hawaii, which is considered to be the server, and the other terminal, the client, is placed in 17 different
cities. The starting time of the simulations is chosen randomly within two of
the intervals: when the end terminals are not separated by the seam and when
they are separated by the seam. The metric visualized in these simulations is the
transfer time of the file.

Figure 9 represents the time needed to transfer 15 MB for terminals located
in different cities, whether they are separated by the seam or not. There does not
seem to be any blatant difference between the values of the transfer time when
the end terminals are separated by the seam and when they are not-separated
by the seam.

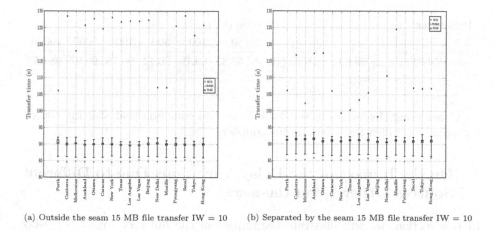

(a) Outside the seam 15 MB file transfer IW = 10   (b) Separated by the seam 15 MB file transfer IW = 10

Fig. 9. Transfer time simulations of a 15 MB file

4.3   Impact of the seam Handover Delay and File Size

Section 4.1 illustrated that the seam handover delay increases the transmission
time of a 9 kB in a non negligible manner. However, Sect. 4.2 illustrated that
this impact can be neglected when the file weighs 15 MB. This section aims at
determining to what extent the seam handover delay impacts a file transfer,
depending on the file size.

Table 4 gathers the Mean Transfer Time (MTT) for a file transfer between
one terminal located in Los Angeles and another located in Hawaii. $MTT_{no\ seam}$
means that the file transfer between the terminals is not affected by the seam
handover delay while it is the case for the MTT_{seam}. This table confirms the
conclusions that have been proposed in the beginning of this section.

Table 4. Mean Transfer Time (MTT) for a file transfer

Parameter	File size	
	9 kB file	15 MB file
$MTT_{no\ seam}$	90.35 ms	89.67 s
MTT_{seam}	179.43 ms	91.02 s
$MTT_{no\ seam}/MTT_{seam}$ (%)	50.35	98.52

We have run several simulations with different file sizes transferred from a server which is located near the Iridium gateway at Hawaii to a terminal client which is placed in 17 different cities. Table 5 presents the mean percentage values of the ratio of the $MTT_{no\ seam}$ and MTT_{seam}.

Table 5. Impact of the **seam** vs File sizes

Parameter	File size (kB)						
	25	50	100	500	1000	5000	10000
mean($MTT_{no\ seam}/MTT_{seam}$)(%)	59.38	59.35	69.79	90.71	96.78	99.97	98.55

Considering the values in the Table 5, we can conclude that starting 100 kB the **seam** has much less effect on file transfer.

5   On the Impact of the Delay Variations Due to Different Sources Other Than the **seam**

In this section, we will illustrate the impact of the different sources of delay variations of Iridium other than the **seam** on a TCP connection. We will also present the results for both low and high throughput configurations to illustrate the impact of the delay variation sources according to the values presented earlier in the Table 3.

5.1   Objective

We have seen that the variation of the delay in LEO constellations involve five phenomena that are unequally frequent, as detailed in the Sect. 2.3. After studying in detail the effect of the **seam**, we now want to see closely the effect of the pendulous behaviour of the other three causes of delay variation on TCP that we could simulate *i.e.* elevation variation denoted by 1, intra-orbital handover delay denoted by 2 and inter-orbital handover delay denoted by 3 on the Fig. 4.

5.2 Details of the Simulation

We have run a simulation for a non-stop CUBIC TCP source which is an end terminal on a boat in the Atlantic Ocean and a receiving terminal in London. The same couple of end terminals that we used in the Sect. 2.3, particularly the Fig. 4. The results shown here are during the steady phase *i.e.* after the slow-start during 51 min19 s starting 12 h21 min. The metrics visualized in this simulation are the *cwnd* and the instantaneous receiving throughput with a 1 second granularity.

The simulation set presented above are valid for both low and high throughput cases.

5.3 Results for the Low Throughput Configuration

On the Fig. 10, we have gathered the 3 different use cases of delay variation stated in the Subsect. 2.3.

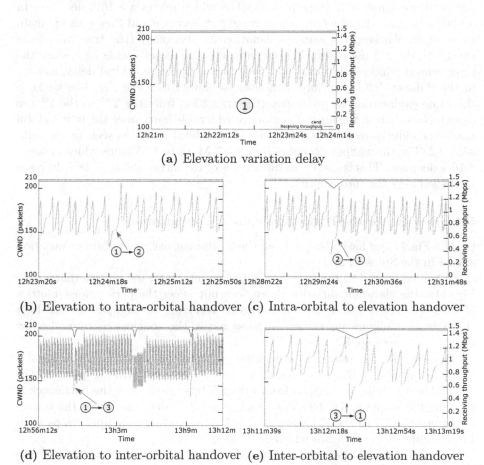

(a) Elevation variation delay

(b) Elevation to intra-orbital handover (c) Intra-orbital to elevation handover

(d) Elevation to inter-orbital handover (e) Inter-orbital to elevation handover

Fig. 10. Impact of different delay sources on *cwnd* and Receiving throughput for low throughput configuration

In the Fig. 10a, we can see that the elevation variation delay does not affect the performance metrics of TCP *i.e.* *cwnd* and the instantaneous receiving throughput. As explained in the Subsect. 2.3, the delay varies smoothly between [2.6 ms; 8.2 ms].

If we focus on the intra-orbital handovers (from the 1st to the 2nd use cases in Fig. 10b), there is not much impact on the throughput even if it impacts the *cwnd* evolution. Since the delay is increasing, then previously sent packets and *acks* take less time to be received which induces the sender in incrementing the *cwnd*. However, in the reverse transition (from the 2nd to the 1st in the Fig. 10c), previously sent packets and ACKs take more time than the ones freshly sent since the delay is decreasing, which results in a decreasing of the *cwnd*, thus the throughput drops from 1.47 Mbps (given that the bottleneck is fixed to 1.5 Mbps) to 1.36 Mbps which is a 7.48% decrease.

If we focus on the inter-handover delay (for the transition from the 1st to the 3rd use case in Fig. 10d), the delay variation has an impact on the throughput as it goes from 1.47 Mbps to 1.35 Mbps which makes a 8.16% decrease. In addition to that, the *cwnd* and the throughput decrease and then pick up again twice after. We keep the same explanation as previously (the transition from the 1st to the 2nd use cases). Yet, the impact is more noticeable here, since the inter-orbital handover induces more delay than the intra-orbital delay, as seen in the Subsect. 2.3. From inter-handover to elevation in the Fig. 10e, we keep the same explanation as previously (the transition from the 2nd to the 1st use cases). Nonetheless, the impact is more considerable here, since the inter-orbital handover induces more delay than the intra-orbital delay, as seen in the Subsect. 2.3. The throughput decreases from 1.47 Mbps to 1.35 Mbps which makes a 8.16% decrease. This is similar to the impact of the intra-orbital (7.48% decrease in the value of the throughput).

5.4   Results for the High Throughput Configuration

On the Fig. 11, we have also gathered the 3 different use cases of delay variation stated in the Subsect. 2.3.

When compared to the low throughput counterpart, we can see that in the Fig. 11a, the elevation variation delay does not affect the performance metrics of TCP (*i.e.* *cwnd*) and the instantaneous receiving throughput for the high throughput configuration either. In these cases, the conclusions from the low throughput cases apply.

However, for the intra-orbital handovers (transition from the 1st to the 2nd use-cases, in Fig. 11b), we notice an impact on both the throughput and the *cwnd*. The throughput dropped from 118.19 Mbps (given that the bottleneck is fixed to 120 Mbps) to 116.69 Mbps which is a 1.27% decrease. From the transition from the 1st to the 2nd use-cases, in Fig. 11c, the throughput drops from 118.18 Mbps to 111.98 Mbps which is a 5.25% decrease.

For the inter-handover transition, (transition from the 1st to the 3rd use case in Fig. 11d), we keep the same explanation as for the intra-orbital handover (transition from the 1st to the 2nd use cases). The impact is slightly more

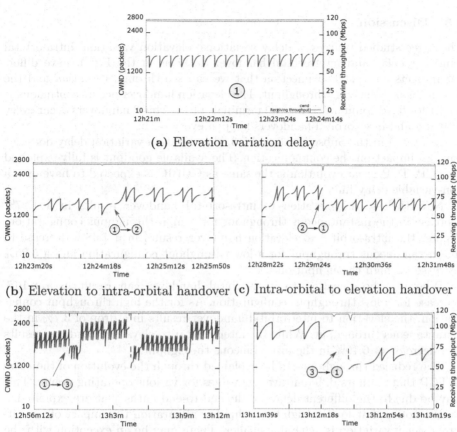

(a) Elevation variation delay

(b) Elevation to intra-orbital handover (c) Intra-orbital to elevation handover

(d) Elevation to inter-orbital handover (e) Inter-orbital to elevation handover

Fig. 11. Impact of different delay sources on *cwnd* and Receiving throughput for high throughput configuration

noticeable here, since the inter-orbital handover induces more delay than the intra-orbital delay, as seen in the Sect. 2.3. The 1 to 3 transition has an impact on the throughput as it goes from 118.18 Mbps to 113.81 Mbps which makes a 3.7% decrease. In addition to that, the *cwnd* and the throughput decrease and then pick up again several times after. For the inter-handover transition (transition from the 3rd to the 1st use case in Fig. 11e), we can notice that the first glitch corresponds to an elevation to intra-orbital handover (the transition from the 1st use case: the elevation, to the 2nd, as in the Fig. 11b). As for the second glitch, we keep the same explanation as previously (the transition from the 2nd to the 1st use cases). Nonetheless, the impact is more considerable here, since the inter-orbital handover induces more delay than the intra-orbital delay, as seen in the Subsect. 2.3. The throughput decreases from 118.19 Mbps to 110.88 Mbps which makes a 6.19% decrease.

5.5   Discussion

The three studied sources of delay variations, elevation variation, intra-orbital handover delay and inter-orbital handover delay as in the Fig. 4, have different impacts on a TCP connection that we can see through the *cwnd* and the instantaneous receiving throughput. The elevation handover occurs continuously, whilst for fixed communicating end terminals intra-orbital handovers occur every ~10 min and inter-orbital handovers happen every ~2 h.

As stated in the Subsect. 5.3 and 5.3, the elevation variation delay does not have an impact on the communication. The available goodput is fully exploited by TCP. TCP *cwnd* evolution is the same as CUBIC is expected to have over a non-variable delay link.

Nevertheless, the elevation to intra-orbital handover results in a 1.27% decrease in the instantaneous throughput for a high throughput configuration. Where, the intra-orbital to elevation handover results in a 7.48% decrease in the instantaneous throughput for a low throughout configuration and a 5.25% decrease for high throughput one.

Whereas, the elevation to inter-orbital handover can result in a 8.16% decrease for a low throughput configuration. As for the high throughput configuration, the elevation to inter-orbital handover results in a drop of 3.7% in the instantaneous throughput. While the inter-orbital to elevation handover results in a decrease of 6.19% in the instantaneous throughput.

The reduced throughput can be explained through the evolution of the *cwnd* of TCP that exhibits different average values for various operating points. This may be due to the different delays of the end-to-end paths that are exploited.

We notice that for the high throughput configuration the impact of the different delay variation is generally smaller. There may be an exception with the elevation to intra-orbital handover.

6   Conclusion

The recent decades have seen a boom in MEO/LEO satellite constellations for broadband purposes. That is why we examined the recent and deployed Iridium LEO satellite in this paper. In our work we focused on the impact of the constellation's topology dynamic on TCP from delay variation point of view. We have seen that there are 5 major sources of delay variation in polar satellite constellations: elevation, intra-orbital handover, inter-orbital handover, orbital seam handover and ISLs changes. All of our tests were conducted for only one single flow at a time to evaluate the impact of the intrinsic characteristics, *e.g.* delay variations induced by the satellite constellation topology on a TCP connection. The consequences of the constellation's behaviour on congestion deserves another in-depth study. We have seen that, using a recent TCP algorithm such as CUBIC TCP, during the orbital seam, which happens three times at most and at least twice during 24 h, the transfer time suffers a significant increase for small flows (66.6% mean), whereas for large flows it is marginal (1.47% mean increase).

As for the other sources of delay variation, we have seen that, through the *cwnd* and the instantaneous receiving throughput, the inter-orbital handover, happening typically every $\sim$ 2 hours, resulted in 8.16% decrease in the throughput from 1.47 Mbps to 1.35 Mbps. While in the high throughput configuration, the elevation to inter-orbital handover resulted in a 3.7% decrease in the throughput from 118.18 Mbps to 113.81 Mbps And the reverse handover resulted in a 6.19% drop in the throughput from 118.19 Mbps to 110.88 Mbps. Whilst the intra-orbital handover, occurring every $\sim$ 10 minutes, resulted in 7.48% decrease in the throughput from 1.47 Mbps to 1.36 Mbps, for a low throughput configuration. Whereas for a high throughput configuration, the elevation to intra-orbital handover resulted in a 1.27% decrease of the throughput from 118.19 Mbps to 116.69 Mbps, and the reverse transition resulted in a 5.25% drop from 118.18 Mbps to 111.98 Mbps. Unlike the elevation delay, which occurs continuously, that did not result in any change on the studied metrics for both of the low and high throughput configurations. These results could be extended to satellite constellations with similar characteristics.

The results that are shown in this paper illustrate that CUBIC TCP is not really impacted by the delay variations in a generic LEO satellite constellation. However, more recent TCP stack include reordering management based on delay variations. Future works include considering more complex stacks to confirm these trends and further confirm that TCP splitting mechanisms may not be needed for LEO constellations.

References

1. FCC NGSO constellations (2017). https://www.fcc.gov/document/cut-established-additional-ngso-satellite-applications
2. Globalstar 1st generation. http://space.skyrocket.de/doc_sdat/globalstar-2.htm. Accessed 12 Mar 2018
3. Globalstar 2nd generation. https://fr.slideshare.net/SambitShreeman/iridium-globalstar-ico-satellite-system. Accessed 12 Mar 2018
4. Globalstar 2nd generation. https://en.wikipedia.org/wiki/Globalstar. Accessed 12 Mar 2018
5. Introduction to satellite constellations. https://savi.sourceforge.io/about/lloyd-wood-isu-summer-06-constellations-talk.pdf. Accessed 15 Apr 2019
6. Iridium. https://en.wikipedia.org/wiki/Iridium_satellite_constellation#Next-generation_constellation. Accessed 06 Mar 2018
7. Iridium. http://www.argo.ucsd.edu/sat_comm_AST13.pdf. Accessed 06 Mar 2018
8. Iridium FCC (2013). http://licensing.fcc.gov/myibfs/download.do?attachment_key=1031348
9. Leosat. http://leosat.com/technology/. Accessed 06 Mar 2018
10. Leosat. http://leosat.com/media/1114/leosat-technical-overview.pdf. Accessed 06 Mar 2018
11. Leosat FCC (2017). http://licensing.fcc.gov/myibfs/download.do?attachment_key=1158225
12. O3b 1st generation. http://spaceflight101.com/ses-orders-super-powered-satellites-from-boeing-to-expand-o3b-broadband-services/. Accessed 06 Mar 2018

13. O3b 2nd generation. https://en.wikipedia.org/wiki/O3b_Networks. Accessed 06 Mar 2018
14. O3b 2nd generation. http://space.skyrocket.de/doc_sdat/o3b-21.htm. Accessed 06 Mar 2018
15. O3b 2nd generation. https://www.ses.com/networks/o3b-mpower. Accessed 06 Mar 2018
16. Oneweb. https://fr.wikipedia.org/wiki/OneWeb#Caract%C3%A9ristiques_techni ques. Accessed 06 Mar 2018
17. Oneweb FCC (2013). https://licensing.fcc.gov/myibfs/download.do?attachment_ key=1134939
18. Oneweb FCC fact sheet (2017). https://transition.fcc.gov/Daily_Releases/Daily_ Business/2017/db0601/DOC-345159A1.pdf
19. Satellite constellation. https://en.wikipedia.org/wiki/Satellite_constellation. Accessed 06 Mar 2018
20. Spacex FCC (2017). https://licensing.fcc.gov/myibfs/download.do?attachment_ key=1190019
21. Telesat. https://www.telesat.com/services/leo. Accessed 12 Mar 2018
22. Telesat. http://www.mit.edu/~portillo/files/Comparison-LEO-IAC-2018-slides. pdf. Accessed 21 Mar 2019
23. Theia. http://www.parabolicarc.com/tag/theia-holdings/. Accessed 12 Mar 2018
24. Viasat. https://www.viasat.com/news/going-global. Accessed 12 Mar 2018
25. Chotikapong, Y., Cruickshank, H., Sun, Z.: Evaluation of TCP and internet traffic via low earth orbit satellites. IEEE Personal Commun. 8(3), 28–34 (2001)
26. Goyal, R., Kota, S., Jain, R., Fahmy, S., Vandalore, B., Kallaus, J.: Analysis and simulation of delay and buffer requirements of satellite-ATM networks for TCP/IP traffic. arXiv preprint cs/9809052 (1998)
27. Henderson, T.R., Wood, L.: ns-2 satellite plot scripts (2000). https://savi. sourceforge.io/sat-plot-scripts/
28. Subramanian, S., Sivakumar, S., Phillips, W.J., Robertson, W.: Investigating TCP performance issues in satellite networks. In: 3rd Annual Communication Networks and Services Research Conference (CNSR 2005), pp. 327–332. IEEE (2005)
29. Wood, L.: Satellite Constellation Networks, pp. 13–34 (2003). https://doi.org/10. 1007/978-1-4615-0431-3_2

Research and Simulation of Rain Attenuation Time Series at Q/V Bands

Jiangtao Yang[1,2], Chen Zhang[1,2(✉)], Yonghua Huang[3], and Gengxin Zhang[1,2]

[1] College of Telecommunications and Information Engineering, Nanjing University of Posts and Telecommunications, Nanjing 210003, China
zhangchen@njupt.edu.cn
[2] National Engineering Research Center for Communication and Network Technology, Nanjing University of Posts and Telecommunications, Nanjing 210003, China
[3] CETC38 China Electronic Technology Group Corporation, Hefei 230088, China

Abstract. The design and optimization of fade mitigation techniques in Q/V bands satellite communications require rain attenuation time series. Methods for synthesizing short-term and long-term rain attenuation time series at Q/V bands are integrated in this paper. Firstly, based on the 'Event-on-Demand' model, the rain attenuation process is transformed into a first-order stationary Markov process after nonlinear transformation. The generation steps of short-term rain attenuation time series are analyzed. Then, the principle of Dirac-lognormal distribution model is analyzed, and the steps of generating long-term rainfall attenuation time series are given. Finally, the short-term and long-term rain attenuation time series at Q/V bands are obtained through simulation. The power spectrum estimation of the series shows the validity of the rain attenuation time series.

Keywords: Satellite communications · Q/V bands · Rain attenuation · Rain attenuation time series

1 Introduction

With the development of satellite communication and the increasing demand of users for data capacity, Q/V (33 GHz–75 GHz) bands satellite system has been paid more and more attention. However, when the frequency exceeds 30 GHz, there is severe rain attenuation in communications [1, 2]. In order to design the satellite communication system at Q/V bands, the traditional method of adding a static link margin in the system is no longer applicable, and the Fade Mitigation Technique (FMT) is needed [3]. The design and optimization of FMT requires a clear understanding of the time characteristics of rain attenuation. Propagation experiments to analyze the dynamic characteristics of

This work is supported by The National Natural Science Foundation of China (No. 61901230, No. 91738201); Key pre-research project for civil space technology (No. B0106 "Research project on VHTS communication technology").

Q. Wu et al. (Eds.): WiSATS 2020, LNICST 357, pp. 227–239, 2021.
https://doi.org/10.1007/978-3-030-69069-4_19

rain attenuation are difficult to achieve and have limited limitations. Simulated synthetic rain attenuation time series are low cost, easy to implement, and highly available [4].

Many researches have been carried out on the simulation and prediction of rain attenuation time series. As early as the 1980s, Maseng and Bakken proposed a model (M-B model) to simulate the dynamic characteristics of rain attenuation based on the first-order Markov theory in literature [5]. This model regards the rain attenuation series as a lognormal distribution, and transforms the series into a first-order Gaussian Markov process by using memoryless nonlinear device. An improved M-B model (E.M-B) was proposed by the French Centre for Aeronautics and National Space Science (ONERA-CNES) in reference [6]. E.M-B model improves the accuracy of prediction, but the problem of generating series on demand has not been solved yet. For this reason, ONERA proposed the 'Event-on-Demand' model in 2009 [7], which is based on the E.M-B model and can generate the corresponding rain series according to the rainfall events. For the long-term rain attenuation time series, the 'Dirac-lognormal' model is proposed in reference [8] to solve the problem. The research on rain attenuation time series in China started late. Reference [9] used E.M-B model to study the rain attenuation time series in typical areas of China, and analyzed the probability of the fading time. However, in this study, the model can not generate rain series according to rainfall events, and the research focuses on 12.5 GHz, which has little reference to the dynamic characteristics of high-frequency. In reference [10], a short-term rain attenuation time series dynamic model based on Markov chains suitable for Ka-band satellite channels is studied. The simulation results reflect the impact of rain attenuation on Ka-band satellite channels, but lack of research on long-term rain attenuation time series.

In view of the lack of research on the high-frequency and long-term rain attenuation time series in China, this paper comprehensively discussed the 'Event-on-Demand' and 'Dirac-lognormal' model, and extended it to the Q/V bands for simulation. Firstly, based on the E.M-B model, the 'Event-on-Demand' rain attenuation model was studied. According to the 'Event-on-Demand' model, the rain attenuation process is transformed into a first-order stationary Markov process after nonlinear transformation. Then we analyzed the steps of generating short-term rain attenuation time series. Secondly the principle of Dirac-lognormal distribution model is analyzed, and the steps of generating long-term rainfall attenuation time series are given. Finally, on the basis of obtaining the rain attenuation distribution, the short-term and long-term rain attenuation time series are obtained by using the two models. The power spectrum estimation of the series shows the validity of the model used.

The rest of the paper is arranged as follows: Sect. 2 gives the principle and implementation steps of the two models; Sect. 3 simulates the proposed model with the actual data of different rain regions in China, and obtains the simulation results; Finally, the paper is summarized in Sect. 4.

2 Rain Attenuation Time Series Model

2.1 Short-Term Rain Attenuation Time Series Based on 'Event-on-Demand' Model

Theoretical Analysis. Under the premise that the rain attenuation values $A(t - t_1)$ and $A(t + t_2)$ at $t - t_1$ and $t + t_2$ are known, the rain attenuation $A(t)$ at t can be calculated by the conditional probability $p(A(t)|A(t - t_1), A(t + t_2))$:

$$p(A(t)|A(t - t_1), A(t + t_2)) = \frac{p(A(t), A(t - t_1), A(t + t_2))}{p(A(t - t_1), A(t + t_2))} \tag{1}$$

Assuming that the rain attenuation $A(t)$ is a moderately stable Markov process, the formula (1) can be transformed into:

$$p(A(t)|A(t - t_1), A(t + t_2)) = \frac{p(A(t + t_2)|A(t)) \cdot p(A(t)|A(t - t_1))}{p(A(t + t_2)|A(t - t_1))} \tag{2}$$

For all time intervals Δt, $p(A(t + \Delta t)|A(t))$ can be expressed by mean and variance of rain attenuation, as shown in formula (3):

$$p(A(t + \Delta t)|A(t)) = \frac{1}{A(t + \Delta t) \times \sigma_{|A(t)}\sqrt{2\pi}} \exp\left(-\left[\frac{\ln(A(t + \Delta t) - \mu_{|A(t)})}{\sigma_{|A(t)}\sqrt{2}}\right]^2\right) \tag{3}$$

Where $\mu_{|A(t)}$ and $\sigma_{|A(t)}$ are as follows:

$$\mu_{|A(t)}(\Delta t) = \mu \cdot (1 - \exp(-\beta|\Delta t|)) + \ln(A(t)) \cdot \exp(-\beta|\Delta t|) \tag{4}$$

$$\sigma_{|A(t)}^2(\Delta t) = \sigma^2 \cdot (1 - \exp(-2\beta|\Delta t|)) \tag{5}$$

Rainfall attenuation condition probabilistic expression (3) is the key to this model. In [11], $p(A(t + \Delta t)|A(t))$ can be obtained by $K_{2A}(A)$:

$$K_{2A}(A) = 2\beta A^2 \sigma^2 \tag{6}$$

Where $K_{2A}(A)$ is the second moment of the known condition of $A(t)$, defined as:

$$K_{iA}(A) = \lim_{\Delta t \to 0} \frac{E\left((A(t + \Delta t) - A(t))^i|A(t)\right)}{\Delta t} \quad i = 1, 2, \ldots \tag{7}$$

For any Δt, $A(t + \Delta t)|A(t)$ follows lognormal distribution, and the probability density function can be derived from formulas (6) and (7):

$$f(A(t + \Delta t)|A(t)) = \frac{1}{\sqrt{2\pi}\sigma_{|A(t)}A(t + \Delta t)} \exp\left[-\frac{(\ln A(t + \Delta t) - \mu_{|A(t)})^2}{2\sigma_{|A(t)}^2}\right] \tag{8}$$

Substituting formula (8) into formula (3), we can know that $A(t)|A(t - t_1), A(t + t_2)$ also follows lognormal distribution, and the mean and variance are:

$$\mu_{\substack{A_1, A_2 \\ t_1, t_2}} = \left\{ \begin{array}{l} (1 - \exp(-2\beta t_1)) \cdot \exp(-\beta t_2) \cdot \ln(A(t + t_2)) \\ +(1 - \exp(-2\beta t_2)) \cdot \exp(-\beta t_1) \cdot \ln(A(t - t_1)) \\ +\mu \cdot (1 - \exp(-\beta t_1)) \cdot (1 - \exp(-\beta t_2)) \\ \cdot (1 - \exp(-\beta(t_1 + t_2))) \end{array} \right\} \Bigg/ (1 - \exp(-2\beta(t_1 + t_2)))$$

$$(9)$$

$$\sigma^2_{\substack{A_1, A_2 \\ t_1, t_2}} = \sigma^2 \cdot \frac{(1 - \exp(-2\beta t_1)) \cdot (1 - \exp(-2\beta t_2))}{(1 - \exp(-2\beta(t_1 + t_2)))} \tag{10}$$

μ and σ are the mean value and standard deviation of the rainfall attenuation value following lognormal distribution, respectively, which can be determined by the attenuation value A_p corresponding to different $p\%$ time rainfall probability [12]:

$$\sigma = \frac{\sum\limits_{i=1}^{N} (p_i - \overline{p_i})(\ln A_{p_i} - \overline{\ln A_{p_i}})}{\sum\limits_{i=1}^{N} (p_i - \overline{p_i})^2} \tag{11}$$

$$\mu = \overline{\ln A_{p_i}} - \sigma \overline{p_i} \tag{12}$$

β is a parameter to describe the dynamic characteristics of rainfall series. From [13], we can get $\beta = \beta_R(0.0053v + 0.002)\theta^{-0.0228v+0.5285}$, where v is the wind speed, unit is m/s, θ is the angle between the link and rainfall direction, take the angle system, β_R is the variation characteristics of rainfall rate. In this paper, β_R is the global general value of $0.001852 \ s^{-1}$[14].

Finally, the expression of event-oriented rain decay sequence model is obtained:

$$p_{\text{demand}}(A(t)|A(t - t_1), A(t + t_2)) = p(A(t)+A_{\text{offset}}|A(t - t_1) + A_{\text{offset}}, A(t + t_2) + A_{\text{offset}}) \tag{13}$$

A_{offset} rain attenuation compensation value, $A_{\text{offset}} = \exp\left(m + \sigma Q^{-1}\left(\frac{p_{\text{rain}}}{100}\right)\right)$, where p_{rain} is the percentage probability of rainfall at the earth station, which can be calculated from [15].

Generation Steps of Short-term Rain Attenuation Time Series. The theory of the 'Event-on-Demand' model has been described in detail. The model mainly uses the log-normal distribution of $A(t)|A(t - t_1), A(t + t_2)$ and interpolates between two rain attenuation values to obtain a more granular rain attenuation series. Suppose it is necessary to simulate a duration of T, the maximum value of rain attenuation is A_{max}, and the maximum time of rain is T_{peak}, the flow chart is as follows (Fig. 1):

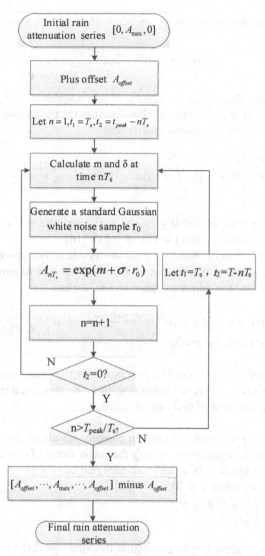

Fig. 1. Flow chart of 'event-on-demand' rain attenuation series synthesis

2.2 Long-Term Rain Attenuation Model Based on Dirac Log-Normal Model

The rain attenuation time series simulated by the 'Event-on-Demand' model introduced earlier is generally short-term. For the long-term rain attenuation time series including rain and no rain, a Dirac log-normal distribution model is introduced. The rain attenuation time series of Dirac log-normal model is obtained based on Dirac and log-normal distribution. First, suppose the rain attenuation probability distribution function PDF

$P(A|A >0)$ is a lognormal distribution function with mean μ and variance δ:

$$P(A|A > 0) = \frac{e^{-\frac{1}{2}(\frac{\ln A - \mu}{\delta})}}{A\delta\sqrt{2\pi}} \tag{14}$$

When the probability distribution function p of rain attenuation is known, the complementary cumulative probability distribution function CCDF of rain attenuation can be expressed as mixed Dirac-lognormal distribution:

$$P(A \geq A_0) = p_0 \int_{A_0}^{+\infty} P(A|A > 0)dA_C = \frac{p_0}{2}(\frac{\ln A_0 - \mu}{\sqrt{2}\delta}) \tag{15}$$

Where p_0 is the rainfall probability of the path, and the mathematical model for calculating p_0 is described in detail in ITU-R P.618 [16].

Secondly, in the Fourier domain, a stationary Gaussian process G(t) with one-dimensional mean value of 0, variance of 1 and correlation function $c_G(\Delta t)$ of any value is generated, then the rain decay time series A(t) is:

$$\begin{cases} A(t) = \exp\left\{\delta\sqrt{2}erfc^{-1}[\frac{erfc(G(t)/\sqrt{2})}{p_0}] + \mu\right\}, G(t) > G_0 \\ A(t) = 0, otherwise \end{cases} \tag{16}$$

Where $G_0 = \sqrt{2}erfc^{-1}(2 \times p_0)$. The generation of the one-dimensional correlation Gaussian process G(t) has a greater impact on the rain attenuation time series A(t), and the specific generation steps of G (t) are as follows:

1. Generate $N/2 + 1$ uncorrelated random complex numbers $(e_k)_{k=0...N/2}$, where the real part and the imaginary part satisfy the mean value of 0 and the variance of 1, and when $k = 0$ and $K = N/2$, the imaginary part of e_k is 0;
2. Define $e_{N-k} = e_k^*$ when $k = \{0, \ldots, N/2\}$;
3. Define $h_k = \begin{cases} 1 & k = 0, k = N/2 \\ \frac{1}{2} & else \end{cases}$;
4. Fourier transform according to correlation function c_G: $\mathcal{F}(G_j) = \frac{1}{N}\sum_{j=0}^{N-1} G_j e^{-\frac{i2\pi}{N}kj}$;
5. Define $a_k = \sqrt{h_k\mathcal{F}(c_G)} \times e_k$;
6. Calculation: $G_j = \mathcal{F}^{-1}(a_k), G(t) = G(j \Delta) = G_j = \sum_{k=0}^{N-1} a_k e^{\frac{i2\pi}{N}kj} = \mathcal{F}^{-1}(a_k)$.

The mean value μ and standard deviation σ of the lognormal distribution of rain attenuation used in the model can be determined by fitting the attenuation values A_p corresponding to different $p\%$ time rainfall probability, and the calculation formulas are (12) and (13).

3 Simulation Results and Analysis

Section 2.1 introduces the specific steps of the 'Event-on-Demand' model, which needs to provide the characteristic parameters of the rain decay time series, including the maximum value, duration and the time of the maximum value. In order to obtain the rain attenuation value of the model at Q/V bands, this section firstly simulates the rain attenuation value in China according to ITU-R p.618-8 standard. The parameters used in the standard are shown in Table 1, and the specific calculation steps are shown in reference [16].

Table 1. Parameters of the ITU-R rain attenuation model

Parameters	Meaning
$R_{0.01}$	Annual average rainfall intensity at 0.01% of time (mm/h)
h_s	Earth station average altitude (km)
θ	Antenna elevation angle(°)
φ	Earth station latitude (°)
F	Frequency (GHz)
R_e	Earth effective radius (8500 km)

Considering the frequency bands recommended by the Federal Communications Commission (FCC) for Q-bands and V-bands: 37.5–40.5 (downlink) and 47.2–50.2 (uplink) for geostationary satellites, and 37.5–38.5 (downlink) and 48.2–49.2 (uplink) for non geostationary satellites, the simulation frequency in this paper are 40 GHz (downlink) and 50 GHz (uplink). The other parameters of the simulation are assumed to be: the GEO satellite is set at 92° E, the annual average 0.01% time and minute rainfall rate $R_{0.01}$ is 58 mm/h [9, 10], the latitude is 39.90° N, the longitude is 116.42° E, and the altitude is 49 m. The simulation results are shown in Fig. 2. In order to further study the rain attenuation of Q/V bands in different regions of China, the rain attenuation of different cities is compared and simulated. The simulation parameters are shown in Table 2. The results are shown in Fig. 3.

Figure 2 shows the rain attenuation values of different rainfall probability for the Q/V bands when the uplink/downlink operating frequency is 50/40 GHz. In the figure, the abscissa is the percentage of time that exceeds the rain attenuation, and the ordinate is the rain attenuation. It can be seen that at the same annual percentage of rainfall, the higher the frequency, the greater the attenuation of rainfall. At 0.01% probability of rain, the rain attenuation at 50 GHz reaches 87.7 dB, and the attenuation at 40 GHz reaches 69.6 dB, which is much higher than that of Ka-band. The rain attenuation of 0.01% time in a year reaches 69.6 dB, which means that the rain attenuation value of 0.01% of the year exceeds 69.6 dB. So the larger the rain attenuation value is, the smaller the annual percentage statistical value is. Figure 3 shows the comparison of rain attenuation in different cities in China at 50 GHz. Comparing Guangzhou and Urumqi, it is found that the annual average rainfall rate difference between the two places is 28 dB, but the

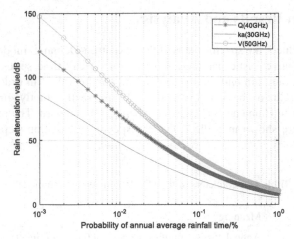

Fig. 2. Q/V bands rain attenuation value and rainfall probability

Table 2. Geographical location and rainfall rate of typical city in China

City	North Latitude	East Longitude	Altitude/(m)	Rainfall rate/(mm/h)
Beijing	39.80°	116.47°	31.2	58
Nanjing	32.00°	118.80°	8.9	81.7
Guangzhou	23.13°	113.32°	6.3	122
Urumqi	43.57°	87.10°	635.5	5

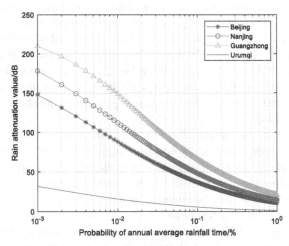

Fig. 3. Comparison of rain attenuation in different cities of china(50 GHz)

difference between the two places is 130 dB. It can be seen that in addition to the rainfall rate, the rain attenuation is also related to the latitude and altitude of the earth station and antenna elevation angle.

Through the above calculations, the distribution of rain attenuation at Q/V bands was obtained. In order to generate a short-term rain attenuation time series for this band in China, the maximum rain attenuation value is 30 dB, the rainfall lasts for 3000 s, and the maximum rain attenuation moment is 1200 s. The result is shown in Fig. 4.

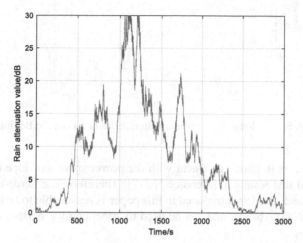

Fig. 4. The Short-term rain attenuation series at 40 GHz in Beijing

It can be seen from Fig. 4 that the generated rain attenuation series has met the requirements in terms of duration, maximum rain attenuation, and maximum rain attenuation time. Based on the detailed introduction of the Dirac log-normal model in Sect. 2.2, the long-term rain attenuation time series of Beijing in China was simulated. The correlation function of the stationary Gaussian process G (t) is selected as $c_G(\Delta t) = 1 \times 10^{-4}(s^{-1})$. According to the steps shown in Sect. 2.2, the parameters $p_0 = 4.79$, $\mu = -1.8221$, $\sigma = 1.6170$ are calculated at the frequency of 50 GHz. The simulation results are shown in Fig. 5.

Power spectrum estimation is one of the main contents of digital signal processing. Power spectrum estimation is to estimate the relationship between the power of the received signal and the frequency through the correlation of the signal. In order to verify the validity of the two models at Q/V bands, fast Fourier transform (FFT) is applied to estimate the power spectrum of rain attenuation time series in Fig. 4 and Fig. 5. The results are shown in Fig. 6 and Fig. 7. In order to compare the difference between the Q/V and Ka bands of the introduced model, the power spectral density of the two models in Ka band is also given by simulation, as shown in Fig. 8 and Fig. 9. Comparing the power spectrum at Q/V and Ka bands, we can see that the slope of the power spectral density of the rain attenuation series is basically parallel to the straight line with a slope of −

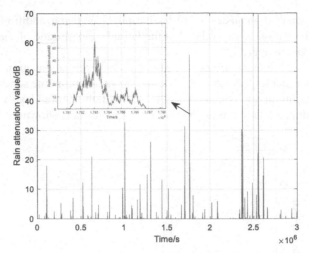

Fig. 5. The long-term rain attenuation series at 50 GHz in Beijing

20 dB/dec, which is in good agreement with the power spectrum slope obtained from the experimental test results in reference [7, 17]. Therefore, the Dirac-lognormal and 'Event-on-Demand' models introduced in this paper is reasonable to be extended from low frequency to Q/V bands, and can be used to generate Q/V bands rain attenuation series.

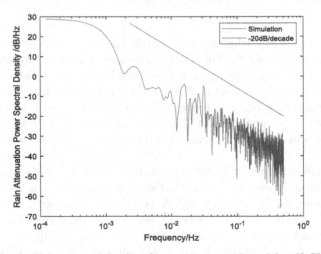

Fig. 6. Power spectral density of 'event-on-demand' model at 40 GHz

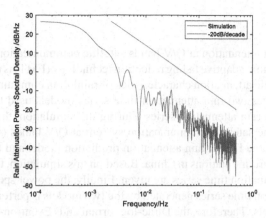

Fig. 7. Power spectral density of 'event-on-demand' model at Ka band

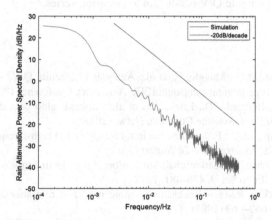

Fig. 8. Power spectral density of dirac-lognormal Model at 50 GHz

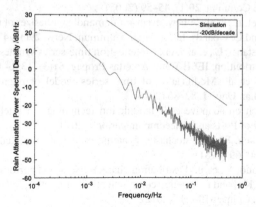

Fig. 9. Power spectral density of dirac-lognormal model at Ka band

4 Conclusion

There is severe rain attenuation at Q/V bands satellite communication link. In order to reduce rain attenuation, adaptive fading reduction technology (FMT) is required, which is based on the dynamic attenuation characteristics of rainfall in communication channels. This paper introduces two rain attenuation time series models used to generate short-term and long-term rain attenuation series. During the simulation, the rain attenuation characteristics of the satellite communication system at Q/V bands (40/50 GHz) were simulated based on the ITU-R rain attenuation prediction model and the actual rainfall rate data of typical ground stations in China. Based on this simulation, the short-term and long-term rain attenuation time series are given. Finally, the power spectrum estimation of the rain attenuation time series generated by the two models is performed to verify the validity of the models. Therefore, the Dirac-lognormal and 'Event-on-Demand' models introduced in this paper is reasonable to be extended from low frequency to Q/V bands, and can be used to generate Q/V bands rain attenuation series.

References

1. Rossi, T., Sanctis, M.D., Maggio, F., et al.: Analysis of satellite Q/V band channel errors based on Italian experimental campaign. IEEE Aerospace Conference (2017)
2. Cornacchini, C., Bernardo, D., Falzini, S., et al.: Alphasat aldo paraboni payload Italian mission segment. Int. J. Satellite Commun. Netw. (2018)
3. Nebuloni, R., Capsoni, C.: Fade mitigation in future Q/V-band high-throughput satellites. In: 32nd URSI GASS, Montreal, 19–26 August (2017)
4. Li, L., Yang, R., Zhao, Z.: Markov chain simulation of rain decline time series in Changchun and Xinxiang. J. Radio Sci. 3, 476–481 (2012)
5. Maseng, T., Bakken, P.M.: A stochastic dynamic model of rain attenuation. IEEE Trans. Commun. 29(5), 660–669 (1981)
6. Lacoste, F., Bousquet, M., Castanet, L., et al.: Improvement of the ONERA-CNES rain attenuation time series synthesizer and validation of the dynamic characteristics of the generated fade events. Space Commun. 20(1), 45–59 (2005)
7. Carrie, G., Castanet, L., et al.: A new 'event-on-demand' synthesizer of rain attenuation time series at Ku, Ka and Q/V bands. Int. J. Satell. Commun. Netw. 29(1), 47–60 (2011)
8. Boulanger, X., Castanet, L., et al.: A rain attenuation time-series synthesizer based on a dirac and lognormal distribution. IEEE Trans. Antettas Propag. 61(3), 1396–1406 (2013)
9. Yang, R., Lu, T., et al.: Modification of time series model of microwave dynamic rain attenuation. J. Xidian Univ. 1, 82–86 (2016)
10. Zhou, R.: Research on adaptive code modulation technology in satellite communication. Beijing University of Posts and Telecommunications (2014)
11. Masen, T.G., Bakken, P.M.: A stochastic dynamic model of rain attenuation. IEEE Trans. Commun. 29(5), 60–69 (1981)
12. Lin, S., Zhu, L., Guo, Y., et al.: Distribution characteristics and performance simulations of rain attenuation at Ka band for satellite communications. In: 2012 5th Global Symposium on Millimeter Waves, China, 579–582 (2012)
13. Kourogiorgas, C., Panagopoulos, A.D., et al.: Dynamic properties of rain attenuation in athens, greece: slant path rain attenuation synthesizer and dynamic diversity gain. Progress Electromagnet. Res. 41, 43–50 (2015)

14. Panagopoulos, A.D., Kanellopoulos, J.D.: On the rain attenuation dynamics: spatial-temporal analysis of rainfall rate and fade duration statistics. Int. J. Satell. Commun. Netw. **21**(6), 595–611 (2003)
15. Characteristics of precipitation for propagation modelling. Recommendation ITU-R P.837–6. (2013)
16. Propagation data and prediction methods required for the design of Earth-space telecommunication systems. Recommendation ITU-R P.618–10 (2009)
17. Lacoste, F., Bousquet, M., Cornet, F., et al.: Classical and on-demand rain attenuation time series synthesis: principle and applications. In: 24th AIAA International Communications Satellite Systems Conference (2006)

An Improved Routing Strategy Based on Virtual Topology in LEO Satellite Networks

Chaoran Sun[1,2(✉)], Yu Zhang[1,2], and Jian Zhu[1]

[1] College of Telecommunications and Information Engineering, Nanjing University of Posts and Telecommunications, Nanjing 210003, China
1218012234@njupt.edu.cn
[2] "Telecommunication and Network" National Engineering Research Center, Nanjing University of Posts and Telecommunications, Nanjing 21003, China

Abstract. With the increasing scale of low Earth orbit (LEO) satellite networks, the satellite network topology may become more and more complex. In order to cope with local congestion and link disruption with the aid of path planning, a virtual topology based improved routing (VTIR) scheme is proposed, which can be considered as a kind of node feedback routing (NFR) To be specific, in the proposed VTIR scheme, the orbit-period is divided into time slices, and the dynamic topology is also converted into a static topology. Moreover, both queue buffer state feedback and connection state feedback are considered in routing-path computation, resulting in that the link cost may be determined by a combination of distance, congestion, and link state. Simulation results show that compared with the conventional snapshot scheme, the proposed VTIR scheme can alleviate local congestion by extending traffic to idle links, without increasing packet loss rate.

Keywords: LEO satellite networks · Virtual topology · Queue buffer · Link cost

1 Introduction

Nowadays, with the widespread application of the internet and high-speed development of space technology, satellite network has played a crucial role in the mobile communication networks [1]. Low earth orbit (LEO) satellite networks, represented by Iridium NEXT [2] and Starlink [3], are designed to supply global coverage and real-time services and contribute to the development of space-ground integrated communication systems [4]. It is suitable for the networks which has wide coverage because it can overcome the problem of long distance and desolate terrains (deserts, oceans, forests, etc.) [5]. Routing strategies are at the core of communication networks [6]. Due to the differences between LEO satellite networks and terrestrial networks, like topology dynamic, LEO satellite networks are difficult to adopt mature routing technologies in terrestrial networks. Meanwhile, the uneven distribution of global services poses significant challenges to satellite communications, such as severe link congestion.

Scholars have proposed a large number of algorithms for the feature of satellite networks, which can be categorized as the Dynamic routing algorithms, virtual node

Q. Wu et al. (Eds.): WiSATS 2020, LNICST 357, pp. 240–250, 2021.
https://doi.org/10.1007/978-3-030-69069-4_20

(VD)-based routing algorithms, and virtual topology (VT)-based routing algorithms. In the Dynamic routing algorithms, the real-time topology can be obtained by exchanging network state information. In [7] and [8], a location-assisted on-demand routing (LAOR) scheme was designed, which can distribute traffic to multiple paths. In the virtual node-based routing algorithm, the Earth's surface is sliced into several regions, each of which is assigned a fixed logic address. Satellites closest to the center of the region have the same logical address as the region. IP-based routing was proposed in [9], which divided the ground into super cellular and cellular, and satellites near the center of cellular were regarded as coverage than cellular. In [10] Ekici proposed a distributed routing algorithm (DRA), which constructed the virtual node by using the orbital plane and the number of satellites. The virtual node-based algorithm conceals the mobility of satellites and is highly adaptable. However, this approach requires a strong regularity of the constellation topology [11]. The virtual topology-based algorithm, which utilizes the periodicity of satellite movement, divided the satellite network period into a series of fixed time slice. Within each relatively small time slice, the satellite's dynamic topology can be considered either as a fixed topology or virtual topology (VT) [12]. This strategy was first proposed by Werner, who separated the dynamic topology of the satellite in a system cycle into a series of static topologies, routing problem can be transformed into virtual path routing calculation under static topology [13]. In [14], a novel routing algorithm based on virtual topology snapshot was proposed and it inherits the advantage of a lower delay in topology snapshot as well as solves the problems of poor robustness and adaptability. Gounder defines the static topology as a snapshot, then every change of inter-satellite links (ISLs) regarded as a new snapshot [15]. Moreover, in [16] and [17], the virtual topology models were used to design and evaluate the algorithm.

Virtual topology-based routing algorithms can convert dynamic topology to static routing, simplifying the conditions for designing routing algorithms and has lower requirements on the processing capability of satellite. However, it has poor adaptability to link failure and congestion, and too much time slice demands more memory space. Focus on these limitations, this paper proposed a node feedback routing (NFR).

The rest of this paper is organized as follows. In Sect. 2, the system model for the routing algorithm has been described. In Sect. 3, the detail of NFR is presented. The simulation results are shown in Sect. 4. Finally, the conclusions are given in Sect. 5.

2 System Model

In LEO satellite networks, the topology changes regularly and repeats periodically, and the number of nodes and constellation structure are usually kept constant. Therefore, the topology of the satellite network is usually represented by an undirected graph. Satellite operational cycles are divided into smaller time slices, with each time slice representing the current satellite network topology. Figure 1 shows the discrete satellite cycle.

Assuming the satellite operation cycle is T, the dynamic network topology is considered as a periodically repeating series of n topology time slices separated by step width $\Delta t = T/n$. Each of the time slices at $t = [k\Delta t, (k+1)\Delta t](k = 0, 1, 2...)$ can be regarded as fixed, which is represented as a graph $G(k) = (V, E(k))$, where $V = \{1, ..., N\}$ is the constant set of nodes and $E(k)$ represents the set of the undirected link $(i, j)_k$ between

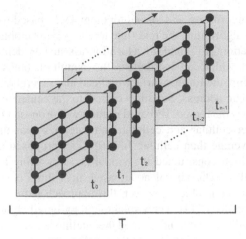

Fig. 1. Discrete-time topology

neighboring nodes i and j, existing at $t = k\Delta t(k = 1, 2, 3...)$. In this paper, the least delay routing is used for the algorithm so that the link cost $C_{i,j}(k)$ is mainly determined by node distance.

In each time slice, the Dijkstra algorithm is used for path planning for all satellites in the static network topology to calculate the shortest path. All satellites only need to store routing tables and switch them at specific times.

3   Analysis of Algorithm

3.1   Conventional Static Routing Based on VT

The VT-based algorithm adopts the model described in Sect. 2. The routing table for each time slice is computed centrally and uploaded to the satellite, thus increasing the simplicity and stability of routing. For the selection of the time slice interval, the first important factor is that the physical topology of the satellite network at the current time should be accurately reflected. Second, the link cost should satisfy formula (1) as much as possible, that is, the variation in link cost within the time slice of the adjacent time should be as small as possible.

$$\frac{C_{i,j}[(k+1)\Delta t] - C_{i,j}(k\Delta t)}{C_{i,j}(k\Delta t)} << 1, \forall (i,j)_k \in E(k) \tag{1}$$

However, the static routing table stored in the satellite is unable to sense sudden changes in the network. When there is link congestion or failure, it cannot respond in a timely manner, resulting in a drastic degradation of network performance. Also, in order to achieve smaller changes in link cost, the duration of time slices should be as small as possible, which conversely requires more storage space. However large time slice interval do not accurately reflect the network topology, thus affecting network performance. Therefore, the length of the time slice is a considerable problem.

3.2 VT Based Node Feedback Routing

An improved algorithm is proposed in this paper mainly focus on the above limitations, named VT based Node feedback routing (VTNFR), which has the following features: (1) The static routing table is no longer stored on the satellite, but the adjacent matrixes, which stores the distance between each satellite nodes and changes dynamically according to the change of node resources; (2) proposed a node feedback mechanism including queue buffer feedback and link interruption feedback, where routing selected based on consideration of not only distance but also queue buffer congestion state and link interrupts.

In the network shown in Fig. 2, assuming that the source node is G and the destination node is C, the routing protocol needs to find the shortest path from node G to node C. Suppose that there are two alternative paths as follows, they are

$$P1 = G, D, E, B, C, P2 = \{G, D, E, F, C\} \tag{2}$$

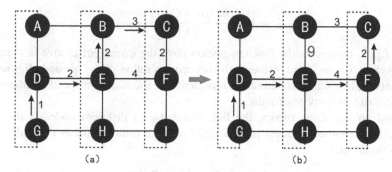

(a)   (b)

Fig. 2. Shortest path diagram

If the distance is used as the link cost only, then the distance of two links is.

$$d_{p1} = 1 + 2 + 2 + 3 = 8, \quad d_{p2} = 1 + 2 + 4 + 2 = 9 \tag{3}$$

$$d_{p1} < d_{p2} \tag{4}$$

The final shortest path is

$$P1 = \{G, D, E, B, C\} \tag{5}$$

As shown in Fig. 2 (a). If congestion occurs on the link between node E and node B, assuming the congestion size is 50% of the queue buffer, that is $Cachestate = 50\%$ (assuming the queue buffer size $CacheSize = 100Kbit$, the ISLs transmission rate $V = 5\,Mbps$), then the queuing time will reach

$$T_{queue} = \frac{CacheSise * CacheState}{V} = 10\,ms \tag{6}$$

Due to the distance is used as the link cost, the delay needs to be converted into a distance. According to the following formula

$$d = T_{queue} * c = 3 \tag{7}$$

Where c is the speed of light, and the value is simplified, which means that the distance from node E to node B needs extra propagation. Then, the cost of the whole path of $P1$ is modified to

$$d_{p1} = 1 + 2 + 2 + 3 + 3 = 11 \tag{8}$$

$$d_{p1} > d_{p2} \tag{9}$$

Obviously, the shortest path from node G to Node C is

$$P2 = \{G, D, E, F, C\} \tag{10}$$

As shown in Fig. 2 (b). Formulas (6) and (7) are combined as follows

$$L_{queue} = [\frac{CacheSise * CacheState}{V}] * c \tag{11}$$

Where L_{queue} represents the link congestion cost, the queue buffer size is expressed as $CacheSize$, $CacheState$ represents the occupation ration of the queue buffer area, V represents the link transmission rate, c represents the transmission speed of information in space, that is, the speed of light.

Based on the above theory, the link cost between different nodes is no longer fixed. The convention shortest path algorithm based protocol treats the link cost as unidirectional, that is

$$L_{cost}(A, B) = L_{cost}(B, A) \tag{12}$$

The Eq. (12) indicates the link cost from node A to node B consistent with the link cost form node B to node A. However, in this paper, the formula needs to be modified as follows based on the existence of the above mechanism

$$L_{cost}(A, B) \neq L_{cost}(B, A) \tag{13}$$

This is because the congestion levels in the queue buffers of node A and node B are not the same. Equation (13) is equal only if there is no congestion between node A and node B.

According to the above mechanism, the generation of the shortest path can be made more flexible and the protocol has stronger adaptability to the congestion situation which can distribute the traffic of the congestion to other relatively idle links.

If the link between the current node and the next node fails during the communication process which leads to data loss. This problem can be addressed by the periodic feedback mechanism. The link in this direction has been broken if no feedback is received within the specified time, then the link cost is modified to infinity in the adjacent matrixes, and the interrupted link can be avoided when calculating the routes. The algorithm flow chart is shown in Fig. 3.

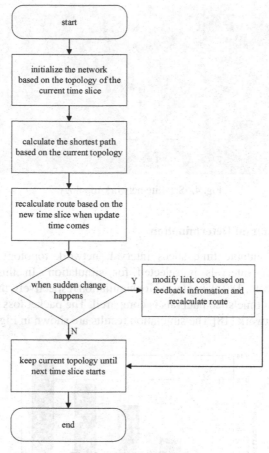

Fig. 3 Algorithm flowchart

4 Simulation and Results

4.1 Simulation Scenario

Simulation results are achieved by superb network simulation software OPNET and the network model built in OPNET is shown in Fig. 4. Referring to the Iridium system, there are 66 satellite nodes evenly distributed in 6 orbits, so that the relative position between the satellites remain essentially the same (ignoring orbital perturbations) and the connections between each satellite can be considered fixed. The altitude of orbits is 780 km and the orbit inclination angle is 86.4°. Meanwhile, each satellite node has four ISLs. Since the satellites on both sides of the reverse seam without ISL, which only have three ISLs.

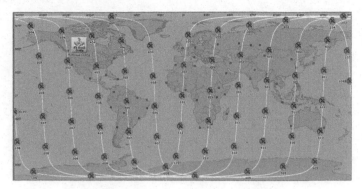

Fig. 4. Satellite network topology

4.2 Time Slice Interval Determination

To determine the suitable time slices interval, network topology structure under different time slice intervals is selected for simulation. In this paper, $\Delta t = \{60\,s, 90\,s, 120\,s, 150\,s, 180\,s\}$ is selected for simulation respectively, the network packet loss rate at different time slice intervals is compared. The packet loss rate indicates the reliability of the network [18] The simulation results are shown in Fig. 5.

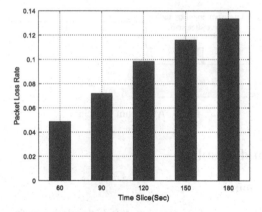

Fig. 5. Different time slice packet loss rate

As is shown in Fig. 5 above, the packet loss rate increases as the time slice interval increases. The smaller the time slice interval, the more accurate the satellite network topology reflected, which means the lower packet loss rate. However, frequent time slice switching causes short-term transmission interruptions and degrades the stability of routing. In addition, due to the large number of time slices, the requirements for storage and computing power are high. It can be seen from the figure that the packet loss rate at the $\Delta t = 120\,s$ is about 10%, while the $\Delta t = 60\,s$ is about 5%, a difference of about 5%. Meanwhile, the number of the time slices at the $\Delta t = 120$ s is half the number of it at the $\Delta t = 60$ s, the requirements for storage and computing power will be half and the routing will be more stable. Considering this, the time slice interval $\Delta t = 120$ s is selected in this paper.

4.3 Evaluation Result of Delay, Path Switch, and Packet Loss Rate

The NFR was compared with the conventional snapshot algorithm. The simulation time was 2 h, the source and destination nodes were selected, and the satellite packets were sent at an interval of 0.05 s. To simulate the local for the congested environment, the generation time of burst traffic is 600 s and the duration is 20 s. The results are as follows.

In Fig. 6, the delay of NFR during congestion is lower than that of the snapshot algorithm. This is because when the network is congested, the snapshot algorithm will transmit packets consecutively on a precomputed path and will not be able to sense the queue buffer congestion, which causes a continuous increase in queue buffer, resulting in a dramatic increase in packet delay. NFR can switch to another idle path in time, thus avoiding the accumulation of data packets in the queue buffer area. At the same time, it can be seen that NFR and the snapshot algorithm have almost the same delay since the basis of the NFR is the snapshot algorithm. Figure 7 shows a schematic representation of path switching, and the ordinate is the satellite number. The next hop for the source node is node 10 and the standby next hop is node 11. It can be seen that the snapshot algorithm does not switch the path when congestion continues to occur. The NFR will promptly switch paths to an idle path 1 s after getting congestion information. When the congestion is cleared, the NFR will switch back to the original path again. The performance of the improved algorithm is verified by simulation to achieve the effect of reducing local congestion.

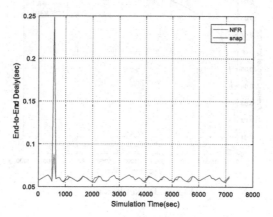

Fig. 6. End-to-end delay

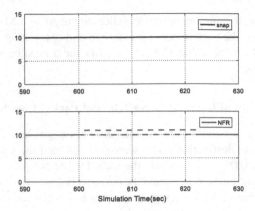

Fig. 7. Path switch

Figure 8 validates the effectiveness of NFR for link disruptions in the polar regions. The results indicate that the snapshot algorithm has an average packet loss rate more than the NFR when the network is stable. The main reason is that the satellites send packets according to the current shortest path during a time slice period, and when the satellites move to the polar region, the inter-satellite link will be closed, but the static routing table calculated according to the current topology cannot detect the link disconnection and is still follows the shortest path, ultimately resulting in a packet loss. The NFR can detect the link on–off state by the link feedback mechanism, and then switch to the normal path to avoid packet loss.

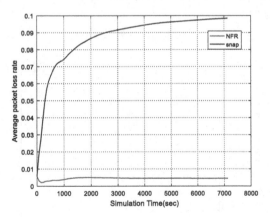

Fig. 8. Packet loss rate

5 Conclusion

In this paper, an improved routing based on virtual topology, called Node Feedback Routing (NFR), is proposed. NFR uses the node feedback mechanism to compute the routing table and feed the state of the queue buffer and link state to the routing protocol. Based on the above mechanism, NFR has strong adaptability to sudden network conditions caused by link congestion and interruptions. At the same time, it inherited the advantages of low end-to-end delay of virtual topology-based routing algorithms.

Acknowledgements. This work presented was partially supported by the National Science Foundation of China (No. 91738201 and 61772287), the China Postdoctoral Science Foundation (No. 2018M632347), the Natural Science Foundation for Jiangsu Higher Education Institutions (No. 18KJB510030 and 16KJB510031), and the Key University Science Research Project of Jiangsu Province (No. 18KJA510004).

References

1. Yin, Z., Zhang, L., Zhou, X.: On-demand QoS multicast routing for triple-layered LEO/HEO/GEO satellite IP networks. J. Commun. **6**(6), 495–508 (2011)
2. Qu, Z., Zhang, G., Xie, J.: LEO Satellite Constellation for Internet of Things. IEEE Access **85**, 18391–18401 (2017)
3. Noschese, P., Porfili, S., Girolamo, S.D.: ADS-B via Iridium NEXT satellites. In: Digital Communications - Enhanced Surveillance of Aircraft and Vehicles (TIWDC/ESAV), 2011 Tyrrhenian International Workshop on. IEEE (2011)
4. Yongtao, S., Liu, Y., Zhou, Y., Yuan, J., Cao, H., Shi, J.: Broadband LEO satellite communications: architectures and key technologies. IEEE Wire. Commun. **26**(2), 55–61 (2019). https://doi.org/10.1109/MWC.2019.1800299
5. Taleb, T., Hadjadj-Aoul, Y., Ahmed, T.: Challenges, opportunities, and solutions for converged satellite and terrestrial networks. IEEE Wirel. Commun. **18**(1), 46–52 (2011)
6. Lu, N., Zhang, H., Ma, J.: A novel inter-satellite routing protocol based on link recognizing. In: International Conference on Cyberspace Technology. IET, pp. 1–4 (2015)
7. Karapantazis, S., Papapetrou, E., Pavlidou, F-N.: On-demand routing in LEO satellite systems. In: ICC 2007, Glasgow, Scotland, United Kingdom: IEEE Press, pp. 26–31 (2007)
8. Papapetrou, E., Karapantazis, S., Pavlidou, F.-N.: Distributed on-demand routing for LEO satellite systems. Comput. Netw. **51**(15), 4356–4376 (2007)
9. Hashimoto, Y., Sarikaya, B.: Design of IP-based routing in a LEO satellite network. In: Proceedings of Third International Workshop on Satellite-Based Information Services (WOSBIS 1998), pp. 81–88 (1998)
10. Ekici, E., Akyildiz, I.F., Bender, M.D.: A distributed routing algorithm for datagram traffic in LEO satellite networks. IEEE/ACM Trans. Netw. **9**(2), 137–147 (2001)
11. Yan, S.: Research on the IP routing in LEO satellite constellation networks. Tsinghua University (2010)
12. Lu, Y., Sun, F., Zhao, Y.: Virtual topology for LEO satellite networks based on earth-fixed footprint mode. IEEE Commun. Lett. **17**(2), 357–360 (2013)
13. Werner, M.: A dynamic routing concept for ATM-based satellite personal communication networks. IEEE J. Sel. Areas Commun. **15**(8), 1636–1648 (1997)

14. Tan, H., Zhu, L.: A novel routing algorithm based on virtual topology snapshot in LEO satellite networks. In: 2014 IEEE 17th International Conference on Computational Science and Engineering, Chengdu, pp. 357–361 2014. doi: https://doi.org/10.1109/CSE.2014.93.
15. Gounder, V.V., Prakash, R., Abu-Amara, H.: Routing in LEO-based satellite networks. In: Wireless Communications and Systems, 2000. 1999 Emerging Technologies Symposium. IEEE (1999)
16. Lu, Y., Sun, F., Zhao, Y., Li, H., Liu, H.: Distributed traffic balancing routing for LEO satellite networks. Int. J. Comput. Netw. Inf. Secur. 1, 19–25 (2014)
17. Fischer, D., Basin, D., Eckstein, K., et al.: Predictable mobile routing for spacecraft networks. IEEE Trans. Mob. Comput. 12(6), 1174–1187 (2013)
18. Li, C., Liu, C., Jiang, Z., et al.: A novel routing strategy based on fuzzy theory for NGEO satellite networks. In: Vehicular Technology Conference. IEEE, pp. 1–5 (2015)

Interference Source Location Based on Spaceborne Multi-beam Antenna

Cen Ruan[1,2], Laiding Zhao[1,2(✉)], Gengxin Zhang[1,2], and Jidong Xie[1,2]

[1] Key Laboratory of Broadband Wireless Communication and Sensor Network Technology, Nanjing University of Posts and Telecommunications, Nanjing 210003, China
zhaold@njupt.edu.cn
[2] "Telecommunication and Network" National Engineering Research Center, Nanjing University of Posts and Telecommunications, Nanjing 210003, China

Abstract. Based on the frequency division multiplexing principle of the multi-beam antenna, this paper proposes a new method for locating interference sources by only one single satellite. According to the antenna pattern function expression of multi-beam antennas, the positioning equations are derived and established by analyzing the link that interfering signal arrives at the spaceborne multi-beam antenna from the ground. Importantly, the gain error is introduced in the positioning process when we evaluate the performance of this positioning method. Considering the difficulty of solving nonlinear positioning equations, a new algorithm combining the Particle Swarm Optimization (PSO) and grid search is proposed. At the same time, in this paper, in order to analyze the feasibility of this new algorithm, we introduce the Monte Carlo method in the process of this experiment. Finally, this new algorithm is compared with the traditional Particle Swarm Optimization in terms of speed and accuracy, which shows the superiority of this new algorithm.

Keywords: Interference source location · Single-satellite · Multi-beam antenna · Gain error · PSO combined with grid-search

1 Introduction

In the recent years, satellite communication has developed rapidly because of its outstanding coverage, wide communication distance, and no geographical restrictions. Nowadays, the application of satellites is not limited to communication, but is permeated in various fields such as navigation, positioning, military reconnaissance, and weather forecasting [1, 2]. For the satellites with large-scale multi-beam antennas, while their sensitivity of the received signal is improving, they are more susceptible to various intentional or unintentional interference, which affect the operation of the satellite systems to a great extent [3]. Therefore, it is extremely urgent to find a quick and effective method to locate the interference source.

Traditional technology for interference source location are based on time difference of arrival (TDOA), frequency difference of arrival (FDOA), and angle of arrival (AOA)

Q. Wu et al. (Eds.): WiSATS 2020, LNICST 357, pp. 251–260, 2021.
https://doi.org/10.1007/978-3-030-69069-4_21

[4–7]. Although these methods have the superiority of high positioning accuracy, fast positioning speed, and low system complexity, however, at least two qualified satellites are required in these positioning systems. In order to avoid the difficulty of selecting qualified satellites and decrease the consumption of orbit resources, a positioning method based on single satellite is proposed. This positioning technology is proposed to positioning the interference source with three co-frequency beams of the multi-beam antenna, according to the frequency division multiplexing principle, which provides a new idea for locating interference sources. At the same time, in order to further improve the positioning accuracy and reduced positioning time, a particle swarm optimization algorithm combined on grid search is proposed in this paper. By introducing the meshing process for the PSO, the PSO can be significantly optimized in terms of positioning error and time complexity.

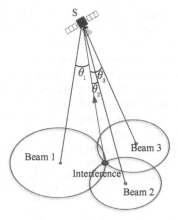

Fig. 1. Positioning model

2 Positioning Principle

Reference [8] gives the function expression of the multi-beam antenna pattern, which proposes that the antenna gain can be approximately calculated by the angle between the signal incident direction and the beam center pointing.

$$G = G_0 \left[\frac{J_1(u)}{2u} + 36\frac{J_3(u)}{u^3} \right]^2 \tag{1}$$

Where J_1 and J_3 are first-order and third-order Bessel function of first kind respectively, $u = 2.07123\sin\theta/\sin(\theta_{3dB})$, $G_0 = \pi^2 D^2 \eta/\lambda^2$ is the beam center gain, θ_{3db} refers to half-power beam width, θ refers to the angle between the incident direction of the interference signal and the center of the beam, D refers to antenna aperture, η refers to antenna efficiency, and λ refers to wavelength of the radiation signal.

For a spaceborne multi-beam antenna, its gain overlap between the co-frequency beam is large. And when the interference signal is strong, the main interfered beam and the co-frequency multiplexed beams that are close to the interference source all can receive this interference signal [9, 10]. The location of the interference source can be acquired by the characteristics that different beams can receive different interference signal strengths. The positioning model is shown in Fig. 1.

2.1 Formula Derivation

In order to obtain the positioning equations, the link characteristics in the Fig. 1 are analyzed below.

It's assumed that the coordinate of the satellite, the coordinates of the center points of *beam* 1, *beam* 2, and *beam* 3 are known. And they are expressed in terms of the vectors r_s, r_1, r_2, and r_3 in the space rectangular coordinate system. The coordinates of interference source is represented as $r_I = (x, y, z)$. For *beam* $i(i = 1,2,3)$, the interference source, satellite, and *beam* i form a triangle. According to the cosine theorem, angle between the incident direction of the interference signal and the *beam* i center pointing can be expressed as

$$\theta_i = \arccos \frac{|r_S - r_i|^2 + |r_S - r_I|^2 - |r_I - r_i|^2}{2|r_S - r_i||r_S - r_I|} \tag{2}$$

Combining the antenna pattern function expression which is given by Eq. 1, the gains of the interference signals in *beam* 1, *beam* 2, and *beam* 3 can be obtained as $G(\theta_1)$, $G(\theta_2)$, and $G(\theta_3)$. $G(\theta_1)$ means that when the incident angle of the radiation signal is θ_1, the intensity of the radiation obtained by *beam* 1 is $G(\theta_1)$.

When interfering signals reach the satellite from the ground, it is assumed that the transmission loss is denoted as L, the transmitting power of the interference source is P_t, and the satellite antenna gain is G_t. For *beam* 1, the interference signal strength received by *beam* 1 is assumed to be P_1. And the link equation can be derived as following.

$$[P_1] = [P_t] + [G_t] + [G(\theta_1)] - [L] \tag{3}$$

The interference signal strengths acquired in *beam* 2 and *beam* 3 are assumed to be P_2 and P_3. Then, the equal gain equations (unit: dB) can be listed as

$$\begin{cases} [P_1] = [P_t] + [G_t] + [G(\theta_1)] - [L] \\ [P_2] = [P_t] + [G_t] + [G(\theta_2)] - [L] \\ [P_3] = [P_t] + [G_t] + [G(\theta_3)] - [L] \end{cases} \tag{4}$$

By eliminating $[P_t]$, $[G_t]$, and $[L]$, and combining the earth ellipsoid model equation in the WGS-84 coordinate system [11], we can get

$$\begin{cases} [P_2] - [P_1] = [G(\theta_2)] - [G(\theta_1)] \\ [P_3] - [P_2] = [G(\theta_3)] - [G(\theta_2)] \\ x^2 + y^2 + \dfrac{z^2}{1 - e^2} = a^2 \end{cases} \tag{5}$$

where a is semi-major axis of the earth ellipsoid mode and e is the first eccentricity of the earth ellipsoid mode under the WGS-84 coordinate system.

3 Error Analysis

3.1 Theoretical Derivation

In the positioning process, the position of the interference source is given by Eq. 5. In this section, we will consider the gain error, beam center position error, and elevation error. Equation 5 can be transformed as

$$
\begin{cases}
\lambda_{21} = f_{21} \\
\lambda_{32} = f_{32} \\
x^2 + y^2 + \dfrac{z^2}{1 - e^2} = a^2
\end{cases}
\tag{6}
$$

Where $\lambda_{21} = [P_2] - [P_1]$, $\lambda_{32} = [P_3] - [P_2]$, $f_{21} = [G(\theta_2)] - [G(\theta_1)]$, $f_{32} = [G(\theta_3)] - [G(\theta_2)]$.

We total differentiate Eq. 6 to get:

$$
\begin{cases}
d\lambda_{21} = \dfrac{\partial f_{21}}{\partial x}dx + \dfrac{\partial f_{21}}{\partial y}dy + \dfrac{\partial f_{21}}{\partial z}dz + \dfrac{\partial f_{21}}{\partial x_1}dx_1 + \dfrac{\partial f_{21}}{\partial y_1}dy_1 + \dfrac{\partial f_{21}}{\partial z_1}dz_1 + \dfrac{\partial f_{21}}{\partial x_2}dx_2 + \dfrac{\partial f_{21}}{\partial y_2}dy_2 + \dfrac{\partial f_{21}}{\partial z_2}dz_2 \\[2mm]
d\lambda_{32} = \dfrac{\partial f_{23}}{\partial x}dx + \dfrac{\partial f_{32}}{\partial y}dy + \dfrac{\partial f_{32}}{\partial z}dz + \dfrac{\partial f_{32}}{\partial x_2}dx_2 + \dfrac{\partial f_{32}}{\partial y_2}dy_2 + \dfrac{\partial f_{32}}{\partial z_2}dz_2 + \dfrac{\partial f_{32}}{\partial x_3}dx_3 + \dfrac{\partial f_{32}}{\partial y_3}dy_3 + \dfrac{\partial f_{32}}{\partial z_3}dz_3 \\[2mm]
da = \dfrac{x}{a}dx + \dfrac{y}{a}dy + \dfrac{z}{a(1 - e^2)}dz
\end{cases}
\tag{7}
$$

Then transform Eq. 7 into a matrix form

$$
dE = W_0 dX + W_1 dX_1 + W_2 dX_2 + W_3 dX_3
\tag{8}
$$

The final positioning error of the interference source can be expressed as

$$
dX = W_0^{-1}(dE - W_1 dX_1 - W_2 dX_2 - W_3 dX_3)
\tag{9}
$$

Where

$$
W_0 = \begin{bmatrix} \frac{\partial f_{21}}{\partial x} & \frac{\partial f_{21}}{\partial y} & \frac{\partial f_{21}}{\partial z} \\ \frac{\partial f_{32}}{\partial x} & \frac{\partial f_{32}}{\partial y} & \frac{\partial f_{32}}{\partial z} \\ \frac{x}{a} & \frac{y}{a} & \frac{z}{a(1-e^2)} \end{bmatrix}, \quad
W_1 = \begin{bmatrix} \frac{\partial f_{21}}{\partial x} & \frac{\partial f_{21}}{\partial y} & \frac{\partial f_{21}}{\partial z} \\ 0 & 0 & 0 \\ 0 & 0 & 0 \end{bmatrix}
$$

$$
W_2 = \begin{bmatrix} \frac{\partial f_{21}}{\partial x_2} & \frac{\partial f_{21}}{\partial y_2} & \frac{\partial f_{21}}{\partial z_2} \\ \frac{\partial f_{32}}{\partial x_2} & \frac{\partial f_{32}}{\partial y_2} & \frac{\partial f_{32}}{\partial z_2} \\ 0 & 0 & 0 \end{bmatrix}, \quad
W_3 = \begin{bmatrix} 0 & 0 & 0 \\ \frac{\partial f_{32}}{\partial x_3} & \frac{\partial f_{32}}{\partial y_3} & \frac{\partial f_{32}}{\partial z_3} \\ 0 & 0 & 0 \end{bmatrix} \quad
dE = \begin{bmatrix} d\lambda_{21} \\ d\lambda_{32} \\ da \end{bmatrix} \quad
dX = \begin{bmatrix} dx \\ dy \\ dz \end{bmatrix}
$$

$$
dX = \begin{bmatrix} dx_i \\ dy_i \\ dz_i \end{bmatrix} i = 1, 2, 3
$$

3.2 Simulation Analysis

In order to discuss the performance of the positioning method proposed above, this section analyzes the influence of some errors on final positioning accuracy. In the simulation, it is assumed that the center position of *beam* 1, 2, and 3 are ($E136.383°$, $N39.9°$), ($E124.067°$, $N30.75°$), and ($E139.283°$, $N26.083°$) respectively. The location of the satellite bottom point is ($E113.383°$, $N29.967°$). The satellite orbital altitude is 35786km and orbital inclination is $0°$.

When the interference source is in different positions, we will discuss the influence of the gain measurement error on the positioning accuracy. Considering the gain measurement error with 1 dB ($d\lambda_1 = d\lambda_2 = 1$ dB), and the results are shown in Fig. 2.

In Fig. 2, it can be seen that when the interference source is close to the center of a certain beam, the positioning error is small. However, when the interference source is close to the center of the area surrounded by these three beams, the positioning error becomes large. Actually, the gain error has a great impact on the final positioning accuracy. When the gain error is 1 dB, the final location will be 10, 000 to 50, 000 m away from the real interference source.

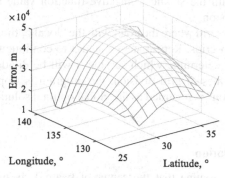

Fig. 2. Gain error

4 Algorithm

4.1 Particle Swarm Optimization Based on Grid Search

Considering that $G(\theta_1)$, $G(\theta_2)$, and $G(\theta_3)$ are non-linear functions, Eq. 5 belongs to a non-linear equation group. For nonlinear equations, Taylor expansion method and Newton iteration method are commonly used, but the solution process is mostly tedious [12, 13]. In order to further improve the positioning accuracy and reduced positioning time, a particle swarm optimization algorithm combined on grid search is proposed. Compared with the traditional particle swarm algorithm [14, 15], this algorithm mainly replaces the search task of some populations by dividing the grid and randomly taking points in these grids. For Eq. 5, the algorithm is described as follows.

1. establish an objective function $f(x, y, z)$:

$$f(x, y, z) = sqrt([(P_2 - P_1) - (G(\theta_2) - G(\theta_1))]^2 + [(P_3 - P_2) - (G(\theta_3) - G(\theta_2))]^2) \quad (10)$$

2. Initialization

Unknown components x and y are randomly generated in the three beam centers, and this is used as the initial position of the population in the particle swarm search. The optimal solution searched by particle swarm algorithm in two-dimensional space is denoted as (x_0, y_0).

3. With (x_0, y_0) as the center point, create a square search area S near (x_0, y_0). In the area S, the grid is continuously refined by repeatedly taking points randomly to find the point closest to the true location of the interference source. The specific method is as follows:

- Step1: Divide the square search area into four sub-grids in a grid
- Step2: Randomly take multiple random points (x, y) in these four sub-grids. The component z is solved by the model equation of the earth ellipsoid $x^2 + y^2 + \frac{z^2}{1-e^2} = a^2$
- Step3: Substitute (x, y, z) into the objective function for analysis and judgment, taking the random point with the smallest objective function value as the "local optimal solution" of this division.
- Step4: Divide the sub-grid where the point with the "local optimal solution" is located into four smaller sub-grids. Repeat steps 2 and 3 to continuously update the "local optimal solution" to determine which sub-mesh will be divided next time. After a certain number of times of grid division, the program is stopped, and the current "local optimal solution" is regarded as the global optimal solution of the interference source.

4.2 Algorithm Simulation

In this simulation, we assume that the center of beam 1, beam 2, and beam 3 are $(E116.383°, N39.9°)$, $(E104.067°, N30.75°)$, and $(E119.283°, N26.083°)$ respectively. It is assumed that the location of the satellite bottom point is $(E113.383°, N29.967°)$, the actual location of the interference source is $(E113°, N29°)$, the satellite orbital altitude is 35786 km and orbital inclination is 0°.

Considering the gain error has a great impact on the positioning accuracy, the gain error with 1 dB is introduced in the process of solving the equations. Based on Monte Carlo Method [15], a hundred simulations were performed, and the simulation results are shown in Fig. 3 and Fig. 4. The Fig. 3 shows the result of 10 iterations and Fig. 4 shows the result of 200 iterations.

The red five-pointed star in these two figures indicates the actual position of the interference source, and these blue points are the optimal solution found in each simulation. With the number of iterations increasing, these blue points become more and more concentrated near the true location of the interference source. The positioning errors of Fig. 3 and Fig. 4 are 36.724 km and 30.115 km respectively.

In order to prove the superiority of this algorithm, it is compared with the traditional particle swarm optimization algorithm.

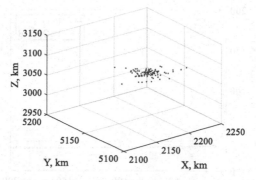

Fig. 3. 10 iterations of the positioning result

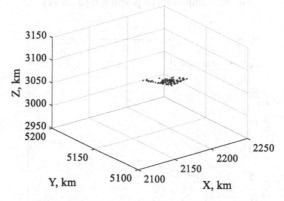

Fig. 4. 100 iterations of the positioning result

When using the traditional particle swarm algorithm to solve the positioning equations, we set the maximum number of iterations to 200 and the population size to 20. However, when using the improved algorithm to solve it, we reduced the population size to 10. For the grid-search part of the new algorithm, the grid is divided five times, and ten points are randomly selected from each sub-grid.

The simulation results are shown in the Fig. 5 and Fig. 6. Figure 5 shows the relationship between iteration times and positioning errors. Figure 6 shows the relationship between iteration times and positioning time. In these two pictures, the red solid line represents the traditional particle swarm optimization algorithm and the blue dotted line represents the improved algorithm.

Taking the simulation parameters of this paper as an example, the convergence speed of the two algorithms is basically the same, and they can basically achieve convergence when iterating 12 times.

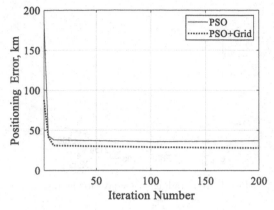

Fig. 5. Comparison of positioning accuracy

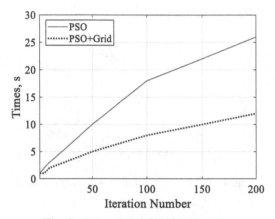

Fig. 6. Comparison of positioning time

In terms of time complexity: the improved algorithm reduces the number of initial populations in the PSO while introducing the process of meshing. By selecting the appropriate number of populations and the number of grid divisions, the speed of the algorithm can be effectively improved.

In terms of solving errors: the improved algorithm meshes within the error range after the convergence of the traditional particle swarm optimization algorithm to meet the requirements of higher positioning accuracy.

Meanwhile, Table 1 shows the positioning errors and positioning time of these two algorithms in 200 iterations.

The results show that both algorithms have strong convergence. After 200 iterations, the positioning time of the improved algorithm is reduced to half that of the traditional particle swarm optimization, and the positioning accuracy of the new algorithm is also improved.

Table 1. Algorithm comparison

	Positioning accuracy (unit: meter)	Positioning time (unit: second)
PSO	3.67e + 04	27
PSO combined with meshing	3.01e + 04	14

5   Conclusion

Single-satellite positioning technology based on the spaceborne multi-beam antenna requires only one satellite, but its positioning accuracy is greatly affected by the gain measurement error. Then we introduce the gain measurement error when we solve the nonlinear positioning equations. Meanwhile, a particle swarm algorithm based on grid search is proposed to assist this experiment. In order to demonstrate the reliability of this new algorithm, we compare it with the traditional particle swarm algorithm in terms of speed and the accuracy, which shows the superiority of this new algorithm.

References

1. Song, X., Ping, X.: Eatures of current foreign satellite communication systems and their developing trend. Commun. Audio Video (2014)
2. Mao-Qiang, Y., Dao-Xing, G., Lu, L.U.: wireless communication technology, 91, 1031–1041 (2012)
3. Vatalaro, F., et al.: Analysis of LEO, MEO, and GEO global mobile satellite systems in the presence of interference and fading. IEEE J. Sel. Areas Commun. 13(2), 291–300 (1995)
4. Liu, C., Yang, J., Wang, F.: Joint TDOA and AOA location algorithm. J. Syst. Eng. Electron. 24(2), 183–188 (2013)
5. Lin, X., You, H.E., Shi, P.: Location algorithm and error analysis for earth object using TDOA FDOA by dual-satellite and aided height information. Chin. J. Space Sci. 26(4), 277 281 (2006)
6. Zhu, W.Q., et al.: Analysis of precision of multi-satellite joint location based on TDOA/FDOA. Syst. Eng. Electron. 31(12), 2797–2800 (2009)
7. Wu, R., et al.: A novel long-time accumulation method for double satellite TDOA/FDOA interference localization. Radio Sci. 53(1), 129–142 (2018)
8. Caini, C., et al.: A spectrum- and power-efficient EHF mobile satellite system to be integrated with terrestrial cellular systems. IEEE J. Sel. Areas Commun. 10(8), 1315–1325 (1992)
9. Sohyeun, Y., et al.: Multibeam reflector antenna for ka-band communication satellite. In: Antennas & Propagation Society International Symposium. IEEE (2012)
10. Matsumoto, Y., et al.: Satellite interference location system using on-board multibeam antenna. Electron. Commun. Japan (Part I: Commun.) 80(11), 22–33 (2015)
11. Yu, Z.Y.: A location method based on WGS-84 earth model using satellites TDOA measurements. J. Astronaut. 24(6) 569–573 (2003)
12. Julier, S., Uhlmann, J., Durrant-Whyte, H.F.: A new method for the nonlinear transformation of means and covariances in filters and estimators. IEEE Trans. Autom. Control 45(3), 477–482 (2000)

13. Yan, G.: A newton method for a nonsmooth nonlinear complementarity problem. Oper. Res. Trans. **15**(15), 53–58 (2011)
14. Van den Bergh, F., Engelbrecht, A.P.: A study of particle swarm optimization particle trajectories. Inf. Sci. **176**(8), 937–971 (2006)
15. Liu, B., et al.: Improved particle swarm optimization combined with chaos. Chaos Solitons & Fractals **25**(5), 1261–1271 (2005)
16. Yeh, W.C., et al.: A particle swarm optimization approach based on monte carlo simulation for solving the complex network reliability problem. IEEE Trans. Reliab. **59**(1), 212–221 (2010)

Research on Signal Separation Technology for Satellite IoT Signal

Yixin Hu[1,2], Ziwei Liu[1,2(✉)], Jing Zeng[1,2], and Gengxin Zhang[1,2]

[1] College of Telecommunications and Information Engineering , Nanjing University of Posts and Telecommunications, Nanjing 210003, China
lzw@njupt.edu.cn
[2] National Engineering Research Center for Communication and Network Technology, Nanjing 210003, China

Abstract. Most of transmitted signals of satellite Internet of Things (IoT) terminals have the characteristics of low baud rate, short packet length and burstiness. The collision of massive access of IoT terminals can be solved by a random multiple access technology in company with an efficient and reliable collision separation method in the receiver. However, most existing signal separation technologies are proposed for continuous signals, and the receiving structure is designed based on the phase-locked loop. In this paper, a short burst signal separation method based on adaptive minimum mean square error (MMSE) filtering is proposed for the classical contention resolution diversity slotted Aloha (CRDSA). The proposed method estimates the frequency and phase difference between copies by amplitude and phase estimation (APES) firstly and cancels the collision signal based on a MMSE filter. The theoretical analysis and simulation results verify the feasibility of the proposed method.

Keywords: Adaptive filtering · Signal separation · Random multiple access · Satellite IoT

1 Introduction

As an important infrastructure of national information network, satellite communication system has great strategic significance in maintaining national security, protecting national economy, and promoting economic development for its wide coverage, flexibility and freedom from geographical and climatic factors. It is of great interests worldwide and is a commanding height of economic and technological competition in various countries [1]. As the terrestrial mobile communication system gradually develops from the

This work was supported in part by the National Natural Science Foundation of China under Grant 61801445, Grant 61801233 and Grant 91738201, in part by the Natural Science Foundation of Jiangsu Province under Grant SBK2017043119, and in part by the Nanjing University of Posts and Telecommunications Science Foundation (NUPTSF) under Grant NY219011 and Grant NY217126.

Q. Wu et al. (Eds.): WiSATS 2020, LNICST 357, pp. 261–272, 2021.
https://doi.org/10.1007/978-3-030-69069-4_22

4G to the 5G, the integration of satellite communications and terrestrial 5G networks has get attention. Among them, massive machine type communications (mMTC) is an important application scene for 5G application [2]. Satellite communication system, as an important complement of terrestrial Internet of Things (IoT), can take advantage of wide coverage and strong system survivability to provide access services for IoT terminals in remote areas. The existing satellite IoT systems in the world at present include the Orbcomm satellite communication system in the United States [3] and the ARGOS system [4] jointly established by France and the United States. Chinese satellite IoT system is planning and developing, BeiDou satellite navigation global system (BDS-3) can offer short message communication services [5], which afford lessons of related techniques or features for satellite IoT system.

Random access of massive user terminals is the first problem should to be solved on the transmission and access side for satellite IoT system. Multiple access schemes in satellite communication system can generally be divided into competitive multiple access and non-competitive multiple access. Typical non-competitive multiple access schemes include time division multiple access (TDMA), frequency division multiple access (FDMA), code division multiple access (CDMA) [6–8], and demand assignment multiple access (DAMA) [9], etc. Satellite IoT services are not connection oriented with certain suddenness and randomness, also the size of packets is very small. In the face of the burst IoT services with frequent requests and resources are frequently requested by IoT terminals, so that the efficiency of the system will be reduced because of the transmission duty cycle is low. Compared with the non-competitive multiple access scheme, the contention-based multiple access scheme usually refers to random access (RA) [10]. Users can preempt communication resources in a competitive manner without scheduling by using RA scheme. Aloha is the earliest random access protocol used in satellite communication systems [11]. Because there is no resource request and scheduling link, users will encounter data packet collision during resource competition will result in access failure, and its channel utilization is only 18%. Slotted Aloha is based on Aloha by introducing the concept of slot, and the collision probability of packets is reduced. Compared with Aloha, the theoretical channel utilization is improved to 36%. With the development of coding technology and digital signal processing technology, researchers put forward some enhanced version of the scheme, such as diversity slotted Aloha (DSA) [12], contention resolution diversity slotted Aloha (CRDSA) [13], CRDSA+ + [14], and irregular repetition slotted Aloha (IRSA) [15]. These techniques send packets in a data frame through time diversity, and employ successive interference cancelation (SIC) to solve the conflict packets at the receiver, so as to improve the throughput.

Most of the transmitted signals of satellite IoT terminals have the characteristics of low baud rate, short packet time and burstiness. The problem of massive access of IoT user terminals can be solved by random multiple access technology in company with an efficient and reliable collision separation method. At present, most existing signal separation technologies are proposed for continuous signals, and the receiving structure is designed based on the phase-locked loop. The separation method for short burst signals is lack of researching in the open literature. A robust physical layer receiving technology still needs to be studied for uplink multiple access of the short burst IoT signals. In most cases, the satellite channel varies slowly and the IoT signals have the characteristics of low baud rate and narrow bandwidth. In CRDSA scheme, the Doppler shift of the copies sent by the same user terminal is small, and the difference exists in complex coefficients introduced by satellite channel. The correlation between the waveforms of copies are still strong if the frequency offset and phase offset of copies can be compensated. Based on the above-mentioned analyses, a short burst signal separation method is proposed in this paper. The proposed short burst signal separation method employs adaptive minimum mean square error (MMSE) filtering combined with amplitude and phase estimation (APES) [16] in the receiver for the CRDSA scheme.

Following this Introduction, Sect. 2 describes the shortcoming of existing multiple access scheme of satellite IoT briefly and the CRDSA scheme. Section 3 describes the received signal model. Section 4 describes the signal separation method and key performance results are provided in Sect. 5. Finally, the conclusions are drawn in Sect. 6.

2 Satellite IoT Access Scenario

Multiple access is designed to divide and allocate system resources from different dimensions. It plays a vital role in improving system resource utilization, reducing terminal access delay, and saving terminal power consumption. In traditional terrestrial mobile communication systems, the multiple access scheme has gradually evolved from TDMA / FDMA of the 2G, CDMA of the 3G, and OFDMA of the 4G to non-orthogonal multiple access. However, multiple access schemes need to be redesigned for satellite IoT system according to its system architecture, service characteristics, etc. The multiple access scenario of satellite IoT is shown in Fig. 1.

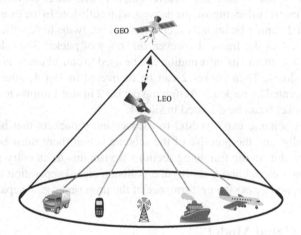

Fig. 1. Satellite IoT multiple access scenarios

User signal collision becomes an inevitable problem in the massive access process of IoT terminals because of large coverage of satellite beams for satellite IoT system. This paper studies the problem of short burst signal collision in the uplink access. The following contents introduces the receiving process of the CRDSA scheme and signal collision scenarios.

The random multiple access has attracted people's favor since it was proposed because of high flexibility and the overhead of signaling is low. An enhanced version of the DSA scheme, which is contention resolution diversity slotted Aloha (CRDSA) has been proposed by Casini et al. [13], in order to solve the problem of low access efficiency of the conventional Aloha schemes. The CRDSA scheme exploits SIC at packet level to recover conflicting packets based on the DSA scheme, which can further improve system throughput and reduce packet loss ratios. The CRDSA access process is shown in Fig. 2.

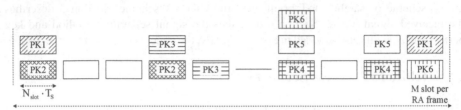

Fig. 2. CRDSA access process

The core idea of the CRDSA scheme is that the same user terminal randomly selects two different time slots to send twins of packet in the same frame, and each packet contains information on the position of all time slots where its copy is located in the same frame. On the access side, the receiver employs SIC based on the copies without collision to successively decompose the packets with collision. In the example presented in Fig. 2, packet 2 cannot be initially recovered as both twins have suffered a collision in slot 1 and slot 4 of the frame. However, one copy of packet 3 (in slot 5) has been successfully recovered and its information can be used to cancel the interference caused by packet 3 in slot 4. Then packet 2 can be recovered in slot 4, after removing the interference generated by packet 3. Removing packet 2 in slot 1 allows to recover packet 1 so that also packet 6 can be decoded in slot M.

The CRDSA scheme exploits SIC to recover more packets that have suffered a collision originally, and the premise of the scheme is that there must be a clean copy of packet in time slot. In the following sections we use this as an entry point, describe the received signal model and a short burst collision signal separation method for the CRDSA scheme, and assess the performance of the proposed signal separation method.

3 Received Signal Model

In this section, the received signal model is described based on the CRDSA scheme. In the following derivations, it is assumed that two user terminals of IoT have sent packets to the satellite, where the packet 1 sent by user terminal in slot m is $s_{0k_1}(t)$, and the copy of packet 1 in slot j is $s'_{0k_1}(t)$. The other user terminal sent packet 2 as $s_{0k_2}(t)$ in slot m, and the copy of packet 2 as $s'_{0k_2}(t)$ in slot $j+i$, where $i \neq 0$ and $j+i \neq m$. Therefore, the packet 1 and packet 2 sent by different user terminals have suffered a collision in slot m, and the received collision signal in slot m at the receiver is

$$r_m(t) = s_{k_1m}(t) + s_{k_2m}(t) + v(t)$$
$$= h_1\sqrt{p_1}s_{0k_1m}(t) + h_2\sqrt{p_2}s_{0k_2m}(t) + v(t)$$
$$= h_1\sqrt{p_1}A_1\cos(\omega_1 t + \varphi(t) + \varphi_1) + h_2\sqrt{p_2}A_2\cos(\omega_2 t + \varphi(t) + \varphi_2) + v(t)$$

$$(1)$$

where h_1, h_2 are channel gains, there just multiply a complex coefficient before signal because of the slowly varying satellite channel and the narrow bandwidth of IoT signals as mentioned in Sect. 1. p_1, p_2 are transmitted signal powers, A_1, A_2 are transmitted signal amplitudes, ω_1, ω_2 are frequencies of the received signal, and φ_1, φ_2 are initial phases of the received signal, $v(t)$ is additive white Gaussian noise.

Since the other copy of packet 1 and the other copy of packet 2 are not sent in the same slot, assuming that a detection result without error of a clean copy of packet 1 is obtained and restored to a waveform without noise after a normal single user detection as

$$x(t) = s_{k_1j}(t) = h_1\sqrt{p_1}s'_{0k_1}(t)$$
$$= h'_1\sqrt{p_1}A_1\cos(\omega' t + \varphi(t) + \varphi'_1)$$

$$(2)$$

where h'_1 is channel gain, which is approximately equal to h_1 in the received signal, p_1 is transmitted signal power, A_1 is the amplitude of the clean copy of packet 1, and ω', φ'_1 represent, respectively, the carrier frequency and phase of the clean copy.

The special characteristic of satellite IoT system is significantly different transmission channel compared with terrestrial IoT system, that is, exploiting communication satellites as relays to achieve the transmission of IoT information. The transmission channel of satellite IoT system is the line-of-sight (LOS) channel or the block fading channel, which has a short term stationary. Combining the characteristics of satellite channel and the rate of IoT signals is very low, the twins sent by the same user terminal are stable in one slot and non-stationary in different slots in CRDSA scheme [17].

In the following sections we derive the signal separation method based on the received signal model combined with the transmission characteristics of satellite IoT channel, and assess the performance of the proposed signal separation method.

4 Signal Separation Method

The separation problem based on reference signals is essentially a parameter estimation and fitting problem. In the following, we assume that the clean copy of packet as reference signal, and make use of the correlation between reference signal and collision signal to study efficient and reliable signal separation methods for the CRDSA scheme. The signal separation principle framework is shown in Fig. 3.

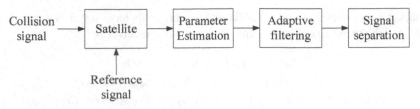

Fig. 3. Signal separation principle framework

The correlation is severely reduced because of the large frequency offset between the clean copy of packet 1 and the packet 1 in collision signal, so that a parameter estimation step needs to be added to achieve short burst signal separation. The received collision signal $r_m(t)$ in (1) is multiplied by the detection result without error $x(t)$ of the clean copy of packet 1 obtained by single user detection in (2) (see Sect. 3). As a result, the channel gain h and transmitted signal power p do not participate in the derivation calculation, and the obtained demodulated signal is

$$
\begin{aligned}
r'_m(t) &= \left(s_{k_1 m}(t) + s_{k_2 m}(t) + v(t)\right) \cdot x(t) \\
&= (A_1 \cos(\omega_1 t + \varphi(t) + \varphi_1) + A_2 \cos(\omega_2 t + \varphi(t) + \varphi_2) + v(t)) \cdot A_1 \cos(\omega' t + \varphi(t) + \varphi'_1) \\
&= \frac{A_1^2}{2}\left[\cos((\omega_1 + \omega')t + 2\varphi(t) + \varphi_1 + \varphi'_1) + \cos((\omega_1 - \omega')t + \varphi_1 - \varphi'_1)\right] \\
&\quad + \frac{A_1 A_2}{2}\left[\cos((\omega_2 + \omega')t + 2\varphi(t) + \varphi_2 + \varphi'_1) + \cos((\omega_2 - \omega')t + \varphi_2 - \varphi'_1)\right] + v(t)
\end{aligned}
\tag{3}
$$

Let $\triangle \varphi = \varphi_1 - \varphi'_1$, the signal $r''_m(t)$ after filtering the high frequency components by low pass filtering is

$$
\begin{aligned}
r''_m(t) &= \frac{A_1^2}{2}\left[\cos((\omega_1 - \omega')t + \triangle \varphi)\right] \\
&\quad + \frac{A_1 A_2}{2}\left[\cos((\omega_2 - \omega')t + \varphi_2 - \varphi_1 + \triangle \varphi)\right] + v(t)
\end{aligned}
\tag{4}
$$

It can be seen from (4) that the signal after low pass filtering does not contain the modulation term, but there is frequency offset and phase offset. In order to use the correlation between the clean copy and the collision signal to separate the collision signals, the frequency and phase must be estimated first and the frequency offset and phase offset are then compensated into the clean copy signal.

Considering that APES algorithm can be employed to estimate frequency offset and phase offset of short burst signal. The amplitude and phase estimation (APES) is a new filter design method proposed by Li et al. [16]. The APES algorithm breaks through the limitations of the traditional fast Fourier transform (FFT) algorithm, and still has a high frequency resolution for short term signals. It can not only accurately estimate the frequency of the signal, but also calculate its amplitude and initial phase angle.

Sampling after low pass filtering signal $r''_m(t)$ of (4) as the input signal of filter, and it is assumed that the frequency of transmitted signals of the two user terminals is the same, that is $\omega_1 = \omega_2 = \omega$. We consider designing M tapped FIR filter so that the signal with the desired angular frequency offset $\triangle \omega = \omega - \omega'$ passes through the filter without distortion, while suppressing other frequency components of signal $r''_m(n)$ and noise as much as possible.

Define the filter weight vector as w. To make the signal with angular frequency offset $\triangle\omega$ pass through the filter without distortion, there should be

$$w^T a(\omega) = 1 \tag{5}$$

where $a(\omega)$ is the signal frequency vector.

The above problem can be transformed into the following constraint optimization problem through calculation:

$$\min_{w,\alpha}\left\{ J(w,\alpha) = \frac{1}{L} \sum_{n=M-1}^{N-1} \left| w^H r''_m(n) - \alpha e^{j\omega n} \right|^2 \right\}, \quad s.t. \quad w^H a(\omega) = 1 \tag{6}$$

where $L = N - M + 1$, ω represents any given frequency, and α is the complex amplitude of the signal which frequency is ω.

Expanding the objective function defined in (6), we get

$$J(w,\alpha) = \left| \alpha - w^H g(\omega) \right|^2 + w^H R w - w^H g(\omega)g^H(\omega)w \tag{7}$$

where

$$g(\omega) = \frac{1}{L} \sum_{n=M-1}^{N-1} r''_m(n)e^{-j\omega n}$$

$$R = \frac{1}{L} \sum_{n=M-1}^{N-1} r''_m(n)r''_m(n)^H \tag{8}$$

We can find that α which minimizes the objective function from (7) is

$$\alpha(\omega) = w^H g(\omega) \tag{9}$$

Substituting (9) into (7), and letting

$$Q(\omega) = R - g(\omega)g^H(\omega) \tag{10}$$

Then the constraint optimization problem (6) can be transformed into

$$\min_{w} w^H Q w, \quad s.t. \quad w^H a(\omega) = 1 \tag{11}$$

The optimal weight vector of the APES algorithm can be obtained by solving the above optimization problem as

$$w_{\text{APES}} = \frac{Q^{-1}(\omega)a(\omega)}{a^H(\omega)Q^{-1}(\omega)a(\omega)} \tag{12}$$

Substituting w_{APES} into (9), the estimation of the complex amplitude α of the signal can be obtained as

$$\alpha(\omega) = \frac{a^H(\omega)Q^{-1}(\omega)g(\omega)}{a^H(\omega)Q^{-1}(\omega)a(\omega)} \tag{13}$$

Note that the complex amplitude estimate $\alpha(\omega)$ is a function of the frequency ω, and the amplitude spectrum of the signal can be obtained from (13), that is:

$$|\alpha(\omega)| = \left| \frac{a^H(\omega)Q^{-1}(\omega)g(\omega)}{a^H(\omega)Q^{-1}(\omega)a(\omega)} \right|, \qquad \omega \in [-\pi, \pi] \tag{14}$$

The frequency offset and phase offset of the clean copy relative to the packet 1 in collision signal can be accurately estimated exploiting APES spectrum estimation, based on the power difference between the clean copy and the packet 1 in collision signal. $|\alpha(\omega)|$ will show a peak at frequency offset $\omega = \Delta\omega$, while $|\alpha(\omega)|$ will be flat at other frequencies. The results of frequency estimation can be substituted into (13) to obtain the amplitude and phase of the signal at the frequency offset $\omega = \Delta\omega$.

The frequency offset and phase offset between the clean copy and the packet 1 in collision signal are compensated into the clean copy after APES spectrum estimation to improve correlation between twins sent by the same user terminal. In the following, we can make use of the correlation to separate the collision signal based on the MMSE criterion.

Let the clean copy of packet 1 after compensating the frequency offset and phase offset as the input signal $x'(n)$ of the MMSE filter, and define the estimation error of the collision signal separation as

$$e(n) = r_m(n) - y(n) = r_m(n) - w^H x'(n) = r_m(n) - x'^H(n)w^* \tag{15}$$

where $r_m(n)$ is the received collision signal, the filter output $y(n)$ is an estimate of the packet 1 in the collision signal, and $y(n) = w^H x'(n) = x'^H(n)w^*$.

Define the average power of the estimation error $e(n)$ as

$$\xi(w) = E\left[|e(n)|^2\right] = E\left[e(n)e^*(n)\right] \tag{16}$$

where $E[\cdot]$ represents mathematical expectation. It is often called $\xi(w)$s as the estimated mean square error (MSE) or cost function. Substituting (15) into (16), we have

$$\begin{aligned}
\xi(w) &= E\left\{\left[r_m(n) - w^H x'(n)\right]\left[r_m(n) - x'^H(n)w^*\right]^*\right\} \\
&= E\left\{|r_m(n)|^2\right\} - E\left\{r_m(n)x'^H(n)\right\}w \\
&\quad -w^T E\left\{x'(n)r_m^*(n)\right\} + w^H E\left\{x'(n)x'^H(n)\right\}w
\end{aligned} \tag{17}$$

Defining the filter weight vector as w is a certain quantity, and it is assumed that the mean value of the expected response $r_m(n)$ is 0, the average power of the first expected response in (17) is also the variance, let $\sigma_r^2 = E\{|r_m(n)|^2\}$.

The twins sent by the same terminal have a strong correlation because of the frequency offset and phase offset between the twins have been compensated by APES algorithm. We can make use of the clean copy and the collision signal to calculate the covariance matrix R and the cross correlation vector p. Where R and p represent, respectively, the covariance matrix of the clean copy, that is, $R = E\left[x'(n)x'^H(n)\right]$, and the cross correlation vector of the clean copy and the collision signal, that is, $p = E\left[x'(n)r_m^*(n)\right]$. The mean square error Eq. (17) can be expressed by using σ_r^2, R, and p as

$$\xi(w) = \sigma_r^2 - p^H w - w^H p + w^H R w \tag{18}$$

To minimize the mean square error equation, find the partial derivative of w in (19). Note that the differential operation of the scalar function on the vector can be expressed by the gradient of the scalar function on the vector. We can get the gradient of (18) as

$$
\begin{aligned}
\nabla_w \xi(w) &= 2\frac{\partial}{\partial w^*}[\xi(w)] = 2\frac{\partial}{\partial w^*}\left[\sigma_r^2 - p^H w - w^H p + w^H R w\right] \\
&= 2\frac{\partial \sigma_r^2}{\partial w^*} - 2\frac{\partial}{\partial w^*}\left(p^H w\right) - 2\frac{\partial}{\partial w^*}\left(w^H p\right) + 2\frac{\partial}{\partial w^*}\left(w^H R w\right) \\
&= 0 - 2\frac{\partial w^T}{\partial w^*}p^* - 2\frac{\partial w^H}{\partial w^*}p + 2Rw \\
&= 0 - 2Op^* - 2Ip + 2Rw \\
&= -2p + 2Rw
\end{aligned}
\tag{19}
$$

where O and I represents the zero matrix and the identity matrix respectively.

The necessary condition for the mean square error $\xi(w)$ to obtain an extreme value at w is $\frac{\partial \xi(w)}{\partial w_i^*} = 0$, $i = 1, 2, \cdots, M$. Let $\nabla_w \xi(w) = 0$, have

$$Rw = p \tag{20}$$

Using R^{-1} to multiply both sides of (20) to get collision signal separation weight

$$w_{MMSE} = R^{-1}p \tag{21}$$

Obviously, the closer the filter output estimated by the separation weight w_{MMSE} is to the packet 1 in collision signal, the closer the separated packet 2 is to the packet 2 sent by user terminal 2.

Finally, the collision signal and the filter output signal are destructively processed to achieve the separation of collision signal. The proposed short burst collision signal separation method can be achieved based on adaptive MMSE filtering through detailed derivation.

5 Simulation Results and Analysis

In this section, the performance results of proposed short burst signal separation method have been provided through an analytical model and Monte Carlo simulations.

The simulation parameters are as follows: the signal-to-noise ratio (SNR) difference between the received signals is 3 dB; the carrier frequency of received signal is 1100 Hz, and initial phase is π; the carrier frequency of the clean copy at the receiver is 1000 Hz, and initial phase is 0; the sampling frequency is 10 kHz, and the remaining parameters described in Table 1 have been used for the simulations.

Table 1. Simulation parameters

Parameter	Value
Packet size	100 bit
Packet rate	1000 bit/s
Modulation	BPSK
Channel type	AWGN
Filter length	1
E_b/N_0	0~10 dB

It is assumed that the packet 2 in the collision signal separated by the proposed signal separation method, and the performance results are obtained after the packet 2 is demodulated. Simulation performance results are shown in Figs. 4 and 5 for APES algorithm and signal separation method, respectively.

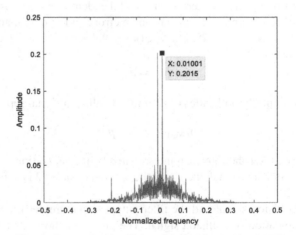

Fig. 4. Spectrum of collision signal estimated by APES

Figure 4 demonstrates the collision signal spectrum after APES algorithm. As it can be seen that the frequency offset between packet 1 in the received collision signal and the clean copy of packet 1 is about 100.1 Hz (the sampling frequency is 10 kHz), which corresponds to a theoretical value. The peak of multiplying the clean copy and the packet 1 after the low pass filter is much higher than the peak of multiplying the clean copy and the packet 2 after the low pass filter at the frequency offset position. The frequency offset and phase offset of the received collision signal can be well estimated by APES algorithm.

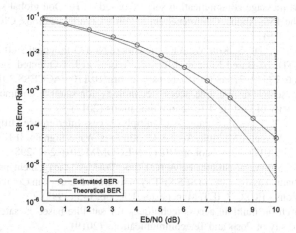

Fig. 5. Collision signal separation performance curve

The collision signal separation performance curve has been derived in Fig. 5 for various E_b/N_0. As shown in Fig. 5, the bit error rate gradually decreases in company with the E_b/N_0 increases. The estimated bit error rate curve and the theoretical bit error rate curve basically coincide with each other at low E_b/N_0, and there is a certain degree of deviation at high E_b/N_0. It can be concluded from the performance result that the proposed short burst collision signal separation can be achieved.

6   Conclusions

In this paper, a short burst collision signal separation method employs adaptive MMSE filtering combined with APES spectrum estimation at the receiver side, based on the correlation between collision signal and clean copy for the CRDSA scheme has been proposed and shown to solve the problem of user signal collision because of massive access process of satellite IoT terminals, and its performance assessed through detailed simulations, which verifies the feasibility of proposed method. Different simulation parameters can be set to further analyze the performance of proposed short burst collision signal separation method in the next work.

References

1. Li, D., et al.: On construction of china's space information network. Geomatics Inf. Sci. Wuhan Univ. **40**(6), 711–s715 (2015)
2. Bockelmann, C., et al.: Massive machine-type communications in 5g: physical and MAC-layer solutions. IEEE Commun. Mag. **54**(9), 59–65 (2016). https://doi.org/10.1109/MCOM. 2016.7565189

3. Tao, X., et al.: The research of orbcomm constellations about its development and new dynamic. Space Electron. Technol. **12**, 9–36 (2015)
4. Song, F., Feng, X.: Present status and development trend of argos system. Mar. Forecasts **29**(6), 98–102 (2012)
5. Liu, H.: Short message communication service based on BeiDou global satellites. In: Proceedings of the 15th Annual Conference on Satellite Communications, CIC, Beijing China, pp. 317–322 (2019)
6. Wang, Q., Ren, G., Gao, S., Kun, W.: A Framework of Non-Orthogonal Slotted Aloha (NOSA) Protocol for TDMA-Based Random Multiple Access in IoT-Oriented Satellite Networks. IEEE Access **6**, 77542–77553 (2018). https://doi.org/10.1109/ACCESS.2018.2883399
7. Chang, R.: Research on multiple access technology for satellite communication system. Beijing University of Posts and Telecommunications (2017)
8. Shen, Y., Wang, Y., Peng, Z., Siliang, W.: Multiple-Access Interference Mitigation for Acquisition of Code-Division Multiple-Access Continuous-Wave Signals. IEEE Commun. Lett. **21**(1), 192–195 (2017). https://doi.org/10.1109/LCOMM.2016.2625298
9. Caruso, M.G., Santo, L., Strano, F.: A real time DAMA management processor for high throughput channel assignment in SESNET system. In: 3rd European Conference on Satellite Communications - ECSC-3, IET, Manchester, UK, pp. 1–5 (1993)
10. Li, P.: Research on multiple access techniques for satellite-based in satellite IoT system. Beijing University of Posts and Telecommunications (2019)
11. Abramson, N.: THE ALOHA SYSTEM: another alternative for computer communications. Fall Joint Comput. Conf. **37**, 281–285 (1977)
12. Choudhury, G., Rappaport, S.: Diversity ALOHA--A Random Access Scheme for Satellite Communications. IEEE Trans. Commun. **31**(3), 450–457 (1983). https://doi.org/10.1109/TCOM.1983.1095828
13. Casini, E., De Gaudenzi, R., Herrero, O.: Contention Resolution Diversity Slotted ALOHA (CRDSA): An Enhanced Random Access Schemefor Satellite Access Packet Networks. IEEE Trans. Wireless Commun. **6**(4), 1408–1419 (2007). https://doi.org/10.1109/TWC.2007.348337
14. Herrero, O.D.R., Gaudenzi, R.D.: A high-performance MAC protocol for consumer broadband satellite systems. In: IET Conference Publications (2009)
15. Liva, G.: Graph-Based Analysis and Optimization of Contention Resolution Diversity Slotted ALOHA. IEEE Trans. Commun. **59**(2), 477–487 (2011). https://doi.org/10.1109/TCOMM.2010.120710.100054
16. He, Z., Xia, W.: Modern Digital Signal Processing and Its Application. Tsinghua University Press Beijing China (2009)
17. Clazzer, F., et al.: Irregular repetition slotted ALOHA over the Rayleigh block fading channel with capture. In: 2017 IEEE International Conference on Communications (ICC), pp. 1–6. IEEE, Paris (2017)

Design of Optimal Routing for Cooperative Microsatellite Swarm Network

Zhi Yang[✉], Dandan Wang, and Yan Zhang

DFH Satellite Co. Ltd., Beijing 100094, People's Republic of China
young_zhi@163.com

Abstract. The cooperative microsatellite swarm network has the advantages of low construction cost, short development cycle, flexible working mode and strong anti-destruction ability. In the network, micro-satellite nodes need to complete network control functions such as link maintenance, state monitoring and routing calculation. The valuable on-board payload and inter-satellite link resources are consumed. In order to reduce the energy consumption of satellite communication transmission, this paper focus on the routing issue in swarm network. A specific routing protocol is proposed, which defines the uniform format of swarm network packets suiting for path addressing based multi-hop transfer and the header deletion technique based packet routing scheme. An algorithm for optimal routing in swarm networks is devised, in which the transmission power consumption and the transfer time delay are chosen as the primarily concerned factors. The routing problem is mathematically formulated as a constrained optimization problem, with the total transmission power consumption of satellites as the optimization objective and with the transfer time delay as the constraint respectively. Then the graph theory approach is utilized as the tool to solve the problem. Examples are used to demonstrate the performance and efficiency of the proposed routing protocol and algorithm.

Keywords: Swarm network · Routing protocol · Routing algorithm · Constrained optimization problem · Graph theory

1 Introduction

With the in-depth development of space exploration, networking and data communication between satellites and other spacecraft have gradually become an important challenge [1]. However, there are some problems in the traditional design methods of satellite constellation network, such as relying on fixed configuration, vulnerable to be attacked, poor network reliability and high construction cost. The swarm network organized by micro-satellites has the advantages of low construction cost, short development cycle, flexible working mode and strong anti-destruction ability. It can complete some tasks such as information collection and observation that can not be completed by large satellites [2]. It has been paid more and more attention by research institutions.

Q. Wu et al. (Eds.): WiSATS 2020, LNICST 357, pp. 273–282, 2021.
https://doi.org/10.1007/978-3-030-69069-4_23

The study of satellite clusters is in its infancy. There are many problems in simulation verification and evaluation technology, network protocol design and optimization technology, multi-satellite cooperative control technology, adaptive task decision technology and so on. The topology of satellite cluster network is different from that of satellite constellation. Its network service requirements are very different from those of satellite constellations. The research on related technologies of swarm network is mainly focused on network topology control algorithm, network capacity research, task resource scheduling and so on [3–5]. More research is focused on the top-level architecture and bottom layer (physical layer and link layer) protocols, but there is no literature research on satellite cluster network routing protocols.

One of the most important functions of network layer quality-of-service (QoS) metrics is to provide guaranteed quality of data exchanging among satellites in an effective manner, which raises the problem of optimal routing in swarm networks. Space network routing techniques have been a research focus for years along with the rapid development of cooperative microsatellite swarm network. A large number of efforts have been made to explore the efficient routing strategies for space networks, and various routing protocols and algorithms have been proposed [6]. But these studies mostly focus on the application scenarios of conventional distributed space systems, such as low earth orbit (LEO) or medium earth orbit (MEO) communication or navigation satellite constellations, which are not directly applicable to swarm networks. For example, the mobility of network nodes (satellites or satellites) constitutes a major difference. The topology of a satellite constellation network is usually deterministic and can be predicted quite accurately, and the complete topology dynamic is periodic [6]. For ad hoc space networks, Shen et al. proposed a flexible routing architecture [7]. However, the proposed routing architecture is mainly oriented to inter planetary missions, in which the spacecraft is deployed in diverse orbits and has sparse and intermittent communication connectivity. So, it does not suit for the cooperative microsatellite swarm network. In a word, efficient routing strategies must consider the specific mission scenarios and optimization objectives of swarm network. Wu et al. proposed an optimization algorithm for signal routing in satellite sensor networks [8]. Although the sensor network mission scenarios in [8] are quite different from the microsatellite swarm network, the optimization objectives discussed in [8] are similar to that discussed in this paper. In [8] the authors transform the sensor network routing optimization problem into a single-objective optimization problem and a tabu search algorithm is used to solve the problem, while in this paper we formulate the swarm network routing optimization problem as a constrained optimization problem and utilize the graph theory based approach to solve the problem. In addition, a specific routing protocol is proposed for the microsatellite swarm network in this paper.

The rest of this paper is organized as follows. Section 2 concerns on routing protocol of swarm networks, in which format and routing scheme of network packets are presented. In Sect. 3, an on-board implementable routing algorithm is devised. In Sect. 4, some examples are studied. Finally, Sect. 5 concludes the paper.

2 Swarm Network Routing Protocol

2.1 Network Packet Format

Network packets are the basic data units being transferred in the swarm network, so all the application data must be encapsulated in network packets for transfer. As we have discussed in the previous sub-section, one of the major functions of network packets is to support the multi-hop transfer of application data in the swarm network. For this purpose, a specific swarm network packet format is defined below, as illustrated in Fig. 1.

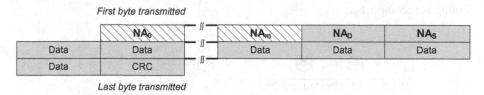

First byte transmitted

| Data | NA₀ | NAₘ | NA_D | NA_S |

Last byte transmitted

Fig. 1. Format of a network packet

In the packet, NA_0 to NA_m are the path address sequence, which define the route to be taken by the packet for transferring across the swarm network. The path address sequence is composed of the network addresses of routers used to guide the packet across the swarm network from the source node to the destination node. Note that, the path address sequence is generated by the router which locates in the same subnet with the source node by using route generation algorithm. NA_D is the destination address, which is specified as the network address of the destination node. NA_S is the source address, which is specified as the network address of the source node. Packet cargo comprises the application data that is encapsulated in the packet for transfer. CRC is an 8-bit cyclic redundancy check code used for packet error detection.

2.2 Packet Routing Scheme

Swarm network is a packet routing network. The routers provide a means of routing packets from the source node to the destination node. As discussed previously, path addressing is used for packet routing. With path addressing, the path address sequence is specified as a list of network addresses of routers that the packet will traverse.

Header deletion is a simple but effective technique designed in this paper to manage the transfer of packets across a swarm network. An intuitional illustration of the header deletion approach is illustrated in Fig. 2. As illustrated, when a packet is received at a router, its leading byte is firstly checked for validity verification. If the leading byte of the packet is not consistent with the NA of the router, it means that the packet should not be handled by this router. Then, the router should terminate the routing process and report the error to higher layers. Else, the router will check the second byte of the packet to determine the next hop to forward this packet to. Two cases are possible for this situation: 1) If the four most significant bits of the second byte is not consistent with the SN of the router, it means that the packet should be forwarded to some other router in the swarm network whose NA is consistent with the second byte. In this case, the leading byte (i.e. header) of the packet should be deleted, and the packet will pass through the router without this leading byte. Then, the routing process has to continue by repeating the above process, and the second byte of the packet which is now the new leading byte will be used for the subsequent routing. 2) If the four most significant bits of the second byte is consistent with the SN of the router, it means that the packet should be sent to a certain node in the current subnet whose CN is consistent with the four least significant bits of the second byte. This node is just the destination node, and till now the packet routing is accomplished.

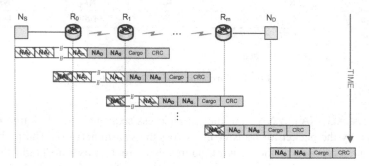

Fig. 2. Header deletion across multiple routers

3   Swarm Network Routing Algorithm

3.1   Routing Problem Formulation

As we known, power resources in cooperative microsatellite swarm network are very precious. Hence, power consumption is the first priority to be optimized in our design. An efficient routing algorithm is required to provide optimal routes in terms of both power consumption and transfer time delay.

Considering the m-hops data transfer process illustrated in Fig. 2, the overall power consumption for transferring the packet across the swarm network is formulated as

$$PC = \sum_{i=0}^{m-1} PC_{i,i+1} \tag{1}$$

where $PC_{i,i+1}$ is the power consumption of router R_i for transferring the packet to the next router R_{i+1}.

Let E_t be the transmitted energy per bit, according to the free space propagation model of signal, the received energy per bit E_r at the receiving end with distance d is

$$E_r = \frac{E_t}{d^\alpha} \tag{2}$$

where α is the signal attenuation factor, whose value is generally 2 for space communication. Assume that the minimum received energy per bit to maintain the required signal-to-noise ratio at the receiving end is E_b. Then, the minimum transmitted energy per bit E_m is

$$E_m = E_b \times d^\alpha \tag{3}$$

Let N be the total number of transmitted bits by router R_0 at the first hop, because of header deletion technique used for package routing, the total number of transmitted bits by router R_i at the $(i + 1)$-th hop should be $N - 8 \times i$. Then, the minimum power consumption of router R_i should be

$$PC_{i,i+1} = (N - 8 \times i) \times E_b \times d^\alpha_{i,i+1} \tag{4}$$

where $d_{i,i+1}$ is the length of wireless link between router R_i and router R_{i+1}, or equivalently the relative distance between satellites that carry routers R_i and R_{i+1}.

According to (1) and (4), we have

$$PC = \sum_{i=0}^{m-1} (N - 8 \times i) \times E_b \times d^\alpha_{i,i+1} \tag{5}$$

Because N is generally much lager than $8 \times i$, (5) can be approximately written as

$$PC = N \times E_b \times \sum_{i=0}^{m-1} d^\alpha_{i,i+1} \tag{6}$$

For the example illustrated in Fig. 1, transfer time delay of the packet from the source node to the destination node is formulated as

$$TD = TD_{S,0} + \sum_{i=0}^{m-1} TD_{i,i+1} + TD_{m,D} \tag{7}$$

where $TD_{S,0}$ and $TD_{m,D}$ is the intra-satellite transfer time delay, and $TD_{i,i+1}$ is the inter-satellite transfer time delay for forwarding the packet from router R_i to router R_{i+1}. Assuming that the upper bound of inter-satellite transfer time delay is τ, we have

$$TD_{\max} = TD_{S,0} + m \times \tau + TD_{m,D} \tag{8}$$

From (6), it is not difficult to find that transferring a packet in a multi-hop manner may remarkably decrease the overall power consumption compared with transferring the packet directly in some cases. For example, assume that the satellites that carry routers $R_0 \sim R_m$ (denoted as $M_0 \sim M_m$) are in a formation of 'string-of-pearls', where M_0 and M_m locate at two ends of the string, and the rest satellites distribute equidistantly between M_0 and M_m. Then, the overall power consumption for transferring a packet successively passing through $M_1 \sim M_{m-1}$ from R_0 to R_m with m-hops is $m^{(1-\alpha)}$ times of that for transferring the packet directly. Although it is effective for power saving, the penalty is that multi-hop transfer will take much more time.

From the designers' point of view, the power consumption is expected to be as low as possible. Meanwhile, the transfer time delay has to meet the strict real-time constraint. Let power consumption be the optimization objective and transfer time delay be the constraint, then the swarm network routing problem can be modeled as a constrained optimization problem, which is formally formulated as:

$$
\begin{cases}
\text{Given} & N_S, N_D \\
\text{Find} & \{R_0, R_1, \ldots, R_m\} \\
\text{Min} & PC = N \times E_b \times \sum_{i=0}^{m-1} d_{i,i+1}^{\alpha} \\
\text{s.t.} & TD_{S,0} + m \times \tau + TD_{m,D} \le TD_C
\end{cases}
\tag{9}
$$

where TD_C is the end-to-end time delay constraint pre-defined according to the task requirement. For N and E_b are constants, (9) is equivalent to

$$
\begin{cases}
\text{Given} & N_S, N_D \\
\text{Find} & \{R_0, R_1, \ldots, R_m\} \\
\text{Min} & \sum_{i=0}^{m-1} d_{i,i+1}^{\alpha} \\
\text{s.t.} & m \le \left\lfloor \frac{TD_C - TD_{S,0} - TD_{m,D}}{\tau} \right\rfloor
\end{cases}
\tag{10}
$$

3.2 Routing Algorithm Implementation

The main purpose of this section is to illustrate the implementation of the algorithm. Main procedure of the algorithm is presented in Algorithm 1 using pseudo code. Giving the graph model $G = <V, E, W(t)>$ of a swarm network, a pre-specified source node v_s, and a hop limitation L_{hop} as inputs, Algorithm 1 is used to compute the optimized routing paths from v_s to each $v_i \in V$ with hop limitation L_{hop}. Here we say that a path is optimized if the path is a minimum weight path between two specific nodes in G with bounded length L_{hop} (Table 1).

Table 1. Routing optimization algorithm.

Algorithm 1. Routing Optimization Algorithm	

1:     **input**: graph model of a swarm network $G=<V, E, W(t)>$; source node v_s;
       hop limitation L_{hop}.

2:     **output**: optimized routing paths from v_s to each $v_i \in V$ with hop limitation
       L_{hop}, i.e. $P_{route} = \{p_{si} \in P_{min}(v_s, v_i, L_{hop}) \mid v_i \in V\}$.

3:         **begin**

4:         /* initialization*/

5:         **for** $i=1$ to $|V|$

6:             $p_{si} = v_s \rightarrow v_i$;

7:             $p'_{si} = p_{si}$;

8:             *improved* = 0;

9:         **end for**

10:        /* main loop*/

11:        **for** $hop=1$ to $L_{hop}-1$**do**

12:            **foreach** p_{si} *whose length is equal to hop* **do**

13:                **foreach** $v_j \in V$ **do**

14:                    **if** $w(p_{si}, t) + w(e_{ij}, t) < w(p'_{sj}, t)$ **then**

15:                        $p'_{sj} = p_{si} \rightarrow v_i \rightarrow v_j$;

16:                    **end if**

17:                **end foreach**

18:            **end foreach**

19:            **for** $i=1$ to $|V|$

20:                **if** $w(p'_{si}, t) < w(p_{si}, t)$ **then**

21:                    $p_{si} = p'_{si}$;

22:                    *improved* = 1;

23:                **end if**

24:            **end for**

25:            **if** *improved*==0 **then**

26:                **break**;

27:            **end if**

28:        **end for**

29:    **end**

4 Examples and Discussions

4.1 Experiment Scenarios and Items

In this section, some examples will be presented to test and evaluate the routing protocol and algorithm we proposed. Assume that the swarm is composed of eight satellites, in which the satellites are required to stay within a bounded range $D_{max} = 10$ km.

The osculating orbital elements of each satellite at the initial time are listed below in Table 2. Data used in the experiments can be calculated from the initial conditions.

Table 2. Osculating orbital elements of satellites at initial time

Satellite no	a (km)	e	i (rad)	Ω (rad)	ω (rad)	M (rad)
1	7044.7770	0.0017655062	1.7135689	0.41960884	0.71080177	5.8878418
2	7044.7959	0.0019333002	1.7141038	0.41978852	0.61962430	5.9790881
3	7044.7543	0.0017789350	1.7136303	0.41962750	0.70051393	5.8983631
4	7044.7585	0.0018306072	1.7137249	0.41966203	0.71456895	5.8840353
5	7044.8015	0.0018911526	1.7138806	0.42000115	0.82386247	5.7748226
6	7044.7924	0.0017659261	1.7135688	0.41970884	0.71606259	5.8830248
7	7044.7999	0.0017710582	1.7135765	0.41961160	0.71162926	5.8867685
8	7044.8003	0.0019047291	1.7138145	0.41967736	0.70718406	5.8914562

As we have stated, the main objective of our network routing algorithm is to minimize the total transmission power consumption of the satellites with the transfer time delay, or equivalently the hop limitation, as constraint. So, the performance for power saving of the algorithm is the first priority to be tested. Normalized power consumption index, denoted as PC_{norm}, is used as the criterion for evaluation, which is defined as

$$PC_{norm} = \frac{PC_{route}}{PC_{direct}} \tag{11}$$

where PC_{route} and PC_{direct} are respectively the total transmission power consumption of satellites in the swarm for transferring the packets with and without multi-hop routing in a specified time interval.

4.2   Results of Centralized Organization

For centralized organization, we assume that all the satellites in the swarm could be selected as the leader. So, there are 8 cases. In each case, the network communication traffic is assumed to be as follows: every second, the leader polls all the followers in the swarm by sending polling packets to them one by one; once a follower is polled by the leader, it replies an acknowledgement packet to the leader immediately. Each packet is transferred from the source to the destination with multi-hops, where the hop limitation could be 2 to 7 according to different real-time demands, and all the packets are assumed to be of the same size in order to simplify the discussion.

The results of PC_{norm} at each second for the 8 different cases are illustrated in Fig. 3. For each case, several curves are plotted according to the experimental data of different hop limitations L_{hop}. On each curve, there are about 3000 samples, which correspond to the results of PC_{norm} at second i ($i = 0, 1, ..., 3000$). From Fig. 3 we can see that, for all the 8 cases (i.e. no matter which satellite is designated as the leader), with hop limitation $L_{hop} \geq 2$, the value of PC_{norm} at each second is less than 1, exactly it is between about 0.4 to 0.8. This means that, using our algorithm can considerably reduce (about 20% to 60% for different situations) the total transmission power consumption of the satellites at each second, with the real-time requirement being considered. For the 8 cases, the optimization degrees of power consumption are different, because their dataflow relations are various. Focusing on a specific one of the 8 cases (i.e. a specific sub-figure in Fig. 3) we can see that, the looser the hop limitation is the better the effect of power saving will be. Besides, for each curve in the sub-figure, its value varies with time because topology of the swarm changes from second to second.

Results in Fig. 3 shows that, the routing optimization algorithm we proposed is well suitable for power saving in the swarm network with centralized organization.

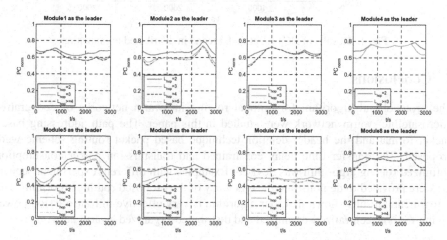

Fig. 3. Results of PC_{norm} at each second for different cases in centralized organization

4.3   Results of Distributed Organization

In a distributed organized swarm, all the satellites are of the same probability to transfer data to the other satellites. So we assume that, in each second there is a mutual communication (i.e. packet transfer) between each pair of satellites, and all the packets are of the same size.

For the network communication specified above, the results of PC_{norm} at each second for different hop limitations are illustrated in Fig. 4, which show that our algorithm performs well in each second for power saving, and the looser the hop limitation is the better the performance will be.

Results in Fig. 4 shows that, the routing optimization algorithm we proposed is well suitable for power saving in the swarm network with distributed organization.

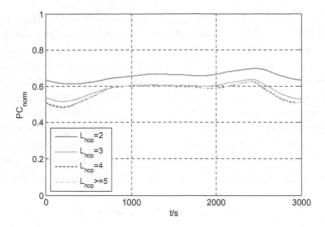

Fig. 4. Results of PC_{norm} at each second in distributed organization

5 Conclusions

The protocol and algorithm for optimal routing in swarm networks of cooperative microsatellite swarm network were studied in this paper. The path addressing based packet format and the header deletion technique based packet routing scheme were proposed. The transfer time delay constrained and transmission power consumption optimized routing algorithm was devised. Examples with different experiment scenarios were provided to demonstrate the efficiency of the proposed routing algorithm. The experimental results shown that, our algorithm is very effective in transmission power saving for both centralized-organized and distributed-organized swarm networks.

References

1. Li, D., Shen, X., et al.: On construction of china's space information network. Geomat. Inf. Sci. Wuhan Univ. **40**(6), 711–715 (2015)
2. Radhakrishnan, R., Edmonson, W., Afghah, F., et al.: Survey of inter-satellite communication for small satellite systems: physical layer to network layer view. IEEE Commun. Surv. Tutor. **18**(4), 2442–2473 (2016)
3. Wang, J., Yu, Q.: System architecture and key technology of space information network based on distributed satellite clusters. ZTE Technol. J. **11**(4), 9–13 (2016)
4. Chen, Q., Zhang, J., Hu, Z.: A topology control strategy with reliability assurance for satellite cluster networks in earth observation. Sensors **17**(3), 445 (2017)
5. Zhang, W., Zhang, G., Dong, F., et al.: Capacity model and constraints analysis for integrated remote wireless sensor and satellite network in emergency scenarios. Sensors **15**(12), 29036–29055 (2015)
6. Alagoz, F., Korcak, O., Jamalipour, A.: Exploring the routing strategies in next-generation satellite networks. IEEE Wirel. Commun. **14**, 79–88 (2007)
7. Shen, C., Sundaram, B., Jaikaeo, C.: A flexible routing architecture for ad hoc space networks. Comput. Netw. **46**(3), 389–410 (2004)
8. Wu, X., Vladimirova, T., Sidibeh, K.: Signal routing in a satellite sensor network using optimisation algorithms. In: 2008 IEEE Aerospace Conference, Big Sky, MT, USA, 1–8 March 2008 (2008)

An Inter-domain Routing Protocol N-BGP for Space Internetworking

Huiwen Chen[⊠], Kanglian Zhao, Jiawei Sun, Wenfeng Li, and Yuan Fang

Nanjing University, Nanjing, China
chenhuiwen@smail.nju.edu.cn

Abstract. Boarder Gateway Protocol (BGP) is mainly used for inter-domain routing in terrestrial internetworking. However, when the traditional BGP is used for space internetworking, inter-domain link interruption might occur more frequently and the time of routing convergence will tend to be long, which would greatly reduce the stability of the network. A new variant of border gateway protocol, N-BGP is proposed in this paper for space internetworking. Firstly, the existing NTD-BGP method are adopted in N-BGP to deal with predictable link changes caused by orbital dynamics of satellites. For the unpredictable link break, BGP finite state machine is modified and a new link break detection mechanism is also introduced. Considering the predictability of satellite motion, the backup routing mechanism is also used to maintain the stability of the network, which realizes the high stability of inter-domain routing. The experimental results show that the improved routing protocol N-BGP is superior to the traditional BGP in reducing the detection time of link interruption and maintaining the network stability.

Keywords: Inter-domain routing protocol · Unexpected link interruption · Space environments

1 Introduction

Typical satellite networks include GEO, MEO, LEO and other satellite systems [1]. In space networks, each satellite system is generally regarded as an independent and complete autonomous system (AS) domain [2]. Within each AS autonomous domain, one or more satellites are selected as the boundary router of this domain to establish inter-domain links with the corresponding boundary routers of other domains to realize information transmission between different autonomous domains.

On the other hand, compared with the topology of space networks which change frequently because of the orbital dynamics of the satellites, the topologies of the terrestrial networks are relatively fixed and the distance between each pair of routers in the link is shorter, which results in shorter transmission delay. Therefore, the traditional BGP protocol and the network topology are tightly coupled in the terrestrial networks. When there is a change in the neighbor relationship, because the traditional BGP is sensitive to the change of link state, so it can detect the unexpected interruption of the link

Q. Wu et al. (Eds.): WiSATS 2020, LNICST 357, pp. 283–296, 2021.
https://doi.org/10.1007/978-3-030-69069-4_24

quickly. Considering the characteristics of the space environment, the topology changes frequently because of the orbital dynamics of the satellites, resulting in the frequent updating of the neighborhood relations, which will cause the huge consumption of the limited onboard resources. Moreover, there are also unpredictable link interrupts, which are usually caused by the radiation interference of the communication channel or the temporary failure of a satellite. When unpredictable interrupts occur, the traditional BGP protocol often requires longer routing convergence time to detect link interruption. However, in space internetworking, the time for route updating can be long, which means the link might change again even if the route has not been updated. In the process from link interruption to link recovery, a large number of packets might be lost, which will not only increase the rate of packet loss, but also greatly reduce the stability of the network. The special situations as mentioned above in space internetworking will bring a series of challenges and burden to the satellites networks with limited bandwidth.

In order to solve the problems with the application of the traditional BGP protocol in the space environment [3], the existing research direction is mainly aimed at the frequent change of spatial topology, and a series of solutions are proposed. Wei Han [4] et al. proposed NCSR which applies network coding to multicast transmission of geographic satellite network BGP in response to environmental interference. Roman Chertov et al. [5] conducted a high-fidelity experimental study on intermittent space/ground links and its impact on BGP peer-to-peer sessions between ground and satellite routers. Fabrice Hobaya [6] et al. analyzed the different ways of deploying BGP in DVB-S2/RCS networks and the opportunities to leverage the reliable multicast transport layer. Eylem Ekici and Chao Chen [7] proposed the BGP-S protocol, which makes the automatic discovery of paths through satellite networks possible.

NTD-BGP [8] takes advantage of the predictability of the orbital dynamics of the satellites, establishes the neighbor relation based on router loopback address, reduces the number of changes in neighbor relations, decouples the mapping relation between network topology and inter-domain neighbor relations and route updates, realizes the fast update of route, and improves the stability of network. However, this kind of scheme only focuses on the predictable change in topology, but it cannot solve a series of problems caused by unpredictable link interruptions.

The scheme presented in this paper utilizes the existing NTD-BGP method to cope with the predictable change of the topologies, while for the unpredictable link interruptions, a new mechanism is introduced to shorten the convergence time and improve the stability of the network for inter-domain routing in space environment.

2   The BGP Protocol

As an inter-domain routing protocol [9], BGP is responsible for the routing among different AS domains. The BGP routers in the same domain maintain the interior boarder gateway protocol (IBGP) neighbor relationship with each other, while the routers in different domains maintain the exterior boarder gateway (EBGP) neighbor relationship with each other. EBGP neighbor relationships require physical links between neighbor bodies, while only logical links are required between IBGP neighbor bodies. The BGP adopts a finite state machine, in which the router starts from the Idle state, exchanges a series of messages, and finally reaches the Established state, successfully establishing the neighborhood body relationship, as shown in Fig. 1.

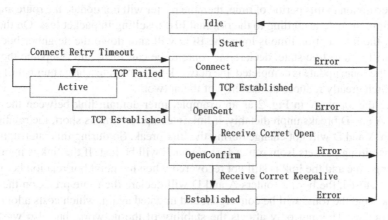

Fig. 1. BGP finite neighbor state machine

After the neighbor relationships are established, the router announces all the routing prefix information to all the neighbors to generate the forward information base (FIB). The state of the link is detected by sending keepalive messages periodically between neighbors (default 60 s), indicating the effectiveness of the link, and a value of hold time (default 180 s) is maintained between the neighbor bodies by default. When routers start exchanging open messages with each other, they will receive the value of send time from each other in the open message and determine the value of hold time and keepalive time after negotiation. The negotiation algorithm is shown in Algorithm 1.

Algorithm 1: time negotiation

1) If (send time from the other router < local hold time)
   local hold time = send time
2) If (local keepalive time < (send time from the other router / 3))
   local keepalive time = send time/3

When the router receives a larger hold time value than its own, no changes will be made. On the contrary, when it receives a smaller time, it will use the received time to replace its own hold time. When the router does not receive the keepalive message sent periodically by the neighbor body including hold time, a link interrupt will be inferred and both sides of the neighbor body will return to the Idle state from the Established state and send the undo route prefix to update the route. For the neighbors, if the hold time is too long, the routing update time will also be too long. If the link is interrupted unexpectedly, the packet loss rate of the link will be greatly increased and the stability of the network will be reduced. However, if the hold time is too small, the link will be updated frequently, resulting in the instability of inter-domain neighbor relations, which consumes the limited computing resources and bandwidth on the satellite networks.

Three keepalive messages without response indicates link interruption in the traditional BGP protocol. On the one hand, when the inter-domain link is interrupted unexpectedly, if the interruption time is short, the traditional BGP protocol cannot detect the link interruption in this period of time, then the router will not update the route and keep forwarding the data according to the original FIB resulting in packet loss. On the other hand, if the interruption time is long, the BGP will shut down the neighbor body. The router will turn to Idle state, declare the route to be canceled, and re-update the route. Before the route update is completed, the network will generate a large number of packet loss, which greatly reduces the stability of the network.

Take the topology in Fig. 2 as an example, inter-domain link between the border routers A and D breaks unpredictably, if link interruption time is short, the relationship between A and D will not change during the link break. So during this interruption, all the transmitting packets from router E to router F will be lost. If the link is interrupted for a long time and the link is still not recovered when the neighbor relation between A and D is closed, the border routers A and D will declare the route prefix on the whole network Sand the route will be convergent and updated again, which costs a lot of time and resources. This not only affects the stability of the network, but also wastes the limited onboard resources.

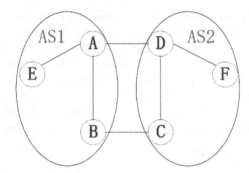

Fig. 2. Link detection mechanism of traditional BGP protocol

3   A New Variant of the BGP Protocol for Space Internetworking

Based on the traditional BGP, a new variant of the BGP protocol, N-BGP, is proposed in this section. Similar to the NTD-BGP protocol, N-BGP copes with the problem of routing updates caused by predictable topology changes. Moreover, in view of the unpredictable link break, N-BGP introduces a new inter-domain link break detection mechanism, which improves the BGP originally limited neighbor state machine itself and greatly shortens the time of detection of accident link breaks. Secondly, N-BGP calculates the corresponding backup routing for the link between each domain and stores in each router. When the new detection mechanism detects the unpredictable break link, the router turns to a new state, amending the routing itself to backup routing and guarantee the stability of the network.

3.1 The Detection Mechanism of the Unpredictable Link Interruptions

In N-BGP, the traditional BGP neighbor state machine is improved with the introduction of new detection mechanism. Hold time is set as 180 s by default while keepalive time is set as 60 s by default. On the border routers, test messages are sent every 10s regularly to detect the state information of inter-domain links. Once the neighbor does not receive the test messages, it judges that the link is down. The modified state machine is shown in Fig. 3.

When the detection mechanism detects a link interrupt, it modifies the router's own FIB to a backup FIB. When it detects the link recovery, it returns to the established state from the backup route state. When the backup route fails to meet the requirements, the traditional BGP route updating mechanism is reactivated. The new detection mechanism of the N-BGP greatly shortens the detection time of link interruption and reduces the consumption of onboard resource for calculation to some extent.

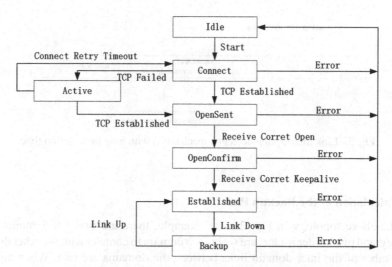

Fig. 3. Improved finite neighbor state machine

Unpredictable link interruptions can be divided into two categories:

1) If the link interruption is short, the link interruption and recovery are completed within the hold time in this situation. Then the neighbor relationship of neighbor body of each inter-domain link will not change. When an unexpected link interruption occurs, it turns to back up routes after receiving the probe message. After the link recovery, the original main route will be restored. As we can see in the following Fig. 4.

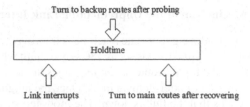

Fig. 4. Link interrupt detection mechanism with short interrupt time

2) If the link interruption time is long, the EBGP neighbor relationships will comes to an end and the routers will change to the Idle state. When the link reconnects, the route will be updated and the original main route will be restored in the routers. As we can see in the following Fig. 5.

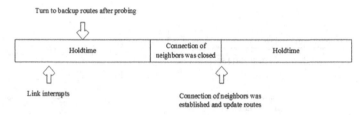

Fig. 5. Link interruption detection mechanism with long interruption time

3.2 Calculation of the Backup Path

Take the above topology in Fig. 2 as an example, there are two AS domains in the topology, and two border routers are set in each domain to connect with the other domain. The number of the inter-domain links between the domains are two. When an inter-domain link is interrupted unexpectedly, the border router replaces the main route with the stored backup route. The calculation of backup route is mainly aimed at the next hop, and the next hop is modified as the backup route. The backup routing mechanism of the N-BGP consists of the following three steps:

Firstly, a table of inter-domain topological relation is introduced, which records the border routers in AS1 and AS2 in real time, as well as the relations between them. The stored table of inter-domain topological relation is shown in Table 1, which has border router A and B in AS1, border router D and C in AS2. And there is an inter-domain link between router A and router D, and an inter-domain link between router B and router C.

Secondly, the inter-domain topology relation table, IGP routing table, and BGP routing table stored in router A is summarized as mentioned above. There are three destinations in AS2 to router A in AS1. Each destination is described as a prefix. To arrive each destination, router D will be its next hop, which is the same as described in the following Table 2. In AS1, there are two destinations except router A. And to reach router E or B, next hop is also shown as in the following Table 3.

Table 1. Table of inter-domain topological relation.

AS1	AS2
A	D
B	C

Table 2. BGP routing table.

Destination	Next hop
Prefix1	D
Prefix2	D
Prefix3	D

Table 3. IGP routing table.

Destination	Next hop
E	E
B	B

Third, backup FIB is summarized as mentioned above (Table 4).

Table 4. Backup FIB.

Destination	Next hop
Prefix1	B
Prefix2	B
Prefix3	B

The principle of the calculation of the backup route is:

1) For any routing table item (destination, next hop), if and only if the next hop is the EBGP neighbor node of the router, the corresponding backup route (destination', next hop) is generated.
2) For any backup route (destination', next hop), destination' router and destination router are in the same AS.

Taking the topology shown in Fig. 2 as an example, there is an inter-domain link between router A and router D, and there is also an inter-domain link between router

B and router C, and EBGP neighbor relationship is established respectively. Router A, router B and router E belong to the same domain AS1 and are the IBGP neighbors to each other. For router A, any destination prefix in domain AS2 can be reached by router D for the next hop, but also can be reached by another border router C in the same domain through router B. So as for router A, it uses path A to D to arrive AS2 as main route while it also uses path A-B-C-D as backup route.

When the link between router A and router D is interrupted unexpectedly, the route on router A and router D is switched to the backup route, which can guarantee the stability of the network during interruption and reduce the packet loss rate. For other routers in the domain, the routing table is kept unchanged and router A or router D is still taken as the next hop to the destination in the other domain. When the link is restored, the backup route is cancelled and switched back to the original route.

3.3   Main Modules of N-BGP Protocol

Main modules of N-BGP protocol are shown in Fig. 6.

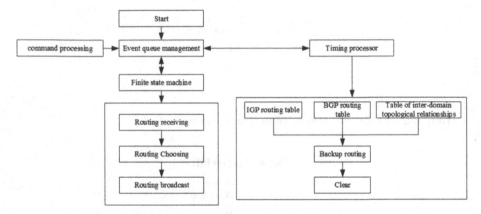

Fig. 6. Main modules of the BGP protocol.

1) The start module mainly completes the initialization.
2) The event queue management module mainly manages the time queue, which is the trigger condition of the state transfer of N-BGP finite state machine and promotes the operation of the module of finite state machine.
3) The command processing module is responsible for processing various commands and calls related functions for processing.
4) The timing processing module handles the event timeout and other behaviors through the timer queue, detects the link state through the timing processing module, and then turns to the backup routing mechanism.
5) The calculation module of backup route is shown in the box, indicating that the backup route is calculated by IGP routing table, BGP routing table and inter-domain topological relation table. In addition, in the space internetworking, when the satellite

motion produces a change in topology, the backup route stored in the original storage is cleared by the clearance mechanism to reduce the overhead of the satellite.

6) The module of finite state machine is responsible for the management of finite neighbor state machine. In the original BGP protocol, there are 13 events that can trigger the state change. When the neighbor relationship is established, a series of processing processes from receiving to sending are completed through the routing receiving, routing selection and routing broadcast modules in the box.

Compared with the traditional BGP protocol, the new protocol N-BGP not only can deal with a series of problems such as longer time of routing convergence caused by frequent changes of the routing update frequently. In view of the unpredictable link break, it introduces a new detecting mechanism, which changes the traditional BGP neighbor finite state machine. The new detection mechanism can be more effective and rapidly detect link interruption, greatly reducing the routing convergence time. On the other hand, the table of inter-domain topological relation is introduced, and the backup route is calculated by the table of inter-domain topological relation, IGP routing table and BGP routing table. When the backup route fails to work, the traditional BGP mechanism is reverted to and the route is re-converged and updated to ensure the effectiveness.

4   Simulation Results

4.1   Experimental Scenarios

In this part, the performance of the proposed N-BGP will be verified in the case of unpredictable link interrupts, especially with the comparison with the traditional BGP. A topology of eight simplified nodes in a certain time slice is assumed, as shown in Fig. 7.

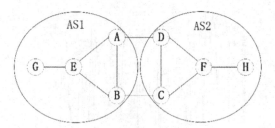

Fig. 7. Test topology.

In this topology, there are two AS domains, each containing four router nodes and two boundary routers. There are altogether four boundary routers in the whole topology, two of which are EBGP neighbor bodies of each other, and there are two interdomain links between the two domains. In order to simulate space environment and verify the validity of the improved inter-domain routing protocol, it uses Docker [12] and the software router Quagga [11] as routers. At the same time, the routers are connected by OVS [13] and it uses OVS flow table to simulate link interruption and recovery, which effectively increases the fidelity of the emulation. Considering the impact of link interruption time on performance, different lengths of the link interruption time are selected here as independent variables to test the performance.

4.2 Performance Analysis

Three metrics are selected to evaluate the performance of the proposed N-BGP and the traditional BGP protocol, which are the detection time of the unexpected link interruption, the routing convergence time and the network stability.

Among them, the detection time of the unexpected link interruption indicates the time required to detect the unpredictable link interruption.

Routing convergence time T, on the other hand, contains two parts. One is convergence time after link interruption is detected. The other is the convergence time after routing recovery. In the test of routing convergence time, the time of routing convergence is mainly tested under different link interrupt times randomly.

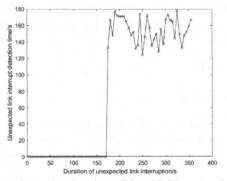

(a) Detection time in traditional BGP protocol

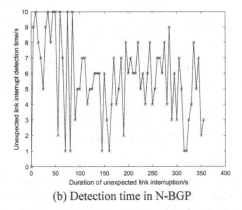

(b) Detection time in N-BGP

Fig. 8. The detection time of the unexpected link interruption.

In Fig. 8, the link interruption time is selected from 5s to 360s, and each 5s is a step length. When the unpredictable link interruption duration is less than 180s, it can

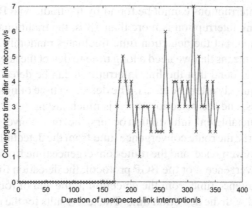

(a) Convergence time of traditional BGP protocol

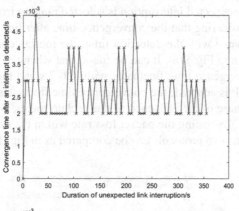

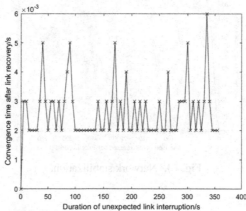

(b) Convergence time of improved protocol

Fig. 9. Routing convergence time.

be found that link interruptions cannot be found by the traditional BGP protocol. When the unpredictable link interruption is more than 180s, the traditional BGP protocol can detect the interruption, but the detection time fluctuates randomly within the scope of 120s to 180s, which means that we need a long time to detect the accidental interruption. In contrast, it can be found that the link interruption can be detected by the improved protocol relatively quickly after about 10s. The detection time of link interrupt fluctuates in the range of 0-10s, and the detection speed is much faster.

When an unpredictable link interruption occurs, the route convergence time is mainly composed of two parts: the route convergence time from the detection of link interruption to the end of route convergence, and the route convergence time from the link recovery to the end of route convergence. For the BGP protocol, the detection time is relatively long and the route convergence time from the detection to the end of routing convergence is negligible compared with the detection time. The test results for the routing convergence time are shown in Fig. 9.

The duration of unexpected interruption is selected ranging from 5 to 360s, and the step length is 5s. Considering that the convergence time after link interruption in BGP can be ignored compared with the detection time, the routing convergence time after link recovery is shown in Fig. 9(a). It can be found that when the protocol detects link interruption, the convergence time fluctuates within 1–7 s and the convergence speed is slow. When N-BGP is adopted, the convergence time fluctuates within the range of 0–10 ms. This is because of the existence of the backup routes, which greatly reduces the convergence time. By testing the packet loss rate within the link interrupt time, the network stability of the two protocols can be compared as in Fig. 10.

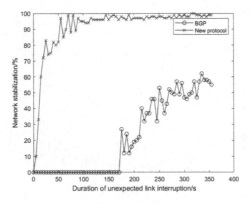

Fig. 10. Network stabilization.

It can be found that the network stability of the BGP protocol is poor, which is less than 50%, and increases gradually with the increases of link interruption duration. However, the N-BGP protocol has better network stability, which increases rapidly with the increases of link interruption duration and maintains about 100% in a long range.

5 Conclusions

In this paper, N-BGP is proposed to solve a series of performance problems caused by frequent topology changes and unpredictable inter-domain link interruptions. N-BGP adopts the scheme of the NTD-BGP protocol and introduces a new detection mechanism to detect the inter-domain link interrupts at a faster speed. In addition, considering the predictability of orbital dynamics of the satellites, a backup routing mechanism is introduced to guarantee the corresponding backup route on the boundary router. When the link interruption is detected quickly, the backup route is switched to ensure the stability of the network. Finally, the new improved protocol was designed and implemented in Quagga. The results of emulation show that the proposed N-GBP protocol greatly improves the network stability by shortening time for link interruption detection and backup routes. However, N-BGP requires a certain amount of space to store routing information on the router, which increases the cost of routing. The future research will be focused on how to reduce the routing cost as well as shorten the routing convergence time and improve the routing stability.

References

1. Roddy, D.: Satellite Communications (2003)
2. Chandra, R., Traina, P., Li, T.: BGP communities attribute. RFC 1997, August 1996
3. Narvaez, P., Clerget, A., Dabbous, W.: Internet routing over LEO satellite constellations. In: Third ACM/IEEE International Workshop on Satellite-Based Information Services (WOSBIS 1998) (1998)
4. Han, W., Wang, B., Feng, Z., et al.: NCSR: multicast transport of BGP for geostationary Satellite network based on network coding. In: 2015 IEEE Aerospace Conference, pp. 1–10. IEEE (2015)
5. Chertov, R., Almeroth, K.: Using BGP in a satellite-based challenged network environment. In: 2010 7th Annual IEEE Communications Society Conference on Sensor, Mesh and Ad Hoc Communications and Networks (SECON), pp. 1–9. IEEE (2010)
6. Hobaya, F., Chaput, E., Baudoin, C., et al.: Reliable multicast transport of BGP for geostationary satellite networks. In: 2012 IEEE International Conference on Communications (ICC), pp. 3239–3244. IEEE (2012)
7. Ekici, E., Chen, C.: BGP-S: a protocol for terrestrial and satellite network integration in network layer. Wireless Netw. **10**(5), 595–605 (2004)
8. Yang, Z., Wu, Q., Li, H., et al.: NTD-BGP: an inter-domain routing protocol for integrated terrestrial-satellite networks. J. Tsinghua Univ. (Sci. Technol.) **59**(7), 512–522 (2019)
9. Hares, S., Rekhter, Y., Li, T.: A Border Gateway Protocol 4 (BGP-4) (2006)
10. Papa, A., De Cola, T., Vizarreta, P., et al.: Dynamic SDN controller placement in a LEO constellation satellite network. In: 2018 IEEE Global Communications Conference (GLOBECOM), pp. 206–212. IEEE (2018)

11. Quagga Routing Suite. https://www.quagga.net/
12. Boettiger, C.: An introduction to Docker for reproducible research, with examples from the R environment. ACM Sigops Oper. Syst. Rev. **49**(1), 71–79 (2014)
13. Open vSwitch. https://www.openvswitch.org/
14. Ramanath, A.: A Study of the interaction of BGP/OSPF in Zebra/ZebOS/Quagga (2004)

Cloud Change Prediction System Based on Deep Learning

Dai Zheng[✉], Zhao Kanglian, and Li Wenfeng

NanJing University, 163 Xianlin Street, Qixia Distirct, Nanjing 210023, Jiangsu, China
1056318647@qq.com

Abstract. In satellite-to-ground laser communications, the laser beam is susceptible to the effects of atmospheric media when it passes through the atmosphere.
The main reason is that the laser beam will be absorbed and scattered by the cloud
when it passes through the cloud, causing the communication link to be blocked.
In order to know the cloud cluster information around the laser beam in advance,
this paper proposes a Cloud Prediction Network (CloudNet) model, which classi-
fies first, then predict the cloud trajectory for the next 100 s by collecting clouds
images over a ground station, so as to reasonably allocating the resources of the link
and select the ground stations. The experimental results show that the prediction
accuracy of the model is up to 81% under the condition of 5% error.

Keywords: Laser communication · Cloud Prediction Network · Cloud sequence
prediction

1 Introduction

Laser communication is the main method of communication technology in future
satellites-to-satellites and satellites-to-ground in space networks. Compared with traditional microwave communication technology, space laser communication takes the
advantages of using laser as a carrier, which can realize large data transmission at
high speed, and has high anti-interference and confidentiality [1]. Compared with inter-
satellite laser links, satellite-to-ground laser links which need to pass through the atmosphere are subject to atmospheric turbulence, clouds, fog, haze and other atmospheric
environments, which seriously attenuates the laser transmission signal. Therefore, it must
be considered that atmospheric factors affect the transmission quality in the satellite-
to-ground laser communication. It can provide important priori information on whether
satellites and grounds are suitable for laser link construction and whether meeting expec-
tations of link quality when learning about the status of cloud clusters over ground stations in advance so as to ensure uninterrupted satellite-to-ground laser communication.
Therefore, in order to know the cloud coverage information around the laser communication link in advance, it is necessary to predict the change trend of the cloud over the
ground station in advance.

Q. Wu et al. (Eds.): WiSATS 2020, LNICST 357, pp. 297–310, 2021.
https://doi.org/10.1007/978-3-030-69069-4_25

The extrapolation methods commonly used in radar image prediction mainly predict radar images on the premise that the system remains stable e.g. linear prediction methods, cross-correlation methods and single centroid methods which extrapolate to match the cloud image based on local feature matching and sequential cloud motion vector. However, linear prediction methods have been rarely used as most of the actual scenarios are non-linear problems. Reference [2] simply predict the cloud cluster position at the next moment based on the cross-correlation method by calculating the cross-correlation coefficient of two adjacent images. However, due to the inherent disadvantages of the cross-correlation method, the algorithm's forecasting ability rapidly decreases with time [3]. The monomer centroid method first needs to identify the monomers, and then scans the images at adjacent moments to perform the matching and tracking of the monomers. This type of algorithm is suitable for easily identified target monomers. For the application scenario of this paper, the cloud in the atmosphere will be deformed or disappear, and new clouds will be generated, so the cloud cannot be used as a single centroid model.

In the case that the traditional extrapolation methods have their own shortcomings, this paper proposes a solution, CloudNet, whose workflow is shown in Fig. 1, including a classification model and an unsupervised prediction model which both based on deep learning for predicting the trend of cloud clusters in the airspace through the laser link. First, a large number of continuous cloud images above the ground station were collected to make a cloud sequence dataset named CloudSequence. Then according to the characteristics of cloud cluster categories and total cloud cover in meteorology, the cloud sequence data set is divided into three categories: few-cloud, cloudy and stratiform clouds. During training, four neural network models need to be trained, namely a classification model and three prediction models corresponding to respective categories. During prediction, the cloud image sequence to be predicted is first classified by a classification model, and then the corresponding prediction model is used to predict the dynamic change trend of the cloud at the next moment according to the classification result.

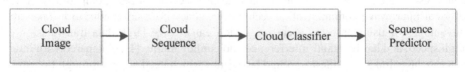

Fig. 1. CloudNet workflow

2 Classification of Cloud Sequences

2.1 Cloud Categories

Currently, clouds are generally divided into low, medium, high and direct expansion clouds as a international tradition. Based on this classification system in China, clouds are specifically divided into three families, ten genera, and 29 categories of clouds by combining observations and actual usage descriptions. Calbó et al. [4] defined 8 cloud categories for different sky conditions while Heinle et al. [5] defined 7. These standards are formulated according to the needs of the scenario. For the use scenario in this article, the purpose of classification is to improve the period of time and accuracy of prediction so as to achieve uninterrupted transmission of the laser link. We attempt to divide the cloud sequences into two categories: few-cloud and cloudy according to the degree of cloud cover [6] by threshold of 1/3 due to the amount of cloud over the link will directly affect the prediction result. Furthermore, We treat stratiform clouds as a separate category and have the highest classification priority as the stratiform clouds are evenly curtain-like, with a large range and long duration among all categories of clouds, which are different from others. Based on the above characteristics, the cloud sequences are divided into three categories: few-cloud, cloudy and stratiform clouds.

2.2 Classification Model

Deep learning method is selected for its great performance in the field of computer vision while VGG16 model shows a graceful accuracy in the fields of image classification and object detection. Therefore, this paper extract features from cloud image sequences using VGG16 model whose structure is shown in Fig. 2.

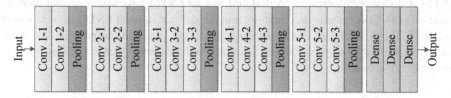

Fig. 2. VGG16 model structure

VGG16 has 13 shareable convolutional layers and three fully connected layers with very small (3 × 3) convolution filters, which shows that a significant improvement on the prior-art configurations can be achieved by pushing the depth to 16–19 weight layers [7]. This article uses pre-trained weight models on ImageNet for transfer learning, which means the trainable parameters of all layers except the last three fully connected layers setting to untrainable and only the parameters of the last three fully connected layers being adjusted.

3   Prediction Model of Cloud Sequences

It is necessary to build an internal model of the object and its motion model in Kinematics if you want to predict the trajectory of an object. But when it comes to the field of deep learning, all models are data-driven, that is, to predict the change trend of cloud clusters over ground stations of satellite-to-ground laser communication links, we do not need to model the changes and movements of cloud clusters, but trains model parameters through a large amount of continuous cloud image sequences.

Taking into account the temporal correlation of cloud sequences which actually are high-dimensional time series, this paper proposes a deeper PredNet model based on the Convolution Long-Short-Term Memory Network (ConvLSTM) as a prediction model. And we compared it with traditional stacked ConvLSTM model. We train these two network models with different types of cloud image sequences as input data to predict the change trend of cloud sequence at the next moment. And compare each other to determine which model better in actual scenario based on the actual testing accuracy.

3.1 Long Short-Term Memory Network

Long short-term memory (LSTM) is a special model of recurrent neural network (RNN) [8] that successfully solves the problem of gradient disappearance and explosion during the training process of back propagation through time (BPTT) of recurrent neural network [9] and can make full use of historical information, modeling the time dependence of signals. At present, LSTM networks show outstanding performance in many sequence prediction tasks, such as time series prediction, natural language processing [10] and so on.

The LSTM structure is shown in Fig. 3. It consists of an input layer, an output layer, and a hidden layer. Compared with the traditional RNN structure, the hidden layer of the LSTM is no longer an ordinary neural unit, but an LSTM unit with a special memory function [11]. Control gate and memory unit are defined in each LSTM unit, as shown in Fig. 4. The control gate includes input gate, forget gate and output gate, which are usually expressed by sigmoid or tanh functions, and the memory unit includes unit state (c_t) and output state (o_t).

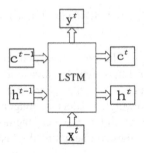

Fig. 3. LSTM structure

The specific working process of the LSTM unit is as follows: At time t, the LSTM input includes the input x_t at the current time, the last hidden state h_{t-1} and the last unit state c_{t-1} at the previous time, that is, retain the useful information in the cloud image sequence at the last moment. x_t and h_{t-1} get the current input unit state $\widetilde{c}_t$ through activation function *tanh*. The current unit state c_t is the sum of the last unit state c_{t-1} passing through the forget gate f_t and the current input unit state $\widetilde{c}_t$ passing through the input gate i_t. Finally, LSTM output h_t is calculated by the current unit state c_t through the activation function and output gate. The calculation formula [12] for each variable

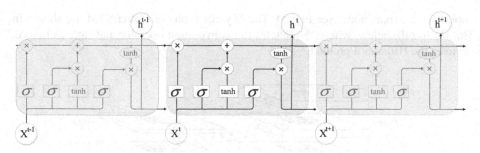

Fig. 4. Four interaction layers in LSTM

is as Eq. (1) to (5):

$$i_t = \sigma_g (W_{xi} \cdot x_t + W_{hi} \cdot h_{t-1} + W_{ci} \cdot c_{t-1} + b_i) \tag{1}$$

$$f_t = \sigma_g \left(W_{xf} \cdot x_t + W_{hf} \cdot h_{t-1} + W_{cf} \cdot c_{t-1} + b_f \right) \tag{2}$$

$$c_t = f_t \otimes c_{t-1} + i_t \otimes \sigma_c (W_{xc} \cdot x_t + W_{hc} \cdot h_{t-1} + c) \tag{3}$$

$$o_t = \sigma_g (W_{xo} \cdot x_t + W_{ho} \cdot h_{t-1} + W_{co} \cdot c_t + b_o) \tag{4}$$

$$h_t = o_t \otimes \sigma_h(c_t) \tag{5}$$

Where: W_{xf}, W_{xi}, W_{xo}, W_{xc} are weight matrices connected to the input x_t while W_{hc}, W_{hi}, W_{ho}, W_{hf} are weight matrices connected to the last hidden state h_{t-1}. W_{ci}, W_{cf}, W_{co} are diagonal matrices connecting the current unit state c_t and the gate function. b_i, b_f, b_c, b_o are offset vectors. σ_g is the activation function, usually tanh or sigmoid function and '$\otimes$' denotes the Hadamard product.

One advantage of using the memory cell and gates to control information flow is that the gradient will be trapped in the cell (also known as constant error carousels [9]) and be prevented from vanishing too quickly, which is a critical problem for the vanilla RNN model [9, 13].

3.2 Convolution Long Short-Term Memory Network

Although the FC-LSTM layer has proven powerful for handling temporal correlation, it contains too much redundancy for spatial data. To address this problem, [14] propose an extension of LSTM called ConvLSTM which has convolutional structures in both the input-to-state and state-to-state transitions. The distinguishing feature of ConvL-STM is that all the inputs X_1, X_2...... X_t, cell outputs C_1, C_2,......,C_t, hidden states H_1, H_2,......,H_t, and gates i_t, f_t, o_t, of the ConvLSTM are 3D tensors whose last two dimensions are spatial dimensions (rows and columns). The ConvLSTM determines the future state of a certain cell in the grid by the inputs and past states of its local neighbors. This can easily be achieved by using a convolution operator in the state-to-state and input-to-state transitions (see Fig. 5). The key equations of ConvLSTM are shown in Eq. (6) to (10) below, where '*' denotes the convolution operator and '⊗', as before, denotes the Hadamard product:

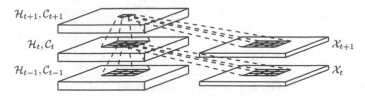

Fig. 5. Struture of ConvLSTM

$$i_t = \sigma_g(W_{xi} * X_t + W_{hi} * H_{t-1} + W_{ci} * C_{t-1} + b_i) \tag{6}$$

$$f_t = \sigma_g\left(W_{xf} * X_t + W_{hf} * H_{t-1} + W_{cf} * C_{t-1} + b_f\right) \tag{7}$$

$$c_t = f_t \otimes C_{t-1} + i_t \otimes \sigma_c(W_{xc} * X_t + W_{hc} * H_{t-1} + c) \tag{8}$$

$$o_t = \sigma_g(W_{xo} * X_t + W_{ho} * H_{t-1} + W_{co} * C_t + b_o) \tag{9}$$

$$h_t = o_t \otimes \sigma_h(C_t) \tag{10}$$

This paper take advantage of ConvLSTM for multilayer stacking (see Fig. 6) which consists of two parts, an encoding network and a decoding network. The encoding ConvLSTM compresses the whole cloud image sequence into a hidden state tensor and the decoding ConvLSTM unfolds this hidden state to give the final prediction by upsampling.

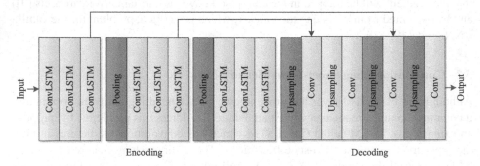

Fig. 6. Stacking ConvLSTM

3.3 Deeper PredNet

PredNet was originally used for short-term video prediction, and it is one of the state-of-art methods in the field of video prediction [15]. In this paper, we propose a deeper cloud sequences nowcasting model based on the PredNet architecture.

The Deeper PredNet model is improved based on the ConvLSTM model with increased stack layers from 4 to 6 and enlarged kernel size from 3 * 3 to 5 * 5 for larger state-to-state kernels are more suitable for capturing spatiotemporal correlations [14]. Each layer is composed of four basic modules: an input convolutional layer (A_l), a recurrent representation layer (R_l), a prediction layer ($\widehat{A_l}$), and an error representation (E_l). As Fig. 7 shows, these modules stacked in a certain relationship instead of simple linear stacking of ConvLSTM. The representation layer, R_l, is a recurrent convolutional network that can generate a prediction, $\widehat{A_l}$, of what the layer input, A_l, will be on the next frame. The network takes the difference between A_l and $\widehat{A_l}$ and outputs an error representation, E_l, which is split into separate rectified positive and negative error populations. The error, E_l, is then passed forward through a convolutional layer to become the input to the next layer (A_{l+1}). The recurrent prediction layer R_l receives a copy of the error signal E_l, along with top-down input from the representation layer of the next level of the network (R_{l+1}) [15].

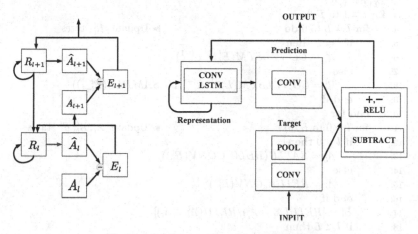

Fig. 7. Module structure of deeper PredNet

Although the model architecture is general with respect to the kinds of data with fixed-size, here we focus on cloud image sequences data x_t. The specific update rules are shown in Eq. (11) to (14). Different from the prednet, the error of each layer uses Huber loss function instead of L1 error [15]. The total loss function is defined as the weighted sum of the prediction errors at each layer and at each timestep, which is listed in Eq. (15), Where λ_t is the error weight at each time, while λ_l is the error weight at each layer, and n_l is the number of units in the lth layer.

The update sequence of each unit in the model is implemented according to the status update algorithm given in Fig. 8. The status is updated by two steps: first, the R_l^t, state is updated by the top-down pass; then the A, A_l^t, and E_l^t states are updated by forward pass. R_l and E_l are initialized to 0 on the account of the nature of the convolutional network, indicating that the original predictions are spatially uniform.

$$A_l^t = \begin{cases} x_t, & if \ l = 0 \\ MAXPOOL(RELU(CONV(E_{l-1}^t))), & l > 0 \end{cases} \tag{11}$$

$$\widehat{A}_l^t = RELU(CONV(R_l^t)) \tag{12}$$

$$E_l^t = \begin{cases} \frac{1}{2}(y - f(x))^2 \ for \ |y - f(x)| \leq \delta, \\ \delta|y - f(x)| - \frac{1}{2}\delta^2, \quad otherwise \end{cases} \tag{13}$$

$$R_l^t = CONVLSTM(E_l^{t-1}, R_l^{t-1}, UPSAMPLE(R_{l+1}^t)) \tag{14}$$

$$L_{train} = \sum_t \lambda_t \sum_l \frac{\lambda_l}{n_l} \sum_{n_l} E_l^t \tag{15}$$

Algorithm 1 Calculation of PredNet state
Input: x_t
1: $A_0^t \leftarrow x_t$
2: $E_l^0, R_0 \leftarrow 0$
3: **for** $t = 1$ to T **do**
4:    **for** $l = L$ to 0 **do**   ▶ Update R_l^t states
5:      **if** $l = L$ **then**
6:        $R_L^t = CONVLSTM(E_L^{t-1}, R_L^{t-1})$
7:      **else**
8:        $R_l^t = CONVLSTM(E_l^{t-1}, R_l^{t-1}, UPSAMPLE(R_{l+1}^t))$
9:      **end if**
10:   **end for**
11:   **for** $l = 0$ to L **do**   ▶ Update $\hat{A}_l^t, A_l^t, E_l^t$ states
12:     **if** $l = 0$ **then**
13:       $\hat{A}_0^t = SATLU(RELU(CONV(R_0^t)))$
14:     **else**
15:       $\hat{A}_l^t = RELU(CONV(R_l^t))$
16:     **end if**
17:     $E_l^t = [RELU(A_l^t - \hat{A}_l^t); RELU(\hat{A}_l^t - A_l^t)]$
18:     **if** $l < L$ **then**
19:       $A_{l+1}^t = MAXPOOL(CONV(E_t^l))$
20:     **end if**
21:   **end for**
22: **end for**

Fig. 8. Algorithm of PredNet state calculation

4   Experiment

The overall model of the prediction system CloudNet structure is shown in Fig. 9. The cloud image sequence to be predicted is first classified by the classifier and then entered into the predictor of the corresponding category. Our implementations of the models are in Python with the help of Keras2.2.4 using tensorflow backend. We run all the experiments on a computer with a single NVIDIA 2080Ti GPU.

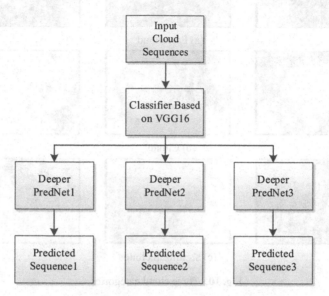

Fig. 9. CloudNet structure

4.1 DataSet

We collected the cloud image sequences over a specific area in Nanjing in March with the cloud infrared imager independently developed by our research laboratory. The infrared imager collected a total of 30291 cloud images as the basic dataset CloudImage by taking pictures every 5 s, all of which are grayscale images with a resolution of 720 × 480. 6,000 cloud image sequences with a time span of 100 s are sampled every 20 s on the CloudImage, and binary serialized after normalization and saved as cloud sequence dataset CloudSequence in hickle format.

4.2 Cloud Sequence Classification

We divided CloudSequence into three categories based on the principles of few-cloud, cloudy and stratiform clouds. As shown in Fig. 10, it is clear that the three categories of clouds have different characteristics. The classification accurancy with VGG16 model is up to 91% after the model being trained for several hours.

4.3 Cloud Sequence Prediction

It is shown in Fig. 11 and Fig. 12 respectively that the prediction results of using PredNet model and CloudNet model, where (a) to (c) are few-cloud, cloudy, and stratiform clouds

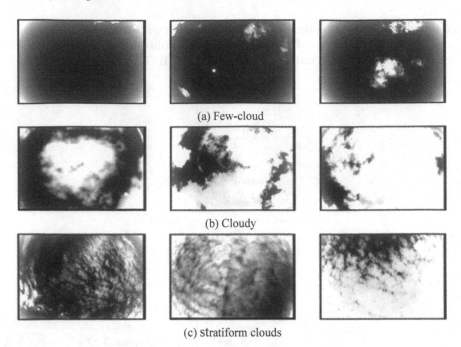

(a) Few-cloud

(b) Cloudy

(c) stratiform clouds

Fig. 10. Three cloud categories

image sequence respectively. In each image sequence, the first row is the ground truth of cloud image sequence, while the second row is predicted cloud image sequence based on the previous timestep. By comparing the predicted images, we can see that both two models can predict cloud image sequences. Under all three conditions, the prediction results of the PredNet model are significantly different from real images in the last several images. In comparison, the prediction result of CloudNet is more consistent with the ground truth.

Table 1, 2 and 3 respectively calculate the mean square error (MSE) and accuracy of the prediction results of PredNet and CloudNet on three conditions of few-cloud, cloudy and Stratiform clouds. In a few-cloud situation, the prediction accuracy will be relatively high for most of the picture is covered by the clear sky while a small part was occupied by cloud. In the case of cloudy, the accuracy of cloud motion prediction is more credible due to it has obvious movement visually and is growing and disappearing over time. Stratiform clouds are evenly distributed, with a large range and a long duration, making it easier for model to extract features, and as a result, the accuracy of prediction is quite acceptable. In actual use, all three cases will occur, so the data sets of the three cases will be used for model training, but the prediction accuracy of cloudy is relatively more credible. We train the model on three sets of data sets, but take cloudy prediction accuracy as the credible accuracy considering the three cases will occur in actual use.

According to the prediction results, CloudNet can predict the cloud status at the next moment more accurately than PredNet. The prediction average accuracy of the which is up to 81% with 100 s prediction interval and a tolerance of 5% error per pixel. Therefore,

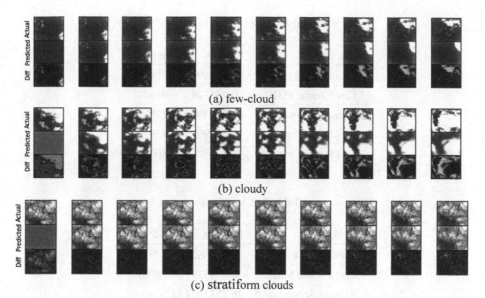

(a) few-cloud

(b) cloudy

(c) stratiform clouds

Fig. 11. Prediction results of PredNet

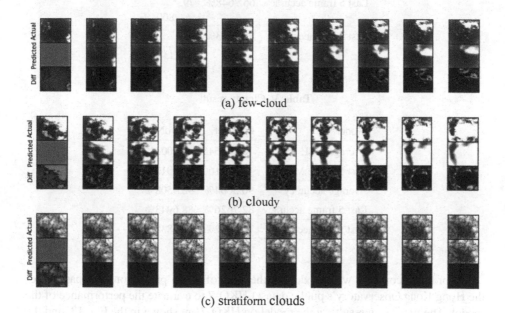

(a) few-cloud

(b) cloudy

(c) stratiform clouds

Fig. 12. Prediction results of CloudNet

we use the CloudNet model that is superior to the other model as the first choice in the scenario of cloud change trend prediction on the satellite-to-ground laser communication link.

Table 1. Few-cloud result

Model	PredNet	CloudNet
Average MSE	0.021499	0.014128
Last 5 frame MSE	0.035378	0.035097
Average accuracy	79.8133%	88.7363%
Last 5 frame accuracy	73.5179%	81.4399%
Last frame accuracy	71.2973%	75.8605%

Table 2. Cloudy result

Model	PredNet	CloudNet
Average MSE	0.022660	0.017616
Last 5 frame MSE	0.054533	0.028306
Average accuracy	76.7533%	81.7590%
Last 5 frame accuracy	66.7648%	79.8004%
Last frame accuracy	57.3893%	75.7755%

Table 3. Cloudy result

Model	PredNet	CloudNet
Average MSE	0.003645	0.000412
Last 5 frame MSE	0.007160	0.001200
Average accuracy	90.3664%	96.4508%
Last 5 frame accuracy	82.7626%	88.6943%
Last frame accuracy	77.3012%	81.6838%

In order to compare with models in the field of video prediction, this paper uses the Hong Kong Observatory's public dataset HKO-7 to evaluate the performance of the model. The prediction results of the model on HKO-7 are shown in the Fig. 13, and the accuracy comparison results are shown in the Table 4. CloudNet has a good performance on satellite cloud images prediction although the it is specifically used to predict infrared cloud images collected from the ground.

Fig. 13. Prediction result of CloudNet on HKO-7

Table 4. HKO-7 result

Model	CloudNet
Average MSE	0.005941
Last 5 frame MSE	0.009553
Average accuracy	86.9808%
Last 5 frame accuracy	86.0788%
Last frame accuracy	84.6634%

5   Conclusion and Future Work

This paper takes the influence of atmospheric cloud clusters on satellite-ground laser links as a starting point, and we have successfully applied the deep learning to the challenging cloud change trend nowcasting problem. We made two cloud datasets, CloudImage and CloudSequence, and proposed a cloud change trend prediction system CloudNet model based on the extension of PredNet to tackle the problem. By incorporating classification model and prediction model into the system, we build an end-to-end trainable model suitable for different weather conditions over the ground station. For future work, we will make a more detailed classification of cloud categories according to Meteorology. Besides, more research will be done on how to improve prediction time such as taking all-sky cloud image sequences as dataset for it has a longer time span.

References

1. Arnon, S., Kopeika, N.S.: Laser satellite communication network-vibration effect and possible solutions. Proc. IEEE **85**(10), 1646–1661 (1997). https://doi.org/10.1109/5.640772
2. Evans, K.F., Wiscombe, W.J.: An algorithm for generating stochastic cloud fields from radar profile statistics. Atmos. Res. **72**(1–4), 263–289 (2004). https://doi.org/10.1016/j.atmosres.2004.03.016
3. Hamill, T.M., Nehrkorn, T.: A short-term cloud forecast scheme using cross correlations. Weather Forecast. **8**(4), 401–411 (2002). https://doi.org/10.1175/1520-0434(1993)008%3c0401:astcfs%3e2.0.co;2
4. Calbó, J., Sabburg, J.: Feature extraction from whole-sky ground-based images for cloud-type recognition. J. Atmos. Ocean. Technol. **25**(1), 3–14 (2008). https://doi.org/10.1175/2007JTECHA959.1
5. Heinle, A., Macke, A., Srivastav, A.: Automatic cloud classification of whole sky images. Atmos. Meas. Tech. **3**(3), 557–567 (2010). https://doi.org/10.5194/amt-3-557-2010

6. Wood, R., Bretherton, C.S.: On the relationship between stratiform low cloud cover and lower-tropospheric stability. J. Clim. **19**(24), 6425–6432 (2006). https://doi.org/10.1175/JCL I3988.1

7. Simonyan, K., Zisserman, A.: Very deep convolutional networks for large-scale image recognition. In: 3rd International Conference on Learning Representations, ICLR 2015 - Conference Track Proceedings, p. 14 (2015)

8. Karpathy, A., Johnson, J., Fei-fei, L.: V Isualizing and, p. 11 (2015)

9. Hochreiter, S., Schmidhuber, J.: Long short-term memory. Neural Comput. **9**(8), 1735–1780 (1997). https://doi.org/10.1162/neco.1997.9.8.1735

10. Narasimhan, K., Kulkarni, T.D., Barzilay, R.: Language understanding for text-based games using deep reinforcement learning. In: Conference Proceedings - EMNLP 2015 Conference on Empirical Methods In Natural Language Processing, p. 11 (2015). https://doi.org/10.18653/v1/d15-1001

11. Gers, F.A., Schmidhuber, J., Cummins, F.: Learning to forget: continual prediction with LSTM. Neural Comput. **12**(10), 2451–2471 (2000). https://doi.org/10.1162/089976600300 015015

12. Yao, K., Peng, B., Zhang, Y., Yu, D., Zweig, G., Shi, Y.: Spoken language understanding using long short-term memory neural networks. In: 2014 IEEE Workshop Spoken Language Technology, SLT 2014 - Proceedings, no. October, pp. 189–194 (2014). https://doi.org/10.1109/SLT.2014.7078572

13. Pascanu, R., Tour, D., Mikolov, T., Tour, D.: On the difficulty of training recurrent neural networks, no. 2

14. Shi, X., Chen, Z., Wang, H., Yeung, D.Y., Wong, W.K., Woo, W.C.: Convolutional LSTM network: a machine learning approach for precipitation nowcasting. In: Advances in Neural Information Processing Systems, vol. 2015-January, pp. 802–810 (2015)

15. Lotter, W., Kreiman, G., Cox, D.: Deep predictive coding networks for video prediction and unsupervised learning. In: 5th International Conference on Learning Representations, ICLR 2017 - Conference Track Proceedings, p. 18 (2019)

Evaluating IP Routing on a General Purpose Network Emulation Platform for Space Networking

Jiawei Sun[1], Peng Zhou[2], Kanglian Zhao[1], and Wenfeng Li[1(✉)]

[1] Institute of Space-Terrestrial Intelligent Networks, Nanjing University, Nanjing, China
2711025503@qq.com, zhaokanglian@nju.edu.cn, leewf_cn@hotmail.com
[2] Advanced Institute of Information Technology, Peking University, Beijing, China
pzhou@aiit.org.cn

Abstract. Driven by lacking of a low-cost, large-scale, flexible and reconfigurable general purpose network emulation platform for space networking, ISTIN laboratory of Nanjing University designed a flexible and fully reconfigurable space network emulation platform supporting emulation of multiple network architectures and network protocols. We have carried out some space network protocol research based on the platform, such as DTN and IP. This paper constructs a spatial network scenario to evaluate OSPF and OSPF+ routing performance on this platform The emulation results indicate the emulation platform has the ability of IP routing emulation, which guarantees considerable reliability and provides a reference for subsequent emulation work of IP protocols.

Keywords: Space Information Networks · Network emulation · OSPF · Quagga

1 Introduction

Space Information Networks (SIN) are the network systems based on space platforms, such as geostationary (GEO) satellites, medium earth orbit (MEO) satellites, low earth orbit (LEO) satellites, stratospheric balloons, etc., which provide services such as communication, positioning and navigation. Due to the enlargement of network scale and diversity of demands, the emulation platform for SIN research needs to be extensible, flexible and reconfigurable.

So far, there exist two schemes for SIN research. One is to carry out research in the real space network, but the experiment cost is relatively high The other scheme is to use existing network simulators (such as OPNET [1] or NS [2], etc.) for simulation. Compared with on-board experiments, software simulation is easy to implement, but it cannot generate real data flow between nodes. Hence, the reliability of the software simulation cannot be guaranteed.

In order to carry out space network research, the Institute of Space-Terrestrial Intelligent Networks (ISTIN) of Nanjing University developed a scalable network emulation platform for space internetworking [3]. On the basis of retaining reliability, the platform

Q. Wu et al. (Eds.): WiSATS 2020, LNICST 357, pp. 311–320, 2021.
https://doi.org/10.1007/978-3-030-69069-4_26

focuses on enhancing the scalability and reconfigurability so that researchers can deploy and switch network scenarios conveniently and rapidly. The platform supports emulation of multiple network protocols and architectures. Some SIN protocols such as DTN and IP have been emulated on this platform.

Based on this platform [3], IP routing protocols OSPF and OSPF+ [4] are emulated in this paper. Then, we compare routing convergence performance with those of NS simulator to verify reliability of emulation.

The OSPF+ protocol was proposed by Mingwei Xu et al. [4]. Considering the periodicity and regularity of satellite motion, Xu et al. classified space link changes into predictable and unpredictable types. Aimed at predictable link changes, topology prediction module was added to the original routing protocol OSPF and the neighbor state machine module was modified.

The rest of the paper is organized as follows. Section 2 introduces design of the network emulation platform. Section 3 describes the detailed design process of research. Section 4 describes the experimental setup and performance evaluation. Session 5 concludes the paper.

2   Emulation Platform Design

As shown in Fig. 1, the architecture of the emulation platform can be divided into three parts: logical plane, control plane, and data plane.

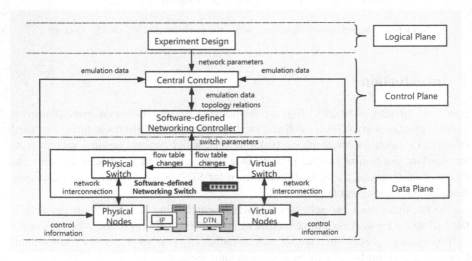

Fig. 1. Architecture of emulation platform.

The function of logical plane is to establish the corresponding network model by modeling software according to the specific SIN scenario. The network model includes connection plans, link states and protocol stacks loaded on the satellites. The Control Plane receives information and parameters from the logical plane and drives the emulations in the Data Plane. The main elements of the Control Plane include central controller and the SDN controller. Data Plane is the principal part of routing emulation, including emulation nodes, switches and other equipments, which is responsible for sending or receiving data, and monitoring the information. The Data Plane mainly includes emulation nodes and devices such as switches.

Various routing protocols or algorithms based on different protocol stacks, such as OSPF and CGR, can be tested and emulated on the proposed emulation platform [3]. The principle of multi-protocol emulation is shown in Fig. 2. Relevant protocol stacks are installed on the nodes according to emulation requirements, and all nodes are connected to the software-defined network switches.

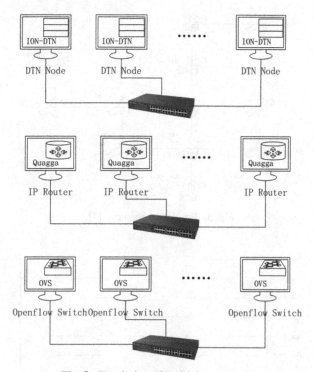

Fig. 2. Emulation of multiple protocols.

3 Routing Emulation Process Design

According to the emulation scheme, the whole emulation testing process can be divided into three phases: experiment preparation, experimental execution and data collection.

3.1 Experiment Preparation

In the experiment preparation stage of emulation, the work is mainly carried out on the logical plane and control plane.

In logical plane, according to the required space routing protocol, an emulation scene from [4] was modeled and the detailed network parameters were obtained. As shown in Fig. 3, a constellation composed by 14 low earth orbit (LEO) satellites is adopted. There are 10 intra-orbit links and 8 inter-orbit links in the constellation. The 10 intra-orbit links are always connected while 8 inter-orbit links are intermittently connected. The link on-off relationships of inter-orbit links in an experiment period (6000s) are illustrated in Fig. 4. A segment represents an interval in the connection state.

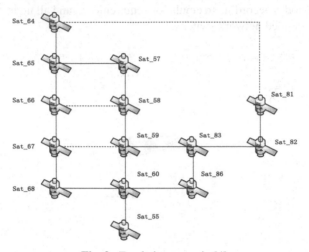

Fig. 3. Emulation scenario [4].

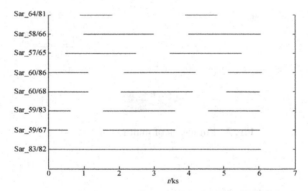

Fig. 4. Connectivity of inter-orbit links [4].

In the control plane, the central controller should be operated and other devices should be available simultaneously before Experiment Execution Phase. Concrete steps are shown in Fig. 5. As mentioned before, network parameters such as connection plans and dynamic link characteristics will be exported to the database of the central controller. Once the network topology changes, it is necessary to carry out Scenario design again and repeat the export steps. In addition, emulation nodes can be constructed from a pre-prepared protocol image and connected to the software-defined network switch. Here, Docker Virtualization Technology (VT) [5] are used to build OSPF/OSPF+ images and nodes. After finishing these preparation work, the central controller is connected to the nodes and switches so that it can send control messages to other devices and collect their feedback.

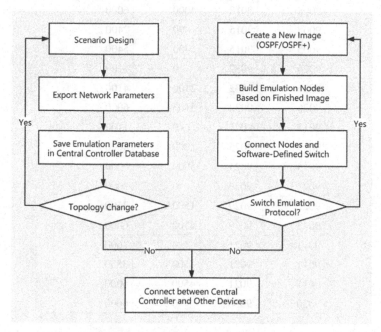

Fig. 5. Concrete steps of experiment preparation.

3.2 Experiment Execution

In the experiment execution stage, the central controller sends the start signal to the emulation devices. After a node receives the signal, it will run the corresponding protocol process. In our experiment, it is referred to as OSPF/OSPF+ protocol process in the open source routing software Quagga [6]. Meanwhile, the software-defined networking controller will also be signaled. When the network topology changes, the software-defined networking controller will send a set of flow table items to the software-defined network switch. This makes switching network topologies flexible and convenient. The flow table [7] in our experiment is shown in Table 1. In every row, the first and second items represent network cards at both ends of an inter-orbit link, and the third and fourth items represent beginning and ending times of a link connection respectively.

Table 1. Flow table.

Source node	Dest node	Start time(s)	Stop time(s)
9002	9034	900	1900
9002	9034	3900	4900
9008	9018	1000	3000
9008	9018	4000	6000
9005	9015	400	2400
9005	9015	3400	5400
9026	9032	0	1100
9026	9032	2100	4100
9026	9032	5100	6000
9013	9025	0	1100
9013	9025	2000	4000
9013	9025	5000	6000
9022	9029	0	600
9022	9029	1500	3500
9022	9029	4500	6000
9011	9021	0	600
9011	9021	1500	3500
9011	9021	4500	6000
9030	9036	0	6000

3.3 Data Collection

After completion of data exchanging, it will enter Data Collection Phase. The data to be collected can be obtained from the software-defined network switch and each node. The switch will feed the real-time traffic information back to the central controller. Certainly, some packet capture software such as Wireshark [8] can be applied to analyze data packets. For example, it counts sending and receiving time of data packets at both ends of an end-to-end transmission to calculate the propagation delay and jitter rate etc.. In addition, by obtaining the statistical information of each route forwarding node, real-time neighbor status, route convergence status, and so on can be obtained.

In our research work, the performance indicators of concern were obtained by calculating the time difference recorded in the log file of OSPF/OSPF+ process. Log files of OSPF/OSPF+ process record the timeing of some key events such as state transitions and SPF calculation (see Fig. 6). The details are described in Sect. 4.

Disruption judgement time of OSPF/OSPF+ can be calculated by the following formula (1) and (2). In formula (1) and (2), $t_{linkoff}$ represents the time at which the link is disrupted. When OSPF detects a predictable link-off event, it will change the neighbor state from Full to Down. The time is marked as $t_{Full \rightarrow Down}$. When OSPF+ detects a

```
2019/05/14  14:44:07  OSPF:  ospf_spf_calculate: Stop. 0 vertices
2019/05/14  14:44:07  OSPF:  ospf_ia_routing():start
2019/05/14  14:44:07  OSPF:  ospf_ia_routing():not ABR, considering all areas
2019/05/14  14:44:07  OSPF:  Pruning unreachable networks
2019/05/14  14:44:07  OSPF:  Pruning unreachable routers
2019/05/14  14:44:07  OSPF:  Route: Router Routing Table free
2019/05/14  14:44:07  OSPF:  SPF: calculation complete
```

Fig. 6. OSPF process log file.

predictable link-off event, it will change the neighbor state from Full to Leaving. The time is marked as $t_{Full \rightarrow Leaving}$. 5 experiments were carried out for each scenario to reduce the test error.

$$\text{Disruption judgement time}_{OSPF} = \sum\nolimits_{i=1}^{5} \left(t_{Full \rightarrow Down} - t_{linkoff} \right)/5 \qquad (1)$$

$$\text{Disruption judgement time}_{OSPF+} = \sum\nolimits_{i=1}^{5} \left(t_{Full \rightarrow Leaving} - t_{linkoff} \right)/5 \qquad (2)$$

Routing stability of OSPF/OSPF+ is defined as proportion of stable routing time (marked as t_{stab}) within two consecutive link disruptions (marked as t_{total}). Excluding the disruption judgement time (marked as t_{judge}), link state information synchronization time (marked as t_{sync}) and routing calculation time (marked as t_{calc}) in t_{total}, the remaining time is stable routing time. So the calculation formula of routing stability can be described as formula (3). Also, 5 experiments were carried out for each scenario, and the average was finally calculated.

$$\text{Routing stability}_{OSPF/OSPF+} = \left(\sum\nolimits_{i=1}^{5} \frac{t_{total} - t_{judge} - t_{sync} - t_{calc}}{t_{total}} * 100\% \right)/5 \qquad (3)$$

4 Performance Evaluation

Predictable link change times are read into the quagga's OSPF+ module in the form of a configuration file so that the OSPF+ neighbor state machine can trigger a state transition at a specified time. Two performance indicators of OSPF and OSPF+ have been tested and calculated in four scenarios. The bandwidth and delay are configured as 1000 Mbps/25 ms, 1000 Mbps/15 ms, 100 Mbps/15 ms, and 10 Mbps/15 ms respectively. The measured OSPF/OSPF+ disruption judgment time and routing stability (the percentage of time that all nodes in the entire area are converged within two consecutive link disruptions) are shown in the following Table 2 and 3, and Fig. 7 and 8 respectively. The left side represents the results of our emulation, and the right side represents those of NS simulator obtained from [4].

It can be seen that the disruption judgment time of OSPF+ is greatly shortened compared with that of OSPF due to the introduction of the topology prediction mechanism, which saves the time (4 Hello message periods) for judging disconnection between the neighbors as shown in Fig. 9. The neighbor structure of OSPF+ is preserved during

Table 2. Disruption judgement time.

Bandwidth/Delay	OSPF(s)	OSPF+ (s)	Bandwidth/Delay	OSPF(s)	OSPF+ (s)
1000 Mbps/25 ms	37.14	0.37	1000 Mbps/25 ms	41.00	1.00
1000 Mbps/15 ms	35.46	0.46	1000 Mbps/15 ms	41.00	1.00
100 Mbps/15 ms	34.68	0.89	100 Mbps/15 ms	41.00	1.00
10 Mbps/15 ms	33.64	0.94	10 Mbps/15 ms	41.00	1.00

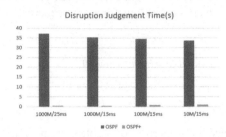 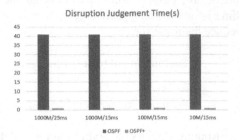

Fig. 7. Disruption judgement time.

Table 3. Routing stability.

Bandwidth/Delay	OSPF	OSPF+	Bandwidth/Delay	OSPF	OSPF+
1000 Mbps/25 ms	88.75%	99.60%	1000 Mbps/25 ms	76%	99.50%
1000 Mbps/15 ms	86.94%	99.63%	1000 Mbps/15 ms	76%	99.50%
100 Mbps/15 ms	86.63%	99.69%	100 Mbps/15 ms	76%	99.50%
10 Mbps/15 ms	87.31%	99.69%	10 Mbps/15 ms	76%	99.50%

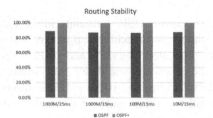 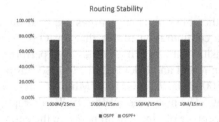

Fig. 8. Routing stability.

the predictable link disruption period. Therefore, when link recovery occurs, the neighbor state machine transforms from Leaving to Exchange directly without handshakes and negotiations. Besides, a new link state database newLSAsList which stores LSAs accepted during the disruption period is added to original OSPF module, so that synchronizing full link state database can be replaced by synchronizing newLSAsList only. These operations reduce the routing reconvergence time by about 14% compared with OSPF when links are restored. The routing stability of OSPF+ is approximately 100%.

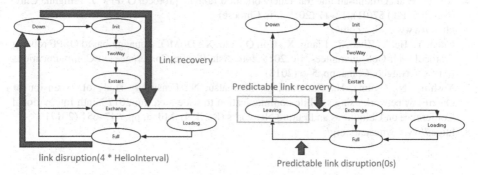

Fig. 9. OSPF/OSPF+ neighbor state machine.

There is a certain gap at the aspect of routing reconvergence time compared with the results obtained from [4]. In the performance evaluation of that paper, routing stability of OSPF is approximately 80% while in our paper the performance indicator is about 85%. Such slight difference can be ignored temporarily being considering the possible differences in software implementation and the introduction of real data flow of the emulation platform. By comparing the simulation results with NS simulation results, it can be seen that the current emulation platform has been able to carry out IP routing emulation, which ensures the reliability to a certain extent.

5   Conclusion

Based on the designed emulation platform, emulation is performed on the newly proposed spatial routing protocol OSPF+. Performance comparison has been made with the traditional intra-domain routing protocol OSPF. It can be seen that for predictable link changes in space network, OSPF+ has a faster link disruption judgment mechanism and shorter routing re-convergence time compared with OSPF. Furthermore, a simple comparison has been carried out between performance indicators obtained from our emulation and NS simulator. Results indicate current emulation platform has the ability of IP routing emulation, which guarantee considerable reliability and provides a reference for subsequent emulation work of IP protocols.

References

1. Zhao, J., Zhu, X.: Research on a hardware-in-the-loop simulation method for wireless network based on OPNET. In: 2015 IEEE Advanced Information Technology, Electronic and Automation Control Conference (IAEAC), Chongqing, pp. 821–825 (2015)

2. Wang, Z., Cui, G., Li, P., Wang, W., Zhang, Y.: Design and implementation of NS3-based simulation system of LEO satellite constellation for IoTs. In: 2018 IEEE 4th International Conference on Computer and Communications (ICCC), Chengdu, China, pp. 806–810 (2018)
3. Lu, T.: An emulation architecture of routing protocol in space information network. Nanjing University (Master's thesis in Chinese) (2018)
4. Xu, M., et al.: Ground-air integrated network intra-domain protocol OSPF+. J. Tsinghua Univ. (Nat. Sci. Ed.) **57**(01), 12–17 (2017). (in Chinese)
5. https://www.docker.com/
6. Chen, Y., He, Y., Zhao, Z., Liang, X., Cui, Q., Tao, X.: DEMO: a quagga-based OSPF routing protocol with QoS guarantees. In: 2018 24th Asia-Pacific Conference on Communications (APCC), Ningbo, China, pp. 5–6 (2018)
7. Yoshino, N., Oguma, H., Kamedm, S., Suematsu, N.: Feasibility study of expansion of OpenFlow network using satellite communication to wide area. In: 2017 Ninth International Conference on Ubiquitous and Future Networks (ICUFN), Milan, pp. 647–651 (2017)
8. https://www.wireshark.org/

Bundles Aggregation of Licklider Transmission Protocol Over Lossy and Highly Asymmetric Space Network Channels

Yu Zhou[1], Ruhai Wang[2(✉)], Lei Yang[1], Siwei Peng[1], and Kanglian Zhao[3]

[1] School of Electronics and Information Engineering, Soochow University, Suzhou, Jiangsu, People's Republic of China
{20195228016,20195228043,swpeng}@stu.suda.edu.cn
[2] Phillip M. Drayer Department of Electrical Engineering, Lamar University, Beaumont, TX, USA
rwang@lamar.edu
[3] School of Electronic Science and Engineering, Nanjing University, Nanjing, Jiangsu, People's Republic of China
zhaokanglian@nju.edu.cn

Abstract. Licklider transmission protocol (LTP) was developed to provide reliable and highly efficient data delivery over unreliable space network channels. Some preliminary studies on LTP's aggregation mechanism in space communication networks have been done. However, the effect on LTP aggregation of data losses caused by lossy space channels has been ignored. Data loss is one of the key features that characterize space networks, and therefore its effect on LTP transmission cannot be left out. In this paper, the LTP aggregation mechanism is studied with focus on its characterization and performance over lossy and highly asymmetric space channels. An analytical model is presented for calculating the minimum number of bundles that should be aggregated within an LTP block for transmission over a lossy channel to avoid report segment (RS) transmission delay caused by highly asymmetric channel rates. The model is validated by realistic file transfer experiments over an experimental testbed infrastructure and packet-level analysis of the results. It is concluded that the aggregation threshold derived from the analytical model functions effectively with respect to resolving RS delay effects and decreasing latency in file delivery, leading to higher transmission efficiency.

Keywords: Space communications · Space networks · Satellite communications · Wireless networks · DTN · Licklider Transmission Protocol (LTP)

1 Introduction

National Aeronautics and Space Administration (NASA) has recognized delay/disruption tolerant networking (DTN) [1] as the only candidate networking technology that approaches the level of maturity required to provide reliable data delivery

© ICST Institute for Computer Sciences, Social Informatics and Telecommunications Engineering 2021
Published by Springer Nature Switzerland AG 2021. All Rights Reserved
Q. Wu et al. (Eds.): WiSATS 2020, LNICST 357, pp. 321–337, 2021.
https://doi.org/10.1007/978-3-030-69069-4_27

service in deep-space communications [2]. As the main data transport protocol of DTN in space networking, the Licklider transmission protocol (LTP) [3, 4] was developed to provide reliable data/file delivery service in unreliable space communications that are characterized by very long propagation delay, frequent link interruptions, and a high data loss rate. The file delivery of LTP is implemented as independent transmissions of LTP data blocks, and each block is fragmented into data segments according to the Maximum Transmit Unit (MTU) at the underlying data link layer. Put simply, the transmission of each LTP block is organized as a "session" which operates as a sequence of data segment exchanges between the sender and the receiver [4].

In additional to a long delay, random link interruptions, and a high data loss rate, asymmetric channel rates is another major feature which characterizes space communications [2]. Channel rate asymmetry in space generally means that the uplink channel rate deployed for acknowledgment (ACK) transmission (from the Earth to the spacecraft or another planet) is much lower than the downlink channel rate deployed for data transmission in the opposite direction [5]. With respect to the operation of LTP, the lower uplink channel rate introduces delay in the transmission of report segments (RSs) (at the receiver) which acknowledge the arrival status of a data block. In other words, it results in a longer RS transmission time and thus, an increase of the round-trip time (RTT) for the block transmission round. For transmission of a very large file conveyed by a large number of LTP blocks, the overall file delivery time will be significantly increased, leading to severe transmission efficiency degradation.

In view of the effect of channel-rate asymmetry in space on LTP, it is reasonable to aggregate multiple bundle protocol (BP) [6, 7] bundles into a single LTP block rather than encapsulating each bundle as an individual block for transmission [3]. A set of preliminary experimental studies on the bundle aggregation mechanism of LTP were done as part of our previous work, mainly with respect to its operation and performance. There are also a few analytical discussions that are supported by the experimental results. This set of work is discussed in Section II—*Related Work*. However, among all these previous studies, the effect of data losses in transmission over lossy space links is completely ignored in analysis. As recognized by the community, data loss is one of the key features that characterize data communications at all levels of space communications. It has especially severe effect over a deep-space channel. Therefore, in practice, the effect of data losses on bundle aggregation in BP/LTP transmission cannot be left out.

In this article, we present an analysis of the LTP aggregation of BP bundles in space communications but focus on its characterization and performance over lossy and highly asymmetric space channels. Analytical modeling is presented for calculating the minimum number of bundles that should be aggregated within a block for transmission over a lossy channel to avoid RS transmission delay caused by highly asymmetric channel rates. The model is validated by realistic file transfer experiments over a testbed infrastructure and packet-level analysis of the experiment results.

2   Related Work

A series of studies have been done for DTN protocols in space, with most of them done jointly by NASA's Jet Propulsion Laboratory (JPL), California Institute of Technology and other research teams. While some of them focus on BP [5, 8–10], numerous studies of LTP examine its design, analysis and performance [11–17]. Among these studies, a set of baseline performance comparisons were conducted between LTP and the most commonly-used TCP/UDP protocols using a statistical analysis method [11]. The comparative evaluations indicate that LTP has a performance advantage for reliable data delivery in a challenging space networking environment. With the joint presence of the very long link delay, highly lossy channel, and highly asymmetric channel rates on the data links, the performance advantage of LTP over other data transport protocols is significant.

As mentioned, some preliminary experimental studies on the bundle aggregation of LTP and its performance in space communications was done in our previous work of DTN in space [18–20]. Most of them focus on an understanding of its operation based on experimental results with a few supported by analytical discussions. However, among this set of previous studies of the bundle aggregation mechanism, the critical effect of data losses in LTP transmission caused by channel error of space channels is completely ignored in analysis. At present, no work has been done in analyzing the bundle aggregation mechanism of LTP with the inevitable effect of data loss taken into consideration for reliable data delivery with asymmetric channel rates.

3   A Scenario of LTP Transmission Over Lossy and Asymmetric Space Channels

As discussed, the file delivery of LTP is implemented as independent transmissions of LTP data *blocks*. To achieve the reliable delivery of the file (i.e., to guarantee all the bytes of the entire file successfully delivered), each block is set as 100% red. The transmission of each block is organized as a "session" which operates as a sequence of data segment exchanges between the sender and the receiver. The last segment of a block is transmitted with a checkpoint (CP) flag. A CP segment is intended to trigger the receiver for checking the arrival status of all the segments of the block for data loss or transmission error. If none of the segments is lost or received with error, the receiver acknowledges to the sender by returning a positive acknowledgment, i.e., an RS, to confirm the successful, cumulative reception for the block. If the RS indicates that any data byte of the block is lost, the segment conveying the data byte is retransmitted.

To ensure reliable delivery of CP and RS, both segments are transmitted with a timer set, leading to two important timers, *CP timer* and *RS timer*. These two countdown timers are set to detect a possible loss of CP and RS, respectively, and retransmit them as necessary upon the expiration of the corresponding timer.

To illustrate the effect of data loss on block transmission over lossy and highly asymmetric channels, a scenario of LTP block transmission is illustrated in Fig. 1 based on the interactive segments exchange between the sender and the receiver over a lossy space channel. For the sake of simplicity, the transmission scenario is shown only for three blocks numbered as $Block_1$, $Block_2$, and $Block_3$. As illustrated, each of three blocks is fragmented into multiple data segments (DSs) numbered as DS_1–DS_n. The last segment of each block, DS_n, is flagged as the CP, and it is named as CP_1, CP_2, and CP_3 for three blocks in Fig. 1, respectively. The blocks and the segments of each block are transmitted in a continuous manner. For transmission of $Block_1$, as soon as CP_1 segment

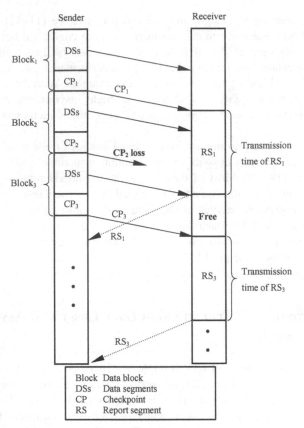

Fig. 1. A scenario of LTP data transmission illustrating the effect of CP loss on block transmission over lossy and highly asymmetric channels.

(which is also a DS) is successfully received, the receiver checks all the segments of Block$_1$ for possible data loss. Assuming that none of the segments of Block$_1$ are lost or corrupted, the RS corresponding to CP$_1$, here named RS$_1$, is immediately transmitted as a positive report of the cumulative reception for the block. The sender then sends a report acknowledgment (RA), RA$_1$, to acknowledge the receipt of RS$_1$, which closes the transmission session of Block$_1$.

Because of the very slow ACK channel rate, the time taken by the receiver in transmitting RS$_1$ is longer than the time taken by the sender in transmitting Block$_1$. In this case, while RS$_1$ is being transmitted, the segments of Block$_2$ are already on the way to the receiver. The last segment of Block$_2$, CP$_2$, is expected to initiate a check of the arrival status of the entire block. The segments of Block$_2$ are expected to arrive at the receiver before the entire RS$_1$ is completely transmitted. Even if all the segments of Block$_2$ are successfully delivered to the receiver without any data loss, RS$_2$ is not sent until RS$_1$ is completely transmitted because of the long transmission time of RS$_1$. In other words, RS$_2$ has to wait for transmission until RS$_1$ is completely transmitted. This is the origin of the RS waiting time and RS transmission queue, leading to an increase of the RTT length for the block transmission round.

However, because the channel is lossy or error-prone, any DS of $Block_2$ can be corrupted by channel error during transmission. Suppose that due to transmission error over the data channel, CP_2 is corrupted or lost while all other DSs are successfully received, as illustrated in Fig. 1. The loss of CP_2 prevents the receiver from responding with an RS on the arrival status of the block. Therefore, the RS in response to $CP_2/Block_2$, named RS_2, is not generated at the receiver for transmission over the ACK channel. A lack of RS_2 for transmission actually relieves the severely constrained ACK channel transmission capacity/rate. This can be observed in Fig. 1 where there is some "free" time at the receiver after RS_1 is completely transmitted. The receiver is "free" because there is no data to send at this time. The receiver keeps itself "free" until the receipt of CP_3 of $Block_3$ which triggers the receiver to generate RS_3 for transmission.

In the light of the earlier discussions, a high LTP block transmission data loss rate resulting from a lossy space channel is expected to reduce the RS waiting time and transmission round-trip time. As a result, it is expected to improve the transmission performance of LTP over links characterized by extremely asymmetric data rates, especially for transmission of a large file which is conveyed by a large number of bundles for which many blocks is more likely transmitted.

4 Analytical Modeling for LTP Aggregation of Bundles Over Lossy Space Channels

The total length of an encapsulated LTP block at the link layer, termed L_{Block_Link}, was formulated as a function of the number of bundles to be aggregated and the fragmented segment size in [18, 20]. The formula is reiterated below

$$L_{Block\_Link} = \frac{N_{Bundle} \times (L_{Bundle} + L_{Bundle\_Head}) \times (L_{Ltp\_Seg} + L_{Frame\_Head})}{L_{Ltp\_Seg}} \quad (1)$$

in which

N_{Bundle} is the number of bundles aggregated within an LTP block,
L_{Bundle} is the length of a bundle,
L_{Bundle_Head} is the header length of each bundle,
L_{Ltp_Seg} is the average length of a fragmented segment, and
L_{Frame_Head} is the total length of the overhead added to a segment because of the encapsulation processes.

The total length of the frame overhead L_{Frame_Head} in (1) is actually the total encapsulation overhead starting from the LTP layer until the link layer. Therefore, it can be simply formulated as a sum of the length of an individual head added at Layer 1 (the link layer) up to the LTP layer, i.e.,

$$L_{Frame\_Head} = \sum_i L_{Head\_Layer(i)} \quad (2)$$

in which $L_{Head\_Layer(i)}$ is the length of head added by the ith layer. In specific, from bottom to top, $L_{Head\_Layer(1)}$ is the head length at the link layer, $L_{Head\_Layer(2)}$ is the head length at the IP layer, $L_{Head\_Layer(3)}$ is the head length at the UDP layer, and $L_{Head\_Layer(4)}$ is the head length at the LTP layer. In fact, the numerical value of L_{Frame_Head} varies depending on the protocol configuration as in some applications, a specific protocol may not be needed.

It is important to note that the formula of L_{Block_Link} in (1) ignores the effect on LTP aggregation of data losses caused by lossy space channels. In other words, the effect of channel loss or error caused by channel noise is not considered. However, as mentioned, data loss caused by channel error is one of the key features that characterize space communications, and its effect on LTP transmission cannot be ignored.

Let $\overline{T_{RS}}$ be the average transmission time of an RS out of the total number of RSs. As discussed, an RS can only be triggered by a successfully delivered CP segment. In other words, the CP segments that are lost or corrupted when received at the receiver do not generate the RSs. Therefore, $\overline{T_{RS}}$ can be formulated as

$$\overline{T_{RS}} = \frac{(1 - p)^{8 \times L_{CP}} \times L_{RS}}{R_{RS}} \tag{3}$$

in which.

p denotes an "effective net channel bit-error-rate (BER)" of the data channel which represents the net overall data loss rate (i.e., the transmission quality of a channel),

L_{CP} is the length of the CP segment in bytes,
L_{RS} is the length of an encapsulated RS at the link layer, and
R_{RS} is the uplink channel rate available for RS transmission.

Denote $\overline{T_{Block}}$ as the average transmission time of a single block out of the total number of blocks for the entire file transmission. Let R_{Data} be the data channel rate available for downloading data from a deep-space craft (i.e., Moon lander or Mars lander). Then, $\overline{T_{Block}}$ can be formulated as

$$\overline{T_{Block}} = \frac{L_{Block\_Link}}{R_{Data}} \tag{4}$$

Because of the "one RS per block" acknowledgment policy of LTP, the total number of RSs transmitted by the receiver is actually equal to the total number of LTP data blocks that the entire file is divided among to convey all the data bytes. In order to avoid RS transmission delay due to channel-rate asymmetry, it is required that during the entire file delivery process, the average transmission time of a block must be greater than or equal to the average transmission time of an RS sent by the data receiver, with each segment serving as a positive report of the cumulative reception for an individual block (i.e., a positive ACK), i.e., $\overline{T_{Block}} \geq \overline{T_{RS}}$. Their relationship can be formulated using different factors as

$$\frac{L_{Block\_Link}}{R_{Data}} \geq \frac{(1 - p)^{8 \times L_{CP}} \times L_{RS}}{R_{RS}} \tag{5}$$

With (5), L_{Block_Link} can be formulated as

$$L_{Block\_Link} \geq \frac{(1-p)^{8 \times L_{CP}} \times L_{RS} \times R_{Data}}{R_{RS}} \qquad (6)$$

L_{Block_Link} in (6) actually means that the total length of an encapsulated LTP block (when passed to the link layer) for transmission over the data channel must be large enough so that the average block transmission time is longer than the average RS transmission time. By this, the RS transmission delay due to the low ACK channel rate can be avoided.

Plugging the formula of L_{Block_Link} in (1) into (6), N_{Bundle} can be written as a function of other factors, and it is shown as

$$N_{Bundle} \geq \frac{(1-p)^{8 \times L_{CP}} \times L_{RS}}{R_{RS}} \times \frac{R_{Data} \times L_{Ltp\_Seg}}{\left(L_{Bundle} + L_{Bundle\_Head}\right) \times \left(L_{Ltp\_Seg} + L_{Frame\_Head}\right)} \qquad (7)$$

The formula of N_{Bundle} in (7) defines the number of bundles to be aggregated within an LTP block so that the delay of RS transmission due to the effect of channel-rate asymmetry can be avoided. Therefore, the threshold numerical value of N_{Bundle} is actually a minimum number of aggregated bundles to be able to avoid the delay of RS transmission. Denote this minimum number of bundles as N_{Bundle_Min}. With the effects of channel-rate asymmetry, channel data loss rate, data fragmentations, and the total overhead taken into consideration, it can be formulated as

$$N_{Bundle\_Min} = \left\lceil \frac{(1-p)^{8 \times L_{CP}} \times L_{RS}}{R_{RS}} \times \frac{R_{Data} \times L_{Ltp\_Seg}}{\left(L_{Bundle} + L_{Bundle\_Head}\right) \times \left(L_{Ltp\_Seg} + \sum_i L_{Head\_Layer(i)}\right)} \right\rceil \qquad (8)$$

5 Numerical Experimental Results and Model Validation

In this section, the numerical results of the file transfer experiments over the testbed are presented to validate the predictions of the analytical model for calculating the recommended minimum number of bundles aggregated within a block. The discussion focuses on a study of whether or not the delay of RS transmission caused by channel-rate asymmetry is avoided; the magnitude of this delay is measured by comparing the measured RTT lengths of the first and last block transmission rounds.

5.1 Overview of Experimental Infrastructure and Configurations

This analysis and the resulting value for the minimum number of bundles aggregated within a block to avoid the delay effect of RS transmission derived in Section IV are validated through file transfer experiments using an experimental infrastructure that emulates communication in a cislunar operational environment. The experimental infrastructure adopted for the proposed file transfer is the PC-based space communication and networking testbed (SCNT) [11]. The SCNT infrastructure was validated through a series of our previous studies in performance evaluation of a protocol suite proposed for space networks and deep-space communications [11–13]. For a detailed description of it, refer to [11].

The protocol implementation, BP/LTP, used for the experiments was adapted from the Interplanetary Overlay Network (ION) distribution v3.6.2. ION is a software implementation of the DTN protocol suite for space networks and deep-space communications developed by NASA's JPL [21]. IP and Ethernet were adopted to serve at the underlying network layer and data link layer, respectively. As the frame length (MTU size) of Ethernet is 1500 bytes, each LTP segment is configured to be 1400 bytes, making it fit within the frame MTU. Bundle size is arbitrarily fixed at 1000 bytes.

A one-way delay of 1.35 s, which is common over a cislunar channel, was introduced to each of the data and ACK channels to emulate the signal propagation delay in deep space. The effect of the channel-rate asymmetry on file transmission was implemented by configuring a high channel speed ratio (CR), 500/1, resulting from a downlink channel rate of 2 Mbps and an uplink channel rate of 4 Kbps. A text file of 1 Mbyte is transmitted from the sender to the receiver by running LTP together with associated protocols to measure the performance of the protocol.

As this study focuses on the effect of data loss on bundle aggregation in LTP, different levels of data loss are imposed as channel loss rate or channel quality for LTP file transmission. Four different effective net BERs (i.e., p in (3)), including 10^{-8}, 10^{-7}, 10^{-6} and 10^{-5}, are configured in our experiments. While the BERs of 10^{-8} and 10^{-7} are introduced to emulate a *less lossy* channel, the BERs of 10^{-6} and 10^{-5} are introduced to emulate a *lossy* channel and a *highly lossy* channel, respectively. The study is mainly concerned with the effect of data loss caused by the channel error on reliable data delivery of LTP. For this reason, each LTP block is declared 100% *red* in our experiments.

Although the size of an LTP segment is fixed at 1400 bytes in this study, the LTP block sizes adopted for the experiments vary drastically. The number of bundles aggregated within a block varies over a wide range. By varying block size in this way, we study how the transmission performance of LTP varies with variations of block size measured in the number of bundles.

5.2   Effect of RS Delay on File Delivery Over Lossy Channels

Figure 2 provides a comparison of the RTT lengths measured for the first and the last block transmission rounds in transmitting a 1-Mbytes file over an emulated cislunar space communication infrastructure having different channel qualities (i.e., with the BERs of 10^{-8}, 10^{-7}, 10^{-6}, and 10^{-5}). The RTT length for the first block transmission round is denoted as RTT_{1st} while it is denoted as RTT_{Last} for the last round. The communication infrastructure is configured with a CR of 500/1 and 5 bundles/block. It is observed that the RTT_{1st} is consistently around 2.9 s at all three channel BERs. This is reasonable provided that the one-way link delay configured for the experiments is 1.35 s to emulate a cislunar communication scenario.

In comparison, RTT_{Last} is much higher than RTT_{1st} at all three channel BERs considered, varying in the range of 22–24 s. This leads to a significant difference between RTT_{1st} and RTT_{Last}, around 20 s, regardless of the channel loss rate. Given that RTT_{1st} is shorter than three seconds, the RTT length difference of more than twenty seconds is a very strong indication that RTT_{Last} has the delay effect of RS transmission over the forward uplink ACK channel and/or delay effect of block transmission over the return downlink data channel. Because block transmission is initiated by the sender without waiting for any signal from the receiver and transmission is therefore continuous, no delay should have been experienced. Therefore, the only delay effect contributing to RTT_{Last} is the delay in RS transmission, which is caused by the channel-rate asymmetry.

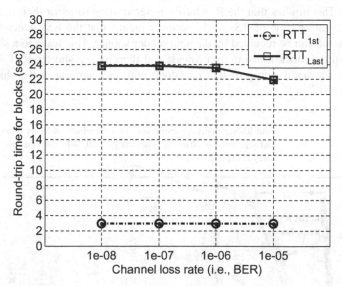

Fig. 2. Comparison of the RTT lengths measured for the first and the last block transmission rounds of LTP in transmitting a 1-Mbyte file over an emulated cislunar space communication infrastructure with highly asymmetric channel rates (with the CR of 500/1) and different channel qualities (i.e., with different loss rates), and LTP configured with 5 bundles/block.

The drastic difference of the RTT lengths can be easily explained by considering the number of bundles aggregated. The testbed is configured to have five bundles aggregated within a single block for this set of transmissions. Five bundles (aggregated within a block) are too few to resolve the delay effect of the RS transmission caused by the very low ACK channel rate. The time difference between RTT_{Last} and RTT_{1st} is so large because the RS delay resulted from each block transmission is accumulated over the transmission rounds of all the blocks. Furthermore, all the delay effects experienced by the previously transmitted blocks add up to the RTT length for the last round, which makes RTT_{Last} extremely long compared to RTT_{1st} (without any delay effect of RS transmission).

It is also observed that along with the channel BER increase, there is a slight decrease of RTT_{Last}. While the decrease is minor for the BER increase from 10^{-8} to 10^{-6}, it is obvious from 10^{-6} to 10^{-5}, around 2 s. This is reasonable according to the discussion in Section IV. Formulated as $1 - (1 - p)^{8 \times L_{CP}}$, the probability that a CP segment of a block is corrupted during file transmission is higher when a higher channel loss rate (p) is experienced. Given that the size of a file for transmission is fixed, the number of blocks is fixed, implying that the number of CP segments is also fixed according to the "one

CP segment per block" policy of LTP. With a higher loss probability for a CP segment, the number of CP segments that are successfully received by the receiver decreases. Following the "one RS per block" acknowledgment policy of LTP [5], the number of RSs generated at the receiver for transmission in response to the arrived CP segments must likewise decrease. With fewer RSs transmitted over the constrained ACK channel, the number of RS in waiting for transmission is reduced, leading to a shorter queue for the RSs. This implies that the RSs have shorter waiting time for their transmission. The shorter waiting time of RSs at the receiver means that the RSs generated for the file transmission can be received by the data sender sooner. This leads to a shorter RTT length for all the block transmission rounds and therefore, a shorter RTT for the last round. This clarifies the drop of RTT_{Last} along with the increase of the channel BER from 10^{-6} to 10^{-5} in Fig. 2.

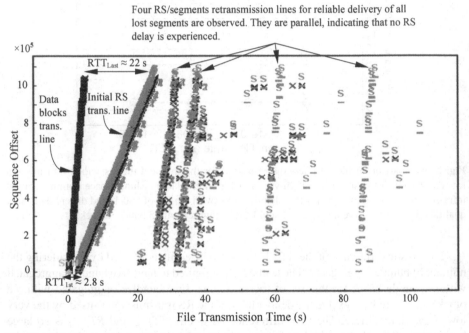

Fig. 3. TSG illustrating the LTP transmission at packet level at the sending node for delivery of a 1-Mbyte file over a highly lossy cislunar channel (with a BER of 10^{-5}) with highly asymmetric channel rates (with a CR of 500/1) and LTP configured with 5 bundles/block.

Figure 3 illustrates the time sequence graph (TSG) [22, 23] for a transmission scenario over a highly lossy channel with a BER of 10^{-5}, i.e., for the transmission which demonstrated a slight decrease of RTT_{Last} in Fig. 2. The original data transmission line and the corresponding initial RS transmission line vary in a linearly increasing pattern but with different slope rates. This leads to significantly different lengths of RTT—RTT_{1st} for the first block has a very short length around 2.8 s, and RTT_{Last} for the last block is very long, around 22 s. The TSG shows various loss and retransmission events starting from the RS transmission line. It is found that around eighty corruption/retransmission events are observed during the entire file delivery. As the transmission is configured with a BER of 10^{-5} and a given file size of 1 Mbyte, this is correct according to the calculation of $10^6 \times 8 \times 10^{-5} = 80$ which is statistically an average number of the data corruption (and retransmission) events.

These corruption events cause either losses of regular data segments or losses of CP segments. The loss events result in retransmission of the segments and even re-retransmission(s) of them. That is why in addition to the initial RS line, four more RS/segment retransmission lines are observed, indicating segments that are retransmitted for four times. Some segments are even retransmitted more than four times. In contrast to the original RS transmission line, these four retransmission lines are parallel, which indicate that there is no RS delay experienced in transmitting them. This is because of the decrease of the number of RSs for transmission along with the increase of the transmission attempts. Each attempt causes additional blocks to be successfully delivered and leaves fewer blocks to be retransmitted in the next attempt. Fewer blocks result in fewer CPs, resulting in fewer RSs sent by the receiver. This can also be observed from the fact that the RS lines are becoming sparser along with the transmission because of the decrease in the number of RSs sent.

The details of the loss of regular segments and the absence of some RSs for transmission over the ACK channel because of the failure of delivery of the corresponding CP segments can be observed from a TSG at LTP segment level. Figure 4 shows a zoom-in view of a selected portion of the TSG for the transmission of two LTP data blocks. The two blocks, numbered as $Block_1$ and $Block_2$, are transmitted in a continuous manner around 2 s. It is observed that the RS for $Block_2$ is received around 10 s while it is unexpectedly not received for $Block_1$. This is an indication that $Block_2$ experiences regular data corruption/loss (not CP loss) due to the high channel error rate of 10^{-5}, and the situation for $Block_1$ is different.

For the transmission of $Block_2$, it is transmitted in four segments in order, and the last segment should be sent as its CP segment. After one round trip, the RS for the block is received around 10 s, showing the RS line corresponding to the sequence numbers for the first, third and fourth (CP) segments. This indicates that these three segments are successfully delivered. But the RS line corresponding to the sequence numbers for the second segment is missing, and it is shown as a gap in the RS line to be filled. This means that the second segment is not successfully delivered because of corruption, and the receiver requests for retransmission of it.

The TSG shows that the second segment is then quickly retransmitted in red (for transmission reliability) as a separate block, and it is eventually successfully delivered. The acknowledging RS for the successful delivery of the second segment (up to the beginning of the block) arrives at the sender around 27 s, signaling the successful delivery of all four segments of the entire block. The mandatory RA with the sequence number aligned with the end of the block is sent immediately by the sender in response to the receipt of the RS. The RA is shown on top of the RS.

For transmission of $Block_1$ illustrated in Fig. 4, the missing of its RS is shown as a gap in the RS line to be filled. It can be inferred that the loss of the RS is caused by the corruption/loss of the CP segment (i.e., the last segment) of $Block_1$ to the receiver.

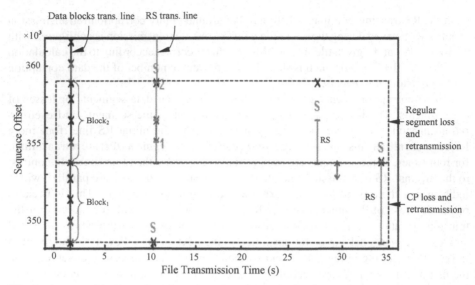

Fig. 4. A zoomed-in view of a selected portion of the TSG in Fig. 3, illustrating transmission of two LTP data blocks of a file—Block₁ having a CP loss and Block₂ having a regular segment loss.

Otherwise, if the CP segment is not corrupted, an RS should be sent to the sender reporting the delivery status, but this does not occur. For all four segments of the block, only the last segment (i.e., the CP) is retransmitted. This is a strong indication that the CP segment of $Block_1$ was corrupted by channel error.

The sender resends the lost CP segment for $Block_1$ upon the expiration of the CP timer around 29 s. As soon as the resent CP is successfully received, the receiver checks all four segments of the block (including the previously received three segments and the resent CP). It is found that all four segments are successfully received, implying a successful delivery of the entire block. Therefore, the RS for the block is sent in response immediately. As shown in the enlarged view, the RS arrives at the sender around 34 s, covering all four segments of $Block_1$. By this, $Block_1$ is successfully delivered and acknowledged.

The numerical value for a minimum number of bundles to be aggregated within a block to avoid the RS delay (i.e., N_{Bundle_Min}) can be calculated from the model using the pre-defined transmission conditions and protocol setting. As mentioned, the encapsulated segment size for transmission at the link layer is around 1440 bytes. So, for transmission over less lossy channels (e.g., with a BER of 10^{-7}), it is calculated that and according to (8), $N_{Bundle\_Min} = 33$. The same value is given at the BER of 10^{-8}.

$$(1 - p)^{8 \times L_{CP}} = \left(1 - 10^{-7}\right)^{8 \times 1440} \approx 99.89\%$$

Similarly, for a transmission over a lossy channel with a BER of 10^{-6}, it is calculated that

$$(1 - p)^{8 \times L_{CP}} \approx 98.86\% \quad \text{and} \quad N_{Bundle\_Min} = 33$$

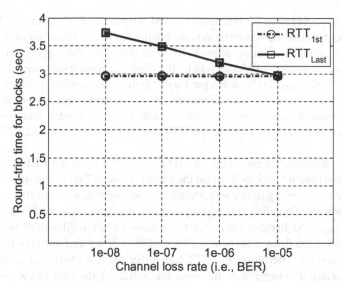

Fig. 5. Comparison of the RTT lengths measured for the first and the last block transmission rounds of LTP configured with 30 bundles/block.

and over a highly lossy channel at the BER of 10^{-5},

$$(1 - p)^{8 \times L_{CP}} \approx 89.12\% \quad \text{and} \quad N_{Bundle\_Min} = 30$$

The calculation result indicates that over less lossy and lossy channels (i.e., with the BERs of 10^{-8}–10^{-6}), the minimum number of bundles to be aggregated within a block to avoid RS delay is equal, 33 bundles/block in each scase. The calculated minimum number of bundles to be aggregated is thirty (i.e., 30 bundles/block) for transmission over a highly lossy channel with a channel BER of 10^{-5}.

As a validation to the model, Fig. 5 presents a comparison of the RTT lengths measured for the first block transmission round and the last block transmission round of a 1-Mbyte file configured with thirty bundles aggregated within a single block, or simply, 30 bundles/block. All the transmission conditions are the same as in Fig. 2 except for the number of aggregated bundles. Comparing with the observations in Fig. 2, the similarities are: (1) RTT_{1st} remains unchanged and low, less than 3 s, at all four channel BERs; (2) RTT_{Last} is longer than RTT_{1st} at the BERs of 10^{-8}–10^{-6}; and (3) RTT_{Last} shows slight decrease with the increase of the channel BER. All these observations are clarified in the discussion of Fig. 2, and the explanations still apply to the results in Fig. 5 even though the number of aggregated bundles is six times greater.

There are two main differences between Fig. 2 and Fig. 5. First, RTT_{Last} with 30 bundles/block in Fig. 5 is much shorter than the RTT_{Last} with 5 bundles/block in Fig. 2. This leads to only minor differences between RTT_{Last} and RTT_{1st} for the transmissions with 30 bundles/block. The second difference is with the transmission at the channel BER of 10^{-5}—while RTT_{Last} is significantly longer than RTT_{1st} with 5 bundles/block, they are roughly equal with 30 bundles/block.

By way of explanation for the first observed difference, RTT_{Last} in Fig. 5 is significantly shorter because the transmissions are configured with a larger number of bundles (30 bundles) aggregated within a block. With so many bundles aggregated, given the fixed file size, the number of blocks sent by the sender to convey the entire file decreases significantly. Following the "one RS per block" policy, the number of RSs generated at the receiver for transmission also decreases. This leads to a much shorter waiting time for the RS transmission over the ACK channel and therefore, a much shorter RTT length for almost every block. As a result, the RTT length for the last block, RTT_{Last}, drops drastically.

The second difference observed, i.e., $RTT_{Last} = RTT_{1st}$ at the BER of 10^{-5}, has a similar explanation: it happens because the transmission in Fig. 5 is configured with 30 bundles/block. According to the aforementioned calculation, with the BER of 10^{-5}, the minimum number of bundles to be aggregated within a block to avoid RS delay is thirty, i.e., $N_{Bundle\_Min} = 30$. In other words, the transmission configured with 30 bundles/block is able to resolve the delay effect caused by the CR of 500/1 and does not impose delay in RS transmission. Therefore, the RTT length for the last block transmission round remains unchanged compared to the ones measured for the first block and all other blocks.

In comparison, RTT_{Last} is slightly longer than RTT_{1st} at the BERs of 10^{-8}, 10^{-7} and 10^{-6}. In other words, there is a minor RS delay effect experienced for these three transmissions. In comparison, RTT_{Last} is slightly longer than RTT_{1st} at the BERs of 10^{-8}, 10^{-7} and 10^{-6}. In other words, there is minor effect of RS delay experienced for these three transmissions. According to the calculation derived above, the minimum number of bundles to be aggregated within a block to avoid the RS delay is thirty-three, i.e., $N_{Bundle\_Min} = 33$, for the transmissions at all three BERs. However, the file transmissions in the experiment were actually configured with 30 bundles/block. So, the aggregated numbers of bundles in the experiment were slightly fewer than the required minimum number of bundles. As a result, the delay effect is resolved significantly but not entirely. In other words, there is still some delay effect experienced for many blocks. The resulting minor delay effects are accumulated toward the last block transmission. This causes RTT_{Last} to be slightly longer than RTT_{1st} as shown in Fig. 5. Note that the delay effect is diminished with the increase of the BER because of the increment in CP loss events that leads to fewer RS for transmission and thus shorter delay of RS, as discussed with Fig. 2.

For an illustration of the LTP transmission at packet level without the effect of RS delay experienced, Fig. 6 presents the TSG for the same transmission of 1-Mbyte file as the one presented in Fig. 3 but configured with a much larger number of bundles aggregated within a block, 33 bundles/block. As calculated from the model, given that a bundle size of 1000 byte and a segment size of 1400 bytes are configured, thirty (30) bundles are the required minimum number of bundles to be aggregated to avoid the RS delay at the BER of 10^{-5}. Therefore, it is expected that a transmission with 33 bundles/block resolves thoroughly the delay of RS transmission and thus, leads to an equal length of the RTT for all the block transmission rounds.

Comparing this figure with the TSG with 5 bundles/block in Fig. 3, the main difference is that both the data line and the corresponding RS line in Fig. 6 increase linearly

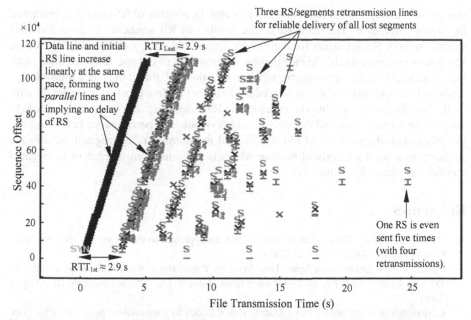

Fig. 6. TSG illustrating the transmission at packet level for delivery of a 1-Mbyte file over a highly lossy cislunar channel (with a BER of 10^{-5}) and LTP configured with 33 bundles/block.

at the same pace, forming two parallel lines. This leads to nearly consistent length of RTT for all the blocks. Both RTT_{Last} and RTT_{1st} are around 2.9 s, as an indication that the configuration of 33 bundles/block resolves the delay effect of RS transmission. This means that the calculated numerical value of N_{Bundle_Min}, 30 bundles/block, is able to overcome the effect of RS delay even over a highly lossy channel. Because of the high data loss events (with a BER of 10^{-5}), three parallel RS/segments retransmission lines are obviously observed in Fig. 6, in addition to the initial RS line. One RS is even retransmitted five times with four retransmission attempts.

6 Conclusions

In this article, an analytical model is presented for the minimum number of BP bundles to be aggregated within an LTP block for transmission over a lossy channel so that the RS transmission delay imposed by highly asymmetric channel rates can be resolved. The model is validated by realistic file transfer experiments over a testbed infrastructure and packet-level analysis of the experimented results. It is found that regardless of the channel loss rate, the minimum number of aggregated bundles derived from the analytical model functions effectively with respect to resolving all the RS delay effect caused by asymmetric channels and achieves high goodput performance.

It is concluded that regardless of the number of bundles aggregated within a block (i.e., block size), along with the increase of channel loss rate, there is slight decrease of RTT. This is because with a high loss rate involved, both the number of CP segments that are successfully delivered to the receiver and the number of RS segments generated in response decrease. The decrease of the number of RS segments leads to a shorter waiting time of RS segments for their transmission and thus, a shorter RTT for all the block transmission rounds. On the other hand, regardless of channel loss rate, along with the increase of the number of aggregated bundles, the RTT for all the block transmission rounds also decreases because of the reduced number of data blocks/CP segments originally sent by the sender. In both cases of the RTT decrease, the transmission leads to shorter file delivery time and thus increase of goodput. The performance keeps improving along with the increase of block size until the number of aggregated bundles are as many as around a threshold number which is the minimum number of aggregated bundles calculated from the model.

References

1. Burleigh, S., et al.: Delay-tolerant networking: an approach to interplanetary internet. IEEE Commun. Mag. **41**(6), 128–136 (2003)
2. Consultative Committee for Space Data Systems: Rationale, scenarios, and requirements for DTN in space. CCSDS 734.0-G-1. Green Book. Issue 1. CCSDS, Washington, DC, August 2010
3. Consultative Committee for Space Data Systems: Licklider transmission protocol for CCSDS. CCSDS 734.1-B-1. Blue Book. Issue 1. CCSDS, Washington, DC, May 2015
4. Ramadas, M., Burleigh, S., Farrell, S.: Licklider transmission protocol specification. Internet RFC 5326, September 2008
5. Sabbagh, A., Wang, R., Zhao, K., Bian, D.: Bundle protocol over highly asymmetric deep-space channels. IEEE Trans. Wireless Commun. **16**(4), 2478–2489 (2017)
6. Scott, K., Burleigh, S.: Bundle protocol specification. IETF request for comments RFC 5050, November 2007. https://www.ietf.org/rfc/rfc5050.txt.
7. Consultative Committee for Space Data Systems: Bundle protocol specifications. CCSDS 734.2-B-1. Blue Book. Issue 1. CCSDS. Washington, DC, September 2015
8. Feng, C., Wang, R., Bian, Z., Doiron, T., Hu, J.: Memory dynamics and transmission performance of bundle protocol (BP) in deep-space communications. IEEE Trans. Wireless Commun. **14**(5), 2802–2813 (2015)
9. Zhao, K., Wang, R., Burleigh, S.C., Sabbagh, A., Wu, W., De Sanctis, M.: Performance of bundle protocol for deep-space communications. IEEE Trans. Aerosp. Electron. Syst. **52**(5), 2347–2361 (2016)
10. Wang, R., Sabbagh, A., Burleigh, S., Zhao, K., Qian, Y.: Proactive retransmission in delay-/disruption-tolerant networking for reliable deep-space vehicle communications. IEEE Trans. Veh. Technol. **67**(10), 9983–9994 (2018)
11. Wang, R., Burleigh, S., Parik, P., Lin, C.-J., Sun, B.: Licklider transmission protocol (LTP)-based DTN for cislunar communications. IEEE/ACM Trans. Netw. **19**(2), 359–368 (2011)
12. Zhao, K., Wang, R., Burleigh, S., Qiu, M., Sabbagh, A., Hu, J.: Modeling memory variation dynamics for the Licklider transmission protocol in deep-space communications. IEEE Trans. Aerosp. Electron. Syst. **51**(4), 2510–2524 (2015)
13. Yu, Q., et al.: Modeling RTT for DTN protocols over asymmetric cislunar space channels. IEEE Syst. J. **10**(2), 556–567 (2016)
14. Lent, R.: Regulating the block loss ratio of the Licklider Transmission Protocol. In: Proceedings of 2018 IEEE 23th International Workshop on Computer Aided Modeling and Design of Communication Links and Networks (CAMAD), Barcelona, Spain, 17–19 September 2018 (2018)

15. Lent, R.: Analysis of the block delivery time of the Licklider transmission protocol. IEEE Trans. Commun. **67**(1), 518–526 (2019)
16. Alessi, N., Caini, C., de Cola, T., Raminella, M.: Packet layer erasure coding in interplanetary links: the LTP erasure coding link service adapter. IEEE Trans. Aerosp. Electron. Syst. **56**(1), 403–414 (2020)
17. Alessi, N., Burleigh, S., Caini, C., de Cola, T.: Design and performance evaluation of LTP enhancements for lossy space channels. Int. J. Satell. Commun. Netw. **37**(1), 3–14 (2019). Special Issue: ASMS/SPSC 2016
18. Wang, R., Wei, Z., Zhang, Q., Hou, J.: LTP aggregation of DTN bundles in space communications. IEEE Trans. Aerosp. Electron. Syst. **49**(3), 1677–1691 (2013)
19. Hu, J., Wang, R., Zhang, Q., Wei, Z., Hou, J.: Aggregation of DTN bundles for space internetworking system. IEEE Syst. J. **7**(4), 658–668 (2013)
20. Yang, Z., et al.: Analytical characterization of Licklider transmission protocol (LTP) in cislunar communications. IEEE Trans. Aerosp. Electron. Syst. **50**(3), 2019–2031 (2014)
21. Burleigh, S.: Interplanetary overlay network design and operation v3.6.2. JPL D-48259, Jet Propulsion Laboratory, California Institute of Technology, CA, March 2019. https://source forge.net/projects/ion-dtn/files/latest/download
22. TCP Connection Analysis Tool: TCPTRACE. https://linux.die.net/man/1/tcptrace
23. Ltptrace Analysis Tool: LTPTRACE. https://ion.ocp.ohiou.edu/content/ltptrace

Reliable Proactive Retransmission of Bundle Protocol for Deep-Space Communications

Lei Yang[1], Ruhai Wang[2(✉)], Yu Zhou[1], Qinglin Xie[1], and Kanglian Zhao[3]

[1] School of Electronics and Information Engineering, Soochow University,
Suzhou, Jiangsu, People's Republic of China
{20195228043,20195228016,20155228003}@stu.suda.edu.cn
[2] Phillip M. Drayer Department of Electrical Engineering, Lamar University,
Beaumont, TX, USA
rwang@lamar.edu
[3] School of Electronic Science and Engineering, Nanjing University, Nanjing,
Jiangsu, People's Republic of China
zhaokanglian@nju.edu.cn

Abstract. In this paper, a new transmission approach is proposed for bundle protocol (BP) of delay/disruption-tolerant networking (DTN) adopted for use in deep-space communications. It is intended to achieve highly reliable deep-space file transfer over unreliable space channel which may experience unpredictable or random link disruption events or any other events that lead to burst data losses. The main idea of the proposed approach is to use a hybrid of the *proactive retransmission* and *active retransmission* during file transfer, with each employing different time intervals for the bundle's custodial retransmission timeout (RTO) timer. The reactive retransmission is to provide additional transmission reliability in case the reliability provided by the proactive retransmission was not achieved due to the unpredictable link disruption events. Analytical modeling is presented for performance analysis of the approach, and the built model is validated by the file transfer experiment.

Keywords: Space communications · Satellite communications · Wireless networks · Protocol design · Performance evaluation

1 Introduction

1.1 Research Background

Developed as an effective networking technology in accommodating the lengthy link disruptions and long link delays that are inevitable in space communications, delay/disruption-tolerant networking (DTN) [1] is a networking architecture which is typically suitable for reliable data/file delivery over unreliable space links. As the main

Q. Wu et al. (Eds.): WiSATS 2020, LNICST 357, pp. 338–351, 2021.
https://doi.org/10.1007/978-3-030-69069-4_28

protocol of DTN for space, bundle protocol (BP) [2] is designed to establish an overlay network for reliable file transfer across highly heterogeneous communication networks. The basic mandatory data transmission method adopted by BP is a "store-and-forward" mechanism. Working together with an "optional" custody transfer method, BP is expected to provide reliable data delivery over an unreliable space channel.

In [3], a general DTN architecture for its use in a typical networking environment (especially in heterogeneous space and wireless communications) is presented in [3]. In the architecture, the adopted reference networking protocols are also suggested. As observed from the architecture, BP establishes a networking overlay to interconnect heterogeneous networks that adopts different data transport technologies Those heterogeneous networks could be operating based on the widely adopted Internet protocols such as Transmission Control Protocol (TCP) and User Datagram Protocol (UDP). They could also be operating based on the recently proposed reliable transmission protocol of DTN, Licklider transmission protocol (LTP) [4, 5]. Depending on the user's requirement, these heterogeneous networks even could be operating based on using a hybrid of these protocols. Working together with the nonvolatile permanent memory for necessary custodial service of data units (named BP *bundles*) at DTN custodial nodes, the mandatory "store-and-forward" and the optional custody transfer method of BP secure reliable data delivery at receiver even in the presence of highly data loss due to strong channel noise and link disruption events over space channel.

1.2 Contributions and Novelty

DTN is consistently considered as the only candidate networking technology to achieve highly reliable communication service in deep-space communications [6] in the past decade. Reliable data/file transmission mechanisms for high performance of BP are presently under development. In this paper, a new transmission approach is proposed for DTN's BP for use in deep-space communications. It is intended to achieve highly reliable deep-space file transfer over unreliable space channel which may experience unpredictable or random link disruption events or any other events that lead to burst data losses. The main idea of this proposed approach is to use a hybrid of the *proactive retransmission* and *active retransmission* during file transfer, with the proactive retransmission followed by the active retransmission.

The *proactive retransmission* and *active retransmission* are designed to have different transmission objectives. The objective of the *proactive retransmission* is to achieve highly reliable data delivery within the first (or simply the single) round-trip time (RTT) interval. The supplemental *reactive retransmission* is to provide additional transmission reliability in case the reliability provided by the proactive retransmission was not achieved on data transmission due to the unpredictable link disruption events or any other link events that may lead to burst data losses.

To implement this hybrid transmission approach, two different intervals are employed for the bundle's custodial retransmission timeout (RTO) timer during the file transfer—one for the proactive retransmission and another for the reactive retransmission. An analytical model is built for performance analysis of the proposed transmission approach, and it is verified based on the file transfer experiment. This study is expected to be practically useful to optimal design and configuration of BP of DTN.

2   Related Work

A lot of work has been done in research and development of DTN architecture/protocols and analysis for their application in space networks and interplanetary communications [3, 7–14]. These studies are done in either theoretical manner and/or experimental manner based on file transfer experiments over a testbed. Among these studies, the aforementioned "proactive" retransmission mechanism is proposed for BP in [14]. For a detailed discussion of the operation and performance analysis of the proposed "proactive" retransmission mechanism, refer to [14].

The "proactive" retransmission mechanism proposed in [14] should work effectively if the communication channel is relatively reliable for which the file transfer unlikely experiences unpredictable or random link disruption events or a very high channel errors that lead to burst data losses. In case of a presence of a lengthy link disruption or any other channel causal events which cause unavailability of data link for a long time, the scheduled multiple proactive retransmission attempts may fail to deliver many or even all the bundles to the receiver but the sender is not aware of it. In this case, the sender assumes that the entire file is successfully delivered at the receiver but is actually not. This results in a catastrophic consequence to the transmission performance of BP for file delivery.

To resolve potentially severe performance issue of the mechanism proposed in [14], we propose to use a hybrid of the proactive retransmission and active retransmission during the file transfer. In other words, in addition to the mentioned proactive retransmission mechanism, the traditional reactive retransmission mechanism is employed for extra transmission reliability to file transfer. The proposed retransmission approach is illustrated and discussed in Sect. 3 in a comparison with the one in [14].

3   Illustration of the Proposed Reliable Proactive Retransmission of Bundle Protocol

Figure 1 illustrates a recreation of a file transmission scenario using the proactive approach proposed in [14]. The operation of the scenario is self-explanatory. For the details of its operation, see [14]. As discussed, in case of a presence of a lengthy link disruption or any other channel causal events which cause unavailability of data link for a long time, the multiple retransmission attempts made within the interval of RTT may fail to deliver many or even all the bundles to the destination.

To resolve the possible catastrophic performance degradation of the approach proposed in [14] in the presence of link disruption event, the approach has been extended for performance enhancement. The bundle-based operation of the enhanced approach of BP is illustrated in Fig. 2. In comparison to the illustration in Fig. 1, the proposed reliable proactive retransmission approach adopts a joint use of the proactive retransmission mechanism and reactive retransmission mechanism. Therefore, following the proactive retransmissions of the file within the first (or simply the single) RTT interval, a supplemental reactive retransmission is implemented. With respect to the operation of the proactive retransmissions of the file in the first phase, it is the same as the retransmission process done within the interval of RTT illustrated in Fig. 1. In other words, each

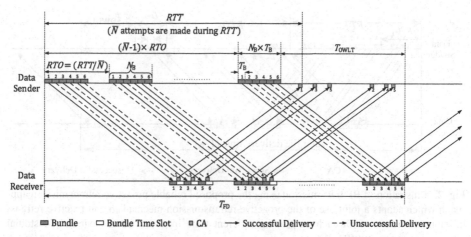

Fig. 1. File transmission of BP in bundles using a proactive retransmission mechanism proposed in [14] with the bundle retransmission controlled by the retransmission timer which is configured according to the length of RTT so that $\overline{N}$ transmission attempts can be made during the interval of RTT.

bundle is retransmitted for specified times following the calculated RTO timer length, termed as RTO_1, without regard to the acknowledgment from the receiver.

As mentioned, the reactive retransmission designed in the second phase is intended to have additional transmission reliability in case the transmission attempts made in the first phase are not successful for any reason. With respect to the time for retransmission of the lost bundles during the reactive retransmission phase, the first reactive retransmission attempt is made as soon as the CA for any bundles sent in the first phase is received. That is, the first reactive retransmission attempt is made right after the first RTT. This is because it generally takes the RTT interval to receiver the acknowledgment from the sender. The CA indicates to the sender that which bundles were not successfully delivered or simply, lost, and thus need to be retransmitted. Then, those lost bundles are retransmitted.

Similar to the operation of many other automatic-repeat-request (ARQ) mechanisms, the reactive retransmission mechanism can retransmit the data bundles based on either the received acknowledgments or as soon as the RTO timer expires. Therefore, the RTO timer is slightly longer than the RTT interval. To differentiate it from the RTO timer length in the first phase, this timer is named as RTO_2. So, if any bundles retransmitted during the reactive transmission phase are lost again, they are re-retransmitted as soon as the CAs are received which is generally done upon expiration of RTO_2.

In comparison to the proactive retransmission approach illustrated in Fig. 1 (i.e., the one in [14]), the extended proactive retransmission proposed in this paper takes a much longer file delivery time. This is the cost for the additional transmission reliability.

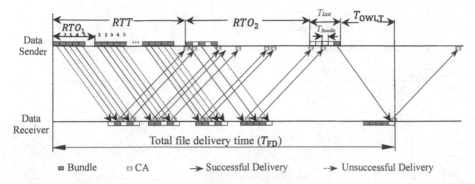

Fig. 2. Illustration of BP transmission using the proposed reliable proactive retransmission approach which adopts a joint use of the proactive retransmission mechanism and reactive retransmission mechanism with each employing different time intervals for the bundle's custodial retransmission timeout (RTO) timer.

4   Performance Modeling for Reliable Proactive Retransmission of BP Over Lossy Space Channels

As discussed, the reliable proactive retransmission approach is proposed based on the proactive retransmission mechanism. Therefore, considering their connection, the performance analysis results for the proactive retransmission in [14] are revisited before the performance modeling for reliable proactive retransmission is presented.

According to the performance analysis in [14] and based on the time components involved in Fig. 1, the total file delivery time of the approach, defined as T_{FD}, can be approximated as a sum of the RTO intervals for the first $(\overline{N} - 1)$ attempts, the bundles' transmission time in the last round, and the one-way propagation time, T_{OWLT}, for the last round. It is reiterated as

$$T_{FD} = (\overline{N} - 1) \times RTO + N_B \times T_B + T_{OWLT} \tag{1}$$

All the symbols presented in (1) are well defined in [14].

The file transmission efforts made by the sender, $\overline{N}$, is derived as

$$\overline{N} = \left\lceil -\log_{1-(1-p)^{8 \times \left[L_B + L_{BHD} + L_{UHD} + \left\lceil \frac{L_B + L_{BHD} + L_{UHD}}{L_{MTU} - L_{IHD}} \right\rceil \times (L_{IHD} + L_{LHD}) \right]}} \left\lceil \frac{L_F}{L_B} \right\rceil \right\rceil \tag{2}$$

in which

p is the channel bit-error-rate (BER) reflecting the net overall transmission quality,
L_F and L_B are the file size and bundle size, respectively, and.

Other notations of L_{xHD} represents the length of the header length at various layers that encapsulate individual bundle.

With the formula for $\overline{N}$ plugged in (1), T_{FD} is reformulated in [14] as

$$T_{FD} = \left\{ \left[\frac{-\log}{1-(1-p)^{8\times\left[L_B+L_{BHD}+L_{UHD}+\left\lceil\frac{L_B+L_{BHD}+L_{UHD}}{L_{MTU}-L_{IHD}}\right\rceil\times(L_{IHD}+L_{LHD})\right]\left\lceil\frac{L_F}{L_B}\right\rceil}} - 1 \right\} \times RTO + \left\lceil\frac{L_F}{L_B}\right\rceil \right.$$

$$\times \frac{L_B + L_{BHD} + L_{UHD} + \left\lceil\frac{L_B+L_{BHD}+L_{UHD}}{L_{MTU}-L_{IHD}}\right\rceil \times (L_{IHD}+L_{LHD})}{R_D} + T_{OWLT} \quad (3)$$

As discussed in [14], there is a maximum value of the time-out retransmission timer, RTO. Therefore, the setting range of RTO has to meet the following requirement

$$\left\{ \frac{L_B+L_{BHD}+L_{UHD}+\left\lceil\frac{L_B+L_{BHD}+L_{UHD}}{L_{MTU}-L_{IHD}}\right\rceil\times(L_{IHD}+L_{LHD})}{R_D} \times \left\lceil\frac{L_F}{L_B}\right\rceil \right\}$$

$$< RTO \le$$

$$\left[\frac{RTT}{\left\lceil\frac{-\log}{1-(1-p)^{8\times\left[L_B+L_{BHD}+L_{UHD}+\left\lceil\frac{L_B+L_{BHD}+L_{UHD}}{L_{MTU}-L_{IHD}}\right\rceil\times(L_{IHD}+L_{LHD})\right]}}\left\lceil\frac{L_F}{L_B}\right\rceil\right\rceil} \right] \quad (4)$$

In Fig. 2, a scenario of BP file transmission using the proposed reliable proactive retransmission approach which adopts a joint use of the proactive retransmission mechanism and reactive retransmission mechanism, with each employing different time intervals for the bundle's custodial RTO timer, is shown. For the sake of simplicity, the scenario is shown for the transmission of file conveyed by five bundles.

As shown in Fig. 2, the file is transmitted three times within the first RTT, and corresponding CA reaches the data sender beyond the first RTT interval. For those bundles that are successfully delivered, since their corresponding CAs are received, the bundles are released at the data sender. The remaining bundles of the file are retransmitted beyond the first RTT. Therefore, the number of bundles transmitted for the fourth time (i.e., the first time after the first RTT) in Fig. 2 is the number of bundles that failed for the first transmission attempt. After the bundle's retransmission time-out timer RTO_2 expires, the data sender will retransmit the remaining bundles until the data receiver receives all the bundles.

Let L_{EACK} be the length of an encapsulated CA at the link layer. Then, L_{EACK} should be simply formulated as the lengths of an encapsulated CA bundle in bytes after being encapsulated by all the layers (underneath BP)

$$L_{EACK} = L_{ACK} + L_{BHD} + L_{UHD} + \left\lceil \frac{L_B + L_{BHD} + L_{UHD}}{L_{MTU} - L_{IHD}} \right\rceil \times (L_{IHD} + L_{LHD}) \quad (5)$$

Then, the probability of error in delivering a CA, P_{ACK}, can be formulated as

$$P_{ACK} = 1 - (1-p)^{8\times L_{EACK}} = 1 - (1-p)^{8\times\left[L_{ACK}+L_{BHD}+L_{UHD}+\left\lceil\frac{L_B+L_{BHD}+L_{UHD}}{L_{MTU}-L_{IHD}}\right\rceil\times(L_{IHD}+L_{LHD})\right]} \quad (6)$$

Similarly, define L_{EB} as the size of an encapsulated data bundle, and the probability of error in delivering an encapsulated data bundle, termed as P_B, can be formulated as

$P_B = 1 - (1 - p)^{8 \times L_{EB}} = 1 - (1 - p)^{8 \times \left[L_B + L_{BHD} + L_{UHD} + \left\lceil \frac{L_B + L_{BHD} + L_{UHD}}{L_{MTU} - L_{IHD}} \right\rceil \times (L_{IHD} + L_{LHD}) \right]}$.

Then, the probability for that both a bundle and its CA are successfully delivered can be written as

$$P_{Round} = (1 - P_B) \times (1 - P_{ACK}) \tag{7}$$

For transmission of multiple bundles over highly asymmetric channels, all the CAs except the first one need to wait to be transmitted because of the delayed transmission of the previous CAs caused by reduced ACK channel rate. Assume that the downlink channel rate available for data transmission is R_D and the uplink channel rate available for CA transmission is R_{ACK}. To avoid the delay of CAs due to channel-rate asymmetry, there is a limit to the minimum bundle size, named L_{B-Min}. According to the previous study [12], L_{B-Min} is formulated as

$$L_{B-Min} = \frac{L_{EACK} \times R_D}{R_{ACK}} - L_{BHD} \tag{8}$$

Let $k = \left\lceil \frac{RTT}{RTO_1} \right\rceil$ and the number of transmission attempts beyond the first RTT is m. Then, the total transmission attempts during the entire file delivery, n, can be written as $n = k + m$.

Let $N_{B(i)}$ be the number of bundles that incur error during transmission round i. Since the CAs of the first k transmission attempts have not reached to the data sender, the number of bundles transmitted for each transmission attempt from the first attempt to the kth attempt are N_B. The CAs of the first transmission attempt arrive at the data sender beyond the first RTT interval, but the CAs of the subsequent transmissions made within the first RTT interval do not arrive the sender by that time. Therefore, the number of bundles transmitted in the $(k + 1)$th attempt can be formulated as $N_{B(k+1)} = N_B \times (1 - P_{Round})$. For the $(k + 2)$th transmission attempt, one RTO_2 timer interval has passed since the $(k + 1)$th transmission made. Therefore, the CAs of the first $(k + 1)$ transmission efforts arrive at the data sender. The bundles transmitted in the $(k + 2)$th attempt are those failed in the first $(k + 1)$ transmission efforts, and it can be formulated as $N_{B(k+2)} = N_B \times (1 - P_{Round})^{k+1}$. Then, for the $(k + m)$th transmission attempt, $N_{B(k+m)}$ can be formulated as $N_{B(k+m)} = N_B \times (1 - P_{Round})^{k+m-1}$. Continuing with this iterative procedure, $N_{B(k+m+1)}$ can be formulated as $N_B \times (1 - P_{Round})^{k+m}$.

Similarly, during the $(k + m + 1)$th transmission attempt, if the bundles released from the sender's memory is fewer than 1, i.e., that is $N_{B(k+m+1)} < 1$ or $N_B \times (1 - P_{Round})^{k+m} < 1$, it implies that the successful delivery of an entire file is achieved by the $(k + m)$th transmission attempt. Let n be the total transmission attempts, and it can be written as

$$n > \left\lceil -log_{(1-P_{Round})} N_B \right\rceil \tag{9}$$

Then, the average transmission attempts made by the sender, N, can be derived as

$$N = \lceil -log_{(1-P_{Round})}N_B \rceil \tag{10}$$

The file delivery time is mainly composed of the first RTT, file retransmission time, one-way file propagation time, and the time sent by the last bundle in the last transmission round. Then, the total file delivery time T_{FDT} for the proposed reliable proactive transmission approach can be approximated as

$$T_{FDT} = RTT + (m - 1) \times RTO_2 + T_{OWLT} + T_{last} \tag{11}$$

in which T_{last} is the transmission time for the last attempt, and it can be formulated as $\frac{1}{N_B} \times \sum_{i=1}^{N_B} \frac{i \times L_B}{R_D}$.

The goodput for the transmission can be written as $\gamma = \frac{L_F}{T_{FDT}}$, and it can be normalized as $\gamma_N = \frac{\gamma}{D_N}$. D_N is the total data load transmitted over the channel after normalized, and it can be written as $\frac{D_{total}}{L_F}$. D_{total} is the total data load (in bytes) which includes the amount of data in the first k transmission attempts, the $(k + 1)th$ transmission attempt, and the subsequent $(m - 1)$ transmission attempts.

Let $D_{(i)}$ be the amount of data that are transmitted in transmission round i. Since the number of bundles for each transmission attempt from the first to the kth are N_B, the amount of data can be calculated as $k \times N_B \times L_{EB}$. The amount of data transmitted in the $(k + 1)$th attempt can be formulated as $D_{(k+1)} = (1 - P_{Round}) \times N_B \times L_{EB}$. For the $(k + 2)$th transmission attempt, the amount of data can be formulated as $D_{(k+2)} = (1 - P_{Round})^{k+1} \times N_B \times L_{EB}$.

Continuing with this iterative procedure, for the $(k + m)$th transmission attempt, $D_{(k+m)}$ can be derived as $(1 - P_{Round})^{k+m-1} \times N_B \times L_{EB}$. Therefore, D_{total} can be formulated as

$$D_{total} = k \times N_B \times L_{EB} + (1 - P_{Round}) \times N_B \times L_{EB} + \sum_{i=1}^{m-1}(1 - P_{Round})^{k+i} \times N_B \times L_{EB} \tag{12}$$

There is a limit to the numerical value of m. In other word, no matter within or beyond the first RTT interval, there will be at least one transmission attempt made, that is $0 < m < n - 1$. At the same time, k should satisfy $\frac{RTT}{RTO_1} \leq k < \frac{RTT}{RTO_1} + 1$. Therefore, the normalized goodput γ_N can be formulated as.

$$\gamma_N = \frac{N_B \times L_B^2}{\left(\lceil \frac{RTT}{RTO_1} \rceil + (1 - P_{Round}) + \sum_{i=1}^{m-1}(1 - P_{Round})^{\lceil \frac{RTT}{RTO_1} \rceil + i} \right) \times L_{EB}}$$
$$\times \frac{1}{RTT + (m - 1) \times RTO_2 + T_{OWLT} + T_{last}} \tag{13}$$

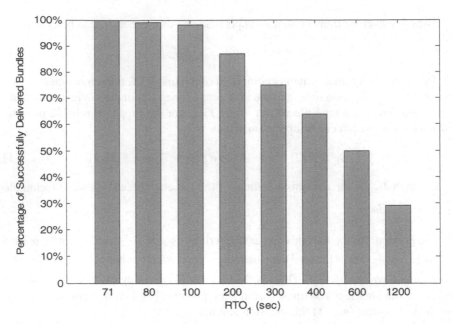

Fig. 3. Comparison of the percentage of successfully transferred bundles with different intervals of RTO_1 over a deep-space channel with a bundle of 30 Kbytes.

5 Numerical Experimental Results and Model Validation

5.1 Overview of Experimental Infrastructure and Configurations

The performance model built in Sect. 4 is validated through file transfer experiments using an experimental infrastructure that emulates communications in a deep-space operational environment. The testbed and the experimented configurations/setting are the same as those in [14]. As done in [14], the protocol implementation of BP was provided by JPL [15]. A one-way link delay was configured as 600 s. Provided that the length of RTT is 1200 s, the interval of RTO_2 is fixed to be slightly higher than 1200 s. However, a wide range of RTO_1 intervals, from 47 s to 1200 s, are experimented.

5.2 Experimental Results and Model Validation

Figure 3 presents a comparison of the percentage of successfully delivered bundles using the proposed reliable proactive retransmission approach in transmitting a 10-Mbyte file with different intervals of RTO_1 over a deep-space channel with link delay of 10 min and a BER of 5×10^{-6}, asymmetric channel ratio of 300/1 and a bundle of 30 Kbytes. It is observed in Fig. 3 that the smaller the file transmission interval RTO_1 within a single RTT is configured, the more transmission attempts within a single RTT time are made. In other words, more attempts are made by configuring a smaller RTO_1 timer interval within a single RTT time. With more transmission attempts made, the higher the percentage of bundle successful transmission at the end of the RTT time is achieved. This means that with k transmission attempts made, more bundles are successfully delivered. As a result, the file delivery time decreases, and the efficiency of file transfer is improved.

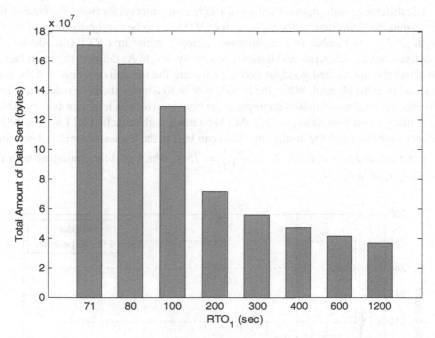

Fig. 4. Comparison of the total amount of data sent with different intervals of RTO_1 and a bundle of 30 Kbytes.

Figure 4 presents a comparison of the total amount of data sent by a file with different RTO_1 timer interval within a single RTT time. It can be observed that as the number of transmissions within a single RTT time increases, the total amount of data sent increases rapidly.

Figures 5 and 6 present sample comparisons of the normalized goodput performance of BP with variations of RTO_1 timer interval, predicted by the model and observed in the experiments with bundle sizes of 30 Kbytes and 58 Kbytes, respectively. Both bundle sizes are larger than the required minimum bundle size,L_{B-Min}, to avoid the ACK delay. The numerical value of L_{B-Min} is 29.6 Kbytes according to (8). It is observed that in both Fig. 5 and Figs. 6, the predicted numerical values of the model match well with those measured from the experiments for all the configured intervals of RTO timer regardless of the bundle size. This indicates that the realistic file transfer experiments validate the model. In addition, the numerical value of the model is slightly higher because some minor delay components such as queue delay and processing delay are ignored when the total file delivery time is modeled.

In comparison, the optimal setting of RTO_1 timer interval which achieves the highest normalized goodput performance of BP is found to be different for two bundle sizes. For the bundle size of 30 KB, the optimal setting of RTO_1 is very short, around equal to 75 s. With the bundle size significantly increased to 58 Kbytes, the optimal setting increases to a much larger value which is around 600 s, a half of the RTT length.

The difference in the optimal setting of RTO_1 timer interval for two different bundles are reasonable. Considering that the length of RTO has to be configured larger than the length of T_F, the number of transmission attempts in the first RTT (i.e., during the proactive retransmission) should not exceed twenty-seven. As defined, the main factors that affect the normalized goodput performance are the file delivery time and the total data load over the channel. When the bundle size is 30 Kbytes, it can be calculated from (10) that the total transmission attempts is seventeen, which is less than twenty-seven. So, as many transmissions as possible should be made within the first RTT so that the file delivery time can reach the minimum which can lead to the highest normalized goodput. It can be calculated that $RTO_1 \approx \left\lceil \frac{1200}{17-1} \right\rceil = 75$ s, which is fully consistent with the variation trend in Fig. 5.

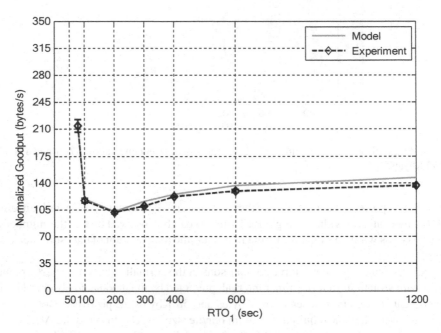

Fig. 5. Comparison of normalized goodput performance of BP with variations of RTO_1 timer interval, predicted by the model and observed in the experiments.

In comparison, for the much larger bundle size of 58 Kbytes, the total transmission attempts are fifty-three which is greater than twenty-seven. Therefore, multiple transmissions must be performed within the first RTT during the proactive retransmission phase and after the first RTT during the reactive retransmission phase. By this, the file delivery time and the total data load over the channel greatly increase. This implies that

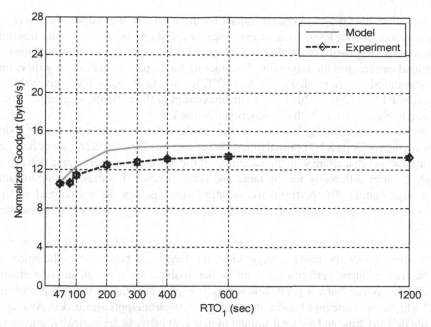

Fig. 6. Comparison of normalized goodput performance of BP with variations of RTO_1 timer interval, predicted by the model and observed in the experiments with a bundle size of 58 Kbytes.

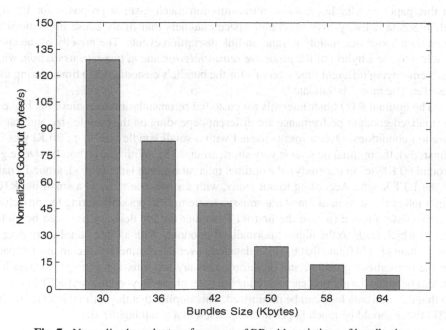

Fig. 7. Normalized goodput performance of BP with variations of bundle size.

the total data load has the greatest impact on the normalized goodput. Therefore, for transmissions with a lossy channel and a reasonably large bundle, as many transmission attempts as possible should be made beyond the first RTT interval so that the total data load can reaches the minimum. Considering the impact of file delivery time, only two transmissions are needed in the first RTT, leading to $RTO_1 = 600$ s given that the length of RTT is 1200 s. This leads to the maximum of the normalized goodput, which is completely consistent with the variation trend in Fig. 6.

As we can see from Fig. 5, the shorter the bundle is, the better the normalized goodput performance is for its RTO optimal timer. This is also true for other RTO_1 timer intervals. Figure 6 shows that along with the variations of the RTO_1 timer interval, the normalized goodput varies differently for the large and small bundles. It varies less significantly for a large bundle. The performance variation indicates that the normalized goodput performance is significantly different when the bundle is larger than when the bundle is smaller.

Figure 7 presents the normalized goodput performance of BP with the variations of bundles. Under the same configuration, the larger the bundle size, the lower the normalized goodput performance. This is reasonable. Given a transmission channel condition, it is true that a larger bundle generally experiences the greater loss probability. With a higher loss rate for a bundle, more retransmission attempts are needed. As a result, the file delivery time and the total amount of data sent increase dramatically, leading to a decrease in normalized effective goodput and degradation of the transmission efficiency.

6   Summary and Conclusions

In this paper, a reliable proactive retransmission mechanism is proposed for BP for reliable data delivery over unreliable space channels that likely cause unpredictable burst data losses due mainly to random link disruption events. The novelty of the approach is to use a hybrid of the *proactive retransmission* and *active retransmission*, with each employing different time intervals for the bundle's custodial RTO timer during file transfer. The model is validated.

The optimal RTO timer intervals for custodial retransmission to achieve the highest normalized goodput performance are different depending on the bundle size and transmission conditions. Over a lossy channel with a small bundle size (e.g., 30 Kbytes in our study), the optimal interval is very short, around 75 s. With a large bundle size (e.g., around 60 Kbytes in our study), the optimal interval is much large (600 s), around a half of the RTT length. According to our study, with a small bundle size, a small the RTO timer interval results in as many transmissions attempts as possible during the proactive retransmission phase (within the first RTT) so that the file delivery time can be minimized which leads to the highest normalized goodput. With a large bundle size over a lossy channel, it is found that the total data load over the channel has the greatest impact on the normalized goodput, and therefore, as many transmission attempts as possible should be made during the reactive retransmission phase (beyond the first RTT interval) so that the total data load can be minimized. This implies that the optimal interval of the RTO timer should be much larger in comparison to a small bundle size.

It is also found that over a lossy deep-space channel, the larger the bundle size is configured, the lower the normalized goodput performance is. This is reasonable because for transmission with a large bundle over a lossy channel, more retransmission attempts are needed to secure successful delivery of a file, leading to a longer file delivery time and thus decrease in normalized goodput.

References

1. Burleigh, S., et al.: Delay-tolerant networking: an approach to inter-planetary Internet. IEEE Commun. Mag. **41**(6), 128–136 (2003)
2. Scott, K., Burleigh, S.: Bundle protocol specification. IETF Request for Comments RFC 5050, November 2007. https://www.ietf.org/rfc/rfc5050.txt
3. Wang, R., Qiu, M., Zhao, K., Qian, Y.: Optimal RTO timer for best transmission efficiency of DTN protocol in deep-space vehicle communications. IEEE Trans. Veh. Technol. **66**(3), 2536–2550 (2017)
4. Ramadas, M., Burleigh, S., Farrell, S.: Licklider transmission protocol specification. Internet RFC 5326, September 2008
5. Consultative Committee for Space Data Systems: Licklider transmission protocol for CCSDS. CCSDS 734.1-B-1. Blue Book. Issue 1. CCSDS, Washington, DC, May 2015
6. The Space Internetworking Strategy Group (SISG): Recommendations on a strategy for space internetworking. IOAG.T.RC.002.V1. Report of the Interagency Operations Advisory Group, NASA Headquarters, Washington, DC, USA, 1 August 2010
7. Wang, R., Burleigh, S., Parik, P., Lin, C.-J., Sun, B.: Licklider transmission protocol (LTP)-based DTN for cislunar communications. IEEE/ACM Trans. Network. **19**(2), 359–368 (2011)
8. Zhao, K., Wang, R., Burleigh, S., Qiu, M., Sabbagh, A., Hu, J.: Modeling memory variation dynamics for the Licklider transmission protocol in deep-space communications. IEEE Trans. Aerosp. Electron. Syst. **51**(4), 2510–2524 (2015)
9. Sabbagh, A., Wang, R., Burleigh, S., Zhao, K.: Analytical framework for effect of link disruption on bundle protocol in deep-space communications. IEEE J. Sel. Areas Commun. **36**(5), 1086–1096 (2018)
10. Sabbagh, A., Wang, R., Zhao, K., Bian, D.: Bundle protocol over highly asymmetric deep-space channels. IEEE Trans. Wireless Commun. **16**(4), 2478–2489 (2017)
11. Wang, R., et al.: Modeling disruption tolerance mechanisms for a heterogeneous 5G network. IEEE Access **6**, 25836–25848 (2018)
12. Feng, C., Wang, R., Bian, Z., Doiron, T., Hu, J.: Memory dynamics and transmission performance of bundle protocol (BP) in deep-space communications. IEEE Trans. Wireless Commun. **14**(5), 2802–2813 (2015)
13. Zhao, K., Wang, R., Burleigh, S., Sabbagh, A., Wu, W., De Sanctis, M.: Performance of bundle protocol for deep-space communications. IEEE Trans. Aerosp. Electron. Syst. **52**(5), 2347–2361 (2016)
14. Wang, R., Sabbagh, A., Burleigh, S., Zhao, K., Qian, Y.: Proactive retransmission in delay-/disruption-tolerant networking for reliable deep-space vehicle communications. IEEE Trans. Veh. Technol. **67**(10), 9983–9994 (2018)
15. Burleigh, S.: Interplanetary overlay network design and operation v3.6.2. JPL D-48259, Jet Propulsion Laboratory, California Institute of Technology, CA, March 2019. https://sorcef orge.net/projects/ion-dtn/files/latest/download

Ground Station Site Selection with Real Cloud Data for Satellite-Ground Optical Networking

Yihua Wang[1,2], Xiaoyong Zhuge[1,2], Shulei Gong[1,2], Kanglian Zhao[1,2(✉)], Wenfeng Li[1,2], and Yuan Fang[1,2]

[1] School of Electronic Science and Engineering, Nanjing University, Nanjing 210023, China
zhaokanglian@nju.edu.cn
[2] School of Atmospheric Sciences, Nanjing University, Nanjing 210023, China

Abstract. Optical communication is an important technology for future space networks. However, compared with inter-satellite optical communication, satellite-ground optical communication is more challenging because of weather, which are mostly cloud factors. To deal with this problem, an effective strategy is to achieve ground station site diversity. In this paper, we propose a method to determine the range of clouds that affects satellite-ground optical links for a certain ground station. Given the number of candidate ground stations, through processing the cloud products of the Himawari-8 GEO satellite, we obtained the cloud coverage data corresponding to each ground station. Then, by calculating the availability probability of possible combinations of ground stations, the network with the highest availability is chosen as the optimal optical ground station network. By calculating the availability probability with real cloud data, the results of ground station site selection in mainland China are obtained.

Keywords: Satellite-ground optical networking · Ground station site selection · Network availability

1 Introduction

Optical communication is one of the most promising communication technologies for the future space networks. Compared with the traditional RF communication technology, optical communication uses optical beams as the carrier, which can not only realize high transmission rate, but also achieve higher anti-interference performance. These characteristics of optical communication allow it to be applied to downlink earth observation data form LEO satellites, or to transmit data to GEO satellites as feeder links, etc. [3]. However, compared with inter-satellite optical links, satellite-ground optical links are subject to weather conditions such as cloud coverage condition, which will seriously attenuate the optical signal and even directly interrupt the optical links.

© ICST Institute for Computer Sciences, Social Informatics and Telecommunications Engineering 2021
Published by Springer Nature Switzerland AG 2021. All Rights Reserved
Q. Wu et al. (Eds.): WiSATS 2020, LNICST 357, pp. 352–361, 2021.
https://doi.org/10.1007/978-3-030-69069-4_29

An effective strategy to solve this problem is to use multiple ground stations to form an optical ground station (OGS) network [2–8]. When some ground stations are covered by clouds and can't communication, site diversity guarantees one or more ground stations with cloud free line of sight to maintain the optical communication and avoid communication disruption. Therefore, the selection of ground stations for an optical ground station network is particularly important for improving the availability of satellite-ground optical networking (Fig. 1).

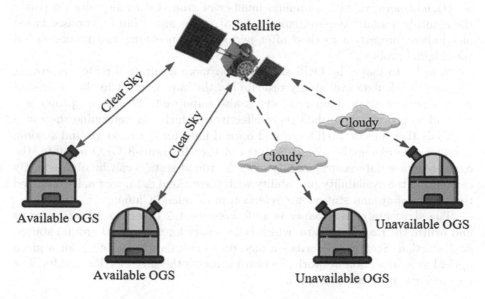

Fig. 1. OGS network of multiple ground stations

In [1], a ground station selection scheme is proposed based on the consideration of geographical and climatic characteristics in mainland China. The effects of atmospheric scattering and atmospheric turbulence on satellite-ground links were simulated. And the satellite tool kit (STK) software was used to analyze the link characteristics between the GEO satellite and five ground stations. However, this work mainly considered the effect of atmospheric environment such as atmospheric turbulence, the effect of cloud coverage was not discussed in depth. Three approximation methods including Monte Carlo sampling, the Lyapunov central limit theorem and Chernoff bound are adopted in [2] to estimate the probability of having a certain number of satellite-ground links fail due to cloud coverage.

An efficient algorithm is proposed in [3] to calculate the availability of an optical ground station network, and used five years of cloud data to simulate the behavior of three networks with different topologies including German, European and intercontinental. In [4], a method is presented to estimate the cloud-free line-of-sight probability of both a single optical ground station and a network of optical ground stations for medium earth orbit (MEO) constellation satellite communication systems. In [5], a mixed integer linear program model and a hierarchical method are presented based on an exhaustive enumeration of the sets of stations and on a dynamic programming algorithm. And a model is presented in [6] to optimally determine the location of optical ground stations to serve LEO missions, considering the trade-offs between minimal cloud probability, minimal latency and proximity to support infrastructure. In [7], the authors investigated the monthly variation of cloud coverage statistics and used them for the optimum selection of network with minimum number of ground stations, which satisfied the monthly availability requirements. In [8], a new algorithm is proposed based on gradient projection method after performing smoothing and relaxation on the original problem.

In order to make the OGS site selection more accurate, besides improving the way to calculate availability probability, the improvement in the method of processing and using cloud products is also important. This paper proposes a method to process cloud data more effectively, which can determine the range of clouds that affects satellite-ground optical links for a certain ground station. Through processing the cloud products of the Himawari-8 GEO satellite, the cloud coverage data corresponding to each ground station can be obtained. By calculating the availability probability with these cloud data, we finally obtained the results of ground station site selection in mainland China.

The structure of this paper is as follows: Sect. 2 describes how to process and utilize the real cloud data, which is necessary for the optical ground station site selection. Section 3 describes a method to calculate availability for a given optical ground station network. Section 4 presents the site selection results. The conclusions are drawn in Sect. 5.

2   Processing and Utilization of Real Cloud Data

At first, in order to achieve OGS site selection, it is necessary to get the cloud coverage data over each candidate ground station. Considering the location of candidate ground stations, we selected the Himawari-8 GEO satellite to get real cloud data. Figure 2 shows the observation range of the Himawari-8 GEO satellite. The resolution of cloud mask products is 5500×2200 pixels, while the spatial resolution 2 km and the temporal resolution is 30 min.

All the data we obtained is the cloud coverage information of every pixel from January 1, 2017 to December 31, 2017 every 30 min. In addition, the data is divided into four values of 0, 1, 2, and 3 according to the cloud coverage, which respectively represent clear, probably clear, probably cloudy and cloudy. The latitude and longitude information of a ground station can be used to find which pixel corresponds to this ground station, and then we can finally obtain the cloud coverage data over this ground station.

However, satellites are rarely directly above ground stations. The more common case is that the optical link between a satellite and a ground station maintains an inclination with the normal direction of ground. Therefore, the factor

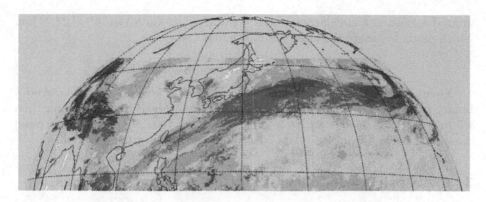

Fig. 2. The observation range of the Himawari-8 GEO satellite

that really affects optical links is not the cloud directly above a ground station, but the cloud at the intersections of cloud layer and optical links. Furthermore, a ground station usually communicates with multiple satellites, thus a ground station can have more than one optical link. Therefore, the cloud area that affects optical links of satellite-ground communication is a range rather than a point. In this case, all the cloud data in this range must be considered.

As discussed in [9], considering the characteristics of optical links, an optical ground station is available for communication only if it has an optical link with an elevation angle to the satellite of more than 20° and the satellite-ground optical link is not blocked by clouds.

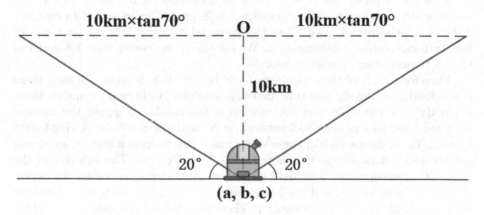

Fig. 3. The range of clouds that needs to be considered

As shown in the Fig. 3, the coordinates of the ground station in the Cartesian coordinate system are (a, b, c), and the height of cloud layer is assumed to be 10 km. Therefore, the range of cloud data that we need to consider for this ground station is a circular area with a radius of $10\,\text{km} \times \tan 70° = 27.47\,\text{km}$, which needs to satisfy the following inequality:

$$\sqrt{(x-a)^2 + (y-b)^2 + (z-c)^2} \leq 27.47\,\text{km} \tag{1}$$

Then, we average all cloud data of the points in this circular area. And a binary process also be done after averaging. If the averaged data is greater than 1.5 and less than 3, we set it to 1, otherwise set it to 0. Finally, the processed data is regarded as the cloud data corresponding to this ground station.

3   Network Availability of Optical Ground Networks

In this section, we introduce an effective method to achieve the optimal OGS network based on the calculation of network availability [3].

As described in Sect. 2, through the processing and utilization of real cloud data, we can get the cloud coverage data of each candidate ground station. To facilitate calculation, for each candidate ground station, a cloud data vector C_i is constructed:

$$C_i = [C_1, C_2, ...C_j, ...C_{N_{Sample}}] \tag{2}$$

There are N_{Sample} elements in this vector, which represents that the number of sample data points is N_{Sample}. The data we obtained is sampled by Himawari-8 GEO satellites every 30 min, and we use the data of one year to calculate the availability probability, so the number of elements N_{Sample} of each cloud data vector is 17520.

It should be noted that C_i is obtained by averaging the original data within a range, which is determined by the method in Sect. 2. The original data contains 4 states, which are 0, 1, 2 and 3, so the averaged data will be a double type. To facilitate calculation, we binarize it. We set the data greater than 1.5 and less than 3 to one, others are set to zero.

Therefore, each of these elements C_i is binary. If it is zero, it means there is no cloud over the sky and this station is available. Otherwise, it means there is cloudy over the OGS, and this station is unavailable. Suppose the number of ground stations in the OGS network is N, and there will be N cloud data vectors. Then, we use each of these vectors as a row to form a matrix, so we can get the cloud data matrix C, whose size is $N \times N_{Sample}$. The i-th row of the matrix C represents the cloud data of the i-th ground station during the period of N_{Sample} time points, and the j-th column of the matrix represents the cloud data of all stations at time sample j. Therefore, for a given network S, which including N OGS, the number of available ground stations at time sample j can be calculated as:

$$a_j = N - \sum_{i \in S} C_{i,j} \tag{3}$$

In order to calculate the availability, in addition to defining the parameter N which represents the number of ground stations included in the network, we also need to define the parameter M, which represents the number of required OGS. That is, the network is available when at least M stations are available. Then, if a_j is greater than or equal to M, set the redefined $a_j{}^*$ to one, otherwise set it to zero. Following [3], the availability of OGS network can be calculated as:

$$A = \frac{1}{N_S} \sum_{j=1}^{N_S} a_j^* \tag{4}$$

In the case that we have a certain number of candidate ground stations, we only need to calculate the network's availability for each possible combination of ground stations. The combination with the highest availability probability can be regarded as the optimal OGS network, that is, the ground station site selection results under the parameters of N and M.

4 Results

First, we selected 15 candidate ground stations as shown in Table 1:

Table 1. Candidate ground stations

Number	Name	Latitude	Longitude
1	Beijing	39.91N	116.39E
2	Xian	34.27N	108.94E
3	Taiyuan	38.50N	111.36E
4	Qingdao	36.07N	120.38E
5	Changchun	43.81N	125.33E
6	Xiamen	24.48N	118.09E
7	Nanning	22.82N	108.35E
8	Jiuquan	40.58N	100.18E
9	Xichang	27.88N	102.21E
10	Kashi	39.48N	75.93E
11	Wenchang	19.61N	110.73E
12	Sanya	18.24N	109.54E
13	Kunming	24.88N	102.83E
14	Urumqi	43.82N	87.53E
15	Ali	31.59N	81.84E

Secondly, calculating the range of clouds that affects satellite-ground optical communications for these candidate ground stations by the method in Sect. 2.

Table 2. OGS site selection results when M is 1

N	Maximum network availability	Selection results
1	61.71%	5
2	83.25%	3, 5
3	91.28%	3, 5, 15
4	95.12%	3, 5, 9, 14
5	97.20%	3, 5, 6, 13, 14
6	98.38%	3, 4, 5, 6, 13, 14
7	99.05%	3, 4, 5, 6, 8, 13, 14
8	99.39%	2, 3, 4, 5, 6, 8, 13, 14
9	99.59%	2, 3, 4, 5, 6, 8, 11, 13, 14
10	99.72%	1, 2, 3, 4, 5, 6, 8, 9, 13, 14
11	99.80%	1, 2, 3, 4, 5, 6, 8, 9, 11, 13, 14
12	99.83%	1, 2, 3, 4, 5, 6, 8, 9, 11, 13, 14, 15
13	99.85%	1, 2, 3, 4, 5, 6, 7, 8, 9, 10, 13, 14, 15
14	99.86%	1, 2, 3, 4, 5, 6, 7, 8, 9, 10, 11, 13, 14, 15

Table 3. OGS site selection results when M is 2

N	Maximum network availability	Selection results
1	0%	/
2	45.55%	1, 3
3	63.27%	1, 3, 5
4	75.18%	1, 3, 5, 15
5	83.83%	1, 3, 5, 14, 15
6	89.65%	1, 3, 5, 6, 14, 15
7	93.18%	1, 3, 5, 6, 13, 14, 15
8	95.20%	1, 2, 3, 5, 6, 13, 14, 15
9	96.57%	1, 2, 3, 4, 5, 6, 9, 14, 15
10	97.68%	1, 2, 3, 4, 5, 6, 9, 12, 14, 15
11	98.40%	1, 2, 3, 4, 5, 6, 8, 9, 13, 14, 15
12	98.81%	1, 2, 3, 4, 5, 6, 8, 9, 12, 13, 14, 15
13	99.06%	1, 2, 3, 4, 5, 6, 8, 9, 10, 12, 13, 14, 15
14	99.20%	1, 2, 3, 4, 5, 6, 8, 9, 10, 11, 12, 13, 14, 15

After that, by processing all the cloud data in this range, as described in Sect. 2, we can obtain the cloud data vector of each candidate ground station, and then the cloud data matrix C can be constructed.

Table 4. OGS site selection results when M is 3

N	Maximum network availability	Selection results
1	0%	/
2	0%	/
3	30.03%	1, 3, 4
4	48.07%	1, 3, 5, 8
5	61.35%	1, 3, 5, 8, 15
6	70.65%	1, 3, 5, 8, 14, 15
7	78.72%	1, 3, 5, 6, 9, 14, 15
8	84.32%	1, 3, 5, 6, 8, 9, 14, 15
9	87.96%	1, 3, 5, 6, 8, 9, 13, 14, 15
10	90.74%	1, 2, 3, 5, 6, 8, 9, 13, 14, 15
11	93.00%	1, 2, 3, 4, 5, 6, 8, 9, 12, 14, 15
12	94.47%	1, 2, 3, 4, 5, 6, 8, 9, 12, 13, 14, 15
13	95.44%	1, 2, 3, 4, 5, 6, 8, 9, 10, 11, 13, 14, 15
14	96.06%	1, 2, 3, 4, 5, 6, 8, 9, 10, 11, 12, 13, 14, 15

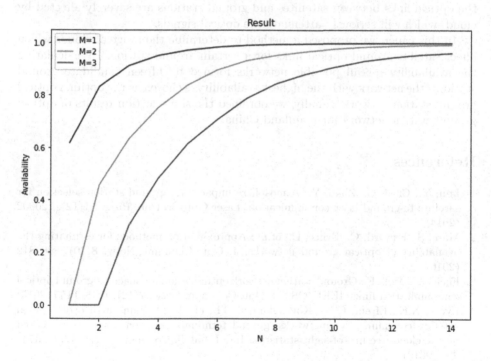

Fig. 4. Maximum availability of network under different N and M

Finally, this matrix is used as an input to the network availability calculation method. As mentioned above, the other two inputs are parameters N and M, where N is the number of all ground stations that make up the network, and M is the number of ground stations that required to be available. For different parameters N and M, by using the method in Sect. 3, we calculated the availability probability for each OGS network combination formed by these candidate ground stations. And the network with the highest availability is considered as the optimal OGS network, that is, the result of ground station network selection.

For the above-mentioned candidate ground stations, the ground station site selection results and the maximum network availability under different N and M are as follows, while the ground stations in the selection result is indicated by its number (Tables 2, 3 and 4).

The maximum availability of OGS network under different N and M is shown in Fig. 4.

5 Conclusion

As a key technology for future space network, satellite-ground optical networking can realize higher transmission rate than traditional RF technology. However, the optical links between satellites and ground stations are severely affected by cloud, which will seriously attenuate the optical signals.

In this paper, we proposed a method to determine the range of clouds which affect satellite-ground optical links for a certain ground station. By calculating the availability for all possible networks formed by fifteen candidate ground stations, the network with the highest availability is chosen as the optimal optical ground station network. Finally, we obtained the site selection results of optical ground station network for mainland China.

References

1. Lou, Y., Chen, C., Zhao, Y.: Atmosphere impact and ground station selection for satellite-to-ground laser communication. Laser Optoelectron. Prog. **51**(12), 120602 (2014)
2. Marc, S., Edward, C., Bruce, C., et al.: Approximation methods for estimating the availability of optical ground networks. J. Opt. Commun. Netw. **8**(10), 800–812 (2016)
3. Fuchs, C., Moll, F.: Ground station network optimization for space-to-ground optical communication links. IEEE/OSA J. Opt. Commun. Netw. **7**(12), 1148–1159 (2015)
4. Lyras, N.K., Efrem, C.N., Kourogiorgas, C.I., et al.: Medium earth orbit optical satellite communication networks: ground terminals selection optimization based on the cloud-free line-of-sight statistics. Int. J. Satell. Commun. Netw. **37**(4), 370–384 (2019)
5. Capelle, M., Jozefowiez, N., Olive, X., et al.: A hierarchical approach for the selection of optical ground stations maximizing the data transfer from low-earth observation satellites. In: IEEE International Conference on Communications (ICC), Paris, France, pp. 1–6 (2017)

6. Sanchez, M., Cameron, B., Crawley, E., et al.: Optimal location of optical ground stations to serve LEO spacecraft. In: IEEE Aerospace Conference, Big Sky, MT, USA, pp. 1–16 (2017)
7. Lyras, N.K., Efrem, C.N., Kourogiorgas, C.I., et al.: Optimum monthly based selection of ground stations for optical satellite networks. IEEE Commun. Lett. **22**(6), 1192–1195 (2018)
8. Gong, S., Shen, H., Zhao, K., et al.: Network availability maximization for free-space optical satellite communications. IEEE Wireless Commun. Lett. **9**(3), 411–415 (2020). ISSN 2162-2337
9. Interagency Operations Advisory Group Optical Link Study Group: Optical link study group final report (2012)

A Base Station Sleep Management Scheme Based on Simulated Annealing Algorithm

Wenchao Yang[✉], Xu Bai, Yulong Gao, and Rui Wang

Harbin Institute of Technology, Harbin 150001, China
wenchaoy@hit.edu.cn

Abstract. With the advent of 5G, the energy consumption of communication industry also increases, among which the base station (BS) energy consumption accounts for 43% of the total energy consumption of mobile communication.In order to reduce the communication energy consumption, the BS sleep technology can make the BS with low load enter the sleep state, realize the energy saving and create the green communication. In this paper, the simulated annealing (SA) algorithm is used to determine the BS closing mode. The switching situation can effectively reduce the energy consumption, which has practical significance and conforms to the expectation. The simulation results show that the sleep strategy can reduce the energy consumption, and the optimization of the algorithm can get a better solution and a simpler traversal process.

Keywords: 5G · Energy consumption · Simulated annealing algorithm

1 Introduction

In the 5G era, the requirements of users are getting more and more, the throughput and the rate is higher and higher, and the energy consumption of the communication industry is also increasing. With the rapid development of the information industry, users' requirement for cellular networks is increasing, and the BS account for 43% of the total energy consumption of mobile communications [1]. In order to meet the requirements of green communication and reduce the communication energy consumption, the research finds that the BS sleep technology can reduce the BS energy consumption by 10% and 60%, and it has great potential in reducing the system energy consumption and operating cost [2].

Chen et al. proposed a heterogeneous campus network protocol with orthogonal frequency division multiple access (OFDMA) [3], which allows a femtocell to completely close its wireless communication-related components without involving effective calls. Ashraf et al. discussed three different sleep strategies [4], namely micro BSl control, core network control and user device control. Deployment of sleep strategy control in different locations has its own advantages and disadvantages. Cho et al. proposed a BS sleep mechanism to set the minimum separation distance between the BS [5]. However, for the 5G dense heterogeneous network, it is difficult to set the minimum separation

Q. Wu et al. (Eds.): WiSATS 2020, LNICST 357, pp. 362–368, 2021.
https://doi.org/10.1007/978-3-030-69069-4_30

distance between base stations.Cai et al. proposed an operation scheme based on the joint location and the user density to achieve the approximate optimality in the polynomial time [6]. In 5G dense heterogeneous network, the use of centralized algorithm may bring very high computational complexity, while distributed algorithm may lead to the bad Qos when some nodes are closed and cannot be perceived. Therefore, it is very important to select the appropriate algorithm for the intensive heterogeneous network.

2 BS Sleep Strategy

The design of the base station switching mechanism is very complicated. The problems we are faced with are the sleeping period and the number of sleeping BS. If too many BS are closed by the wrong threshold estimation in the mechanism, the available resources in the network will be greatly reduced, resulting in the shortage of bandwidth resources and longer waiting time of users, which cannot meet the communication needs of users. In addition, if too many BS are closed, the distance between each service BS will be greatly increased, and all users cannot be guaranteed to be within the service BS area. As a result, the coverage performance of the network will be deteriorated, and the data transmission efficiency of users and system spectrum efficiency will be reduced correspondingly due to the increase of link delay.

This paper propose an adaptive BS management scheme based on energy balance, and a better BS sleep strategy is solved by using a centralized sleep algorithm in heterogeneous cellular network scenarios. In this paper, the simulated annealing (SA) algorithm was applied to the dormancy strategy, through to the BS and the connection between the users to solve the problem of abstraction and modeling, in view of the BS closed cover blind area and network terminal problem, and frequent closed questions, the BS is put forward in the heterogeneous network management scheme based on energy balance. It is a good way to improve the network energy consumption situation by using the simulated annealing algorithm.

The SA algorithm was proposed by Professor Kirkpatrick in 1982, inspired by the solid annealing process in thermodynamics. The SA algorithm is based on the Monte Carlo iterative solution strategy, with the global search function, good adaptability and robustness. In general, the initial high temperature is set first. In the process of gradual temperature decline, the probability jump can be used to jump out of the local optimal solution and approach the global optimal solution [7].

According to the Boltzmann ordering principle, the annealing process follows the law of thermodynamics, and the spontaneous change of the state of the system is always in the direction of the reduction of free energy. When the free energy reaches the minimum, the system reaches the equilibrium state. If E is the micro state energy of the system, the probability that the system is in state I is:

$$P_i = A \exp(-\frac{E_i}{kT})$$ (1)

From $\sum_i P_i = 1$, that is $\{T, \emptyset, \cdots, \emptyset\}$. Let $Z = A \sum_i \exp(-\frac{E_i}{kT})$, we get $A = \frac{1}{Z}$. The Eq. (1) can be obtained:

$$P_i = \frac{1}{Z} \exp(-\frac{E_i}{kT})$$ (2)

Where, K is Boltzmann constant, T is absolute temperature, and $\exp(-\frac{E_i}{kT})$ is Boltzmann factor.

The inner loop of SA algorithm adopts Metropolis criterion, that is to accept the new state with probability. When the temperature is T, the new state j is generated from the current state i. The energy of the two is E_i and E_j respectively. If $E_j < E_i$, the new state j will be accepted as the current state. Otherwise, if the probability $P_i = \exp(-\frac{E_j - E_i}{kT})$ is greater than the random number in the interval $[0,1]$, the new state j will be accepted as the current state. If the above conditions are not true, i will be retained as the current state.

3   BS Sleep Scheme Based on SA Algorithm

In this paper, a model of random distribution of base stations is adopted to simulate the actual situation. Matern-like Point Progress (MLPP) improves the Poisson point distribution model [8]. It is mainly that when the distance between two points is less than a given value, one of the points is removed according to certain rules and the Poisson point distribution process is diluted.

(1) The first step is to generate a Poisson point process with a probability density of λ_P. In the finite set $A \subset R^2$(A is the area of some range within the region), the number of points follows Poisson's distribution, and the mean is $\lambda|A|$.

$$P(\theta(A) = n) = \exp(-\lambda|A|)\frac{(\lambda|A|)^n}{n!} \tag{3}$$

$\theta(A)$ is the number of midpoints in A. Meanwhile, for two disjoint finite sets in the region $A \subset R^2$ and $B \subset R^2$, the number of points in A and B is not correlated, so the Poisson point process is only correlated to λ.

(2) For any point $x \in \theta(A)$ in $\theta(A)$, add a tag($m_x \in U[0, 1]$) to each point that is independent of each other.

(3) For each point in the circle $B(x, R)$, if the mark of $x \in \theta(A)$ is the smallest, the point is retained and the rest points are deleted. $U[0, 1]$ is the uniform distribution between 0 and 1. R is the dilution radius that is the given minimum distance, and the point selection process can be expressed by Formula (4).

$$\psi = \{x : x \in \theta(A),\ m_x \le m_y, \forall y \in B(x, R) \cap \theta(A)\} \tag{4}$$

In the Formula (4), ψ represents the last remaining points in the circle $B(x, R)$ which are selected to be retained. According to this method, a reservation can be selected from the points in the close distance, and the distribution model formed by the points left after the steps above is the distribution process model of Matern-like points.

In the actual BS deployment, the microcell has the low power consumption, the small coverage and the strong randomness. Therefore, in this scheme, Poisson point distribution is directly adopted for micro BS and Matern-like point distribution is adopted for macro BS. The simulated area of 5 km is shown in Fig. 1.

The specific steps of the scheme are:

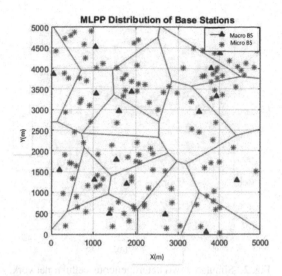

Fig. 1. Heterogeneous cellular network based on MLPP

(1) Initialization: according to the complexity of the problem, set the initial temperature T, initial solution state S, and the number of internal iteration L.
(2) perform steps (3) to (6) for $k = 1,2,…, L$.
(3) A disturbance is generated in the original state to find the value of the current optimization function.
(4) Calculate the increment $\Delta T = C(S_1) - C(S)$, $C(S)$ is the evaluation function.
(5) If $\Delta T < 0$, S_1 is accepted as the current latest solution. If $\Delta T > 0$, S_1 is accepted as the new current solution with probability $\exp(-\Delta T/T)$.
(6) If the termination condition is satisfied, the current solution is output as the optimal solution.
(7) Set the network topology according to the optimal solution, close the the zero-load BS.

4 Simulation Analysis

In a two-layer heterogeneous network, there are three sectors in a macro BS, and two micro BS are deployed in each sector. The distance from the micro BS to the macro BS is three-quarters of the coverage radius of the macro BS. Assume that the coverage radius of the macro BS is 500 m and that of the micro BS is 100 m. Users within the coverage area of the micro BS have priority access to the micro BS, while other users have access to the macro BS. The BS sleep algorithm is the SA. When the BS with low load is closed, the users in its cell are reconnected to the nearest macro BS, and the micro BS can only connect the users within its coverage area.

The simulated cellular network is shown in Fig. 2. This two heterogeneous cellular network includes 19 macro BS, each of which is surrounded by six micro BS evenly distributed.

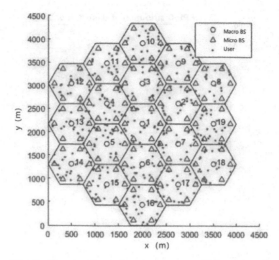

Fig. 2. Simulated two heterogeneous cellular network.

Table 1 shows the energy consumption comparison between the SA algorithm and the typical particle swarm optimization (PSO) algorithm from 0:00 a.m. to 8:00 a.m. it can be seen that the results of the two algorithms are close when the user flow is low, but at 7:00, the energy consumption of the SA algorithm is about 1 kW lower than that of the PSO algorithm. This reason is that random factors are introduced into the search process of the SA algorithm, there is some probability to accept the worse solution in the inner loop, which can make the algorithm jump out of the current optimal solution in the execution process, and find the global optimal solution. As the data in the table shows, the PSO algorithm has good stability, but it will fall into the local optimal solution. The SA algorithm introduces random factors, and can jump out of the current solution at some times to obtain the overall optimal solution.

Table 1. Comparison of energy consumption between SA and PSO (W)

Time	0 a.m	1 a.m	2 a.m	3 a.m	4 a.m	5 a.m	6 a.m	7 a.m	8 a.m
SA	63469	49956	38584	30279	25638	25571	30068	38531	50171
PSO	63077	49934	38168	30551	25845	26014	29991	39408	50258

The energy efficiency is equal to the throughput of the system divided by the total energy consumption. By comparing the energy efficiency of the SA algorithm and the PSO algorithm to verify the green of the algorithm, the energy efficiency comparison between the two algorithms is shown in Fig. 3.

It can be seen from the figure that the energy efficiency of the SA algorithm at 3–4 a.m. is higher than that of the PSO algorithm, and at other time the energy efficiency of the PSO algorithm is slightly higher or close to that of the SA algorithm.

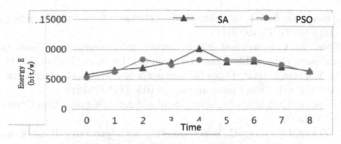

Fig. 3. Energy efficiency comparison.

Figure 4 and Fig. 5 respectively count the time consumed to execute the algorithm of the two algorithms and the number of active BS.

In Fig. 4, the SA algorithm takes much less time to solve than the PSO algorithm. It can be seen from the simulation results that the SA algorithm can search for the optimal solution quickly. In Fig. 5, the number of the BS opened with the SA algorithm is less than that of PSO algorithm in most cases. That means the SA algorithm can better closed the BS with light load. From the global perspective, it can close the BS with the low load under the condition of ensuring the communication quality of users, and achieve the purpose of the energy consumption balance. By applying the BS sleep algorithm to the actual scene, achieve the purpose of green communication in the 5G environment.

5   Conclusion

This paper focuses on the energy consumption of the BS in the communication system, and use a BS sleep scheme with the SA algorithm, which can quickly solve the large-scale combination optimization problem. With a two-layer heterogeneous cellular network model based on materne like point distribution process, this scheme is compared with the typical PSO method from energy consumption, energy efficiency, algorithm consumption time etc. The simulation results show that in the case of the similar performance, the SA algorithm can get the global optimal solution, and its energy consumption can be saved 500–1000 watts. Its' algorithm speed is 15% faster than PSO algorithm. Under the condition of ensuring the quality of user communication, the SA algorithm can sleep the low load base station and achieve the green communication in 5G environment.

References

1. Auer, G., Godor, I., Hevizi, L., et al.: Enablers for energy efficient wireless network sf. In: IEEE Vehicular Technology Conference Fall (VTC 2010-Fall), 2010 IEEE 72nd. 2010, Ottawa, ON, Canada, pp. 1–5 (2010).
2. Humar, I., Ge, X., Xiang, L., et al.: Rethinking energy efficiency models of cellular networks with embodied energy. IEEE Network **25**(2), 40–49 (2011)
3. Chen, C.S., Nguyen, V.M., Thomas, L.: On small cell network deployment: a comparative study of random and grid topologies. In: IEEE Vehicular Technology Conference (VTC Fall), 2012 IEEE, 2012, pp. 1–5, Quebec City, QC, Canada (2012).

4. Ashraf, I., Boccardi, F., Ho, L.: Sleep mode techniques for small cell deployments. IEEE Commun. Mag. **49**(8), 72–79 (2011)
5. Cho, S., Choi, W.: Coverage and load balancing in heterogeneous cellular networks with minimum cell separation. IEEE Trans. Mob. Comput. **13**(9), 1955–1966 (2014)
6. Cai, S., Che, Y., Duan, L., et al.: Green 5G heterogeneous networks through dynamic small-cell operation. IEEE J. Sel. Areas Commun. **34**(5), 1103–1115 (2016)
7. Zhu, H.D., Zhong, Y.: A kind of renewed simulated annealing algorithm.Comput. Sci. Appl. **19**(06), 32–35 (2009).
8. Ren, C.M., Zhang, J.F., Wang, C., et al.: Modeling heterogeneous cellular networks based on Matern-like point process model. J. Appl. Sci. **32**(05), 486–492 (2014)

Adaptive Particle Swarm Optimization for Harmonic Impedance Matching in 5G Power Amplifier Design

Chengxi Bian, Weiqing Dong, Wa Kong, and Jing Xia[✉]

School of Computer Science and Communication Engineering, Jiangsu University, Zhenjiang 212013, China
2221908005@stmail.ujs.edu.cn, Jingxia@ujs.edu.cn

Abstract. This paper proposes an optimization-oriented design method for harmonic tuned power amplifier (PA) using particle swarm optimization (PSO). Optimal source and load impedances for achieving high efficiency are obtained at the package plane of a Wolfspeed CGH40010 transistor. PSO is employed to optimize matching networks for fitting the desired trajectories of impedances. The designed PA with optimized matching networks was simulated in Keysight's advanced design system for verification. The results showed that the saturation efficiency of the PA reaches 75% at 3.5 GHz with associated output power of 42 dBm, which verified that the method can be used to design high efficiency PA for 5G mobile communication systems.

Keywords: 5G · Class-F · Particle swarm optimization · Harmonic impedance · High efficiency · Power amplifier

1 Introduction

Future wireless communication systems require higher data rates and efficient energy consumption, which will increase the requirements for power amplifiers (PAs). How to achieve highly efficient operation of the power amplifier is an important issue in wireless communication system design. In the past few decades, many different types of power amplifiers have been developed to meet these requirements, such as Class E, Class F and Class F-1. Class F power amplifiers achieve high efficiency due to their non-overlapping drain voltage and current waveforms [1]. However, achieving good control of harmonic waveforms has higher requirements on the design of matching networks [2]. Although there are multiple technologies used in the design of high-efficiency power amplifiers [3, 4], it is necessary to further optimize the matching network to control harmonic impedance. Therefore, it is useful to use excellent optimization algorithms to design and optimize the matching network.

Particle swarm optimization (PSO) algorithm is a simple and powerful optimization algorithm, which has a strong applicability when solving continuous function optimization problems [5, 6]. If there is a definite matching network structure and a clear

Q. Wu et al. (Eds.): WiSATS 2020, LNICST 357, pp. 369–378, 2021.
https://doi.org/10.1007/978-3-030-69069-4_31

optimization goal, the optimization can be completely handed over to the intelligent algorithm.

This paper proposes an optimization-oriented design method for harmonic tuned power amplifier using PSO. The theoretical basis of the adaptive particle swarm optimization algorithm was given and then used to analyze the input and output matching network of the power amplifier to obtain the corresponding fitness function. A 3.5 GHz high-efficiency power amplifier is optimally designed with the load impedance value obtained by using load-pull as the goal. The optimization result was evaluated and the best matching network was selected for the design. The feasibility of the proposed method provides a useful design for high efficiency power amplifiers.

2   Theoretical Analysis of Adaptive Particle Swarm Optimization

The particle swarm optimization algorithm is an evolution algorithm based on swarms, which is developed by the bird's foraging behavior [7]. Each particle in the particle swarm represents a possible solution to a problem. All particles have a position attribute and a velocity attribute. The position attribute is the position of the particle in the solution space, and the velocity attribute is used to determine the direction of the next movement of the particle and speed. In each iteration, the particles in the population change their own speed attributes by sharing their own information, and eventually all particles in the population will approach the optimal solution.

The algorithm used in this paper is an adaptive particle swarm optimization (APSO) algorithm. The following will introduce some necessary formulas in this algorithm in order to understand the adaptive particle swarm optimization algorithm.

Suppose that in an S-dimensional target search space, m particles form a group, and the i-th particle is represented as an S-dimensional vector $\vec{x}_i = (x_{i1}, x_{i2}, \cdots, x_{iS})$, $i = 1, 2, \cdots, m$, and the position of each particle is a potential solution. The fitness value can be calculated by substituting $\vec{x}_i$ into an objective function, and the merits of the solution can be measured according to the fitness value. The speed of the i-th particle is an S-dimensional vector, denoted as $\vec{V} = (V_{i1}, V_{i2}, \cdots V_{iS})$. The best position searched so far for the i-th particle is the best position $\vec{P}_{gS} = (P_{gS}, P_{gS}, \cdots, P_{gS})$.

Assuming $f(x)$ is the objective function of minimization, the current best position of particle i is determined by the followings:

$$P_i(t+1) = \begin{cases} P_i(t) \rightarrow f(x_i(t+1)) \geq f(P_i(t)) \\ X_i(t+1) \rightarrow f(x_i(t+1)) < f(P_i(t)) \end{cases} \tag{1}$$

The particle can be operated by

$$v_{is}(t+1) = v_{is}(t) + c_1 r_{1s}(t)(p_{is}(t) - x_{is}(t)) + c_2 r_{2s}(t)(p_{gs}(t) - x_{is}(t)) \tag{2}$$

$$x_{is}(t+1) = x_{is}(t) + v_{is}(t+1) \tag{3}$$

where $i = [1, m]$, $s = [1, S]$, and learning factors c_1 and c_2 are non-negative constants. And, r_1 and r_2 are independent pseudo-random numbers, which subject to uniform distribution on $[0, 1]$. $v_{is} \in [-v_{max}, v_{max}]$, and v_{max} is a constant, set by the user.

It can be seen from above equations that c_1 regulates the step size of particles flying towards their best position, and c_2 regulates the step size of particles flying towards their global best position. In order to reduce the possibility of particles leaving the search space during evolution, v_{is} is usually limited to a range, that is $v_{is} \in [-v_{max}, v_{max}]$. If the search space is in the middle of $[-x_{max}, x_{max}]$, $v_{max} = kx_{max}$ can be set, where $0.1 \leq k \leq 1.0$.

To improve the optimization performance, (2) can be improved as

$$v_{is}(t+1) = \omega v_{is}(t) + c_1 r_{1s}(P_{is}(t) - x_{is}(t)) + c_2 r_{2s}(t)(P_{gs}(t) - x_{gs}(t)) \quad (4)$$

where ω is a non-negative number (called a dynamic constant), which controls the effect of the previous speed on the current speed. When ω is larger, the previous speed has a greater impact and the global search ability is stronger. When ω is smaller, the previous speed has a smaller effect, the local search ability is stronger. By adjusting the size of ω, the local minimum can be jumped out.

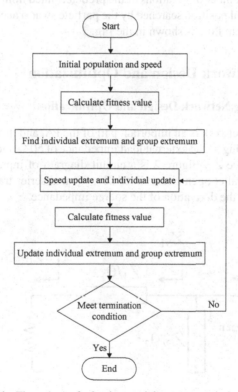

Fig. 1. Flow chart of adaptive particle swarm optimization.

In order to balance the global search ability and local improvement ability of the PSO algorithm, a nonlinear dynamic inertia weight coefficient formula can be given as follows:

$$\omega = \begin{cases} \omega_{max} - \dfrac{(\omega\,max - \omega\,min) * (f - f_{min})}{f_{avg} - f_{min}}, f \leq f_{avg} \\ \omega_{max}, f > f_{avg} \end{cases} \tag{5}$$

where ω_{max} and ω_{min} represent the maximum and minimum values of ω, f represents the current target function value of the particles, and f_{avg} and f_{min} represent the current average target value and minimum target value of all particles, respectively. In this algorithm, ω is called adaptive weight because the inertia weight changes automatically with the target function value of particles. So, the improved PSO algorithm is called APSO.

The termination condition of the adaptive particle swarm optimization algorithm takes the maximum number of iterations or the predetermined minimum threshold value satisfied by the optimal position searched by the particle swarm according to the specific problem. The algorithm flow is shown in the Fig. 1.

3   Matching Network Design and Optimization

3.1   Input Matching Network Design and Optimization

The input matching network is an important part of the PA, and its purpose is to achieve the impedance matching of the external load impedance of 50 Ω and the power amplifier tube source impedance Z_S. Figure 2 is a circuit diagram of input matching network, which consists of parallel open circuit lines (Z_2, θ_2) and series transmission lines (Z_1, θ_1). The following is the derivation of the source impedance.

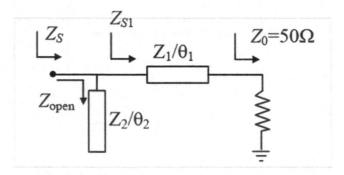

Fig. 2. Circuit diagram of input matching network.

The target source impedance of the Wolfspeed CGH40010 transistor at 3.5 GHz can be determined to be 7-j16 Ω by using source-pull simulation in Keysight's advanced design system (ADS).

Normalized frequency is used for source impedance calculation in fitness function. According to the transmission line impedance transformation formula, Z_{S1} can be obtained, as follows:

$$Z_{S1} = Z_1 \frac{(Z_0 + jZ_1 \tan(\theta_1 \frac{\pi}{180}))}{(Z_1 + jZ_0 \tan(\theta_1 \frac{\pi}{180}))} \tag{6}$$

Similarly, the impedance Z_{open} of the open transmission line can be calculated

$$Z_{open} = Z_2 \frac{(\infty + jZ_2 \tan(\theta_2 \frac{\pi}{180}))}{(Z_2 + j\infty \tan(\theta_2 \frac{\pi}{180}))} = Z_2 \frac{1}{j \tan(\theta_2 \frac{\pi}{180})} \tag{7}$$

It can be obtained from the circuit schematic diagram in Fig. 2 that Z_S is the parallel connection of Z_{S1} and Z_{open}, which can be expressed as:

$$Z_S = Z_{S1} // Z_{open} = \frac{Z_{S1} \cdot Z_{open}}{Z_{S1} + Z_{open}} \tag{8}$$

When the target source impedance Z_{s_target} is 7-j16 Ω, the fitness function can be expressed as the sum of the absolute values of the impedance difference between the real and imaginary parts:

$$F = |9 - real(Z_S)| + |16 + imag(Z_S)| \tag{9}$$

The variables in APSO optimization are Z_1, θ_1, Z_2 and θ_2. The APSO optimizes the source impedance that meets the requirements according to the fitness function above.

In the optimization algorithm, the population size is 10 individuals, and the evolutionary generation is 60 generations. In order to observe the change trend of fitness, the optimization program was run 10 times. Figure 3 shows the relationship between the value of the objective function (fitness value) and the evolutionary generation during optimization operation. It can be seen from Fig. 3 that the blue line in the figure represents the fitness value of the best individual, and the red dotted line represents the average fitness value optimized 100 times. As the number of iterations increases, the fitness value of the best individual keeps decreasing from around 1 and finally stabilizes at around 0; and the average fitness value also shows a downward trend, which is stable at around 0 between 30 and 40 generations.

Figure 4(a) and Fig. 4(b) give the changes of various parameters (Z_1, Z_2, θ_1 and θ_2) and real(Z_{L1}) and imag(Z_{L1}) in the optimal optimization. The results show that these parameters and results are deviate greatly from the expected value in the early stage, but with the increase of the number of iterations, they quickly turn to the optimal value. The optimal solution is $Z_1 = 43.7$ Ω, $\theta_1 = 47.4°$, $Z_2 = 57.7$ Ω, $\theta_2 = 70.6°$. The fitness data is close to 0, indicating that the difference between the current impedance and the target impedance can be minimized, which means that the input matching network is optimized.

3.2 Output Matching Network Design and Optimization

The output matching network is an important part of the PA, which achieves the impedance matching of the external load impedance 50 Ω and the optimal load

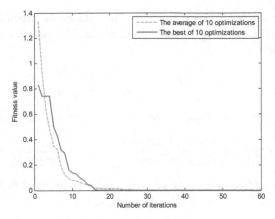

Fig. 3. The fitness value changes with the number of iterations.

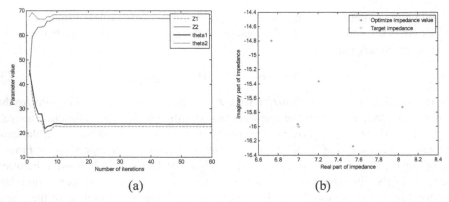

(a)   (b)

Fig. 4. (a) The values of Z_1, Z_2, θ_1 and θ_2 with algebra (b) Changes in impedance during optimization.

impedance ZL of the power amplifier tube. Figure 5 is the circuit diagram of the output matching network, which consists of two-stage parallel open-circuit transmission line and 4-stage series transmission line. The parameters of the output matching network are (Z_1, θ_1), (Z_2, θ_2), (Z_3, θ_3), (Z_4, θ_4), (Z_5, θ_5) and (Z_6, θ_6). The target load impedance value can be obtained from the load-pull simulation results. The target fundamental frequency $Z_{L\_target\_1}$ is $16.2 - j0.4$ Ω, the 2nd harmonic frequency $Z_{L\_target\_2}$ is j36 Ω and the 3rd harmonic frequency $Z_{L\_target\_3}$ is $-j293$ Ω.

According to the transmission line impedance transformation formula, Z_{L1} can be calculated as follows:

$$Z_{L1} = Z_6 \frac{(z_0 + jz_6 \tan(\theta_6 \frac{\pi}{180}))}{(z_6 + jz_0 \tan(\theta_6 \frac{\pi}{180}))} \tag{10}$$

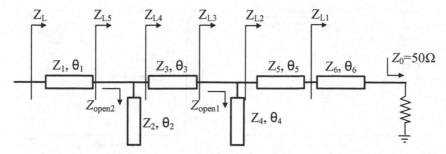

Fig. 5. Circuit diagram of output matching network

Taking into account (10), Z_{L2} are expressed as

$$Z_{L2} = Z_{L5} \frac{(z_{L1} + jz_5 \tan(\theta_5 \frac{\pi}{180}))}{(z_5 + jz_{L1} \tan(\theta_5 \frac{\pi}{180}))} \tag{11}$$

Similarly, the input impedance of the open line Z_{open1}, Z_{open2} can be given by

$$Z_{open1} = Z_4 \frac{1}{j \tan(\theta_4 \frac{\pi}{180})} \tag{12}$$

$$Z_{open2} = Z_2 \frac{1}{j \tan(\theta_2 \frac{\pi}{180})} \tag{13}$$

According to (10) and (11) and combined with the circuit schematic, Z_{L3} can be calculated as follows:

$$Z_{L3} = Z_{L2} // Z_{L\_open1} = \frac{(z_{L2} \cdot z_{L\_open1})}{(z_{L2} + z_{L\_open1})} \tag{14}$$

Therefore, Z_{L4} can be retrieved:

$$Z_{L4} = Z_3 \frac{(z_{L3} + jz_3 \tan(\theta_3 \frac{\pi}{180}))}{(z_3 + jz_{L3} \tan(\theta_3 \frac{\pi}{180}))} \tag{15}$$

From (14), Z_{L5} can be obtained:

$$Z_{L5} = Z_{L4} // Z_{L\_open2} = \frac{(z_{L4} \cdot z_{L\_open2})}{(z_{L4} + z_{L\_open2})} \tag{16}$$

Z_L can finally be calculated:

$$Z_L = Z_1 \frac{(z_{L5} + jz_1 \tan(\theta_1 \frac{\pi}{180}))}{(z_1 + jz_{L5} \tan(\theta_1 \frac{\pi}{180}))} \tag{17}$$

When the target fundamental load impedance $Z_{L\_target\_1}$ is $16.2 - j0.4\ \Omega$, the fitness function can be expressed as the sum of the absolute values of the impedance difference between the real and imaginary parts:

$$F_{1st} = |16.2 - real(Z_L)| + |0.4 + imag(Z_L)| \tag{18}$$

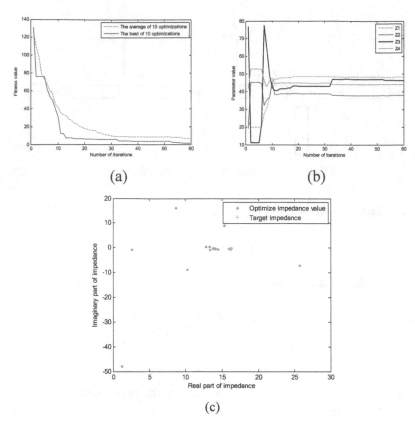

Fig. 6. (a) The fitness value changes with the number of iterations. (b) The values of Z_1, Z_2, Z_3 and Z_4 with algebra (c) Changes in impedance during optimization.

The calculation of the target 2nd and 3rd load impedance is similar to the above fundamental wave calculation, and can be calculated as follows:

$$F_{2nd} = |0 - real(Z_L)| + |36 + imag(Z_L)| \tag{19}$$

$$F_{3rd} = |0 - real(Z_L)| + |293 - imag(Z_L)| \tag{20}$$

After the impedance at three frequencies is used as the optimization target, the optimization output results are shown in Fig. 6. The results show that the values of the parameters sought are $Z_1 = 39.9\ \Omega, Z_2 = 33.5\ \Omega, Z_3 = 45.3\ \Omega, Z_4 = 32.0\ \Omega, Z_5 = 27.4\ \Omega, Z_6 = 25.0\ \Omega, \theta_1 = 32.1°, \theta_2 = 30.6°, \theta_3 = 59.3°, \theta_4 = 35.8°, \theta_5 = 48.9°, \theta_6 = 80.2°.$ The fitness is at least 1.6, which is approximately the goal.

4   Power Amplifier Simulation

After using the above-mentioned adaptive particle swarm optimization to design the input and output filter matching network, the power amplifier can be designed and simulated

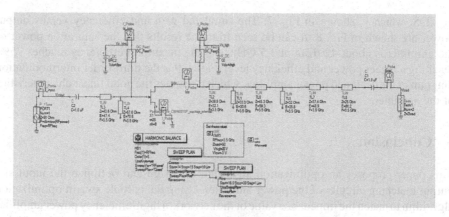

Fig. 7. Power amplifier simulation schematic

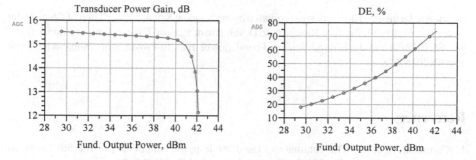

Fig. 8. Gain and efficiency of power amplifier simulation at 3.5 GHz

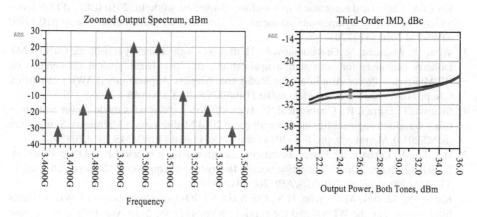

Fig. 9. Third-order intermodulation diagram of power amplifier

in ADS, which is shown in Fig. 7. The simulated gain and efficiency versus output power are shown in Fig. 8. It can be seen from the results that the saturation power of the amplifier is about 42 dBm at 3.5 GHz, and the maximum efficiency reaches 75%, reaching a higher power and efficiency level. Figure 9 is the third-order intermodulation diagram of the designed power amplifier, which illustrates the good linear characteristics of the amplifier.

5 Conclusion

This paper proposes an optimization algorithm to design and optimize the input and output matching circuits of the power amplifier. Using the particle swarm optimization algorithm to match the impedance value of the network, a high-efficiency power amplifier is designed and optimized. Simulation results show that the amplifier can achieve higher efficiency, indicating that the method has practical reference value for the design of PAs.

Acknowledgement. This work was supported by the National Science Foundation of China under Grant No. 61701199, the Key Research & Development Plan of Jiangsu Province under Grant No. BE2018108 and the Natural Science Foundation of Jiangsu Province of China under Grant No. BK20150528.

References

1. Carrubba, V., et al.: The continuous class-f mode power amplifier. In: The 5th European Microwave Integrated Circuits Conference, Paris, pp. 432–435 (2010)
2. Stameroff, A.N., Pham, A., Leoni, R.E.: High efficiency push-pull inverse class F power amplifier using a balun and harmonic trap waveform shaping network. In: 2010 IEEE MTT-S International Microwave Symposium, Anaheim, CA, pp. 521–525 (2010). https://doi.org/10.1109/MWSYM.2010.5517720
3. Wong, J., Watanabe, N., Grebennikov, A.: High-power high-efficiency broadband GaN HEMT Doherty amplifiers for base station applications. In: 2018 IEEE Topical Conference on RF/Microwave Power Amplifiers for Radio and Wireless Applications (PAWR), Anaheim, CA, pp. 16–19 (2018). https://doi.org/10.1109/PAWR.2018.8310055.
4. Sharma, T., Darraji, R., Ghannouchi, F.: High efficiency continuous mode power amplifiers using waveform engineering. In: Proceedings of 2014 Mediterranean Microwave Symposium (MMS2014), Marrakech, pp. 1–4 (2014). https://doi.org/10.1109/MMS.2014.7088978.
5. Hoorfar, A., Lakhani, S.: Faster antenna optimization using a hybrid EP-PSO algorithm. In: 2009 IEEE Antennas and Propagation Society International Symposium, Charleston, SC, pp. 1–4 (2009). https://doi.org/10.1109/APS.2009.5171498
6. Kahng, S., Khattak, M.K., Kim, H.S., Oh, S.H.: A PSO-optimized, compact UWB bandpass filter suppressing the WLAN and the spurious harmonics. In: 2015 Asia-Pacific Microwave Conference (APMC), Nanjing, pp. 1–4 (2015). https://doi.org/10.1109/APMC.2015.7411625
7. Chiang, J., Chou, Y., Hsu, W., Liao, S.: PSO and APSO for optimal antenna locations in indoor environment. In: 2014 International Conference on Intelligent Green Building and Smart Grid (IGBSG), Taipei, pp. 1–4 (2014). https://doi.org/10.1109/IGBSG.2014.6835259.

A New Method to Construct Non-binary QC-LDPC Codes Based on ACE Value

Xinting Wang[1] , Kegang Pan[1(✉)] , Rong Lv[2] , and Ruixiang Zhao[1]

[1] College of Communication Engineering, Army Engineering University of PLA, Nanjing, China
wangxinting_wxt@163.com, pankg@163.com
[2] The Sixty-third Research Institute, National University of Defense Technology, Nanjing, China
lvrong17@nudt.edu.cn

Abstract. This paper presented a method for constructing NB-QC-LDPC (non-binary quasi-cyclic LDPC) codes. First, the initial base matrix of NB-QC-LDPC code was constructed by two arbitrary subsets in a finite field. Then, by combining the number and connectivity of cycles jointly, the new masking method was proposed to construct a type of NB-QC-LDPC codes with larger ACE average values. The simulation illustrates that proposed codes have better error correction performance compared with binary LDPC codes and other NB-LDPC codes.

Keywords: Non-binary (NB) quasi-cyclic (QC) LDPC codes · Code constructed · Masking · The approximate cycle EMD (ACE)

1 Introduction

As one of the famous channel coding techniques, low-density parity-check (LDPC) codes [2] were proposed in 1962 to concrol errors in communication and data storage system due to their capacity-approaching performances and efficient parallel decoding mechanism.

Until 1998, Davey and Mackey firstly discovered non-binary (NB) LDPC codes [1] and put forward a q-ary sum product algorithm (QSPA) for decoding at the same time. Compared with binary LDPC codes, NB-LDPC codes do have the advantage of correcting random and burst errors that happened simultaneously in channels. In a higher finite field, NB-LDPC codes with much longer code length could approach the Shannon Limit. However, the higher computational complexity in coding and decoding makes it impractical. Therefore, NB-LDPC codes deserve more attention and research effort.

Similar to binary LDPC codes, there are two types of construction methods for NB-LDPC codes, including random construction method and structural construction method. For the former, given a degree distribution, the progressive

Suppported by National Natural Science Foundation of China, No. 61671476.

edge growth (PEG) algorithm [14] generates a parity-check matrix by column in which all connecting labels are randomly selected. In particular, the approximate cycle extrinsic message degree (ACE) algorithm [12] can reduce the error floor performance at high signal-to-noise ratios (SNRs) by ensuring the ACE value of some cycles is bigger than a given value. However, random methods take up a large amount of memory space to store the stochastic parity-check matrix.

The latter methods include algebraic approach [4,5,8,18,19], matrix theory [13,15–17], etc., are used to generate a type of quasi-cycle (QC) LDPC codes [9]. Codes based on finite fields GF(q) are called NB-QC-LDPC codes, which are given by the null space of an array H of sparse circulant matrices of the same size. The sparse circulant matrices in the parity-check array H are circulant permutation matrices (CPMs), which can save hardware storage space and simplify the coding and decoding process. To improve the error correction performance and reduce the computation complexity, several measures was proposed, such as eliminating short cycles [10], maximizing girth, improving Hamming distance [7], improving connectivity of cycles [3], etc.

In this paper, we combine the number with the connectivity of cycles to improve performance. Since not all short cycles are harmful to performance, selectively eliminate cycles with bad connectivity can make a excellent cycle condition [11]. The new masking technique is proposed to construct an irregular NB-QC-LDPC code with short and long code lengths. The simulation results show that the codes with larger ACE average values have excellent decoding performance.

The rest of paper is organized as follows. The basic theory of NB-QC-LDPC codes over a finite field is briefly introduced in Sect. 2. Section 3 describes our model and masking algorithms for constructing NB-QC-LDPC codes. Meanwhile, Sect. 3 illustrates with some examples. Simulation results and analysis will be discussed in Sect. 4. Finally, we conclude the paper in Sect. 5.

2   NB-QC-LDPC CODES

2.1   Definitions and Concepts

QC-LDPC codes given by the null space of an array of sparse circulant permutation matrices (CPM) of the same size over a finite field GF(q) (q > 2) is called NB-QC-LDPC codes. While $q = 2$, they become to binary QC-LDPC codes. As for any positive integer r, let Q be a $r \times r$ CPM in GF(q) with columns and rows labeled from 0 to $r - 1$.

There are two categories of Q. If all nonzero elements in Q is single, such Q is called the q-ary CPM and has the following structural characteristics: (1) the first row contains a single nonzero element in GF(q), at position between 0 and $r - 1$; (2) each row in Q is a cyclic right shift of the previous row and the first row is obtained from the last row shift to right. All nonzero elements in q-ary CPM are same, but are different in positions.

Another structure is called α^λ-multiplied CPM, in which all nonzero elements are different in both. To be specific, each row, except the first row, is obtained by cyclic right shift of the previous row and the single nonzero value which alse belongs to GF(q) is the single nonzero value in the above row multiplied by α. Furthermore, q-ary CPM is much simpler in coding and decoding process. Thus, we will take q-ary CPMs as examples.

In the parity-check matrix $\boldsymbol{H}$, a cycle is a closed path that consists of a set of horizontal and vertical lines alternately, in which each vertex is a nonzero element. The length of a cycle must be even. For example, two rows and two columns can form a cycle whose length is 4. The shortest cycle is called girth. Cycle is an important factor during iterative decoding. Reducing short cycles and maximizing girth are common approaches to improve performance.

Various structures of LDPC code have to satisfy the row-column (RC) constraint [6]: no two rows (or two columns) have more than one position where they both have nonzero entries, which ensures the Tanner graph of the code with girth at least 6. In this paper, we are mainly concerned of RC-constrained NB-QC-LDPC codes.

2.2   Construction Principles and Masking

Suppose a finite field GF(q), q $= 2^s$. Let α be a primitive element, and all elements in GF(q) are represented as $\{\alpha^{-\infty}, \alpha^0, \alpha^1, \cdots, \alpha^{q-2}\}$. This section explains a construction method of the base matrix $\boldsymbol{B}$ of NB-QC-LDPC codes by using two random subsets in GF(q).

Let $S_1 = \{\alpha^{i_0}, \alpha^{i_1}, \cdots, \alpha^{i_{m-1}}\}$ and $S_2 = \{\alpha^{j_0}, \alpha^{j_1}, \cdots, \alpha^{j_{n-1}}\}$ are two random subsets, with $i_k, j_l \in \{-\infty, 0, 1, \cdots, q-2\}$, $0 \leqslant k < m$, $0 \leqslant l < n$, and $i_0 < i_1 < \cdots < i_{m-1}$, $j_0 < j_1 < \cdots < j_{n-1}$. Then we can use following rule to generate a base matrix $\boldsymbol{B}$ [4,5]:

$$\boldsymbol{B} = \left[\gamma\alpha^{i_k} + \alpha^{j_l}\right]_{0 \leqslant k < m, 0 \leqslant l < n} \tag{1}$$

The constructed base matrix has the following characteristics: (1) all the entries in the row (column) are different elements in GF(q); (2) each row (or column) contains at most one zero element; (3) no two rows (or two columns) have the same item in the same position; (4) any submatrix is nonsingular. According to the structure properties (2) and (4), $\boldsymbol{B}$ satisfies the RC constraint. γ is called the multiplier of $\boldsymbol{B}$.

The parity-check matrix $\boldsymbol{H}$ is generated by extending each element in $\boldsymbol{B}$ with q-ary CPMs of size $r \times r$, $r = q - 1$, whose generator has α^j as its single nonzero component at the position j, which makes sure the Tanner graph of it has girth at least 6 if the maximum value of j is less than r. The key to construct a QC-LDPC code is to design an optional base matrix $\boldsymbol{B}$ of which a number of structural properties determines the iterate decoding performance. Thus, the replacement results in replacing some nonzero elements by zero which means an $r \times r$ q-ary CPM is replaced by an $r \times r$ ZM (zero matrix), which is refered to as masking. The masking matrix $\boldsymbol{M}$ which only consists of "0" and "1" elements can be performed on $\boldsymbol{B}$ to obtain a masked based matrix $\boldsymbol{B}_{\text{mask}}$:

$$\boldsymbol{B}_{\text{mask}} = \boldsymbol{M} \otimes \boldsymbol{B} = \left[\boldsymbol{I}\left(m_{k,l} b_{k,l}\right)\right]_{0 \leqslant k < m, 0 \leqslant l < n} \tag{2}$$

If $m_{k,l} = 1$, $m_{k,l}b_{k,l} = b_{k,l}$; else if $m_{k,l} = 0$, $m_{k,l}b_{k,l} = 0$.

2.3 Cycles and ACE Value

Each column (row) in a base matrix B corresponds to a variable (check) node, and each element in B represents a connecting edge between two types of nodes. The total number of connecting edges of a node is called the node degree.

A cycle is composed of alternate connecting edges between variable nodes and check nodes, which influnce the error floor. The total degree of variable nodes in cycle determines the connectivity of cycle. Larger degree can increase decoding accuracy, which means more parity-check equations could be used to control errors and it can utilize more nodes to exchange useful information during decoding.

In general, the approximate cycle extrinsic message degree (ACE) of a cycle is one of the important characteristics, which used to roughly measure the connectivity of cycle. The ACE values in cycle g are defined as follows [4]:

$$ACE^g = \sum_i (d_i - 2) \tag{3}$$

d_i is ith node's degree in cycle g, $i = 1, 2, ..., g$. The ACE value of the variable node with degree d can be considered as $d - 2$ and the ACE value of the check node is 0.

From (3), the ACE value of cycle is directly determined by the total degree of variable nodes. A LDPC code with larger ACE value usually exhibits better error correction performance than a code with small ACE value. Hence, removing cycles with low connectivity and keeping the high may improve the error correction performance. When the short cycles is removed by masking, the ACE value of the remaining cycles will also be reduced. Making a compromise between them is what we have to discuss next.

3 Masking Algorithm Based on ACE Value

Cycle is an important factor affecting the performance of QC-LDPC codes, particularly length of 4. However, cycles with different length may have different effects on performance. Not only the number of short cycles, but also the connectivity of cycles plays an important role. Remaining cycles with high connectivity rather than reducing short cycles for increasing girth blindly could improve error-floor effectively. The masking algorithm is prensented to distinguish and select more harmful cycles to make a better cycle condition.

In this paper, we emphasize the importance of ACE value and give priority to removing cycles with smaller ACE values, despite the number of cycles may be increased. Therefore, the mathematical model is proposed by jointly considering both the number and connectivity of cycles to choose one place reasonably if there are more than one nonzero position that could be turned to zero.

The entire masking process is showen in Fig. 1, If there is only one maximum in D, turn the element in this position to zero and calculate the number of cycle g of the new base matrix B; if not, we need to consider the ACE value of cycle g^* to get a base matrix with larger ACE average value.

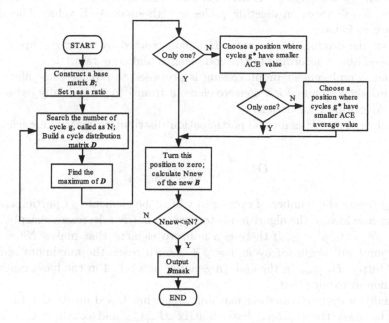

Fig. 1. Masking process

The mathematical model is as follows:

$$B_{\text{mask}} = \arg\max\left(\overline{ACE}^{g^*}\right) \tag{4}$$

$$s.t. \begin{cases} N^g \leqslant \eta N^g_{\text{init}} \\ N^{g'} = 0, g' < g \\ g^* = \begin{cases} g & 0 < \eta \leqslant 1 \\ g+2 & \eta = 0 \end{cases} \end{cases} \tag{5}$$

In (4), B_{mask} is a masked base matrix; $\overline{ACE}^g$ is a ACE average value of cycle g. A masked base matrix B_{mask} that has the highest ACE average of cycle g^* is expected to get. However, if all cycles g^* are eventually eliminated, it is meaningless to control its ACE value. Therefore, according to the ratio η, we divide g^* into two situations to discuss.

The parameters in formulas are explained in (5). N^g is the total number of cycle g; $N^{g'}$ is the total number of cycle g', $g' < g$; N^g_{init} is a initial number of cycle g; η is a ratio of number, $\eta = N^g/N^g_{\text{init}}$; g_{end} is a stopped length. The ratio η determines whose ACE value we should focus on during this process. When $0 < \eta \leqslant 1$, there are some cycles g left after finished, and $N^g > 0$. Thus cycles g with small ACE value need to be elimitated to ensure the final masked base matrix $\boldsymbol{B}_{\text{mask}}$ has large ACE average. In addition, when $\eta = 0$, $N^g > 0$ after finished, it will focus on deleting cycles g with small ACE value. The specific steps are as follows:

First, the original base matrix $\boldsymbol{B}$ is constructed by using the approach as mentioned above according to the code length and code rate.

Then, a replacement preprocessing is proposed to replace some elements in $\boldsymbol{B}$ by orderly searching for a nonzero element from 1 to p to initially reduce cycle g. See Algorithm 1 for details:

In algorithm, $\boldsymbol{D}^g$ is a cycle participation distribution matrix of cycle g.

$$\boldsymbol{D}^g = \left[d^g_{k,l}\right]_{0\leqslant k<m,0\leqslant l<n} \tag{6}$$

$d^g_{k,l}$ represents the number of cycle g in which the element $b_{k,l}$ participates.

The core idea of the algorithm is to ensure that N^g decreases sharply, meanwhile, $N^{g'} = 0$, $g' < g$. If there is a nonzero element that makes $N^g = 0$, the next round will begin for cycle $g = g + 2$ until reach the maximum searching time. Output $\boldsymbol{B}_{\text{replace}}$ in the end. In general, no cycle 4 in the basis matrix is a fundamental requirement.

Finally, a cycle elimination masking algorithm based on ACE value is proposed to mask the replaced basis matrix $\boldsymbol{B}_{\text{replace}}$ and continue to eliminate cycles. Masking a position means all cycles related to it are removed and the ACE value of cycles that the other positions in the same row or same column participated in are decreasing. Therefore. It is crucial to choose a rational place to eliminate cycles with smaller ACE value. Two cases are going to be discussed.

When set $\eta = 0$ for cycle g. In this condition, we need to keep cycle $g+2$ with larger ACE value. Find the biggest value in $\boldsymbol{D}^g$ by row and save its position. If there are several candidate positions, compare their ACE minimum values and ACE average values of cycle $g+2$. Choose a place whose ACE minimum value is the smallest at first. Then choose the smallest ACE average value if all the above conditions are the same. Stop masking cycle g and $g = g + 2$ until it satisfies condition $N^g = 0$. When $g > g_{\text{end}}$, output $\boldsymbol{B}_{\text{mask}}$

When set $0 < \eta < 1$ for cycle g. We need to selectively keep cycle g with ACE value as large as possible because cycle g still exists in the end. The basic selection principle is as same as in the first case. Stop reducing cycle g until it satisfies condition $N^g = \eta N^g_{\text{init}}$ and $g = g + 2$. When $g > g_{\text{end}}$, output $\boldsymbol{B}_{\text{mask}}$ in the end. See Algorithm 2 for details:

A few examples are given below to explain validity of algorithms.

E.g.1: Let α be a primitive element in a finite field GF(16). Let $\boldsymbol{S}_1 = \{\alpha^1, \alpha^2, \alpha^5\}$ and $\boldsymbol{S}_2 = \{\alpha^6, \alpha^7, \alpha^9, \alpha^{10}, \alpha^{12}, \alpha^{14}\}$ be two arbitrary subsets of GF(16). Set $\gamma = 1$. We get a 3×6 base matrix over GF(16) in the form given by (1).

Algorithm 1. A Replacement Preprocessing Algorithm

Input: B, r, maxtime
Output: B_{replace}
1: Set $B_{\text{replace}} = B$;
2: **for** $t = 1$ to maxtime **do**
3:     Calculate D^g and N_{init}^g. Find the maximum in D^g by global searching and save its row and column positions as $Index$
4:     **for** $k = 1$ to length($Index$) **do**
5:         **for** $z = 1$ to p **do**
6:             Let $B_{\text{replace}}(Index(k)) = z$. Calculate D^g and $D^{g'}$ of the new B_{replace}
7:             **if** $N^{g'} = 0$ && $\min(N^g)$ **then**
8:                 Record all alternative values z in Z
9:             **end if**
10:         **end for**
11:         **if** $\sim$isempty(Z) **then**
12:             If there are multiple alternative values, select v at random and set $B_{\text{replace}}(Index(k)) = q$
13:             break
14:         **else**
15:             continue
16:         **end if**
17:     **end for**
18: **end for**
19: output B_{replace}

Set $\eta = 0$ of cycle 6. Algorithm 1 and 2 are used to generate a masked base matrix $B_{1,\text{mask}}$. The parity-check H is generated by extending the masked base matrix $B_{1,\text{mask}}$ with 16-ary CPMs and ZMs of size 15×15. It is a NB-QC-LDPC code over GF(16) whose length is 90 symbols and rate is 0.5. The structure of $B_{1,\text{mask}}$ is as follows:

$$B_{1,\text{mask}} = \begin{bmatrix} \alpha^{11} & \alpha^{14} & 0 & \alpha^8 & \alpha^{13} & 0 \\ 0 & \alpha^{12} & \alpha^{11} & \alpha^4 & \alpha^7 & \alpha^{13} \\ \alpha^9 & \alpha^{13} & \alpha^6 & 0 & \alpha^{14} & 0 \end{bmatrix}$$

For comparison, another masked base matrix $B_{2,mask}$ of NB-QC-LDPC code in GF(16) is generated with girth is at least 10. The structure of $B_{2,mask}$ is as follows:

$$B_{2,\text{mask}} = \begin{bmatrix} \alpha^{11} & \alpha^{14} & 0 & \alpha^8 & 0 & 0 \\ 0 & 0 & \alpha^{11} & \alpha^4 & \alpha^7 & \alpha^{13} \\ \alpha^9 & \alpha^{13} & \alpha^6 & 0 & \alpha^{14} & \alpha^{12} \end{bmatrix}$$

E.g.2: Let α be a primitive element over a finite field GF(64). Let $S_1 = \{\alpha^7, \alpha^8, \alpha^9, \alpha^{10}\}$ and $S_2 = \{\alpha^{53}, \alpha^{54}, \alpha^{55}, \alpha^{56}, \alpha^{57}, \alpha^{58}, \alpha^{59}, \alpha^{60}\}$ be two arbitrary subsets of GF(64). Set a $\gamma = 1$. The base matrix B_1 is given by (1).

Set $\eta = 0$ for cycle 6 and $\eta = 0.2$ for cycle 8. A masked base matrix $B_{3,\text{mask}}$ that is generated by Algorithm 1 and 2 has a handle of cycle 8 with larger ACE

Algorithm 2. A Cycle Elimination Masking Algorithm based on ACE Value

---

Input: B_{replace}, g_{end}, η

Output: B_{mask}

1: Set $B_{\text{mask}} = B_{\text{replace}}$, $[m, n] = \text{size}(B_{\text{replace}})$;

2: Based on η, set $g^* = \begin{cases} g + 2 & \eta = 0 \\ g & 0 < \eta < 1 \end{cases}$

3: Calculate N_{init}^g of B_{mask}.

4: **while** $(g < g_{\text{end}})$ **do**

5:    Calculate D^g and N^g of B_{mask}

6:    **for** $j = 1$ to m **do**

7:       Find the maximum in D^g and save its position as *col*

8:       **if** length(col) ≥ 1 **then**

9:          Calculate the ACE minimum value and average value of cycle g^* in which the nonzero elements in the same row or column participate. Choose a position s where the former value is minimum at first, then the last one is minimum

10:      **else**

11:         continue

12:      **end if**

13:      Set $B_{\text{mask}}(j, s) = 0$. Calculate D^g and N^g for the next round

14:      **if** $N^g \leqslant \eta N_{\text{init}}^g$ **then**

15:         $g = g + 2$

16:         Set new η and g^*

17:      **end if**

18:   **end for**

19: **end while**

20: output B_{mask}

---

average value. The H is generated by extending $B_{3,\text{mask}}$ with 64-ary CPMs and ZMs of size 63×63, whose code length is 504 symbols and rate is 0.5.

$$B_{3,\text{mask}} = \begin{bmatrix} \alpha^{37} & 0 & \alpha^{15} & \alpha^{45} & 0 & 0 & \alpha^{21} & 0 \\ 0 & \alpha^{38} & 0 & 0 & \alpha^{46} & \alpha^{30} & \alpha^{61} & 0 \\ 0 & \alpha^{18} & \alpha^{39} & \alpha^{26} & 0 & 0 & \alpha^{31} & \alpha^{62} \\ \alpha^{49} & \alpha^{47} & \alpha^{19} & \alpha^{40} & \alpha^{27} & \alpha^{18} & 0 & \alpha^{32} \end{bmatrix}$$

For comparison, the base matrix $B_{4,\text{mask}}$ is generated with girth is at least 10. The structure of $B_{4,\text{mask}}$ is as follows:

$$B_{4,\text{mask}} = \begin{bmatrix} \alpha^{37} & 0 & \alpha^{15} & 0 & \alpha^{29} & \alpha^{60} & \alpha^{21} & \alpha^{58} \\ 0 & \alpha^{38} & 0 & \alpha^{16} & 0 & \alpha^{30} & \alpha^{61} & \alpha^{22} \\ \alpha^{46} & 0 & \alpha^{39} & \alpha^{26} & \alpha^{17} & 0 & \alpha^{31} & 0 \\ 0 & \alpha^{47} & \alpha^{19} & \alpha^{40} & 0 & \alpha^{18} & 0 & \alpha^{32} \end{bmatrix}$$

At present, most of works focus on constructing binary QC-LDPC codes by eliminating short cycles and maximum girth of the Tanner graph [13,15], which are unilateral if just consider a single factor. In [8], a class of LDPC codes proposed by using different combinations of the scyclotomic cosets in a finite field performed better than some EG-LDPC codes. In [5], a very large class of q-ary CPM QC-LDPC codes were constructed based on two arbitrary subsets of a finite field. Then, through masking by a masking matrix M, the masked base matrix had a good cycle distribution. The result demonstrated a phenomenon that a larger girth does not necessary to a better error performance. Thus, not only the number of short cycles, but also the connectivity may influence the error correction performance.

The number and The ACE average value of cycles in NB-QC-LDPC code under different code lengths and finite fields are mentioned in Table 1.

Table 1. The number and The ACE average value of cycles in NB-QC-LDPC Code under different code lengths and finite fields

Type	Source	Number of cycle 4	Number of cycle 6	Number of cycle 8	ACE value 1	2	3	4	5	ACE value average
GF(16) (90,45)	$B_{1,mask}$	0	0	180	0	3	4	5	0	3.167
	$B_{2,mask}$	0	0	0	0	0	0	0	0	0
	In [8]	0	0	150	4	4	2	0	0	1.800
GF(64) (504,252)	$B_{3,mask}$	0	0	189	0	0	1	2	0	3.667
	$B_{4,mask}$	0	0	0	0	0	0	0	0	0
	In [5]	0	0	252	0	1	1	2	0	3.250

Since the base matrix $B_{1,mask}$ satisfies the RC-constraints when $r = 15$, it has girth at least 6. From Table 1, it also has the number of cycles of length 8 is 180 with ACE average value is 3.167. A masked base matrix $B_{2,mask}$ over GF(16) is constructed for comparation, whose Tanner graph has girth at least 10. The codeword in [8] has girth at 6 and the number of cycles of length 8 is 150 with ACE average value is 1.800. It could be seen that although the number of cycles 8 has increased, the ACE average value is higher.

Similarly, the masked base matrix $B_{3,mask}$ satisfies the RC-constraints when $r = 63$. The length of cycle is at least 8. Table 1 illustrates that it has the number of cycles 8 is 189 with ACE average value is 3.667. A masked base matrix $B_{4,mask}$ over GF(64) is constructed for comparation, whose Tanner graph has girth at least 10. As for [5], it has some cycles 6 with ACE average value is 3.250. It could be seen that those methods in this paper make a reasonable compromise between the number and the connectivity of cycles.

4   Result and Discussion

The block error performance of NB-QC-LDPC codes are simulated in BPSK modulation and AWGN channel, which are decoded with 50 iterations of the FFT-QSPA in Fig. 2 and Fig. 3.

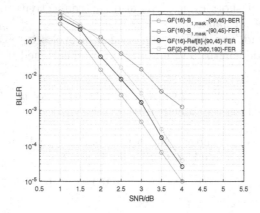

Fig. 2. Block error performance of the 16-ary (90,45) code.

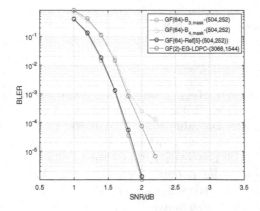

Fig. 3. Block error performance of the 64-ary (504,252) code.

Shown in Fig. 2 the block error performance of the codeword constructed in this paper is the best. For the codeword with code length of 90 symbols and rate of 0.5, the block error performance of codeword constructed by $B_{1,\mathrm{mask}}$ is far superior to the codeword constructed by $B_{2,\mathrm{mask}}$, which means that blindly increasing girth does not necessarily to bring performance improvement. Then, the performance of codeword constructed by $B_{1,\mathrm{mask}}$ is about 0.4 dB better than that of codeword in [8] when BLER is 10^{-4}, which shows the superiority of LDPC codes under larger ACE values. It is also about 0.5 dB better than the binary LDPC code [8] when BLER is 10^{-4}. This phenomenon shows that NB-LDPC codes have stronger error correction capabilities than binary LDPC codes.

In addition, Fig. 3 illustrates that for code length of 504 symbols and rate of 0.5, the block error performance of codeword constructed by $B_{3,mask}$ in this paper is much better than that of codeword constructed by $B_{4,mask}$ which exists error floor when BLER is 10^{-4}. This fully demonstrates the feasibility of improving performance by eliminating poorly connected cycles. Meanwhile, the performance of codeword constructed by $B_{3,mask}$ is a little better than that of the codeword in [5] when BLER is 10^{-4} because both codewords have good ACE values, but the constructed codeword is larger. Similarly, the comparison with binary EG-LDPC codes in [9] also illustrates the superiority of NB-LDPC codes.

5 Conclusion

In this paper, we presented a simple and flexible masking method for constructing irregular NB-QC-LDPC codes. The proposed method aimed to ensure that the left cycles in a masked base matrix have larger ACE average value under the constraint of the number of cycles. Examples in different range of lengths and finite fields were presented to illustrate the advantage of this feature. Simulation results showed that the codewords constructed in paper have better block error performance.

References

1. Davey, M.C., MacKay, D.J.C.: Low density parity check codes over gf(q). In: 1998 Information Theory Workshop (Cat. No.98EX131), pp. 70–71 (1998)
2. Gallager, R.: Low-density parity-check codes. IRE Trans. Inf. Theory **8**(1), 21–28 (1962)
3. Han, G., Guan, Y.L., Kong, L.: Construction of irregular QC-LDPC codes via masking with ace optimization. IEEE Commun. Lett. **18**(2), 348–351 (2014)
4. Li, J., Liu, K., Lin, S., Abdel-Ghaffar, K.: Algebraic quasi-cyclic LDPC codes: construction, low error-floor, large girth and a reduced-complexity decoding scheme. IEEE Trans. Commun. **62**(8), 2626–2637 (2014)
5. Li, J., Liu, K., Lin, S., Abdel-Ghaffar, K.: A matrix-theoretic approach to the construction of non-binary quasi-cyclic LDPC codes. IEEE Trans. Commun. **63**(4), 1057–1068 (2015)
6. Liu, K., Huang, Q., Lin, S., Abdel-Ghaffar, K.: Quasi-cyclic LDPC codes: construction and rank analysis of their parity-check matrices. In: 2012 Information Theory and Applications Workshop, pp. 227–233 (2012)
7. Liu, L., Huang, J., Zhou, W., Zhou, S.: Computing the minimum distance of nonbinary LDPC codes. IEEE Trans. Commun. **60**(7), 1753–1758 (2012)
8. Lu, M., Zhang, L.: Constructions of irregular nonbinary QC-LDPC codes: cyclotomic coset approach. In: 2012 IEEE 11th International Conference on Signal Processing, vol. 2, pp. 1468–1472 (2012)
9. Ryan, W., Shu, L.: Channel codes classical and modern (2009)

10. Tao, X., Feng, D., Zhang, Y., Huang, A.: Construction of non-binary LDPC codes with very large girth. In: 2012 8th International Conference on Wireless Communications, Networking and Mobile Computing, pp. 1–4 (2012)
11. Tian, T., Jones, C.R., Villasenor, J.D., Wesel, R.D.: Selective avoidance of cycles in irregular LDPC code construction. IEEE Trans. Commun. **52**(8), 1242–1247 (2004)
12. Vukobratovic, D., Djurendic, A., Senk, V.: Ace spectrum of LDPC codes and generalized ace design. In: 2007 IEEE International Conference on Communications, pp. 665–670 (2007)
13. Wang, D., Wang, L., Chen, X., Fei, A., Ju, C., Wang, Z.: Construction of QC-LDPC codes based on pre-masking and local optimal searching. IEEE Commun. Lett. **22**(6), 1148–1151 (2018)
14. Hu, X.-Y., Eleftheriou, E., Arnold, D.: Irregular progressive edge-growth (peg) tanner graphs. In: Proceedings IEEE International Symposium on Information Theory, p. 480 (2002)
15. Xu, H., Feng, D., Luo, R., Bai, B.: Construction of quasi-cyclic LDPC codes via masking with successive cycle elimination. IEEE Commun. Lett. **20**(12), 2370–2373 (2016)
16. Xu, J., Chen, L., Djurdjevic, I., Lin, S., Abdel-Ghaffar, K.: Construction of regular and irregular LDPC codes: geometry decomposition and masking. IEEE Trans. Inf. Theory **53**(1), 121–134 (2007)
17. Yang, F., Wang, L., Wang, D., Chen, X., Cui, M.: Construction of irregular QC-LDPC codes via arbitrary degree distribution masking algorithm. In: 2018 Asia Communications and Photonics Conference (ACP), pp. 1–3 (2018)
18. Zeng, L., Lan, L., Tai, Y.Y., Song, S., Lin, S., Abdel-Ghaffar, K.: Transactions papers - constructions of nonbinary quasi-cyclic LDPC codes: a finite field approach. IEEE Trans. Commun. **56**(4), 545–554 (2008)
19. Zhou, B., Kang, J., Tai, Y.Y., Lin, S., Ding, Z.: High performance non-binary quasi-cyclic LDPC codes on Euclidean geometries LDPC codes on Euclidean geometries. IEEE Trans. Commun. **57**(5), 1298–1311 (2009)

A Local High-Capacity LEO Satellite Constellation Design Based on an Improved NSGA-II Algorithm

Chao Zheng(✉)[iD], Bing Zhao[iD], and Daoxing Guo[iD]

Army Engineering University of PLA, Nanjing 21007, Jiansu, China
1599974708@qq.com

Abstract. As we all know, satellite communication has the advantages of wide coverage, large communication capacity, etc. compared to terrestrial communication, and is not easily affected by geographical natural disasters. But the coverage of one satellite is limited, so we often need a constellation satellite communication system composed of multiple satellites to communicate. Also, the cost of satellites is relatively high, and the satellite constellation usually needs to consider both cost and communication performance, how to use the least cost to achieve a best communication performance. We construct a design multi-objective optimization model of satellite constellation for a local high capacity, using the improved NSGA-II algorithm to solve model, using STK software to simulate the results of the solution.

Keywords: Constellation satellite communications design ·
Multi-objective optimization · Improved NSGA-II

1 Introduction

Compared with a single satellite, constellation satellites have the characteristics of orbit diversification, strong system survivability, short communication delay, large communication capacity, and wide coverage [1]. Various constellation design schemes have been proposed in different countries, and some constellation satellite communication systems have also been established. The primary commercial constellation satellite communication systems built and operated are Iridium, Globalstar, OneWeb system, SpaceX Starlink and Hongyan constellation of China.

According to the different satellites in the design scenario, the optimization of satellite constellation is mainly divided into two situations for local high capacity and wide-area supplementary coverage. Scholars have conducted a lot of research on these two design scenarios, and have proposed corresponding constellation design and optimization schemes. Literature [2,3] proposed a global-oriented constellation design scheme, in which literature [2] proposed an improved algorithm to utilize the minimum number of satellites to achieve a stronger satellite constellation coverage performance; literature [3] based on navigation accuracy and satellite orbit parameters , based on the Walker constellation, proposed an optimized design scheme for the global navigation satellite constellation. References [4,5] and [6] proposed an area-oriented constellation design scheme. Reference [4] divided the target area into three parts according to latitude and longitude, combined with the satellite constellation coverage multiple, minimum coverage requirements and the total number of satellites. The optimization problem is solved by using genetic algorithm, and finally the regional-oriented constellation design scheme is given; In [5], the maximum value is given by combining the satellite orbit and the average communication elevation angle. The constellation design scheme that minimizes the coverage factor and minimizes the semi-major axis of the orbit; [6] gives an optimization algorithm for inter-satellite routing, and a satellite network design scheme based on multi-layer satellites.

We can see that the satellite constellation is the basis of the satellite communication system. The constellation design need to consider how to meet the QoS of different communication services, the coverage of this constellation, the way of satellite access and switching, communication delay and throughput, etc., and the need to minimize construction costs must also be considered because the design needs to achieve the trade-off between multiple goals, so this satellite design problem can be regarded as Multi-objective optimization problem. It was proposed by Italian economist Pareto and was first used to solve the trade-off problem in political economy. The multi-objective optimization problem can be defined as determining the vector composed of decision variables in the feasible domain so that a set of conflicting objective function values reach the maximum value at the same time. There are many methods for solving multi-objective optimization problems, for example, ant colony algorithm, simulated annealing, genetic algorithm, tabu search, combinatorial optimization algorithm, etc. [7].

The design and optimization of the constellation satellite constellation for the local high-capacity LEO satellite communication system are aimed at reducing the deployment cost of the satellite constellation and building a more convenient and economical satellite communication system. The traditional satellite communication design focuses on the optimization of communication performance such as satellite coverage multiple, average communication elevation angle, lack of consideration for the needs of ground users and deployment costs, resulting in excessive waste of satellite-related orbits, frequencies, and other resources. We chose China as the target area, longitude range: 73°E to 135°E, latitude range: 3°N to 53°N. The letter is mainly for the design of high-capacity low-orbit satellites for the target area. In the design and optimization process of this constellation, the constellation design is closely combined with the actual needs of users, under the dual conditions of communication quality and cost efficiency, giving a feasible constellation deployment solution for a local high-capacity satellite communication system. Also, in this optimized design, We chose the walker constellation as the basic configuration, continue to optimize the number of satellites, the number of orbits, satellite orbit period, orbit tilt angle, and other parameters.

NSGA-II is an algorithm for searching the optimal solution derived from simulating biological genetics and evolution theory. We use the improved NSGA-II algorithm to solve the satellite design, which involves multiple optimization parameters, the optimal solution and use STK software to simulate and evaluate the performance of the satellite constellation scheme, and compare with Globalstar to verify the effectiveness of this constellation design.

The rest of the letter is organized as follows. In Sect. 2, the system model is described. Section 3 introduces the improved NSGA-II algorithm, and the model is solved. The results are simulated by STK software and compared with Globalstar. Conclusions are drawn in Sect. 4.

2 System Model

According to the previous discussion, we need to achieve a balance between the performance and cost of the constellation. It can generally be modeled as a multi-objective optimization problem. Assuming that there are q optimization goals, and these q optimization goals may conflict with each other, the mathematical model can usually be expressed by the following formula:

$$\begin{cases} minF = [f_1(x), f_2(x), ..., f_q(x)] \\ s.t.g_i(x) \le 0, i = 1, 2, ..., m \end{cases} \tag{1}$$

In the formula, $x = (x, x, ..., x,)^T$ is an n-dimensional decision vector, and its space is called the decision space, where each variable x_n, which is the decision variable, affects the performance of the optimization goal: $(f_1(x), f_2(x), ..., f_q(x))$ are q-dimensional target vectors, and their space is called the target space. Each target function $f_q(x)$ corresponds to the sub-goal to be optimized; $g_i(x) \le 0$ is the inequality constraint condition, which means the constraint condition to be met by the variables in the decision space. In this letter, we divided the entire constellation design optimization target into performance target and cost target. In the performance target, the coverage N of the satellite to the target area and the communication capacity C of the constellation are mainly considered. The coverage of the constellation is an important indicator to measure the performance of the constellation. High coverage rate is an important factors to achieve seamless connection for ground terminals and ground stations. The communication capacity of the constellation mainly refers to the ability of the constellation to serve the target area. In summary, the performance objective function is expressed as increasing communication capacity and coverage as much as possible. In the cost targe, since the total cost of a single satellite is still relatively high, reducing the cost of satellite constellation is also the focus of research.

2.1 Performance Target

Since the Walker constellation coverage performance is stronger than the polar orbit constellation, and the design of the regional constellation is not troubled by the establishment of the ground station, the Walker is selected as the basic configuration of the constellation design. Divide into small grids according to 1 ° of latitude and longitude, and the points on the grid are the feature points. Assuming that the total number of feature points is n, then it is considered to be measured every minute within an orbital period to calculate the constellation coverage at the current time. The rate is m/n, and the average constellation coverage of one orbit period is our optimization goal, which is expressed as follows:

$$C = \frac{1}{[P]} \sum_{k=1}^{[P]} \frac{m_k}{n_k} \qquad (2)$$

In the formula, [.] indicates rounding down, C indicates the average coverage rate of the target area at the kth measurement, the number of covered feature points is m_k, the total number of feature points in the target area is n_k, and p is the orbital period.

Analysis of constellation satellite capacity requires comparison with the user needs to form a constraint. The constellation capacity we define here refers to the service capability of the satellite constellation for the target area, that is, the number of satellites that the constellation can serve for the target area. The mathematical model established is as follows:

First, the capacity of a single satellite is as follows:

$$C_{sat} = \frac{P_{sat}G_{sat}GL_fL_M - I}{SNRkTR_{user}} \qquad (3)$$

L_M represents the rain attenuation of the signal in free space, R_{user} represents the user rate of a single user, P_{sat} represents the transmission power of the satellite to the user, G_{sat} represents the satellite antenna gain, G represents the user antenna gain, and L_f represents the signal when the signal propagates in free space Path loss. SNR represents the required signal-to-noise ratio of the user, k represents the Boltzmann constant, T represents the noise temperature of the user terminal, and R_{user} represents the data rate of the user terminal. In the process of serving users, the satellite receives interference from other satellites as follows:

$$I = \sum_{j \in N and j \neq i} P_{sat,j}G_{sat,j}G_j \left(\frac{\lambda}{4\pi d_j}\right)^2 \qquad (4)$$

N represents the number of satellites in this constellation, of which m satellites interfere with the target satellite, where $P_{sat,j}$ represents the transmission power of the satellite labeled j, and $G_{sat,j}$ represents the satellite labeled j for the user's antenna gain, G_j represents the user terminal's reception gain for the interfering satellite marked j, and the last part represents the path loss of the satellite marked j in free space.

The total satellite capacity of the constellation is calculated as follows:

$$C_{total} = N_pN_{sat}C_{sat}\frac{S_t}{S_c} \qquad (5)$$

N_p represents the number of orbits, N_{sat} represents the number of satellites in each orbit, S_t represents the area when the target area is mapped into space, depends on the periods of the satellite constellation orbit and the area of the target area, S_c represents the size of the constellation coverage area, the value depends on satellite constellation orbit period P and orbit inclination angle i [8].

Demand of users is represented by the number of satellite communication users in the target area. Therefore, the user demand model is mainly to establish the relationship between the population of the target area and the size of the communication market and the number of satellite communication users. First of all, the population of the target area can be calculated by the density of the ground population and the population distribution. In this model, the actual population mainly refers to the statistical results of NASA's International Earth Science Center. Based on the relevant information on the website, the population density of the ground can be calculated. We use population density data for 2020, see the Fig. 1. The scale of the communication demand mainly depends on the economic development of the target area and the user's acceptance of satellite communication. These indicators are reflected in the user demand model.

Fig. 1. Global 2020 population density of NASA's International Earth Science Center

We have previously calculated the coverage rate and divided the target area into several small grids. We directly obtained the population density of each small grid from the data, and then normalized the population density. The normalized formula is as follows:

$$\sum_{grid=1}^{N_g} D(grid) = 1 \tag{6}$$

N_g represents the number of all grids, $grid$ represents the number of the grid, and $D(grid)$ represents the normalized population density distribution. Therefore, the satellite communication users in each grid are as follows:

$$DM(grid) = f_{sat} M_{number} D(grid) \tag{7}$$

2.2   Cost Target

Due to the complexity of satellite cost calculation, there is currently a variety of satellite cost calculation methods. This letter mainly calculates based on the cost model given in Reference [9]. To simplify the calculation, this letter focuses on analyzing the deployment cost of the space segment. The total cost of a satellite communication system includes satellite cost, launch cost, maintenance cost, number of satellites, satellite power, and satellite quality. Therefore, the cost is as follows:

$$COST = N_P * N_{sat} * (1+\beta) * (1+\alpha + 0.00049 * ((((\frac{T}{2\pi})^2 * GM)^{\frac{1}{3}} - r)^{0.43}) * W_{sat} \quad (8)$$

β represents the proportion of insurance costs, α represents the ratio of the weight of the aircraft to the weight of the loader, W_{sat} represents the weight of the satellite.

$$W_{sat} = (1 + \alpha)(W_{array} + W_{battery} + W_{tran} + W_{antenna})$$

$W_{arag} \approx 0.1 \times P_{total}$ represents the weight of the solar array, $W_{batten} \approx 0.125 \times P_{total}$ represents the weight of the battery, $W_{ren} \approx 0.075 P_{rotal} + 50$ represents the weight of the on-board transponder, and $W_{antema} \approx \frac{(\frac{GM}{(\frac{2\pi}{P})^2})^{\frac{1}{3}}}{200}$ represents the weight of the on-board antenna. P_{total} represents the total power of the satellite.

In summary, we unified the performance target and the cost target to make the performance target as large as possible and the cost target as small as possible. We proposed a multi-objective optimization model for the local high-capacity satellite constellation optimization model. This constellation design is to use the minimum satellite deployment cost to achieve a low-orbit satellite constellation that meets the needs of users in the target area. The Walker constellation is used as the basic constellation. The orbit altitude is limited to [500, 2000] kilometers. The minimum communication elevation angle when it is not greater than 60, deploy a low-orbit satellite constellation that serves users in the target area. Therefore, the optimization model is as follows:

$$\min_{N_p, N_{sat}, P, \theta} (COST, -C_{total}, -C)$$

$$s.t. \begin{cases} C_{total} \geq \sum_{grid=1}^{N_p} DM(grid); \\ C \geq 90\%; \\ N_{p\,max} \geq N_p \geq N_{p\,min}; \\ N_{sat\,max} \geq N_{sat} \geq N_{sat\,min}; \\ 2\pi \sqrt{\frac{(r+2000)^2}{GM}} \geq P \geq 2\pi \sqrt{\frac{(r+500)^2}{GM}}; \\ \theta_{max} \geq \theta \geq \theta_{min} \end{cases} \quad (9)$$

In order to achieve better economic benefits and optimization effects, the number of satellites in the constellation and the orbit period need to be controlled within a certain range. Walker is the basic configuration in the design process of this constellation, so the orbital inclination is limited to between 40 and 60. It can be seen that the design of satellite constellation for local high capacity is an optimization process that includes multiple optimization goals. From the objective function, it can be seen that the satellite deployment cost, satellite constellation coverage, and satellite capacity are mutually restricted. As the number of satellites increases, the coverage of the satellite constellation increases, and the satellite constellation capacity increases first and then tends to be flat. However, the increase in the number of satellites will increase the cost of satellite deployment. The traditional mathematical optimization solution method is not suitable for solving such multi-objective optimization problems, so we will use the improved NSGA-II algorithm [10] to solve the optimization problem in the next section.

3   Improved NSGA-II Algorithm to Solve the Model

Given the shortcomings of NSGA, Deb et al. proposed NSGA's improved algorithm-non-dominated set sorting genetic algorithm with elite strategy (NSGA-II). NSGA-II is a genetic algorithm based on Pareto optimal concept. Compared with NSGA, NSGA-II has made the following improvements [11]:

(1) Using the fast non-dominated sorting method, the computational complexity is reduced from $O(kN^3)$ to $O(kN^2)$. Where k is the target number and the number of individuals in the N-group.
(2) The crowded distance is adopted to maintain the diversity of the population.
(3) Introduce elite strategies to prevent the loss of excellent solutions.

Experiments show that the results of NSGA-II are better than several other representative algorithms, but the performance of the SBX (Simulated Binary Crossover) cross operator is relatively weak, which limits the search performance of the algorithm to a certain extent. Besides, NSGA-II has yet to be improved in terms of convergence rate and maintaining the diversity of the population.

Lei Peng et al. applied the reverse learning mechanism to the population's initialization process and obtained good results [12]. Because it considers both population P and reverses population P*, it is larger than simple random initialization. The probability is close to the optimal goal of the problem. Apply reverse learning mechanism to genetic process. In the genetic process of each generation, the reverse population P* of its population P is calculated, and N optimal individuals are selected from the population P and the reverse population P* as the evolutionary population of the next generation. However, considering the significance of solving the inverse later in the algorithm, it reduces the speed of the algorithm. Therefore, the following method is adopted: In each generation of the evolution process, its population P is calculated with a certain probability O_r (opposite rate) of its reverse population P*, and during the evolution process, it decreases linearly, namely:

$$O_r = \max O_r - \frac{g}{MGG}\left(\max O_r - \min O_r\right) \tag{10}$$

where MGG is the maximum genetic generation, g is the current generation, and $maxO_r$ and $minO_r$ are the maximum and minimum values of O_r, respectively. In the way, the reverse learning mechanism can accelerate the convergence of the algorithm. To maintain the diversity of the population in the evolution process, when the individual $x_{ij}(g)$ and the individual $ox_{ij}(g)$ of the reverse population are not dominated by each other, ox_{ij} (accept rate) is accepted with a certain probability. Similarly, the probability of $accR$ is also linearly decreasing:

$$accR = \max accR - \frac{g}{G}(\max accR - \min accR) \tag{11}$$

Considering that in the genetic process, it is hoped that individuals with better distribution (low-rank value) and better distribution (large dist value) will occupy a larger proportion of the genes of individual offspring, for this reason, The crossover operator is as follows:

$$\alpha = \begin{cases} \frac{B \cdot rank}{A \cdot rank + B \cdot rank}, A \cdot rank \neq B \cdot rank \\ \frac{A \cdot dist}{A \cdot dist + B \cdot dist}, A \cdot rank = B \cdot rank \end{cases} \tag{12}$$

$A \cdot rank$ represents the non-dominated ranking of individual A of the current generation, and $A \cdot dist$ represents the crowded distance of individual A of the current generation. In the later stage of the algorithm, the genes of the better-distributed individuals are better preserved, and thus improved algorithms [10] is as follows:

Algorithm 1. Improved NSGA-II algorithm

Random initialization of population P and calculate opposite population $P*$
Selecting N fittest individuals from P and $P*$ as initial population
Evaluate initial population
while the halting criterion is not satisfied **do**
    Tournament Selections routines
    Arithmetic Crossover routines
    Polynomial Mutation routines
    Evaluate population P
    if $(rnd(0, 1) < O_r)$ **then**
        Compute opposite population $P*$
        Select PopSize fittest Individuals from P and $P*$
    end if
end while

The flowchart of satellite constellation optimization is as Fig. 2.

Some notes on algorithm solving:

a) In the entire constellation design, the decision variables are the number of satellite constellation orbits, the number of satellites in a single orbit, the satellite orbit tilt angle, the satellite orbit period, and the satellite minimum

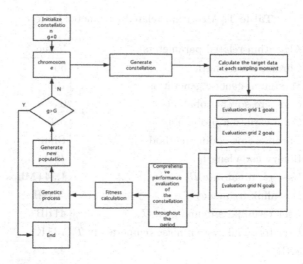

Fig. 2. Satellite constellation optimization flowchart

communication elevation angle. In this scenario, the value range and precision range of each decision variable determine its length in the chromosome. Also, the minimum communication elevation angle is directly taken as $10°$ according to the Globalstar system. The coding method of each chromosome is as follows:

$$X = [N_P/N_{sat}/i/P]$$

b) For each set, each individual has a multi-dimensional optimization target value, sort the optimization target values separately, adjust the individual's level according to the sorting result, and solve the crowding degree.

c) The characteristics of the elite strategy are that the excellent individuals in the parent directly enter the offspring, avoiding the loss of the optimal solution caused by chromosome crossover and gene mutation. First, eliminate the infeasible solutions in the parent; secondly, according to the results of non-dominated sorting, add individuals to the new population in descending order until the new population size exceeds the initial population size. Sort the population from large to small to fill the new population and build a new parent.

d) Select individuals from each generation according to the roulette wheel selection method. In general, the probability of individual inheritance depends on the size of the individual's crowding degree, and the probability that an individual with a large crowding degree inherits the next generation is greater. As shown in the following formula.

$$P_i = \frac{f_i}{\sum_{j=1}^{N} f_j} \tag{13}$$

e) The selection table of some related parameters is shown in the Table 1.

Table 1. Algorithm related parameter table

Algorithm related parameters	Value
Chromosome length	50
Maximum genetic generation	100
Gene crossover probability	0.8
Gene variation probability	0.3
Chromosome coding method	Binary
Binary code length	48
User terminal rate R_0	1.544 Mbps
Downlink frequency f	40 GHz
User terminal antenna gain G	41 dB
User terminal system noise temperature T	135 K
SNR	4.8 dB
Rain attenuation and other losses L_M	−5 dB

f) To ensure the cost of constellation design, the total number of constellation satellites is limited to 100, the number of orbits does not exceed 10, and the number of satellites in each orbit does not exceed 10. Besides, the inclination angle range of the track is limited to 30 to 60.

According to the proposed optimization scheme, the improved NSGA-II algorithm is used to solve the satellite constellation design of the target area. The results are as follows. The satellite constellation uses the Walker constellation as the basic configuration and consists of 35 low-orbit satellites with a total of 5 orbital inclination angles. It is a 48° orbital plane, and there are 7 evenly distributed satellites in each orbit, with a satellite orbit period of 110 min. The constellation illustration simulated by stk software are shown in Fig. 3 and Fig. 4.

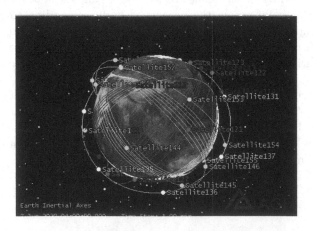

Fig. 3. 3D illustration of satellite constellation

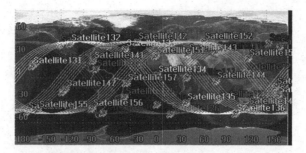

Fig. 4. 2D illustration of satellite constellation

To verify the effectiveness of the LEO satellite constellation scheme given for the target area in this paper, we mainly compare it with the Globalstar system.

First of all, we use the STK coverage analysis module to analyze coverage rate, and use our design and Globalstar to calculate coverage rate for the same small area. The results are shown in Fig. 5 and Fig. 6.

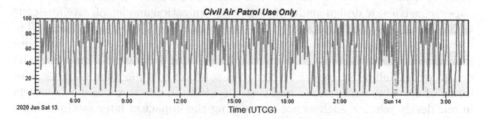

Fig. 5. Coverage rate of our designed scheme

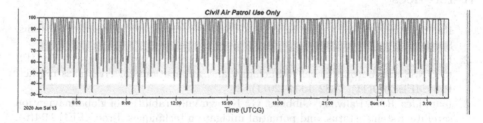

Fig. 6. Coverage rate of Globalstar

The coverage rate of our design is more concentrated in 100%, which shows that the solution is more stable than Globalstar.

Then the cost analysis. In our design, there is only 35 satellites and Globalstar has 48 satellites. In terms of space segment deployment cost, the overall cost of the constellation we design is lower than Globalstar, which just meets the design goals of this article and greatly saves Constellation deployment costs.

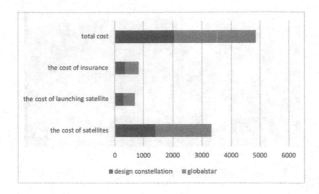

Fig. 7. Cost comparison analysis

4   Conclusion

In this letter, the constellation design problem for the target area is proposed. In order to achieve a compromise between cost and performance of satellites, this paper construct a design multi-objective optimization model of satellite constellation and use the improved NSGA-II algorithm to solve model, using STK software to simulate the results of the solution. But, the letter should be more innovative, our solution just compare the design with Globalstar. Comparing the design with Globalstar, we can see that our solution is better than Globalstar in terms of coverage performance and cost. In addition, due to some shortcomings in our design scheme, such as not considering the impact of inter-satellite links, not considering the ground cost, etc., we will improve it in future work.

References

1. Re, E., Ruggieri, M. (eds.): Satellite Communications and Navigation Systems. Springer, New York (2007)
2. Fernandez-Prades, C., Presti, L.L., Falletti, E.: Satellite radiolocalization from GPS to GNSS and beyond: novel technologies and applications for civil mass market. Proc. IEEE **99**(11), 1882–1904 (2011)
3. Ioannides, R.T., Pany, T., Gibbons, G.: Known vulnerabilities of global navigation satellite systems, status, and potential mitigation techniques. Proc. IEEE **104**(6), 1174–1194 (2016)
4. Meziane-Tani, I., Métris, G., Lion, G., Deschamps, A., Bendimerad, F.T., Bekhti, M.: Optimization of small satellite constellation design for continuous mutual regional coverage with multi-objective genetic algorithm. Int. J. Comput. Intell. Syst. **9**(4), 627–637 (2016)
5. Mo, Y., Yan, D., You, P., Yong, S.: Comparative study of basic constellation models for regional satellite constellation design. In: 2016 Sixth International Conference on Instrumentation & Measurement, Computer, Communication and Control (IMCCC), pp. 171–176. IEEE (2016)

6. Soterroni, A.C., Galski, R.L., Ramos, F.M.: Satellite constellation design using the qG global optimization method. In: 2015 Third World Conference on Complex Systems (WCCS), pp. 1–6. IEEE (2015)
7. Deb, K.: Multi-objective optimization. In: Burke, E., Kendall, G. (eds.) Search Methodologies, pp. 403–449. Springer, Boston (2014) https://doi.org/10.1007/978-1-4614-6940-7_15
8. Asvial, M., Tafazolli, R., Evans, B.G.: Satellite constellation design and radio resource management using genetic algorithm. IEE Proc. Commun. **151**(3), 204–209 (2004)
9. Lei, L., Qiongqing, Y., Dongtang, M.: Cost analysis and comparison of constellation satellite mobile communication systems. Ph.D. dissertation (2007) (in chinese)
10. Xiao, B., Liu, Y., Dai, G.: Improved nsga-ii algorithm and its application in optimization of satellite constellation. Comput. Eng. Appl. **48**(10), 47 (2012)
11. Deb, K., Pratap, A., Agarwal, S., Meyarivan, T.A.M.T.: A fast and elitist multi-objective genetic algorithm: NSGA-II. IEEE Trans. Evol. Comput. **6**(2), 182–197 (2002)
12. Peng, L., Wang, Y., Dai, G.: A novel opposition-based multi-objective differential evolution algorithm for multi-objective optimization. In: Kang, L., Cai, Z., Yan, X., Liu, Y. (eds.) ISICA 2008. LNCS, vol. 5370, pp. 162–170. Springer, Heidelberg (2008). https://doi.org/10.1007/978-3-540-92137-0_18

Modulation Recognition Based on Neural Network Ensembles

Xiaobo Ma[1], Bangnig Zhang[1], Daoxing Guo[1]([⊠]), Lin Cao[1],
Guofeng Wei[1], and Qiwei Ma[2]

[1] Army Engineering University of PLA, Chongqing 210007, China
elfin_cao@163.com, xyzgfg@sina.com
[2] Huawei Technologies Co., Ltd., Shenzhen, China
maqiwei@huawei.com
https://www.zj-huawei.com

Abstract. This paper studies the modulation recognition of digital communication signals based on neural networks. The BP neural network ensembles method is put forward, which is a linear composition of the BP neural networks. The recognition accuracy of ten different modulation formats is given according to the model above in feature extraction. The approach presented is superior to a neural network algorithm in existing articles. The result shows that the method proposed can recognize complex signal modulation formats availably. The overall recognition accuracy is basically up to 100% in the sample data of this paper when the SNR is more than 8 dB.

Keywords: Non-cooperative communication · Modulation recognition · Neural network ensembles · Feature extraction

1 Introduction

Nowadays, communication is the primary way for humans contact to obtain information. Modulation formats are various and sophisticated, no matter whether they are communication countermeasures and electronic warfare in the military or mobile communication in public life. Digital communication signal modulation is thus increasingly complex because of a higher communication accuracy and transmission rate, which brings real difficulties for signal demodulation. Modulation recognition is a process between reception and demodulation [14] and lays a foundation for signal demodulation, monitoring, interference, etc. It aims to identify the modulation format of the modulated signal with noise after receiving the message. There are two kinds of modulation recognition algorithms [7]: maximum likelihood estimation (MLE) hypothesis test based on decision theory and pattern recognition based on feature extraction in the published papers

Supported by Jiangsu Provincial Natural Science Foundation of China, No. BK20-191328.

on modulation recognition [4]. The advantage of MLE is that, theoretically, the classification is optimal under the Bayes tiniest miscalculation cost criterion [25]. But it needs a lot of prior knowledge, and big calculation due to the complex expressions of statistics caused by unknown parameters [18], which is difficult to process in real-time [22]. Instead, pattern recognition based on attributes and classifiers selected to classification training is relatively less complicated than MLE, in which the accuracy of classifiers can test classification performance [5].

Thus this paper takes advantage of the neural network algorithm for modulation recognition based on the pattern recognition of feature extraction. However, there are always more or less different flaws in the existing articles by the neural network algorithms. The paper studies modulation recognition based on the combined feature parameter and modified probabilistic neural network [26]. But the accuracy of the model is not pretty during low SNR. The paper specializes in modulation recognition based on the combined feature parameter and modified probabilistic neural network [27]. However, the method is challenging to apply because of complex feature parameters and a large amount of calculation. Although the paper [24] adopts a tree-structured neural network to modulation recognition, the approach has no comparison between the layers of different neural networks, and the astringency of the method is inadequate.

This paper digs into research on the above issues, and the approach offered performs well in the excellent accuracy of recognition, simple feature extraction, and small calculation. The contribution of this paper is as follows.

i. This paper develops a new model of neural network ensembles by a combination of the BP neural networks.
ii. The model presented is trained by a dataset of the novel and simple feature extraction of this paper.
iii. The model performance assessed by the testing set is impressive.

The rest of the paper is organized as follows. The feature extraction is clearly stated in Sect. 2. A brief overview of the neural network ensembles and algorithm flow is clarified in Sect. 3. Section 4 analysis results of the experiment simulation. Conclusions and the value of engineering are presented in Sect. 5.

2 Features Extraction

The method based on higher-order cumulant [6] has better adaptability to noise among all kinds of modulation recognition algorithms. The higher-order statistics of the modulation signal have batter anti-fading characteristics. At present, researches have been published in the succession of higher-order cumulant [8,15,19,28]. High-order cumulants, as the stable characteristics for modulation recognition, of all kinds of features are significant [9,13,21,29]. Based on the fourth-order cumulant, the identification of BPSK, QPSK, 4PAM, and 16QAM is carried out, and the effects of SNR and sample number on the recognition performance are discussed [19]. BPSK, 4PSK, and 8PSK are identified based on fourth-order cumulants, and unknown parameters of signals are estimated [29].

2ASK, 4ASk, 8ASK, 4PSK, and 8PSK are classified based on fourth-order cumulants and support vector machines [21]. It is concluded that the sixth-order cumulant has stronger benefits of anti-interference by comparing the performance of
the higher-order cumulants and the cyclic spectrum for MPSK modulation signals of the mixed recognition algorithm [15]. The signal is differentiated, and then
the higher-order cumulant is calculated to realize the MFSK signal recognition
[13]. BPSK, QPSK, OQPSK, 8PSK, π/4DPSK, 16APK, 16QAM, and 32QAM
are identified based on higher-order cumulants [8]. The theoretical basis of the
high-order cumulant of the modulation signal [19] is given mainly including the
definition of the high-order moment and high-order cumulant as follows.

2.1   Cumulant of a Random Variable

x is a continuous random variable, $f(x)$ is probability density function, eigenfunction is defined as:

$$\phi(\omega) = \int_{-\infty}^{+\infty} f(x)e^{j\omega x}dx = E[e^{j\omega x}]. \tag{1}$$

the cumulant generating function is defined as:

$$\psi(\omega) = ln(\phi(\omega)). \tag{2}$$

The $k-$moment of random variable x is defined as:

$$m_k = E[k] = \int_{-\infty}^{+\infty} x^k f(x)dx. \tag{3}$$

If $m_k(k = 1, 2, ..., n)$ exists, the relationship between the $k - th$ moment of x and
the eigenfunction is:

$$m_k = (-j)d^k \frac{\phi(\omega)}{(d\omega)^k}|(\omega = 0) = (-j)^k \phi(\omega)^k (k \le n). \tag{4}$$

The $k-$order cumulant of random variable x is defined as:

$$c_k = (-j)^k \frac{d^k \phi(\omega)}{(d\omega)^k}|_{\omega=0} = (-j)^k \psi^k(0)(k \le n). \tag{5}$$

2.2   Cumulant of the Random Process

$x(n)$ is the zero mean $k-$order stochastic stationary process, the $k-$order
moment of the process is defined as:

$$m_{kx}(\tau_1, \tau_2, ...\tau_{k-1}) = mom(x(n), x(n + \tau_1), ..., x(n + \tau_{k-1})). \tag{6}$$

The $k-$order cumulant of $x(n)$ is:

$$c_{kx}(\tau_1, \tau_2, ...\tau_{k-1}) = cum(x(n), x(n + \tau_1), ..., x(n + \tau_{k-1})). \tag{7}$$

$mom(\cdot), cum(\cdot)$ are united moment and united cumulant respectively.

For stationary complex random sequences $x(n)$, the moment and cumulant are defined as:

$$M_{p+q,q} = E[x^p(n), (x^*(n))^q],\tag{8}$$

$$C_{p+q,q} = cum[x(n), ...x(n), x^*(n), ..., x^*(n)],\tag{9}$$

where the number of $x(n)$ and $x^*(n)$ are p and q respectively.

2.3 High Order Cumulant Characteristic Parameters

The higher-order cumulants of the communication signals with Gaussian white noise are equal to the sum of the higher-order cumulants of the communication signals and Gaussian noise from the properties of higher-order cumulants [28]. The higher-order cumulant (more than 2-order) of Gaussian noise is equal to zero, so the higher-order cumulant has excellent anti-noise performance. In this paper, the second, fourth, sixth, and order cumulants are selected, referring to previous articles.

- the expressions of second order cumulants are:

$$C_{20} = cum(x(n), x(n)) = M_{20}.\tag{10}$$

$$C_{21} = cum(x(n), x*(n)) = M_{21}.\tag{11}$$

- the expressions of fourth order cumulants are:

$$C_{40} = cum(x(n), x(n), x(n), x(n)) = M_{40} - 3M_{20}^2.\tag{12}$$

$$C_{41} = cum(x(n), x(n), x(n), x*(n)) = M_{41} - 3M_{20}M_{21}.\tag{13}$$

$$C_{42} = cum(x(n), x(n), x*(n), x*(n))$$
$$= M_{42} - M_{20}M_{21} - 2M_{21}^2.\tag{14}$$

- the expression of sixth order cumulants are:

$$C_{60} = cum(x(n), x(n), x(n), x(n), x(n), x(n))$$
$$= M_{60} - 15M_{40}M_{20} + 30M_{20}^3.\tag{15}$$

$$C_{61} = cum(x(n), x(n), x(n), x(n), x(n), x*(n))$$
$$= M_{61} - 5M_{40}M_{21} - 10M_{41}M_{20} + 30M_{21}M_{20}^2.\tag{16}$$

$$C_{63} = cum(x(n), x(n), x(n), x*(n), x*(n), x*(n))$$
$$= M_{63} - 6M_{41}M_{20} - 9M_{42}M_{21}$$
$$+ 18M_{21}M_{20}^2 + 12M_{21}^3.\tag{17}$$

According to the calculation method of the theoretical value of the higher-order cumulant, the notional value of each digital modulation signal's cumulant is obtained, as shown in Table 1 [15]. The signal energy is E.

Table 1. The theoretical value of the cumulant of different modulations

Modulation	C_20	C_21	C_40	C_42	C_60	C_61	C_63
4ASK	E	E	$-1.36E^2$	$-1.36E^2$	$-8.32E^3$	$8.32E^3$	$8.32E^3$
2FSK	0	E	0	$-E^2$	0	0	$4E^3$
MSK	0	E	$-0.8E^2$	$-E^2$	0	$3.3E^3$	$4E^3$
BPSK	E	E	$-2E^2$	$-2E^2$	$-16E^3$	$16E^3$	$16E^3$
QPSK	0	E	E^2	$-E^2$	0	$4E^3$	$4E^3$
8PSK	0	E	0	$-E^2$	0	$4E^3$	$4E^3$
16QAM	0	E	$-0.68E^2$	$-0.64E^2$	0	$2.08E^3$	$2.08E^3$
32QAM	0	E	$-0.62E^2$	$-0.43E^2$	0	$0.74E^3$	$0.74E^3$
OFDM	–	–	0	0	0	0	0
CPM	0	E	0	$-E^2$	$0.36E^3$	E^3	E^3

2.4 Feature Parameters Selection

Considering that the higher-order cumulant will be affected by many factors such as signal amplitude and reference phase, besides, the cumulant of below the second-order Gaussian noise is not zero, this paper constructs the characteristic parameters are as follows based on the article [15].

$$F_1 = \frac{|C_{40}|}{|C_{42}|}. \tag{18}$$

$$F_2 = \frac{|C_{63}|^2}{|C_{42}|^3}. \tag{19}$$

$$F_3 = \frac{|C_{61}|^2}{|C_{42}|^3}. \tag{20}$$

The value of F_2, F_2, F_3 can be calculated according to the Table 1 and formula (18–20), as shown in Table 2 to Table 4.

Table 2. The value, F_1 of different modulations

Modulation	F_1	Modulation	F_1
CPM	0	2FSK	0
4ASK	1	MSK	0.8
BPSK	1	OFDM	0
QPSK	1	16QAM	1.06
8PSK	0	32QAM	1.49

Table 3. The value, F_2 of different modulations

Modulation	F_2	Modulation	F_2
CPM	1	2FSK	16
4ASK	27.52	MSK	16
BPSK	32	OFDM	0
QPSK	16	16QAM	13.76
8PSK	16	32QAM	6.89

Table 4. The value, F_3 of different modulations

Modulation	F_3	Modulation	F_3
CPM	1	2FSK	0
4ASK	27.52	MSK	10.89
BPSK	32	OFDM	0
QPSK	16	16QAM	13.76
8PSK	16	32QAM	6.89

Signals can be divided seven groups: {OFDM}, {4ASK}, {2FSK, MSK, QPSK, 8PSK}, {CPM}, {BPSK}, {32QAM}, {16QAM} by, F_2, from Table 3. QPSK, 8PSK, 2FSK, and MSK can be classified as {2FSK}, {MSK}, and {QPSK,8PSK} with parameter F_3, from Table 4. Finally, QPSK and 8PSK is recognized by parameter F_1.

3 Model of the Neural Network Ensembles

The researches show some problems with the prediction model for a neural network to digital communication signals modulation recognition [1–3,20,23]. First, the number of hidden layer nodes in a neural network will increase greatly on complex modulation signals, which will lead to training difficulties on account of difficulties of parameter setting and fast multiplication of training time [20]. Second, a neural network will cause an "overfitting" phenomenon due to the excessive pursuit of training accuracy [2]. Third, the defects of weak robustness and generalization in a neural network perform significant differences in the prediction of unknown data, which can not guarantee the accuracy of modulation recognition of digital communication signals [1]. But the neural network ensemble can improve performances by making the most of the information in multiple independent networks [3].

The neural network ensemble (NNE) [2] refers to the combination of multiple neural networks to complete the same training task. The output of each neural network determines the production of ensembles in the input samples.

This paper proposes a model named BP neural network ensembles (BPNNE) based on the BP neural network [11]. The mode is divided into two levels: the first level consists of T neural networks, and the second level is composed of S NNE. The individuals on the first level are trained by the feature parameters F_2, F_2, and F_3 extracted from different modulation signals. The output of the NNE on the last level is a linear combination of the output of the first level. Weight distribution is a typical optimization problem solved by a quantum immune algorithm [10]. Assuming that the last output of input x is y, there is a functional expression, g, between x and y. Based on a testing set, $V(x_i, y_i)(i = 1, 2, \cdots, N)$, and training set, $D_i(i = 1, 2, \cdots, T)$, T neural networks are trained independently to form a set, $H = h_t(t = 1, 2, \cdots, T)$. Each element h_t of H is an approximation of function g. The purpose of optimization is to improve the generalization ability of the neural network ensemble, which is to reduce the generalization error. That is, the neural network ensemble with a smaller generalization error is better than others. The generalization error can be expressed as the expected risk of ensemble optimization. The mean square error of the neural network ensemble on a given data set can be used as an estimation of generalization error. According to the criteria of minimum mean square error of neural network ensembles, the objective function of weight optimization is the mean squared error:

$$f_{2min}(\omega) = \sum_{i=1}^{N}[y_i - \sum_{s=1}^{S} NNE_s(x_i)/S]^2/N, \tag{21}$$

$$NNE_s(x_i) = \sum_{t=1}^{T} \omega_{st} h_t(x_i), \tag{22}$$

where $\omega = \omega_s t(s = 1, 2, \cdots, S; t = 1, 2, \cdots, T)$, $\omega_s t$ is the weight of the s-th ensemble with the $t-$th independent neural network, y_i is theoretical output of the $i-$th NNE, $NNE_s(x_i)$ is the $s-$th ensemble output, x_i is the $i-$th input. In the process of weight optimization, the value range of weight is usually limited to $[0, 1]$, and the sum of weight is set to 1, to reduce the influence of collinearity and noise [16]. The specific structure is shown in Fig. 1.

Figure 1 The structure partitioning policies: *S ensembles* and *1 ensemble*. *S ensembles* indicates the first ensemble, *1 ensemble* manifests the last ensemble.

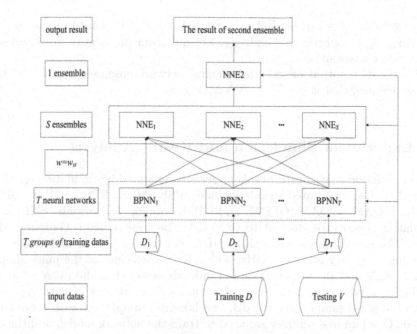

Fig. 1. Structure of BPNNE.

3.1 Algorithm Flows

The algorithm exploits neural network ensemble to optimize performance, and the implementation steps are as follows:

Step 1: The input dataset of the model offered is formed by extracting feature parameters.

Step 2: Divide the input dataset into a training set, D, and testing set, V, according to the proportion, and divide training set, D, into T groups randomly and equally, that is, $D_i(i = 1, 2, \cdots, T)$.

Step 3: According to the training data, $D_i(i = 1, 2, \cdots, T)$, of neural network sets, $P_j(j = 1, 2, \cdots, T)$ neural networks are trained independently by changing the number of hidden layers and nodes. And, the first level neural network set, $H = h_t(t = 1, 2, \cdots, T)$, consists of the neural networks selected in each set, P_j, with the best performance based on MSE.

$$f_{1min} = \sum_{i=1}^{N}[y_i - \sum_{p=1}^{P} h_p(x_i)/P]^2/N, \tag{23}$$

where h_p is the training output of neural network set $H = h_t(t = 1, 2, \cdots, T)$.

Step 4: The secondary neural networks are obtained by the weighted sum of the set, $H = h_t(t = 1, 2, \cdots, T)$, referring to formula (22). The weights of the secondary neural networks are optimized according to the MSE minimum principle. The optimization employs the quantum immune algorithm [12] which makes weights, $\omega = \omega_{st}(s = 1, 2, \cdots, S; t = 1, 2, \cdots, T)$, map to quantum code, $p = \{\alpha_{\mathbf{st}}, \beta_{\mathbf{st}}\}^{\mathrm{T}}$, where, α_{st}, and, β_{st}, are quantum probability amplitudes, T represents transposition.

Step 5: The output of secondary neural network ensemble is obtained by a simple average, that is $\bar{y} = \sum_{s=1}^{S} NNE_s(x_i)/S$.

4   Experiment Simulation and Result Analysis

The modulation signals used in this paper are generated by simulation on MAT-LAB [17]. The modulated signals include 2FSK, MSK, BPSK, QPSK, 8PSK, 4ASK, 16QAM, 32QAM, OFDM, and CPM, totaling ten formats. SNR of the simulation signal varies from 0 dB to 15 dB. The noise added is Gaussian white noise. The carrier frequency is three GHz. The symbol rate is one GB/S. The sampling frequency is sixteen GHz. The roll off coefficient of the pulse shaping filter is 0.25, and the initial phase is randomly selected in the range of $[0, 2\pi]$. MATLAB randomly generates signal symbols. The amount of data generated is two thousand samples every 1 dB, two hundred samples for each modulation format. One hundred samples are used to train the network model, and the others are used to test the model. Therefore, there are sixteen thousand samples of training data and sixteen thousand samples of test data, and each sample contains one thousand and two hundred symbols. The algorithm is implemented on MATLAB [11]. Each BP neural network contains the input layer, the hidden layer, and the output layer. The number of nodes in the input layer and the output layer is 3 and 10, respectively. And the number of the hidden layer's nodes is denoted by M, which can be obtained according to the empirical formula given by the paper [23], $M = \sqrt{I + O} + K$, where I, O, and L are the number of input nodes, output nodes, and hidden layers, while K is an integer between 1 and 10. The maximum of neural network ensembles epochs is 500. The value of the neural network set P_j, on the first level is set to ten. And the model proposed is trained by the different parameters above. The results of the experiments are shown in the following figures.

Figure 2 The above figure is the recognition accuracy curves of 10 modulation formats under different SNR of the BPNNE.

Figure 2 shows the curves of recognition accuracy of ten different modulation formats mentioned above with different SNR when the hidden layer's nodes is ten, and epochs are eighty. The probability of the correct recognition of ten formats is over 94% when SNR is 5 dB from Fig. 2. The BPNNE model proposed can recognize the ten modulated signals infallibly when SNR is 8 dB during the sample sets of the paper. However, the performance of the BPNNE model is inadequate near 0 dB.

Figure 3 The above figure is the recognition accuracy curves of 10 modulation formats with different hidden layer's nodes of the best BP neural network.

Figure 4 The above figure is the recognition accuracy curves of 10 modulation formats with different hidden layer's nodes of the best BP neural network.

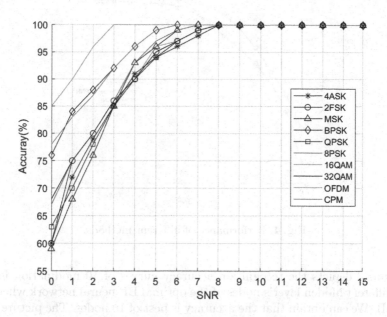

Fig. 2. Curves of accuracy with SNR.

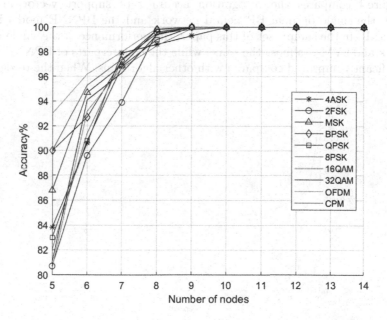

Fig. 3. Curves of accuracy with different nodes of the hidden layer.

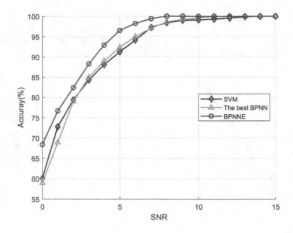

Fig. 4. Performance of different methods.

Figure 3 depicts the recognition accuracy curves of 10 modulation formats with different hidden layer's nodes of the optimal BP neural network when SNR is 15 dB. We can obtain that the accuracy is best of 10 nodes. The picture above also indicates property of the correct recognition is not improved any more. In other words, the hidden layer's nodes are not the more the better. Besides the figure exhibits The best BP neural network is inferior to the BPNNE model.

Figure 4 compares the recognition accuracy of support vector machine (SVM), the single optimal BP neural network and the BPNNE model in different SNR. In the sample set of this paper, the performance of the single neural network and SVM is almost the same, while the counterparts of BPNNE model is significantly improved compared with other algorithms. When the recognition

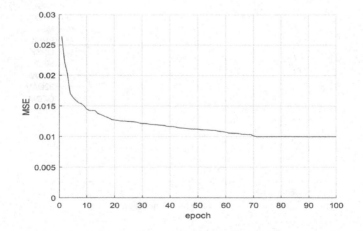

Fig. 5. MSE of BPNNE with Epochs.

accuracy is 98%, BPNNE model is 2 dB better than SVM and the single neural network.

Figure 5 The above figure diplays the minimum mean square error (MSE) of the BPNNE model with epochs when the SNR is 5 dB, and the nodes of the hidden layer are 10.

Figure 5 is mainly used to characterize the generalization performance of the BPNNE model. It can be seen from the above picture that MSE converges to 0.01 when epoch is 70, which indicates that the generalization error of the model can reach 10^{-2}, showing good generalization ability.

5   Conclusions

In this paper, a method of modulation recognition based on neural network ensembles is proposed on the foundation of the BP neural network. The characteristic parameters are simulated and verified by BP neural network ensembles. The experimental results manifest ten modulation formats are identified efficiently, including the complex modulation signals such as OFDM and CPM. The algorithm presented has high accuracy, and the extracting features are simple, which is not complicated for engineering applications.

References

1. Bragagnolo, L., da Silva, R., Grzybowski, J.: Artificial neural network ensembles applied to the mapping of landslide susceptibility. CATENA **184**, 104240 (2020). https://doi.org/10.1016/j.catena.2019.104240, http://www.sciencedirect.com/science/article/pii/S0341816219303820
2. Carney, J.G., Cunningham, P., Bhagwan, U.: Confidence and prediction intervals for neural network ensembles. In: Proceedings of International Joint Conference on Neural Networks (Cat. No.99CH36339), IJCNN 1999, vol. 2, pp. 1215–1218 (1999)
3. Choi, J.Y., Lee, B.: Ensemble of deep convolutional neural networks with Gabor face representations for face recognition. IEEE Trans. Image Process. **29**, 3270–3281 (2020)
4. Chung-Yu Huan, Polydoros, A.: Likelihood methods for MPSK modulation classification. IEEE Trans. Commun. **43**(2/3/4), 1493–1504 (1995)
5. Dobre, O.A., Abdi, A., Bar-Ness, Y., Su, W.: Survey of automatic modulation classification techniques: classical approaches and new trends. Commun. IET **1**(2), 137–141 (2007)
6. Dobre, O.A., Bar-Ness, Y., Wei Su: higher-order cyclic cumulants for high order modulation classification. In: IEEE Military Communications Conference 2003, MILCOM 2003, vol. 1, No. 1, pp. 112–117 (2003)
7. Fontes, A.I.R., Martins, A.D.M., Silveira, L.F.Q., Principe, J.C.: Performance evaluation of the correntropy coefficient in automatic modulation classification. Expert Syst. Appl. **42**(1), 1–8 (2015)
8. Han, Y., Wei, G., Song, C., Lai, L.: Hierarchical digital modulation recognition based on higher-order cumulants. In: 2012 Second International Conference on Instrumentation, Measurement, Computer, Communication and Control, pp. 1645–1648 (2012)

9. Li, P.H., Zhang, H.X., Wang, X.Y., Nan, X.U., Xu, Y.Y.: Modulation recognition of communication signals based on high order cumulants and support vector machine. J. China Univ. Posts Telecommun. **19**, 61–65 (2012)

10. Liu, J., Wang, H., Sun, Y., Li, L.: Adaptive niche quantum-inspired immune clonal algorithm. Natural Comput. **15**(2), 297–305 (2015). https://doi.org/10.1007/s11047-015-9495-4

11. Liu, L., Chen, J., Xu, L.: Realization and application research of BP neural network based on MATLAB. In: 2008 International Seminar on Future BioMedical Information Engineering, pp. 130–133 (2008)

12. Liu, X.H., Shan, M.Y., Zhang, R.L., Zhang, L.H.: Green vehicle routing optimization based on carbon emission and multiobjective hybrid quantum immune algorithm. Math. Probl. Eng. **2018**, (2018)

13. Mingzhu, L., Yue, Z., Lin, S., Jingwei, D.: Research on recognition algorithm of digital modulation by higher order cumulants. In: 2014 Fourth International Conference on Instrumentation and Measurement, Computer, Communication and Control, pp. 686–690 (2014)

14. Nandi, A.K., Azzouz, E.E.: Algorithms for automatic modulation recognition of communication signals. IEEE Trans. Commun. **46**(4), 431–436 (1998)

15. Pedzisz, M., Mansour, A.: Automatic modulation recognition of MPSK signals using constellation rotation and its 4th order cumulant. Digit. Signal Proc. **15**(3), 295–304 (2005)

16. Shang, R., Du, B., Dai, K., Jiao, L., Esfahani, A.M.G., Stolkin, R.: Quantum-inspired immune clonal algorithm for solving large-scale capacitated arc routing problems. Memetic Comput. **10**(1), 81–102 (2018)

17. Shilin, Q., Zhifeng, S., Huifang, F., Kun, L.: BP neural network for the prediction of urban building energy consumption based on Matlab and its application. In: 2010 Second International Conference on Computer Modeling and Simulation, vol. 2, pp. 263–267 (2010)

18. Su, W., Xu, J.L., Zhou, M.: Real-time modulation classification based on maximum likelihood. IEEE Commun. Lett. **12**(11), 801–803 (2008)

19. Swami, A., Sadler, B.M.: Hierarchical digital modulation classification using cumulants. IEEE Trans. Commun. **48**(3), 416–429 (2000)

20. Wang, C., Ji, Z., Wang, Y.: A novel memetic algorithm based on decomposition for multiobjective flexible job shop scheduling problem. Math. Prob. Eng. **2017**, (2017)

21. Wang, L., Ren, Y., Rui-Hua Zhang: algorithm of digital modulation recognition based on support vector machines. In: 2009 International Conference on Machine Learning and Cybernetics, vol. 2, pp. 980–983 (2009)

22. Wei, Z., Hu, Y.: Automatic digital modulation recognition algorithms based on approximately logarithm likelihood method. In: 2006 International Conference on Communications, Circuits and Systems, vol. 2, pp. 834–838 (2006)

23. Wong, M., Nandi, A.: Automatic digital modulation recognition using artificial neural network and genetic algorithm. Signal Proc. **84**(2), 35–365 (2004). https://doi.org/10.1016/j.sigpro.2003.10.019, http://www.sciencedirect.com/science/article/pii/S0165168403002846, special Section on Independent Component Analysis and Beyond

24. Yiqiong, X., Lindong, G., Bo, W.: Digital modulation recognition method based on tree-structured neural networks. In: 2009 International Conference on Communication Software and Networks, pp. 708–712 (2009)

25. Xu, J.L., Su, W., Zhou, M.: Likelihood function-based modulation classification in bandwidth-constrained sensor networks. In: 2010 International Conference on Networking, Sensing and Control (ICNSC), pp. 530–533 (2010)
26. Yulong Gao, Z.Z.: Modulation recognition based on combined feature parameter and modified probabilistic neural network. In: 2006 6th World Congress on Intelligent Control and Automation, vol. 1, pp. 2954–2958 (2006)
27. Zhang, Y.G.Z.: Modulation recognition based on combined feature parameter and modified probabilistic neural network. In: 2006 6th World Congress on Intelligent Control and Automation, vol. 1, pp. 2954–2958 (2006)
28. Zhao, X.: Mixed recognition algorithm for signal modulation schemes by high-order cumulants and cyclic spectrum. Dianzi Yu Xinxi Xuebao/J. Electron. Inf. Technol. **38**(3), 674-680 (2016)
29. Zhijin, Z., Tao, L.: A mpsk modulation classification method based on the maximum likelihood criterion. In: Proceedings 7th International Conference on Signal Processing, 2004. Proceedings. ICSP 2004, vol. 2, pp. 1805–1808 (2004)

An Infrared Cloud Imaging System for Satellite-Earth Laser Communications

Zhang Zhi-yong$^{(\boxtimes)}$, Zhao Kang-lian, Fang Yuan, and Li Wen-feng

Nanjing University, Nanjing 210023, China
zhiyonglove@hotmail.com

Abstract. This paper designs an infrared cloud imaging system for satellite-to-earth laser communications. The imaging system provides a reliable service for establishing an effective satellite laser communication link by collecting the cloud images over a ground station site, processing and analyzing the time and space statistics of the cloud, and acquiring the optical depth of the cloud. To realize day and night automatic monitoring of cloud state information, the infrared cloud imager designed in this paper can effectively observe the fixed viewpoint of the sky, and the uncooled infrared focal plane array calibration model considering the working temperature effect of the detector can meet the radiation setting of sky cloud monitoring, which provides cloud state data information with higher temporal and spatial resolution. Preliminary observation experiments show that the infrared cloud imaging system proposed in this paper can get required real-time cloud image and information for space-terrestrial laser communications.

Keywords: Satellite-to-Earth laser communication · High-Rate-Data · Cloud infrared imager · Radiation calibration

1 Introduction

With the increasing demand for space data communication, the microwave communication technology used between traditional satellites and grounds has been difficult to meet the increasing data transmission requirements due to the relatively lower transmission rate. The use of laser communication technology have becoming the future development trend of communication between satellites and grounds [1].

There are many factors that need to be considered in the process of building a satellite-earth laser link, including clouds, atmospheric attenuation, atmospheric turbulence, etc., where cloud coverage is one of the key factors that affect the performance of the link or even the broken link. In recent years, scientists from various countries have made many efforts to study the characteristics of clouds, and have conducted corresponding studies using various observation methods, including satellites, ground radiation, lidar, ground imagers and infrared cloud imaging [2–6]. The ideal instrument for measuring cloud characteristics requires to provide continuous day and night cloud image spatiotemporal data, with high spatial resolution and temporal resolution. Although there are many ways to detect cloud coverage, most of the current methods are designed for specific needs and cannot fully meet the requirements of satellite-to-earth laser communication

© ICST Institute for Computer Sciences, Social Informatics and Telecommunications Engineering 2021
Published by Springer Nature Switzerland AG 2021. All Rights Reserved
Q. Wu et al. (Eds.): WiSATS 2020, LNICST 357, pp. 418–428, 2021.
https://doi.org/10.1007/978-3-030-69069-4_35

applications. The spatial and temporal resolution of satellite observation is limited; lidar is mainly used for fixed-point zenith direction observation; visible light imaging is not suitable for night observation; artificial observation is influenced by empiricism and subjective judgment. Since the clouds have the same infrared radiation characteristics in the infrared (8–14 μm) band regardless of day or night, it is possible to consider using infrared imagers to continuously observe the sky day and night [7].

The attenuation of optical signals by clouds varies greatly with the optical properties of the clouds. The thick cloud layer attenuates the laser signal strong enough to completely cut off the laser communication link. Optical thin clouds, especially cirrus clouds, mainly eliminate the energy of the signal propagation path and reduce the signal quality by scattering and attenuating the light beam. In order to make the satellite-earth laser communication link feasible and reliable, it is necessary to accurately measure the presence or absence of clouds and their optical characteristics between the links. Especially when the satellite has several ground stations as candidates to establish a satellite-earth laser link for communication, the appropriate ground station can be selected based on the observed real-time cloud status information over the candidate ground station, or even predicting the cloud change trend in advance Perform chain building.

Therefore, in order to guarantee the uninterrupted laser communication mission of the satellite and earth, it is very important to obtain the changing trend of the cloud clusters above the ground station in advance, which can be realized mainly through two aspects of work. The first part is to observe the cloud image above the ground station to obtain the optical characteristics of the cloud. The second part is to use machine learning and other technologies and a large number of spatial-temporal data of the cloud map over the ground station to predict the cloud state over the ground station to achieve to predict in advance and actively switch the purpose of the communication link. This paper focuses on the construction of the first part. Since the actual operation of laser communication ground stations requires the use of miniaturized, day and night observation, high spatial and temporal resolution instruments [8] to describe the characteristics of clouds, this paper developed an infrared cloud imager for continuous day and night ground measurement of cloud Statistical characteristics.

2   System Design of Infrared Cloud Imager

The prototype of the infrared cloud imager designed in this paper is mainly composed of optical module, temperature control module, communication master control module and power supply module. Its main structural diagram is shown in Fig. 1. Use a microcomputer to control the uncooled infrared camera to obtain sky radiation data, and obtain the real-time working temperature information of the imager through the temperature sensor for calibration processing, so as to obtain the infrared radiation distribution cloud image of the sky. After further processing, the required cloud statistical characteristics can be obtained. Cloud statistics based on real-time data can be used in the neural network model training set to predict cloud state information and cloud variation trends.

2.1   Optical Module

In the infrared cloud imager designed in this paper, the role of the optical module is to collect the infrared images of the sky. Its core is a microwave radiant heat engine camera based on FLIR TAU2, which can provide a diagonal field of view of 110°. The camera uses a sealed housing design, an uncooled focal plane array, no need for an external thermoelectric cooler, internal heaters and related control circuits, an embedded fan to ensure internal air circulation, and the camera's spectral response is between 8 μm and 14 μm.

The ground station of laser link is usually established at a high altitude, and its temperature difference between day and night is relatively large. The operating temperature range of this camera reaches −40 °C − + 80 °C, which meets the temperature requirements of the actual working scene. However, since it is an uncooled focal plane array camera, its response will drift with temperature, and the camera response needs to be corrected. The specific correction method is shown in Sect.2.

(a)   the infrared cloud imager.

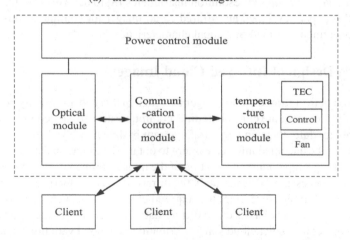

(b) Block diagram for the structure of the infrared cloud imager.

Fig. 1. Infrared cloud imager.

2.2 Temperature Control Module

In order to ensure the imager can work effectively for a long time, a temperature control module is designed to stabilize the temperature inside the imager chassis and prevent instrument failure caused by excessive temperature. The temperature control module is mainly composed of semiconductor (TEC) refrigerator, temperature controller and fan.

Using the temperature sensor inside the camera, the real-time temperature information of the camera is read from the camera serial port through the microcomputer. When the temperature of the camera reaches a predetermined upper threshold, the temperature controller will automatically activate the TEC cooler built in the chassis to cool the interior of the chassis, and use the fan to maintain the air circulation inside the chassis to keep the camera temperature at about 25 °C. The acquired real-time temperature information also supports the camera's radiation calibration.

2.3 Communication Control Module

The main function of the communication control module is to manage the normal operation of the imager and as an interface for interconnection with users.

Infrared cloud imager integrates a microcomputer to control and access to data. Using the server-client mode, it can accommodate multiple users to access the server and download real-time data at the same time. Users can set the time to take cloud pictures according to their own needs at intervals and send the captured observation data in 8-bit PNG format to the local client via the server. Figure 2 is a typical cloud image obtained by the infrared imager during the day (a) and night (b) obtained by the client.

3 Radiation Calibration Treatment

Radiation calibration is the process of converting the brightness gray value of the image acquired by the sensor into absolute radiation brightness. In the infrared cloud imager designed in this paper, because the optical module uses a camera based on an uncooled focal plane array, although it has the advantages of miniaturization, low cost, and fast response, its response is not only dependent on the source radiation or temperature, but also affected by the temperature of the focal plane array and the ambient temperature. Therefore, the radiometric calibration needs to establish a relationship between the output of the camera and the temperature radiation of the scene source, and relies on compensation for this, otherwise the camera cannot maintain stable radiometric calibration.

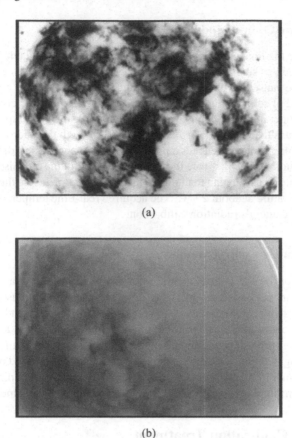

(a)

(b)

Fig. 2. Observations on 27 March 2019.

Figure 3 shows the processing of radiometric calibration. First, the scene image and the focal plane array temperature at the time of shooting are obtained, and the corresponding output when the camera is stabilized at the reference temperature is obtained by using the calibration coefficient that eliminates the dependence of the focal plane array temperature. Finally, the gain and offset measured at the reference temperature are used to convert the FPA stable data into the required comprehensive radiation value [9].

To verify the temperature dependence of the microwave bolometer camera, we placed a FLIR TAU2 camera and a face black body source in an environmental cavity.

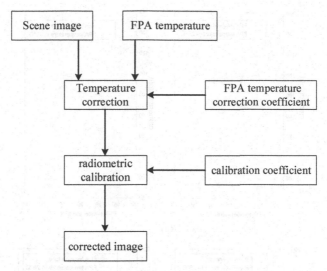

Fig. 3. Flow chart of the radiation calibration.

The temperature in the environmental cavity rose from 15 °C to 35 °C, and the temperature of the black body was maintained at 10 °C, 20 °C, and 30 °C, respectively. The results are shown in Fig. 4. In Fig. 4(a)–Fig. 4(c), the left graph is the actual temperature corresponding to the DN value of the camera response output, and the right graph is performed 3 times.

The result after fitting. The red line represents the camera's response to the blackbody source as the ambient temperature gradually increases. The blue line represents the camera response at different blackbody temperatures when the ambient temperature is stable at 25 °C. It can be seen that for this camera, as the focal plane array (FPA) temperature increases, the response to the blackbody scene decreases.

In order to correct the uncooled infrared camera, many patent documents have proposed a variety of calibration methods for thermally unstable cameras. For example, a fourth-order polynomial curve fitting method is used; by changing the camera integration time, reading bias, or other camera parameters to compensate for the corresponding response change of the sensor caused by the temperature change of the focal plane array [10]. The temperature dependence method of the modified focal plane array used in this paper is a correction method based on mathematical principles proposed by P.W. Nugent and J.A. shaw et al. [11]. Mathematical modeling is used to determine the parameters needed to stabilize the camera output when the camera temperature changes.

In this method, the corrected camera response output is mainly determined by two factors, one is the original response output containing the error, and the other is the difference between the current focal plane array temperature (the reference temperature The center of the range, this article is 25 °C). The camera's output response can be expressed as:

$$D_N = G(T)L_t + B(T) \tag{1}$$

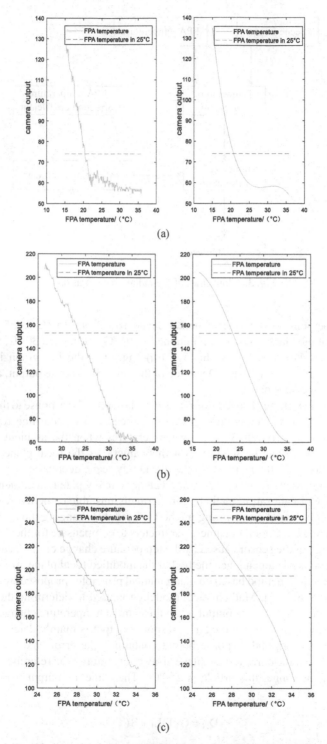

Fig. 4. The relationship between the camera's output response and ambient temperature changes. (a.blackbody temperature in 10 °C; b.blackbodytemperature in 20 °C ; c.blackbody temperature in 30 °C) (Color figure online)

Where $G(T)$ is the temperature-dependent gain, Lt is the scene radiation, and $B(T)$ is the temperature-dependent offset. The temperature correction equation of the camera is:

$$D_{Nc} = \frac{D_N - b(\Delta T)}{1 + m(\Delta T)} \tag{2}$$

Where D_{Nc} is the output value of the temperature correction of the focal plane array, ΔT is the difference between the FPA temperature and the reference temperature of 25 °C, $b\,(\Delta T)$ is the temperature-related deviation correction, which is described as a polynomial function with three temperatures condition and a constant bias.

$$b(\Delta T) = b_1 \Delta T + b_s \Delta T^2 + b_s \Delta T^3 - o_1 \tag{3}$$

$m(\Delta T)$is the temperature-dependent gain correction, which is described as a scalar multiplied by FPA temperature difference.

$$m(\Delta T) = m_1 \Delta T \tag{4}$$

Among them, m1 is a scalar corresponding to each camera. Then the relationship between the modified DN value and the scene radiation value is:

$$L_{sky} = g \left[\frac{D_N - b_1 \Delta T - b_s \Delta T^2 - b_s \Delta T^3 + o_1}{1 + m_1 \Delta T} \right] + b \tag{5}$$

Through the experimentally collected focal plane array temperature and corresponding camera output, the parameters of the camera used in this paper were subjected to Moore-Penrose pseudo-inversion [10]. Each pixel has a corresponding set of parameters for correction.

The data before and after correction of the focal plane array temperature (black) and the data after correction (red) are shown in Fig. 5. The blue dotted line is the output response when the camera focal plane array temperature stabilizes at 25 °C. The calibrated camera response reduces the relative error of the radiation output of the scene source to about 5%. Using the camera output response after eliminating the temperature dependence of the focal plane array, the radiation calibration of the uncooled infrared camera can be determined.

4 Data Processing

The cloud optical depth algorithm uses the atmospheric transmission model to calculate the total radiation value of the atmospheric path in the infrared band from 7.5 μm to 13.5 μm from the cloud height to the ground and the average transmittance of the atmosphere. Use formula:

$$\varepsilon = \frac{L_{cld} - L_a}{\tau L_{bb}} \tag{6}$$

Able to calculate the emissivity of the cloud. Where ε is the emissivity of the cloud, L_{cld} is the cloud radiation value acquired by the infrared cloud imager, L_a is the total

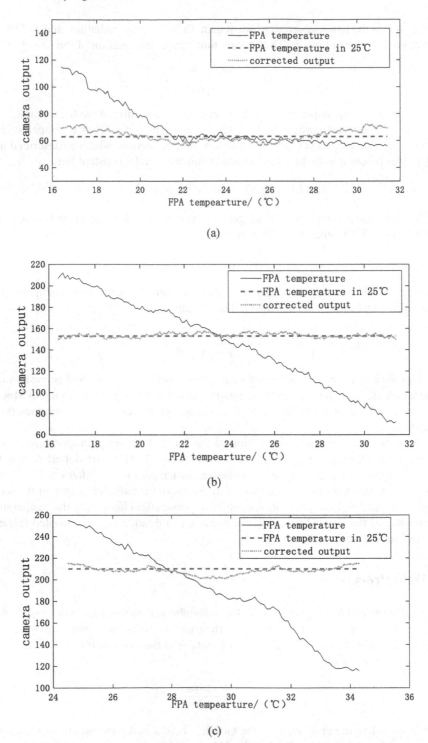

Fig. 5. Corrected camera output response at different blackbody temperatures (Color figure online)

radiation value under the local atmospheric path, τ is the average transmittance under the atmospheric path, and L_{bb} is at the same temperature The radiation value of the black body.

According to the relationship between cloud emissivity and optical depth [12]:

$$\sigma = \frac{\ln(1 - \varepsilon)}{-0.79} \tag{7}$$

Finally, an optical depth image of the cloud can be obtained (see Fig. 6).

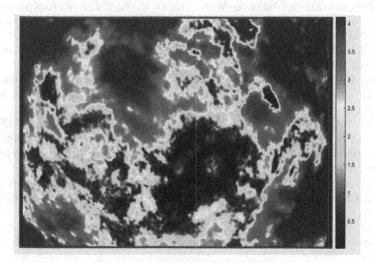

Fig. 6. Optical depth image of the cloud.

5   Conclusion

In this paper, the calibration model of the uncooled infrared focal plane array is determined to determine its calibration model, which solves the problem of radiation calibration measurement, analyzes how to obtain the optical depth image of the cloud, and on this basis, a ground-based remote sensing for cloud is developed. The infrared cloud imager realizes continuous day and night observation of clouds, and provides a means for obtaining objective and quantitative cloud observation data.

Over the designated area in Nanjing, infrared cloud imager observation is continuing, and quasi-continuous data has been obtained in recent months. A series of studies on the hardware of observation instruments and the characteristics of clouds are constantly being updated and improved. Analysis and processing of the already acquired sky radiation observation data, and further acquisition of cloud cover and cloud height are also in progress.

References

1. Nugent, P.W., Shaw, J.A., Piazzolla, S.: Infrared cloud imaging in support of Earth-space optical communication . Opt. Express **17**(10), 7862–7872 (2009)

2. Wojcik, G.S.: Deep-space to ground laser communications in a cloudy world. Proc. SPIE-Int. Soc. Opt. Eng. **5892**, 589203 (2005)
3. Long, C.N., Ackerman, T.P., Gaustad, K.L., et al.: Estimation of fractional sky cover from broadband shortwave radiometer measurements. J. Geophys. Res. Atmos. **111**(D11) (2006)
4. Thurairajah, B., Shaw, J.A.: Cloud statistics measured with the infrared cloud imager (ICI) . IEEE Trans. Geosci. Remote Sens. **43**(9), 2000–2007 (2005)
5. Long, C.N., Slater, D.W., Tooman, T.: Total sky imager model 880 status and testing results. Office Sci. Tech. Inf. Tech. Rep. (2001)
6. 章文星, 吕达仁, 宣越健等. 利用扫描式红外亮温仪对天空云量的试验观测[J]. 气象学报, **68**(6), 808–821 (2010).[Zhang, W.-X., , Lv, D.-R., Yi, Y.-J., et al.: Experimental observation of sky cloud amount using scanning infrared brightness meter. J. Meteorol. **68**(6), 808–821 (2010)]
7. Shaw, J.A., Nugent, P.W.: Physics principles in radiometric infrared imaging of clouds in the atmosphere. Eur. J. Phys. **34**(6), S111–S121 (2013)
8. Nugent, P.W., Shaw, J.A., Piazzolla, S.: Infrared cloud imager development for atmospheric optical communication characterization, and measurements at the JPL Table Mountain Facility. Interplanetary Netw. Progress Rep. **42**(192), 1–13 (2013)
9. 孙学金, 高太长, 翟东力等. 基于非制冷红外焦平面阵列的全天空红外测云系统[J]. 红外与激光工程, **37**(5) (2008).[Sun, X.-J., Gao, T.-C., Zhai, D.-L., et al.: All-sky infrared cloud measurement system based on uncooled infrared focal plane array. Infrared Laser Eng. **37**(5) (2008)]
10. Wang, J., Gou, J., Wu, Z.M., et al.: Design and imaging application of room-temperature terahertz detector with micro-bolometer focal plane array. Electron. Technol. J. **14**(2), 98–102 (2016)
11. Nugent, P.W., Shaw, J.A., Pust, N.J.: Correcting for focal-plane-array temperature dependence in microbolometer infrared cameras lacking thermal stabilization . Opt. Eng. **52**(6), 061304 (2013)
12. Nugent, P.W.: Deployment of the third-generation infrared cloud imager A two-year study of Arctic clouds at Barrow, Alaska.Montana State University - Bozeman, College of Engineering, 113 (2016)

Collaborative Interference Source Search and Localization Based on Reinforcement Learning and Two-Stage Clustering

Guangyu Wu[1](✉)(iD), Yang Huang[2,3](iD), and Simeng Feng[2](iD)

[1] College of Computer Science and Technology, Nanjing University of Aeronautics
and Astronautics, Nanjing 210016, China
GYWu9908@163.com
[2] Key Laboratory of Dynamic Cognitive System of Electromagnetic Spectrum Space,
Ministry of Industry and Information Technology, Nanjing University of Aeronautics
and Astronautics, Nanjing 210016, China
{yang.huang.ceie,simeng-feng}@nuaa.edu.cn
[3] National Mobile Communications Research Laboratory, Southeast University,
Nanjing 210000, China

Abstract. Exploiting unmanned aerial vehicles (UAVs) to locate the
position of interferences has attracted intensive research interests, due to
UAVs' flexibility and the feature of suffering less multi-path interference.
However, in order to find the position of an interference source, off-the-
shelf Q-learning-based schemes require the UAV to keep searching until
it arrives at the target. This obviously degrades time efficiency of localization. To balance the accuracy and the efficiency of searching and localization, this paper proposes a collaborative search and localization approach, where search and remote localization are iteratively performed with
a swarm of UAVs. For searching, a low-complexity reinforcement learning
algorithm is proposed to decide the direction of flight (in every time interval) for each UAV. In the following remote localization phase, a two-stage
clustering algorithm is proposed to estimate the position of the interference
source, by processing intersections of the extensions of UAVs' trajectories. Numerical results reveal that in the proposed collaborative search and
localization scheme, the proposed reinforcement-learning-based searching
can benefit the collaborative localization, in terms of the accuracy of localization. Moreover, compared to the Q-learning-based approach, the proposed approach enables remote localization and can well balance accuracy,
the robustness and time efficiency of localization.

This work was supported in part by the National Natural Science Foundation of China
under Grant 61631020, 61827801 and 61901216, the Natural Science Foundation of
Jiangsu Province under Grant BK20190400, the open research fund of National Mobile
Communications Research Laboratory, Southeast University (No. 2020D08).

Keywords: Reinforcement learning · Clustering · Unmanned aerial
vehicle · Localization · Wireless communications

1   Introduction

Interference sources not only occupy growing spectrum resources illegally but
also have brought grave implications to many fields such as railway communications, broadcast channel and IoT communications. The demand of an efficient and accurate search and location method to locate interference source
is soaring [3]. Nevertheless, locating interference source in practice always suffers from unknown but dynamic surroundings, e.g. random background noise,
such that detected signals remain changing over time intervals. Therefore, it
is urgent to find out an interference source localization method which can be
adaptive to varying environments instead of relying on a prior knowledge of the
environments.

Unmanned aerial vehicles (UAVs) are capable of performing effective interference source localization [5], due to the fact that trajectories of UAVs can be
flexibly planned to avoid obstacles in semistructured or unstructured environments. Moreover, signal processing devices and sensors, e.g. electronic scanning
antennas, carried by UAVs suffer less multi-path interference, such that the position achieved by localization can be more accurate and reliable. In the meanwhile, attempts were made to employ multiple UAVs for a collaborative search
and localization of interference sources. In [6], the authors proposed a received
signal strength (RSS) value based localization method using multi-UAV. However, such a method is applicable only in scenarios where transmit power and
propagation parameters of the interference source are known.

Instead of relying on a prior knowledge of the environments, reinforcement
learning [2,9] is able to exploit samples and function approximation to optimize performance in dynamic environments. Recently, some researches studied
reinforcement-learning-based interference source localization with UAVs [1,11,
12]. In these works, a single UAV is exploited to locate interference source in
unknown dynamic environments. Searching the interference source only based
on reinforcement learning may require the UAV to keep searching until it arrives
at the target. Apparently, such a search heavily degrades time efficiency. It is
also inapplicable to the scenario where performing localization from a distance
is necessary. On the other hand, remote localization may suffer from multi-path
effect and therefore mitigation in the accuracy performance.

Against this background, this paper proposes a novel collaborative search and
localization approach based on reinforcement learning and two-stage clustering,
where the search and localization could benefit from synthesizing individual
decisions within a swarm of UAVs. Briefly, in the proposed method, a searching
phase and a localization phase are alternatively performed. During the searching
phase of a certain time interval, each UAV in the swarm can decide and evaluate
direction of searching through reinforcement learning. Then, in the following
localization phase of the time interval, by developing a novel two-stage clustering

algorithm, Individual estimates of the position of the interferer achieved by UAVs are synthesized, by processing intersections of extensions of the trajectories. The contributions of this paper are listed as follows.

Firstly, a novel collaborative search and localization scheme based on reinforcement learning and two-stage clustering is presented for a swarm of UAVs to locate an interference source. Basically, the design of the proposed scheme aims at benefiting from the accuracy of localization and intelligence resulted from reinforcement-learning-based searching, as well as time efficiency of the remote localization. To this end, the proposed scheme merges reinforcement-learning-based searching and collaborative remote localization by alternatively performing a search phase and a localization phase over time intervals.

Secondly, for the search phase, a low-complexity reinforcement learning algorithm is proposed. During this phase, each UAV in the swarm can decide and evaluate its own direction of searching through reinforcement learning. In the localization phase, a novel two-stage clustering algorithm is proposed to find out the potential position of the interference source. Firstly, the two-stage clustering algorithm clusters UAVs' trajectories' intersections and decides whether to move a certain intersection into a candidate queue by performing the weighted clustering. Then, by performing the secondary clustering, the position of the interference source can be estimated.

Thirdly, in-depth simulation results are presented to demonstrate the performance of the proposed method. The effectiveness of the proposed collaborative search and localization scheme is confirmed. Numerical results show that compared to the Q-learning-based scheme, the proposed scheme is more time-efficient and can perform remote localization. It is also shown that by integrating reinforcement-learning-based searching with two-stage-clustering-based localization, the proposed scheme can improve the robustness and accuracy of the remote localization.

The remainder of this paper is organized as follows. Section 2 presents the system model. Section 3 proposes a collaborative interference source search and localization method, based on reinforcement learning and two-stage clustering. Simulation results are presented and analyzed in Sect. 4. Conclusions are drawn in Sect. 5.

2   System Model

In this paper, we aim at designing a time-efficient and accurate approach which applies a swarm of UAVs to search and locate a certain interference source, without a prior knowledge of the interference source model or the noise model. In the swarm, each UAV is equipped with an electronic scanning antenna which can be used to measure power of received signals from different directions. An example of the studied system is presented in Fig. 1.

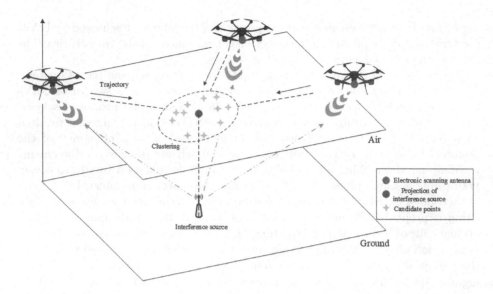

Fig. 1. Collaborative interference source search and location system with a swarm of UAVs.

2.1   Trajectory Model of UAVs

Suppose that in the swarm, the number of the UAVs is n. The time-varying coordinate of a certain UAV U_i at time interval $j-1$ can be designated as $(x_{j-1}^{(i)}, y_{j-1}^{(i)}, z_{j-1}^{(i)})$. The initial coordinate of a certain UAV U_i (for $i = 1, \ldots, n$) can be written as $(x_0^{(i)}, y_0^{(i)}, z_0^{(i)})$. We assume that each UAV flies in a straight line between two adjacent time intervals, and stays at a constant altitude $z_0^{(i)}$. Hence, the position of U_i at time interval j can be expressed as

$$x_j^{(i)} = x_{j-1}^{(i)} + l_j^{(i)} \cos \lambda_j^{(i)}, \tag{1}$$

$$y_j^{(i)} = y_{j-1}^{(i)} + l_j^{(i)} \sin \lambda_j^{(i)}, \tag{2}$$

$$z_j^{(i)} = z_0^{(i)}, \tag{3}$$

where $l_j^{(i)}$ represents the horizontal distance between horizontal coordinates $(x_{j-1}^{(i)}, y_{j-1}^{(i)})$ and $(x_j^{(i)}, y_j^{(i)})$; $\lambda_j^{(i)}$ is the angle between the x-axis and the direction UAV U_i flies towards. In this paper, we assume that $l_j^{(i)}$ is equal to l $\forall i, j$.

2.2   Receive Power Model of Electronic Scanning Antenna

In the studied scenario, each UAV is equipped with a three-demensional electronic scanning antenna to measure power of receive signals from horizontal,

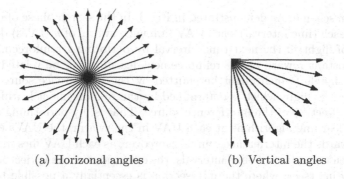

(a) Horizonal angles   (b) Vertical angles

Fig. 2. The detection range of an electronic scanning antenna.

as well as vertical, directions. Each electronic scanning antenna is able to measure u horizontal directions $\{\theta_1, \theta_2, \theta_3, \cdots, \theta_{u-1}, \theta_u\}$ and v vertical directions $\{\varphi_1, \varphi_2, \varphi_3, \cdots, \varphi_{v-1}, \varphi_v\}$, as shown in Fig. 2.

In our study, a UAV flies at a constant altitude and directions of flight vary only in the horizontal plane. Therefore, given a horizontal angle θ_i, although power of signals from different vertical angles $\{\varphi_1, \varphi_2, \varphi_3, \cdots, \varphi_{v-1}, \varphi_v\}$ can be different, only the maximum can be applied to making decisions on the horizontal direction of flight, which should be in the direction of the signal source. Therefore, let a set of $P_d(\theta_i, :)$ collects receive power values obtained at horizontal angle θ_i and all the vertical angles $\{\varphi_1, \varphi_2, \varphi_3, \cdots, \varphi_{v-1}, \varphi_v\}$, the final power value $P_f(\theta_i)$ (with respect to (w.r.t.) the horizontal angle θ_i) for making decisions on horizontal directions of flight can be defined as

$$P_f(\theta_i) = \max(P_d(\theta_i, :)), \forall \theta_i \in \{\theta_1, \theta_2, \theta_3, \ldots, \theta_{u-1}, \theta_u\}. \tag{4}$$

Benefit from the extended dimension (i.e. scanning in vertical directions), three-dimensional electronic scanning can achieve a higher detection accuracy than the two-dimensional electronic scanning, however, introducing higher computational complexity for further signal processing. By performing (4), the search of the direction of an interference source can be restricted to the range of horizontal angles.

3 Collaborative Search and Location

In this section, we propose and design a collaborative search and localization scheme, which consists of a search phase and a localization phase. As depicted in Fig. 3, the search phase and the localization phase are alternatively performed, where the former is based on reinforcement learning while the latter is based on two-stage clustering.

Prior to elaborating on the design of the reinforcement learning and the two-stage clustering algorithms, we concisely outline the collaborative search and localization scheme. As demonstrated in Fig. 3, in the search phase of every iteration (i.e. each time interval), each UAV (among a swarm of n UAVs) decides the direction of flight in the next time interval by performing reinforcement learning. The instant reward of the reinforcement learning can be related to power of receive signals (which might be emitted by the interference source). Hence, the direction of flight which is determined by the reinforcement learning can be a possible direction of the interference source. That is, by performing such reinforcement learning algorithms at each UAV in the swarm, the UAVs can search and fly towards the interference source. Moreover, as each UAV flies in a straight line between two adjacent time intervals, the extensions of the trajectories of two UAVs may intersect, where the intersection is essentially a possible position of the interference source. Due to the fact that the searching may suffer from noise and possibly multi-path interferences, extending the trajectories of the UAVs may achieve a large number of intersections. To find out the potential position of the interference source, the aforementioned intersections are processed by the proposed two-stage clustering algorithm during the localization phase. The two-stage clustering algorithm first cluster the intersections and make a decision whether to move a certain intersection into the candidate cluster. Then, by performing the secondary clustering, the position of the interference source can be estimated. The search phase and the localization phases will implement until the estimated position meet the terminating condition which is elaborated in the subsequent sections.

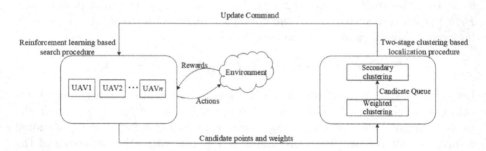

Fig. 3. The framework of collaborative search and localization based on reinforcement learning and two-stage clustering.

3.1   Reinforcement Learning Based Search

Searching According to Measured Power. Interference signals can be received by the UAV's electronic scanning antenna, and changes in measured power of the receive signals can indicate whether the distance between the UAV and the interference source is reduced. Therefore, for each UAV, in order to find out the position of the interference source, the direction of flight in each time interval can be selected according to measured power. Such a search problem (or decision problem on directions of flight in each time interval) can be equivalent to maximizing the expected long-term measured power, where the long-term measured power can be formulated as the discounted sum of all future rewards (i.e. measured power) at current time t. Such a problem can be modeled as a Markov Decision Process (MDP) problem [8], which aims at finding the optimal policy $\pi^{(i)}$ for each UAV U_i, so as to maximize the expectation of discounted sum of all future measured power, i.e. [7]

$$\max_{\pi^{(i)}} \mathbb{E}_{\pi^{(i)}} \left\{ \lim_{\mathcal{T} \to \infty} \sum_{t=0}^{\mathcal{T}} \gamma^t r^{(i)}(s^{(i)}, a^{(i)}) \right\}, \tag{5}$$

where $\gamma \in [0,1]$ denotes a discount factor; $a^{(i)}$ and $s^{(i)}$ represent UAV U_i's action and state, respectively. The action $a^{(i)} \in \{1, 2, 3, \cdots u\}$ selects direction of flights from a set of u possible flight directions $\{\theta_1, \theta_2, \cdots, \theta_u\}$, as shown in Fig. 2. The state $s^{(i)}$ is the direction selected by UAV U_i in the previous time interval, e.g. state $s_j^{(i)}$ in time interval j is the action $a_{j-1}^{(i)}$ in time interval $(j-1)$

$$s_j^{(i)} = a_{j-1}^{(i)}. \tag{6}$$

In (5), the reward $r^{(i)}(s^{(i)}, a^{(i)})$ is defined as

$$r^{(i)}(s^{(i)}, a^{(i)}) = \frac{1}{N} \sum_{k=1}^{N} D_k(s^{(i)}, \theta_{a^{(i)}}), \tag{7}$$

where $D_k(s^{(i)}, \theta_{a^{(i)}})$ is equal to measured power of a sample of signals received by the electronic scanning antenna at state $s^{(i)}$ and direction $\theta_{a^{(i)}}$ (which results from action $a^{(i)}$). As shown in (7), in order to alleviate effect of noise on measured power, power of N samples are averaged such that $\frac{1}{N} \sum_{k=1}^{N} D_k(s^{(i)}, \theta_{a^{(i)}})$.

Reinforcement Learning Algorithm. In order to solve problem (5), we propose a reinforcement learning algorithm based on Q-learning, which is a lookup-table-based approach [7]. By this means, the expectation of discounted sum of all future measured power can be recursively approximated. In this paper, in order to accelerate the convergence of Q-learning, we simultaneously update action values $Q^{(i)}(s^{(i)}, :)$ with various actions for a given state $s^{(i)}$. Hence, different from the conventional Q-learning, the update rule is given as

$$Q^{(i)}(s^{(i)}, :) \leftarrow Q^{(i)}(s^{(i)}, :) + \alpha[r^{(i)}(s^{(i)}, :) + \gamma Q^{(i)}(s^{'(i)}, :) - Q^{(i)}(s^{(i)}, :)], \tag{8}$$

where $Q^{(i)}(s^{(i)}, :)$ collects action values ranging from $Q^{(i)}(s^{(i)}, \theta_1)$ to $Q^{(i)}(s^{(i)}, \theta_u)$, which are the action values with current state $s^{(i)}$ and all possible actions. Similarly, $Q^{(i)}(s^{'(i)}, :)$ collects qualities of actions w.r.t. the previous state $s^{'(i)}$. In contrast to the reward in the conventional Q-learning [7], $r^{(i)}(s^{(i)}, :)$ in (8) collects not only the reward $r^{(i)}(s^{(i)}, a^{(i)})$, which results from taking action $a^{(i)}$, but also average power of samples measured at other directions by the electronic scanning antenna, i.e. $\frac{1}{N} \sum_{k=1}^{N} D_k(s^{(i)}, \theta)$ for all $\theta \neq \theta_{a^{(i)}}$

but belonging to $\{\theta_1, \theta_2, \cdots, \theta_u\}$. It means that by taking action $a^{(i)}$, the UAV arrives at a certain position and achieves the reward $r^{(i)}(s^{(i)}, a^{(i)})$ (for which the electronic scanning antenna receive signals from the direction of $\theta_{a^{(i)}}$); afterwards, signals from directions $\theta \neq \theta_{a^{(i)}}$ are detected by the electronic scanning antenna to obtain $r^{(i)}(s^{(i)}, :)$. Note that in this paper, we consider the scenario where γ and α for all UAVs are identical.

Once action values $Q^{(i)}(s^{(i)}, :)$ is updated, each UAV find the optimal action by performing

$$a^{(i)*} = \arg\max_{a^{(i)}} Q^i(s^{(i)}, a^{(i)}). \tag{9}$$

After action $a^{(i)*}$ is chosen at time interval j, each UAV flies in its direction $\theta_{a^{(i)}*}$ for a distance of l. The horizontal coordinate of each UAV is then updated as $(x_j^{(i)}, y_j^{(i)})$. The trajectory at time interval j for each UAV satisfies

$$y^{(i)} = \tan\theta_{a^{(i)}*}(x^{(i)} - x_j^{(i)}) + y_j^{(i)}, \tag{10}$$

where $\tan\theta_{a^{(i)}*}$ is related to the $\lambda_j^{(i)}$ in (1) and (2), while $(x_j^{(i)}, y_j^{(i)})$ stands for the UAV's current position.

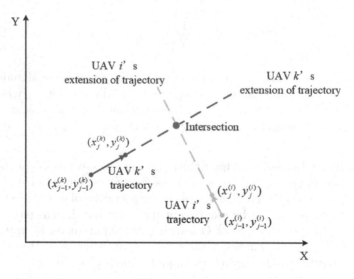

Fig. 4. Intersection of UAVs' trajectories at time interval j.

For a certain pair of UAVs, the extensions of their trajectories can intersect at time interval j, as shown in Fig. 4. Since UAVs fly towards the direction that can maximize the expectation of discounted sum of measured power, the intersection is essentially a potential position of the interference source. In general, the intersection of the extension of UAV U_i's trajectory and that of U_k's trajectory can be obtained by

$$p^{(i,k)} = \left(\frac{x_j^{(i)} \cdot \tan\theta_{a^{(i)*}} - x_j^{(k)} \cdot \tan\theta_{a^{(k)*}} + y_j^{(k)} - y_j^{(i)}}{\tan\theta_{a^{(i)*}} - \tan\theta_{a^{(k)*}}}, \right.$$

$$\left. \frac{\tan\theta_{a^{(i)*}} \cdot \tan\theta_{a^{(k)*}} \cdot (x_j^{(i)} - x_j^{(k)}) + \tan\theta_{a^{(i)*}} \cdot y_j^{(k)} - \tan\theta_{a^{(k)*}} \cdot y_j^{(i)}}{\tan\theta_{a^{(i)*}} - \tan\theta_{a^{(k)*}}} \right).$$

$$(11)$$

A weight is defined for each intersection, and the weight can be obtained as

$$w^{(i,k)} = \frac{Q^{(i)}(s^{(i)}, a^{(i)*}) \cdot Q^{(k)}(s^{(k)}, a^{(k)*})}{Q_0^{(i)}(s_0^{(i)}, a_0^{(i)*}) \cdot Q_0^{(k)}(s_0^{(k)}, a_0^{(k)*})}, \tag{12}$$

where $Q^i(s^{(i)}, a^{(i)*})$ and $Q^k(s^{(k)}, a^{(k)*})$ represent the maximum action values of U_i and U_k respectively at current state $s^{(i)}$ and $s^{(k)}$. $Q_0^{(i)}(s_0^{(i)}, a_0^{(i)*})$ and $Q_0^{(k)}(s_0^{(k)}, a_0^{(k)*})$ denote U_i and U_k's maximum action values obtained at the first state.

The intersections form a candidate set $\{p^{(i,k)}\}$ $(i, k \in [1, n], i < k)$ which is used as the input of the two-stage clustering algorithm for localization alone with the weight set $\{w^{(i,k)}\}$ $(i, k \in [1, n], i < k)$. The proposed reinforcement learning algorithm is summarized as a part of Algorithm 1.

3.2   Two-Stage Clustering Based Localization

Localization Based on Searching Results. As UAVs fly in straight line between two adjacent time intervals, the extensions of the trajectories of arbitrary two UAVs can intersect, where the intersection essentially constitutes a possible position of the interference source. In this paper, we study the scenario where there is only one interference source. Intuitively, in the ideal case, the intersection of the extensions of trajectories of UAVs is unique. Unfortunately, due to the noise, multi-path effect, etc., there can be a large number of intersections.

Thus, aiming at estimating the most possible position of the interference based on the intersections found in the search phase, the localization problem boils down to a clustering problem [4,10] , which can be cast as

$$\min_{P^T} \frac{1}{|C|} \sum_{(i,k)\in C} w^{(i,k)} \cdot \left\| P^{(i,k)} - P^T \right\|, \tag{13}$$

where P^T is an estimate of the position of the interference source; and P^T minimizes the weighted sum of Euclidean distance between an arbitrary intersection point $p^{(i,k)}$ and P^T. In (13), the set C collects all potential $p^{(i,k)}$ found in the search phase; and $|C|$ is the cardinality of C.

Algorithm 1. The proposed collaborative search and localization

1: Initialize the number of UAVs n;
2: Initialize flight direction set $d = \{1, 2, 3 \cdots, u\}$;
3: Initialize learning rate α, discount factor γ and step length l;
4: Set iteration number $j = 1$, operation command $f = false$;
5: **for** $i = 1 \rightarrow n$ **do**
6:    Initialize UAV U_i's position $\left(x_0^{(i)}, y_0^{(i)}, z^{(i)}\right)$;
7:    Initialize $Q^{(i)}(:,:)$ and $r^{(i)}(:,:)$ to $\mathbf{0}$ (i.e. a zero matrix);
8:    Select an initial state $s_0^{(i)} = randi(d)$;
9: **end for**
10: **repeat**
11:    **for** $i = 1 \rightarrow n$ **do**
12:       Obtain measured values and update reward table r^i according to (26);
13:       Update action values $Q^{(i)}(s^{(i)}, :)$ according to (8);
14:       Select action $a^{(i)*} = \arg\max_{a^{(i)}}(Q^i(s^{(i)}, a^{(i)}))$;
15:       Update current state $s^{(i)} \leftarrow a^{(i)*}$;
16:       Update U_i's position $\left(x_j^{(i)}, y_j^{(i)}, z^{(i)}\right)$ according to (1) and (2);
17:       Compute U_i's trajectory according to (9);
18:    **end for**
19:    $j = j + 1$;
20:    Obtain candidate set $\left\{p^{(i,k)}\right\}(i, k \in [1, n], i < k)$ and weight set $\left\{w^{(i,k)}\right\}(i, k \in [1, n], i < k)$ according to (11) and (12) for two-stage clustering based localization;
21:    **do** two-stage clustering (which is shown in **Algorithm 2**);
22:    Obtain operation command f;
23: **until** $f = true$

Two-Stage Clustering Algorithm. The proposed two-stage clustering algorithm is performed provided the UAV's reward $r^{(i)}(s_j^{(i)}, :)$ (which collects measured power of signals in directions of $\theta_1, \ldots, \theta_u$) satisfies a constraint in the coefficient of variation:

$$\frac{\overline{r^{(i)}(s_j^{(i)}, :)}}{\sigma(r^{(i)}(s_j^{(i)}, :))} < \lambda, \tag{14}$$

where $\sigma(r^{(i)}(s_j^{(i)}, :))$ and $\overline{r^{(i)}(s_j^{(i)}, :)}$ represent the standard deviation and the mean of $r^{(i)}(s_j^{(i)}, :)$, respectively. The coefficient of variation i.e. the ratio of $\frac{\overline{r^{(i)}(s_j^{(i)}, :)}}{\sigma(r^{(i)}(s_j^{(i)}, :))}$ evaluates volatility of $r^{(i)}(s_j^{(i)}, :)$ at time interval j. Given a small value of λ, a certain $r^{(i)}(s_j^{(i)}, :)$ satisfying (14) means that $r^{(i)}(s_j^{(i)}, :)$ suffers less noise or multi-path interference. As a consequence, the direction (i.e. action $a^{(i)*}$) of flight obtained by the reinforcement-learning-based searching algorithm can be (nearly) aligned with the direction of the interference. Therefore, at a certain time interval j, only in the case where both $r^{(i)}(s_j^{(i)}, :)$ and $r^{(k)}(s_j^{(k)}, :)$ (of UAVs U_i and U_k, respectively) satisfy (14), can the intersection $p^{(i,k)}$ resulted from extensions of the trajectories of UAV U_i and U_k be collected in the set C and reliable for localization.

Prior to the clustering, in each time interval, an estimate of the position of the interference source is obtained. At a certain time interval j, the estimate can be achieved by

$$P_j = \frac{1}{|C|} \sum_{(i,k) \in C} p^{(i,k)} . \tag{15}$$

Each P_j is associated with a weight ω_j, which can be obtained by

$$\omega_j = \frac{1}{1 + e^{-\frac{1}{N} \sum_{(i,k) \in C} w^{(i,k)} + 1}}, \tag{16}$$

where $w^{(i,k)}$ is obtained by computing (12). Equation (16) suggests that ω_j is essentially a normalized weight achieved by processing $\frac{1}{N} \sum_{(i,k) \in C} w^{(i,k)}$ with a sigmoid function. By applying the sigmoid function, the value of the $w^{(i,k)}$ can be limited in the range of $(0.5, 1)$. We define sets C' and W' to respectively collect P_j (which is obtained by (15)) and ω_j (which is obtained by (16)) computed in each time interval j.

Weighted Clustering. In order to perform weighted clustering, a weighted distance matrix M is firstly defined and computed with elements in sets C' and W'.

$$M = \begin{pmatrix} \frac{\|P_\varphi - P_\varphi\|}{\sqrt{\omega_\varphi \cdot \omega_\varphi}} & \cdots & \frac{\|P_\varphi - P_\eta\|}{\sqrt{\omega_\varphi \cdot \omega_\eta}} \\ \vdots & \ddots & \vdots \\ \frac{\|P_\eta - P_\varphi\|}{\sqrt{\omega_\eta \cdot \omega_\eta}} & \cdots & \frac{\|P_\eta - P_\eta\|}{\sqrt{\omega_\eta \cdot \omega_\varphi}} \end{pmatrix}, \tag{17}$$

where $P_\varphi, P_\eta \in C'$ for $\varphi < \eta$. Row i (for $i \in [0, \eta - \varphi]$) of matrix M collects distances between element a certain $P_i \in C'$ and all the elements in C'. For instance, as shown in the first row (i.e. $i = 1$) of matrix M in (17), P_1 w.r.t. row 1 is equal to P_φ. Elements in each row of M is arranged in ascending order. In order to evaluate the possibility that P_i $\forall i$ is equal to the coordinate of the interference source, we define a metric for each row, i.e.

$$\varepsilon_i = \sum_{k=0}^{\lceil \phi \cdot (\eta - \varphi) \rceil} M(i, k), \tag{18}$$

where ϕ is a decimal. Equation (18) illustrates that for row i, ε_i is equal to the sum of elements in columns $0, 1, \ldots, \lceil \phi \cdot (\eta - \varphi) \rceil$. We perform (18) for each row. Then, according to the ordering of ε_i $\forall i$ (which are then sorted in ascending order), in the matrix M, we can find κ^l rows which correspond to the κ^l smallest ε_i values among all the ε_i values. By this means, we essentially find κ^l potential positions (or coordinates) of the interference source. We then compute the centroid of the κ^l potential coordinates by performing

$$ P_j' = \frac{1}{\kappa^l} \sum_{i=1}^{\kappa^l} P_i, \tag{19} $$

where P_i denotes the coordinate w.r.t. the ith smallest ε_i value. Moreover, P_j' is the result of weighted clustering at time interval j.

Secondary Clustering. In order to further improve the accuracy of localization, we propose the method of secondary clustering. In the proposed secondary clustering, a candidate queue q is defined. Once the weighted clustering achieves an estimate of the position P_j' of the interference source at time interval j, P_j' is collected in candidate queue q for secondary clustering with the size of k_q. The diagram of candidate queue q is shown in Fig. 5.

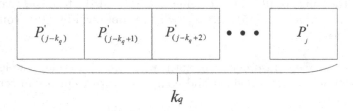

Fig. 5. Candidate queue collects outputs of the weighted clustering, where the maximum length of the queue is equal to k_q.

Suppose that the number of elements in candidate queue q is k_e. In the presence of $k_e < k_q$, P_j' achieved by the weighted clustering at time interval j can be directly pushed into queue q. Otherwise, the queue will firstly be popped before P_j' is pushed. Thus, candidate queue q can be viewed as a cluster of points obtained within the latest k_q intervals.

Similarly to matrix M in (17), a distance matrix M' is computed with elements in queue q. In the matrix, each element is equal to the distance between arbitrary two coordinates in candidate queue q. Matrix M' is obtained as

$$
M' = \begin{pmatrix} \left\| P'_{(j-k_e)} - P'_{(j-k_e)} \right\| & \cdots & \left\| P'_{(j-k_e)} - P'_j \right\| \\ \vdots & \ddots & \vdots \\ \left\| P'_j - P'_{(j-k_e)} \right\| & \cdots & \left\| P'_j - P'_j \right\| \end{pmatrix} \tag{20}
$$

where k_e (for $k_e \leq k_q$) stands for the number of elements collected in queue q at time interval j. We then sort elements in each row of M' in ascending order. Similarly to (18), we define a metric to evaluate the possibility of coordinates in queue q being the position of the interference source. Such a metric can be defined as

$$
\varepsilon'_i = \sum_{k=0}^{\lfloor k_t \rfloor} M'(i, k). \tag{21}
$$

Equation (21) illustrates that for row i of matrix M', ε'_i is equal to the sum of elements in columns $0, 1, \ldots, \lfloor k_t \rfloor$. By performing (21) for each row, we can find the κ' smallest ε'_i values. According to the definition of M', each one of the κ' smallest ε'_i values corresponds to a coordinate of P'_i in the candidate queue q. Hence, by finding the κ' smallest ε'_i, we basically find κ' coordinates which are close to each other and therefore can be used to estimate the position of the interference source. We then compute the centroid of the κ' coordinates, yielding

$$
P^T_j = \frac{1}{\kappa'} \sum_{i=1}^{\kappa'} P'_i. \tag{22}
$$

Hence, P^T_j is the result of secondary clustering at time interval j. P^T_j is selected as estimated coordinate of the position of the interference source when P^T_j converges over iterations (i.e. time intervals). In this work, if the standard deviation σ w.r.t. the latest three estimated coordinates $\left\{ P^T_j, P^T_{(j-1)}, P^T_{(j-2)} \right\}$ satisfies

$$
\sigma \left(\left\{ \left\| P^T_j - P^T_{(j-1)} \right\|, \left\| P^T_j - P^T_{(j-2)} \right\|, \left\| P^T_{(j-1)} - P^T_{(j-2)} \right\| \right\} \right) \leqslant \beta, \tag{23}
$$

the collaborative search and localization terminates, and P^T_j is output as an estimate of the position of the interference source. The proposed two-stage clustering is summarized in Algorithm 2.

Algorithm 2. Two-stage Clustering Algorithm

1: Obtain the result of the reinforcement learning: candidate set $\left\{p^{(i,k)}\right\}(i,k \in$
   $[1,n], i < k)$ and weight set $\left\{w^{(i,k)}\right\}(i,k \in [1,n], i < k)$;
2: Obtain current iteration number j and operation command f;
3: **for** $i = 1 \to n$, $k = i + 1 \to n$ **do**
4:    **if** UAV U_i and U_k satisfy (14); **then**
5:       $C = C \cup \{(i,k)\}$;
6:       $flag = true$;
7:    **end if**
8: **end for**
9: **if** $flag$ **then**
10:    Compute P_j and w_j by performing (15) and (16);
11:    $C' = C' \cup P_j, W' = W' \cup \omega_j$;
12:    Compute the weighted distance matrix M by performing (17);
13:    Sort elements in each row of M in ascending order;
14:    Evaluate each row's metric ε_i through (18);
15:    Find the κ^l smallest metric avlues ε_i and the corresponding κ^l coordinates
       belonging to C';
16:    Obtain the output P_j' of the weighted clustering by performing (19);
17:    **if** $length(q) = k_q$ **then**
18:       Pop candidate queue q;
19:    **end if**
20:    Push P_j' into candidate queue q;
21:    Form distance matrix M' by performing (20);
22:    Sort elements in each row of M' in ascending order;
23:    Evaluate each row's metric ε_i' through (21);
24:    Find the κ' smallest metric avlues ε_i' and the corresponding κ' coordinates
       belonging to queue q;
25:    Obtain the output P_j^T of the secondary clustering by performing (22);
26: **end if**
27: **if** P_j^T satisfies the stopping criterion (23) **then**
28:    $f = true$;
29: **end if**

---

4   Simulation Results

In the simulations, we consider an interference source located at (5000 m, 2885 m, 0 m) with transmit power of 20 W and a swarm of three UAVs. Initial positions of the UAVs are set as (0 m, 0 m, 200 m), (5100 m, 8660 m, 190 m) and (10000 m, 0 m, 190 m), respectively. Each UAV is equipped with an electronic scanning antenna to locate the interference source. The electronic scanning antennas have the same radiation characteristic (as shown in Fig. 6), which is given by

$$F(\theta) = \cos(\frac{\pi}{2}\sin\theta) \cdot \cos(\pi\sin\theta) \cdot \cos[\frac{\pi}{4}(\cos\theta - 1)]. \tag{24}$$

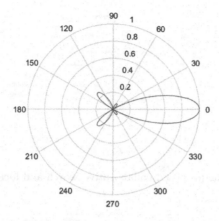

Fig. 6. Horizontal direction characteristics of the antennas.

Therefore, the receive gain $G_R(\theta)$ of each electronic scanning antenna for the horizontal angle θ and elevation angle φ is represented as follows:

$$G_R(\theta) = \frac{4\pi\eta F^2(\theta)}{\int_0^{\frac{\pi}{2}} \int_0^{2\pi} F^2(\theta) \sin\varphi d\varphi d\theta}, \tag{25}$$

where $\varphi \in [0, \frac{\pi}{2}]$, $\theta \in [0, 2\pi)$ and the antenna efficiency $\eta = 1$. Thus, received power at each antenna can be obtained as

$$P_R(\theta) = \frac{P_T G_T G_R(\theta)\lambda^2}{(4\pi)^2 d^2 L} + n^2, \tag{26}$$

where P_T and G_T represent transmit power of the interference source and transmit antenna gain, respectively. The wave length λ is set as 3 m; the loss factor L is set as 1; n^2 stands for power of noise signal, which is a random variable with an average value of -38 dBm. In Algorithm 1, the learning rate α and discount factor γ in (8) are set as 0.9 and 0.1, respectively. In the two-stage clustering, λ in (14) is set as 2, and k_q for secondary clustering in Algorithm 2 is set as 30.

Two baseline schemes are considered in our study. The first one performs searching based on the reinforcement learning algorithm proposed in Sect. 3.1. This baseline is designated as Q-learning for simplicity in the subsequent discussions. The other scheme integrates Maximum-dimensional-based Search (MRS) with Two-Stage-Clustering-based Localization (TSCL). That is, similarly to the proposed collaborative search and localization, this baseline scheme consists of a search phase and a localization phase. However, in each time interval of the search, each UAV measures power of signals in different directions. Then, the UAV flies towards the direction w.r.t. the maximum measured power. In the localization phase, the UAV performs two-stage clustering as in Algorithm 2. This baseline scheme is then designated as MRS-TSCL.

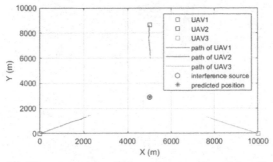

(a) The proposed collaborative search and location.

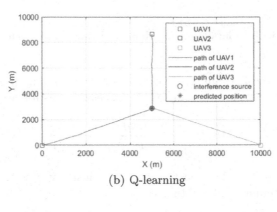

(b) Q-learning

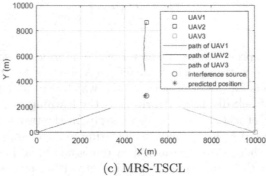

(c) MRS-TSCL

Fig. 7. UAVs' trajectories achieved by different approaches.

Figure 7 depicts UAVs' trajectories achieved by different approaches. The comparison of Fig. 7(a) and Fig. 7(b) indicates that although Q-learning-based search can find the interference source, the proposed collaborative search and location based on reinforcement learning and two-stage clustering can be more time-efficient, in terms of locating the interference source.

Additionally, it can be seen that compared to the proposed collaborative search and location scheme, MRS-TSCL suffers from a longer flight distance and degradation in the accuracy of localization. This suggests that the proposed reinforcement learning as in Algorithm 1 can benefit the localization phase, in terms of the accuracy of localization.

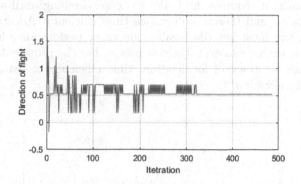

Fig. 8. Directions of flight as a function of number of iterations.

Figure 8 investigates directions (which are horizontal angles) of flight as a function of iterations. It is shown that the direction of flight w.r.t. a certain UAV converges as the number of iterations increases. This confirms the convergence of the proposed reinforcement learning. Moreover, it can be seen from Fig. 8 that the proposed reinforcement learning algorithm terminates before 500 iterations, since the stopping criterion has been reached. This implies that the prerequisite of the two-stage clustering algorithm termination is the convergence of the proposed reinforcement learning approach.

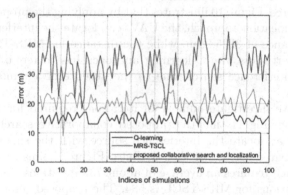

Fig. 9. Localization error of different approaches.

Figure 9 compares the proposed collaborative search and localization approach to baseline schemes, in terms of localization error. As shown in Fig. 9, we
repeat simulation 100 times. The numerical results indicate that the localization
error achieved by the proposed collaborative search and localization approach,
Q-learning and MRS-TSCL is 20.39 m, 14.94 m and 32.98 m, respectively. It is
worth noting that although the Q-learning approach yields the best localization
error performance, it requires the UAVs to keep searching until arriving at the
interference source and therefore degrades time efficiency. Additionally, it can
be found that the most volatile localization error performance is achieved by
MRS-TSCL. Hence, we can draw the conclusion that the proposed approach can
well balance the accuracy of localization, time efficiency of searching and the
robustness of localization.

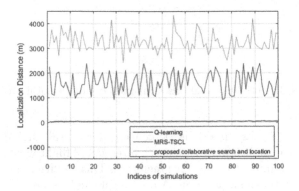

Fig. 10. Localization distance of different approaches.

Figure 10 studies the localization distance, which is the distance between the
interference source and the position (of a UAV) where the UAV can locate the
interference source. Figure 10 illustrates that by applying the proposed collaborative search and location approach, the UAVs can locate the interference source at
an average distance of 3225.98 m, while the distance for MRS-TSCL is around
1687.64 m. Nevertheless, the Q-learning approach has to require the UAVs to
arrive at the interference source, due to the absence of a remote localization
method.

In Fig. 11, we investigate number of iterations required for localization. It
can be seen from Fig. 11 that the proposed collaborative search and localization approach can locate the interference source with the smallest number of
iterations, compared to that of the baselines. Figure 11 illustrates that the Q-
learning approach requires an average of about 733 iterations, while the average
number of iterations for MRS-TSCL is 584. The proposed collaborative search
and localization approach, on the other hand, requires only an average of about
378 iterations.

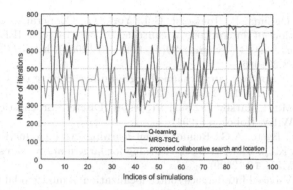

Fig. 11. Number of iterations required for localization.

5 Conclusion

In this paper, we have proposed a novel collaborative search and localization scheme, which exploits a swarm of UAVs to locate an interference source. The proposed approach iteratively performs search and remote localization. In the search phase of each time interval, a computationally efficient reinforcement learning algorithm is proposed to decide the trajectory of each UAV. In the following localization phase of the time interval, a two-stage clustering algorithm has been developed to process the intersections of the extensions of UAVs' trajectories, so as to estimate the position of the interference source. Simulation results have revealed that the proposed approach can accurately locate the position of a interference source from a distance, while the conventional Q-learning can achieve slightly higher localization accuracy at a significant cost of time efficiency. Moreover, by integrating reinforcement learning with two-stage clustering, the accuracy of remote localization can be improved.

References

1. Bayerlein, H., Kerret, P., Gesbert, D.: Trajectory optimization for autonomous flying base station via reinforcement learning, pp. 1–5, June 2018. https://doi.org/10.1109/SPAWC.2018.8445768
2. Jiang, C., Zhu, X.: Reinforcement learning based capacity management in multilayer satellite networks. IEEE Trans. Wireless Commun. **19**(7), 4685–4699 (2020)
3. Lemic, F., Bsch, J., Chwalisz, M., Handziski, V., Wolisz, A.: Infrastructure for benchmarking RF-based indoor localization under controlled interference. In: 2014 Ubiquitous Positioning Indoor Navigation and Location Based Service (UPINLBS), pp. 26–35, November 2014. https://doi.org/10.1109/UPINLBS.2014.7033707
4. Macqueen, J.: Some methods for classification and analysis of multivariate observations. In: Proceedings of Berkeley Symposium on Mathematical Statistics & Probability (1965)
5. Maeda, K., Doki, S., Funabora, Y., Doki, K.: Flight path planning of multiple UAVs for robust localization near infrastructure facilities. In: IECON 2018–44th Annual Conference of the IEEE Industrial Electronics Society, pp. 2522–2527 (2018)

6. Pack, D.J., DeLima, P., Toussaint, G.J., York, G.: Cooperative control of UAVs for localization of intermittently emitting mobile targets. IEEE Trans. Syst. Man Cybern. Part B (Cybern.) **39**(4), 959–970 (2009). https://doi.org/10.1109/TSMCB.2008.2010865

7. Powell, W.B.: Approximate Dynamic Programming: Solving the Curses of Dimensionality, vol. 703. Wiley, Hoboken (2007)

8. Puterman, M.L.: Markov Decision Processes: Discrete Stochastic Dynamic Programming. Wiley, Hoboken (1994)

9. Sutton, R.S., Barto, A.G.: Reinforcement learning: An introduction (1998)

10. Weinberger, K.Q.: Distance metric learning for large margin nearest neighbor classification. JMLR **10** (2009)

11. Wu, G.: UAV-based interference source localization: a multimodal Q-learning approach. IEEE Access **7**, 137982–137991 (2019)

12. Wu, S.: Illegal radio station localization with UAV-based Q-learning. China Commun. **15**(12), 122–131 (2018)

A New Joint Tracking Method of BeiDou B1C Signal and Its Influence on Signal Quality Evaluation

Zhenyuan Hao[1,2], Chengyan He[1(✉)], Ji Guo[1,3], Xiaochun Lu[1,3], Yongnan Rao[1], and Meng Wang[1,2]

[1] National Time Service Center, Chinese Academy of Science, Xi'an 710600, China
hechengyan@ntsc.ac.cn
[2] School of Electronics, Chinese Academy of Science University, Beijing 101408, China
[3] School of Astronomy and Space Science, University of Chinese Academy of Sciences, Beijing 100098, China

Abstract. Aiming at the problem of low accuracy of traditional open-loop tracking and long time-consuming of closed-loop tracking, this paper proposes a joint open-loop and closed-loop tracking method of BeiDou B1C signal, which not only ensures the tracking accuracy but also greatly reduces the time-consuming of signal tracking. To verify the effectiveness and feasibility of the proposed algorithm, this paper uses the 40-m large aperture antenna system of Haoping observation station to collect the measured satellite signal data for verification and makes in-depth analysis from tracking time-consuming, correlation peak, correlation loss, zero-crossing deviation of S-curve, code and carrier phase consistency, etc. The results show that under the condition of the same tracking parameters when the data length ratio of the open-loop and the closed-loop parts is 9:1, the time of the method is saved about 90% compared with the closed-loop tracking method; at the same time, the difference of the three evaluation parameters is within 1%, which verifies the effectiveness and feasibility of the proposed method. The research results can provide a theoretical basis and technical support for parallel processing of navigation signals and automatic quasi-real-time signal quality monitoring and evaluation in the future.

Keywords: Open-closed-loop joint tracking · Closed-loop tracking · BeiDou B1C navigation signal · Signal quality evaluation

1 Introduction

As the link between satellite and user, the performance of the satellite navigation signal directly determines the service performance of the satellite navigation system, such as positioning, navigation, timing, and so on. Navigation signal quality monitoring and evaluation can provide important technical means and support for navigation system signal design and key technology on-orbit verification, and provide decision support

Q. Wu et al. (Eds.): WiSATS 2020, LNICST 357, pp. 449–467, 2021.
https://doi.org/10.1007/978-3-030-69069-4_37

information for system performance maintenance and management. It is an important means to ensure the safety, integrity, stability, and reliability of the satellite navigation system. Therefore, the monitoring and evaluation of navigation signal quality are one of the important links in the design and operation of the satellite navigation system.

To realize the interoperability with GPS L1C and Galileo E1: OS signals, the Bei-Dou B1C signal adopts Quadrature Multiplexed Binary Offset Carrier(QMBOC) modulation, the power spectral density, and autocorrelation function of QMBOC signal are the same as that of TMBOC signal, compared with the Time-Multiplexed Binary Offset Carrier(TMBOC) modulation signal, the receiver of QMBOC eliminates the switching circuit of time-division multiplexing locally, and they have the same performance under the condition of matching reception;

The design of Composite Binary Offset Carrier (CBOC) modulation signal determines that the power of its pilot component and data component is equal, while the power ratio of QMBOC signal components among different channels can be different, only the total power can meet the definition of normalized power spectral density of Multiplexing Binary Offset Carrier(MBOC) modulation signal, and its implementation mode is more flexible.

Before demodulating and fine analysis of satellite navigation signals, it is necessary to capture and track the signals. The tracking accuracy and time consuming directly affect the subsequent analysis and processing accuracy and data processing efficiency. Conventional closed-loop tracking takes the signal master code period as the loop phase and frequency identification period, and periodically adjusts the frequency and phase of carrier and code. Due to the loop input and output of data in each cycle, this method has high tracking accuracy, but the huge amount of computation and long-time consumption are not conducive to quasi-real-time signal analysis. The traditional open-loop tracking is based on the code phase shift and Doppler frequency shift obtained in the acquisition phase. The frequency and phase of carrier and code are directly used in the signal tracking phase through the least square estimation, Kalman filter, and other methods fitting. The computation is small and the time is short, but the error of various fitting models leads to poor tracking accuracy. In literature [1], the least square method and Kalman filtering method were used to optimize the estimation of the carrier frequency and the rough value of the code phase, which improved the estimation accuracy to a certain extent, but still could not achieve good stable tracking of the measured data. A JOINT GPS/Galileo tracking method based on maximum likelihood estimation was proposed in the literature [2]. Kalman filter is used to reduce noise and improve loop stability by using the error of code phase and frequency estimation generated by MLE, but the actual performance is not analyzed. Literature analyzes closed-loop serial processing and open-loop parallel processing [3] and verifies by combining INS and GPS deep combination system. Compared with the closed-loop system, the accuracy is not improved, but the complexity of the algorithm is increased. Literature adopts the methods of open-loop capture and closed-loop tracking to ensure tracking accuracy [4], but it takes a long time. To make up for these shortcomings, a new BeiDou open-closed-loop joint tracking method for the B1C signal is proposed. This method not only has good tracking accuracy but also can greatly improve the computing efficiency.

2 BeiDou B1C Signal Characteristics

The B1C signal is no longer a single signal, but a composite signal containing data and pilot channels. Among them, the data channel modulation has navigation message data, which can be used for pseudo-range measurement and navigation information solution, while the pilot channel does not modulate navigation information, but is only composed of spread spectrum code modulated by the carrier. In this way, the design can increase the coherence integration time at the receiving end and be used for pseudo-range measurement with higher accuracy [5]. B1C signal has higher tracking accuracy and anti-multi-path, anti-interference ability.

The power ratio of the B1C data component S_d and the pilot component S_p signal is 1:3. The data component was modulated with BOC(1, 1), and the pilot channel was modulated with QMBOC(6, 1, 4/33) orthogonal multiplexing of the high-frequency component BOC(6, 1) and the low-frequency BOC(1, 1) [6]. B1C signal structure is shown in Table 1 below:

Table 1. Signal structure of B1C

Component	Modulation		Phase relationship	Power ratio
$s_{B1C\_data}(t)$	Sine BOC (1, 1)		0	1/4
$s_{B1C\_pilot\_a}(t)$	QMBOC (6, 1, 4/33)	Sine BOC (1, 1)	90	29/44
$s_{B1C\_pilot\_b}(t)$		Sine BOC (6, 1)	0	1/11

B1C signal baseband form can be expressed as:

$$S_{B1C}(t) = \frac{1}{2}S_d + j\frac{\sqrt{3}}{2}S_p = \frac{1}{2}D_d \times C_d \times sign(\sin(2\pi fS\_dt))$$
$$+ \sqrt{\frac{1}{11}}C_p \times sign(\sin(2\pi fS\_bt))$$
$$+ j\sqrt{\frac{29}{44}}C_p \times sign(\sin(2\pi fS\_at)) \qquad (1)$$

Where $D(t)$ is the navigation data stream, $C_d(t)$ is the data component spread spectrum code, $C_p(t)$ is the pilot component spread spectrum code, fS_a is the subcarrier frequency of narrow-band S_{pa}, and fS_b is the subcarrier frequency of narrow-band S_{pb}. $sign(\cdot)$ is a sign function.

3 Software Receiver Tracking Method

3.1 Principle of Open-Loop Tracking

The principle of open-loop tracking is shown in Fig. 1. $s_{IF}(n)$ is the input digital intermediate frequency signal, τ is the code phase offset of the input signal, f is the Doppler frequency offset of the input signal, φ is the estimated carrier phase error value, i is the resulting signal of I-branch mixing, i_p is the correlation result, I_p is the coherent integral value, and f_{clock} is the driving clock frequency.

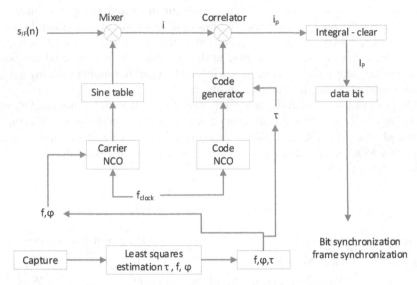

Fig. 1. Schematic diagram of open-loop tracking

The input signal is acquired by traditional acquisition to obtain rough Doppler frequency and code phase estimation value. Then, the least square criterion is used to fit the quadratic polynomial, and the peak value of the fitting curve is selected as the correction value of the Doppler frequency and code phase. The modified Doppler frequency, code phase, and carrier phase are output to the subsequent bit synchronization, frame synchronization, and other processing modules as the result of open-loop tracking [7].

The amplitude of the complex coherent integral value is:

$$V(\tau_e, f_e) = aR(\tau_e)|\sin c(f_e T_{coh})| + \varepsilon_n \tag{2}$$

Where, T_{coh} is coherent integration time, τ_e and f_e are doppler frequency and code phase estimation errors respectively, $R(\cdot)$ is code autocorrelation function, and $\sin c(\cdot)$ is energy fading function caused by Doppler frequency error. For the estimation of the Doppler frequency shift. It can be seen from the formula of complex coherent integral value that the profile of coherent integral value at any code phase is the result of function superposition noise, so the quadratic polynomial of linear least square fitting is used for parameter fitting.

3.2   Closed-Loop Tracking Principle

After the satellite signal is captured, the rough estimates of carrier frequency and code phase of the current satellite signal are obtained. However, due to the change of Doppler effect caused by the relative motion between satellite and receiver and the change of relative acceleration, as well as the frequency offset between satellite clock and receiver clock crystal oscillator, the carrier frequency and code phase of the received satellite signal will change unpredictably with time. Therefore, it is necessary to process the satellite signal in the loop, that is, code tracking and carrier tracking. The specific tracking principle is shown in Fig. 2.

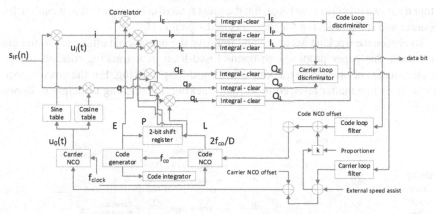

Fig. 2. Schematic diagram of closed-loop tracking

Carrier loop and code loop work simultaneously and coordinate with each other. Carrier loops with higher accuracy will carry out carrier assistance to the code loops at the frequency discrimination result, to eliminate the dynamic stress on the code loops and realize better loop tracking [8]. carrier loop is generally composed of a discriminator, loop filter, and Numerical Control Oscillator (NCO). THE Digital IF signal s_{IF} at I, Q is multiplied by sine and cosine respectively on the two branches, mixed with the local duplicated carrier signal (multiplied) to realize carrier separation, then the output signal is sent to the carrier loop discriminator for frequency identification, then it enters the filter to filter, finally, the output result is sent to the carrier NCO to calculate the phase difference, to adjust the local duplicated carrier signal and connect the local duplicated signal The phase difference between the received signals is always 0 to keep the continuous tracking of the signals. In the navigation receiver, Costas phase-locked loop is generally used, which is not sensitive to modulation data.

In the stage of carrier loop and code loop processing, the data of one main code cycle length is read each time for data analysis, and finally, the carrier phase difference is obtained to adjust the local recurrence signal of each loop and the received signal phase time to be consistent. The advantage of closed-loop in tracking is that the data of each main code cycle length is frequently discriminated against to ensure a high tracking accuracy.

3.3 Open-Closed-Loop Joint Tracking Mode

At present, the commonly used software and hardware receivers for satellite navigation signal processing are all based on the closed-loop tracking mode, which has the advantage of being able to achieve high-precision and stable tracking of signals. However, the loop calculation is large and time-consuming, which is not conducive to quasi-real-time data analysis. Compared with the traditional closed-loop tracking method, the biggest difference of open-loop tracking is that the τ, f and φ obtained from the least square estimation are directly used for the tracking of subsequent data, rather than the feedback of the code phase and Doppler frequency output value to the tracking loop for frequency discrimination correction and output [9, 10]. The biggest advantage of open-loop tracking is that it saves a lot of time and cost, but the most fatal disadvantage is that it can't achieve accurate and stable tracking for the measured signal [11].

To ensure the tracking accuracy and improve the operational efficiency to the greatest extent, this paper proposes an open-closed-loop joint tracking method based on the advantages of open-loop tracking and closed-loop tracking. For the convenience of explanation, hereinafter referred to as joint tracking, the tracking principle is shown in Fig. 3.

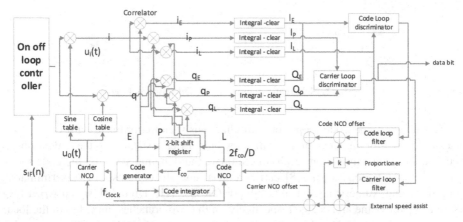

Fig. 3. Schematic diagram of open-closed-loop joint tracking mode

Generally, since the difference of carrier phase and the adjustment parameters of the code loop are very small for the data of tens or hundreds of milliseconds after the signal enters the stable tracking stage, a loop controller can be added to the feedback loop of the code loop and the carrier loop to realize the joint tracking of open-loop and closed-loop tracking. Because the frequency discrimination times of carrier loop and code loop are reduced, the tracking time of the signal is greatly reduced.

The loop control principle is shown in Fig. 4. First, set the open-loop interval according to the signal characteristics and data quality, for example, 100 ms. The loop input signal $s_{IF}(n)$ first judges the tracking mode adopted by the data of the period length of the main code through the loop controller. If the open-loop tracking is adopted, the loop output parameters of the previous closed-loop tracking will be assigned to the current open-loop tracking. If the closed-loop tracking is adopted, the normal tracking will be conducted according to the flow shown in Fig. 2, and finally a complete loop will be formed. The main function of the closed-loop tracking is to adjust the phase and frequency of the locally repeated carrier and code through the periodic output of the loop, so that it is strictly consistent with the frequency and phase of the input signal, to achieve a high-precision tracking effect.

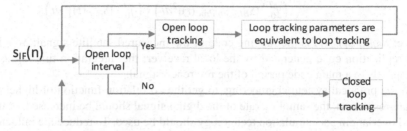

Fig. 4. Schematic diagram of the loop controller

The input and output signals of the loop are expressed as follows:

$$u_i(t) = U_i \sin(\omega_i t + \theta_i) \tag{3}$$

$$u_0(t) = U_0 \sin(\omega_0 t + \theta_0) \tag{4}$$

$u_i(t)$ and $u_0(t)$ represent the input and output signals of the loop discriminator respectively, and U_i, U_0 represent the signal amplitude of the input and output signals of the loop discriminator respectively. The angular frequency ω_i and the initial phase θ_i of the input signal and the angular frequency ω_0 and the initial phase θ_0 of the output signal are both functions of time.

The open-loop tracking and closed-loop tracking are organically combined by the open-closed-loop controller. The closed-loop tracking part ensures the tracking accuracy, and the open-loop tracking part reduces the tracking time. The advantages of the two are combined by the open-closed-loop controller.

4 Main Parameters of Signal Quality Evaluation

4.1 Correlation Peak

The distortion of the received navigation satellite signal chip waveform is not only reflected in the amplitude attenuation of the correlation output but also causes the deformation of the correlation function [12]. The pseudo-range error caused by the distortion of the received signal can directly reflect the abnormality of the correlation function. Using the correlation curve, we can evaluate the correlation power loss caused by channel band limit and distortion and its influence on navigation performance. Firstly, according to the output of the tracking loop of the software receiver, carrier stripping, and Doppler removal are carried out for the received navigation satellite signal, and the measured signal ranging code is obtained by equalizing the measured channel transmission characteristics. The normalized cross-correlation between the measured signal and the local reference code is calculated. The definition is as follows:

$$CCF(\tau) = \frac{\int_0^{Tp} S_{BB-PreProc}(t) \cdot S_{Ref}^*(t - \tau)dt}{\sqrt{\left(\int_0^{Tp} |S_{BB-PreProc}(t)|^2 dt\right) \cdot \left(\int_0^{Tp} |S_{Ref}(t)|^2 dt\right)}} \tag{5}$$

Where: $S_{BB-PreProc}(t)$ is the ranging code of the measured satellite signal; S_{Ref} is the ideal replication code generated by the local receiver; the integration time T_p usually corresponds to a main code period of the reference signal.

In the practical system engineering, to get the correlation function of higher time-domain resolution, the sampling rate of the digital signal should be increased, or multi-period overlapping accumulation technology should be used. To reduce the influence of noise, the correlation function can be averaged in multiple code periods.

4.2 Correlation Loss

Correlation loss refers to the difference between the received signal power in the designed frequency band bandwidth and the recovered signal power in the ideal correlation receiver in the same frequency band bandwidth. In the ideal correlation receiver, the input is the ideal signal waveform, the filter is the bandwidth designed for the signal, and the inner phase of the bandwidth is the linear ideal sharp cut-off filter.

The correlation loss is calculated as follows:

$$P_{CCF}[dB] = \max_{\substack{aver \\ all}} \left(20 \cdot \log_{10}(|CCF(\varepsilon)|)\right) \tag{6}$$

$$CL_{\text{Distortion}}[dB] = P_{CCF}_{IdealS_{Input}}[dB] - P_{CCF}_{RealS_{Input}}[dB] \tag{7}$$

Where P_{CCF} represents signal power, $P_{CCF}_{IdealS_{Input}}$ represents ideal signal power, $P_{CCF}_{RealS_{Input}}$ represents received signal power, and $CL_{\text{Distortion}}$ represents correlation loss.

The lower the correlation loss, the higher the pseudo-range measurement accuracy, and the lower the receiver threshold [13]. When using the above formula to calculate the correlation loss, we should also consider the influence of the relative change of power distribution between different bandwidth signal components caused by the actual band-limited filter on the calculation results.

4.3 Zero Crossing Deviation of S-Curve

Theoretically, the Zero crossing point of the receiver code loop frequency discrimination curve (S-curve), that is, the lock point of the code loop, should be located at the point where the code tracking error is zero. In fact, due to the influence of channel transmission distortion and multipath, the frequency discrimination curve of the code loop is often locked in the place with phase deviation [14].

Taking the noncoherent lead-lag power frequency discriminator as an example, if the lead-lag distance of the correlator is δ, the S-curve can be expressed as follows:

$$SCurve(\varepsilon, \delta) = \left|CCF\left(\varepsilon - \frac{\delta}{2}\right)\right|^2 - \left|CCF\left(\varepsilon + \frac{\delta}{2}\right)\right|^2 \tag{8}$$

The deviation of the locking point $\varepsilon_{\text{bias}}(\delta)$ satisfies:

$$SCurve(\varepsilon_{\text{bias}}(\delta), \delta) = 0 \tag{9}$$

In particular, when there is more than one zero-crossing (such as BOC modulation signal), the zero-crossing nearest to the maximum correlation power shall be selected.

S-curve deviation is defined as:

$$SCB = \max_{\substack{over \\ all\delta}}(\varepsilon_{\text{bias}}(\delta)) - \min_{\substack{over \\ all\delta}}(\varepsilon_{\text{bias}}(\delta)) \tag{10}$$

The value range δ is $[0, \delta_{\max}]$ and the value of $\delta_{\max}$ is as follows:

$$\delta_{\max}[\text{chips}] = \begin{cases} \frac{1.5}{4\frac{m}{n}-1} & BOC(m, n) \text{ signal} \\ 1.5 & BPSK - n \text{ signal} \end{cases} \tag{11}$$

From the expression of S-curve and the deviation of the locking point $\varepsilon_{\text{bias}}(\delta)$, we can draw the curve of the deviation of the locking point $\varepsilon_{\text{bias}}(\delta)$ with the distance δ. Besides, to minimize the impact of noise, average processing can be performed in multiple code cycles. At the same time, to reduce the influence of cross-correlation between different signal components, it is necessary to average for different cross-correlation situations. In the calculation process, the influence of uncertainty and instability introduced by the measurement system itself should be avoided as far as possible.

4.4 Code and Carrier Phase Consistency

By evaluating the consistency of ranging code pseudo-range and carrier phase pseudo-range, the relative jitter between code and carrier in the modulation process of the satellite navigation signal is measured. Because the output value of the carrier phase observation of the receiver is not the absolute carrier phase output, but relative to the relative carrier phase output at a certain time, at present, the consistency evaluation is mainly to evaluate the relative stability of the code and the carrier phase.

$$\Delta\rho_N = \rho_{N+1} - \rho_N$$
$$\Delta\Phi_N = \Phi_{N+1} - \Phi_N$$
$$\Phi_N = \psi_N \times C/(f_0 + f_{Ndpp})$$
$$\Delta = \Delta\rho_N - \Delta\Phi_N \tag{12}$$

The ρ_N and ψ_N represents the code pseudo distance and the carrier phase output of the receiver, c represents the speed of light, the value is 299792458 m/s, f_0 represents the signal center frequency, f_{Ndpp} represents the Doppler frequency shift, and Δ represents the pseudo-range difference between the code and the carrier phase in units of distance.

5 Open-Closed-Loop Tracking Test Results

Using the 40-mlarge aperture antenna system at Haoping observation station in Luonan, Shaanxi Province, to observe and collect the satellite downlink signal data, taking the

BeiDou Global System MEO-2 satellite as an example, the acquisition card parameters are set with the sampling rate of 250 MHz, the acquisition time of 3 s, and the data of 2–3 s that the signal enters the stable tracking are taken for the comparison and signal quality evaluation of the two tracking methods (1) the closed-loop tracking parameters are set with the carrier loop bandwidth 20 Hz, damping factor $\sqrt{2}/2$, code loop bandwidth 5 Hz, damping factor $\sqrt{2}/2$, correlator interval 0.1, loop cycle 10 ms; (2) the joint tracking parameters are consistent with the closed-loop, and the loop cycle of three components B1Cd, B1Cpa and B1Cpb is 100 ms.

In the following, the time-consuming and the impact of signal quality evaluation results are compared and analyzed in depth.

5.1 Time-Consuming Comparison

The loop period of 10 ms is adopted for the closed-loop tracking of the BeiDou B1C signal, and 100 ms is adopted for the joint tracking. The two concentric rings represent the output of the loop result, the phase discrimination of the loop, and the time-consuming proportion of the filtering from the outside to the inside; the first and second sectors represent the joint tracking and the closed-loop tracking respectively from 0 degrees clockwise. The time-consuming statistics are as follows:

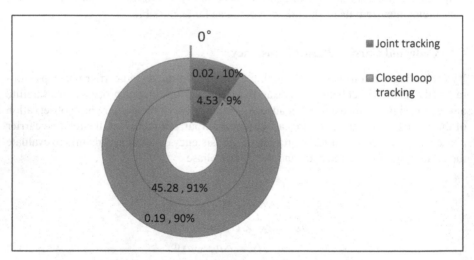

Fig. 5. Open closed-loop tracking time chart (time/s)

The actual data analysis results show that:

The signal tracking process is mainly composed of carrier and pseudo code separation, loop phase discrimination, and filtering, and the time ratio of joint tracking and closed-loop tracking is about 1:10. The separation process of carrier and pseudo code is the most computationally intensive and takes up the most time. The total time of joint tracking is 4.554 s, and the total time of closed-loop tracking is 45.535 s, which saves about 90% of the time compared with closed-loop tracking.

5.2 Comparison of Signal Evaluation Results

Comparison of Tracking Results

Figure 6, 7 and 8 shows the tracking results of three signal components of B1C. The dotted line represents closed-loop tracking and the solid line represents joint tracking. Compared with the closed-loop tracking, the overall trend of the output value of the loop discriminator and the output value of the loop filter in the open-closed-loop tracking method is basically consistent with that of the traditional closed-loop tracking method, which shows that this method can realize the stable tracking of the signal.

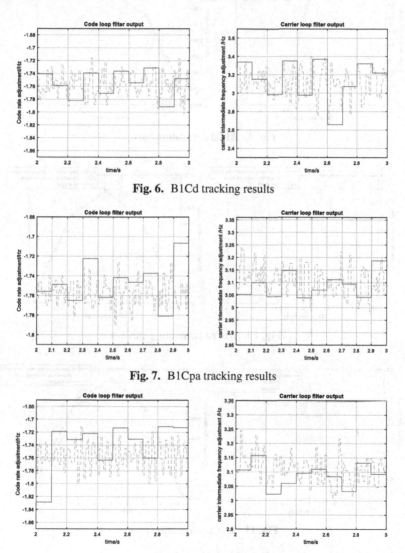

Fig. 6. B1Cd tracking results

Fig. 7. B1Cpa tracking results

Fig. 8. B1Cpb tracking results

Comparison of Signal Quality Evaluation Results

Correlation Curve

Figure 9, 10 and 11 shows the correlation curve of three signal components of B1C calculated by Eq. (5). In these figures, the solid line represents the ideal signal, the dotted line represents the closed-loop tracking signal, and the triangle solid line represents the joint tracking signal. The right figure is the amplification diagram at the correlation peak.

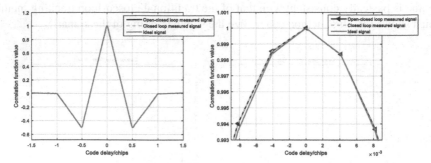

Fig. 9. B1Cd correlation curve

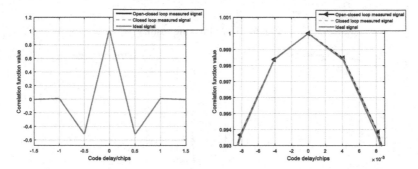

Fig. 10. B1Cpa correlation curve

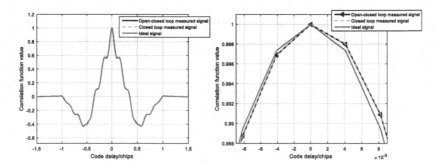

Fig. 11. B1Cp correlation curve

To analyze and compare the symmetry, smoothness, and coincidence degree of the curves, the whole correlation curve is moved to 0 chip.

From the comparison of Fig. 9, 10 and 11, it can be seen that the joint tracking method basically coincides with the correlation curve of the traditional closed-loop tracking.

Table 2 shows the mean value and standard deviation of the correlation curve difference between the two tracking methods of each component.

Table 2. Correlation curve differences

Signal component	Mean value	Standard deviation
B1Cd	−2.8002e−07	5.4571e−06
B1Cpa	−1.4064e−07	1.3141e−05
B1Cp	−1.0715e−07	1.1267e−05

According to Table 2, the difference between the two tracking methods of each component is very small, and the curve coincidence is high.

Correlation Loss

Figure 12, 13 and 14 shows the correlation loss figure of each component calculated once every 50 ms in two tracking methods, with a total of 20 times. The horizontal line with a value of 0.3 represents the evaluation index. Take the mean value and get the correlation loss evaluation results in Table 3 through correlation calculation.

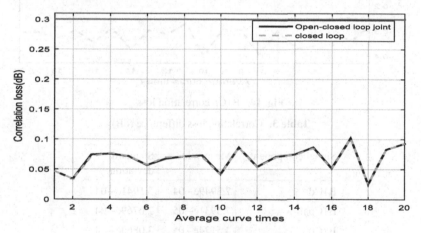

Fig. 12. B1Cd correlation loss

It can be seen from Fig. 12, 13 and 14 that the correlation loss of the three signal components is less than the index requirement of 0.3 dB in the BeiDou ICD document and the variation degree of each correlation loss value is small.

Table 3 shows the mean value and standard deviation of the correlation loss difference of each component in two tracking methods.

From Table 3, it can be seen that the difference between the two tracking methods of each component is very small, and the curve coincidence is high.

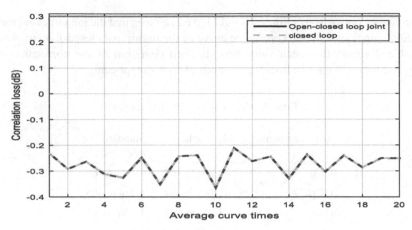

Fig. 13. B1Cpa correlation loss

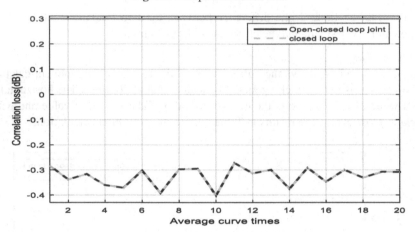

Fig. 14. B1Cp correlation loss

Table 3. Correlation loss difference (dB)

Signal component	Mean value	Standard deviation
B1Cd	2.3949e−04	3.1941e−04
B1Cpa	7.5931e−05	2.6769e−04
B1Cp	4.5124e−05	3.0863e−04

Table 4 shows the correlation loss values corresponding to the two tracking methods of each component, and the index requirements are not more than 0.3 dB

Table 4. Correlation loss (dB)

Signal component	Index	Closed-loop	Joint tracking
B1Cd	≤0.3	0.066587	0.066827
B1Cpa		−0.274641	−0.274566
B1Cp		−0.325460	−0.325415

From Table 4, it can be seen that the variation range of the correlation loss value of joint tracking is within 0.4% compared with that of closed-loop tracking, and the difference between the two is very small.

Zero Crossing Deviation of S-curve

Figure 15, 16, 17 and 18 shows the Zero crossing deviation of the S-curve of each component in two tracking modes. The difference between the maximum value and the minimum value of the curve in these figures is the Zero crossing deviation of the curve in Table 5. B1cp 0.16–0.36 chip peak skew summit results in a large range deviation, which will be abandoned as an evaluation index. Figure 17 shows the SCB value at b1cp 0.01–0.15 chip and Fig. 18 shows the SCB value at b1cp 0.37–0.46 chip.

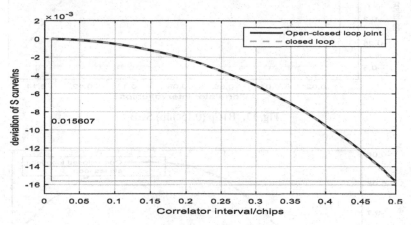

Fig. 15. B1Cd SCB

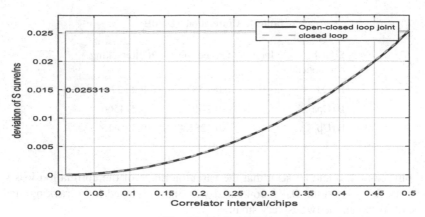

Fig. 16. B1Cpa SCB

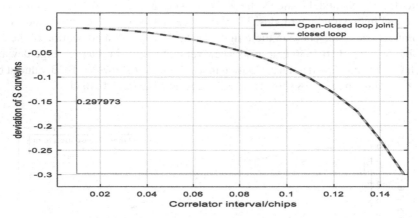

Fig. 17. B1Cp (0.15chip) SCB

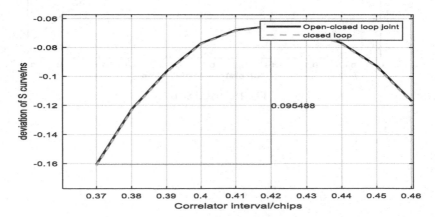

Fig. 18. B1Cp(0.46chip) SCB

Table 5. S zero-crossing deviation difference of curve (ns)

Signal component	Mean value	Standard deviation
B1Cd	2.8776e−05	2.9175e−05
B1Cpa	−5.4799e−05	5.1520e−05
B1Cp (0.15chip)	2.8763e−04	3.2261e−04
B1Cp (0.46chip)	7.8407e−04	3.9641e−04

It can be seen from Fig. 15, 16, 17 and 18 that the SCB curves of the two tracking modes of each component are coincident.

Table 5 shows the mean value and standard deviation of the zero-crossing deviation of the S-curve of each component in two tracking methods.

It can be seen from Table 5 that the difference between the two tracking methods of each component is very small and the curve coincidence is high.

Table 6 shows the zero-crossing deviation value of S-curve corresponding to the two tracking methods of each component and meets the index requirements of no more than 0.5 ns.

Table 6. Zero-crossing deviation of S-curve (ns)

Signal component	Index	Closed-loop	Joint tracking
B1Cd	≤0.5	0.015707	0.015607
B1Cpa		0.025482	0.025313
B1Cp (0.15chip)		0.299040	0.297973
B1Cp (0.46chip)		0.095802	0.095488

From Table 6, it can be seen that the value range of SCB of each component of joint tracking is within 0.7% compared with that of closed-loop tracking, and the difference between them is very small.

Code and Carrier Phase Consistency

Table 7 shows the average consistency of code and carrier phase corresponding to the two tracking methods of each component and meets the requirement of no greater than the index 1°.

It can be obtained from Table 7 that there is basically no difference in the result of phase consistency between each component code and carrier phase of joint tracking compared with closed-loop tracking.

Table 7. Consistency average of code and carrier phase (°)

Signal component	Index	Closed-loop	Joint tracking
B1Cd	≤1	−0.024899	0.025039
B1Cpa		−0.075774	−0.077376
B1Cp		−0.230170	−0.307586

6 Conclusion

This paper first introduces the principle and characteristics of traditional open-loop tracking and traditional closed-loop tracking. Because the traditional open-loop tracking takes less time and the traditional closed-loop tracking method has high tracking accuracy, this paper makes full use of the advantages of the open-loop tracking and the closed-loop tracking, proposes a new open-closed-loop joint tracking method for the BeiDou B1C signal, and makes use of the BeiDou total collected by Haoping observation station The validity and feasibility of the proposed method are verified by analyzing the measured data of the downlink signal of MEO-2 satellite. Taking the data of 2–3 s that the signal enters into the stable tracking to compare the two tracking methods and evaluate the signal quality, the research results show that:

1. Under the condition of the same measured signal and the same receiver tracking parameters, the data length ratio of open-closed-loop tracking of Joint tracking is 1:9, and the tracking time of the open-closed-loop joint tracking method is about 90% less than the traditional closed-loop tracking method.
2. The mean and standard deviation of the difference between the two correlation curves are very small, and the degree of curve coincidence and the symmetry of the left and right overall are relatively high.
3. The change range of correlation loss values of the two tracking methods is within 0.4%, the difference between them is very small, and both are less than the 0.3 dB index requirements in the BeiDou ICD document.
4. The coincidence degree of SCB curves of the two tracking methods is very high, and the value range of SCB is within 0.7%, which meets the index requirements of 0.5 ns.
5. There is basically no difference between the code and carrier phase consistency mean results of the two tracking methods.

Therefore, the open-closed-loop joint tracking method proposed in this paper can greatly improve the efficiency of data processing based on ensuring the tracking effect.

The next step is to further study the method of intelligent control and adjustment of loop controller parameters by a loop feedback mechanism, and analyze whether the joint tracking sensitivity of different signal components to the same time is the same.

References

1. Lv, F.: Open-loop tracking design and performance analysis of the satellite navigation receiver. Beihang University (2015)
2. Won, J., Pany, T., Eissfeller, B.: Design of a Unified MLE tracking for GPS/Galileo software receivers (2006)
3. Van, G.F., Soloviev, A., Uijt, D.H.M., et al.: Closed-loop sequential signal processing and open-loop batch processing approaches for GNSS receiver design. IEEE J. Select. Top. Sig. Process. 3(4), 571–586 (2009). https://doi.org/10.1109/jstsp.2009.2023350
4. Han, C., Bai, Y., Si, J.: Carrier synchronization algorithm of joint open-loop acquisition and closed-loop tracking in a highly dynamic environment. J. Northwest. Polytech. Univ. 36(06), 1232–1235 (2018)
5. Guo, Y.: Research on high precision tracking and evaluation technology of the BeiDou B1C signal. UCAS(NTSC) (2019)
6. Academic exchange center of China Satellite Navigation System Management Office.: Bei-Dou Navigation Satellite System Signal In: Space Interface Control Document Open Service Signal B1C (Version 1.0). Beijing: China Satellite Navigation System Management Office (2017)
7. Li, Z., Zhang, T., Yan, K., et al.: A phase prediction method for improving carrier phase continuity of GPS receiver. J. Geodesy Geodyn. 38(12), 1280–1284 (2018). https://doi.org/10.14075/j.jgg.2018.12.013
8. Feng, Z.: Study on LEO-LEO occultation signal receiving technology. UCAS(NTSC) (2018)
9. Jing, S.: Research on performance evaluation and auxiliary enhancement technology of GNSS space service airspace. Shanghai Jiao Tong University (2017)
10. Han, S., Wang, W., Chen, X., et al.: High dynamic carrier tracking loop based on the UKF quasi-open loop structure. Acta Aeronaut. ET Astronaut. Sin. 31(12), 2393–2399 (2010)
11. Yan, K.: Research on scalar deep combined baseband technology for GNSS high precision positioning in urban complex environment. WuHan University (2018)
12. He, C., Lu, X., Guo, J.: A new method to evaluate the waveform distortion of the satellite navigation signal. J. Electron. Inf. Technol. 41(05), 1017–1024 (2019)
13. Hauschild, A., Montenbruck, O.: A study on the dependency of GNSS pseudorange biases on correlator spacing. GPS Solutions 20(2), 159–171 (2014). https://doi.org/10.1007/s10291-014-0426-0
14. He, C., Lu, X., Guo, J., et al.: Initial analysis for characterizing and mitigating the pseudo-range biases of the BeiDou navigation satellite system. Satell. Navig. 1(11) (2020). https://doi.org/10.1186/s43020-019-0003-3

Spectrum Sensing for Weak Signals Based on Satellite Formation

Yu Zhang[1,2], Xiaojin Ding[2(✉)], Chaoran Sun[1,2], Jian Zhu[1], and Gengxin Zhang[1,2]

[1] College of Telecommunications and Information Engineering, Nanjing University of Posts and Telecommunications, Nanjing 210003, China
[2] Telecommunication and Network National Engineering Research Center, Nanjing University of Posts and Communications, Nanjing 210003, China
dxj@njupt.edu.cn

Abstract. In this paper, we investigate the spectrum sensing of a weak signal based on multiple low earth orbit (LEO) satellites in the presence of a spectrum-sharing node, which can generate the interference imposed on the sensing LEO satellites. In order to improve the sensing ability of the weak signal, a cooperative spectrum sensing method relying on satellite formation is proposed. Specifically, firstly, some satellites will be chosen from multiple LEO satellites for formation purposes, where the specific number of satellites chosen can be adjusted by evaluating the probability of detection weak signal, as detailed later. Then, considering the object that both restraining the interference and magnifying the weak signal, the weighted value of each satellite for beamforming may be optimized with the aid of genetic algorithm, and the receive gains of the weak signal and the interference can be achieved. Finally, the probability of detecting the weak signal can be evaluated by calculating the signal to interference plus noise ratio (SINR), and the number of the chosen satellites can be decided accordingly. Simulation results show that the proposed method not only can suppress the interference imposed on the sensing satellites, but also can increase SINR of sensing satellites for the weak signal, resulting in improving the probability of detection.

Keywords: Spectrum sensing · Multi-satellite collaboration · Beamforming · Satellite formation

1 Introduction

Spectrum sensing is one of the key technologies in cognitive radio technology, which is mainly used to monitor the frequency usage of primary users. Traditional spectrum sensing technology is mainly divided into two categories: single node spectrum sensing and multi-node cooperative spectrum sensing. The most basic spectrum sensing methods include spectrum sensing based on energy, spectrum sensing based on cyclic-stationary characteristics and spectrum sensing based on matched filter detection [1]. Among these spectrum sensing methods, the energy sensing method is the simplest one, because this method does not need any prior information characteristics of the transmitted signal, and

Q. Wu et al. (Eds.): WiSATS 2020, LNICST 357, pp. 468–479, 2021.
https://doi.org/10.1007/978-3-030-69069-4_38

it is the most widely used spectrum sensing technology at present [2]. At the beginning of the emergence of cognitive radio technology, the research is based on the ground network, that is, the cognitive users and primary users both are nodes in the ground network, and so far, the research of cognitive radio technology in the ground network has been quite mature [3]. However, due to the fact that the ground network can't solve the problem of communication obstacles caused by the desert, ocean and other terrain areas, and the high cost of setting up base stations in sparsely populated and remote areas, people have to consider the development of the satellite network [4]. Satellite communication becomes more concentrated because of its large coverage, wide coverage, high communication quality, and it can overcome the communication obstacles caused by the desolate terrain encountered by the ground network [5]. As an extension and supplement of the ground network, satellite network has become one of the leading technologies of the next generation of mobile communication system to construct the satellite ground integrated system and realize the seamless coverage of wireless mobile communication [6]. With the advantages of large carrying capacity of ground system and wide coverage of satellite system, the satellite ground integrated system can provide users with seamless coverage services. At the same time, with the development of the satellite ground integrated system, it is inevitable to face the problem of spectrum resource shortage, so it is necessary to apply cognitive radio technology to the satellite ground integrated system.

Spectrum sensing in the satellite ground integrated system will face another problem. That is, due to the long-distance transmission between the ground network and the satellite, the low signal-to-noise ratio will seriously affect the performance of spectrum sensing [7]. Especially for the proposed scenario, when the satellite perceives a weak signal with strong signal interference, the SINR of the weak signal received by the satellite will be lower. Therefore, the low signal-to-noise ratio of satellite spectrum sensing will become a hot topic. At present, some scholars have also studied related problems, such as in Ref. [8], the author has studied the optimization of different spectrum sensing parameters by using genetic algorithm in the case of low SNR. The simulation results show that this method provides a better practical solution for cognitive radio network. Another example, in Ref. [9], the author proposed an improved energy detection method based on gradient for the change of noise power and low SNR. The simulation results show that the performance of spectrum sensing is improved based on this method.

However, there are few researches on the spectrum sensing of a weak signal based on multiple low earth orbit (LEO) satellites in the presence of a spectrum-sharing node, which can generate the interference imposed on the sensing LEO satellites. In this paper, a multiple satellite cooperative spectrum sensing model is proposed, and beamforming technology is introduced to improve the received signal-interference-noise ratio (SINR) of the weak signal when there is strong signal interference on the ground. According to the relevant research, beamforming technology can be used to solve the problem of interference, for example, a scenario of beamforming technology application proposed in Ref. [10], and the simulation results show that beamforming technology plays an important role in canceling the influence of fading and interference. At the same time, in Ref. [11], the author puts forward another application scenario of beamforming technology, and the simulation results show that the design method of beamforming can find the best combination of beamforming, and can deal with interference management problems well, so it is feasible to apply beamforming technology to the scenario proposed in this paper. The method proposed in this paper is to make the satellite form the pattern in the form of formation. In the direction of weak signal, the manifold vectors of each satellite are superposed in the same phase, and in the direction of strong signal, the manifold vectors of each satellite are eliminated in the reverse direction as much as possible, so as to improve the signal-interference-noise ratio (SINR) of satellite reception. The main innovations of this paper are as follows:

1) The system model of satellite sensing weak signal in the presence of strong interference is proposed;
2) Beamforming technology is introduced to improve the received signal-interference-noise ratio (SINR) of satellite;
3) Simulation results show that this method can effectively improve the performance of satellite spectrum sensing.

The rest of this paper is arranged as follows: Sect. 2 is the introduction of the proposed system model and energy perception. In Sect. 3, the beamforming technology proposed in this paper is introduced, and the calculation formula of signal- interference-noise ratio (SINR) of satellite receiving under this technology is given. Section 4 is performance evaluation, and Sect. 5 concludes this paper.

2   The System Model

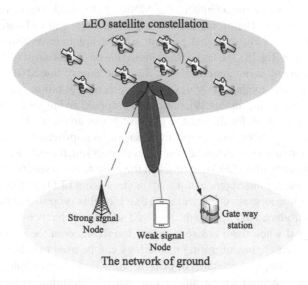

Fig. 1. Illustrative of cooperative sensing model for satellite communications

The model in Fig. 1 is based on a satellite-ground integration scenario in which the satellite acts as a cognitive user to perceive weak signal node on the ground in the presence of strong signal interference. In this scenario, the ground network has a strong signal transmitting node and a weak signal transmitting node as well as a signal gateway for satellite transmitting and receiving signals. The LEO satellites over the nodes are grouped in formation to form a cluster to sense the weak signal node in the ground network when there is strong signal interference. Based on the above model, it is assumed that the transmitting signal of the weak signal node on the ground is s_1, the transmitting power is P_{T1}, the transmitting gain is G_{T1}, and the channel gain between the weak signal node and the satellite i is h_{1i}. Accordingly, the transmitting signal of the strong signal node is s_2, the transmitting power is P_{T2}, the transmitting gain is G_{T2}, the channel gain between the strong signal node and satellite i is h_{2i}, assuming the satellite's receiving gain is G_R, then the received signal of satellite i can be given by the following formula:

$$y_i = \sqrt{G_{T1} \cdot P_{T1} \cdot G_R} \cdot h_{1i} \cdot s_1 + \sqrt{G_{T2} \cdot P_{T2} \cdot G_R} \cdot h_{2i} \cdot s_2 + n_0, \quad 1 \leq i \leq N \quad (1)$$

The channel gain of ground nodes to each satellite is approximately considered to be equal because of the mode array of satellite formation. It means that h_{1i} and h_{2i} all are the same, assuming that, after Gauss decline, the channel gain's mean is 0, and the variance is 1, then that satisfies $h_{1i} = h_{2i} = 1$, and n_0 represents Additive white Gaussian noise. Then after satellites forming, the signal-interference-noise ratio (SINR) of the weak signal by satellite i can be expressed as:

$$SINR_i = \frac{P_{T1} G_R G_{T1} \left(\frac{c}{4\pi d_{jif}}\right)^2}{P_{T2} G_R G_{T2} \left(\frac{c}{4\pi d_{jif}}\right)^2 + KBT} \quad j = 1,2 \quad (2)$$

Where K is Boltzmann constant, T represents the equivalent noise temperature of the receiver, and B represents the transponder bandwidth, c is the light speed, d_{ji} denotes the distance between the satellite i and the node j, f is the center frequency of the spectrum bands.

According to Ref. [12], the relationship between the correct detection probability of a single satellite perception and SINR is shown in Fig. 2. From Fig. 2, it can be seen that the correct detection of conventional energy sensing method will decrease sharply when SINR is below -4 dB, in the scenario shown in Fig. 1, the SINR will be much lower than -4 dB when the transmitted power of the sensing signal and the Interference signal are 10 dBm and 30 dBm, respectively, there is an urgent need to explore a new perception method to meet the needs of weak signal perception.

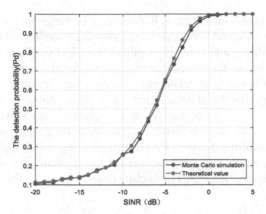

Fig. 2. Single user detection probability varies with SINR in energy perception

3   Spectrum Sensing Based on Multi-satellite Array

3.1   Model of Satellite Array

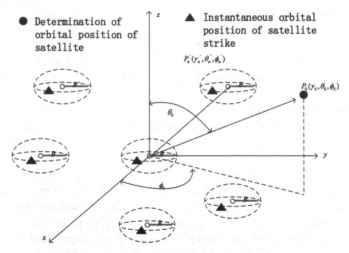

Fig. 3. Distributed satellite cluster array model

As shown in Fig. 3, it is the distributed satellite cluster array model, the orbital position information determined by the nth satellite is set as $P_n(\gamma_n, \theta_n, \phi_n)$, γ_n is the distance from the origin of coordinates of the nth satellite, and the elevation Angle and azimuth Angle of the satellite meet $\theta_n \in [0, \pi]$ and $\phi_n \in [0, 2\pi)$ respectively. Because of the perturbation force, the position of the satellite will wobble randomly. In consideration of satellite wobble, it is assumed that the instantaneous actual position of the nth satellite is randomly distributed in a sphere with determined position information $P_n(\gamma_n, \theta_n, \phi_n)$ as its center and radius B, and the actual coordinates of the satellite are denoted by $P_n'(\gamma_n', \theta_n', \phi_n')$. After the satellite array is assumed, the desired spatial azimuth direction of the main lobe of its orientation graph is set as $P_0(\gamma, \theta_0, \phi_0)$. Based on [13], the following assumptions are also made:

(1) The satellites in the distributed satellite cluster use the same type of antenna, and the array pattern function conforms to the pattern multiplication theorem.
(2) The distance between the distributed satellite cluster and the ground node is much larger than that between the satellites in the distributed cluster, so the electromagnetic signal path attenuation between the ground node and the satellite array elements is roughly the same.
(3) The LOS is the main link for each satellite element to reach the ground node, and only the additive white Gaussian noise channel is considered, not the multipath, fading or shadow caused by reflection or scattering.
(4) The array satellite is perfectly synchronized in carrier frequency, phase and time.

3.2 Cooperative Beamforming Pattern Function

The following is a brief description of the relevant formulas of distributed satellite array pattern function based on random antenna array theory.

$$
A_n(\theta, \phi) = \overbrace{\exp\left[jk\gamma_n'\left(cos\psi_n' - cos\psi_{n,0}'\right)\right]}^{\text{random term}} \cdot \overbrace{\exp(jk\gamma_n cos\psi_n)}^{\text{fixed term}}
$$

$$
= \exp\left\{jk\left(\gamma_n'\left(cos\psi_n' - cos\psi_{n,0}'\right)+\gamma_n cos\psi_n\right)\right\} \qquad n = 1, 2, ...N \qquad (3)
$$

Where, $k = \dfrac{2\pi}{\lambda}$ and λ is wavelength, $n = 1, 2, ...N$ (N is the number of satellites). Substitute through the following formula:

$$
cos\,\psi_n' = sin\,\theta\,sin\,\theta_n'\,cos(\phi - \phi_n') + cos\theta cos\theta_n' \qquad (4)
$$

$$
cos\,\psi_n = sin\,\theta\,sin\,\theta_n\,cos(\phi - \phi_n) + cos\theta cos\theta_n \qquad (5)
$$

$$
cos\,\psi_{n,0}' = sin\,\theta_0\,sin\,\theta_n'\,cos(\theta_0 - \varphi_n') + cos\theta_0 cos\theta_n' \qquad (6)
$$

$$
\rho_0 = \sqrt{(sin\theta cos\phi - sin\theta_0 cos\phi_0)^2 + (sin\theta sin\phi - sin\theta_0 sin\phi_0)^2} \qquad (7)
$$

$$
cos\,\delta = \rho_0^{-1}(sin\theta cos\phi - sin\theta_0 cos\phi_0) \qquad (8)
$$

$$
sin\,\delta = \rho_0^{-1}(sin\theta sin\phi - sin\theta_0 sin\phi_0) \qquad (9)
$$

$$
cos\,\gamma = \rho_0^{-1}(cos\theta - cos\theta_0) \qquad (10)
$$

$$
\delta = tan^{-1}[\frac{sin\,\theta\,sin\,\phi - sin\,\theta_0\,sin\,\phi_0}{sin\,\theta\,cos\,\phi - sin\,\theta_0\,cos\,\phi_0}] \qquad (11)
$$

$$I_n = R_n \sin\theta'_n \cos(\phi'_n - \delta), \qquad -1 \le I_n \le 1 \tag{12}$$

$$Q(\theta, \phi) = 2\pi\beta\rho_0 \tag{13}$$

$$T_n = R_n \cos\theta'_n, \qquad -1 \le T_n \le 1 \tag{14}$$

$$G(\theta) = 2\pi\beta\rho_0 \cos\gamma \tag{15}$$

$$L_n = \frac{\gamma_n}{\lambda} \tag{16}$$

Where $R_n = \gamma_n/B$, $\beta = B/\lambda$ represents the normalization of wavelength by perturbation radius of array satellite, and L_n represents the normalization of wavelength by the distance from the nth satellite to the origin of coordinates. After the above formula is substituted, the average manifold vector formula of the nth satellite is obtained as follows:

$$\overline{A_n}(\theta, \phi) = 6tinc(Q(\theta, \phi))jinc(G(\theta)) \times$$
$$\exp[j2\pi L_n(\sin\theta \sin\theta_n \cos(\phi - \phi_n) + \cos\theta \cos\theta_n)] \tag{17}$$

Where $tinc(x) = J_1(x)/x$, $jinc(x) = j_1(x)/x$, $J_1(x)$ denotes the first spherical Bessel function of the first order, and $j_1(x)$ denotes the first Bessel function of the first order. Then the corresponding average beam pattern function of a distributed cluster can be expressed as:

$$F(\phi) = \frac{1}{N} \sum_{n=1}^{N} w_n \overline{A_n}(\phi) \tag{18}$$

Where w_n is the weighted value of the nth satellite array, $w_n \in C(C$ denotes the complex field). The corresponding average power pattern formula is as follows:

$$S(\phi) = |F(\phi)|^2 \tag{19}$$

3.3 A Spectrum Sensing Method Based on Satellite Array

The above two sections introduce the satellite array model and the relevant knowledge of the beam pattern function. In order to apply this beamforming method to the proposed model, the expected direction of the main lobe of the average power pattern of the satellite cluster array should be aligned with the direction of the weak signal node in the model. In this direction, the manifold vectors of each satellite participating in the array are superimposed in the same phase. So the weighted value of each satellite should meet formula (20):

$$w_n = \exp(-j2\pi L_n \sin\theta_n \cos(\phi_0 - \phi_n)), \qquad n = 1, 2, ...N \tag{20}$$

The formula (20) can be substituted into the above formula (10) for the average power pattern, and the final formula for the average power pattern can be obtained. In order to improve the SINR of the weak signal node, the null region direction of the array satellite pattern is aligned with the direction of the strong signal node on the ground and the genetic algorithm is combined to make the value as small as possible. So as to maximize the signal- interference-noise ratio (SINR) of satellite reception. For convenience, we set the desired direction of the array (direction of weak ground signal) as $(\theta_0, \phi_0) = (90°, 0°)$, then the formula of the average power beam pattern can be expressed as follows [14]:

$$S(\phi) = \frac{1}{N^2} \left| \sum_{n=1}^{N} 3tinc(\alpha(\phi) \cdot \exp(j2\pi L_n \sin\theta_n[\cos(\theta - \theta_n) - \cos\phi_n]) \right|^2 \quad (21)$$

Where $\alpha(\phi) = 4\pi\beta \sin(\phi/2)$. Assuming that the satellites in the array are in the same perturbation condition (the perturbation of the satellites is taken into account), the perturbation radius of the satellites is set to be 15, it satisfies $\beta = 15$. In order to improve the performance of the satellite array, we can select suitable satellites to participate in the formation. The detailed selection process is as follows:

(1) According to the distribution structure of the formation satellites, the first step is to initialize the position information of the formation satellites.
(2) Given the location information of both strong signal node and weak signal node on the ground.
(3) Given the number of satellites participating in the collaboration. In the progress of determining the number of satellites, we can adjust the number of satellites by evaluating the probability of detection weak signal. Objective function is to maximize the received power in the direction of weak signal node and to minimize the received power in the direction of strong signal node, the satellite nodes with the best position information are selected from the satellite formation by genetic algorithm to co-operate to detect the weak signal node in the presence of strong signal interference.

In the above process, the purpose of minimizing the receiving power of strong signal node and maximizing the receiving power of weak signal node is to improve the signal-interference-noise ratio (SINR) of array satellites when they perceive weak signal with strong signal interference.

After optimizing, when the main lobe of the array is aligned to the direction of weak signal, the manifold vector of the array are superimposed in the same phase, and null region gain is generated in the direction of strong signal. In this process, when the number of array satellites is N, it will get N times of gain in the desired direction of the received signal, correspondingly, it will also have a gain of N^2 times in power value of the received signal. That is, the receiving power gain of the sensor signal and the jamming signal are $G_s = N^2$ and G_{R2} respectively. Then the signal-interference-noise ratio (SINR) of the corresponding array satellites cluster receiving weak signal with strong signal interference can be further expressed as:

$$SINR = \frac{G_{T1}P_{T1}N^2 G_R(\frac{c}{4\pi df})^2}{G_{T2}P_{T2}G_R G_{R2}(\frac{c}{4\pi df})^2 + KBT} \tag{22}$$

Supposing the null region direction of the pattern formed by the array satellites (the direction of the strong signal on the ground) is $(\theta, \phi) = (90°, 0.3°)$. Under the above conditions, when $L = 2000$, $M = 500$ and $N = 5$, the patterns of the formation of the array satellites and the curves of the nulls in the pattern with the number of the array satellites are shown in Figs. 4(a) and (b) below respectively:

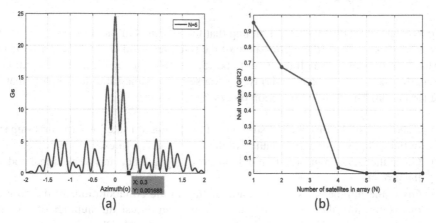

Fig. 4. Experimental simulation results

In Fig. 4(a), it can be seen that when the number of array satellites in the satellite cluster is N = 5, the null region of the beam pattern is about $1.6e - 3$. In addition, it can be seen from Fig. 4(b) that the null region of the beam pattern decreases with the increase in the number of array satellites, which means that with the increase in the number of array satellites, the satellite cluster is more capable of suppressing strong signal.

4   Performance Evaluation

Based on the above formula, the parameter setting table is given (Table 1):

The value of the unknown quantity G_{R2}, in the formula of signal-interference-noise ratio (SINR) is obtained by combining genetic algorithm with the given number of satellites participating in formation. The implementation is described in the previous section, so we will not repeat it again. In order to highlight the proposed method that can improve the SINR of the weak signal node when the satellite perceiving with the strong signal interference on the ground. The following data show the comparison diagram of the spectral sensing method proposed in this paper and the "Or criterion" used in multi-satellite coordination. About the "Or criterion", this paper, due to limited space, will not be repeated, more details can be seen in Ref. [15].

Table 1. Relevant parameter settings of SINR calculation

Parameter	Value
Satellite orbit height	1000 km
Satellite antenna revenue	$G_R = 25$ dbi
Satellite quality factors	$G/T = 5$ dBk^{-1}
Transmission frequency	2 GHZ
Transmitting power of weak signal node	$P_{T1} = 10$ dBm
Transmitting power of strong signal node	$P_{T2} = 30$ dBm
Signal transmission bandwidth	30 MHZ
Transmission gain of weak signal node	$G_{T1} = 1$
Transmitting gain of strong signal node	$G_{T2} = 1$
K (Boltzmann constant)	$K = -228.6$(dB)
N	Number of satellites participating in satellite array

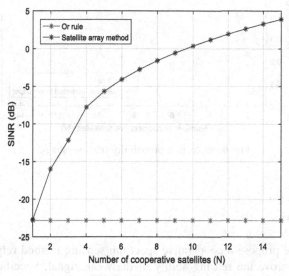

Fig. 5. SINR versus N

In Fig. 5, Compared with the "Or criterion" method in the multi-satellite cooperative spectrum sensing, you can see that under the same conditions, the method proposed in this paper has obvious advantages in the signal-interference-noise ratio (SINR) of weak signal node in the presence of strong signal interference on the ground. Besides that, with the increase of the number of cooperative satellites, the SINR of the satellite receiving weak signal with strong signal interference is gradually increasing. Finally, the detection probability under different number of cooperative satellites is researched, and the method proposed in this paper is compared with the traditional "Or criterion" method, as shown in Fig. 6. Although the "Or criterion" can't improve the SINR, according to its fusion rules $P_D = 1 - \prod_{i=1}^{M} (1 - P_{d,i})$, the detection probability of satellites will increase with the increase of cooperative satellite nodes. Figure 6 shows that there is a big gap between the proposed method and the "Or criterion", which is mainly due to the introduction of beamforming in the multi-satellite cooperative spectrum sensing scenario, this method improves the receiving power gain of the weak signal and decreases the receiving power gain of the strong interference signal, and improves the whole spectrum sensing performance of the array satellites. The simulation result is as follows:

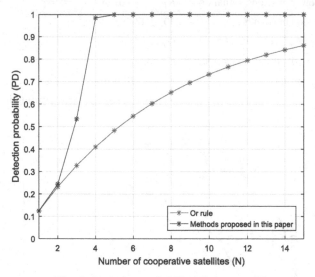

Fig. 6. Detection probability (P_D) versus N

5   Conclusions

In this paper, we propose a cooperative spectrum sensing method relying on satellite formation to improve the sensing ability of the weak signal. Specifically, firstly, we select some LEO satellites to form a formation, and adjust the specific number of selected satellites by evaluating the detection probability of weak signal. Furthermore, by using genetic algorithm to optimize the beamforming weight of each satellite, the receive gains of the weak signal and the interference can be obtained. Finally, the detection probability of the weak signal is evaluated by calculating the SINR after the satellite formation, and the number of selected satellites is determined accordingly. Simulation results show that the proposed method not only can suppress the interference imposed on the sensing satellites, but also can increase SINR of sensing satellites for the weak signal, resulting in improving the probability of detection.

Acknowledgement. This work presented was partially supported by the National Science Foundation of China (No. 91738201 and 61772287), the China Postdoctoral Science Foundation (No. 2018M632347), the Natural Science Foundation for Jiangsu Higher Education Institutions (No. 18KJB510030 and 16KJB510031), and the Key University Science Research Project of Jiangsu Province (No. 18KJA510004).

References

1. Alom, M.Z., Godder, T.K., Morshed, M.N.: A survey of spectrum sensing techniques in Cognitive Radio network. In: 2015 International Conference on Advances in Electrical Engineering (ICAEE), pp. 161–164. Dhaka (2015)
2. Qu, Z., Song, Q., Yin, S.: Optimal spectrum sensing in energy harvesting cognitive radio systems. J. Signal Process. Syst. **11**(05), 83–90 (2014)
3. Hinman, R.D.: Application of cognitive radio technology to legacy military waveforms in a JTRS (Joint Tactical Radio System) Radio. In: MILCOM 2006–2006 IEEE Military Communications Conference, Washington, DC, pp. 1–5 (2006)
4. Banerjee, J., Naskar, M.K., Biswas, U., Alfandi, O., Hogrefe,D.: Leader selection in wireless sensor networks — An energy efficient approach. In: Proceedings of The 2014 International Conference on Control, Instrumentation, Energy and Communication (CIEC), Calcutta, pp. 508–512 (2014)
5. Anpilogov, V.R.: Satellite communication and broadcasting systems in the 21st century. In: 3rd International Conference on Satellite Communications (IEEE Cat. No.98TH8392), Moscow, Russia, pp. 144–145 (1998)
6. Zhou, G.: Future earth observing satellites. In: 2001 International Conferences on Info-Tech and Info-Net, Proceedings (Cat. No.01EX479), Beijing, China, pp. 1–5 (2001)
7. Li, H., Li, J.: Wavelet transforms detection of spectrum sensing in the space network. In: 2015 Science and Information Conference (SAI), London, pp. 978–984 (2015)
8. Chatterjee, S., Ray, S., Dutta, S., Roy, J.S.: Performance analysis of spectrum sensing in cognitive radio at low SNR environment[C]. In: 2017 1st International Conference on Electronics, Materials Engineering and Nano-Technology (IEMENTech), pp. 1–4. Kolkata (2017)
9. Koley, S., Mirza, V., Islam, S., Mitra, D.: Gradient-Based Real-Time Spectrum Sensing at Low SNR. IEEE Commun. Lett. **19**(03), 391–394 (2015)
10. Salah, M., Kostanic, I.: Performance evaluation of 5G downlink under different beamforming and scheduling methods. In: 2019 IEEE 9th Annual Computing and Communication Workshop and Conference (CCWC), pp. 778–782. Las Vegas (2019)
11. Kwon, H.J., Lee, J.H., Choi, W.: Machine learning-based beamforming in two-user miso interference channels. In: 2019 International Conference on Artificial Intelligence in Information and Communication (ICAIIC), pp. 496–499. Okinawa, Japan (2019)
12. Digham, F.F., Alouini, M.S., Simon, M.K.: On the energy detection of unknown signals over fading channels. IEEE Trans. Commun. **55**(1), 21–24 (2007)
13. Li, Y., Yuan, Y., Yu, Q., Zhang, W., Liu, P.: A survey of the application of genetic algorithms in optimization problems. In: Shandong industrial technology, pp. 242–243. Shandong (2019)
14. Yu, L., Cheng, Y., Hong, T., Zhang, G.: Research on collaborative beamforming for a distributed satellite cluster based on Convex Optimization. In: 2019 International Symposium on Advanced Electrical and Communication Technologies (ISAECT), pp. 1–5. Rome, Italy (2019)
15. Liu, Q., Gao, J., Chen, L.: Optimization of energy detection based cooperative spectrum sensing in cognitive radio networks. In: 2010 International Conference on Wireless Communications & Signal Processing (WCSP), pp. 1–5. Suzhou (2010)

Beam Hopping Resource Allocation for Uneven Traffic Distribution in HTS System

Xudong Zhao[1,2], Chen Zhang[1,2(✉)], Yejun Zhou[3], and Gengxin Zhang[1,2]

[1] College of Telecommunications and Information Engineering, Nanjing University of Posts and Telecommunications, Nanjing 210003, China
zhangchen@njupt.edu.cn
[2] National Engineering Research Center for Communication and Network Technology, Nanjing University of Posts and Telecommunications, Nanjing 210003, China
[3] Institute of Telecommunication Satellite, China Academy of Space Technology, Beijing 100081, China

Abstract. Recently beam hopping technique is considered as a potential key technology in the next generation of high throughput satellite (HTS) systems for its flexible resource allocation. This paper is focused on the downlink resource allocation of beam hopping in the HTS System. Firstly, the user traffic model which varies in geography and time is built. Then with the proposed uneven traffic distribution model, the beam hopping time slot optimization algorithm is provided based on fairness objective function. Finally, the beam hopping pattern is designed to be combined with precoding to suppress co-channel interference. The simulation results show that compared with the traditional methods, the proposed algorithm can dynamically adjust the resource allocation with the change of the traffic requirements, and eliminate the co-channel interference of the beam as much as possible to meet the traffic requirements of each beam, thus improving the capacity of the satellite network.

Keywords: Traffic modeling · High-throughput satellite · Beam hopping · Resource allocation

1 Introduction

In the last few years, as a resource allocation method in high-throughput satellites (HTS), beam hopping (BH) technology has become a research hotspot in academia. The core concept of BH is to employ time-slicing method: not all beams are illuminated at the same time, only part of them are activated on demand. Compared to the traditional resource allocation methods, BH can flexibly allocate resources in dimensions of time, space, frequency, and power [1], which improves the system resource utilization [2].

This work is supported by The National Natural Science Foundation of China (No. 61901230, No. 91738201); Key pre-research project for civil space technology (No. B0106) "Research project on VHTS communication technology".

According to the objective function of the allocation algorithm and whether the co-channel interference (CCI) is considered, the existing resource allocation algorithms of the beam-hopping satellite system are divided into three categories: heuristic genetic algorithm, iterative algorithm and convex optimization algorithm. In order to meet the users' traffic demand, [3, 4] proposes the genetic algorithms for BH resource allocation. Focused on the influence of CCI of the beam-hopping satellite system, two iterative algorithms, minCCI and maxSIRN, was proposed to meet users' traffic demand [5, 6]. However, both the above-mentioned heuristic genetic algorithm and iterative algorithm have the problems of large amount of calculation and long calculation time, and are not suitable for scenarios where users' traffic demand changes dynamically. Although the convex optimization algorithm saves calculation time in resource allocation, it is not suitable for scenarios with severe CCI [7]. In addition, these previous researches lack the relatively real user traffic demand model.

In order to solve these problems, with the goal of service-driven and on-demand coverage, this paper is focused on the downlink resource allocation of beam hopping for uneven traffic distribution in the HTS system. Firstly, through grid division and comprehensive consideration of economic development and population density, the user traffic demand model which varies in geography and time is built. Secondly, based on the proposed uneven traffic model, a fair objective function is established and solved through integer programming method. Finally, the beam hopping pattern is designed to combing with precoding to suppress co-channel interference [8–12].

2 Beam Hopping Satellite System

The model of the beam-hopping system is illustrated in Fig. 1. This paper focuses on the forward link of HTS system, because the forward link is the main direction of traffic [13]. The forward link consists of the uplink between the gateway ground station and the satellite and the downlink between the satellite and the user terminals. The downlink adopts Time Division Multiplexing (TDM). According to the beam hopping time slot table, beam switched by the Hopping-beam Controller on satellite to meet the traffic demand of terminals.

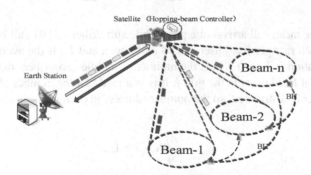

Fig. 1. Beam hopping system model

In order to accurately describe the beam-hopping satellite system, this paper assumes that the total power of the satellite is P_{tot}, the total bandwidth is B_{tot}, and the number of beams is N_B. Besides, constrained by the payload, the BH period is set to T_H, the time slot length is set to T_{slot}, the window length is defined by $N_t = T_H/T_{slot}$, and the maximum number of beams are illuminated simultaneously is N_{mat}^{st}. The beam-hopping time slot allocation model is illustrated in Fig. 2, different colors represent different beams, and the number of the same color represents the number of time slots allocated to the beam by the system.

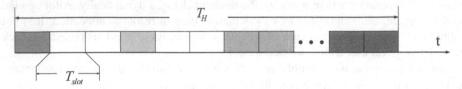

Fig. 2. Model of time slot allocation for beam-hopping

3   Traffic Demand Model

3.1   Spatial Model

Affected by factors such as economy and population density, the traffic demand of different regions is uneven. The region under the satellite coverage is divided into 559 grids, each gird has a longitude width of about 1.5° and latitude width of about 1.25°. The grid' distribution is illustrated in Fig. 3. For convenience, this paper takes China as the research object and builds its traffic demand model, but the method of building the traffic demand model is also applicable to other countries.

According to [14], the traffic intensity $\rho(j)$ inside the grid j is given by

$$\rho(j) = \lambda_1 T_m \sum_j n_{1j} + \lambda_2 T_m \sum_j n_{2j} \tag{1}$$

Where λ_1 is the mean call arrival rate per mobile subscriber (=0.01 call/hour), λ_2 is the mean call arrival rate per fixed user (=0.04 call/hour), and T_m is the average unencumbered call duration (=2 min). $n_{1,j}$ is the number of mobile subscribers in the grid j. $n_{2,j}$ is the number of fixed users in the grid j. It is assumed that the number of users in each province is evenly distributed, so the number of users in each grid can be calculated by the area ratio:

$$n_{i,j} = \frac{A_j}{S_k} N_{i,k} \quad i = 1, 2 \tag{2}$$

Where, if $i = 1$, $N_{i,k}$ is the mobile subscribers in province k, if $i = 2$, $N_{i,k}$ is the fixed users in province k. A_j is the area of grid j. S_k is the area of province j, which got by

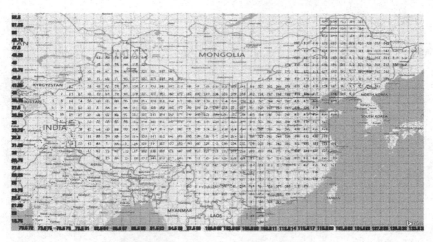

Fig. 3. Spatial traffic grid distribution

adding area of all grids belong to province k. $N_{i,k}$ and A_j are calculated by the following steps.

Calculation of the number of users:

$$N = GPM \times P_r \times T_p \tag{3}$$

Where GPM is the determination of the gross potential market, expressed in GDP (Gross Domestic Product), P_r is the popularity of satellite services, and T_p is the take-up rate of satellite services, expressed in population density. When estimating the number of users, this paper only considers GPM and T_p, GDP and population density are from [15].

Calculation of grid area:

$$A \approx l_m l_n = R_E^2 \times \frac{\pi}{120} \times \frac{\pi}{144} \cos(\theta)$$
$$= R_E^2 \times \frac{\pi^2}{17280} \times \cos(\theta) \tag{4}$$

Where l_m is the length of each grid in the longitude direction, l_n is the length of each grid in the latitude direction, θ is the latitude of the center of each grid, and $R_E = 6378$ Km.

The spatial model is related to the position of the beams. The beams coverage and arrangement are illustrated in Fig. 4.

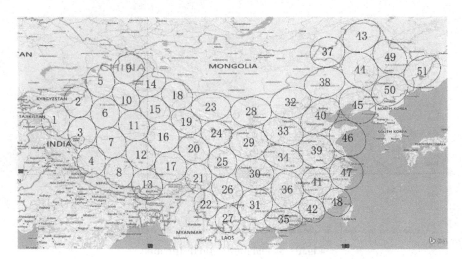

Fig. 4. Beam distribution

The peak traffic demand of each beam calculated by the following steps:

(1) Calculate the traffic demand intensity in each grid by formula (1);
(2) Calculate the coordinate of the beam;
(3) Calculate and sum the traffic demand intensity of all grids, which belong to the same beam;
(4) Repeat steps 1–4 for all beams in turns, the peak traffic demand intensity of all beams can be obtained.

This paper multiplies the peak traffic demand intensity with the PCM30/32 channel group rate (2.048 Mbps) to get the peak traffic demand (in Mbps) [16]. (Note that, if other services are considered, such as Internet services, multimedia services, the corresponding service rate should be chosen.)

After the above process, the spatial model of peak traffic demand is built. As illustrated in Fig. 5.

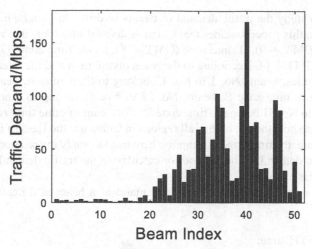

Fig. 5. Peak traffic demand of all beams

3.2 Time Varying Model

In order to analyze the change of traffic demand affected by time and describe the change of traffic demand within one day, a normalized time weighting factor was proposed. Within a day (24 h), according to people's daily habits, a time weighting factor was assigned to each period. This model is applied to all regions, as depicted in Fig. 6. The local time of each spot beam is obtained by GMT (Greenwich Mean Time).

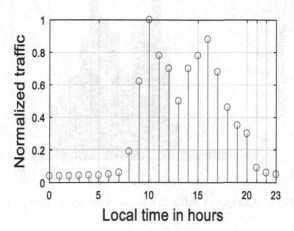

Fig. 6. Diurnal variation model

In order to study the traffic demand of beams in different geographic locations at different times, this paper assumes that China is divided into four time zones, namely A time zone (GMT + 9), B time zone (GMT + 8), and C time zone (GMT + 7) and D time zone (GMT + 6). According to the beam distribution and the international time zone division rules, beams No. 1 to No. 13 belong to time zone A, beams No. 14 to No. 27 belong to time zone B, beams No. 28 to No. 42 belong to time zone C, and beams No. 43 to No. 51 belong to time zone D. The beam in same time zone composes a cluster. (Please note that, in reality, all regions in China use the Eastern Eighth time as the standard time, the time zone assumption here used to study the relationship between time and traffic demand.). The method for calculating the traffic demand of a beam at different times is as follows:

The method for calculating the traffic demand of a beam at different times is as follows:

(1) Identify GMT time;
(2) Calculate the time weighting factor of the time zone to where the beam belongs;
(3) Multiply the peak traffic demand of the beam by the weighting factor.

Through the above steps, the change of the traffic demand of a beam in one day is built. Here, the change of traffic demand of beam No. 40 in one day are given, as illustrated in Fig. 7.

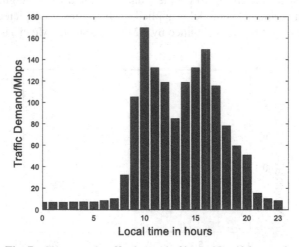

Fig. 7. Changes of traffic demand of beam No. 40 in one day

4 Beam Hopping Resource Allocation and Pattern Design

4.1 Resource Allocation by Beam Hopping

According to Sect. 3, the traffic demand model has the characteristics of time-varying and uneven distribution. Compared with the traditional resource allocation method, the beam-hopping technology can improve the resource utilization of the satellite system. According to the traffic demand of each beam and with the objective of maximizing the traffic offered to each beam, a method of allocating beam-hopping time slots is established. The specific method is as follows.

Firstly, according to the traffic demand of each beam, the fairness objective function is established to calculate the number of timeslots of each beam. As following:

$$\max \prod_{k=1}^{N_B} \left(\frac{r_k}{d_k} \right) \tag{5}$$

$$\text{s.t. } r_k \leq d_k \tag{6}$$

$$\sum_{k=1}^{N_B} N_k \leq N_{max}^{st} N_t \tag{7}$$

$$N_k \geq 0, N_k \in \text{integer} \tag{8}$$

Where, N_k is the number of timeslots allocated to beam k. d_k is the traffic demand of beam k and r_k is the capacity allocated to beam k, which can be calculated by (9). The rest parameters can be got form Sect. 2.

$$r_k = \frac{N_k}{N_{slot} \times T_{slot}} B_{tot} \log_2(1 + SNR_k) \tag{9}$$

Secondly, we reform the objective function of Eq. (5) into a convex optimization problem by the logarithmic equivalent transformation:

$$\max \sum_{k=1}^{N_B} \ln(\frac{r_k}{d_k}) \tag{10}$$

Finally, the established optimization problem is an integer programming, therefore integer programming solution package of CVX is employed to obtain beam hopping time slot schedule matrix $\mathbf{T} = [\mathbf{T}_1, \mathbf{T}_2, ... \mathbf{T}_{N_B}]^T$ [17], where $\mathbf{T}_i = [n_{i1}, n_{i2}, ... n_{iN_t}]$, $\forall n_{ij} \in [0, 1]$. And $n_{ij} = 1$ indicates that the beam i is allocated to the time slot j.

4.2 Beam Hopping Pattern Design

By arranging the illuminated order of each beam, the beam-hopping pattern can avoid partial interference between beams. However, for those inevitable interferences, it is necessary to introduce a new interference avoidance strategy. The specific measures are as follows:

Firstly, the time-slot allocation schedule of beam hopping is analyzed to search out the beams suffering serious co-frequency interference in the same time slot. Secondly, in the non-ideal channel, the MMSE precoding is used to suppress the co-frequency interference. According to [18], the non-ideal channel matrix is composed by the channel state information estimation matrix and the channel estimation error matrix, as shown in (11):

$$\mathbf{H} = \hat{\mathbf{H}} + \Delta H \tag{11}$$

Where $\hat{\mathbf{H}}$ is the channel estimation matrix and ΔH is the channel estimation error matrix. Each element in ΔH are assumed to be complex Gaussian, with zero mean and a variance of σ_ε^2. According to [19], the elements in $\hat{\mathbf{H}}$ is

$$\left[\overline{\mathbf{H}}\right]_{k,n} = \frac{G_T G_R B_{kn} e^{j\psi}}{4\pi \left(\frac{D_k}{\lambda}\right)^2} k = 1, \ldots N_B; n = 1, \ldots N_B \tag{12}$$

Where G_T is the antenna transmission gain, G_R is the antenna reception gain, B_{kn} is the gain factor of the co-channel interference of the user in the $n - th$ beam to the $k - th$ beam, ψ is the time-varying phase, D_k is the distance from the user in the $k - th$ beam to the satellite, λ is the wavelength.

According to the MMSE, the smaller the difference between the transmitted and received signals, the smaller the interference received by the users. According to this, the objective function and constraints are as follows:

$$\arg \min E\left[\left\|\hat{a} - a\right\|^2\right]$$
$$s.t. E\left[\|Fa\|^2\right] \le P_T \tag{13}$$

Where $\hat{a} = HFa + \beta^{-1}n$, $\beta = \sqrt{\frac{P_T}{E[\|Fa\|^2]}}$, For the optimization problem in (13), detailed theoretical derivation and calculation is given in[18], which is not calculated here. Finally, the precoding matrix expression as shown in (14):

$$\mathbf{F} = \hat{\mathbf{H}}\left(\hat{\mathbf{H}}\hat{\mathbf{H}} + K\sigma_\varepsilon^2 I + \xi I\right)^{-1} \tag{14}$$

5   Simulation Results and Analysis

The simulation parameters in this paper are illustrated in Table 1. In addition, in order to better compare the experimental results, two indicators of traffic unsatisfied and traffic satisfaction are used. The two definitions are as follows:

traffic unsatisfied:

$$U_s = r_k - \min\{r_k, d_k\} \tag{15}$$

Table 1. Simulation parameters

Parameter	Value
Satellite longitude	105° east (GEO)
Satellite total on-board power	$P_{tot} = 200W$
Downlink carrier frequency	$f_{down} = 20$ GHz
Number of beams	$N_B = 51$
Maximum number of beams are illuminated simultaneously	$N_{max}^{st} = 4$
Total bandwidth	$B_{tot} = 200$ MHz
Duration of one time-slot	$T_{slot} = 1.4$ ms
Beam hopping period	$T_H = 512T_{slot}$
Transmit antenna gain	$G_T = 40$dBi
Receive antenna gain	$G_R = 50$ dBi
Variance of ΔH	$\sigma_\varepsilon^2 = 0.1$

traffic satisfaction:

$$\rho_j = \frac{\sum_{k=1}^{K} \bar{r}_k}{\sum_{k=1}^{K} d_k} \tag{16}$$

Where $\bar{r}_k = \min(r_k, d_k)$, r_k, d_k is the same as the definition in Sect. 4. This article compares four resource allocation algorithms: the Proposed Algorithm is the algorithm proposed in this paper, it cooperates all clusters for beam-hopping pattern design and uses precoding algorithms to suppress inter-beam interference. The Joint Cluster algorithm refers to the design of hopping beam pattern by spatial isolation and time isolation, which is employed in [11]. The Only BH refers to the design of hopping beam pattern by time isolation only, which is employed in [2]. The Uniform Timeslot algorithm refers to that system resources are evenly allocated.

As illustrated in Figs. 8 and 9, the Uniform Timeslot algorithm evenly divides the satellite's bandwidth and power to each spot beam, which cannot meet the high traffic demand of the beam. The Only BH algorithm avoids the intra-cluster interference through time isolation method, but it cannot avoid the inter-cluster interference. The Joint Cluster algorithm reduces some inter-cluster interference by increasing spatial isolation method. The Proposed Algorithm effectively suppresses intra-cluster interference and inter-cluster interference, making full use of on-board resources.

As illustrated in Figs. 10 and 11, when the traffic demand of beam No.40 is small, the beam needs fewer time slots and has less interference with other beams, therefore the traffic satisfaction of the four algorithms is close to 1. However, when the traffic demand of the beam is large, the Uniform Timeslot algorithm lacks flexibility to optimize the allocation of satellite resource. The Only BH algorithm can allocate more time

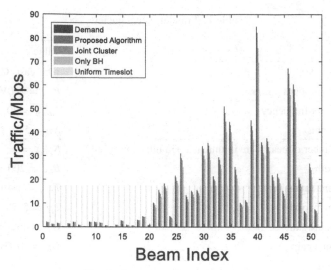

Fig. 8. System traffic at GMT = 6

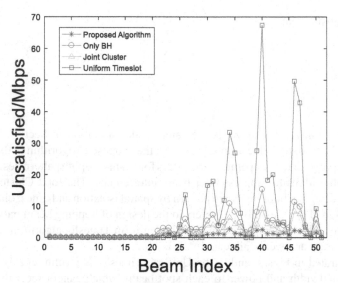

Fig. 9. System traffic unsatisfied at GMT = 6

slots to No. 40 as the traffic demand increases, but at the same time, it increases the interference between the No.40 beam and its neighboring beams. The Joint Cluster algorithm can reduce some interference of adjacent beams through the beam-hopping pattern design method. Compared with previous algorithms, the Proposed Algorithm has a better performance.

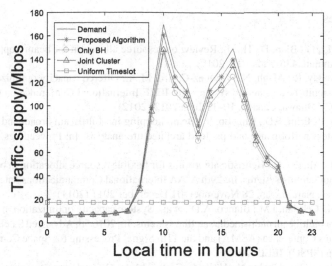

Fig. 10. System traffic supply for the 40th beam in a day

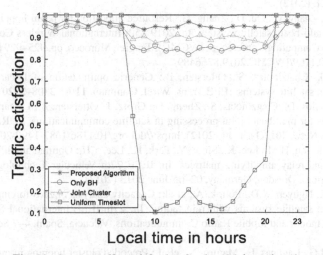

Fig. 11. System traffic satisfaction for the 40th beam in a day

6   Conclusion

In this paper, two kinds of traffic demand model, spatial model and time-varying model, are established, which make the beam hopping communication system more complete. To improve the efficiency of on-board resource utilization in HTS, beam hopping pattern is designed to combing with precoding to suppress co-channel interference. Simulation results clarify that the proposed algorithm can dynamically adjust the resource allocation with the change of the traffic requirements, and eliminate the co-frequency interference of the beam as much as possible.

References

1. Tang, J., Li, G., Bian, D., Hu, J.: Review on resource allocation for beam-hopping satellite. Mob. Commun. **43**(05), 26–31 (2019)
2. Alegre-Godoy, R., Alagh, N., Vazquez-Castro, M.A.: Offered capacity optimization mechanisms for multi-beam satellite systems. In: IEEE International Conference on Communications (ICC), Ottawa, Canada, 10–15 June 2012 (2012)
3. Angeletti, P., Prim, F.D., Rinaldo, R.: Beam hopping in MultiBeam broadband satellite systems: system performance and payload architecture analysis. In: Proceedings of the AIAA (2006)
4. Alegre, R., Alagha, N.: Heuristic algorithms for flexible resource allocation in beam hopping multi-beam satellite systems. In: 29th AIAA International Communications Satellite Systems Conference, Nara, Japan, 28 November–01 December 2011 (2011)
5. Alberti, X., Cebrian, J.M., Bianco, A.D., et al.: System capacity optimization in time and frequency for multibeam multi-media satellite systems. In: 2010 5th Advanced Satellite Multimedia Systems Conference (ASMA) and the 11th Signal Processing for Space Communications Workshop (SPSC). IEEE (2010)
6. Alegre-Godoy, R., Alagha, N., Vázquez-Castro, M.A.: Offered capacity optimization mechanisms for multi-beam satellite systems. In: IEEE International Conference on Communications. IEEE (2012)
7. Wang, L., Zhang, C., Qu, D., Zhang, G.: Resource allocation for beam-hopping user downlinks in multi-beam satellite system. In: 2019 15th International Wireless Communications & Mobile Computing Conference (IWCMC), Tangier, Morocco, pp. 925–929 (2019). https://doi.org/10.1109/IWCMC.2019.8766489
8. Zheng, G., Chatzinotas, S., Ottersten, B.: Generic optimization of linear precoding in multibeam satellite systems. IEEE Trans. Wirel. Commun. **11**(6), 2308–2320 (2012)
9. Christopoulos, D., Chatzinotas, S., Zheng, G., Grotz, J., Ottersten, B.: Linear and nonlinear techniques for multibeam joint processing in satellite communications. EURASIP J. Wirel. Commun. Netw. **2012**(1), 1–13 (2012). https://doi.org/10.1186/1687-1499-2012-162
10. Kim, H., Kwon, H.M., Lee, K., Shim, Y., Park, H., Lee, Y.H.: Optimal amplify-and-forward precode and relay amplifying matrices. In: IEEE 77th Vehicular Technology Conference (VTC Spring), Dresden, Germany, 02–05 June 2013 (2013)
11. Ahmad, I., Nguyen, K.D., Pollok, A., et al.: Capacity analysis of zero-forcing precoding in multibeam satellite systems with rain fading. In: 27th IEEE International Symposium on Personal, Indoor and Mobile Radio Communications, Valencia, Spain, 4–7 September 2017 (2017)
12. Kibria, M.G., Lagunas, E., Maturo, N., et al.: Precoded cluster hopping in multi-beam high throughput satellite systems. https://arxiv.org/abs/1905.1162, May 2019
13. Alberto, G., Emiliano, R., Pantelis-Daniel, A.: Joint beam hopping and precoding in HTS systems. In: 9th International Conference on Wireless and Satellite Systems, Oxford, UK, 14–15 September 2017 (2017)
14. Hu, Y.F., Sheriff, R.E.: Satellite-UMTS traffic dimensioning and resource management technique analysis. IEEE Trans. Veh. Technol. **47**, 1329–1341 (1998)
15. Statistics Bureau of the people's Republic of China. China Statistical Yearbook. China Statistics Press, Beijing (2019)
16. ITU-T Rec. G.747 (11/88) Second order digital multiplex equipment operating at 6312 kbit/s and multiplexing three tributaries at 2048 kbit/s
17. Grant, M., Boyd, S.: CVX: Matlab Software for Disciplined Convex Programming, version 2.0 beta. https://cvxr.com/cvx, September 2013

18. Dabbagh, A.D., Love, D.J.: Precoding for multiple antenna broadcast channels with channel mismatch. In: Fortieth Asilomar Conference on Signals, Systems & Computers, Pacific Grove, pp. 1601–1605, October 2006
19. Perez-Neira, A.I., Vazquez, M.A., Maleki, S., et al.: Signal processing for high throughput satellite systems: challenges in new interference-limited scenarios. IEEE Signal Process. Mag. **36**(4), 112–131 (2018)

Author Index

Printed in the United States
By Bookmasters